Counseling
Assessment
and Evaluation

Counseling and Professional Identity

Series Editors: Richard D. Parsons, PhD, and Naijian Zhang, PhD

COUNSELING and
PROFESSIONAL IDENTITY

Counseling Assessment and Evaluation

Fundamentals of Applied Practice

Joshua C. Watson
Texas A&M University–Corpus Christi

Brandé Flamez
Walden University

Los Angeles | London | New Delhi
Singapore | Washington DC

Los Angeles | London | New Delhi
Singapore | Washington DC

FOR INFORMATION:

SAGE Publications, Inc.
2455 Teller Road
Thousand Oaks, California 91320
E-mail: order@sagepub.com

SAGE Publications Ltd.
1 Oliver's Yard
55 City Road
London EC1Y 1SP
United Kingdom

SAGE Publications India Pvt. Ltd.
B 1/I 1 Mohan Cooperative Industrial Area
Mathura Road, New Delhi 110 044
India

SAGE Publications Asia-Pacific Pte. Ltd.
3 Church Street
#10-04 Samsung Hub
Singapore 049483

Acquisitions Editor: Kassie Graves
Editorial Assistant: Carrie Baarns
Production Editor: Melanie Birdsall
Copy Editor: Sarah J. Duffy
Typesetter: C&M Digitals (P) Ltd.
Proofreader: Susan Schon
Indexer: Judy Hunt
Cover Designer: Candice Harman
Marketing Manager: Sheri Countryman

Printed in the United States of America

Library of Congress Cataloging-in-Publication Data

Watson, Joshua C.

Counseling assessment and evaluation : fundamentals of applied practice / Joshua C. Watson, Texas A&M University–Corpus Christi, Brandé Flamez, Walden University.

pages cm— (Counseling and professional identity)
Includes bibliographical references and index.

ISBN 978-1-4522-2624-8 (pbk.)

1. Counseling psychology. 2. Counseling psychologists. 3. Counseling psychologist and client. 4. Behavioral assessment. I. Flamez, Brandé. II. Title.

BF636.6.W37 2014
158.3—dc23   2014008524

This book is printed on acid-free paper.

SFI label applies to text stock

14 15 16 17 18 10 9 8 7 6 5 4 3 2 1

Brief Contents

Detailed Contents

2 Basic Assessment and Statistical Concepts

3 Reliability

4 Validity 83

5 Selecting, Administering, Scoring, and Reporting Assessment Results 103

8   Achievement and Aptitude Assessment   197

9   Standardized Methods of Personality Assessment   235

10   Projective Methods of Personality Assessment   281

11   Behavioral Assessment

15   Assessment Issues With Diverse Populations

16   Ethical and Legal Issues in Assessment

To my family who stood by me throughout the writing process,
I cannot begin to thank you enough for all the support you gave me. April, Kaylee, and Cara,
I love you each more than you probably know.

—Joshua

To my family—who always loves, supports, and believes.
I love you more than all the sand on the beach and the stars in the sky.

—Brandé

Editors' Preface

Counseling Assessment and Evaluation: Fundamentals of Applied Practice, by Joshua C. Watson and Brandé Flamez, is a text that will demonstrate that the processes of assessment and evaluation are more than simply a good idea—they are truly a response to our professional codes and ethics and an essential tool guiding effective practice.

Throughout the pages to follow, you will come to understand that *Counseling Assessment and Evaluation* addresses more than the testing or gathering of information that occurs at the time of client intake. Assessment and evaluation when employed by the ethical counselor engages processes by which a counselor gains not only a more comprehensive and accurate understanding of the client and his or her reasons for seeking counseling services, but also clarity about the strategies that provide the best opportunity for success and the data essential to the monitoring progress and goal achievement. When used as directed by its authors, *Counseling Assessment and Evaluation* IS fundamental to applied practice.

Counseling Assessment and Evaluation: Fundamentals of Applied Practice is a text that is clear, cogent, and comprehensive. However, beyond the explication of the core concepts of counseling assessment and evaluation, the text, with its rich use of case illustrations and guided practice exercises, helps each reader personalize the material presented and begin to incorporate that information into the development of his or her own professional identity and skill set.

As is obvious, any one text, or any one learning experience, will not be sufficient for the successful formation of your professional identity and practice. Becoming and being a counselor will be a lifelong process—a process that we hope to facilitate through the presentation of this text along with the creation of our series: Counseling and Professional Identity.

Counseling and Professional Identity is a new, fresh, pedagogically sound series of texts targeting counselors in training. This series is not simply a compilation of isolated books matching that which is already in the market. Rather, each book, with its targeted knowledge and skills, will be presented as but a part of a larger whole. The focus and content of each text serves as a single lens through which a counselor can view his or her clients, engage in his or her practice, and articulate his or her own professional identity.

Counseling and Professional Identity is distinctive not just in that it is a "packaged" series of traditional text, but also in that it provides an integrated curriculum targeting the formation of the readers' professional identity and efficient, ethical practice. Each book in the series is structured to facilitate the ongoing professional formation of the reader. The materials found in each text are organized to move the reader to higher levels of cognitive, affective, and psychomotor functioning, resulting in his or her assimilation of the materials presented into both his or her professional identity and approach to professional practice. While each text targets a specific set of core competencies (cognates and skills), competencies which have aligned with those identified by the Council for Accreditation of Counseling and Related Educational Programs as essential to the practice of counseling, each book in the series will emphasize each of the following:

- assimilation of concepts and constructs provided across the texts in the series, thus fostering the reader's ongoing development as a competent professional
- blending of contemporary theory with current research and empirical support
- focus on the development of procedural knowledge, with each text employing case illustrations and guided practice exercises to facilitate the reader's ability to translate the theory and research discussed into professional decision making and application
- emphasis on the need for and means of demonstrating accountability
- fostering of the reader's professional identity and with it the assimilation of the ethics and standards of practice guiding the counseling profession

We are proud to have served as co-editors of this series, feeling sure that each book in it will serve as a significant resource to you and your development as a professional counselor. Let your journey begin!

—Richard D. Parsons, PhD

—Naijian Zhang, PhD

Titles in Counseling and Professional Identity Series

CACREP Standards	Sangganjanavanich, *Introduction to Professional Counseling*	Watson, *Counseling Assessment and Evaluation*	Conyne, *Group Work Leadership*	Parsons, *Becoming a Skilled Counselor*	Parsons, *Counseling Theory*
1. PROFESSIONAL ORIENTATION AND ETHCIAL PRACTICE	1a 1b 1d 1e 1f 1g 1h 1i 1j	1j	1b 1j	1b 1d 1e 1j	1j
2. SOCIAL AND CULTURAL DIVERSITY	2c 2f 2g	2g	2d 2e 2g	2b 2c 2g	2c 2e 2g
3. HUMAN GROWTH AND DEVELOPMENT			3f		3b
4. CAREER DEVELOPMENT		4f			
5. HELPING RELATIONSHIPS	5a 5b 5c 5f 5g 5h		5b 5c 5d 5e	5a 5b 5c 5d	5b 5c 5d 5e 5g
6. GROUP WORK		6a 6b 6c 6d 6e			
7. ASSESSMENT		7a 7b 7c 7d 7e 7f 7g	7b	7b	
8. RESEARCH AND PROGRAM EVALUATION					

(Continued)

Titles in Counseling and Professional Identity Series (Continued)

CACREP Standards	Wong, Counseling Individuals Through the Lifespan	Duan, Becoming a Multiculturally Competent Counselor	Wright, Research Methods for Counseling	Tang, Career Development and Counseling	Scott, Counselor as Consultant	Sheperis, Ethical Decision Making for the 21st Century Counselor
1. PROFESSIONAL ORIENTATION AND ETHCIAL PRACTICE	1j	1j	1j	1b 1j	1b 1j	1b 1d 1e 1f 1h 1i 1j
2. SOCIAL AND CULTURAL DIVERSITY	2a 2b 2c 2d 2e 2g	2c 2e 2f 2g	2g	2g	2d 2g	2c 2e 2f 2g
3. HUMAN GROWTH AND DEVELOPMENT	3a 3b 3c 3d 3e 3f 3g	3d 3e		3e		3g
4. CAREER DEVELOPMENT				4a 4b 4c 4d 4e 4f 4g	4c	
5. HELPING RELATIONSHIPS	5b	5b 5e		5b 5c	5b 5c 5f 5g 5h	5b 5d 5h
6. GROUP WORK						6d 6e
7. ASSESSMENT	7f		7c 7d 7e			
8. RESEARCH AND PROGRAM EVALUATION			8a 8b 8c 8d 8e			8d

Preface

MOTIVATION FOR THIS PROJECT

The motivation to write this book stems from our personal passion for assessment. In our professional careers, as both clinicians and academicians, we each have experienced the positive role assessment can play in the counseling process. Through the years, our interest in assessment has led us to become involved in various assessment-related organizations, especially the Association for Assessment in Research in Counseling (AARC). Our participation in AARC, whether through serving on committees or serving in leadership positions, has allowed us to connect with and learn from many talented and gifted counselors around the country who share our passion for the assessment process. Our interactions with these professionals has enabled us to see the vast potential for assessment in the helping professions. In writing this book, our goal was to help create this passion for assessment in you. As the next generation of counselors, your willingness to embrace assessment and actively utilize assessment techniques in an appropriate fashion will be of vital importance as the counseling profession continues to evolve its identity and more effectively serve those in our society who are most in need.

As counselor educators, we are keenly aware of the fact that testing and assessment courses are not among the more popular in counselor training programs. At the beginning of each semester, students routinely share with us how they are skeptical of testing and do not see a scenario in which they can envision themselves using assessment in their counseling work. For many, this course is simply a requirement they need to satisfy to graduate. However, what we often find is that these opinions are usually based on misperceptions about what assessment really is and how it can be effectively used. Consequently, we spend a great deal of time early in the semester helping students see how, when you think about it, assessment really is what we do when we counsel someone. Counselors are always gathering information about their clients and using it to inform their conceptualization of presenting problems. Did the client show up on time? Does the client look distressed? What does the client's lack of eye contact mean? These are all forms of assessment. Beginning with our initial impression of clients, and continuing through the duration of our work together, we constantly assess clients to better understand how what we are doing is helping them reach their goals. So you see, assessment is much more than just the use of standardized tests. While testing receives the most attention, primarily due to the manner in which its results are used, it really constitutes only a portion of the full scope of assessment activities a counselor uses on a daily basis. Once you open your mind and view assessment from this broader perspective, you will be able to fully appreciate its value to you.

OVERVIEW AND ORGANIZATION

As we were formulating our vision for this book, we decided early on that we wanted it to be a resource that would really speak to our readers. Specifically, we wanted to create a book that helped counselors see how assessment could be integrated into the counseling process in many practical applications. As such, we have adopted a more conversational tone throughout the book that speaks to the ways you can use the material we present in any number of counseling settings. Additionally, case illustrations and guided practice exercises are included in every chapter to help you begin to see the many ways assessment practices can be used with all types of clients.

The first section of the book provides a more global overview of counseling assessment. In Chapter 1 we describe the process of counseling assessment and share the multiple purposes assessment serves in the counseling relationship. We also provide you with a historical perspective of assessment to illustrate how it has evolved throughout the years into the practices counselors use today. Knowing where we have been in the past helps us better understand why we do what we do today and where we need to go in the future. In Chapter 2, we introduce basic principles of assessment and score reporting that should help you develop a comfort level with common concepts and terminology. Chapters 3 and 4 address two important psychometric components of assessment: reliability and validity. When assessment is unreliable and invalid, the results obtained serve little purpose and do not inform the counseling process. In Chapter 5 we take you step by step through the process of selecting tests and assessments to use. The value of the data derived from an assessment rises significantly when informed decisions are made. These chapters all lead up to Chapter 6, where we begin talking about the many ways counselors can integrate assessment throughout the counseling process.

In the second section of the book, our focus shifts from a global overview to a more specific review. The chapters in this section were written to expand on the information presented in Section I and illustrate how assessment is performed in various domains. In this section, chapters specific to the assessment of intelligence, ability, achievement, aptitude, personality, behavior, and career and vocational interests and aptitudes are all included as they represent the predominant domains in which assessment occurs. In each chapter readers will gain an understanding of the assessment process as it relates to these constructs and be introduced to the most frequently used assessment instruments in these areas.

The final section includes chapters related to the use of assessment for specific applications. In Chapter 13 an overview of the clinical assessment process is provided, including the appropriate steps involved with diagnosing clients who present with mental disorders. Chapter 14 introduces readers to the practices of program evaluation and outcome assessment, two growing areas in today's era of evidence-based practice. Finally, this section concludes with chapters dedicated to an examination of sound applications of assessment practice. In Chapters 15 and 16, a review of the practice standards, professional regulations, and state and federal laws governing the use of assessment in an ethical and culturally competent manner is included to help ensure that you follow best practices in your assessing of clients.

ACKNOWLEDGMENTS

Completing a project of this scope could not have been accomplished without the support and assistance of many individuals. To each of you, we extend our sincere appreciation for helping us create a product we believe to be a true asset to the counselor-training profession. To our families, we thank you for your love and support as the many long hours we spent invested in this project were certainly made easier by your positivity and well-timed words of encouragement. To our friends and colleagues, especially those in the Association for Assessment and Research in Counseling, thank you for stimulating our creative process and supporting our writing efforts. Because of you, the practice of assessment remains a visible and important part of the counseling process in all settings. Specifically, we would like to thank our colleagues Ashley Clark, Melinda Haley, and Gary Szirony for their time and effort spent reviewing our manuscript and sharing their insights throughout the process. To Rick Parsons and Naijian Zhang, thank you for allowing us to be part of this project and contributing to this timely series. Finally, we would like to thank those at Sage who helped shepherd our vision into reality, especially our acquisitions editor, Kassie Graves, whose constant enthusiasm, patience, and commitment to the project did not go unnoticed.

Last, we would be remiss if we did not mention the many individuals who reviewed our manuscript throughout the process: Patricia Andersen, Midwestern State University; John C. Clements, Webster University; Charles R. Crews, Texas Tech University; Mark Dewalt, Winthrop University; Yolanda Dupre, University of Louisiana at Monroe; Connie Kane, California State University, Stanislaus; Wendy Killam, Stephen F. Austin State University; David M. Kleist, Idaho State University; Jason Kushner, University of Arkansas at Little Rock; Jessica Lester, Indiana University; Bill McHenry, Texas A&M University-Texarkana; Jessica Nina, Indiana University; Susan Schaeffer, Chadron State College; Nancy E. Sherman, Bradley University; and Jeffery M. Smith, Creighton University. The feedback we received from these talented counselor educators definitely helped us produce a more polished product in the end.

PUBLISHER'S ACKNOWLEDGMENTS

SAGE gratefully acknowledges the contributions of the following reviewers:

Gregg Allinson, Beaufort County Community College

Desalyn De-Souza, SUNY Upstate Medical University

Stephen Dougherty, University of New England

Janet Ford, University of Kentucky

Robert Hard, Albertus Magnus College

Elaine Johannes, Kansas State University

SECTION I

Principles and Foundations of Counseling Assessment

Introduction to Counseling Assessment

As you continue your training as a professional counselor, you are no doubt beginning to realize that there is no "one-size-fits-all" counseling approach that can be applied to all clients. If there were, counselor training programs would require far less coursework to complete. The reason we as counselors have such a variety of approaches, techniques, and interventions at our disposal is that each client who seeks counseling is unique. Every individual presents with his or her own set of issues and circumstances that allow him or her to experience life differently. What may be viewed as a source of great distress for one person may not even register as a concern for another. Because each client's situation is different, it is important for counselors to acquire as much information about their clients as possible so that they can provide them with treatment options tailored to their specific needs.

Assessment is the process by which counselors gather the information they need to form a holistic view of their clients and the problems with which they present. As a counselor, you will regularly assess your clients throughout the counseling process, especially in the early stages. Consider for a moment the following scenario: A female client presents for counseling tearful and distraught. She states that her life feels like it is falling apart, and she does not know what to do or where to turn for help. As a counselor, you probably have many questions you would need answered before you could begin to help this woman. For example, why is she so despondent? What has happened to make her feel like her life is falling apart? How long has she felt this way? Does she have any resources or support to help her through this trying time? Your ability to find answers to these questions will determine how the counseling process unfolds and how successful it ultimately will be. With so many questions needing answers, it becomes important to know how to effectively employ appropriate assessment techniques and procedures. In this chapter we will introduce you to the practice of counseling assessment and present an overview of the assessment process. In addition, we will examine the historical role assessment has played in both clinical and nonclinical settings. Learning about the important developments and advances that have helped shape assessment practices and procedures throughout history will help you appreciate how we have reached our current understanding of client assessment.

WHAT IS ASSESSMENT?

Before beginning our discussion of assessment, we believe it would be most beneficial to present an operational definition of the term. In 1985, members from the American Educational Research Association (AERA), the American Psychological Association (APA), and the National Council on Measurement in Education (NCME) got together to produce a document known as the *Standards for Educational and Psychological Testing* (herein referred to as the *Standards*). The *Standards*, written for both a professional and layperson audience, is a collection of best practices that describe how tests should be developed as well as appropriate uses of tests in various educational, psychological, and employment settings. The intent of this group of professionals was to create a frame of reference to which clinicians and test administrators could turn to ensure that they were making and using tests appropriately. The *Standards* have been revised twice since their original publication date. In the third and most current edition, the term **assessment** is defined as "a process that integrates test information with information from other sources (e.g., information from other tests, the individual's social, educational, employment, health, or psychological history)" (AERA, APA, & NCME, 1999, p. 3). As you can see, this definition highlights the broad nature of the assessment process. By collecting client data from various sources, using a combination of formal and informal techniques, counselors are able to formulate a more comprehensive and accurate understanding of the client and his or her reason for presenting for counseling services (Drummond & Jones, 2010). How does this definition compare to how you previously thought of counseling assessment? Guided Practice Exercise 1.1 invites you to think about how you conceptualize the assessment process.

GUIDED PRACTICE EXERCISE 1.1

Understanding Counseling Assessment

For many counselors, the term *assessment* conjures up images of standardized tests and rigid scoring protocols that place labels on clients. In this chapter we hope to dispel this myth and show you that counseling assessment encompasses much more than standardized testing and can actually be a useful tool for you to successfully advance the counseling process. Imagine that you are scheduled to see a new client this afternoon for the first time. All you know is that the client was referred to you to discuss an issue with anger management. Assessment could be used to help you better understand the scope of the problem. What information would you like to have about the client and the presenting problem to more accurately understand the situation and begin formulating an effective treatment plan?

Throughout the professional literature you will see the term *assessment* used interchangeably with other terms such as *appraisal* and *evaluation*. Although these may seem like they are the same, there are subtle nuances that differentiate the activities. Like assessment, both appraisal and evaluation also make use of various methods of formal and informal data collection. However, a noted difference is in how the collected information is used. When counselors assess clients, their goal is to document and describe what is going on with the clients. Thus assessment is largely an objective activity. On the other hand, appraisal and evaluation both involve a process whereby counselors are asked to make judgments based on the evidence that they collect. These activities are more subjective in nature. Considering the reasons you need to acquire information about your client's presenting problem will help you understand which activity you actually are conducting.

Another term you might see used in the literature is *psychological testing*. A **psychological test**, as defined by Anastasi and Urbina (1997), is an objective, standardized measure of behavior. In the first half of the 20th century, counseling professionals were known to use tests fairly regularly in their work with clients. In fact, educational and vocational counselors, as well as trait-and-factor theorists, employed a variety of tests to learn more about their clients and tailor their treatment approach to best meet the needs of their clients. Consequently, many people interpreted assessment and testing as referring to the same practice (Leppma & Jones, 2013). However, as noted in the latest revision of the *Standards*, assessment encompasses much more than testing. In reality, the modern scope of assessment activities goes far beyond the exclusive use of standardized tests (McQuaid et al., 2012). Assessment activities include the collection of data from direct (client) and indirect sources (family, friends, co-workers) using both formal and informal methods. Included in the list of assessment methods are such interventions as observation, interviewing, screening, and standardized testing (see Case Illustration 1.1). As you can see, tests represent only one source of information for counselors to use. As a result, the use of the word *testing* to refer to any and all assessment activities has primarily ceased. Instead, we view the practice of assessment in a more holistic sense to refer to the collection of ways through which we begin to know more about our clients and the issues for which they present for counseling services.

CASE ILLUSTRATION   1.1

A school counselor has been contacted by a teacher for assistance with a student who is having difficulty in class. The teacher informs the school counselor that the student is disruptive and is preventing other students from learning. The school counselor agrees to intervene and work with the student to see what may be going on. To better understand the nature of the disruptive behavior, the school counselor may employ several assessment strategies to gather additional information. The school counselor might sit in on a class session and observe the student directly to see what the disruptive behavior actually looks like, what precedes the behavior, and what if any reaction the student receives from exhibiting the behavior. The school counselor might also talk to the student to see what benefit the behavior serves. Other teachers might be consulted to see if this behavior exists in other classes, or the student's parents might become involved to assess whether this type of behavior is exclusive to school or is one that the parents see occurring at home as well. In this case illustration the school counselor is using several assessment methods to gain as much information as possible to begin working on a solution to the problem with the student. Without this information the counseling process would be a lot less directed and focused and may not be successful.

Purposes of Assessment

Assessment plays an integral role throughout the counseling relationship. From the moment we first meet a client through the last session we have together, counselors are always assessing and gathering data. The more information we have about a client, the better we are able to help the client achieve a successful outcome. Depending on where we are in the counseling process with a client, the scope and goals of assessment practices vary. Generally speaking, assessment serves four primary purposes in the counseling process: (a) screening, (b) diagnosis, (c) treatment planning and goal identification, and (d) progress evaluation (Erford, 2006). A more in-depth discussion of each of these purposes can be found in Chapter 6.

Having now provided you with a better idea of what counseling assessment entails, we will present a brief historical look at how assessment practices have evolved through the years. Our reason for including the following section is twofold. First, program accreditation standards mandate that students be taught this information. The Council for the Accreditation of Counseling and Related Educational Programs (CACREP, 2009) directs counselor training programs to include in their curriculum a discussion of the "historical perspectives concerning the nature and meaning of assessment" (p. 12). Second, examining the past is a great way to help understand the present and shape the future. Accreditation standards aside, having a basic working knowledge of the history of assessment will not only allow you to better understand current assessment issues and practices (Drummond & Jones, 2010), but also help you to avoid repeating past mistakes related to the misuse of assessment procedures and interventions. When used in an informed and valid manner, assessment activities can be useful tools for a counselor to employ.

HISTORICAL OVERVIEW OF ASSESSMENT PRACTICES

The history of psychological assessment and testing is one that is marked by necessity and innovation (Geisinger, 2000). As a result, assessment and testing practices feature prominently in several vocational, educational, and clinical settings. In this section, we will highlight some of the major events and milestones in the history of assessment. While it is generally accepted that the modern assessment era begins with the 20th century, there is recorded evidence of assessment practices being used as many as 4,000 years ago. An introduction to these early usages will help you better understand how assessment helps us today in the various settings in which counselors might work.

Assessment Practices in Ancient Times (BCE)

One of the earliest recorded uses of assessment practices was in China around 2200 BCE. At that time the Chinese empire was rapidly expanding in both size and scope. To maintain order and control throughout the empire, the emperor required a large number of officials to assist in governing the people. Individuals who held these positions were held in high regard and paid quite well. Many government officials were able to support their entire family for years to come with the salary they received. As a result, they were highly sought-after positions. To assist in selecting the most qualified individuals to serve in these important positions, the Chinese government initiated a civil service examination. The examination was a grueling affair, lasting for three full days and testing individuals on a variety of topics, including civil law, military affairs, agriculture, revenue, geography, music, archery, horsemanship, and writing. To be successful, potential candidates needed to spend a great deal of time studying in preparation for the examination. In theory the examinations were open to all citizens, allowing for individuals to be selected based on their own merits rather than any family or political connections they might have had. However, the time and expense associated with preparing for the examination typically resulted in officials being selected predominantly from the wealthiest families. Although many took the examination, only about 3%–5% passed and became government officials. Despite the fact that testing conditions were not ideal (participants were kept isolated for long hours and asked to complete several grueling tasks), the civil service examination remained in use until 1905. Despite its flaws, this early usage still incorporated many of the assessment practices we use today, including standardized test administration and documenting content validity. A more detailed discussion of these topics will appear in subsequent chapters.

The Ancient Greeks provide us with another example of early assessment usage. For the Greeks, testing was an established adjunct to the educational process (Anastasi & Urbina, 1997). In 500 BCE Socrates developed philosophies that emphasized the use of assessment in educational planning. He advocated for the importance of assessing an individual's competencies and aptitudes prior to vocational selection. Socrates' original ideas also are seen in the work of perhaps his most famous student, Plato. In his most well-known book, the *Republic*, Plato (circa 380 BCE) suggested that people should work at jobs consistent with their abilities and endowments. In other words, the career choice individuals make should be based on a thorough analysis of who they are as individuals, including what they believe and value as well as what skills and talents they currently possess. Plato was a firm believer that matching skill and aptitude with career choice was essential in building a strong and reliable workforce. Despite the innovative approaches used by the ancient Chinese and Greeks, much is lost to antiquity and little recorded history of the usage of assessment exists for the next 2,000 years. It is not until the 1500s that we again begin to see assessment play a functional role in society.

Assessment Practices in the Middle Ages (1500s)

In the 1500s a Spanish physician by the name of Juan Huarte began studying and researching the human faculties of memory, intelligence, and imagination. Huarte believed that people use different faculties to address problems that arise in their lives. While some people may use imagination to conjure solutions for an existing problem that might work, others rely on memory and apply prior remedies that have proved to be effective in the past at solving problems. Each approach has its own merits. The selection of which faculty to activate is unique to the individual. Huarte's work in human intelligence led him to publish an influential textbook in 1575 called *Examen de los Ingenios Para las Scienzias*, which translated into English reads *The Trial of Wits: Discovering the Great Differences of Wits Among Men and What Sort of Learning Suits Best With Each Genius*. In his book, Huarte posits that all students should be assessed prior to the beginning of their academic training. Based on the results of this assessment, students should be placed in programs that prepare them for careers that best match their intellectual capabilities as determined by their assessment. In so doing, Huarte effectively called for the first usage of mental or intelligence testing. Consequently, his work is widely regarded as being a precursor for the modern field of educational psychology. These early examples laid the foundation for the period of rapid growth and development of assessment practices known as the modern testing movement.

Around the same time, the Jesuits began expanding assessment practices by introducing the use of the written examination. In 1540, Jesuit universities were administering written examinations to students across Europe. The results of these examinations were then used for screening, placement, and evaluative purposes. While the use of written examinations was seen as an improvement over existing methods of evaluating students and their acquisition of knowledge, there were inherent biases in the approach. According to Crusan (2010), "since literacy was the exclusive privilege of nobility and the clergy, the use of written examinations served as a means of social control" (p. 20). In other words, only the social elite would have the means to succeed at a written examination. Nevertheless, the use of written assessments became quite popular and represents one of the primary assessment strategies used in educational settings today.

The Modern Testing Movement (1800s)

The origins of the modern testing movement can be traced back to the Victorian era and the work of English biologist Francis Galton in the 1800s. Inspired by the work of his cousin Charles Darwin, Galton began studying heredity. Specifically, he examined variations in human ability; hypothesizing that successful individuals were those who had inherited superior qualities from their parents and previous generations. His work is recorded in his book *Hereditary Genius,* published in 1869. To test his hypothesis, Galton sought to compare the abilities of biologically related and unrelated individuals. Based on the premise that individuals learn based on their interactions with the environment around them, he employed a series of sensory discrimination tests. The more perceptive an individual's senses, the more information that person would be able to derive from the surrounding environment and the better equipped that person would be to make intelligent decisions. Galton's research led him to conclude that human mental abilities and personality traits were largely inherited (D. Seligman, 2002). Additionally, Galton's work led to the development of several statistical concepts used in measurement and research today, including the normal curve and correlational analyses. In fact, it was Galton who encouraged his student Karl Pearson to develop an appropriate way to indicate the strength of association between two variables. The commonly used Pearson product-moment correlation coefficient (r) is the result of their work.

Wilhelm Wundt stands as another pioneer in the assessment and testing movement. Regarded as the "father of experimental psychology," Wundt established the first psychological laboratory at the University of Leipzig in Germany, in 1869. Wundt and his colleagues also were drawn to studying human intelligence. In particular, they were interested in identifying the factors associated with intelligence. Their experiments were largely focused on sensory phenomena. Wundt and colleagues assessed participants' sensitivity to various visual, auditory, olfactory, and tactile stimuli by measuring simple reaction time. However, unlike Galton, they were more interested in identifying those characteristics that made humans similar than those that made them different. As Anastasi and Urbina (1997) note, the early experimental psychologists were more concerned with the formulation of generalized descriptions of human behavior than they were with measuring individual differences. To best illustrate the purpose of Wundt's work, consider the following experiment. An individual is asked to place a hand in a bucket filled with ice. The frigid temperature of the ice would cause most people to recoil their hand from the bucket. Experimental psychologists would measure the time it took for you to remove your hand and compare the results. The focus here is on the fact that removing your hand is the appropriate response that would be common for all participants. Those who did not remove their hand and were able to endure the cold temperatures of the ice were accepted as statistical outliers in the study and excluded from further analysis. The work of Wundt and others at the university laboratory highlighted the importance of rigorous control of experimental conditions. This emphasis led to the development of standardization procedures that play a prominent role in modern assessment practices.

A discussion of the early testing movement would not be complete without mentioning the work of James McKeen Cattell. An American psychologist, Cattell was actually a doctoral student of Wundt's at the University of Leipzig. Following his graduation he accepted a postdoctoral fellowship in London and had the opportunity to study in the laboratory of Francis Galton. In 1888 he returned to the United States and accepted a position as professor of psychology at the University of Pennsylvania. It was here that he established the first American experimental psychology laboratory. In 1891 he accepted a faculty position at Columbia University, where he served as a professor and department head for the next 26 years, training the next generation of American psychologists.

In addition to starting the experimental psychology movement in America, Cattell also is well known for his early work in human intelligence. In a paper published in 1890, Cattell introduced the term **mental test** for the first time in the professional literature. In his paper Cattell described a process by which a series of tests could be administered annually to college students to assess their intellectual level. Representing his view of intelligence as being multifaceted, his mental tests were designed to measure several human characteristics, including muscular strength, speed of movement, sensitivity to pain, keenness of vision and hearing, weight discrimination, reaction time, and memory (Anastasi & Urbina, 1997). The inclusion of memory as a tested characteristic of intelligence was a pioneering innovation of Cattell's. While he believed he was pioneering the assessment of intelligence by measuring these constructs, subsequent researchers found no discernible relationship between performance on Cattell's mental test battery and academic performance. In the late 1890s and early 1900s, the work of psychologists Alfred Binet and Victor Henri would render the mental tests developed by Cattell irrelevant.

The work of early researchers like Galton, Wundt, and Cattell helped establish a base understanding of how standardized testing and observation could be applied to gain additional knowledge about people. Their efforts led to rapid growth and expansion for the assessment field during the 20th century. Because of the many practical applications associated with being able to measure differences between and among people, assessment practices were applied in many different directions, including the assessment of intelligence, achievement, and personality (see Guided Practice Exercise 1.2). The following sections detail some of the seminal developments in assessment in the modern era.

GUIDED PRACTICE EXERCISE 1.2

Historical Influences on Modern Practice

Discuss how the work of Galton, Wundt, and Cattell influenced the development of modern testing. Discuss some key historical events that influenced how modern-day assessments are used.

Assessment in the Modern Era (1890s–1910s)

In the 1890s French psychologists Alfred Binet and Victor Henri began publishing in the area of human intelligence. They believed that the previously held views of intelligence were focused too heavily on sensory aspects and that intelligence involved more complex functions then those originally identified by Cattell and Galton. The two published a paper together in 1895 in which they defined intelligence in terms of a collection of complex mental abilities such as memory, abstraction, judgment, analytic processing, and reasoning. The full extent of their findings would not be realized until nearly a decade later. In 1904 the Minister of Public Instruction in Paris commissioned a group to study "educationally retarded" children. The committee, of which Binet was an appointed member, was charged with finding a means to differentiate mentally retarded from normal children so that alternative education could be provided for those most in need. The work of this committee resulted in the publication of the initial Binet-Simon scale of intelligence (Binet & Simon, 1905). Binet and Simon envisioned intelligence as a learned entity. As a result, their instrument was developed to assess an individual's intelligence based on his or her age. The individually administered test consisted of 30 items designed to assess judgment, comprehension, and reasoning. Items increased in complexity throughout the test. An example of a simple task would be for a child to shake hands with the examiner. A more complex task would require the child to point to various body parts named by the examiner. The most complex tasks asked children to repeat back a series of seven random digits or provide rhyming words for a given word. Revisions to the test were made in both 1908 and 1911. The 1908 revision included the introduction of the term **intelligence quotient (IQ)**. The intelligence quotient was a ratio of a person's mental age and chronological age. Mental age was the level at which a child could pass all of the tasks deemed appropriate for a given age. For example a 6-year-old child who was able to successfully complete all tasks usually passed by 8-year-olds would have a mental age of 8.0. A more detailed description of the Binet-Simon intelligence tests appears in Chapter 7.

In 1916, an educational psychology professor at Stanford University by the name of Lewis Terman published a revised version of the Binet-Simon intelligence scale. In addition to translating the instrument into English, Terman performed several statistical analyses and conducted numerous normative studies on the original scale. The result of these efforts led to the replacement of many of the tests of mental ability at age levels other than those for which they originally were designed. In addition, Terman added several new subtests he both created himself and borrowed from other sources. His revisions have proved to be successful, and for this reason the test is now referred to as the Stanford–Binet test of Intelligence.

The advent of World War I in the 1910s saw the military also begin applying the assessment of intelligence to its recruiting efforts. As World War I began and it became apparent that the United States would be entering the fray, Robert Yerkes, then serving as president of the American Psychological Association, urged the membership of his society to get involved in the war effort. The result was the publication of the Army Alpha and Beta tests in 1917. Developed by a group of psychologists specializing in the study of human intelligence, the tests were designed to assess intellectual and emotional functioning of recruits entering the military and to assist in the selection of officers and the assignment of recruits to specific military occupations or units. Because of the large number of recruits that needed to be screened in a relatively short period of time, these tests were designed to be group-administered rather than individually administered tests. The **Army Alpha** was a test that measured verbal ability, numerical ability, ability to follow directions, and knowledge of information. The **Army Beta** was the nonverbal counterpart to the Army Alpha. It was used to evaluate the aptitude of illiterate, unschooled, or non-English-speaking recruits. Both instruments used a multiple-choice response format, a relatively new innovation pioneered by Arthur S. Otis. Although Otis gave permission to administer his mental tests to over 1.75 million soldiers, the war came to an end before they could be put to use in the selection and assignment of new recruits. Although not used in an official context during World War I, the Army Alpha and Army Beta tests were released to the public following the war and served as the foundation on which subsequent military screening instruments were built. In addition, these tests provided the prototype for most other group-based tests used to assess a variety of constructs (e.g., achievement, intelligence, specific aptitude, psychopathology). Figure 1.1 illustrates examples of items appearing on the Army Beta test.

A discussion of the early part of the 20th century would not be complete without mentioning the advent of the vocational guidance movement. Two of the leading figures in this movement were Frank Parsons and Jesse B. Davis. Often referred to as the father of guidance, Parsons is best known for his work with the Boston Vocational Bureau. It was here that he developed his three-step model of career counseling. His model required counselors to (1) gather information about the person, (2) gather information about the world of work, and (3) match the person to the appropriate occupation in the world of work. While Parsons did not develop any specific strategies or tools for assessing these three areas, his ideas were important in the development and construction of many career and vocational inventories that would follow. Jesse B. Davis was one of the first individuals to establish a systematic school guidance program. As a high school principal in the Chicago area, Davis encouraged his faculty to begin integrating career assessment into their curriculum. The vocational guidance movement led to the development of the school counseling specialization currently practiced.

Figure 1.1   Sample Questions on the Army Beta Test of Intelligence

Source: United States War Department.

Assessment in the Modern Era (1920s–1930s)

Although the intelligence tests developed by Binet and Simon and the Army Alpha and Beta tests developed by Yerkes and the APA served social purposes (educational and military selection and assignment), they largely were developed without any real theoretical foundation. In the 1920s and 1930s, a focused effort was made to develop a strong theoretical understanding of what intelligence really was and how it could best be measured. To this end, a number of prominent psychologists began developing their theories on intelligence. Charles Spearman (1927) proposed one of the earliest theories of intelligence. Spearman believed that intelligence actually comprised two factors: general intelligence (g) and specific intelligence (s; see Figure 1.2). General intelligence referred to an individual's overall intellectual ability. It is evident across many different tasks and activities. In his research, Spearman found that those individuals who scored highly in a particular intellectual task tended to score high on other tests of mental ability. An example of an individual with a high *g* factor would be a student on the Dean's list in college. The high grade point average required to be on this list would indicate that the student is able to perform at a high level in all classes, be they math, language arts, or science. The other factor represents specific intelligence. This is the mental ability needed to perform well at a distinct task that may not be generalizable to other areas. I might be able to understand tax codes and prepare my own income tax returns each year, but I may have no idea how to change the oil in my car.

Figure 1.2   Charles Spearman's Conceptualization of Global (G) and Specific (s) Intelligences

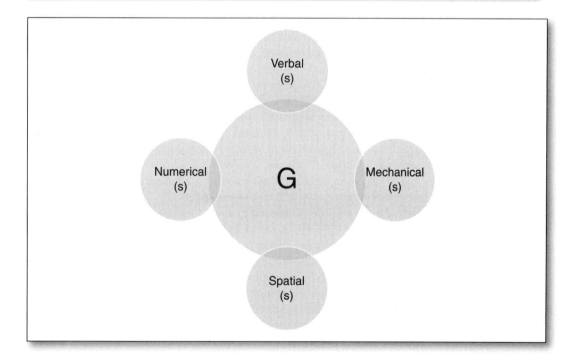

In the 1930s Louis Thurstone argued that the *g* factor proposed by Spearman did not exist and was in fact just a statistical artifact created by the mathematical analyses used to study it. In its place, Thurstone (1938) identified seven independent factors, called **primary abilities**, which constituted human intelligence: word fluency, verbal comprehension, spatial visualization, number facility, associative memory, reasoning, and perceptual speed.

In 1939 David Wechsler, a clinical psychologist at Bellevue Psychiatric Hospital in New York City, introduced a new assessment instrument designed to measure adult intelligence. His instrument, known as the Wechsler-Bellevue Intelligence Scale, featured a battery of intelligence tests. The scale was designed to measure the "global capacity of the individual to act purposefully, to think rationally, and to deal effectively with his environment" (Wechsler, 1939, p. 3). His tests became extremely popular and led to several revisions. In 1955 he revised the test and renamed it the Wechsler Adult Intelligence Scale (WAIS). The WAIS has since been revised in 1981, 1997, and its most current version (WAIS-IV) in 2008. Wechsler's test provided a couple of important advances that have helped shape our understanding of intelligence and how it can be measured. First, his test consisted of several subtests that measured various aspects of mental ability. Combined, these subtests provide a global measure of one's intelligence. Second, he introduced the use of a deviation IQ score. The deviation IQ score, unlike the ratio IQ score used in the Binet-Simon test, allows for comparisons to be made between individuals. An average score of 100 was established with a standard deviation of 15.

In the 1920s and 1930s, interest in assessment was not limited to examinations of individual intelligence (Whiston, 2009). In 1921 Hermann Rorschach developed the Rorschach Inkblot Test under the title *Psychodiagnostik*. The Rorschach Inkblot Test includes 10 inkblot cards that feature ambiguous stimuli. Test takers are asked to describe what they see in the image. Their responses are then interpreted based on the determinants (form and color of the shape) and localized details of the stimulus that triggered their response. Another personality test developed during this time was the Thematic Apperception Test (1935), in which test takers were presented with a picture and asked to tell a story about it. Their story was to include a depiction of what was going on, what happened previously, and what was likely to follow. Their responses were examined and themes were identified. A further discussion of these and other projective personality tests is provided in Chapter 10. Following up on the work of Parsons and the career counseling movement, standardized vocational inventories were developed. The Strong Vocational Interest Inventory (1927) and Kuder Preference Record–Individual (1932) emerged as viable instruments to use in assessing individual interests and aligning those interests with vocational careers.

The rapid growth of the assessment field led to a need to classify the instruments and inventories being developed. In the 1930s Oscar Buros set forth to establish a reference source that would list available assessment instruments and evaluate their structure and uses. He titled his reference the *Mental Measurements Yearbook* (*MMY*). The first *MMY* was published in 1938 and, according to Buros, it allowed "leading scholars to publish candidly critical reviews of commercially available tests designed to serve the interests of both practitioners and the public at large" (Buros Center for Testing, 2014). The *MMY* is published every 2–3 years and the current edition, the 19th, was published in 2013.

Assessment in the Modern Era (1940s–1950s)

In the 1940s, the fascination with personality assessment increased. Researchers looked to add to the existing projective instruments available by creating more standardized and formal measures. One noteworthy event in this period was the development and publication of the Minnesota Multiphasic Personality Inventory (MMPI) in 1943. The MMPI was developed to provide an objective measure of psychopathology. At the time, personality tests were projective in nature (e.g., Rorschach Inkblot Test, Rotter Incomplete Sentence Blank), and the subjective scoring of these instruments led to much variability in clinical diagnoses among professionals. The authors of the MMPI, Starke R. Hathaway and J. C. McKinley, sought to make an objective measure that featured criterion keying of items. This means that the items on the test were selected based on their ability to accurately tap and assess various signs and symptoms of many diagnostic labels. The MMPI became a universally popular instrument and has been used in many settings. Revised in 1989, the MMPI-II remains one of the most widely used personality assessments by counselors and other mental health clinicians.

The increase in the use of tests during this period led to a need for a more systematic way of managing the assessment process. In an effort to address growing criticism of assessment practices, the American Psychological Association developed a set of standards that outlined the appropriate selection and usage of tests. These standards would be revised in later years and evolve into the *Standards for Educational and Psychological Testing* jointly published in 1985 by APA, AERA, and NCME. In addition to the development of professional standards, advances in scoring methods also took place. The formation of the Educational Testing Service (ETS) led to the development of electronic scoring methods. These new methods greatly reduced the number of scoring errors that were common using hand-scoring methods and allowed for more complicated scoring procedures to be employed.

Assessment in the Modern Era (1960s–1970s)

By the 1960s, testing and assessment had become common practice in a variety of fields. Educational, vocational, and military applications had millions of individuals being tested and placed in various programs based on the results of their tests. The widespread use led many to begin questioning the validity of the testing process. In particular, there were many complaints that testing and assessment were flawed practices inherently filled with many biases. In particular, assessment instruments were scrutinized for ethnic bias, fairness, and accuracy (Whiston, 2009). This increased scrutiny revealed many problems with existing instruments. It was noted that many instruments were normed using samples that were not representative of the larger population, and therefore gender and ethnic biases existed. As a result several legal precedents were established that helped shape the way assessment was practiced. Among the more notable legal challenges was the 1967 case *Hobson v. Hansen*. In this case, a federal court ruled that group-administered ability tests were discriminatory and biased against minorities. As a result, these tests could no longer be used as the sole source of data in determining special education placement in the schools.

The Era of Discontent, a term Maloney and Ward (1976) used to refer to this period, also brought about a change in the way assessment was to be practiced. The noted problems led to a call for greater training and control over the use of tests and assessment measures. Minimum competencies were established to provide a standard of care and regulate who was allowed to administer various testing instruments. Besides increased standards, the 1970s also saw passage of the Family Educational Rights and Privacy Act (FERPA) in 1974 and the Education for All Handicapped Children Act of 1975 (PL 94-142). FERPA had several components that related to the practice of testing and assessment. In addition to giving parents and children over the age of 18 access to their own records, FERPA also specified topics that could and could not be assessed without parental or, for students over 18, student consent. PL 94-142 led to the widespread use of intelligence and achievement tests in the schools. Together, the events of the 1960s and 1970s helped tighten the testing process and further establish the credibility of the assessment process.

Assessment in the Modern Era (1980s–1990s)

In response to some of the concerns raised in the 1970s, the 1980s saw revisions made to many of the more popular assessment instruments. These revisions primarily dealt with increasing the diversity of the sample groups used to norm the instruments. This practice enabled these instruments to be used more effectively with an increasingly diverse client population. Among the many revised instruments released during this decade were the Minnesota Multiphasic Personality Inventory-II (1989), the Wechsler Intelligence Scale for Children-III (1989), and the Wechsler Adult Intelligence Scale-Revised (1981) and Wechsler Adult Intelligence Scale-III (1997). In addition, new assessment instruments that were designed to be more sensitive to the cultural differences in a diverse society were created. Most notable among this group of new instruments was the Kauffman Assessment Battery for Children released in 1983.

The 1990s saw a rise in authentic assessment. **Authentic assessment** refers to assessment tasks that test student abilities by measuring how well students perform in real-life contexts. In this approach, teachers assessed students using measures consistent with the instructional area being taught and gathered multiple indicators of student performance in order to assess student success. The use of authentic assessment changed the way teachers evaluated their students in school. Now, student success was determined by their ability to not only *recall* important information presented in class, but also *apply* it to a real-world setting. Using a variety of assessment measures ensured that a student's performance was accurately being represented in the test results and was not simply an artifact of the type of test being used. In other words, authentic assessment allows students who may not be the best test takers to demonstrate their knowledge and ability in other ways such as projects, essays, reports, or case studies.

Current Assessment Practices (2000–Present)

Current testing practices are being influenced heavily by the use of computers and technology. These innovations have helped facilitate the testing process and allow for greater precision in score reporting and interpretation. As Scalise and Gifford (2006) note, the use of computer-based assessment measures vastly expands assessment possibilities beyond the limitations of traditional paper-and-pencil instruments. As Internet access increases, the ability of counselors and educators to reach previously unreachable populations will expand and influence the way services are delivered (see Guided Practice Exercise 1.3).

Continual revisions to existing instruments have been made in response to new knowledge and technologies. Revised versions of the Strong Interest Inventory (2004), the Wechsler Intelligence Scale for Children-IV (2003), and the Wechsler Adult Intelligence Scale-IV (2008) have all been released, and more are planned for the coming years. Although the future of the practice of assessment is difficult to predict, it no doubt will include a greater push to be more inclusive and sensitive to individual differences.

GUIDED PRACTICE EXERCISE 1.3

Identifying Assessment Instruments Currently Used

The types of assessment instruments you are most likely to use in your counseling practice will depend largely on the setting in which you work, the age of the clients you see, and the problems you are likely to encounter. To help you better prepare for working in your chosen field, contact a counselor in that field (a school counselor or licensed professional counselor), and ask that person to share with you the assessment instruments he or she most often uses or is required to be able to interpret in his or her work as a counselor. You can then get a head start on your career by reading more about and gaining additional exposure to these instruments.

ASSESSMENT COMPETENCIES REQUIRED OF PROFESSIONAL COUNSELORS

To conduct assessment properly, there are several competencies counselors are required to possess. These competencies are included in several sources and should be reviewed by counselors before engaging in assessment-related activities. A review of the assessment competencies counselors should possess, as well as the source of these competencies, is included in this section.

American Counseling Association (ACA) *Code of Ethics*

The ACA *Code of Ethics* is a document that establishes the principles defining ethical behavior and best practices in counseling. All ACA members are required to practice in accordance with the *Code of Ethics*. The *Code of Ethics* contains eight main sections and is revised every 7–10 years. In the 2014 *Code of Ethics*, the most recent version at the time of this writing, Section E is devoted entirely to evaluation, assessment, and interpretation. Included in Section E is a discussion of the competencies needed to use and interpret assessment instruments, informed consent in assessments, release of data to qualified professionals, diagnosis of mental disorders, instrument selection, conditions of assessment administration, multicultural issues, scoring and interpretation of assessments, assessment security, obsolete assessments and outdated results, and forensic evaluation. These standards help ensure that counselors are using sound assessment procedures in a professional manner that is appropriate to the situation and beneficial to the client.

In addition to acting in accordance with the ACA (2014) *Code of Ethics*, counselors should become familiar with a number of additional standards designed to help guide assessment practices. In 1985, the Joint Committee on Testing Practices (JCTP) was established by AERA, APA, and NCME as a consortium of professional organizations and a forum for counseling and education-related associations to improve test use through education. Despite disbanding in 2007, the JCTP published several useful documents related to testing and assessment such as the *Code of Fair Testing Practices in Education, Responsibilities of Users of Standardized Tests, Standards of Qualifications of Test Users,* and the *Rights and Responsibilities of Test Takers: Guidelines and Expectations.* Each of these documents is still used and referenced by assessment specialists. A brief description of each of these valuable assessment resources is provided below.

Code of Fair Testing Practices in Education

Originally developed by the JCTP in 1988, the *Code of Fair Testing Practices in Education* describes the primary obligations test developers and administrators have toward test takers. A revised version was published in 2004 to address advances in assessment practice. Included in the code are 31 standards that provide guidance for both test developers and test users in four key areas: developing and selecting appropriate tests, administering and scoring tests, reporting and interpreting results, and informing test takers. Although initially developed to address testing and assessment in education settings, the principles presented are applicable to counselors as well.

Responsibilities of Users of Standardized Tests

In 2003, the Association for Assessment in Research Counseling (AARC; formerly known as the Association for Assessment in Counseling) developed the *Responsibilities of Users of Standardized Tests* (RUST). The RUST statement outlined what professionals needed to be aware of in terms of effectively integrating standardized tests into the assessment process. The RUST statement includes standards in seven categories: "qualifications of test users, technical knowledge, test selection, test administration, test scoring, interpreting test results, communicating test results" (p. 1). Adherence to these standards is seen as a way to ensure responsible testing practices among counselors and educators.

Standards of Qualifications of Test Users

The *Standards of Qualifications of Test Users* (AAC, 2003b), based on the *Standards for Educational and Psychological Testing*, RUST, ACA and American School Counselor Association (ASCA; a division of ACA) ethical standards, were developed by the ACA Standards for

Test Use Task Force to address qualifications of counselors to use assessment instruments and defined seven competencies in the following areas: skill and knowledge of theory as applied to testing; understanding of test theory, construction, reliability, and validity; working knowledge of sampling techniques, norms, and descriptive correlational and predictive statistics; ability to review, select, and administer test appropriately; administration and interpretation of test scores; cross-cultural and diversity considerations; and knowledge of standards and ethical codes.

Rights and Responsibilities of Test Takers: Guidelines and Expectations

The *Rights and Responsibilities of Test Takers: Guidelines and Expectations* (JCTP, 2000) clarifies "the expectations that test takers may reasonably have about the testing process, and the expectations that those who develop, administer, and use tests may have on other test takers" (p. 1). This document was designed to help address some of the confusion people may have about tests and the role they play in the assessment process. Whereas the RUST statement describes what counselors should do, the *Rights and Responsibilities of Test Takers* describes what clients need to do in the counseling process.

AARC Assessment Competency Standards

As a division of ACA, AARC regularly collaborates with other divisions to produce assessment competency standards in various counseling specialty areas. These competency standards provide a description of the knowledge and skills counselors aspire to possess in order to be effective in assessment and evaluation. Counselors can now access competencies for assessment in career counseling; marriage, couple, and family counseling; mental health counseling; multicultural counseling; school counseling; and substance abuse counseling. For example, AARC and ASCA (1998) created the *Competencies in Assessment and Evaluation for School Counselors* that outlines nine competencies and skills listed under each competency. According to the second competency, school counselors can identify, access, and evaluate the most commonly used assessment instruments:

- They know which assessment instruments are most commonly used in school settings to assess intelligence, aptitude, achievement, personality, work values, and interests, including computer-assisted versions and other alternate formats.
- They know the dimensions along which assessment instruments should be evaluated; including purpose, validity, utility, norms, reliability and measurement error, score reporting method, and consequences of use.
- They can obtain and evaluate information about the quality of those assessment instruments. (pp. 1–2)

These standards merely describe a set of best practices that can be employed by counselors employed in the schools. School counselors should also act in accordance with the ASCA (2010) *Ethical Standards for School Counselors*.

More recently, the International Association of Marriage and Family Counselors collaborated with AACE to form the Marriage, Couple, and Family Counseling Assessment Competencies (Garrett et al., 2011). As outlined in the second competency, counselors understand basic concepts of standardized and nonstandardized testing and other assessment techniques. Marriage, couple, and family counselors can

- explain the differences between norm-referenced and criterion-referenced assessment,
- articulate the need for and use of environmental assessment,
- understand and use performance assessments,
- understand the use of individual and group test and inventory methods,
- effectively make and document behavioral observations during assessment, and
- understand the limitations of computer-managed and computer-assisted assessment methods. (p. 1)

Assessment-Related CACREP Accreditation Standards

In addition to the aforementioned assessment competencies, an accrediting body has established assessment standards. Established in 1982, CACREP grants accreditation to graduate counseling programs that have met the standards set forth by the counseling profession. The purpose of the CACREP (2009) *Standards* is to establish educational excellence and ensure that students develop a counselor professional identity and master the knowledge, skills, and dispositions to practice effectively (CACREP, 2009).

In a CACREP program, students are required to complete eight core curricular areas of study, one of which is assessment. Standard II.G.7 Assessment in the CACREP (2009) *Standards* outlines the specific curricular experience required of every student in the program. Assessment includes studies that provide an understanding of individual and group approaches to assessment and evaluation in a multicultural society. In regard to Standard II.G.7 Assessment, students should demonstrate knowledge and skills related to

- historical perspectives concerning the nature and meaning of assessment;
- basic concepts of standardized and nonstandardized testing and other assessment techniques, including norm-referenced and criterion-referenced assessment, environmental assessment, performance assessment, individual and group test and inventory methods, psychological testing, and behavioral observations;
- statistical concepts, including scales of measurement, measures of central tendency, indices of variability, shapes and types of distributions, and correlations (see Chapter 2);
- reliability (i.e., theory of measurement error, models of reliability, and the use of reliability information; see Chapter 3);
- validity (i.e., evidence of validity, types of validity, and the relationship between reliability and validity; see Chapter 4);

- social and cultural factors related to the assessment and evaluation of individuals, groups, and specific populations; and
- ethical strategies for selecting, administering, and interpreting assessment and evaluation instruments and techniques in counseling (see Chapter 5). (pp. 13–14)

The 2009 Standards also suggest that in addition to the assessment-related core curricular experiences outlined in Section II.G.7, programs (addictions counseling; career counseling; clinical mental health; marriage, couple, and family counseling; school counseling; and student affairs and college counseling) must provide evidence that students possess knowledge and skills related to practice in six broad areas: (1) foundations; (2) counseling prevention and intervention; (3) diversity and advocacy; (4) assessment; (5) research and evaluations; and (6) diagnosis. Under each aforementioned broad area, certain objectives in terms of knowledge and skills related to practice are outlined. The assessment category under each degree is divided into sections G (knowledge) and H (skills). For example, students seeking a master's degree from a CACREP-accredited school counseling program should possess assessment *knowledge* in the following areas:

- understands the influence of multiple factors (e.g., abuse, violence, eating disorders, attention deficit hyperactivity disorder, childhood depression) that may affect the personal, social, and academic functioning of students
- knows the signs and symptoms of substance abuse in children and adolescents, as well as the signs and symptoms of living in a home where substance abuse occurs
- identifies various forms of needs assessments for academic, career, and personal/social development (CACREP, 2009, pp. 42–43)

Students must also demonstrate the following *skills* related to assessment:

- assesses and interprets students' strengths and needs, recognizing uniqueness in cultures, languages, values, backgrounds, and abilities
- selects appropriate assessment strategies that can be used to evaluate a student's academic, career, and personal/social development
- analyzes assessment information in a manner that produces valid inferences when evaluating the needs of individual students and assessing the effectiveness of educational programs
- makes appropriate referrals to school and/or community resources
- assesses barriers that impede students' academic, career, and personal/social development (CACREP, 2009, p. 43)

The professional competencies and the CACREP (2009) *Standards* describe the knowledge and skills that counselors need in the areas of assessment (see Guided Practice Exercise 1.4). The appropriate use of assessment results informs recommendations and effective treatment planning. Thus, as defined by both professional competencies and ethical codes, counselors are expected to have knowledge, skills, and training in assessment.

GUIDED PRACTICE EXERCISE 1.4

Personalizing the CACREP Standards

The professional competencies and the CACREP (2009) *Standards* describe the *knowledge* and *skills* that counselors need in the areas of assessment. After reviewing the CACREP standards related to assessment, what areas in terms of both knowledge and skills can you identify as areas of strength? Which specific standards do you hope to improve or gain more knowledge?

CONTROVERSIAL ISSUES IN COUNSELING ASSESSMENTS

Assessment continues to be a crucial and controversial issue in counseling. One of the more controversial issues is the use of tests with culturally diverse clients. Counselors must continually evaluate whether the assessment practices they use with clients are appropriate to use with diverse populations (see Chapter 15 for a more in-depth examination of the use of assessments with diverse populations). In addition, the use of test results to make high-stakes decisions also receives plenty of attention. As you will see in Chapter 16, a long history of important decisions related to educational and career access and placement has been based on data and test results that are both unreliable and invalid for the purposes they were being used. Because of these gross misuses, many individuals are hesitant to participate in assessment activities for fear of how the results may be used to their detriment. Finally, the use of computers and technology in counseling and assessment also is a source of much controversy. Computers are now being used to administer, score, and interpret test results. While these practices have certainly made the role of the counselor easier in some aspects, there is still much debate over how these instruments compare to traditional methods of assessment and how their use in the counseling process may affect clients.

KEYSTONES

- Assessment is a process of data collection that integrates test information with information from other sources. Key processes include identifying the reason for referral/stated concern, gathering background information, conducting observations of the client, interpreting test results in light of all other information known about a client, and generating a list of potential interventions that could be employed based on all available information.
- Assessment practices have been in use for thousands of years and have played a major role in structuring our social and educational systems.
- World War I was a major event in world history that had a profound impact on interest in individual differences and sparked the rapid development of numerous intelligence tests.

- Counselors are responsible for following a number of standards to help guide assessment practice, including the ACA (2014) *Code of Ethics, Code of Fair Testing Practices in Education, Responsible Test Use,* and *Rights and Responsibilities of Test Takers: Guidelines and Expectations.*
- The professional competencies and the CACREP (2009) *Standards* describe the knowledge and skills that counselors need in the areas of assessment.

KEY TERMS

assessment	authentic assessment	primary abilities
Army Alpha	intelligence quotient (IQ)	psychological test
Army Beta	mental test	

ADDITIONAL RESOURCES

Websites to Assessment-Related Organizations

- American Counseling Association
  www.counseling.org
- American Educational Research Association
  www.aera.net
- American Evaluation Association
  www.eval.org
- Association for Assessment and Research in Counseling
  http://aarc-counseling.org
- National Center for Research on Evaluation, Standards, and Student Testing
  www.cse.ucla.edu
- National Council on Measurement in Education
  www.ncme.org

Assessment and Testing Documents

- ACA Position Statement on High Stakes Testing
  http://aarc-counseling.org/assets/cms/uploads/files/High_Stakes.pdf
- Code of Fair Testing Practices in Education
  http://aarc-counseling.org/assets/cms/uploads/files/codefair.pdf

- Responsibilities of Users of Standardized Tests

  http://aarc-counseling.org/assets/cms/uploads/files/rust.pdf

- Standards for Qualifications of Test Users

  http://aarc-counseling.org/assets/cms/uploads/files/standards.pdf

- Rights and Responsibilities of Test Takers

  http://aarc-counseling.org/assets/cms/uploads/files/rights.pdf

Student Study Site: Visit the Student Study Site at **www.sagepub.com/watson** to access additional study tools, including quizzes, web resources, and journal articles.

Basic Assessment and Statistical Concepts

LEARNING OBJECTIVES

After reading this chapter, you will be able to

- Explain the difference between descriptive and inferential statistics
- Describe the concept of a variable and how it is used in counseling assessment
- Define the scales of measurement used to summarize data
- Summarize and organize data using frequency distributions
- Calculate the various measures of central tendency and variability
- Interpret standard scores

In Chapter 1, you learned that assessment is an important activity a counselor performs throughout the counseling process. Whether it is gathering initial intake data, assessing the severity of a client's presenting problem, measuring treatment progress, or conducting program evaluations, the collection of data is paramount to the work counselors do. The challenge becomes deciphering what all of the data collected means in a way that can benefit the counseling process. To do so in an effective manner, counselors need to gain proficiency in understanding, interpreting, and communicating assessment results. To do so, a basic understanding of the statistical concepts that are used in conjunction with the development and interpretation of tests and test scores is needed (Hood & Johnson, 2009).

In this chapter we introduce you to a number of basic statistical concepts that will help you organize, summarize, and interpret assessment data. Although a cursory overview of the statistical computations behind these concepts is presented, the primary focus of this chapter is to show you how these concepts relate to the work of professional counselors in all of the different settings in which they function. Additional information regarding the theory and calculation of these statistical concepts can be found in most introductory statistics textbooks. Specifically, this chapter describes (a) the types of statistics used to gather data on client variables, (b) scales of measurement used to classify data, (c) frequency distributions, (d) measures of central tendency and variability, and (e) standard scores and the normal curve.

STATISTICS: A TOOL FOR DESCRIBING, ORGANIZING, AND INTERPRETING DATA

Throughout the counseling process counselors are constantly collecting data to better understand the clients with whom they work. This data can become quite voluminous at times and overwhelming to the counselor. To assist in cases such as this, counselors can employ a variety of statistics to make the process of understanding client data easier. **Statistics** are defined as a set of tools and techniques used for describing, organizing, and interpreting information. They serve three primary purposes. First, they describe and display data. Statistics tell us what is happening, how frequently it is happening, and to which clients. Second, statistics help explain relationships. In addition to knowing what is happening to our clients, it is important to know what might be affecting or be affected by certain factors. If a client reports feeling depressed for the past month, it would be helpful for a counselor to know what may have happened a month ago to cause the onset of the depressive symptoms or what may be continuing in the client's life that is worsening the problem and causing the client to feel more depressed. Finally, statistics allow counselors to make conclusions and inferences based on collected data. If we determine that the client suffered a marital separation, lost a job, and had to foreclose on a home a month ago, we could infer that these factors might be contributing to the client's current depressed mood. The ability to make inferences then allows us to structure treatment plans aimed at addressing these related factors that are causing the client to be depressed. In so doing, we are able to treat the root causes and not just client's response (depression) to these root causes.

There are many different types of statistics that can be used to better our understanding of data collected. These can be grouped into two basic categories: descriptive and inferential statistics. **Descriptive statistics** are statistics that can be used to organize and describe the characteristics of a set of data. Descriptive statistics tell us what is occurring, how often it is occurring, and to whom it is occurring. Examples of descriptive statistics include averages, percentages, total frequencies, and measures of variability. **Inferential statistics** are statistics used to draw inferences from a smaller group of data (sample) that then can be applied to a larger group (population). Inferential statistics encompass many of the statistical techniques used in data analysis, including correlations, mean comparisons, and hypothesis testing (see Case Illustration 2.1). Throughout the remainder of this chapter we will focus primarily on descriptive statistics and the manner in which they can be computed and used by counselors to guide the counseling process.

CASE ILLUSTRATION   2.1

The 16-Personality Factor (16-PF) Questionnaire is a personality assessment instrument used by counselors in a variety of counseling settings. It is designed to discover and measure the source traits of human personality. Clients are administered the questionnaire and asked to respond to a number of behavioral situations with how they think they might respond. Scores are provided on 16 primary personality scales and 5 global personality scales. Raw scores and sten scores are produced for each individual who takes the test. The raw scores represent how the individual did on the test. They can be summed, averaged, or divided into frequencies. These raw scores would be classified as descriptive statistics. The sten scores are standardized scores that show how this individual scored in relation to the norm group for this instrument. Sten scores are inferential statistics because they are used to compare the individual to the greater population in a way that is meaningful.

An important concept to understand when using descriptive statistics is that of a variable. A **variable** is any construct that can assume multiple values. Variables are defined using either numeric values or categories. Variables defined using numeric values are referred to as **quantitative variables**. For example, we can collect data regarding income level by asking a client to report his or her yearly earnings. The client's response will be a numeric value and thus represent a quantitative variable. Quantitative variables can be either discrete or continuous. **Discrete data** are units of measurement that cannot be divided or broken down into smaller units. The number of children a person has is a measure of discrete data. Answers to this question can only be whole numbers (nobody has 3.2 children despite what statistics say constitutes the average American family). **Continuous data** can be subdivided infinitely as they are more approximations based on available data. Depending on the precision of your measuring instrument, time can be measured down to milliseconds and nanoseconds. Opposite of quantitative variables are the variables defined by categories known as **qualitative variables**. They are nonnumeric in nature. We could gather data on client income level using a qualitative variable by asking the client to select the appropriate category in which his or her annual income falls ($19,999 and under; $20,000–$49,999; $50,000–$79,999; over $80,000). These variables can be created for all types of client information. Sometimes the variables we assess can be observed and measure directly (see Guided Practice Exercise 2.1). For example, we can see how tall an individual is and even measure the person's height directly. However, there are many variables that counselors have interest in that are not observable. These variables, often referred to as latent variables, cannot be directly measured. They may be inferred from the presence of other variables or self-reported from clients (see Case Illustration 2.2). An example of a latent variable would be a client's level of happiness. Happiness is an intangible construct that cannot be measured, but we could assess how happy a client is based on other factors that may be present (mood, interaction with others, etc.). With so many different types of variables to measure, we need some type of organizational system to help accurately classify these variables.

GUIDED PRACTICE EXERCISE 2.1

Collecting Quantitative and Qualitative Data

To help you become familiar with the collection of quantitative and qualitative data, we invite you to collect data on yourself. For the next week keep a record of the number of hours you watch television. Whenever the television is on and you are watching a program, record the number of minutes spent watching. At the end of the day, tally a total for the number of minutes spent watching television. In addition to documenting the number of hours of television watched (quantitative data), provide a brief commentary on your opinions of the program watched (qualitative data). Did you like the show? Was it interesting? Would you watch it again? At the end of the week, you should be able to see how much television you watch on average per day and the types of programs that most appeal to your interests.

CASE ILLUSTRATION   2.2

A mental health counselor is working with a client who appears to be depressed. Depression is really an abstract construct. Since depression cannot be seen or held, it cannot be measured or observed in a traditional sense. To address this issue, researchers have identified symptoms associated with the latent variable of depression. These symptoms are what we see and record. To properly diagnosis his client as being depressed, the counselor could administer the Beck Depression Inventory-II (BDI-II) to his client. The BDI-II provides a quantitative score that is used to determine the level of depression with which a client may be struggling based on the presence of certain psychosomatic symptoms associated with a diagnosis of major depression as listed in the *Diagnostic and Statistical Manual* (DSM). Based on the client's score on the BDI-II, the counselor can assess whether the depressed state the client is experiencing would be considered mild, moderate, or severe. The test score provides a piece of data that can be communicated by the counselor to the client to help develop a common language of what the client is experiencing. The "score" allows both the counselor and client see the severity of the issue and also determine how effective treatment is at reducing depressive symptoms by comparing follow-up scores to this initial baseline score.

SCALES OF MEASUREMENT

Throughout the counseling process counselors are constantly collecting data to measure various aspects of the clients with whom they work. This process of *measurement* involves the application of a specific set of procedures to assign quantitative values (i.e., numbers) to various objects, traits, and behaviors known collectively as variables (Drummond & Jones, 2010). The variables we measure can range from how old the client is to how depressed the client feels on a depression rating scale. Regardless of the type of variables being measured, a set of logical rules governs how the measurement should be performed.

These rules provide for uniformity in the measurement process so that all who view or interpret the data can have a similar understanding of what is being reported. For example, if we are measuring the distance between two points of interest and are measuring that distance in miles, we can be certain that a mile represents 5,280 feet regardless of the time or place the measuring occurs or who is doing the measuring. A mile is a mile. The rules used for measuring variables are dependent on two characteristics: the amount of information being provided by the outcome measure and the precision of the scale of measurement being used.

There are four scales of measurement used to summarize measured data: *nominal, ordinal, interval,* and *ratio.* Any variable a counselor might assess or measure involves one of these four scales. Each scale is identified by the presence or absence of a set of properties: identification, magnitude, equal intervals, and the presence of an absolute zero point. These properties are defined in Table 2.1. Data collected using different scales of measurement convey different types of information (R. J. Cohen & Swerdlik, 2005). Developing a working knowledge of each of these scales allows counselors to select appropriate assessment instruments and evaluate the results of these assessments as they relate to their work with clients. A description of each of the four scales of measurement follows.

Nominal Scale

The most basic of the measurement scales is the **nominal** scale. The nominal scale is used to classify or categorize data into groups that have different names but are not related to each other in any other systematic way. Derived from the Latin word *nomin,* meaning "name," the nominal scale allows us only to name or identify the object being measured. Therefore the nominal scale satisfies only the identification property of measurement. Although the categories on a nominal scale are not quantitative values, numbers often represents them. An example of a variable measured using a nominal scale would be a client's marital status where 1 = single, 2 = married, 3 = separated, 4 = divorced, and 5 = widowed. In this example the differences between scores are in quality rather than quantity. Values assigned are used to represent variable categories and have no numeric value. Because data

Table 2.1   Measurement Scale Properties

Property	Description
Identification	Each value on the measurement scale has a unique meaning.
Magnitude	Values on the measurement scale have an ordered relationship to one another.
Equal intervals	An equal number of scale units exist between each value along the measurement scale.
Absolute zero point	The measurement scale has a true absolute zero point below which no values exist.

collected on the nominal scale are purely descriptive in nature, we are unable to perform many of the basic statistical analyses that we could with other types of data (Whiston, 2009). The value of nominal data lies simply in its ability to provide us with percentages and frequencies of scores or clients who may fall into particular categories.

Ordinal Scale

Building on the nominal scale, the **ordinal** scale has the properties of both identification and magnitude. Variables measured on the ordinal scale are rank ordered along some type of continuum so that each value on the scale has a unique meaning and appears in an ordered relationship to every other value on the scale in terms of size and magnitude. This allows us to now compare scores or clients and determine such conditions as better, larger, stronger, and so on. An example of a variable measured using an ordinal scale would be an Olympic track race where gold, silver, and bronze medals are awarded to the first-, second-, and third-place finishers, respectively. The ordinal scale allows us to say that the gold medal winner finished ahead of the silver medal winner who in turn finished ahead of the bronze medal winner. However, we are unable to determine *how much* better each medal winner did in comparison to the others. The race may have come down to a photo finish or it may have been won going away. Ordinal data allows us to make general comparisons between the magnitudes of data (greater or less than operations), but we cannot comment on the size of the intervals between the different cases.

Interval Scale

The **interval** scale is a higher order level of measurement than the ordinal scale. It includes the measurement properties of identification, magnitude, and equal intervals. Variables measured on the interval scale are categorized, rank ordered, and arranged so that an equal interval unit appears between each of the scores. The inclusion of equal intervals between scores allows for logical measurement to take place. In other words, we now can make definitive statements about an individual's position on a continuum as well as the positioning relative to others in the group. An example of a variable measured on the interval scale is intelligence (as noted by IQ score). We know that the difference between an IQ score of 125 and 130, 5 points, is the same 5-point difference we would find between IQ scores of 85 and 90. On interval scales, the score of 0 does not represent the absence of the variable being measured. To grasp the importance of an absolute zero point, think of measuring temperature on the Fahrenheit scale. The temperature 0 degrees does not represent the absence of measured temperature; there can be below 0 temperatures (–20 degrees, for example). Absent an absolute zero point, we can only add and subtract values, not multiply them or create ratios (Drummond & Jones, 2010). In other words, we can say that 80 degrees is 20 more than 60 degrees, but it is not 33% more.

Ratio Scale

The highest order measurement scale is the **ratio** scale. The ratio scale satisfies all four of the properties of measurement: identification, magnitude, equal intervals, and presence of an absolute zero point (see Table 2.2). As a result, this scale allows for all types of mathematical calculations, including multiplication and division. For variables measured using the ratio scale, the value of zero represents the absence of the variable being measured. An example of a variable measured on the ratio scale would be weight. An object can be weightless but it cannot have a negative weight. Therefore, 0 pounds represents the absence of weight; it is a meaningful data point. Because there is an absolute zero point, we can make comparisons between variables on the ratio scale. An object that weighs 100 pounds weighs twice as much as an object that weighs 50 pounds and half as much as an object that weighs 200 pounds.

Guided Practice Exercise 2.2 is provided as a way of helping you apply these concepts to variables encountered throughout your life.

Table 2.2 Measurement Properties Satisfied by Each Measurement Scale

Measurement Scale	Properties Satisfied
Nominal	Identification
Ordinal	Identification, magnitude
Interval	Identification, magnitude, equal intervals
Ratio	Identification, magnitude, equal intervals, absolute zero point

GUIDED PRACTICE EXERCISE 2.2

Identifying Measurement Scales

For each of the following variables, determine the measurement scale that is most applicable. It may help to discuss your thoughts with a colleague or classmate. The correct answers are provided.

  A. Family size (number of siblings)
  B. Political party affiliation (e.g., Democrat, Republican)
  C. Beverage sizes at a local fast food restaurant
  D. Average value of homes in your neighborhood
  E. Scores on a personality measure

ANSWERS:

  A. Ratio. Zero siblings represent the absence of any brothers or sisters.
  B. Nominal. These represent nondescript categories of the variable measured.

(Continued)

(Continued)

  C. Ordinal. Sizes are ordered from small to large, but the difference in volume between the sizes is not equivalent.

  D. Ratio. Zero value represents the absence of value to the home.

  E. Interval. Scores are typically reported as standard scores with equivalent intervals existing between each data point.

FREQUENCY DISTRIBUTIONS

In large amounts, data can be difficult to interpret and use. It needs to be collated in a manner that allows for patterns and trends to be noted and easily communicated to others. One of the most common procedures for condensing a large set of data into a more manageable display is to place the scores in a frequency distribution. A **frequency distribution** orders a set of disorganized raw scores and summarizes the number of times each of the different scores occurs within a sample of scores. Frequency distributions often are presented as tables or graphs. In both forms the same two elements must be present: (a) a listing of the categories that make up the original measurement scale and (b) a record of the number of individuals classified in each category. For example, a community mental health clinic is preparing a report to illustrate how it is meeting the needs of the community. Included in the report will be a description of the different demographics of clients served. A frequency distribution table could be created to show the demographic breakdown of clients by ethnicity serviced by this clinic. Whether you use a table or graph, frequency distributions have great utility for counselors. They present you with a visual representation of how individual scores are distributed on a measurement scale. In so doing, they allow you to identify trends within the distribution by showing where the majority of scores lie and compare individual clients with whom you might be working to the larger population to see how they relate. Comparing an individual's score to the population can highlight client strengths or deficits that might factor into your treatment planning and decision-making processes.

Simple Frequency Distribution Table

The most commonly used frequency distribution is a simple frequency distribution table that presents data in two columns. In one column, each of the individual scores found in the distribution are listed in descending order from highest to lowest. In the other column the number of times that particular score occurred in the distribution is recorded as a frequency count. An example of a frequency distribution table is provided in Table 2.3.

Once you have constructed a frequency distribution table, there are a number of mathematical operations you can perform on the data presented. You can determine the total number of individuals or scores in the distribution by summing each of the frequency values listed in the second column ($\Sigma f = N$). You also can calculate this total value by multiplying each X-value by its frequency and then summing those products together ($\Sigma f(X)$). Both methods require you to use all of the information provided to you in the table (both the X-value and frequency columns).

Frequency distributions also can be used to calculate proportions and percentages. These measures can be used to further describe the distribution of scores. Proportions and percentages measure the fraction of the entire distribution that is attributed to a single score or value. In Table 2.3 there were 67 students who had a grade of B out of a total distribution of 273 students. The proportion of students earning a B in the class would be 67/273 or .245. To calculate percentage, we take this value and multiply it by 100 to get (.245)(100) = 24.5%. These two values, proportions and percentages, can be added to the simple frequency distribution table by adding two additional columns. In a third column you would include the proportion (p) data, and in a fourth column you would include the percentage (%) data. Table 2.4 takes the same table data used earlier and adds these two new columns.

Table 2.3 Grade Distribution for a Class of Students ($N = 273$)

Grade	Frequency
A	31
B	67
C	112
D	44
F	19

Grouped Frequency Distribution Tables

The rationale behind creating frequency distributions is to present a large amount of data in a more manageable format so that interpretations can be made. If the distribution is as cumbersome as the original set of raw data, it is of no use to counselors. One way that a frequency distribution can become too distracting is when a large number of X-values are present in the distribution. When this is the case, you might be better served

Table 2.4 Extended Grade Distribution for a Class of Students ($N = 273$)

Grade	Frequency	Proportion	Percentage
A	31	.113	11.3%
B	67	.245	24.5%
C	112	.410	41.0%
D	44	.161	16.1%
F	19	.069	6.9%

by using a grouped frequency distribution. A **grouped frequency distribution** is a distribution in which individual X-values are combined into sets known as intervals. Frequencies are then counted for each of these intervals. An example of a grouped frequency distribution is a score distribution for clients who have been administered the Minnesota Multiphasic Personality Inventory-2nd Edition (MMPI-2) at a local counseling center. For each of the clinical scales assessed on the MMPI-2, clients receive a scale score (t-score) that is used to determine whether there is any need for clinical concern in that area. For t-scores, there is the possibility that 100 separate t-values can be present. A table with 100 separate t-values could be daunting. Intervals can be created for scores so that we now have t-values that represent values from 100–90, 89–80, 79–70, 69–60, 59–50, 49–40, 39–30, 29–20, 19–10, and 9–0. Our t-value column would now have 10 entries instead of 100, a much easier amount to read and interpret which clinical scales had the most elevated scores.

Certain rules need to be applied when creating intervals for a grouped frequency distribution. First, your total number of intervals used should be kept to a minimum. A good rule of thumb is that there should not be more than 10 intervals in a distribution table. Second, the width you choose for the intervals should be a simple number. Usually, multiples of five are used (5, 10, etc.) because they are easy to understand and calculate. Third, your intervals all need to be the same size. Notice in the above example for the class grade distribution the intervals were all 10-point width intervals. It would not be appropriate to have intervals of 100–72, 71–61, 60–40, 39–0. Finally, the bottom number of your interval needs to be a multiple of the interval width. In using the 10-point width interval, each of our intervals should begin with a multiple of 10 (10, 20, 30, 40, 50, etc.).

Using the above rules, creating intervals for a grouped frequency distribution is a relatively easy process. To begin, identify the highest and lowest scores appearing in the distribution. This gives you the range of scores. Then take that range and divide it by an interval width of your choosing. You may need to experiment with several different interval widths to see what gives you the most efficient number of intervals. You want to make sure your lowest interval includes the lowest score in the distribution. Once you determine your intervals, list them in the X-value column of your table. Totaling the number of scores that fall between the parameters of a given interval then populates your frequency column. Let's look at the example in Case Illustration 2.3.

CASE ILLUSTRATION   2.3

Ms. McAlpin, the school counselor, was looking at the scores reflecting her students' performance on a test she distributed following a classroom guidance lesson on alcohol and its abuse. She had the students' answer sheets spread out, and in looking over all 25 sheets she became a bit confused as to how to make sense of how well they did. The scores were 55, 47, 67, 91, 59, 75, 93, 95, 82, 50, 45, 33, 72, 91, 86, 44, 56, 39, 82, 77, 61, 32, 49, 60, and 85. She finally decided to organize the data into a grouped frequency distribution. The following are the steps Ms. McAlpin took to create the grouped frequency distribution.

Step 1: She first had to determine the interval width she wanted to use. She felt that a width of 10 would work since grades are typically awarded on a 10-point scale.

Step 2: Next she needed to determine how many intervals she had in her distribution. To do this she identified the lowest (32) and highest (95) scores in the distribution and found the difference between them. She took this distance, 63, and divided it by the interval width of 10 she selected in Step 1. This gave her an answer of 6.3. Rounding up to the nearest whole number, Ms. McAlpin determined that her distribution would have seven intervals. Since the lowest score was 32, the lowest interval needed to begin with 30 (to keep it a multiple of the interval width of 10).

Grade	Frequency
90–99	
80–89	
70–79	
60–69	
50–59	
40–49	
30–39	

Step 3: Next she began populating the frequency column by adding up the number of scores that fall within each interval and placing that value in the second column. There were four scores in the 90s in our distribution (91, 91, 93, and 95), so she put 4 as the frequency for scores in the interval 90–99. She continued this process, putting the frequencies for scores in the 80s, 70s, 60s, 50s, 40s, and 30s intervals.

Grade	Frequency
90–99	4
80–89	4
70–79	3
60–69	3
50–59	4
40–49	4
30–39	3

(Continued)

(Continued)

Step 4: Now she was able to add the third (proportion) and fourth (percentage) columns to complete the full distribution table. For the proportion column (P) she divided the frequency for that interval by the total number of observations in the distribution ($N = 25$). She then multiplied the result by 100 to determine the percentage (%) value found in column four.

Grade	Frequency	P	%
90–99	4	.16	16%
80–89	4	.16	16%
70–79	3	.12	12%
60–69	3	.12	12%
50–59	4	.16	16%
40–49	4	.16	16%
30–39	3	.12	12%

As previously mentioned, frequency distributions also can be presented as graphs. **Graphs** are pictorial representations of the data and information that appear in frequency distribution tables. Several different types of graphs can be constructed to illustrate the data collected. Commonly used graphs include histograms, bar graphs, polygons, and smooth curves.

A **histogram** is a graph that uses vertical bars to represent the frequencies of a set of variables. The measured values found within the distribution are listed on the horizontal axis (x-axis) found at the bottom of the graph. Frequency counts are placed on the vertical axis (y-axis). The height of the bar represents the number of times that particular value occurred in a distribution. Histograms are used to represent data collected on the ordinal, interval, or ratio scale. Because the data collected from these scales is continuous, the bars on a histogram touch one another. Figure 2.1 shows a histogram.

Bar graphs are similar to histograms in that measured values are found along the x-axis and frequency counts on the y-axis. The difference between the two is that the bars in a bar graph do not touch one another. When used to represent nominal data, the gap between the bars signifies that the data represents discrete values. When used to represent ordinal data, the gap tells the reader that we cannot be certain that the width of each interval is equivalent. An example of data plotted using a bar graph is found in Figure 2.2.

A **frequency polygon** is a variation of a histogram. Instead of having frequencies denoted by a series of vertical bars, a line is drawn to connect the midpoint for each of the different measured variables in the distribution. Frequency polygons are so named because the straight lines used to connect the midpoints create a geometric plane (with the horizontal x-axis forming the bottom). They are often used instead of histograms when you want to compare data from two different sets of scores. Figure 2.3 demonstrates how a frequency polygon can be used to represent the data presented in Figure 2.1.

A final graph we can look at is the smooth curve. **Smooth curves** are used to display the distribution of numeric scores obtained from either an interval or ratio scale. Instead of a series of straight lines between data points, a continuous line is created. Smooth curves are used when large amounts of data are being plotted and the values form a continuum rather than standing alone as discrete values. The most frequently referenced smooth curve is the normal curve, as shown in Figure 2.4. Clearly, counselors have many choices in terms of how to present their data. Guided Practice Exercise 2.3 is designed to help you understand how to pick the correct visual representation based on the data you have collected.

Figure 2.1   Histogram

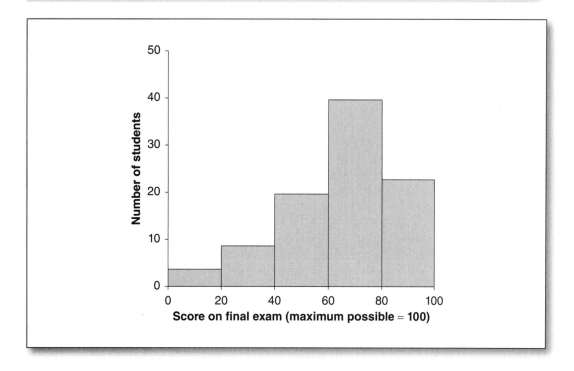

Figure 2.2 Bar Graph

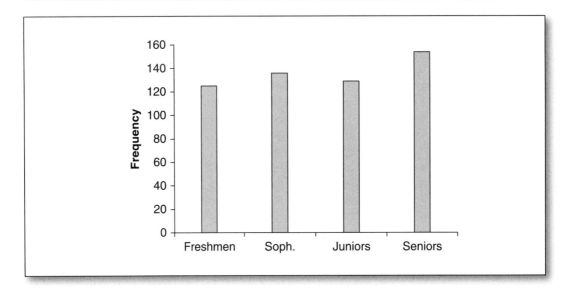

Figure 2.3 Frequency Polygon

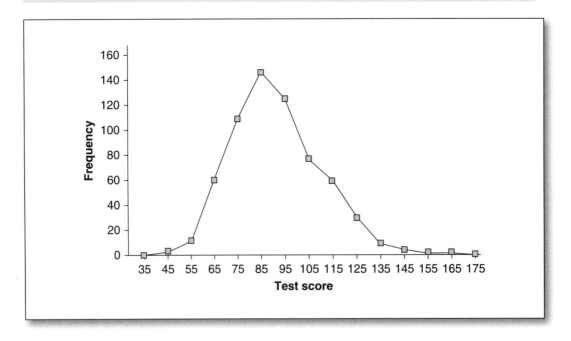

Figure 2.4   Normal Curve

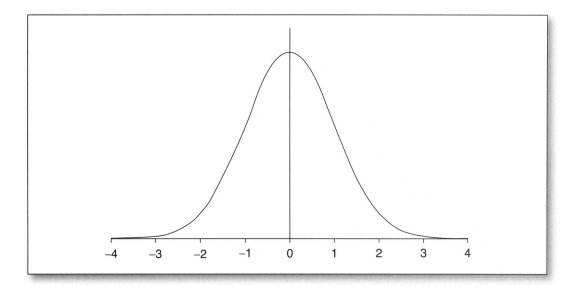

GUIDED PRACTICE EXERCISE 2.3

Visual Representations of Data

In Case Illustration 2.3 we saw Ms. McAlpin construct a grouped frequency distribution for the scores on the classroom guidance test she gave following her presentation on the effects of alcohol usage. Using the data she obtained, construct a visual representation of the data that could be presented at a faculty meeting or to the school administrator to show the efficacy of the school guidance program. Determine whether a histogram, bar graph, frequency polygon, or smooth curve would be most appropriate to depict the data collected.

ANSWER:

Because the data collected is quantitative and continuous, a histogram would be the best choice to use to represent the data.

THE SHAPE OF FREQUENCY DISTRIBUTIONS

When frequency distributions are plotted, their shape can be either symmetrical or asymmetrical. In symmetrical distributions, each side of the curve is a mirror image of the other. In these distributions, the majority of scores are clustered in the center of the distribution, close to the mean score. The distribution thins out as it moves away from the mean and the number of outlying scores decreases. In asymmetrical distributions, the scores are skewed or distorted to one side of the distribution. Both positively and negatively skewed distributions can occur.

In a **positively skewed** distribution the majority of scores fall on the low end of the distribution. The asymmetrical tail extends into the positive side of the graph. When a distribution is **negatively skewed,** the majority of scores fall on the high end of the distribution. Skewness occurs because the mean of the distribution is pulling the tail in a particular direction. If you are having a hard time interpreting whether a graph is positively or negatively skewed, think of the tail. In a negatively skewed distribution the tail is located on the negative side of the graph. In a positively skewed distribution the tail is located to the far right on the positive side of the graph. A simple mnemonic you can use to help you remember whether you are looking at a positively or negatively skewed distribution is *the tail tells the tale.* When the extreme scores (tail portion) in a distribution fall on the right side of the graph, it is positively skewed. When the extreme scores fall on the left side of the distribution, it is negatively skewed. Figure 2.5 illustrates symmetrical, positively skewed, and negatively skewed distributions.

While skewness describes measure of symmetry, the term **kurtosis** is used in assessment to describe the peakness or flatness of a frequency distribution. Both skewness and kurtosis provide a quick visual description of a distribution of test scores. Three main types

Figure 2.5   Symmetrical, Positively Skewed, and Negatively Skewed Distributions

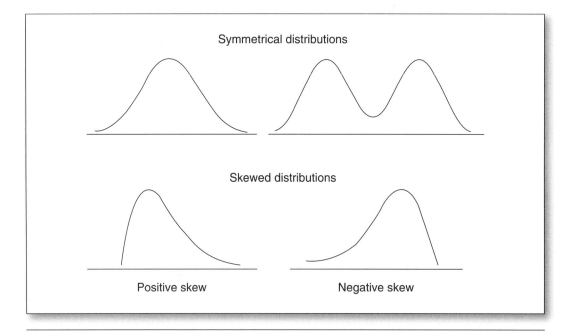

Source: Gravetter & Wallnau (2007, Figure 2.11, p. 50).

of curves are leptokurtic (relatively peaked), mesokurtic (somewhere in the middle), and platykurtic (relatively flat). Platykurtic distributions are flatter because scores are more evenly spread out. Guided Practice Exercise 2.4 is designed to help you interpret the shape of the distribution of a set of scores collected.

GUIDED PRACTICE EXERCISE 2.4

Interpreting Frequency Distributions

The following distribution of scores depicts the number of sessions a college counselor spent with each of his clients this past semester. Plot the data using one of the frequency distribution graphs discussed in this chapter. Would you describe the distribution as symmetrical, positively skewed, or negatively skewed? What allows you to make your decision?

X	f
6	1
5	1
1	4
2	2
8	1

ANSWER:

The distribution is positively skewed. You should notice that there are several low scores in comparison to high scores in the distribution.

MEASURES OF CENTRAL TENDENCY

Central tendency is a statistical measure that indicates the center or the middle of the distribution. There are several ways to describe the center of a distribution. In this section we will review three measures of central tendency widely used in assessment and score reporting: mean, median, and mode. Why is central tendency important? Imagine you are working as a college counselor and Rich, a freshman at the Naval Academy, comes to you and is wondering about his college major. He is interested in becoming a pilot after he graduates. Obtaining a pilot position depends on his GPA. He enjoys both history and political science but wants to choose a major that will allow him to achieve high grades. Last semester he had a 79 average in one of his history courses and an 83 average in a political science course. How would you advise Rich? What additional information would you need? The additional information you need is how Rich's scores compare to those of his fellow classmates. Central tendency allows us to make comparisons between groups and individuals. The following sections describe each of these measures in further detail.

Arithmetic Mean

The **arithmetic mean** is the sum of all the scores divided by the total number of scores. Often referred to as the mean or average, it is denoted by the symbol $\bar{X}$ (pronounced X bar). The formula for calculating the mean is written as:

$$\bar{X} = \sum \frac{X}{N}$$

The symbol $\sum$ is known as the Greek uppercase letter sigma, which simply means sum. X represents the single score and N is the total number of scores. Thus the mean is the summation of all the raw scores divided by the total number of scores in a distribution.

Example: Find the mean of the following scores: 10, 6, 4, and 8.

$$\text{Mean} = \bar{X} = \sum \frac{X}{N}$$

Step 1: First sum all the scores:

$$10 + 6 + 4 + 8 = 28$$

Step 2: Then divide by the total number of scores (N).

$$\frac{28}{4} = 7$$

Thus the mean is 7. $\bar{X} = 7$

Although the mean is often used to report central tendency, it should not be used when dealing with extreme outliers. Why? The mean is not a robust statistic. In other words, the mean is greatly influenced by outliers.

Imagine you are a counselor working with a group of married couples who are having difficulty communicating effectively. The group consists of five couples. During intake you speak with each group member individually and assess his or her perceptions of how satisfied that person is with the communication in his or her marriage. On a scale of 1–20, each member is asked to rate the effectiveness of communication in his or her marriage. Looking over the results, you see that most members had similar scores, but there did appear to be one person who felt much differently than the rest of the group. You could take these ratings and average them together to find the mean level of satisfaction with the current marital communication style for these group members. Do you think this statistic will be truly representative of how the members feel about their communication with their spouse? If you answered no, you are on track. Let's work out the example.

Example: Calculate the mean using a frequency distribution.

Satisfaction Rating	f
20	5
19	2
18	2
2	1

Step 1: Calculate Σ X by summing all the raw scores.

$$\Sigma X = 20 + 20 + 20 + 20 + 20 + 19 + 19 + 18 + 18 + 2 = 176$$

(Notice how the ranking of 20 appears five times and the rankings of 19 and 18 appear twice each? Remember the frequency tells us the number of times the value occurs.)

Step 2: Divide by N, which is the total number of raw scores. There were 10 family members who provided ratings of satisfaction.

$$\Sigma \frac{X}{N} = \frac{176}{10} = 17.6$$

Now thinking about this example, is 17.6 a statistic that really represents how satisfied any of the group members really are? No, as you can see the mean in this case is not the best statistical measure to determine a single score that defines the center of the distribution. Especially when you have a small sample size, the mean is heavily influenced by extreme values. The average rating for this group was lower than what the majority of members rated and much higher than what the one outlying member rated. When you have extreme outliers, use the median rather than the mean to describe the central tendency.

Median

The second measure of central tendency we will discuss is the median. The **median** is defined as the middle score or the score that divides the distribution exactly in half. The median is also equivalent to the 50th percentile, because exactly 50% of the participants have scores at or below the median. The median can be found by arranging the total number of scores in either ascending or descending order and then picking the middle score. When you have an odd number of scores, the median will be the middle number. Again, 50% of the scores will lie above this midpoint number and 50% will lie below.

Example: Find the median of the following scores.

X	f
6	1
5	1
1	4
2	2
8	1

Step 1: Arrange the scores from lowest to highest or highest to lowest.

1, 1, 1, 1, **2**, 2, 5, 6, 8

Step 2: Identify the middle score.

The middle score is 2.

Median = 2

However, when you have an even number of scores, there is no single middle value and the midpoint is the value between these two numbers. Thus you will have to sum the two middle scores and divide by two.

Let's use the same numbers from an earlier example. Recall that we were asked to find the mean for the following scores: 10, 6, 4, and 8. We determined that the mean ($\bar{X}$) was 7.

Example: Now find the median of the following scores: 10, 6, 4, and 8.

Step 1: Arrange the scores from lowest to highest or highest to lowest.

4, 6, 8, 10

Step 2: Identify the middle score.

In the example there are two middle scores: 6 and 8.

Thus add the two scores and divide by 2.

$$\frac{14}{2} = 7$$

Median = 7

Previously we used the example of how satisfied group members were with the level of communication in their marriage to illustrate how the mean can be affected by outlying scores. Recall that we were asked to find the mean for the following scores:

Satisfaction Rating	f
20	5
19	2
18	2
2	1

We found that $\bar{X} = 17.6$.

What is the median?

Step 1: Arrange the scores from lowest to highest or highest to lowest.

2, 18, 18, 19, 19, 20, 20, 20, 20, 20

Step 2: Identify the middle score.

In the example there are two middle scores: 19 and 20.

Thus add the two scores and divide by 2.

Median = 19.5

Since we have a very small sample size and an outlier, the median value of 19.5 is more representative of the sample than the mean is.

Mode

Thus far we have discussed two measures of central tendency: the mean and the median. Next we will consider the third measure of central tendency: the mode. The **mode** is the score that has the greatest frequency in a distribution. The mode identifies the peak in a frequency distribution graph. No calculations are needed to determine the mode. You simply count the scores and report the score that occurs most frequently.

In a previous example, we were asked to find the mean for the following scores: 10, 6, 4, and 8. And we determined it to be $\bar{X} = 7$. We then found the median = 7.

Example: What is the mode for the following scores: 10, 6, 4, and 8?

Notice how each score occurs once. Thus we have four modes: 4, 6, 8 and 10.

Example: In the previous example we were asked to find the mean and the median for the following scores:

Satisfaction Rating	f
20	5
19	2
18	2
2	1

We found the $\bar{X} = 17.6$ and the median was 19.5.

What is the mode?

Step 1: Determine which score appears most often.

As we can see, five group members rated their satisfaction as a 20. The mode would be 20.

However, let's now pretend the group expands and three new couples enter. They too are asked to rate their level of satisfaction. The scores of these new group members are added to the distribution of scores for the group.

Satisfaction Rating	f
20	5
19	5
18	2
16	3
2	1

We now have two modes: 19 and 20. Because there are two scores that are tied with having the highest frequency, this distribution would be called **bimodal** because it contains two modes. A distribution with three or more modes is called **multimodal**. Recall in our earlier example we had a distribution that contained scores of 10, 6, 4, and 8. Because each number occurred once, we discovered there were actually four modes. In this scenario, the shape of the graph takes on a rectangular distribution. When might we use the mode, rather than the mean or the median, as a measure of central tendency? In our earlier discussion of nominal scales, we learned that at this level of measurement, scales measure only the quantity of data represented by names and labels rather than numeric scores (e.g., single, married, divorced, widowed). Because you cannot calculate a mean or median for nominal data, the mode is often used to describe central tendency for this measurement scale (see Table 2.5).

Table 2.5 Central Tendency Measures Used for Each Scale of Measurement

Scale of Measurement	Central Tendency Measure Used
Nominal	Mode
Ordinal	Median and mode
Interval	Mean, median, and mode*
Ratio	Mean, median, and mode

* If the distribution is skewed or representative of a small sample, use the median rather than the mean.

Modes are also useful when describing discrete variables. Both nominal and ordinal data are discrete variables. As you have now learned, discrete variables are those that differ in kind rather than magnitude (e.g., gender, nationality, marital status). Sometimes, discrete variables can be represented by numbers and a mean is calculated. However, in these cases the values are merely for discussion purposes only and do not really exist. For example, on average people have 3.2 kids and own 2.2 cars. Can you really have 3.2 kids? In this example, the mode (the most common item) would be more useful to describe central tendency.

Modes are often used in conjunction with the mean and the median to represent the shape of a distribution. Because the mode is the most frequent item that occurs, the mode is the peak in frequency distribution graphs. We will discuss this in more detail when we cover the concept of distribution skewness. Guided Practice Exercise 2.5 is designed to help you see how the different measures of central tendency can be used in practice.

GUIDED PRACTICE EXERCISE 2.5

Describing Class Member Course Credits

Interview members of your class and gather data that reflect the number of course credits they have earned to date in their program. Once you have those numbers, compute the mean, the median, and the mode for the class. Do you fall above the class average or below it?

MEASURES OF VARIABILITY

As you have just read, the measures of central tendency (mean, median, and mode) can be useful. However, when using assessments with our clients we also want to understand how their scores compare to other people's scores. **Variability** is a quantitative measure that describes how spread out or clustered together scores are in a distribution. When we use statistics that describe the amount of variation in a distribution, we call these **measures of variability**. Some measures of variability are range, inclusive range, standard deviation, and variance.

Range and Inclusive Range

The **range** is the difference between the highest and the lowest value in a distribution and should be used only with interval and ratio data. To calculate the range, subtract the highest score from the lowest score. For example, imagine in your assessment class the highest score on Exam 1 was 100 and the lowest score on Exam 1 was a 40. The range would be equal to $100 - 40 = 60$. Although the range is an easy measure of variability to calculate and gives us a quick description of the spread of scores, its use is limited. Imagine you earned a 95 on Exam 1 in assessment. The range does not provide us with information to interpret your score. You may come across the term *inclusive range*. The **inclusive range** is calculated by subtracting the highest score minus the lowest score and adding 1. For example, the inclusive range for exam scores ranging from 100 to 40 would be $100 - 40 + 1 = 61$. For our purposes we will refer to the range as the highest score minus the lowest score.

Standard Deviation

As we discussed, the problem with using the range is that it depends solely on two scores: the maximum and the minimum score. The range does not take into consideration all the scores in the distribution. Standard deviation is the most commonly used measure of variability. Standard deviation is the most important measure of variability because *each* individual score's distance from the mean is considered. As counselors it is important that we can describe how our clients vary from the mean. **Standard deviation** is the average of amount by which scores vary from the mean. In other words, are the scores near or far from the mean? Are they clustered near or scattered from the mean? We use standard deviation in interpreting our clients' scores. Is a client's score above the mean, below the mean, or close to the mean? Standard deviations also provide useful information to the counselor in regards to variability. Is the standard deviation large, meaning the scores deviate or varied more from the mean? Or is the standard deviation small, meaning most of the scores deviate close to the mean? The symbol for standard deviation is often represented by s, S, SD, or σ (Greek letter sigma). For our purposes we will refer to the standard deviation as SD. Recall X stands for the raw score, $\bar{X}$ is the mean, and N is the total number of scores.

$$SD = \sqrt{\sum \frac{(X - \bar{X})^2}{N - 1}}$$

One should note that there is a debate whether to use $N - 1$ or N as the denominator. We will use $N - 1$, which is known as the unbiased estimate of the population value. Some authors recommend to use $N - 1$ only when you are dealing with sample data and N when using N when the data constitutes a population. In this text we will use the formula $N - 1$ in our calculations.

Variance

Variance (symbolized by a lowercase s^2) is mean squared deviation. In other words, variance is the mean of the squared deviation scores.

$$s^2 = (SD)^2$$

$$\text{Standard deviation} = \sqrt{\text{variance}}$$

Example: Calculate variability: range, standard deviation, and variance.
Recall that in previous examples, we were asked to find three measures of central tendency—mean, median, and mode—of the following scores: 10, 6, 4, and 8.

$$\text{Mean} = \bar{X} = \sum \frac{X}{N} = \frac{10+6+8+4}{4} = 7$$

$$\text{Median} = \frac{8+6}{2} = \frac{14}{2} = 7$$

$$\text{Mode} = 10, 8, 6, \text{ and } 4.$$

Now let's calculate three measures of variability: range, standard deviation, and variance.

1. **Calculate the range.**

To calculate the range, take the highest score in the distribution and subtract from it the lowest score.

$10 - 4 = 6$

Range $= 6$

2. **Calculate the standard deviation.**

To calculate the standard deviation, use the following equation:

$$SD = \sqrt{\sum \frac{(X - \bar{X})^2}{N-1}}$$

We suggest setting up a chart in the specific order displayed below and working from left to right. We also suggest writing out every step as we have done below so you can trace your work backward if you miscalculate. We are going to work from left to right of the SD equation, focusing on the numerator of the equation first. Note that you should already have identified the mean for the distribution.

Starting with the left-hand side, write down all of your scores in the first column. In the second column, write down the mean that you calculate above. In the third column we are going to solve $(X - \bar{X})$. For each score, subtract the mean from it and note your result. Notice that if you were to add of the scores going down the row for $(X - \bar{X})$, the sum would be 0. Do not be alarmed, the sum of this column will always be 0. Why? Remember that the mean is the average of a distribution of scores. The total number of differences above the mean will be equal to the total number of differences below the mean. Remembering that the deviation scores total 0 when added is a great place to stop and make sure you are solving the SD equation correctly. In the fourth column you now take the values found for column three and square them. This addresses the $(X - \bar{X})^2$ expression. Thus far we have calculated $(X - \bar{X})^2$ but remember we have the symbol $\sum$ in front of the equation, which means summation. Therefore we need to sum all the values of $(X - \bar{X})^2$.

Score (X)	Mean ($\bar{X}$)	Deviation (X − $\bar{X}$)	Deviation Squared (X − $\bar{X}$)²
10	7	10 − 7 = 3	(3)² = 9
6	7	6 − 7 = −1	(−1)² = 1
4	7	4 − 7 = −3	(−3)² = 9
8	7	8 − 7 = 1	(1)² = 1
		Σ = 0	Σ = 20

We have now calculated all the information needed for the top part of the SD equation.

$$SD = \sqrt{\sum \frac{(X - \bar{X})^2}{N-1}} = \sqrt{\frac{20}{N-1}}$$

Now we are going to focus on the bottom part of the equation, known as the denominator. Recall that we already discovered the value of N when calculating the mean. We determined that four scores were reported; thus $N = 4$. Remember, we have to subtract 1 from N. Also note that we did this before square rooting our answer.

$$SD = \sqrt{\frac{20}{4-1}} =$$

Next we want to divide the numerator by the denominator.

$$\sqrt{\frac{20}{3}} = \sqrt{7}$$

Now take the square root.

$$\sqrt{7} = 2.58$$

Putting all our steps together, we found the SD:

$$SD = \sqrt{\frac{20}{4-1}} = \sqrt{\frac{20}{3}} = \sqrt{7} = 2.58$$

3. **Calculate the variance.**

To calculate the variance, square the standard deviation.

$$s^2 = (2.58)^2 = 6.67$$

Now that we have shown you how these various measures of central tendency and variability are calculated, we encourage you to try computing them on your own (see Guided Practice Exercise 2.6).

GUIDED PRACTICE EXERCISE 2.6

Computing Descriptive Statistics From Frequency Distributions

In Guided Practice Exercise 2.4 you were asked to plot the number of sessions spent with each client for a college counselor's caseload last semester. Using the same data used in Exercise 2.4, compute the mean, median, mode, range, variance, and standard deviation for this counselor's client data. Is there much variability between the total number of sessions he spends with each client, or is he fairly consistent?

X	f
6	1
5	1
1	4
2	2
8	1

ANSWERS:

Mean = 3, Median = 2, Mode = 1, Range = 7, Variance = 7, Standard Deviation = 2.6. This counselor is quite varied with the amount of time he spends with each client. The large standard deviation means that there is a great deal of variability in the sessions he spends with each client.

STANDARD SCORES

Another way that we can organize our data to more easily interpret it and make treatment decisions based on these results is to create standard scores. **Standard scores** indicate the distance an individual's raw score is above or below the mean of the reference group in terms of standard deviation units. In other words, a standard score is a raw score that has been placed on a distribution with a set mean and standard deviation. To help understand the importance of standardizing scores, let's revisit Rich, our client from earlier in the chapter who came in and told you he had a 79 average in his history class and an 83 average in a political science course. Once we convert his raw score to a standard score, we can see his position of performance relative to the other students in his class. We are able to make these comparisons because standard scores describe how many standard deviations an individual's score is from the mean of that particular distribution. Various standard scores are commonly used in counseling assessment, and each is unique in terms of the mean and standard deviation established for the distribution. In this section we will discuss some standard scores, including *z*-scores, t-scores, percentiles, and stanines. However, we will first look at the normal curve, as all standard scores are based on the normal curve.

Normal Curve

The **normal curve** (also called the bell-shaped curve) is a distribution of scores that has three basic characteristics. First, the normal curve represents a distribution in which the mean, median, and mode all share the same value. These values are all represented by the peak or highest point in the center of the distribution. When the mean, median, and mode are not represented by the same value, the distribution is skewed. The relationship between the mean, median, and modal scores in a positive and a negative skewed distribution are shown in Figures 2.6 and 2.7. Second, the normal curve is perfectly symmetrical. The values on one side of the distribution mirror those on the other side. Fifty percent of the scores fall above the middle point and 50% fall below. The third and final characteristic is that the tails of the curve approach the horizontal axis but never actually touch it, resulting in the curve being asymptomatic.

Figure 2.6   Mean, Median, and Mode Placement in a Positively Skewed Distribution

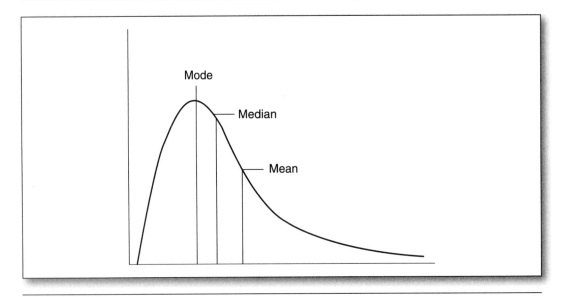

Source: Morris & Maisto (1998, Figure A-5).

Figure 2.7   Mean, Median, and Mode Placement in a Negatively Skewed Distribution

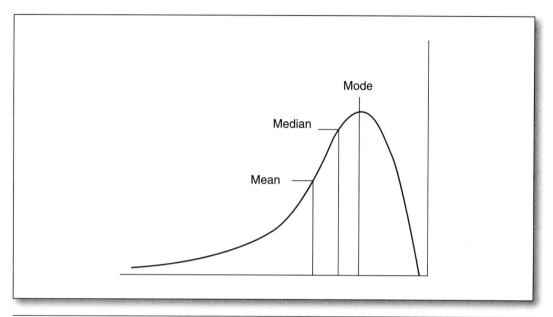

Source: Morris & Maisto (1998, Figure A-4).

The value of the normal curve is great. It provides a useful way for counselors to understand client scores on measures and how those scores compare to others on the same measure. The structure of the normal curve is such that we can predict with great accuracy approximately how many scores fall between certain points on the distribution. For example, looking at the graph in Figure 2.8, you will notice that approximately 68% of all scores occur between one standard deviation below the mean and one standard deviation above the mean. As counselors this data tells us that two-thirds of our test takers score within one standard deviation of the mean. You also can see that approximately 95% of all scores occur between the mean and two standard deviations and roughly 99% of all cases fall between the mean and three standard deviations in either direction. These percentages are fixed and will not change based on the type of standardized score used. In other words, each of the standard scores introduced in this section can be plotted on a normal curve and the same percentages apply.

Z-Scores

All standard scores are based on the z-score. The z-score is the most common standard score produced. The mean of all z-scores is always equal to 0, and the standard deviation for z-scores is always 1. To obtain a z-score, you convert a raw score into a number that

Figure 2.8   The Normal Curve Distribution of Scores

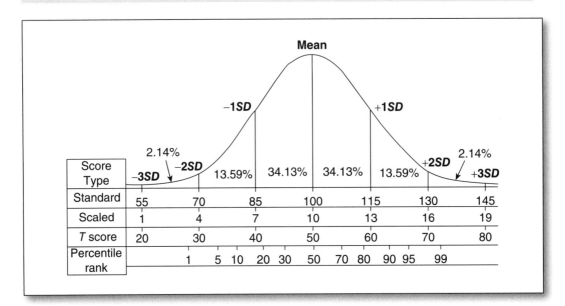

represents how many standard deviations the raw score is above or below the mean. The z-score formula is written as:

$$z = \frac{X - \bar{X}}{SD}$$

In this formula, X represents the individual's raw score, $\bar{X}$ is the mean of the distribution, and SD is standard deviation of the distribution. The following example demonstrates the step-by-step process of taking raw data and computing a z-score.

Example problem: Your client's raw score is 120. The instrument has a mean of 100 and a standard deviation of 10. What is your client's corresponding z-score?

The first step is to write down the information you were given in the problem. You know $X = 120$, $\bar{X} = 100$, and SD = 10.

Next set up your equation for z-scores.

$$z = \frac{X - \bar{X}}{SD} = \frac{120 - 100}{10} = \frac{20}{10} = 2$$

Note that in this example your client had a positive z-score. The sign is equally as important as the actual number computed. The positive sign tells us that the individual had a standard score above the mean. A negative standard score would denote a score below the mean.

T-Scores

T-scores are another type of standard score. The distribution of t-scores has a mean of 50 and a standard deviation of 10. Unlike z-scores, t-scores cannot be negative values and typically eliminate decimal numbers. Thus, t-scores are typically used over z-scores. To calculate a t-score, you multiply the z-score computed by 50 and then add 10 to your result (T = 10z + 50).

Example problem: A client has a z-score of 3. What is her t-score?

$$T = 10z + 50$$

$$T = 10(3) + 50$$

$$T = 30 + 50 = 80$$

In this example, a client with a z-score of 3 would have a corresponding t-score of 80. Earlier we noted that there are various standard scores and that all of them are based on z-scores. As a result, you should see that you cannot calculate a t-score without knowing a client's z-score. For additional practice see Guided Practice Exercise 2.7.

GUIDED PRACTICE EXERCISE 2.7

Computing Standard Scores

Evelyn is being tested for possible inclusion in her school's gifted program by her school counselor. As part of the assessment, she is administered the Wechsler Intelligence Scale for Children-4th Edition (WISC-IV). Her score on the test is 115. The school counselor reads the manual for the WISC-IV and notes that the average for the test is 100 and the standard deviation is 15. Based on this information, what would be Evelyn's z-score and t-score?

ANSWER:

Evelyn's z-score would be 1 and her t-score would be 60. To compute her z-score you would take her raw score (115), subtract the mean for the test (100), and divide the remainder by the standard deviation (15). This gives you (115 − 100)/15 = 1. To compute her t-score you would take her z-score (1), multiply it by 10, and then add 50. This gives you (10)(1) + 50 = 60.

Stanine

Another way of conceptualizing how clients performed is to use stanines. The **stanine** scale converts raw scores into one of nine possible scores and is fairly easy to use. Developed during World War II, this standard score takes the normal curve and slices it into nine segments of equal length; hence stanine comes from a combination of the words *standard* and *nine*. A benefit of this scale is that you do not need to convert your score to obtain a stanine. A stanine scale ranges from 1 to 9, with 1 being the lowest and 9 being the highest. The fifth stanine straddles the mean and each stanine is one-half standard deviation wide. This tells us that half of the fifth stanine is above the mean and half is below the mean. In simple terms, the fifth stanine indicates performance that would place an individual in a range that is one-quarter standard deviation above and one-quarter standard deviation below the mean. It is one-quarter on either side because one-quarter is half of one-half. Thus the fifth stanine extends from −.025 z to +.025 z. The other stanines extend .5 standard deviations from the middle interval. My suggestion is to start at the fifth stanine and work your way forward or backward. For example, if you are at the sixth stanine you can see that the lower boundary on the curve is .25, and if you add .5 standard deviation you can see this puts you at .75. If you keep moving forward you can see that the seventh stanine lower limit is .75 (notice this also is the sixth stanine upper limit) and the upper boundary is 1.25. The distribution of stanine scores is seen in Figure 2.9.

Figure 2.9   Distribution of Stanine Scores

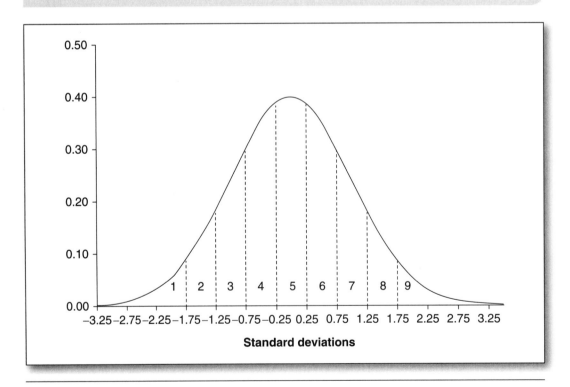

Percentiles

A **percentile score** indicates the percentage of people in a reference group that fall at or below the individual's raw score. A percentile score of 95 means that the individual's score is higher than 95% of the scores among people in the normative group. Imagine you took the National Counseling Examination as part of the process required for licensure as a counselor in your state. You receive your results and they show that you scored in the 95th percentile. This means that for this administration of the exam, your score was better than 95% of the people who took the exam. In other words, you did quite well! Note that percentile and percentage are not the same. Percentile is a type of normative test score, while **percentage** is a portion in relation to a whole, such as percentage of items answered correctly. When you indicate a percentile to a client, you are comparing him or her to a norm group. Scoring a 90% on an exam would mean that you answered 9 out of 10 questions correctly. No information is given as to how your score compares to others who took the same exam.

Let's turn our attention back to our client, Rich. Last semester Rich had a 79 average in his history course and an 83 average in his political science course. You discovered that the average grade in his history class was M = 77 and the class distribution had an SD = 1. After speaking with his political science instructor, you learned the average grade in this class was M = 82 with an SD = 2. What are Rich's z-scores for both the history course and the political science course? What are his t-scores? What is his percentile rank in each class?

We will look at how he performed in his history class first. Start with computing the z-score.

$$z = \frac{X - \bar{X}}{SD}$$

We know $X = 79$, $\bar{X} = 77$, and SD = 1, thus

$$z = \frac{79 - 77}{1} = \frac{2}{1} = 2$$

Rich's z-score is equal to +2 in his history class.

Now we can calculate his t-score using our knowledge of his z-score and the t-score formula.

T = 10z + 50 = 10(2) + 50 = 70. Here we see that Rich's t-score is 70. In both cases, Rich was at a standard score representative of two standard deviation units above the mean. Note that his relative position to the class distribution remains the same regardless of the standard score we choose to report.

Now let's see how he fared in his political science class. Again we begin by computing a z-score, only this time we will use the mean and standard deviation provided for this class.

$$z = \frac{X - \bar{X}}{SD}$$

We know $X = 83$, $\bar{X} = 82$, and SD = 2, thus

$$\frac{83-82}{1} = \frac{1}{1} = 1$$

Rich's z-score is equal to +1 in his political science class.

$$T = 10z + 50$$

$$T = 10(1) + 50 = 60, \text{ so Rich's score is equal to } 60.$$

				Political Science		History	
Z-score	−3	−2	−1	0	+1	+2	+3
T-score	20	30	40	50	60	70	80

Based on Rich's computed z-scores and t-scores, and our knowledge of the distribution of scores in a normal curve, we can now determine his percentile rank. Both Rich's z-scores and t-scores indicate a position that is one standard deviation above the mean. From Figure 2.8 we see that a position of one standard deviation above the mean equates to a percentile of 84. A total of 84% of Rich's classmates scored at or below his score.

When we have data from multiple distributions or measures, we can use standard scores to make comparisons. Although history and political science are two completely different subjects, and knowledge of one does not necessarily translate to success in the other, standard scores can be used to compare Rich's performance in these two classes. In both classes we know his performance is above average because his z-scores were positive (+2 and +1) and his t-scores were both above the average of 50 (70 and 60). Because his score in the history class placed him at a standard score farther from the mean than did his political science score, we can say that his performance was more impressive, relative to his classmates, in the history class. The farther to the right a score is from the mean (the higher the *positive* z-score), the better a person did. The farther a score is to the left (the higher the *negative* z-score), the poorer the student did in relation to the distribution of scores to which he or she is being compared.

KEYSTONES

- Statistics are defined as a set of tools and techniques used for describing, organizing, and interpreting information. They can be either descriptive or inferential.

- There are four scales of measurement used to summarize measured data: nominal, ordinal, interval, and ratio. Each scale is identified by the presence or absence of a set of properties: identification, magnitude, equal intervals, and the presence of an absolute zero point.
- Frequency distributions order a set of disorganized raw scores and summarize the number of times each of the different scores occurs within a sample of observations. They can be presented as either tables or graphs. Examples of frequency graphs include histograms, bar graphs, polygons, and smooth curves.
- Distributions can be either symmetrical or skewed in shape. Positively skewed distributions have the majority of their scores in the negative (low) end of the distribution, and negatively skewed distributions have the majority of their scores in the positive (high) end of the distribution.
- Central tendency refers to a statistical measure that indicates the center or middle of the distribution. The three commonly reported measures of central tendency are the mean, median, and mode.
- Variability is a quantitative measure that describes how spread out or clustered together scores are in a distribution. Some measures of variability are the range, inclusive range, standard deviation, and variance.

KEY TERMS

arithmetic mean	interval	range
bar graphs	kurtosis	ratio
bimodal	measures of variability	smooth curves
central tendency	median	standard deviation
continuous data	mode	standard scores
descriptive statistics	multimodal	stanine
discrete data	negatively skewed	statistics
frequency distribution	nominal	variability
frequency polygon	normal curve	variable
graphs	ordinal	variance
grouped frequency distribution	percentage	
histogram	percentile score	
inclusive range	positively skewed	
inferential statistics	qualitative variables	
	quantitative variables	

ADDITIONAL RESOURCES

Counselors may find the following books helpful as each presents the statistical concepts discussed in this chapter in a nontechnical manner and is designed to be used by practitioners.

Lyman, H. B. (1998). *Test scores and what they mean* (6th ed.). Boston, MA: Allyn & Bacon.

MacCluskie, K. C., Welfel, E. R., & Toman, S. M. (2002). *Using test data in clinical practice: A handbook for mental health professionals.* Thousand Oaks, CA: Sage.

Salkind, N. J. (2013). *Statistics for people who think they hate statistics* (5th ed.). Thousand Oaks, CA: Sage.

Vogt, W. P., & Johnson, B. (2011). *Dictionary of statistics and methodology: A non-technical guide for the social sciences* (4th ed.). Thousand Oaks, CA: Sage.

Student Study Site: Visit the Student Study Site at **www.sagepub.com/watson** to access additional study tools, including quizzes, web resources, and journal articles.

CHAPTER 3

Reliability

LEARNING OBJECTIVES

After reading this chapter, you will be able to

- Explain classical test theory and its influence on the psychometric properties of tests and other assessment instruments
- Define the concept of reliability and explain its relevance to counseling assessment
- Identify sources of measurement error that could compromise reliability
- Describe the methods by which reliability can be estimated
- Interpret and evaluate computed reliability coefficients
- Define the concept of standard error of measurement and discuss its relationship to reliability
- Explain the factors that affect reliability measures

The process of assessment is critical to the success achieved in the counseling relationship. For a counselor to effectively help a client work through his or her presenting issues, the assessment activities used to gather information about the client, be they formal or informal, need to be useful and clinically beneficial. Specifically, the instruments or techniques used by the counselor need to be trustworthy and reliable. In fact, the reliability of an instrument is one of the most important characteristics a counselor should examine before choosing to use a particular instrument or approach. The term *reliability* refers to the consistency or reproducibility of test scores or assessment data. When an assessment is found to be reliable, counselors can use it with a sense of confidence, knowing that the results they obtain are dependable and thus meaningful.

When evaluating the reliability of an instrument, there are a number of statistical methods a counselor can employ. These methods can be used to assess reliability over time, between instruments, and between the individual items on a single instrument. In this chapter we will look at each of the methods commonly used to assess reliability, providing ample examples to help you appreciate the importance of this psychometric property of tests and assessment practices. In addition, we will examine the factors influencing reliability and discuss the concept of standard error of measurement.

RELIABILITY DEFINED

As you begin looking at various assessment instruments to use in your counseling practice, one of the more important characteristics you will need to consider is the reliability of the results that instrument will provide. The term **reliability** refers to the ability of test scores to be interpreted in a consistent and dependable manner across multiple test administrations. Consider the example of a counselor administering the WISC-IV to a student to assess the cognitive ability of a child. If the counselor administered the WISC-IV to the child and noted an overall IQ score of 75 on one day and an overall IQ score of 115 on a subsequent administration two days later, the counselor would have just cause to question the reliability of these results. A 40-point difference in scores on the WISC-IV would not be expected for any child being assessed. In this example, the counselor should obviously not put much faith in these unreliable test results. For results to have any meaningful significance in the counseling process they need to be stable and reliable. Before we begin our discussion of reliability, we thought it prudent to present some caveats to properly understanding how to interpret estimates of reliability.

First, reliability is a property that resides with the scores on an assessment test and not with the test itself. In the above example it was not the intelligence test itself that was unreliable; rather it was the results that test produced that were under question. Second, reliability estimates are specific to the type of reliability being assessed. As we will discuss later in this chapter, there are different measures of reliability that can be computed. A test may have a high level of internal consistency, but that does not mean it also will have a high level of test-retest reliability. Finally, the scores obtained from administration of a test are rarely, if ever, consistent all of the time. As Urbina (2004) has noted in the past, all instruments are subject to some degree of error or fluctuation. Understanding how to interpret reliability coefficients allows counselors to select the most stable and consistent measures to use with their clients. As Onwuegbuzie and Daniel (2002) note, the fact that many counseling decisions are made from the counseling research base underscores the importance of obtaining reliable information from clients.

Because measurement errors play a key role in determining the overall reliability of the results obtained from the administration of a test, we will begin our discussion of reliability by examining the causes of measurement error and how they can be accounted for in our evaluation of test results.

CLASSICAL TEST THEORY

We know that tests scores are never completely consistent and that there will always be at least some degree of variance in them. To help you understand better the concept of measurement error, we introduce you to Classical Test Theory (CTT). CTT, often referred to as the true score model, describes a set of psychometric procedures that can be used to test the reliability, difficulty, and discriminatory properties of test items and scales. It is a theory that describes how measurement error impacts our understanding of an individual's true ability level on a test or measure. The fundamental principle underlying CTT is that the total test score achieved by an individual actually comprises multiple items (Kline, 2005). These items are the raw score (X), true score (T), and any random error (E) not accounted for by the test. CTT posits that a person's achieved score (the raw score) actually comprises his or her true score plus any added measurement error (see Case Illustration 3.1). Thus the formula for CTT is expressed as follows:

$$X = T + E$$

Let's take a moment to explore the implications of this formula. As a student you no doubt have taken countless examinations throughout your academic career. On each examination you received a score indicating your mastery of the subject matter being assessed. But what does this score truly mean? Is it a definitive statement of your level of knowledge regarding the subject you were being tested on? It might surprise you to know that the answer is no, your score is *not* a definitive statement of your knowledge; rather it is merely an estimate of your true knowledge of the subject. Your true score, were you actually able to ascertain it, would be the average score you would get on the same test if you had taken the test an infinite number of times. Since it would be impractical, and not favored by many students, to take a test an infinite number of times, teachers rely on the score obtained on a single test administration as the best estimate of how well the student has mastered the content being tested. Unfortunately, there is always some amount of error associated with this score.

CASE ILLUSTRATION 3.1

On a recent midterm examination comprising 50 multiple-choice items, you receive a score of 84. This score of 84 represents your true score (X) plus some margin of error (E) that was not accounted for in the initial measurement (the examination). In theory, there are several sources of error that could have contributed to the score you received. For one, you could have been sick the day of the examination and thus not performing as well as you might have been able to in better health. Alternatively, you might have been stumped on a few items and fortunately you were able to correctly guess the right answer. Furthermore, there could have been a problem with the way the question was worded or how the question was keyed that caused you to provide the incorrect answer. As you can see, there are many sources of potential error that could have factored into the grade of 84 you received. The 84, then, represents an estimate of how much you know about the subject matter being tested, taking into account these sources of error. On a subsequent administration of the same examination, or a reasonably similar version, your score would be expected to vary slightly. Then you might score an 82 or an 85.

Thinking back to the CTT true score formula, we see that a person's raw score is made up of a combination of his or her true score and an error component. It is this error component that varies the raw score from the true score that would have been obtained under ideal testing conditions and across infinite test administrations. Error can come from many different sources. Plainly speaking, error can be thought of as any factor entering into the process that is not directly relevant to the construct being measured (R. J. Cohen & Swerdlik, 2005). As test administrators, it is our responsibility to limit the amount of error in the testing process as best as we possibly can. When we do so, the scores our clients achieve on assessment tests are more like what their true score should be on the test. In other words, when error is minimized a test produces more reliable scores.

There are various sources of measurement error that can affect the reliability of test scores. These sources could be related to the test itself and how it was constructed, administered, and scored. Other sources may be related to the individual characteristics of the person taking the test. Collectively these sources can be grouped into the two broad categories of systematic and unsystematic measurement error. **Systematic error** occurs when a test is being used and it consistently measures something other than the trait it was designed to assess (Gregory, 2007). In psychometric theory, systematic error is also known as imperfect construct validity (Hunter & Schmidt, 2004). An example of systematic error could be found in the results of a client administered an online screening assessment. Should the client not be too computer savvy, the requirement of completing the assessment online may be quite anxiety provoking. As a result, the test may actually be measuring client anxiety more than it is measuring any of the constructs for which the intake assessment was designed to measure. Because systematic error is seen more as a validity issue, it will be discussed further in Chapter 4.

The other type of measurement error is known as unsystematic error. **Unsystematic error**, also called random error, represents the collection of factors that contribute to the variation in scores noted across administrations of a test or instrument. These factors could be related to the test itself and how it was constructed, administered, and scored. Other sources may be related to the individual characteristics of the person taking the test. Because unsystematic error and the random component of error are issues impacting score reliability (Feldt & Brennan, 1989), they will be explored further in this chapter. In the following section we will examine some common sources of measurement error. However before we proceed, take a moment to look at Guided Practice Exercise 3.1 to see if you can identify any sources of measurement error that may be impacting the data you obtain.

GUIDED PRACTICE EXERCISE 3.1

Identifying Potential Sources of Measurement Error

You are working as a private practice counselor with a client who presented for counseling following a recent divorce. Through your conversations with your client you conceptualize that this client may be clinically depressed. To validate your hypothesis you decide to administer a depression screening inventory. Your client completes the Beck Depression Inventory-II and scores a 23, which would classify the client as being "moderately depressed." What are some sources of measurement error that you would need to consider when interpreting this test result? Remember to consider both systematic and unsystematic sources of measurement error.

SOURCES OF MEASUREMENT ERROR

As noted above there are several sources of error that can contribute to the variation in test scores. Individually, each of these factors can contribute to the unreliability of test scores and should be considered when interpreting test results.

Time Sampling Error

Time sampling errors result from repeated administrations of a test to the same individual. When an individual takes the same test multiple times, the scores obtained will most likely vary. How much they vary will depend largely on the construct being measured. According to Urbina (2004), instruments that assess constructs related to personality traits or individual abilities are less likely to vary because they assess more stable attributes. Constructs that are more transient, such as emotional states, are likely to exhibit a greater amount of variance in scores from one administration to another. When assessing the impact of time sampling, counselors should consider the construct being measured and how likely it is to vary naturally. An individual's mood is more likely to vary from day to day than is his or her intelligence or personality.

When discussing time sampling error, it is important to note the time interval in place between test administrations. The length of time that passes between administrations can produce a number of issues that should be noted. One such issue that is known to have a positive effect on test scoring is carryover effect. **Carryover effect** occurs when an experimental treatment continues to affect a participant long after the treatment is administered (Foley, 2004). In terms of testing, this means that an individual's score on the first administration of a test influences the scores that person receives on subsequent administrations of the same test. An example of a carryover effect is when a client remembers the answers provided previously and answers the same as before. Another issue that might cause scores to increase relates to practice effect. **Practice effect** occurs when individuals improve their scores across test administrations as a result of increased familiarity and comfort with a test and the content that is being assessed. The more exposure a person has to the test and the types of questions being asked, the more likely he or she will perform better in the future. Because some skills improve with practice, counselors should expect to observe increased scores on certain tests.

Time sampling errors also may contribute to test scores varying in a negative fashion. Fatigue is one such issue that might lead to a decrease in scores. **Fatigue** occurs when clients tire from multiple administrations of a test. Their performance decreases as they grow weary of the testing process and are perhaps not as alert and responsive as they might have been on previous items or test administrations. Fatigue is typically an issue on long assessment instruments or in situations where clients are repeatedly tested over a short period of time. For example, a test like the MMPI-2 might produce a fatigue effect. The test contains 567 items and clients may tire or lose interest toward the end of the administration, thus compromising the reliability of their score.

Content Sampling Error

Content sampling errors are related to the development and construction of tests. Also referred to as domain sampling errors, content sampling errors occur when test items are selected that do not adequately assess the construct the test was designed to assess. In some cases it would be near impossible to create a test with enough items to sufficiently assess every aspect of a dimension or construct being assessed. Imagine what an intelligence test would look like if one could be developed to adequately assess all aspects of intelligence. The test would be quite long, assuming researchers could ever fully define the construct of intelligence and how it should be measure and assessed. Since we often find that tests used in the practice of counseling contain an insufficient number of items to assess the entire domain of a given construct, Drummond and Jones (2010) have noted that content sampling errors are viewed as the most common source of error observed in test scores. Combating the effects of content sampling error requires test designers to fully develop the construct they wish to evaluate and operationalize ways it can be assessed and measured.

Test Administration Error

The process of administering a test might also contribute to the random error noted in an individual's score. When the standardized administration protocol for a test is not followed as specified, the reliability of the results may become compromised. Similarly, unforeseen events that occur during the test also might affect performance and scoring. Examples of unforeseen events may include power outages, medical emergencies, fire drills, and so on. To lessen the chance of any administration-related error, test administrators should work to ensure that test takers are given a comfortable testing environment in which to test. For example, counselors could include checking to see that the room is set at a comfortable temperature, the lighting is adequate, and outside noises and distractions are kept to a minimum.

Test Taker Variables

The final source of error we will discuss can be referred to collectively as test taker variables. These include the individual differences in clients and test takers that cannot always be accounted for by the test administrator. Every client you assess will approach the testing process with a different mindset. Some may be more motivated to participate, believing that their results will help both of you better understand the current issue troubling the client. Others may have less of an interest in the testing process and therefore exhibit less effort. Individual variables such as motivation, fatigue, anxiety, test-taking ability, illness, and current mood state should all be taken into account when interpreting test results. When these variables are overlooked, the results may not be completely reliable and counselors might make treatment decisions that are not entirely accurate or appropriate for the client in that particular situation.

MEASURING RELIABILITY: THE CORRELATION COEFFICIENT

You now know that reliability refers to the consistency of a measure or set of scores. The more consistent the scores (whether they be over time, across individuals, or across multiple measures), the more reliable the data we are using to make decisions about our clients. But how do we know how reliable our data are? Fortunately, there is a procedure we can use to compute a numeric value to quantify the reliability of a score or set of scores. This procedure is known as **correlation**. Correlation is a statistical technique used to measure and describe a relationship between two variables. For example, consider the relationship between the amount of time spent studying for an exam and the actual score achieved on said exam. The more hours spent studying for an exam, the better the score will be. A rise in one variable (hours spent studying) is related to a rise on the other variable (exam score). As you interpret this relationship it is important to note that correlation describes only the direction of the relationship. A cause-and-effect relationship cannot be established. While increased amount of time studying appears to be related to improved performance on the exam, we cannot definitively state that the increased amount of time spent studying is directly responsible for the grade earned. Other factors such as fatigue, guessing, and test format may play a role.

Correlations between variables can be either positive or negative. A positive relationship means that the scores on each of the two variables move in the same direction. In this case, both sets of scores either increase or decrease. A negative relationship means that the scores move in opposite directions. Here we see a situation where as scores on one variable increase, scores on the other variable decrease. An example of a negative correlation would be the relationship between the number of depressive symptoms a client exhibits and that client's subjective rating of current mood level. The more symptoms exhibited (value increases), the lower the client's rating of current mood (value decreases). Figure 3.1 shows how positive and negative correlations would look if the data collected on the two variables were plotted on a line graph.

When computing a correlational analysis, the resulting value is called a **correlation coefficient**. The correlation coefficient is a numeric value that indicates the strength of the relationship between two variables. For reliability analyses, the resulting statistic is known as a reliability coefficient. The reliability coefficient represents a ratio between an observed score and true score variance. The formula for a reliability coefficient is as follows:

$$r = \frac{S_r^2}{S_x^2}$$

r = reliability coefficient

S_r^2 = variance of the true scores

S_x^2 = variance of the observed scores

Figure 3.1   Positive and Negative Correlations

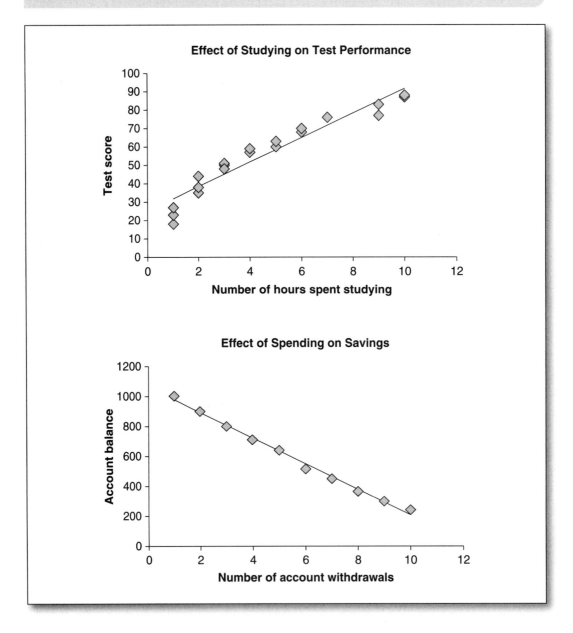

Notice that in the above formula we refer to the true and observed scores in the plural form. This is because reliability coefficients always are computed for groups of scores, not for individual scores. If you were to read that the reliability coefficient for a particular test you were considering using was 0.83, that means that this is the reliability that was computed for multiple administrations of a test with multiple test takers. This value also tells us that 83% of the variance in observed scores is attributed to real differences, not some form of measurement error. The value of the reliability coefficient provides us with a good deal of information that can be used to interpret the suitability of using a particular test in a counseling situation with a client.

The values of a correlation coefficient can range between −1.00 and +1.00. A computed value of −1.00 indicates a perfect negative correlation. Similarly, a value of +1.00 indicates a perfect positive correlation. A perfect correlation means that each and every change in one variable is met with a consistent change in the other variable. Parents may reward their children for maintaining good academic standing in school by offering $5 for every A grade earned. One A earns a child $5, two A's earns $10, three A's earns $15, and so on. As the number of A grades increases by one, the amount of money the student earns increases by an increment of $5. This is an example of a perfect positive correlation because both variables are moving in the same direction (rising). A coefficient of zero indicates that there is no discernible relationship between the variables.

The strength of a correlation is determined by its placement relative to the polar caps of the coefficient range. The closer the coefficient value is to −1.00 or +1.00, the stronger the relationship. When interpreting correlation coefficients, keep in mind that it is the numeric value and not the sign (− or +) that is most telling. A coefficient of −0.95 represents a stronger degree of relationship between variables than a coefficient of +0.85 does. Because we know that reliability coefficients can never exceed +1.00 or −1.00, we can find the percentage of variance attributed to measurement error by subtracting our computed reliability coefficient from 1. The remaining value is our error percentage. Earlier we gave the example of a test that had a reliability coefficient of 0.83. We could subtract that value from one (1 − 0.83) and get a value of 0.17. This tells us that 17% of the variance in observed scores is most likely attributed to some form of measurement error.

METHODS OF ESTIMATING RELIABILITY

Knowing that all assessment instruments have varying degrees of unreliability and are affected by measurement error, we can begin discussing the methods that can be used to estimate the reliability of a test score. There are four primary methods through which reliability can be assessed. These methods are: (a) test-retest, (b) alternate forms, (c) internal consistency, and (d) inter-rater reliability.

Test-Retest Reliability

Perhaps the most commonly used method for assessing reliability is the test-retest method. This approach is used when you are interested in assessing how reliable or stable scores on an instrument are over time (Salkind, 2006). The process of assessing test-retest reliability is straightforward. A set of participants is tested using the same test on two separate occasions. The observed scores of the participants on each test administration are then compared and a reliability coefficient is calculated. In this design, instability over time can be viewed as the primary source of measurement error. Because test-retest reliability is a measure of stability over time, you also may see it sometimes referred to as temporal stability (Erford, 2013). The test-retest reliability method is useful in situations where performance is expected to remain somewhat stable across time (for example, personality traits or intelligence).

Despite its popularity, a challenge with using test-retest reliability is selecting an appropriate length of time between test administrations. Carryover effect is a significant concern when conducting test-retest reliability analyses. When the length of time between test administrations is short, there is a greater likelihood that scores on the second administration of a test may be more related to memory or practice than true ability. A second-grade child is learning his multiplication tables. His teacher tells him that $5 \times 5 = 25$. She then asks him what 5×5 produces, and he says 25. Did the child actually learn to multiply 5×5, or did he simply repeat what he had just heard the teacher say? Alternatively, when the length of the time is too long, there is a risk that maturation or memory loss may adversely impact reliability. The same student is now in college. Presumably his math skills are now more advanced and his ability to complete multiplication problems would be much better than when he was in second grade. One would not expect there to be much consistency between the scores on these two administrations of a math multiplication test. An example of how carryover effect can impact test-retest reliability in a counseling context is provided in Case Illustration 3.2.

When looking at test-retest reliability it is important to consider the construct being assessed and how it is expected to change over time (see Guided Practice Exercise 3.2). For some constructs we would expect to find very stable measures across time, like for personality traits. For others, such as learned knowledge or treatment progress, we would expect there to be great variance from one test administration to another. If consistency is not expected, it may not be practical to rely on test-retest reliability estimates as an indicator of a good instrument to use. Table 3.1 presents the test-retest reliability estimates of some popular commonly used assessment instruments.

Table 3.1   Test-Retest Reliability Estimates of Popular Assessment Instruments

Instrument	Reliability Estimate
Minnesota Multiphasic Personality Inventory-2nd Edition (MMPI-2)	.67 − .92
Millon Clinical Multiaxial Inventory-3rd Edition (MCMI-III)	.82 − .96
Wechsler Adult Intelligence Scale-4th Edition (WAIS-IV)	.74 − .96
Wechsler Intelligence Scale for Children-4th Edition (WISC-IV)	.67 − .89
Personality Assessment Inventory (PAI)	.83
Strong Interest Inventory (SII)	.80 − .92
16 Personality Factors (16-PF)	.69 − .87
Beck Depression Inventory-2nd Edition (BDI-II)	.93

CASE ILLUSTRATION   3.2

A high school counselor has been working with Lisa, a junior, on her test anxiety issues for the past month. Initially, Lisa presented for counseling with concerns that she was unable to perform well on tests in school due to the amount of anxiety she felt when taking tests. From what Lisa described, the counselor concluded that she was suffering mild panic attacks during exams. To check his assumption, the counselor administered an anxiety screening inventory to Lisa. The results of this assessment revealed that she was indeed experiencing many symptoms of anxiety. Over the course of therapy the counselor worked with Lisa to change her cognitions and help her work on anxiety-reduction strategies. On subsequent administrations of the anxiety inventory, a decrease in Lisa's scores was noted. While this typically would indicate poor test-retest reliability, both Lisa and her counselor are encouraged by this trend. Why is this the case? When treatment is working, we have an expectation that our clients will get better, otherwise counseling would hold little value for clients. As a result, their presentation and scores on assessment instruments designed to assess symptoms reported should look noticeably different from how they looked when they first came to counseling. In this case, Lisa's change in scores are an indication that counseling has been helpful to her.

GUIDED PRACTICE EXERCISE 3.2

Predicting Stability or Instability

Consider the following traits or constructs that could be assessed in the counseling process. Would you expect the results from a test-retest reliability analysis to indicate consistent or inconsistent scoring? Why do you think this particular construct would be likely to change over time? In considering the following examples, assume that a standard 2-week period was used between the two testing administrations.

A. Introversion/extraversion

B. Achievement (high school English class)

C. Depression

D. Self-esteem

Alternate Forms Reliability

Alternate forms reliability is a way of assessing stability using different, but equivalent, versions of a test. To create alternate forms of a test, individual items are selected from a pool of test questions designed to assess a given construct. These forms should have similar score means, variances, item difficulty, and correlations with other measures. An example of a test using alternate forms would be the examination counselors are required to take to become a nationally certified counselor. The certification examination is offered twice a year. The same test is not used for each administration. Instead, parallel forms are constructed using items developed to best represent the domain of skills counselors are expected to show competence in. Although the tests are different in look and content, the skills and knowledge assessed on each is equivalent. Because samples of scores are taken using different sets of items, alternate forms reliability may also be referred to as item sampling (Salkind, 2006).

Because a large pool of items is needed to construct alternate forms of a test, this type of reliability estimate is best used when the construct being measured is an ability, aptitude, or specific academic skill (Erford, 2013). These types of constructs lend themselves well to alternate forms reliability because it is easier to develop additional items to measure it. A teacher can develop several multiple-choice items to assess your knowledge of a particular counseling theory. These questions can assess your knowledge of the origins of the theory, specific terms and concepts related to the theory, populations for which the theory can best be applied, and any techniques and interventions associated with the theory. From this pool of items different versions of the test can be created. However, for some constructs, like personality and mood state, there is a more finite number of test items that can be created. As a result, your ability to create two separate forms of a test is challenged. Before considering alternate forms reliability, it is important to consider the construct you are trying to assess, how narrowly defined that construct is, and the breadth and depth of the content domain of that construct from which items will need to be developed.

When alternate forms can be created, this represents a great way to overcome some of the limitations of test-retest reliability analyses. The use of separate forms in many ways mitigates the impact of carryover effect. The items are different, so test takers are not able to simply remember the answers they provided on the previous test administration. Although carryover effects are lessened when using alternate forms, there still might be some lingering effects to note. Because the tests are different in form, any test anxiety a test taker experienced when first seeing the test is likely to be repeated because the novelty of the new test is present. Unlike in the test-retest scenario, the client does not know what the test will look like, so a comfort level is not established. To minimize any carryover effect tests should be developed so that the items are exactly similar in task demands or difficulty and a 2-week interval is used in between the two test administrations.

Internal Consistency

Internal consistency is a little different than the two previous methods of reliability estimation discussed. In internal consistency you are looking at individual items to see if those items are consistent with one another and thus represent a singular construct or trait that is being assessed by the test. This method is used to determine whether errors associated with content sampling are present (Drummond & Jones, 2010). If you were to develop a 20-item test to assess for symptoms of attention deficit hyperactivity disorder (ADHD), you would hope that each of the items on the test assessed some aspect of ADHD. If there were items that assessed for hallucinations and other psychotic features, the test would have very little internal consistency reliability. There are three primary methods for assessing internal consistency: split-half method, Kuder-Richardson formulas, and coefficient alpha.

Split-half reliability. Split-half reliability is accomplished by taking a test and dividing it into two comparable halves. The entire test is administered at once, and a correlation is computed between the results of the two halves. The split-half reliability essentially allows you to create two parallel forms of a test. The benefit lies in the fact that you are able to administer both forms in the same administration. The more highly correlated these two halves are, the greater the internal consistency for the entire test.

To compute the split-half reliability, the **Spearman-Brown prophecy formula** is used. This formula represents an adjusted version of the correlation coefficient formula presented earlier. The adjustment is made to account for the fact that the correlation is being computed between two halves of a test rather than two full-length versions of a test. The result is a variable that provides an estimate of what the reliability coefficient would have been had whole tests been used. The Spearman-Brown prophecy formula is as follows:

$$\frac{2r}{1+r}$$

In this formula r represents the correlation between the two equivalent halves of the test. An example of how this variable should be interpreted is presented in Case Illustration 3.3.

CASE ILLUSTRATION   3.3

A school counselor is evaluating the results of a recent schoolwide assessment of self-esteem as part of a character-building program. The instrument was developed by the school counselor, and she is trying to determine whether the instrument is internally consistent. The instrument contained 30 items, which the school counselor divided into two equal 15-item halves. The correlation coefficient computed for the two equivalent halves was found to be $r = 0.75$. To estimate what the correlation coefficient would have been had two full-version tests been used, the school counselor applies the Spearman-Brown prophecy formula to her results.

$$\frac{2(0.75)}{1+0.75} = 0.86$$

This means that a reliability estimate of 0.86 would be estimated for the full test when the two 15-item test halves are correlated at 0.75. At this level, it could be stated that the test produces reliable and consistent results.

When splitting a test into equivalent halves, you should make note of the how items are arranged and whether they are presented in terms of increasing difficulty level. For tests where the items become progressively more difficult and advanced, it is best to split the test by using odd- and even-numbered items. The odd-even method helps ensure that you are creating two halves that are roughly equivalent in terms of difficulty. Had you divided the test in half where the first set of questions were one form and the second set made up the other form, you would have two halves with noticeably different difficulty levels. This would most certainly compromise your results and possibly lead you to conclude that the instrument had low internal consistency.

Kuder-Richardson formulas. The Kuder Richardson formulas were developed to serve as an alternative to the split-half method of assessing internal consistency. Like in the split-half approach, a single test is administered in a single session. The difference is that rather than arbitrarily dividing the test into two equivalent halves, a statistical process is applied to determine the split-half reliability of all possible combinations of test halves that can be created by separating the items. There are two versions of the Kuder-Richardson formula: KR-20 and KR-21. The KR-20 method uses actual scores on each item (see Case Illustration 3.4), whereas the KR-21 uses mean scores on the entire test in its calculations.

While the KR-20 and KR-21 take the subjectivity out of splitting items and creating test halves that are equivalent in item difficulty and the domain assessed, there is a drawback to this approach. The Kuder-Richardson formulas can be applied only when you have test items that have a dichotomous response set. In other words, questions should provide test takers with the opportunity to respond as either *yes* or *no,* or *true* or *false.* When questions have a dichotomous response set, the KR-20 and KR-21 formulas provide an advantage over the split-half method of estimating reliability.

CASE ILLUSTRATION   3.4

The Self-Directed Search (SDS) is a career assessment instrument developed by John Holland that is designed to help individuals learn about themselves and their career options. It is used frequently in career counseling settings. The SDS includes questions related to an individual's aspirations, activities, competencies, and interest in various occupations and fields of work. An SDS summary code (based on Holland's RIASEC model) is generated. To assess the internal consistency of the instrument, Holland (1994) applied the KR-20 technique and was able to document substantial reliability for the SDS summary scales. KR-20 values ranging between .90 and .94 were noted for each of the summary scales.

Cronbach's alpha. Cronbach's alpha (also referred to as the coefficient alpha) is used when there is no right or wrong answer to a test item. An example of such an item is one that asks the test taker to rate his or her level of agreement with a given statement using a scale from 1 (*strongly disagree*) to 5 (*strongly agree*). Denoted by the symbol α, the formula for computing Cronbach's alpha is as follows:

$$\alpha = \frac{N}{N-1}\left(\frac{s^2 - \sum s_i^2}{s^2}\right)$$

N = number of items

$\sum s_i^2$ = the sum of all the variances for each item

s^2 = variance associated with the observed score

Similar to the Kuder-Richardson formulas, the advantage of Cronbach's alpha is that we now can assess the internal consistency of tests that use multiple-response sets instead of being limited to only looking at items with dichotomous response sets.

Although measures of internal consistency are widely used, they are not sensitive to specific or transient errors (Heppner, Wampold, & Kivlighan, 2008, p. 319). An instrument may demonstrate a great deal of internal consistency, but that consistency may exist only in certain settings or specific to a particular client. A counselor-in-training may complete a counseling skills assessment inventory and produce consistent results. However, once this same student begins moving away from simulated practice sessions and seeing real clients for the first time, the results of this same skills inventory are far less consistent. When used in the controlled training environment, the instrument was reliable and internally consistent, but when used with counselors in their field placement experiences (practica and internships), results were far less consistent.

Inter-rater Reliability

Each of the previously discussed forms of reliability has dealt with the instrument and its items. Now we will look at how the reliability of the test administrator can be assessed. Inter-rater reliability is used when we want to assess the level of agreement between two or more raters in their evaluation of a particular outcome. The most effective way to assess inter-rater reliability is to correlate the scores obtained independently by each of the raters by using the following formula:

$$inter\text{-}rater\ reliability = \frac{number\ of\ agreements}{number\ of\ disagreements}$$

To demonstrate how inter-rater reliability is computed, consider the example in Case Illustration 3.5. When estimating inter-rater reliability counselors should keep in mind that they are assessing only the consistency of raters to rate an item the same. Nothing is said in relation to any measurement error as a result of content sampling or time sampling. To increase inter-rater reliability, raters should be provided with thorough training in which they are taught what they are observing and how it should be rated (see Guided Practice Exercise 3.3). In Table 3.2 we summarize the reliability estimates discussed along with the purpose that each estimate serves.

Table 3.2 Types of Reliability Estimates

Reliability Estimate	Purpose
Test-retest reliability	Used to measure the reliability obtained by administering the same assessment instrument twice over a period of time to the same group of individuals
Alternate forms	Used to measure the relatedness of two different assessment instruments designed to assess the same latent construct
Internal consistency reliability	Used to evaluate the degree to which individual test items designed to assess the same construct produce similar results
Inter-rater reliability	Used to measure the degree to which different raters or observers agree in their assessment decisions

CASE ILLUSTRATION 3.5

Two faculty members in a counselor education program are reviewing skill demonstration tapes submitted by students in an introductory counseling skills course. The instructors are asked to complete a rating sheet for each student. On the rating sheet they are to rate each student on a scale from 1 to 4, with 4 representing masterful implementation of the skill being observed. The rating sheet includes 10 different skills that are to be evaluated. The class average ratings of the two counselor educators are as follows:

Counseling Skill	Instructor 1	Instructor 2
Listening	4	3
Empathy	4	4
Genuineness	3	4
Unconditional positive regard	2	3
Concreteness	3	3
Open questions	4	2
Counselor self-disclosure	2	4
Interpretation	1	1
Summarizing	3	3
Information giving	3	4

To compute the inter-rater reliability, we take the number of items where there was agreement between the two raters (4) and divide that by the number of items where there was disagreement between the raters (6). The result is an inter-rater reliability value of 0.67.

GUIDED PRACTICE EXERCISE 3.3

Calculating Inter-rater Reliability

Partner up with a classmate and look at the following list of counseling theories. Based on your professional opinion, rate each of these theories on how effective you believe they are at helping clients achieve change in their lives using the following scale: 1 = *not effective at all*, 2 = *minimally effective*, 3 = *somewhat effective*, and 4 = *very effective*. First rate each of the theories individually, and then share your results with your partner. Using both of your ratings, compute an inter-rater reliability coefficient. How consistent were the two of you in your ratings?

Theory	Your Rating	Your Partner's Rating
Psychoanalysis		
Individual psychology		
Gestalt therapy		
Person-centered therapy		
Existential counseling		
Behavioral therapy		
Cognitive-behavioral therapy		
Solution-focused therapy		
Reality therapy		
Narrative therapy		

The issue of inter-rater reliability is frequently raised in school settings. School counselors often work with, and rely on information from, administrators, teachers, and parents to shape the work they do with students. Each of these sources may have a different criteria they rely on when assessing a student. As a result, there likely will be little agreement between these sources. One way school counselors can overcome this issue is by working closely with these other stakeholders and training them on what they should be looking for and how a student's behavior should be interpreted. In Chapter 11 we will more closely look at how school counselors can address issues related to reliability in behavioral assessments.

EVALUATING RELIABILITY COEFFICIENTS

Each of the above methods will provide you with a reliability coefficient. Knowing how to correctly interpret that piece of data will be important in your work as a counselor. Earlier we discussed the properties of the correlation coefficient and talked about how scores could range between −1.00 and +1.00, with scores closer to these polar ends being more reliable. But what amount of reliability is considered sufficient? Unfortunately, there is not a clear-cut answer to this question. Whether a test produces scores that are reliable enough for you to use will depend on a number of factors.

One factor to consider is the type of reliability estimate being reported. The test manuals of most instruments include a section on reliability. Here the authors share the results of any reliability analyses they or others may have conducted. Often more than one reliability coefficient is presented. These coefficients could be the result of a test-retest study or an analysis of internal consistency. Counselors should be aware of how reliability was assessed and determine if the methods tested are similar to how they will use the test with their own clients. Because several reliability coefficients will be presented in the test manuals, you are encouraged to consider them all and not make any decisions based on one single piece of data alone. That single score could represent reliability only in a specific type of test administration, or there might have been measurement errors in that analysis that compromised the results. As a result, it is better to consider the whole picture concerning the reliability of test scores across all methods for which reliability was assessed.

A second factor to address is the purpose for which the test is being administered (Whiston, 2009). In other words, how will the results be used? If the decisions made based on the client's scores have higher stakes (program admission, treatment decisions), counselors should opt to use tests with as high a level of reliability as possible. When determining whether a client who presents with thoughts of self-harm meets criteria for an inpatient hospitalization, highly reliable instruments should be used so you can be more confident in the treatment decisions you make based on the test scores. As a general rule of thumb, reliability coefficients in the 0.90s are preferable and indicate a high degree of reliability. Reliability coefficients in the 0.80s are acceptable, but in some situations you may want to acquire corroborating evidence from other sources to support your decisions. The closer the reliability coefficient gets to 0.50, the more likely the tests scores are to be a product of chance than they are any true score variance. Coefficients below 0.50 indicate that the observed score is heavily influenced by measurement error and thus not very reliable at all (see Table 3.3).

A third factor that should be addressed is the individual characteristics of the client being tested. There are several client variables that may influence the reliability of test scores. Age, gender, ethnicity, cultural differences, socioeconomic status, and educational background are but a few client variables that might influence the reliability of test scores. Test users are urged to read test manuals carefully before introducing a test into the counseling process. Is the test you are considering appropriate for the type of client with whom you are working? Have any reliability studies been

Table 3.3   Evaluating Reliability Coefficients

Evaluation	Computed r value
Very high	greater than 0.90
High	between 0.80 and 0.89
Acceptable	between 0.70 and 0.79
Questionable	between 0.60 and 0.69
Unacceptable	less than 0.59

Source: Adapted from Drummond & Jones (2010, Table 5.2, p. 94).

conducted specific to this client population? Knowing the answers to these questions will help you more confidently select appropriate tests and interpret the resulting test scores.

STANDARD ERROR OF MEASUREMENT

There are two additional assumptions of classical test theory (CTT) that bear mentioning at this point. The first is that the distribution of scores observed for an individual on repeated administrations of the same test should be normal. In other words, if you were to plot each score the person achieved with enough test administrations, your plot should resemble a normal curve. The second assumption is that the standard deviation of this normal distribution would be the same for each member of the treatment group or class that was tested. The standard deviation of the normal distribution is called the **standard error of measurement** (SEM).

In Chapter 2 you learned about some of the properties of the normal curve. The same properties apply here. Between +1 SEM and −1 SEM, we can expect to find approximately 68% of the scores in a distribution. Between +2 SEM and −2 SEM, we can expect to find about 95% of the scores. We can use this information to help in constructing confidence intervals. For example, to find a 95% confidence interval we would take an individual's observed score and both add 2 SEM units to it and subtract 2 SEM units from it. The resulting interval allows us to say with 95% confidence that the test taker's true score most likely falls between these two end values. For example, a client scores a t-value of 65 on the paranoia scale (scale 6) of the MMPI-2. If the SEM computed for the clients receiving care at this particular treatment center was calculated to be 3, we could state with 95% confidence that the client's true score would most likely fall in the range of 62 − 68 on this scale.

To compute an SEM you need a couple pieces of information (see Case Illustration 3.6 for additional information). You need to know both the reliability (r_{xx}) and the standard deviation (σ_x) for the set of observed scores. These variables can then be plugged into the following formula:

$$SEM = \sigma_x \sqrt{1 - r_{xx}}$$

CASE ILLUSTRATION 3.6

A school counselor is reviewing the IQ scores computed for students in an accelerated learning class at a local high school. Each of the students was administered the WISC-IV prior to admission into this class. The reliability for the full-scale WISC-IV score is a reported 0.97. The standard deviation for IQ scores is 15. With this information the school counselor can conduct an SEM that can be used to construct confidence intervals for the scores of the students in the accelerated learning class.

(Continued)

(Continued)

$$SEM = 15\sqrt{1 - 0.97}$$

$$SEM = 15\sqrt{0.03}$$

$$SEM = 15(.17)$$

$$SEM = 2.55$$

To find the 68% confidence interval, the school counselor would add and subtract 2.55 from each student's observed IQ score. To find the 95% confidence interval, she would add and subtract 5.10 (2.55 × 2) to each student's observed score. To find the 99% confidence interval, she would add and subtract 7.65 (2.55 × 3) to each observed score.

Small SEM values produce small confidence intervals. The smaller the SEM, the less variance there is among scores, resulting in a higher degree of reliability. As a result, an inverse relationship exists between SEM and reliability. The more reliable the test, the smaller the SEM computed. Although a smaller SEM means you have more reliability in your scores, the confidence you have in the corresponding confidence intervals constructed using that SEM will be lessened. Counselors therefore are cautioned to consider what a greater priority is for them in their given situation. Determining whether it would be preferable to be more accurate (small confidence interval) or confident (larger confidence interval) would help determine how SEM is used in interpreting observed test scores.

FACTORS AFFECTING RELIABILITY

To increase the likelihood of being able to reproduce a set of test scores under differing conditions and situations, there are several steps test developers and users can take to improve reliability and reduce measurement error. The first is to increase the length of the test. The more questions that are included on a test, the more reliable the scores obtained on said test will be. Lengthening the test increases the internal consistency of the test provided that the questions added are of an equivalent difficulty level and the number of items added is not so large as to produce test taker fatigue. Imagine an intelligence test that asked clients to answer a single math problem. Would their resulting IQ score be very reliable? As a result, most intelligence tests include many items and test several different elements that make up the construct known as intelligence.

A second approach counselors can take to increase reliability is to make sure the test or instrument used is designed for the population being assessed. Make sure the reading level is appropriate for your clients based on their age, vocabulary, and level of education. In a study of adolescent reporting of their experiences in counseling, the reliability of adolescent reporting was found to be strongly influenced by question characteristics such as sentence complexity and vocabulary level (Santelli, Klein, Graff, Allan, & Elster, 2002).

Another way to increase test score reliability is to increase the heterogeneity of the group used to norm the instrument. The more similar test takers are, the more likely their scores will be the same. When the scores are similar, there is little error to observe. The ideal situation would be to have a group that was identical in all characteristics other than the one that was being assessed by the test. This would allow you to more confidently state that any variance noted was in fact representative of true score variance.

Finally, reliability can be increased by using an optimal time interval between test administrations. As discussed earlier when we introduced test-retest reliability, the time interval used between tests plays a role in how reliable the results are. An interval that is too short may produce a situation in which test takers are simply remembering what they just answered and their scores are a product of recall more so than ability. Time intervals that are too long may result in a situation where additional variables may come into play that may change a person's scores on a test. If you were to screen a client for depressive symptoms on a weekly basis over the course of 2 months, you would expect to find somewhat consistent results. However, if you tested the same client once every 6 months, the results may not be as consistent. Circumstances in the client's life may have changed for the better, or counseling may have been effective in enhancing mood. Knowing the correct length of time to wait between test administrations is not an exact science and should be determined taking into account the construct being assessed and how the results will be used to forward the counseling process.

KEYSTONES

- Reliability refers to the consistency, dependability, and stability of test scores.
- Reliability is a property of test scores and not the instruments used to produce those scores.
- Test scores are never 100% consistent. Unsystematic (random) error exists and produces the variation noted between an individual's true and observed score on a test.
- Several measures of reliability can be used to assess the consistency of a test score. These measures include test-retest reliability, alternate forms reliability, internal consistency, and inter-rater reliability.
- Acceptable levels of reliability will vary depending on the construct being measured, the way test scores are used, and the method employed for assessing reliability.
- Although measurement error exists in all tests, test developers and administrators can take steps to mitigate the effects of unsystematic error and increase the reliability of test scores so that these scores can be integrated more effectively in counseling practice.

KEY TERMS

carryover effect

correlation

correlation coefficient

fatigue

internal consistency

practice effect

reliability

Spearman-Brown prophecy formula

standard error of measurement

systematic error

unsystematic error

ADDITIONAL RESOURCES

- Research Methods Knowledge Base

  http://www.socialresearchmethods.net/kb/reltypes.php

This website describes various types of reliability estimates and offers illustrations for how they can be obtained.

- National Center for Research on Evaluation, Standards, & Student Testing

  http://www.cse.ucla.edu

- National Council on Measurement in Education

  http://ncme.org

Student Study Site: Visit the Student Study Site at **www.sagepub.com/watson** to access additional study tools, including quizzes, web resources, and journal articles.

CHAPTER 4

Validity

LEARNING OBJECTIVES

After reading this chapter, you will be able to

- Define the concept of validity and explain its relevance to counseling assessment
- Explain the relationship between reliability and validity
- Describe the four primary facets of validity
- Interpret the magnitude of validity coefficients
- Identify the major threats to validity (both internal and external)

As a counselor, it is imperative that you develop the ability to select appropriate assessment instruments to use with your clients. The current accountability movement in education and healthcare necessitates that counselors be able to justify their choices related to instrument selection when it comes to assessment practice. One way counselors can do this is by selecting instruments that are psychometrically sound. In Chapter 3 you learned about an important psychometric property of tests and assessments known as reliability. In this chapter you will learn about a concept equally as important: validity.

Simply stated, validity is a measure of an assessment's accuracy. In other words, validity is concerned with how accurately an instrument or assessment procedure evaluates the trait or variable that it was designed to assess. To illustrate this point more clearly, consider the following example. As a counselor, you could administer an intelligence test (e.g., the Wechsler Adult Intelligence Scale) to a client every week over the course of 2 months of counseling. Although scores might improve slightly due to the effects of practice and **test familiarity**, the client's scores would very likely be quite consistent and thus demonstrate a good deal of reliability. However, if you were interested in assessing whether the client was experiencing symptoms associated with clinical depression, the intelligence test you were administering would probably be of little value to you. Knowledge about the intelligence of an individual does not help you assess that person for depression. In this scenario, you would be using the intelligence test in an incorrect, and invalid, manner.

In this chapter you will learn how the concepts of reliability (discussed in Chapter 3) and validity are interrelated and often reported as complimentary measures. In addition, you will be introduced to a number of methods for gathering evidence of validity commonly used in counseling and psychological assessment. Becoming familiar with these methods will help you become a more accountable and skilled clinician. In addition to introducing the basic types of validity evidence, this chapter also will teach you how to assess for evidence along these types of validity. Finally, this chapter will show you how to detect potential threats to validity and how these threats can be minimized throughout the counseling process.

WHAT IS VALIDITY?

In the introduction to this chapter we described validity as being a measure of an instrument's ability to accurately assess a given trait or variable. As we begin our exploration into the concept of validity, we believe it would be helpful to provide a standard operational definition of the term. There are several definitions put forth for the concept of validity. Perhaps the best definition for validity can be found in the *Standards for Educational and Psychological Testing* (American Educational Research Association [AERA], American Psychological Association [APA], & National Council on Measurement in Education [NCME], 1999). In these standards, **validity** is broadly defined as "the degree to which evidence and theory support the interpretations of test scores entailed by proposed uses of tests" (p. 9). In other words, a test or instrument is valid to the extent that inferences made from it are appropriate, meaningful, and useful to the counselor administering it. Throughout the remainder of this chapter, when we refer to validity, this is the definition we will be basing our discussions on.

As you consider the concept of validity, it is important to note that the validity or accuracy of a measure is not absolute. Instruments by themselves are neither valid nor invalid. Instead, it is the *application* of these instruments and how the results they produce can be interpreted that is validated. As noted by Whiston (2009),

> validity is not a quality that an instrument either has or does not have, rather it is a description of the situations in which it would be appropriate for a counselor to use the particular instrument and how the results should be interpreted. (p. 67)

Think back to our example above where the counselor was administering the intelligence test to a client and trying to assess for depression. Although the test used may be a widely used measure of intelligence, it certainly was not valid in this context. Knowing that a client has a WAIS-IV IQ score of 112 does little to help you understand the client's current mood state. While the intelligence test may not have been a valid measure in this situation, there are other situations in which it might be a completely valid instrument to use. Had the counselor been working in a school setting and attempting to determine placement in a gifted program for a student, the intelligence test would likely be viewed as a valid assessment to administer. The intelligence test itself is not valid or invalid; it is the specific usage of the test and how its results will be used that determine validity. Similarly, the validity of a measure is also contextually specific. What is valid for one population or culture may not be for another (see Guided Practice Exercise 4.1).

GUIDED PRACTICE EXERCISE 4.1

Discussing the Validity of Standardized Admission Tests

Throughout your academic career you have no doubt taken multiple standardized tests (ACT, SAT, GRE, GMAT, etc.) as part of your academic experience. The scores you make on these tests are used to assess your ability to successfully complete undergraduate or graduate degree programs. Despite their widespread use, there are many who question the validity of these tests and whether they really help predict future academic success. What are your thoughts on the utility of these types of tests? Do you believe they are valid measures of future success? How have the scores you made on these tests correlated with your success in your undergraduate and graduate degree programs?

A second important aspect to note is that validity estimates are often expressed in terms of magnitude or the degree to which validity is present. Validity should not be viewed as an all-or-nothing property of an assessment. Depending on the individual circumstances of the situation in which an assessment is being applied, the degree of validity can vary. Modifiers such as *low*, *moderate*, and *high* often are used to describe the validity of an assessment. Like you saw in our discussion of reliability in Chapter 3, a numeric score, in this case known as a validity coefficient, can be computed to assess the relative strength of an assessment's validity. The larger the coefficient value computed, the more valid the use of the assessment test or procedure.

Why Is Validity Important for Counselors?

Validity speaks to the *truthfulness* of data. When the information counselors gather about their clients is truthful and accurate, they are able to provide more effective services. Counselors, therefore, should strive to use only those assessment measures that have been empirically studied and found to be valid. Using valid assessments, counselors are able to more accurately diagnosis client presenting problems and formulate more well-informed treatment plans.

At a more macro-level, validity helps advance the field of counseling. Valid assessment is used to demonstrate that the services counselors provide are as efficacious as many controlled outcome studies of psychotherapy efficacy (McAleavey et al., 2012). The ability to document the effectiveness of services offered not only helps foster consumer confidence in the work that counselors do, but also benefits local and national advocacy efforts designed to advance the counseling profession and remove barriers to mental health services that many people in our communities face on a daily basis.

Relationship Between Validity and Reliability

Reliability and validity are not mutually exclusive concepts; rather they are intimately related (McGoey, Cowan, Rumrill, & LaVogue, 2010). For an assessment to be considered valid, it must first be proved to be reliable. To assess your knowledge of the material presented in this book, your instructor could administer to you an examination testing your knowledge of assessment practices. If your scores on repeated administrations of the exam vary widely, this might be an indication that the questions on the examination are not accurately representing the material presented in this book. Thus the examination, in this context, is invalid. On the other hand, an assessment can be proved to be reliable but not necessarily be considered valid. As we saw in the introduction to this chapter, repeated administrations of the WAIS-IV intelligence test could yield consistent (reliable) results, but this test would hardly be considered a valid method for assessing a client's level of depression. Because of the unique relationship between reliability and validity, reliability is generally viewed as being a *necessary* but *not sufficient* condition for validity (see Guided Practice Exercise 4.2).

To help you visualize the relationship between reliability and validity, look at the three targets presented in Figure 4.1. The center of the target represents the construct you are trying to measure. In this case, let's assume we are trying to assess for the presence of attention deficit hyperactivity disorder (ADHD). In the first target we see a situation where the instrument used to assess ADHD was reliable but not valid. Although the assessment results remained consistent from administration to administration, the instrument used did not accurately assess whether the client had ADHD. In the center target we see a situation where the assessment was valid but not reliable. Scores close to the center indicate that the instrument was able to successfully identify ADHD for some clients but not all. While the test was able to assess the construct which it was designed to assess (validity), it did not do so in a consistent fashion. The final target shows an example of an assessment that was both reliable and valid. Not only did the instrument accurately assess ADHD, it also did so consistently. Case Illustration 4.1 is meant to help you further your understanding of the importance of using valid instruments.

CASE ILLUSTRATION 4.1

A school counselor is interested in assessing the behavior of a student whose teacher reports that he has been acting out in class recently. Specifically, the counselor is interested in determining whether the student in question may have attention deficit hyperactivity disorder (ADHD). If the school counselor chose an instrument that only rated behaviors related to an attention deficit, the instrument would not have much content validity. There would be no questions that focused on hyperactivity. The instrument would not include items that covered all symptoms of ADHD and thus would be a poor choice to use as a diagnostic tool. What could the counselor do to ensure that the instrument selected accurately represents the entirety of the construct being assessed?

Figure 4.1 Relationship Between Reliability and Validity

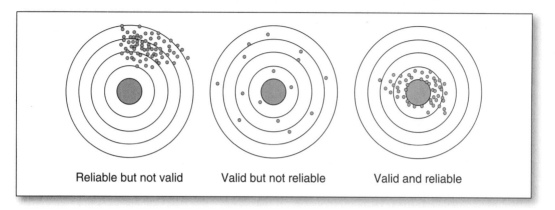

Reliable but not valid   Valid but not reliable   Valid and reliable

Source: Columbia Center for New Media Teaching (2002–2003).

GUIDED PRACTICE EXERCISE 4.2

Comparing Reliability and Validity

Reliability and validity are both important properties of sound assessments. In terms of their relationship, reliability is seen as a *necessary* but *not sufficient* condition for validity. What does this mean to you? Why is it not enough to for an instrument that has demonstrated reliability to also be considered valid?

How Is Validity Assessed?

Now that you know the application of an assessment instrument is what is being evaluated for validity, we can begin looking at the process through which validity is established. Throughout the years, our understanding of validity has changed based on evolving research and study. In the early 1900s validity was largely criterion-based. According to Kane (2001),

> much of the early discussion of validity was couched within a realist philosophy of science, in which the variable of interest was assumed to have a definite value for each person, and the goal of measurement was to estimate this variable's value as accurately as possible. (p. 319)

This approach was based on the premise that a criterion that provided a true measure of the value or amount of a given variable of interest existed. Tests were considered valid when they produced results that were accurate estimates of the established criterion. Though there were noted benefits to using the criterion-based approach toward establishing validity, problems arose when a clearly defined and demonstrably valid criterion could not be produced. This challenge led to a change in the way validity was conceptualized.

In the 1950s, an increased emphasis was placed on scientific rigor and the advancement of psychometrically sound research methodologies. It was during this time that *classical test theory* was developed and actively promoted as the framework of choice to guide the assessment of validity data in research and test development. In classical test theory, the concept of validity is described as occurring in one of three distinct forms: content validity, criterion validity, and construct validity. In this theory it was hypothesized that each of these three types of validity could be assessed independently to determine both the rigor and appropriateness of an assessment instrument (Erford, 2013). Essentially, they were seen as equal but distinct entities. Despite the objections of many researchers to this conceptualization of validity, the tripartite view was included in the original *Standards for Educational and Psychological Testing* (APA, 1966) as well as the subsequent second (1974) and third (1985) editions.

Beginning with the fourth edition (AERA et al., 1999), a new approach to viewing validity was presented. Rather than separating these aspects of validity into three distinct entities, content, criterion, and construct validity were now presented as elements of a single unified construct. Supporting this unified perspective, Messick (1989) contends that all validity is essentially really about the construct being assessed and the meaning of those scores obtained to measure it (see Table 4.1). According to Messick, if the construct itself cannot be accurately identified and clearly defined, any subsequent attempts to measure or assess either its presence or absence in clients would be futile. Case Illustration 4.2 is included to help illustrate Messick's concept of unified validity.

Table 4.1 Aspects of Validity Assessed in the Unified Validity Theory

Aspect	Description
Content	Assesses the relevance, representativeness, and technical quality of an assessment instrument
Substantive	Assesses the theoretical rationale for the observed consistencies in responses to assessment items
Structural	Assesses whether the internal structure of the assessment instrument is consistent with what is known about the internal structure of the construct domain being assessed
Generalizability	Assesses the ability of assessment information to generalize within a population and across other populations
External	Assesses both convergent and discriminant evidence of validity
Consequential	Assesses the actual and potential consequences of using an assessment instrument

Source: Adapted from Dimitrov (2012, pp. 41–51).

CASE ILLUSTRATION   4.2

The following example is designed to help illustrate Messick's point regarding the unified aspect of validity. Imagine that you have been tasked with developing a career assessment instrument to be used by potential employers to assess job candidates who may be best suited for long-term success at a company. Your goal is to design an instrument that could be used to take the subjectivity out of the hiring process. Everyone has his or her own definition of what success is and what qualities make an employee successful. Some may point to workplace productivity, while others may reference personality traits that enable the employee to get along well with coworkers. Because success is such a subjective construct, it would be difficult to try to assess its presence in quantifiable terms that everyone who read them would agree with. How would you go about the process of developing a measure of employee success? What components would make up your construct of success, and how would you ensure that the instrument you create could have universal applicability (in other words, be able to be used across multiple careers and employers)?

In this new unified validity theory, the different types of validity (content, criterion, and construct) introduced in the classical test theory are conceptualized as being facets of (or types of evidence for) a singular measure of validity rather than distinct forms of validity. Through the process of validation (see Guided Practice Exercise 4.3), counselors are tasked with collecting as much validity evidence as they can along these facets that supports the intended interpretation of test scores for the proposed purpose for which the scores were collected (Hubley & Zumbo, 2011). For this reason, the term *construct validity* is commonly used to refer to the entire body of accumulated validity evidence about a test or assessment (Lyman, 1998). The following sections provide a description of each of the three facets of validity and describe how counselors can go about the process of collecting evidence of their existence in a given situation.

GUIDED PRACTICE EXERCISE 4.3

Collecting Evidence of Validity

Imagine that you recently were asked to assess the efficacy of a therapeutic group for individuals who have recently been through a divorce. Based on your understanding of the various forms of validity that can be evidenced, how would you go about determining the accuracy or validity of your assessment?

SOURCES OF VALIDITY

In this section we will present an overview of the three primary types of validity: content, criterion, and construct. Although they are now viewed as being equal parts of a global concept of validity, they are presented individually as the terms are still widely referenced in various test manuals, textbooks, and other professional resources in this manner.

Content Validity

Content validity refers to the ability of an instrument to fully assess or measure a construct of interest. An instrument is content valid when its questions or items sufficiently sample from the entire universe of items for which the instrument was designed to sample. The issue of content validity is mostly a sampling issue (Bausell, 1986). How well did the developers of the instrument select items that represented the full spectrum of possible items that could have been selected to represent the given construct? If the items selected for the instrument represent only a fraction of the possible choices that could have been made, the instrument most likely would not have much content validity. In other words, the instrument oversamples some areas and underrepresents others.

The process of collecting evidence of content validity is largely an imprecise activity. However, according to Erford (2013), "determining the content validity of a test requires a systematic evaluation of the test items to determine whether adequate coverage of a representative sample of the content domain was measured" (p. 149). Beginning with instrument development, content validation is a process that progresses through a series of steps. These steps do not require any intense or complicated computations. Rather, they are based on a logical approach to defining and assessing a variable of interest.

The first step in the content validation process is to make sure that a well-established construct is being used. Drummond and Jones (2010) note that the definition of the construct is important because it determines the subject matter being assessed and the items that are to be included on the instrument assessing that subject. To determine whether an instrument includes a group of items that sufficiently samples the full range of possible items that could be chosen, it is important that a narrowly defined construct be used. For instance, creating an instrument to measure mood would be difficult to do because there are several different moods that can be experienced. The corresponding instrument would need to have an inordinate number of items to ensure that it captured all possible mood states. A better approach would be to select a more specific construct to measure. For example, assessing depression is more specific than assessing mood. When the construct is better defined, it is certainly easier to determine whether the items included on the assessment are representative or not.

After defining a construct, the various domains or subcategories of that construct are identified. These domains are identified through a review of the relevant professional literature, examining existing instruments, or aligning the instrument with existing standards or criteria. An assessment of suicide would include domains related to ideation, intent, and access to means as these are the various components of suicide that are assessed with a client. Items are then collected for each of these domains. The number of items selected for each domain should be proportionate to the importance of that domain to the overall construct. In educational settings, teachers can increase the content validity of their examinations by making sure that the number of questions drawn from each chapter in the textbook that appear on the exam represents the amount of class time spent on each chapter. Including three questions from a chapter that took three weeks to cover and nine questions from a chapter that took a week to cover would not represent a good distribution of items.

Once the instrument has been developed, there are a couple of approaches that can be used to further assess its content validity (see Table 4.2). Perhaps the simplest approach would be to use a panel of experts. The panel of experts can be used to determine content validity by having them review the instrument to see if it is a fair and balanced assessment. Individuals chosen for this panel should include both field experts and lay experts (Rubio, 2005). Field experts are those who have researched and published in the field or encountered the construct in their clinical practice. Lay experts are those nonprofessionals who have personal experience with the construct being assessed (think a client diagnosed with a particular disorder). Creating an instrument to assess anxiety, you would solicit researchers, clinicians, and clients who deal with anxiety to serve on your panel of experts. The benefit of using field and lay experts is that they have the knowledge and expertise in their field or personal experiences to know if the instrument has any glaring omissions or if its items focus too heavily on any one particular area. This approach has been used to validate the disorders listed in the *Diagnostic and Statistical Manual of Mental Disorders* (DSM) that most clinicians use to diagnose a client's presenting problem(s).

A more scientific approach to establishing content validity is through statistical methods. Using advanced analytic techniques, researchers have sought to establish an objective, quantifiable measure of content validity that could be used to directly compare instruments and assessment techniques. One such measure is the **content validity ratio** (CVR) developed by a vocational psychologist named C. H. Lawshe (1975). The CVR is a ratio of the number of raters (from your panel of experts) who evaluate an item and the number of raters who deem an item to be an essential component of the construct being measured. Raters are asked to review each item included on a measure. They then are asked to rate each item as being either essential, useful but not essential, or not necessary

Table 4.2 Method for Establishing Evidence of Content Validity

Step 1	Conduct a task analysis to identify the essential duties, knowledge areas, skills, and abilities related to the task.
Step 2	Link these duties, knowledge areas, skills, and abilities to the associated test construct or component that it is intended to assess.
Step 3	Use content-area experts to affirm the duties, knowledge, skills, and abilities to be assessed in the test, and evaluate the appropriateness and fidelity of the questions or scenarios that will be used.
Step 4	Document that the most essential duties, knowledge areas, skills, and abilities were assessed, and offer a rationale for why less essential knowledge and fewer skills may have been excluded.

Source: Adapted from Industrial Organizational Solutions (2010).

to the construct under examination. Frequencies for each of these response options are recorded and entered into the following equation:

$$CVR = \frac{n_e - \dfrac{N}{2}}{\dfrac{N}{2}}$$

CVR = the content validity ratio

n_e = the number of raters

N = the total number of raters

A CVR value is computed for each item on an instrument. Negative CVR values indicate that the item does not appear to be an essential component of the construct being measured. Positive values indicate that the item does appear to be a good indicator of a construct. To interpret the CVR value computed, Lawshe created a table of critical values by which a test evaluator could determine the size of a calculated CVR necessary, given a specific number of raters, to exceed chance expectation. Due to some potential computation errors in this original table, Wilson, Pan, and Schumsky (2012) calculated a revised table. In both tables, the higher the CVR value, the better the item is at assessing an essential component of the construct of interest. Let's look at Case Illustration 4.3 to see how this formula works.

CASE ILLUSTRATION   4.3

Computing a Content Validity Ratio (CVR) for a Test Item

A school counselor is interested in creating an instrument to assess the extent of bullying behaviors in her school. She creates a set of 10 items that reference various forms of bullying behavior she has found in the professional literature. The school counselor then recruits a panel of experts to review her instrument and provide feedback on the items included. Her panel includes the school principal, four teachers, and five students who serve in leadership positions in the school. The panel is asked to review each item and rate it as being either essential, useful but not essential, or not necessary. For the first item, seven reviewers rate the item as being an essential component of bullying.

$$CVR = \frac{7 - \dfrac{10}{2}}{\dfrac{10}{2}} = 0.40$$

Note that the CVR value computed is positive, indicating that the item is deemed to be an essential component of bullying.

For the second item, only two of the reviewers rate the item as an essential component of the bullying construct.

$$CVR = \frac{2 - \frac{10}{2}}{\frac{10}{2}} = -0.60$$

Note that the CVR value computed for this item is negative. This indicates that the item is determined to be an unnecessary component of bullying.

This process would continue for each of the 10 items selected for the instrument. The school counselor could then examine these CVR values and decide which to keep and which to remove from the instrument.

A term you may hear used in conjunction with content validity is *face validity*. **Face validity** basically assesses whether an instrument appears to look like it measures what it is meant to measure. You would expect a math test to include items with numbers and equations much the same way you would expect a depression inventory to include questions related to the signs and symptoms of depression. However, unlike content validity, there is no empirical way to assess face validity. As a result, the term is no longer included in the *Standards for Educational and Psychological Testing* (AERA et al., 1999) as a legitimate form of validity evidence to collect. In addition to the lack of empirical support for face valid items, the relative straightforward nature of items may result in inaccurate results when test takers may not want to share their true thoughts or feelings on an item.

Although it is no longer seen as a viable source of validity, we mention face validity here primarily to familiarize readers with the term as it is still used in some contexts and literature.

Criterion-Related Validity

Criterion-related validity assesses whether a test reflects a certain set of abilities. To measure the criterion validity of an instrument, test scores are compared to a known standard or outcome measure. This standard or outcome measure is referred to as a **criterion**. A criterion is typically a score on a separate test or instrument that purports to measure the same construct or set of abilities as the test in question. Criterion-related validity is assessed when researchers are interested in understanding the degree to which an assessment instrument predicts a specific outcome measure or criterion. For example, tests like the SAT and ACT are designed to predict future performance in college. Criterion validity can be evidenced by comparing scores on these tests to students' actual performance in college as measured by grade point average (GPA). In this example, the students' GPA is the criterion measure. Because the assessment of criterion validity requires the collection of quantitative data, it is said that this approach more appropriately demonstrates empirical validity than theoretical validity (Hood & Johnson, 2009).

Under the heading of criterion-related validity there are two different approaches to obtaining validity evidence. The decision regarding which approach to use depends on how and when the criterion performance score will be collected. **Concurrent validity** is assessed when the test score and criterion performance measure are collected at approximately the same time. An example is when a counselor conducts an intake interview. The counselor collects data from you regarding your signs and symptoms and uses them to assess what your diagnosis is at the given moment. The counselor then compares your description of how you are feeling to known and established disorders to find a potential match (see Case Illustration 4.4). In this example, it is your description of how you are feeling that is being validated. When the criterion will take place at some point in the future after test scores have been collected, **predictive validity** is what counselors assess.

The previous example describing the purpose of the SAT and ACT tests is an example of predictive validity. The tests, usually taken during the last 2 years of high school, are used to predict college success even though the student has yet to enroll in or complete any collegiate coursework. For criterion validity to be present, only one of these approaches need be assessed. The approach used depends on the purpose of the test and the decisions that need to be made from the data collected. A further discussion of each of these criterion-related validity approaches follows in this chapter, but first it is important that we talk more about criterion measures and how they are selected.

CASE ILLUSTRATION   4.4

In a study published in the *Journal of Counseling Psychology,* Dr. Stephen Sprinkle and his colleagues (2002) assessed the criterion validity of the Beck Depression Inventory-II by pairing blind BDI-II administrations with the major depressive episode portion of the Structured Clinical Interview for DSM-IV Axis I Disorders in a sample of 137 students receiving treatment at a local university counseling center. Their results indicate that student BDI-II scores correlated strongly ($r = 0.83$) with the number of SCID-I depressed mood symptoms reported. The relationship between BDI-II scores and symptoms reported indicate that the use of the BDI-II for assessing depression exhibited strong criterion validity.

Characteristics of a Sound Criterion

You just saw that a criterion is an outcomes measure against which a test is validated. The criterion can be any number of variables and is created at the discretion of test developers. Although there is a great deal of freedom given in selecting criterion measures, there are some best practice guidelines that help ensure that the criterion selected is appropriate and useful. In particular, a sound criterion should be relevant and useful, reliable, free from bias, and free from contamination.

A sound criterion is *relevant and useful*. The variable of interest selected should allow for decisions or behavioral changes to be made based on it. In other words, the criterion should not be abstract or tangential; it should truly represent a variable of interest. Included as a separate standard in the *Standards for Educational and Psychological Testing* (AERA et al., 1999) is the following: "All criterion measures should be described accurately, and the rationale for choosing them as relevant criteria should be made explicit" (p. 16). For example, if you were to design an instrument to assess for the presence of a personality disorder, establishing as your criterion how the person dresses would probably not be the best choice. Fashion sense has little if any connection to personality disorders, and the determination of the criterion would be highly subjective. In addition, knowing how a person dressed would not in any useful way help us work with that person to address issues related to his or her diagnosed personality disorder. Guided Practice Exercise 4.4 gives you an opportunity to begin developing valid criteria for a local mental health residential treatment program.

GUIDED PRACTICE EXERCISE 4.4

Developing Valid Program Admission Criteria

As a counselor at a local community mental health center, you have been placed in charge of a new residential treatment program for individuals who have been dually diagnosed (presence of a concurrent substance use and psychiatric disorder). As the director, your responsibility is to develop the admission criteria for this program. What criteria would you include? How would you go about assessing for these criteria? How can you justify to your administrators, interested stakeholders, and the community at large that the criteria you have decided to use are both reliable and valid?

A sound criterion should be *reliable*. There should not be a large degree of unsystematic error in the measurement of the criterion. The presence of a significant amount of unsystematic error is an indication that the measure lacks consistency. When the criterion lacks consistency, it makes it nearly impossible for researchers to compare test scores to it. Suppose each counselor was allowed to individually determine the criteria used for diagnosing depression. Every counselor would have a slightly different idea of what depression would look like and how it would be assessed. Some counselors might establish their own personal criteria for depression that were more lenient than existing diagnostic criteria, and others might establish criteria that were more stringent. Existing depression inventories such as the Beck Depression Inventory-II (Beck, Steer, & Brown, 1996) would become irrelevant because there no longer would be a singular criterion (DSM diagnostic criteria for depression) to which scores on these inventories could be compared. A diagnosis of depression would depend on the counselor assessing the individual.

A sound criterion is *free from bias*. An objective measure of the skill or ability being assessed should be reported by the criterion. Outside influences should not interfere with the interpretation of the criterion. When there is outside influence, the accuracy of the criterion is called into question. Consider the following scenario as an example. A college professor is grading student term papers. The professor has a rubric by which student work will be evaluated. As he is grading, the professor comes across the paper of a student who has been tardy for several classes and generally disruptive when present in class.

Despite having a clearly defined rubric to guide him, the frustration this student has caused the professor may influence his rating of the submitted paper, resulting in a lower score than may have been warranted. In this scenario the criterion was not free from bias because the professor considered past interactions with the student when assigning a grade for a submitted paper.

A sound criterion measure is *immune from contamination*. Contamination occurs when previous knowledge influences the gathering of criterion data. A client presents for a psychiatric evaluation at a local hospital emergency room. The attending physician notes that the patient has a rather large chart that documents several previous emergency room visits that have resulted in the patient being hospitalized. This knowledge may contaminate the physician's thought process. The physician may enter the examination room with a preconceived notion about the patient and look for evidence to support this notion. In this situation, the decision made on the patient's behalf was based more on past history than current presentation. It could be the case that hospitalization was not warranted in this situation and instead the patient should have been referred back to a current counselor.

Construct Validity

Anastasi and Urbina (1997) define **construct validity** as the extent to which a test may be said to accurately and thoroughly measure a particular construct or trait. According to Eysenck (1987), a **construct** is an abstraction that cannot be seen directly but is valued because it helps organize the myriad of potential observations in the real world. An example of a construct is intelligence. We know intelligence exists but we can neither see it nor touch it. It is more theoretical than anything else. The construct of intelligence was created to describe the set of interrelated variables we commonly associate with intelligence, namely memory recall, spatial ability, and verbal fluency. Because there is no exact definition of what constitutes a construct (for example, what really makes up a person's intelligence?), it is hard to operationally define the term in a manner that allows for accurate measurement. Thus, you will see that construct validity is one of the most difficult types of validity evidence (see Guided Practice Exercise 4.5).

GUIDED PRACTICE EXERCISE 4.5

Defining and Measuring Constructs

One of the challenges researchers face is developing objective definitions of constructs that then can be assessed and measured. For each of the following constructs, develop an objective definition that can measured. Share your definitions with others in class, and see whether they agree with your definition. Discuss what components of your definition were agreeable to others and which were debatable.

CONSTRUCTS:

Love

Wisdom

Anxiety

Depression

Happiness

The term *construct validity* became popular in the 1950s as a result of the work of the American Psychological Association's Committee on Psychological Tests. The committee noted that many psychological constructs had no fully valid criterion measure or adequate specification of the content domain (Hoyt, Warbasse, & Chu, 2006). Since content and criterion validity would be hard to establish, something new needed to be developed. In establishing construct validity, researchers establish the construct of interest and collect data over a period of time to determine whether a test actually measures the given construct. In essence, construct validity allows us to develop an understanding of the meaningfulness of both a test and the rationale that lies behind the test (Lyman, 1998). According to Borsboom, Mellenbergh, and Van Heerden (2004), establishing construct validity is predicated on two conditions: (a) the construct refers to an existing phenomenon, independent of how it is measured, and (b) the phenomenon causes response variation both in the real world and in the phenomenon's measures. In other words, the construct being measured must exist and cause variations among individuals. An example would be the assessment of intoxication. Intoxication refers to the buildup of alcohol in the system that results in the person reaching an inebriated state. Intoxication is a construct that exists and is medically supported. In addition, it is possible to assess variance in intoxication level. While some people may require only a drink or two to feel intoxicated, others may require a much larger amount to produce the same impaired state. There are multiple methods for assessing construct validity. These methods include test homogeneity, convergent and discriminant validity, group differentiation, developmental changes, and factor analysis.

Test homogeneity refers to the degree to which all items on a test appear to be measuring the same construct. The validity of an instrument is enhanced when its items all work in concert to assess the same variable. The homogeneity of a test can be assessed using a number of different procedures known collectively as **item analysis**. One way that this can be accomplished is by demonstrating high internal consistency. Individual items are correlated with one another and an overall internal consistency coefficient is computed. The higher this value, the greater the likelihood that they are indeed all referencing the same construct. Another approach to measuring the homogeneity of a test is item discrimination. In this process, the individual scores on each test item are correlated with the overall score on the entire test. The higher the correlation coefficient computed, the more discriminating the item. Highly discriminating items mean that those who answer a certain way on them are likely to have a certain overall score. An individual who selects "often" when referencing the frequency with which he or she has thoughts of self-harm would most likely score highly on a depression screening and thus need to be referred for counseling services. When items have very little discriminant value, it is suggested that they be dropped from the test as they add very little to the overall measurement of a construct. These correlation coefficients range between −1.00 and +1.00, and a *good* discriminant item has a value greater than 0.20.

Another way to assess construct validity is to gather evidence of convergent and discriminant validity. In **convergent validity**, scores on a test are compared to scores obtained on other tests believed to measure the same construct. To establish the convergent validity of a depression-screening test I created, I could administer to a sample of clients my new instrument as well as established instruments designed to assess for depression, such as the Beck Depression Inventory-II (Beck et al., 1996) and the Reynolds Depression Screening Inventory (W. M. Reynolds & Kobak, 1998). Consistency among the scores would be an indication of convergent validity. An individual that was truly depressed would score high on each of these scales. The opposite of convergent validity is **discriminant validity**. Discriminant validity is established when scores on a test are found to be uncorrelated to scores on other instruments designed to assess alternate constructs. A lack of consistency in scores would be expected if the two tests were indeed measuring separate constructs. I would not expect the scores on my test designed to screen for depression to correlate highly with scores on other instruments designed to measure positive emotional health. The lower the correlation between these seemingly divergent measures, the greater the evidence for discriminant validity.

Counselors also can use group differentiation studies to assess construct validity. In this approach, an instrument is administered to a group of people known to be in two distinct (clinical and nonclinical) groups and their scores are compared. A counselor could administer a personality inventory such as the Minnesota Multiphasic Personality Inventory-II (MMPI-II; Butcher et al., 2001) to a group of psychiatric inpatients as well as a group of undergraduate college students. The scores of the psychiatric inpatients should look more or less like one another, while the scores for the college undergraduates should look markedly different. In this approach, the counselor is trying to determine whether a test can differentiate between different groups of people in a way predicted by theory (Drummond & Jones, 2010). For example, we would expect individuals hospitalized in a mental health facility to have certain signs and symptoms that we would not see in a nonclinical sample of college students (see Table 4.3).

Similar to the group differentiation approach, you also could conduct a developmental change study. In this approach the validity is evidenced by demonstrating how scores change as test takers age. As individuals mature and develop, their abilities increase. For example, we would expect a college student to have a more expanded vocabulary than a first-grade student. When conducting developmental change studies, researchers are looking for correlations between test scores and theoretically explained developmental abilities. While the presence of developmental changes is necessary, they are not sufficient conditions of construct validity by themselves (Erford, 2013). In the above example, we would expect students to expand their vocabulary with additional schooling, but that vocabulary test would not be a construct valid instrument if we were using it to assess math ability.

Finally, we can look at assessing construct validity using a process called factor analysis. **Factor analysis** is a statistical technique used to determine how well items mathematically group together, thus indicating similarity and the measurement of a common construct. The goal of factor analysis is to determine whether a test is unidimensional or multidimensional. In other words, do the items all measure the same construct or might there in fact be multiple constructs being assessed in the same instrument? The MMPI-II (Butcher et al., 2001) contains questions that assess the presence of 10 different clinical diagnoses. There are two primary factor analytic methods: exploratory and confirmatory. In exploratory factor analysis the researcher does not know how the items on the test relate or whether they assess the same construct or multiple constructs. On the other hand, confirmatory factor analysis is used when the factor structure of a test is known and researchers are trying to see if that structure holds true for a particular group or sample of individuals. The process for conducting a factor analysis is complex; fortunately for you, though, these analyses have been conducted for many commonly used instruments and are reported in test manuals and scientific journals.

Table 4.3   Types of Validity Evidence

Validity Type	Purpose	Example
Criterion validity	To assess whether scores obtained for a participant are related to a criterion outcome measure	Do GRE scores predict graduate school performance?
Content validity	To assess whether the content and composition of an instrument are appropriate given what it is intended to measure	Do the items on a career interest inventory sufficiently cover the various aspects of different careers?
Construct validity	To assess whether an instrument is measuring the correct construct	Does the SASSI-3 truly detect the presence of a substance use disorder?

INTERPRETING VALIDITY COEFFICIENTS

Like we saw in the previous chapter on reliability, statistical procedures can be used to determine a quantitative measure of the validity of an assessment instrument. This value, known as the **validity coefficient**, is a measure of how accurate a measure actually is. While there are no standard benchmarks that identify those measures that should be deemed valid and those that should not, there are some criteria you could look to in making your interpretations. For one, you want the coefficient you compute to at least be

Table 4.4   Guidelines for Interpreting Validity Coefficients

Very high	> .50
High	.40 – .49
Moderate	.21 – .39
Low	< .20

Source: Adapted from Drummond & Jones (2010, Table 6.3, p. 108).

statistically significant at the level of significance you determine (e.g., .01, 05). A statistically non-significant coefficient would represent a measure that was not at all valid at predicting a given construct and thus should not be used to make any clinical decisions. When a statistically significant result is found, this means that a relationship between the test score and the criterion has been established. In situations like this, the competent researcher must then establish the strength or size of this relationship.

Compared to reliability coefficients, validity coefficients are often expected to be lower. The reason for these lowered scores is that the constructs often assessed in clinical settings are abstract and thus cannot truly be measured with complete accuracy (what is intelligence really, and how can we know we are accurately assessing it in our clients?). Whereas reliability estimates are expected to be in the .80 and above range, validity coefficients in the .40 to .70 range are quite common and considered to be strong evidence of an instrument's validity in the given context (see Table 4.4).

KEYSTONES

- Validity refers to the ability of an instrument to accurately assess a given trait or variable. The more valid an instrument, the stronger the inferences a counselor can make from the data obtained.
- Validity is contextual. It refers to the manner and situations in which an instrument is used and not the instrument by itself. An instrument can be highly valid in one setting but invalid in another.
- Although current theory views all issues of validity as being construct-oriented, there are multiple facets of validity that can be assessed to gather evidence on an instrument's overall validity. These facets include content, criterion, and construct validity.
- Reliability is a necessary but insufficient condition of validity. An assessment that produces inconsistent results can never be deemed valid. On the other hand, an assessment producing consistent results may not always be considered valid.
- Validity coefficients must be interpreted in the context from which they were acquired. Attention should be paid to the diverse backgrounds of clients and the situations in which data were collected when reviewing validity data and making interpretations.

KEY TERMS

concurrent validity

construct

construct validity

content validity

content validity ratio

convergent validity

criterion

criterion-related validity

discriminant validity

face validity

factor analysis

item analysis

predictive validity

test familiarity

validity

validity coefficient

ADDITIONAL RESOURCES

- Standards for Educational and Psychological Testing
  http://teststandards.org
- American Evaluation Association
  http://www.eval.org

Student Study Site: Visit the Student Study Site at **www.sagepub.com/watson** to access additional study tools, including quizzes, web resources, and journal articles.

CHAPTER 5

Selecting, Administering, Scoring, and Reporting Assessment Results

In previous chapters we provided an overview of the basic elements of assessment. Hopefully you now have a greater appreciation for how assessment plays a vital role in the counseling process and in helping us serve clients to the best of our abilities. In this chapter, we shift our focus and begin looking at the more applied aspects of assessment. Specifically, we will introduce you to the various stages of the assessment process, from method selection to the reporting of results, and demonstrate best practices to follow at each of these stages. To this point we have attempted to portray assessment in its broadest context;

however, in this chapter we focus primarily on the use of objective assessments (i.e., tests). Tests can be used in many different counseling situations. While we will discuss specific applications of assessment testing in Section II of this text (Chapters 7–12), you will find the guidelines and principles outlined in this chapter applicable to all types of testing and assessment.

Our goal in this chapter is to walk you through the steps involved with responsibly using tests as part of your overall assessment process. We will start at the beginning and discuss how counselors select tests to use by finding out about possible tests available for them to use and what considerations must be addressed before the decision to ultimately use a specific test instrument can be made. Next, we will cover the process of orienting clients to the testing process, administering, and eventually scoring a test. For many instruments, a specific procedure is in place to ensure that the results you obtain are valid and reliable, and can be generalized to the larger population of interest. Finally, we will discuss the process of reporting results to a client. For a test to be a useful tool in the counseling process, the results generated by it must be of utility to the counselor *and* the client. In other words, results need to be presented using nontechnical language and in a manner that empowers clients. While you undoubtedly will develop your own personal style as a counselor, the information presented in this chapter will assist you in making sure you practice in a competent and ethical manner.

SELECTING ASSESSMENT INSTRUMENTS

As a counselor you may choose to include an assessment test as part of the counseling process for a number of reasons. A situation might arise in which the use of a particular test could be used to confirm your hypothesis about the true nature of a client's presenting issue or assist in the diagnosis of a particular disorder. You also could use tests to find out more about your client, including the client's areas of strength and weakness, salient personality characteristics, and learning style. No matter what the purpose or your testing needs, a variety of instruments exist for your potential usage. Given this variety, how do you know which instrument to use? In this section we will examine the considerations that should be made when selecting a test to use.

The first stage of the assessment process is test selection. According to Watson and Sheperis (2010), the appropriate selection of a test is an important element in the assessment process. As a result, careful attention should be given to the selection of a test instrument. The choice of which test to use depends on many factors, including the needs of the client, the counseling setting, resources available, decisions to be made based on the test results, and the skill and qualifications of the counselor administering the test. Additionally, the choice of tests to use should be a collaborative effort. Counselors should consult with clients and allow them input into the selection process. After all, the client is the one who will be completing the test, so it should be one that he or she is comfortable taking.

Selecting an appropriate test can be a challenge for some counselors. Fortunately, there are guidelines that a counselor can use to help ensure that the correct test is being selected and ultimately used. These guidelines are questions you should ask yourself prior to introducing a test into the counseling process. Careful attention at the beginning of the process will help ensure that the entire testing experience is received positively by the client and is beneficial to all parties involved. The guiding questions you should be looking to answer include the following:

- What decisions or judgments need to be made?
- What information is needed to make the decision or judgment?
- What information is already available?
- How should additional information be obtained?
- What methods should be used to collect information?
- How will the assessment results be used?
- How will aspects of culture and diversity be addressed?

What Decisions or Judgments Need to Be Made?

In Chapter 1 you saw that there are several reasons why counselors use assessment procedures. These reasons include such activities as screening, diagnosis, treatment planning, goal identification, and progress evaluation. In beginning to choose an assessment instrument, a counselor should first establish what it is that he or she is trying to accomplish. In other words, the counselor needs to clarify the purpose of assessment for the client and then identify instruments that have a strong likelihood of being able to measure the constructs related to the client's presenting needs (Sampson, 2000). Keep in mind that even the most reliable and valid instrument will appear ineffective if it does not measure what you are trying to assess with a particular client. For example, the need to diagnose a client with a particular disorder requires a different set of information than would be needed to set and monitor treatment goals. As a result, the instruments available to you to use will vary. Consider the example presented in Case Illustration 5.1 to see the importance of accurate test selection.

CASE ILLUSTRATION 5.1

A school counselor is asked to see a 10-year-old fourth-grade student. The teacher informs the school counselor that the student has been disengaging when the class begins reviewing their mathematics lesson. The teacher explains that the student has been refusing to participate and has even begun disrupting other students in the class. This behavior appears to only occur when the class is working on their mathematic exercises. At other times of the day, the teacher reports having no problems with this student. The teacher has tried multiple times to help the student and correct the disruptive behavior, but has been unsuccessful to date. After reviewing the student's record, the school counselor notes that this is the student's first year in the school, so there is not a record of any problems in previous

(Continued)

(Continued)

classes. Prior to selecting a test to use, the school counselor realizes she will first need to identify a goal for her work with this student. Since there are no past incidences of this type of behavior, and it only appears to occur during one subject period, the school counselor sets out to learn more about the problem and the circumstances surrounding its occurrence. What the school counselor conceptualizes as the student's salient need in this situation will help guide the selection of an appropriate assessment test to administer. Identifying antecedents to negative behaviors would require the use of a different type of test than would be used to assess for a potential learning disability.

What Information Is Needed to Make the Decision or Judgment?

Once you have established a decision that will need to be made, you can begin looking at the information needed to support that decision. For example, if you were looking to screen a client to see if there was a need for acute psychiatric care at the inpatient level, what information would be needed to help you make this decision? Information on presenting signs and symptoms, presence of any psychotic features, and any verbalization of threats to harm self or others would be supportive of your decision to admit this client to an inpatient care facility. You may find the process of working backward helpful, first considering your desired outcome and then identifying what artifacts will be needed to warrant that particular outcome. What would you need to know to determine whether a client has met established goals? How would you determine whether progress had been made or if the client might be able to transition to an alternative level of care? In Case Illustration 5.1 you read about a school counselor working with a 10-year-old student referred for disruptive classroom behavior. If the school counselor in this scenario believed that the student had a learning disability that affected his performance in the mathematics lesson, what data would she need to acquire to support her hypothesis? She may determine that a measure of the student's intelligence or mathematical ability is required and thus begin looking for a psychometrically sound instrument to assess these constructs.

What Information Is Already Available?

Many times the information we need to make a decision is already available to us. It is not necessary to continually repeat assessments if the needed data already exist. Available information can be found in a client's chart or medical record. Information also can be found by reviewing previous session case notes. Establishing the information you already have is an exercise in efficiency. Time and resources are not wasted covering areas in which relevant information has already been accumulated. Before beginning the test selection process, determine what it is you already know about a client that might help you make the decision you are trying to make. The information you might be able to get from a test administration could be available through other means. Once you are able to quantify what you already know, you can look to select a test that helps you fill in the gaps and address those areas where you have an incomplete picture of the client or presenting situation.

How Should Additional Information Be Obtained?

The majority of the information we gather about a client will come from the client directly. However, this does not mean that the client is the only source of information. In some cases, the client may not even be the best source of information. Additional sources may need to be explored to gain a better perspective of the true nature of the problem. For example, a school counselor may request to speak with the parents to understand how a child behaves at home. By asking the parents, the school counselor may get a more accurate representation of the child's behavior and any issues that may be affecting that behavior. Other sources of information counselors may consider using include past records or evaluations completed by teachers, peers, supervisors, or employers.

Thinking back on our earlier example of the disruptive 10-year-old, what other sources of information could the school counselor have considered using to better understand the current difficulty this student is having in class? The student's parents might be able to provide information that will allow the school counselor to determine the true scope of the problem. After talking to the parents, the school counselor might learn that this behavior has been occurring for several years or that this behavior has been noted to occur at home as well. In addition, she may consider obtaining a release from the parents to talk to teachers or counselors at the student's previous school to learn more about the history of the problem and how it may have been managed in the past.

What Methods Should Be Used to Collect Information?

The decision regarding the type of assessment instrument to use will depend on a number of factors (see Guided Practice Exercise 5.1). Client characteristics will play a significant role in determining the assessment method used. Is the client cognitively able to provide reliable information? Is the client actively engaged in the counseling process, or is there resistance toward participation? Does the client have any motive to provide inaccurate or partial information? These are all questions you will need to ask yourself prior to selecting an instrument. For some clients, a survey or screening questionnaire might be effective, whereas for others an interview or observation might be more appropriate. In addition to client variables, external variables also may factor into your decision. Examples of external variables include, but are not limited to, the following:

- Setting (are you working in a school, hospital, or community mental health agency)
- Timing (are results needed to make an immediate decision or to further long-term care)
- Finances (which instrument makes the most economic sense for all parties involved)
- Legal involvement (is there any judicial or legal oversight of the testing process)

The school counselor's decisions regarding assessment tests to use should be based on her understanding of the student and will be determined by the information she already knows about this student and some of the external variables known to play a role in the student's life. For example, in talking with the student the school counselor may learn that he has a history of difficulty with standardized tests. Knowing that this is a weakness for the student, she might opt to select instruments that are more projective in nature. Similarly, the school counselor may have a restricted budget at her school, so her ability to purchase tests and equipment may be limited. As a result, her choices may be based more on cost and availability than on therapeutic utility.

GUIDED PRACTICE EXERCISE 5.1

Assessing What You Know and What You Need to Know

Imagine that you are working as an intake counselor at a local mental health facility. A new client presents for services. The client states that he has been depressed for quite some time and recently began having thoughts of suicide. How would you determine what type of treatment (inpatient or outpatient) would be most beneficial for this client? As you ponder your decision, think about the information you already have and the additional information you would like to have. What assessment methods would be most helpful to you in gathering the additional information you would like to have to formulate an accurate treatment plan?

How Will the Assessment Results Be Used?

How assessment results will be integrated into the counseling process factors into your decision on which instrument to use as well (Hood, 2001). Will the results be part of an extensive psychiatric battery, or will the results be used informally to verify an initial conceptualization of the client's presenting problem? Depending on who will be viewing the results and the decisions that will be made based on them, your decisions may vary. This is another reason why it is ultimately important to carefully select instruments that are appropriate for your need given the client and circumstance, are psychometrically sound, and are well supported in the professional counseling literature.

How Will Aspects of Culture and Diversity Be Addressed?

Problems can arise when measurement instruments that have been developed by a dominant group are applied to groups for which they were not originally intended (Mushquash & Bova, 2007). In fact, the issue of cultural bias in testing has existed for many years, dating back to the initial work of Binet and Simon in the early 1900s. When counselors review tests for their potential use, they need to make sure that the tests are responsive to cultural diversity and appropriate for the clients with whom they will be used. Specific considerations that need to be made include whether the test was normed for groups similar to those represented in the clients served and how cultural factors mediate clients' responses to test items (Solano-Flores, 2011). The test manual and extant literature describing the test are good sources of information that will help you determine the appropriateness of an instrument with diverse client populations.

LOCATING ASSESSMENT INSTRUMENTS

Once you have made the decision that your work with a particular client will benefit from the use of an assessment test, you will need to begin the process of determining the best instrument to use. This will require you to review and evaluate a number of instruments to see which fits most with your particular client and your needs for the test. Prior to reviewing these tests, knowledge of how to locate tests and information about their usage will be important in helping you make a more informed selection. Although this may seem like a daunting task, finding information may be easier than you think. There are several sources you can access to learn more about existing tests and their various advantages and disadvantages across counseling settings. In this section we introduce you to some of the more commonly used sources of information counselors refer to when selecting an assessment instrument to use.

Mental Measurements Yearbook

A popular source of information on tests and other assessment instruments is the **Mental Measurements Yearbook** (*MMY*). First published by Dr. Oscar Buros in 1938, the *MMY* includes timely, consumer-oriented test reviews designed to promote informed test selection. The purpose of the *MMY* is to provide potential users with objective reviews of tests by those who actually use them in their counseling practice. To accommodate the number of new instruments continually being developed, a new version of the *MMY* is published every few years. Now published by the Buros Center for Testing at the University of Nebraska, the *MMY* is in its 18th edition. To date, over 4,000 tests have been reviewed in the *MMY* series.

Each entry in the *MMY* collection contains descriptive information about the test as well as one or more professional reviews written by content experts in the given field. To be reviewed and included in the *MMY*, a test must be commercially available, published in English, be new or significantly revised since its last appearance in the *MMY* series, and provide sufficient documentation of its technical quality and clinical efficacy. The *MMY* can be accessed in a number of ways. In addition to the published hardback copy of the yearbook, test reviews also can be found online. On the Buros Center for Testing website (http://buros.org), test reviews can be accessed individually exactly as they appear in the published version of the *MMY* for a small fee. The benefit of this online delivery method is that counselors need to pay only for the reviews they wish to read and the access to these reviews is immediate. In Guided Practice Exercise 5.2, we encourage you to familiarize yourself with the process of locating test information in the *MMY*.

GUIDED PRACTICE EXERCISE 5.2

Locating Tests Using the *Mental Measurements Yearbook*

Using either the printed version or the online version, search the *Mental Measurements Yearbook* for two instruments that can be used to diagnosis depression in a client. How do the two instruments compare? Is there a situation in which you would use one more than the other (consider types of clients served and the clinical setting).

Tests in Print

Tests in Print is another resource you might consult for information on tests available for you to use. Like the *MMY*, *Tests in Print* also is published by the Buros Center for Testing. It differs from the *MMY* in that it is a bibliography of all known commercially available tests currently in print in English. The citations for each test provide readers with descriptive listings of tests and include such information as the name of the test, author, publisher, intended purpose, price structure, intended population, and amount of time required to administer. Unlike the *MMY*, comprehensive reviews are not included in *Tests in Print*. In lieu of the actual reviews, readers are guided to reviews that may appear in any of the *MMY* editions available. First made available in 1961, the eighth and most recent version of *Tests in Print* was published in 2011.

Tests

Tests is a reference guide published by PRO-ED. It includes information on over 2,000 tests from more than 164 publishers in the areas of psychology, education, and business. The entries in *Tests* provide readers with basic descriptive information that can help make an informed selection. Comprehensive reviews or evaluations are not included. Unlike the *MMY* or *Tests in Print*, tests catalogued in *Tests* can be either English or Spanish language instruments. A simple, easy-to-read format is followed for each entry in *Tests*. The following information is included for each test:

- Test title
- Authors' names
- Copyright date
- Primary publisher
- Population for which test is intended
- Purpose statement
- Brief description highlighting the test's major features
- Format information
- Scoring method
- Relevant cost and availability information (Maddox, 2008)

The most recent edition is the sixth edition, published in 2008. In reading *Tests*, you will gain a better understanding of the available tests currently on the market that might apply to the specific needs you have with a client. Ordering information for *Tests* can be found on the PRO-ED website at www.proedinc.com.

Professional Organization Websites

Professional organization websites also can be used to find information on tests to use in the counseling process. These sites offer information on tests and reviews to benefit their members or the general public. While there are many more that can be consulted, two that provide a great deal of information are the websites of Educational Testing Services (ETS) and the Association for Assessment and Research in Counseling

(AARC). The ETS Test Collection site is a database of over 25,000 tests and other assessment instruments. Tests published since the early 1900s both in the United States and abroad are indexed in the database. Technical information and the availability of the test are included in the entry. AARC is a division of the American Counseling Association that was chartered in 1965. The mission of AARC is to promote and recognize excellence in assessment, research, and evaluation in counseling. To promote this mission, AARC publishes test reviews in its member newsletter, *Newnotes*. These test reviews also are archived on the division website. The reviews follow a similar format as those included in the *MMY* and are available to the general public.

Test Publisher Websites

In addition to seeking information from published handbooks or searching online, counselors interested in learning more about tests might consider looking directly at test publisher websites. These sites typically contain information similar to what would be found in the aforementioned resources. An added feature that these sources include is the ability to view sample questions and scoring reports generated by using these tests. These references can further help a counselor identify whether the test itself or the information gained from it will be of benefit to the client and whether it should be considered for usage. A drawback to using the test publisher websites directly is that you will have access to only a limited number of tests available in a particular category. You also should keep in mind that these publishers are interested in marketing their commercially available instruments, so the reviews included on these sites may not be completely objective. When you find an instrument that might be a fit for your current need, see if you can find additional information about that test from other sources or if the test has been used in previous research. Some of the more prominent test publishers and their website URLs are listed in Table 5.1.

Table 5.1 Test Publisher Websites

Publisher	Website
CTB McGraw-Hill	www.ctb.com
Mind Garden	www.mindgarden.com
Multi-Health Systems	www.mhs.com
PAR (Psychological Assessment Resources)	www.parinc.com
Pearson Assessments	www.pearsonassessments.com
PRO-ED	www.proedinc.com
Riverside Publishing	www.riversidepublishing.com
Sigma Assessment Systems	www.sigmaassessmentsystems.com
Western Psychological Services	www.wpspublish.com

Literature Reviews

A less widely used, but still effective, method of locating tests that you potentially could use is to review the current literature in your field of interest. Here you will find a number of research studies conducted to expand the knowledge base in a particular area. A review of these research studies should give you some idea of the types of instruments used most often in working with a particular population or to address a specific counseling need or presenting problem. A review of databases that index counseling, education, psychology, social work, and business journals might prove useful to you in locating information about potential instruments to use with your clients. Although you will need to uncover additional information about these tests using the other sources discussed in this section, a review of the literature will at least help you develop a working list of tests used in a particular field. From there you can add or remove tests from your potential list as you become more knowledgeable about them. To help you become familiar with the process of searching the existing literature base for ideas on tests and instruments to use, we refer you to Guided Practice Exercise 5.3.

GUIDED PRACTICE EXERCISE 5.3

Reviewing Existing Literature to Find Test Information

Choose a particular client issue or problem that you might expect to encounter in your work as a counselor. Review the existing literature, and find three potential instruments or assessment techniques you could use to assess that issue or problem in your future clients. As you conduct your search, be sure to check various sources such as the Internet and the holdings at your local library either in print or through its electronic databases.

TEST USER QUALIFICATIONS

Now that you have seen the various sources where information on tests can be found, let's look at some of the considerations that go into selecting a test. Although numerous assessment instruments are available, not every one of these instruments may be appropriate for you to use (Turner, DeMers, Fox, & Reed, 2001). As counselors, we have an ethical and legal obligation to not practice beyond the scope of our competencies. This obligation includes the use of tests and other instruments. When choosing a test, counselors should ensure that they are qualified to competently administer a given test. Qualifications needed to administer tests are included in the professional standards of many national counseling organizations (see Chapter 16). A summary of these qualifications is included in Table 5.2. As you can see in the table, the determination of a test user's qualifications depends on a number of factors, including the individual's knowledge, skills, abilities, training, experience, and credentialing.

Table 5.2   Assessment Qualifications of Professional Organizations

Qualifications	ACA	CACREP	NBCC	FACT	ATP	NCME	ACA–M[a]
Course work in appraisal, assessment, and testing	×	×	×	×	×	×	×
Master's, Specialist, or doctorate in counseling or related field	×	×	×	×	×	×	×
Obtain passing score on the National Counselor Examination			×				
Qualifying experience under supervision	×	×	×	×	×	×	×
Appropriate levels of training for specific tests	×	×	×	×	×	×	×
Need for assessment to assist with accurate diagnosis, treatment planning, and intervention	×	×	×	×	×	×	×

Source: Naugle (2009, Table 1, p. 34).

Note: All information obtained via appropriate organization's website. ACA = American Counseling Association; CACREP = Council for Accreditation of Counseling and Related Educational Programs; NBCC = National Board for Certified Counselors; FACT = Fair Access Coalition on Testing; ATP = Association of Test Publishers; NCME = National Council on Measurement in Education.

a. Model legislation for state licensure.

In addition to professional standards, test publishers also provide guidance on qualified test usage. For some tests, counselors can become qualified to administer them by simply reading the accompanying test manual and becoming familiar with the test. For other tests, the qualifications needed may be greater. In these cases, you might be required to demonstrate specific coursework you have had or document the completion of a terminal degree in your field. To assist you in determining what instruments you are qualified to use, most test publishers have designated different levels of qualification to monitor the competencies of those who purchase and use their products (Naugle, 2009). The qualification levels you are most likely to see are levels A, B, and C.

Level A. Level A tests are those that are designated for general use. They do not require advanced training or education. To administer a Level A test, users would need to familiarize themselves with the administration, scoring, and result reporting protocols for the instrument. This information is typically found in an accompanying test manual. An example of a Level A test would be the Self-Directed Search (Holland, 1994). Although the tests are designated for general use, users are often asked to verify that they work for a recognized organization or institution before the publisher will ship the test materials. This is to ensure that the test is in fact being used in a clinically valid manner by an individual who is guided by an ethical code and standards of practice.

Level B. Level B tests require users to possess technical knowledge related to the practice of assessment. This includes an understanding of instrument development, psychometric issues (reliability and validity), test score properties, and appropriate test usage. Individuals interested in using Level B tests should have completed graduate coursework in assessment as part of their master's degree in counseling, psychology, or a related field. Most test publishers also require those interested in using these tests to document that they have appropriate licensing and credentialing in their field. Examples of Level B assessments are the Myers-Briggs Type Indicator and the 16-Personality Factor Questionnaire. When you begin your career as a counselor following the completion of your master's degree, these are the level tests you most likely will be using.

Level C. The highest level of qualification is Level C. Level C tests require advanced education and training. An earned doctorate in counseling, psychology, education, or a related field is required. In addition to the general assessment coursework required for Level B tests, potential users must also have had coursework in either a specific instrument (e.g., Wechsler Adult Intelligence Scale-Fourth Edition) or a class of instruments (intelligence testing). An example of a Level C test would be the Minnesota Multiphasic Personality Inventory-Second Edition (MMPI-2). Counselors interested in using Level C tests in their practice should check to see if there are any state laws or regulations that may limit their use of certain assessments or tests from this level. In some states, the use of testing is protected and only members of certain professions (counselors, psychologists, social workers, etc.) can use specified tests.

Although multiple test publishers use the level designation system, some publishers have developed their own classification system. The specific criteria for each of these companies may vary slightly. As a result, you should review the administration criteria for the specific company from whom you are looking to purchase an instrument to make sure that you are fully qualified to administer and score the instrument.

ADMINISTRATION PROCEDURES

As a counselor, you will undoubtedly be called on to use assessment tests and instruments at some point in your career. Now that you have seen where counselors can find information on available tests and make the determination as to which test would be best to use in a given situation, we will turn our attention to discussing the process of administering a test. The test administration process is a multi-stage process that expands beyond the actual time spent in direct face-to-face contact with the client. In this section we will look at all that is involved in administering a test, from the initial selection of a test to the collection of testing materials and client debriefing following a test administration. To assist you in understanding your ethical responsibilities as a test user, we have divided our discussion into three sections: before administration, during administration, and after administration (see Table 5.3). For additional information on your responsibilities as a test user, we encourage you to familiarize yourself with the *Responsibilities of Users of Standardized Tests* (commonly referred to as the RUST statement; Association for Assessment in Counseling [AAC], 2003a). The RUST statement outlines all of the tasks and duties test users are responsible for to ensure that a test is appropriately selected, administered, scored, and interpreted. A copy of the RUST statement can be found on the Association for Assessment and Research in Counseling (AARC) website (see additional resources at end of this chapter for the URL).

Table 5.3   Test User Responsibilities During Test Administration (RUST Statement)

Before administration it is important that relevant persons

- are informed about the standard testing procedures, including information about the purposes of the test, the kinds of tasks involved, the method of administration, and the scoring and reporting;
- have sufficient practice experiences prior to the test to include practice, as needed, on how to operate equipment for computer-administered tests and practice in responding to tasks;
- have been sufficiently trained in their responsibilities and the administration procedures for the test;
- have a chance to review test materials and administration sites and procedures prior to the time for testing to ensure standardized conditions and appropriate responses to any irregularities that occur;
- arrange for appropriate modifications of testing materials and procedures in order to accommodate test takers with special needs; and
- have a clear understanding of their rights and responsibilities.

During administration it is important that

- the testing environment (e.g., seating, work surfaces, lighting, room temperature, freedom from distractions) and psychological climate are conducive to the best possible performance of the examinees;
- sufficiently trained personnel establish and maintain uniform conditions and observe the conduct of test takers when large groups of individuals are tested;
- test administrators follow the instructions in the test manual, demonstrate verbal clarity, use verbatim directions, adhere to verbatim directions, follow exact sequence and timing, and use materials that are identical to those specified by the test publisher;
- a systematic and objective procedure is in place for observing and recording environmental, health, emotional factors, or other elements that may invalidate test performance and results; deviations from prescribed test administration procedures, including information on test accommodations for individuals with special needs, are recorded; and
- the security of test materials and computer-administered testing software is protected, ensuring that only individuals with a legitimate need for access to the materials/software are able to obtain such access and that steps to eliminate the possibility of breaches in test security and copyright protection are respected.

After administration it is important to

- collect and inventory all secure test materials and immediately report any breaches in test security and
- include notes on any problems, irregularities, and accommodations in the test records.

Source: AAC (2003).

Before Administration

Once you have made the decision to employ an assessment instrument in your work with a client, the first step is to become familiar with the instrument. Counselors should have a strong working knowledge of a test before they actually use it in session with a client. This means that counselors should be familiar with the technical qualities of the test (reliability, validity, normative information) and its appropriateness for various client populations (Sampson, 2000). Reading the test manual and any other ancillary material provided for the test is a good place to start. The manual will provide information on how the test should be administered, how scores are derived, and how those scores should be interpreted. The more familiar you are with the test, the better you will be able to address any client questions or detect any abnormalities in the testing process. In addition to reading through the materials provided by the test publisher, you also should look for any reviews published on the test. These reviews can provide you with additional information on the strengths and weaknesses associated with the test so that you can better use it effectively in your work with the client.

After familiarizing yourself with the test you intend to use, you will need to make sure that you have available all the necessary testing materials. These may include test booklets, answer sheets, manipulatives, visual aids, or other accessories. For group administrations you will want to ensure that an appropriate number of testing materials are available to accommodate each client being tested. In most cases test publishers will require you to keep all testing materials in a secure location until the time of the test administration to protect the integrity of the test. Refer to the test manual or publisher website for proper procedures related to storage of test materials.

After preparing yourself it is important to prepare the client for the testing process. For many clients the process of testing may be an anxiety-provoking experience (remember the feeling you had taking exams in school?). To help ease client anxiety, counselors should work to establish rapport before introducing testing into the counseling relationship. The topic of testing is best addressed once a comfort level and a sense of trust are established between the counselor and client. Keep in mind that between the two of you, you are the trained professional in the relationship. Most clients probably have very little knowledge of assessment and what it is designed to accomplish. Negative perceptions of the testing process may cause clients to be reluctant toward testing. To combat these negative perceptions, it is incumbent on you to provide the client with as much information about the testing process as possible (see Case Illustration 5.2). In fact, prior to engaging in any assessment activities, counselors have an ethical responsibility to obtain and document informed consent (American Counseling Association, 2014). For clients to be able to give informed consent, they must be provided with several pieces of information about the test and the process in which they are about to engage. Information that should be included as part of the informed consent process includes the following:

- Purpose of the test (and process)
- Criteria used for selecting the test to be used
- Testing conditions that will be made available
- Skills, abilities, or characteristics to be measured
- Administrative procedures to be used

- Number and type of questions that might be seen
- Time allotted to complete the assessment
- Scoring methods to be implemented

Upon providing clients with an overview of the testing process, it is appropriate for you to answer any questions they might have. The more informed clients are, the more at ease they will be during the testing process (see Guided Practice Exercise 5.4). In some cases you might even present clients with sample test items or a practice test to help them acclimate to how questions will be worded and what they will be asked to do during the actual test administration. The administration instructions accompanying the test you intend to use should provide guidance as to whether sample items are available and how they should be presented to the test taker. An additional resource you could provide to your clients is a document called the *Rights and Responsibilities of Test Takers: Guidelines and Expectations* (Joint Committee on Testing Practices, 2000; see additional resources at the end of this chapter for the URL). This document, drafted by the Test Takers Rights and Responsibilities Working Group of the Joint Committee on Testing Practices, provides clients with a description of what is expected of them as participants in the assessment process as well as any rights they may have as participants.

During Administration

Your primary responsibilities during the actual administration of the test include making sure that the test administration protocol is followed. Depending on the test selected, there may be a standardized format for its administration. **Standardization** establishes

---

CASE ILLUSTRATION 5.2

When Sarah was younger she dreamt of being a teacher. Both of her parents were in education and she thought that was the ideal career for her. In college she majored in elementary education with a concentration in biology. After her first 2 years she had a GPA of 3.3 (on a 4.0 scale) and her professors thought she had potential to be a successful educator. Now in her junior year, Sarah is beginning to think education might not be the career she wants. While she enjoys working with children, she has become discouraged by the lack of prospects she sees in teaching as a profession. At this time she is not sure what to do. She realizes she is nearing graduation and should have a better sense of what she is going to do by now. Recently, Sarah has even thought about taking some time off from school, but she doesn't really have any idea what she wants to do. Before making any further decisions on her future, she decides to visit the career counseling center on campus. Following an initial intake, both Sarah and her counselor agree that assessments such as the Strong Interest Inventory and Myers-Briggs Type Indicator might help her better understand where her interests lie. After taking the tests, Sarah and her counselor meet to go over the results. During the session, the counselor allows Sarah to discuss how she believes the results relate to her situation. This collaborative approach allows Sarah to personalize the results and use them to develop a plan for what to do after college.

GUIDED PRACTICE EXERCISE 5.4

Constructing an Informed Consent Document

Draft an informed consent document that you could present to your client before administering the Wechsler Adult Intelligence Scale-Fourth Edition intelligence test. What information would you include in your consent document? How would you ensure that the client fully understands what he or she is being asked to do as part of this assessment process?

uniform procedures for using an assessment so that the observation, administration, equipment, materials, and scoring rules remain the same for all who are administered the test (Millman & Greene, 1993). When all clients are tested under the same conditions, their scores are a result of their own effort and ability and not some external factor. According to Zucker (2004), the process of "standardization attempts to control these external factors to the greatest degree possible so that the assessment is a valid measurement tool that produces meaningful results" (p. 2).

Standardized administration protocols especially are important when using norm-referenced tests. In norm-referenced tests, an individual's score is compared to the average performance of others who took the same test previously. For this to be a fair and valid comparison, we need to ensure that each individual assessed was tested in a similar fashion. When this is the case, the differences noted between tested individuals can be attributed to individual differences rather than external factors. During the administration of a test, counselors should observe their clients to note if any problems arise that might affect the validity of the test results. For example, a client may be struggling to understand a particular question or section of questions on the test, or might be exhibiting signs of distress as a result of the testing process. In situations like these, the counselor should consult with the test manual to see what is recommended practice. Though not common, counselors may need to discontinue the assessment process in the interest of client welfare.

In addition to adhering to the designated administration protocol for the test you select, you also are responsible for making sure that any special accommodations are made for clients who may need assistance. Both the No Child Left Behind Act (2001) and the Individuals with Disabilities Act (1975) specify that test administrators are required to make changes to an assessment to accommodate the needs of individuals with disabilities. **Accommodation** can take many forms. According to Phillips (1993), acceptable test accommodations can include changes in format, response, setting, timing, or scheduling. Counselors should be careful in making accommodations for individuals during the testing process. For one, you need to be sure that the accommodation you make does not significantly impact the score the individual achieves on the test. Second, you need to ensure that the accommodation does not preclude you from comparing a client's score to other scores in a valid manner. You are encouraged to review the administration manual for the test you are using to see how the test authors address the process of accommodating clients with special needs and what types of accommodations can be offered.

After Administration

After you have administered a test to a client, your responsibilities include bringing closure to the experience for the client and securely storing all test materials. In terms of closure, a counselor will often debrief a client following a test administration. During this debriefing period the counselor may ask the client to share his or her thoughts or feelings regarding the test and the testing process. Information shared during this debriefing period can be used to provide context to the client's test scores. Counselors may also take this opportunity to remind the client how the results will be calculated and used to advance the counseling process. If deception was used this would be the time for the counselor to divulge the true meaning of the test and what it was intended to measure. Though not common, sometimes deception is used when the results of a test may be skewed had the client known the true intent of the test. It is primarily used to generate accurate responses and not harm the client in anyway.

Counselors also need to ensure that all testing materials have been collected and accounted for. For instruments that will be scored on site, the materials need to be kept in a secure location to maintain test integrity and protect the confidentiality of the client. Instruments that will be sent off site for scoring will need to be packaged and mailed to the scoring center as directed in the instructions provided by the testing center. As a rule of thumb, counselors should make copies of materials sent off to be scored as a safeguard should something happen in transit and the original answer sheets and testing materials become lost. This will prevent clients from having to recreate their answers from a previous administration.

SCORING AND INTERPRETATION

The scoring of tests is an important part of the assessment process. Without accurate scoring, the results generated are rendered meaningless and of no use to the counselor or client. So what is a test score? By definition, **test scores** are the numerical results of a test administration (Erford, 2013). It is a way of quantifying how a person rates on a particular construct. These scores can then be used to compare the individual to other test takers, to his or her past performance, or to some defined standard or criterion. Several scoring methods are used to derive a test score. Tests may include questions where a single correct answer exists. In this case, a test taker's response is scored as either correct or incorrect. Response choices can be either dichotomous (only two answer choices provided) or polytomous (multiple answer choices provided). Examples of questions using these types of response choices can be found in Table 5.4. You may also encounter questions in which a qualitative rating scale is provided. Clients are asked to either rate their level of agreement (*strongly agree, agree, disagree, strongly disagree*) or offer a subjective rating (on a scale from 1–10, with 1 being the worst and 10 being the best). To best understand what a test score means, you should be familiar with the response options provided to the test taker, what the score quantifies, and how it can be used to assess a particular construct.

Table 5.4   Examples of Dichotomous- and Polytomous-Response Test Questions

Question	Response Options
What is your gender?	Male or female (dichotomous)
Are you married?	Yes or no (dichotomous)
Are you employed?	Yes or no (dichotomous)
What grade are you in?	1st, 2nd, 3rd, 4th, . . . (polytomous)
How often do you have difficulty sleeping?	1–2 nights/week, 3–4 nights/week, every night (polytomous)
What is your ethnicity?	African American, Asian, Caucasian, Hispanic (polytomous)

There are several methods by which test scores can be computed. Whereas some tests provide users with options regarding how they can be scored, others have a defined scoring procedure that must be followed. Generally speaking, scoring methods can be grouped into three categories: hand scoring, computer scoring, and optical scan scoring. A description of each is provided below.

Hand Scoring

Hand scoring is perhaps the most common scoring method used by test users. It involves a process whereby an individual manually scores an instrument by either tallying responses or counting the number of correct responses on a test. Depending on the instrument and the complexity of the scoring procedure, tests can be hand-scored by a counselor or client. In situations where there are a large number of items to score or the individual items collectively provide scale scores, a template can be used. These templates are often placed over an individual answer sheet and the appropriate item responses to record are highlighted.

The benefit of the hand scoring method is that it is low cost and can be conducted by either the counselor or the client. Results can be obtained quickly and the test scorer can look to see if there are any discrepancies in the answers provided by the client. A drawback to this approach is that the chance for a scoring error to take place is greater than one would find for the other scoring methods. Test users may sometimes need to score an instrument a second time to make sure they are reporting the correct score.

Computer Scoring

There are two basic ways in which a test can be computer-scored. The first is through a manual entry method. First a test is administered in a paper-and-pencil format. When completed, the test user then takes the client's answers and manually enters them into a test scoring software package obtained from the test publisher. The software then calculates the appropriate scale scores that can then be reviewed and interpreted by the counselor. A second method is for the client to be administered the test on a computer directly. In this approach the client is seated at a computer terminal and the questions appear on the screen for the client to answer. Like the manual entry approach, the computer converts raw scores into scale scores and issues the test user an interpretive report. The benefit of using the computer scoring approach is that results are provided instantly and can be discussed with the client more quickly. When using a computer to test clients, counselors should make sure that clients are not able to access any outside information that might assist them in completing the test and thus compromising the integrity of their results.

Optical Scan Scoring

Optical scanning requires the use of an optical mark reader and machine-scorable answer sheets. Clients mark their response to each item on the answer sheet and the completed sheet is then fed through the reader. The reader quickly scans each answer sheet and tallies up the number of correct responses depending on how the answer key was coded for the reader. This type of test is often used in academic settings where several individuals need to be tested at a single time.

Optical scan tests can either be scored on site or mailed/faxed to a test publisher for scoring. When using on-site scoring, the test administrator needs to make sure that the correct scoring software has been purchased. The software is used to score the answer sheets and also produce an interpretive report based on the results of the test. This report can be used to generate discussion in session with clients as it relates to their responses on the test. Mail or fax service scoring is used when the completed answer sheets are sent to the test publisher for scoring. Once scored, the publisher sends interpretive reports for each individual client. Test publishers often charge a fee for each answer sheet scored and report generated.

The primary benefit of using an optical scan scoring approach is that it is quick and easy to run. Reports can be generated in a matter of minutes. This is particularly helpful when several tests are being administered at a given time. In addition, the risk of human error in calculating scores is mitigated. However, there also are drawbacks to using this scoring method. Purchasing the requisite optical mark reader and scoring software, as well as sending sheets off to be scored, can be costly. There also is the matter of training staff in the correct use of the scanning equipment so that answer sheets are processed correctly and valid reports are generated. Counselors should weigh the advantages and disadvantages of this approach given their current testing needs to determine if this is the best approach to use.

Now that you have learned a little more about the various test scoring methods, we encourage you to begin thinking about the work you hope to do as a counselor and the clients with whom you will work in order to begin understanding which methods might be most appropriate to use. To help stimulate your thinking, we encourage you to look at Guided Practice Exercise 5.5 with your classmates.

GUIDED PRACTICE EXERCISE 5.5

Selecting the Appropriate Test Scoring Method

In this chapter you learned that there are various test scoring methods. In a small group discuss the advantages and disadvantages of the hand, computer, and optical scan scoring approaches. Are there certain types of clients (age, setting, presenting problem) for which a particular scoring approach would be more beneficial to use? Thinking about the types of clients you hope to one day work with, is there an approach that you believe might not be an effective choice to use with that population?

REPORTING ASSESSMENT RESULTS

Once a test has been scored and interpreted, it is time for the counselor to share the results with the client. These results can be shared informally by discussing them with the client during a counseling session or they can be shared more formally in a prepared assessment report (in Chapter 6 the assessment report format will be further discussed). Whether you choose to use the formal or informal method, there are some key areas that you should cover with your client to help him or her process the experience.

Use Appropriate Language

When you share the results of a test with a client, it is important to use language appropriate to the client. Many clients and parents are uninformed about assessment practices (Barber, Paris, Evans, & Gadsden, 1992). When tests include technical jargon, the terminology may not be immediately recognized or understood by someone not in the profession. Therefore, for these results to be meaningful to the client, you should try to explain the results and what they mean in a manner that the client can understand. For example, instead of reporting that a client had a t-score of 70, it might be more practical to talk about how the client scored higher than most people who have taken this test on this construct. A t-score might not be a term a client can relate to, but stating what that t-score means (higher than average) communicates the same essential information more effectively. You will need to use your own intuition to determine what is appropriate for each client and how results can be reported and accurately understood.

The language you use to convey test results also will depend on the age of your client. For children, it will be important that you use language appropriate for that age group. Speaking on the child's level will help the child better understand the results and feel more invested in the counseling process. To help a child understand what it means to score in the 90th percentile, you could ask the child to picture his classroom and then tell him that his score is one that probably only two or three people would get. Creating a visual image works well with children.

Put Results in Context

A score is just a snapshot picture of how a client thinks, feels, acts, or performs in a given moment in time. It is by no means a definitive statement of who a client is as a person. As a result, test scores should not be reported to a client in a vacuum. There should be some context that accompanies the scores presented. Imagine that I administer to you a new intelligence test I have developed. After completion of the test, I score your responses and report to you that your intelligence score is 5. What does a score of 5 mean? There is no context provided. Is 5 a good score or a poor one? How many people score 5 or better? Without proper context, a score has little meaning, especially to a client. If I were to tell you that the average score on my intelligence test is a 2.5 and a score of 5 places you in the 95th percentile, you would feel much better about your performance. When sharing scores with clients, you should share how this score compares to the average for this instrument and how it compares to the performance of others if a norm-referenced criterion is available.

In addition to putting scores in context, it is important to put the test in context. The test is one form of assessment that is used to learn about a client. It should be interpreted in collaboration with other assessments such as interviews, observations, and other instruments you may have administered. Evaluating multiple sources of information gives you a clearer picture of the client and the issues being experienced. When sharing results with clients, it is a good idea to share how the test results support or differ from what you have gathered from other forms of assessment (see Case Illustration 5.3). You could tell your client that her personality type as determined by the Myers-Briggs Type Indicator appears to support some of the personality characteristics you have noted in your work together.

CASE ILLUSTRATION 5.3

A single piece of information should never be used to make important decisions. Rather, as much information as possible should be gathered and considered collectively. When you applied to graduate school, you most likely were asked to submit a number of items as part of your application packet. These items may have included a copy of your undergraduate transcripts, standardized test scores (e.g., GRE), letters of recommendation, a purpose statement, or a writing sample. You also may have had to participate in an admissions interview. The admissions committee used all of these pieces of information to make a decision about whether to admit you to the program. Imagine if they had used only one piece of information, such as your GRE score? Would that have been a fair assessment of your ability to successfully complete a counselor training program?

Share Limitations

When reviewing scores with clients, it also is a good idea to discuss the limitations of the test. This is where you can explain the concepts of reliability and validity to the client in terms that are easily understandable to nonprofessionals. Clients should also be informed that most test scores are not representative of future performance or behavior. Just because a client may perform at a certain level currently, that does not mean this is what he or she can expect in the future as well. As noted above, test scores are mere snapshots of how a client is currently functioning. They provide both the counselor and client with a starting point or reference point to guide future work together. Helping clients see that scores are not absolute will help motivate them to work in the counseling process.

Throughout the debriefing process the counselor should monitor the client and assess how well the information presented is being received. When it appears that clients are confused by the information they are receiving, the astute counselor should pause and offer clarification. Perhaps there is another way to phrase what it is you are trying to convey, or maybe you will need to offer an example to help illustrate your point. As the counselor you also should allow the client plenty of opportunities to ask questions. Your goal should be to end the assessment process with the client feeling informed and comfortable with the results presented. At times clients may not know what questions to ask, so it may be incumbent on you to stimulate these questions. You can do so by either using incomplete sentences for the client to finish (Whiston, 2009) or sharing with your client some questions that other clients typically have about this experience. The more you are able to share with the client, the better the information will be received and the more beneficial the testing process will be to the overall counseling experience for you and your client.

KEYSTONES

- The decision about which test to use should be made after carefully considering what it is that needs to be assessed, what is already known, and the best way to gather any remaining unknown information.
- Tests are only one source of information about a client. Counselors should always attempt to place test results in context and consider how they relate to other information obtained about the presenting problem from other sources.
- When selecting assessment instruments to use, counselors are legally and ethically obligated to use only those instruments which they are qualified to administer. To determine the criteria for qualified users, counselors should consult with the professional organizations to which they belong and also review the qualified user guidelines provided by individual test publishers.
- When administering tests make sure the appropriate administration protocol is followed so that results are valid and can be interpreted correctly.
- Tests can be scored using a variety of methods: hand, computer, and optical scan scoring. Counselors should be aware of the advantages and disadvantages of using each of these methods and share this information with clients during the informed consent process.
- An important part of the testing process is debriefing clients after the test has been administered and scored. This is the time for sharing results with clients and helping them understand what the results mean and how they can help clients better understand the nature of their presenting problem or issue. Counselors should remember to use common language, put results in context, and discuss any limitations of the test used when debriefing clients either verbally or in writing.

KEY TERMS

accommodation

standardization

Tests

Mental Measurements Yearbook

test scores

Tests in Print

ADDITIONAL RESOURCES

- Association for Assessment in Counseling and Research (Division of ACA)
  http://aarc-counseling.org
- Educational Testing Service (ETS) Database of Tests
  http://www.ets.org/test_link/find_tests
- Responsibilities of Users of Standardized Tests (RUST; 3rd edition)
  http://aarc-counseling.org/assets/cms/uploads/files/rust.pdf
- Test Taker Rights and Responsibilities
  http://aarc-counseling.org/assets/cms/uploads/files/rights.pdf

Student Study Site: Visit the Student Study Site at **www.sagepub.com/watson** to access additional study tools, including quizzes, web resources, and journal articles.

CHAPTER 6

Integrating Assessment Into Counseling Practice

LEARNING OBJECTIVES

After reading this chapter, you will be able to

- Identify the various forms of assessment strategies used to gather initial information from a client
- Describe the role of diagnosis in the counseling process
- Discuss the process of case conceptualization based on the results of assessment practices and instruments administered
- Demonstrate an ability to use assessment results to formulate an effective treatment plan specific to the client with whom you are working
- Assess client success at meeting established counseling goals
- Assess treatment outcomes using both summative and formative data
- Write a professional assessment report to present to clients or other stakeholders

Throughout this first section of the book we have presented you with an overview of the assessment process and described for you how assessment instruments can be selected, evaluated, administered, and scored. This knowledge will help you make informed decisions and apply assessment practices in an ethical and competent manner. But what do you do with the information obtained from assessing a client? What do the scores and numbers you derive mean? When examined individually these data points provide us with a limited picture of the client with whom we are working and the issue for which counseling was sought. However, when pieced together, the results of our assessment efforts allow us to better understand the client. Furthermore, it is this understanding that allows us to begin structuring a therapeutic strategy that can be used to help the client address his or her presenting problem most effectively.

In this final chapter of Section I, we begin exploring the many ways counselors can start using the results of their assessment activities to inform the practice of counseling. Specifically, we focus our attention on how assessment results can be utilized in the many stages of the case conceptualization process, from a counselor's initial assessment of a client to the various stages of the counseling process—including the initial building of rapport, conceptualizing the presenting problem, setting goals, and planning treatment—to finally measuring treatment outcomes. In each of these stages, assessment results can help counselors better understand where the client has been, where the client is currently, and where the client needs to go in the future. Our hope as you read this chapter is that you begin to see that when properly integrated, assessment data can be a valuable tool for directing the focus of counseling and maximizing the therapeutic benefits of the process for you and your clients.

ASSESSMENT AS A VITAL COMPONENT OF THE COUNSELING PROCESS

Assessment is a ubiquitous aspect of counseling. As we highlighted repeatedly in earlier chapters, nearly all we as counselors do with clients involves some assessment-related activity. In Chapter 1 we noted that assessment serves a number of primary purposes in counseling, including screening, diagnosing, case conceptualizing, treatment planning and goal identification, and evaluating client progress. From the moment we first begin working with clients through our final interactions with them, we constantly are assessing to determine whether we are providing the best possible services and clients are experiencing the change they desire. In the following section we will describe these primary purposes of assessment and how they help to advance the counseling relationship.

Screening and Initial Assessments

According to Urbina (2004), the first stage in the counseling process is to screen the client and identify that individual's problems and reason(s) for being assessed. The screening process is designed to allow counselors to develop a quick and cost-effective snapshot of a person and the issues with which he or she may be dealing. This knowledge can then be used to make informed decisions about treatment, including reducing time spent on waiting lists for clients whose needs appear to be more urgent (Smith, Rosenstein, & Granaas, 2001). Additionally, we as counselors screen potential clients because not every person who seeks out counseling services may actually need further assessment or treatment.

Screening therefore helps to determine the next step that might need to be taken in helping a person. An example of how screening can benefit the treatment process is described in Case Illustration 6.1.

CASE ILLUSTRATION   6.1

When an individual presents for services at a hospital emergency room, he or she often is seen by a triage nurse before being called back into a treatment room. The triage nurse asks a variety of questions to get a better sense of what the individual's presenting complaint is and some potential diagnoses to consider given the individual's presenting condition. The information gathered by the triage nurse is then relayed to the attending physician that the individual eventually sees for follow-up and additional assessment. The purpose of this brief encounter with the triage nurse is to get a better sense of the initial presenting problem so that proper treatment protocols can be implemented. Areas where individuals are determined to be at risk are assessed in more depth using more sophisticated techniques and procedures. The same process applies to counselors. Initially, the goal of the counselor is to triage the client and determine what his or her immediate need may be. A client may require immediate hospitalization for medical stabilization or to prevent risk of imminent harm to self or others. This initial triaging of client presenting problems helps counselors better formulate the best possible plan of action for the client and involve the necessary treatment providers to maximize the likelihood of a successful treatment outcome.

Skilled counselors begin the process of screening their clients almost immediately. From the moment a client enters the office, counselors begin assessing to gain a better understanding of the person and his or her presenting issues. Was the client on time? Does the client appear to have a positive attitude about the counseling process? Where does the client sit? Does the client maintain eye contact? The answers to these questions provide us with clues about who our clients are as people and how they are perceiving the situation. Whether they realize it or not, clients' presentation, body language, gestures, and even tone of voice can tell a lot about the problems they are experiencing and why they are seeking counseling at this particular time. In fact, before even asking a single question, counselors can potentially gain insight into their client's problems if they are able to interpret nonverbal communication.

Nonverbal communication is an interesting phenomenon. Since the work of Dr. Albert Mehrabian in the 1960s, researchers have sought to develop a better understanding of how people convey messages and communicate nonverbally. Although difficult to pinpoint an exact percentage, most researchers agree that the vast majority of the communication spectrum occurs nonverbally, with estimates generally in the 70%–93% range. Given the importance of unspoken communication, counselors would be wise to pay attention to clients' nonverbal behavior and assess for clues their clients might exhibit that help explain their current problems (see Guided Practice Exercise 6.1). A description of some nonverbal cues that counselors should assess are included in Table 6.1.

Table 6.1   Nonverbal Cues to Observe

Appearance—How is the client's appearance? Counselors should assess whether the client appears to be neatly dressed and hygienic or if the client looks disheveled and inappropriately dressed.

Activity/motor skills—How is the client's movement? Counselors should assess how the client acts and note whether the client is lethargic and slow to respond or animated and frenetic.

Motivation—Is the client motivated to participate in counseling? Does the client appear willing to share information freely, or must the client be prompted or coaxed to share with the counselor?

Who presents with the client?—Who accompanies the client to counseling can be very telling. If the client presents alone, it might indicate a lack of support or a situation in which others are unaware that a problem exists. When the client is accompanied by others, it should serve as a clue for the counselor as to where the client's support resides and who else might be a source of information or a resource in future treatment planning.

Is the presentation voluntary or involuntary?—Assessing the circumstances surrounding the client's presentation for counseling can help the counselor assess the scope of the problem. When a client presents involuntarily or under duress, it could be a sign that the client does not recognize the existence of a problem. Further assessment will be needed to determine if this lack of insight is intentional or unintentional (a possible sign of cognitive impairment).

GUIDED PRACTICE EXERCISE 6.1

Communicating Nonverbally

Divide into groups of three students. In your group, assign the roles of counselor, client, and observer. Role-play a scenario in which a client is presenting for counseling for the first time (feel free to choose your own presenting issue) and the counselor is about to begin conducting an initial assessment. For a period of 5 minutes, the student playing the role of the client is not allowed to speak. All information is to be communicated nonverbally by the client. The counselor is tasked with gathering as much information as possible regarding the client's presenting problem. At the end of the 5 minutes, the counselor will share his or her assessment and the client will now have an opportunity to discuss whether the counselor accurately assessed the presenting problem. The observer should take notes during the 5-minute initial assessment and comment on any nonverbal cues that may have been missed by the counselor. If time permits, you can repeat the activity and change the roles of each student. At the completion of the exercise, discuss with your group some of the challenges related to interpreting nonverbal cues, how you were able to make sense of the nonverbal cues and identify what the client was trying to communicate, and in what areas you will need to improve your skills when it comes to assessing nonverbal communication.

In addition to the information a counselor gains from his or her observations of clients and assessment of nonverbal cues, additional information can be collected about the client and the client's presenting issue using more formal methods. An example of such a method is the intake interview, also referred to as a psychosocial interview. Most professional counseling relationships between a counselor and a client begin with an intake interview (Freeburg & Van Winkle, 2011). When administered correctly, the intake interview is a great way to better understand clients and their presenting issues. Generally speaking, the **intake interview** is an assessment technique that provides counselors with information about clients' past functioning and how it relates to their current situation and the problems they are facing. In addition to helping counselors identify, evaluate, and explore their clients' presenting issues, intake interviews also aid counselors in identifying the client's interpersonal style, interpersonal skills, and personal history so that an appropriate level of care can be identified for the client. Although a single standard format does not exist, most intake interviews include questions in several common core areas. Each of these areas is important to assess because they provide information that can help a counselor better understand the nature and scope of a client's presenting problem. In total, there are eight core areas most often addressed in an intake interview using a series of open-ended questions:

Demographic information. This section collects basic descriptive data about a client, including name, gender, age, marital status, race or ethnicity identified with, employment status, and living situation.

Referral reasons. This section solicits information from clients as to why they are seeking counseling at this particular time, including the symptoms experienced that led them to believe it was time to get help. Knowing what led an individual to seek counseling at this time, as opposed to last week or a week from now, can help counselors understand how the problem may be exceeding their current coping strategies.

Current situation. Clients are asked to provide a brief description of how the problem currently factors into their life. How often they are troubled by the problem, how they cope with the problem when it emerges, and the impact of the problem on their quality of life are all issues counselors ask about in order to better understand the current situation. The approach a counselor takes with a client who has been dealing with a problem for 3 or 4 weeks would be markedly different than the approach taken with a client who has been dealing with the same problem for over 2 years.

Previous counseling experience. These questions are designed to ascertain whether the client has ever sought professional help for their problems in the past. Clients are asked to report on all forms of help they may have sought, including individual therapy, group therapy, family therapy, medication, outpatient programs, or inpatient hospitalization. Here it is helpful to get as much information as possible, including any specific information (dates, locations, treatment providers) on these past treatment attempts. This information allows counselors to see what approaches may have been effective in the past. These strategies could be replicated, and those that had proved to be ineffective could be avoided. Additionally, there may be a need in the future to contact and consult with previous providers, so knowing who was seen and for what purpose is useful information to have.

Birth and developmental history. In this section questions are asked of clients to understand their past. Specifically, counselors inquire as to whether there were any noteworthy issues or complications surrounding the client's birth or whether any significant developmental milestones may have been missed. This information potentially can help to explain the current functioning and abilities of a client. When clients may not know the answers to these questions, they could ask family members to help provide the requested information.

Family history. Clients are asked to describe their family constellation. Who is in their immediate family and with which extended family members do they maintain active relationships? The questions in this section also explore whether the client's presenting problem may have been experienced by other family members as well. Several mental disorders have a strong genetic component to them. Knowing what illnesses run in a client's family may help identify particular disorders that should be screened for or ruled out.

Medical history. Clients share information related to past or current medical conditions and any treatment sought for those conditions. Additionally, clients are asked to describe any past surgeries or major illnesses and any known drug allergies they may have. In assessing a client's medical history it is important to identify any medications a client may currently be taking, as these medications may be contraindicated with any medications that might be prescribed to help deal with the current issue for which they are seeking counseling.

Educational and/or vocational background. Questions typically found in this section of the intake interview include the following: What is the highest grade completed or degree earned by the client? What kind of student is/was the client? Is the client currently employed, and if so who is the employer, what is the job the client performs, and how long has the client been employed in this position? Any prolonged absences from the workforce also should be noted.

Conducting an effective intake interview requires counselors to establish rapport with their clients (Ivey, Ivey, & Zalaquett, 2010). When a trusting relationship is established, the client feels more comfortable sharing personal information and the counselor is able to gain a much richer understanding of what the client is experiencing (see Guided Practice Exercise 6.2). Counselors should take time to explain to their clients what the interview will cover and how the information gathered will be used to help them in the counseling process. A sample intake interview form is included in Figure 6.1; however, different settings may have their own policies and procedures for how and when intake interviews are to be administered.

GUIDED PRACTICE EXERCISE 6.2

Conducting an Intake Interview With a New Client

Clients who present for counseling for the first time often do so with some anxiety and trepidation. They may be unsure of what to expect or unclear about what they should say or share about themselves. Think about how you would go about introducing the intake interview to such a client. What would you say or do to help build rapport and trust so that the client is willing to actively participate and share during the interview process? How would your approach to the interview process vary when working with clients from a cultural background different than your own?

Figure 6.1   Sample Intake Interview Form

MidState
Behavioral Health Services

ADULT PSYCHOSOCIAL ASSESSMENT
INTAKE INTERVIEW

Counselor: _____   Date: _____

Client Name: _____   SS#: _____

Date of Birth: _____   Age: _____   Race: _____   Gender: _____

Next of Kin: _____   Relationship to client: _____

Address: _____   Telephone: _____

Information obtained from: ☐ Client   ☐ Family Member   ☐ Parent/Spouse   ☐ Employer

INITIAL REASON FOR SEEKING TREATMENT (PRESENTING PROBLEM):

_____

_____

_____

_____

PRECIPITATING FACTORS:

_____

_____

_____

CURRENT SYMPTOMS: *(mark all that apply)*

☐ abnormal thoughts	☐ elevated mood	☐ mania	☐ self-injurious behavior
☐ anger or aggressiveness	☐ euphoria	☐ missing school / work	☐ severe mood swings
☐ anxiety	☐ hallucinations	☐ obsessions / compulsions	☐ sleep disturbances
☐ appetite disturbance	☐ hopelessness / helplessness	☐ oppositional	☐ substance abuse (current)
☐ cognitive impairment	☐ hyperactivity	☐ orientation / memory	☐ substance abuse (past)
☐ decreased energy	☐ grief	☐ panic attacks	☐ tearfulness
☐ delusions	☐ guilt	☐ paranoia	☐ treatment noncompliance
☐ depression	☐ impulsivity	☐ poor concentration	☐ withdrawal symptoms
☐ disruption of thoughts	☐ insight / judgment	☐ pressured speech	☐ worthlessness
☐ dissociative states	☐ irritability	☐ problems with ADLs	☐ other

FUNCTIONAL IMPAIRMENTS: *(specify severity and note any recent changes)*

_____

_____

_____

Copyright © 2007 MBHS, LLC   Page 1 of 5

(Continued)

Figure 6.1   (Continued)

TREATMENT HISTORY:

Have you had previous counseling / therapy experience?   ☐ Yes   ☐ No   Psychiatric hospitalization?   ☐ Yes   ☐ No

If yes, please indicate when: _____ therapist's name: _____

What types of therapy/counseling have you experienced? _____

_____

_____

Has a helping professional ever recommended you take medications?   ☐ Yes   ☐ No   Did you take them? ☐ Yes   ☐ No

What medications were recommended and who made the recommendation? _____

_____

Do you believe that the medication was helpful?   ☐ Yes   ☐ No   If no, why not? _____

DEVELOPMENTAL HISTORY:

How old was mother when you were born? _____   Were there labor and delivery problems?   ☐ Yes   ☐ No

Were you born: ☐ early   ☐ on time   ☐ late   ☐ don't know   What was your birth weight? _____

Were there any problems with language development? _____

Were developmental milestones achieved at the appropriate ages? _____

Any difficulties encountered during development? _____

FAMILY HISTORY:

Family of Origin:

Parent's marital status: ☐ married   ☐ separated   ☐ divorced   ☐ widowed

Relationship with mother: _____

Relationship with father: _____

Siblings:

Name	Sex	Age	Current Relationship with Client

Marital Status:

☐ single / never married   ☐ married   ☐ separated   ☐ divorced   ☐ widowed

Age when married: _____   Number of years married: _____   Number of years separated / divorced: _____

Children:

Name	Sex	Age	Residing at home?

Type of dwelling family resides in: (house, apartment, etc., include # of bedrooms): _____

Is there a history of mental illness in the family?   ☐ Yes   ☐ No   If yes, specify: _____

Are any family members deceased: ☐ Yes   ☐ No   If yes, specify: _____

EDUCATIONAL HISTORY:

Highest grade completed in school: _____   Year graduated: _____

Type of student: _____

_____

Did client have any school-related problems?   ☐ Yes   ☐ No   If yes, please explain: _____

Was client ever suspended (at-home or in-school)?   ☐ Yes   ☐ No   If yes, please explain: _____

EMPLOYMENT HISTORY:

Is client currently employed?   Yes / No   If yes, name of employer: _____

Describe job duties: _____

Number of years at current job: _____   Satisfaction with job: ☐ Excellent ☐Good ☐ Fair ☐Poor

Does client find it difficult to maintain employment? _____

MEDICAL HISTORY:

Have you ever had any serious illnesses, injuries, or surgery? (Please specify) _____

_____

Please list all current medications you are taking: (prescribed or over-the-counter) _____

_____

Who prescribes your medication for you?   _____

Doctor's telephone number: _____   Office address: _____

Do you have any known allergies? ☐ Yes   ☐ No   If yes, please list: _____

Have you ever been pregnant? _____   Have you ever had a miscarriage? _____

(Continued)

Figure 6.1 (Continued)

RISK ASSESSMENT:

Have you ever had any involvement with legal authorities? ☐ Yes ☐ No If yes, please explain: _____

Do you have any pending legal issues (probations, upcoming hearings, etc.)? _____

Have you ever been abused: ☐ physically ☐ emotionally ☐ mentally ☐ other ☐ no abuse

If yes to any of the above, please describe: _____

_____

Are you sexually active? ☐ Yes ☐ No If yes, at what age did you become active? _____

How many partners have you had? _____ Do you practice safe sex or use birth control? ☐ Yes ☐ No

Have you ever used drugs or alcohol? ☐ Yes ☐ No If yes, at what age did you start using? _____

Substance:	Amt:	Freq:	How long using:

Do your parents drink or use drugs? ☐ Yes, current use ☐ No, never ☐ Previous usage ☐ Not Sure
Do your friends drink or use drugs? ☐ Yes, current use ☐ No, never ☐ Previous usage ☐ Not Sure

INTERPERSONAL HISTORY:

Social Relationships:

How easy is it for you to make friends? ☐ very easy ☐ about average ☐ very difficult

How easy is it for you to keep friends? ☐ very easy ☐ about average ☐ very difficult

How many close friends do you have? _____

Leisure Activities:

How do you like to spend your free time? _____

_____

What are your hobbies, interests? _____

Spiritual / Religious Beliefs:

Do you practice a particular religion? ☐ Yes ☐ No If yes, what is your religious affiliation? _____

Strengths or support: _____

Problems or weakness: _____

Any recent changes: _____

_____

SELF ASSESSMENT

What do you see as your greatest strengths or characteristics? _____

_____

_____

What are the areas that you would most like to improve about yourself? _____

_____

_____

Who will be your greatest supports or allies throughout your counseling experience? _____

_____

_____

_____	_____	_____
Counselor Signature	*Credentials*	*Date*
_____	_____	_____
Counselor Signature	*Credentials*	*Date*
_____	_____	_____
Psychiatrist Signature	*Credentials*	*Date*

In addition to needing to establish rapport with their clients, counselors also will need time to conduct an intake interview. By its very nature, the intake interview is designed to be inclusive. Information is gathered across many dimensions. While the focus of the intake interview may seem at first glance to be quite broad in scope, all of the information acquired by the counselor could prove to be essential to the overall success of the counseling process. Because of the inclusive nature of the interview, it is not uncommon for the process to stretch out over multiple settings (Zunker, 2008). The exact length of time it takes to administer an intake interview depends on the format of the interview and the characteristics of the client (age, cognitive ability, presenting problem) being assessed.

Diagnosis

Following the screening stage, counselors proceed to the diagnosis stage. The goal of this stage varies depending on the purpose and setting of the counseling relationship. In general, **diagnosis** refers to the process of learning more about the client and his or her problem. Counselors aim to develop a more in-depth understanding of the problem that might have been identified in the screening stage. Among the areas counselors assess are the history of the client's presenting problem, the developmental history of the problem, any precursors and consequences related to the problem, and the existence of any strengths or weaknesses the client possesses that may need to be highlighted or addressed in counseling. Sometimes the purpose of diagnosing a client is more clinical in nature. When this is the case, and a documented mental disorder is thought to exist, a more technical and standardized approach may be needed.

Clinical diagnosing typically involves classifying the client's presenting problem into preset categories using information gathered through a thorough assessment process. For most counselors, clinical diagnosing will involve use of the *Diagnostic and Statistical Manual*. This book contains a listing of all clinical psychological disorders. The DSM also includes the diagnostic criteria of each of these disorders, listing the signs and symptoms clients must be experiencing to be diagnosed as having a particular disorder. The current version of the DSM, the fifth edition, was released in 2013. Diagnosing clients for the potential presence of DSM-5 disorders includes the use of multiple assessment procedures. Formal tests are administered to assess clients and compare their current state to those of others who have similar problems. The example presented in Case Illustration 6.2 demonstrates how counselors can conduct a clinical assessment.

CASE ILLUSTRATION   6.2

A counselor has been working with a client for a number of sessions now and suspects that the client may have a depressive disorder. To validate his hypothesis the counselor selects a formal assessment instrument to help determine whether the client actually has a clinical depression. He administers to the client the Beck Depression Inventory-2nd Edition. The BDI-II is a self-report instrument that asks clients to respond to a set of 21 items. Each item is a list of four statements arranged in order of increasing severity about a particular symptom of depression. The counselor scores the instrument and learns what symptoms the client may be experiencing. These symptoms are then compared to those listed in the DSM-5 to determine whether the client meets diagnostic criteria. The results of the BDI-II are corroborated using other assessment methods such as observation and interview. Diagnosing the client with depression according to the DSM-5 provides an objective picture of the client's problem that can be addressed much more easily than the client's subjective reporting of "feeling sad or blue." Counselors now have an established symptom set for the client that can be reevaluated in the future to assess the impact treatment is having on symptom presentation. When counseling is working, a counselor would expect the client to report having fewer symptoms than before counseling began.

An accurate diagnosis of a client's problems is important to the overall success of the counseling process. The diagnosis assigned to a client helps counselors identify the treatment approach that should be applied to help that client, the individuals who should be involved in the treatment process, and the prognosis that can be expected for a successful resolution to current problems. In addition, diagnoses allow counselors to conceptualize their clients' problems in a systematic manner that allows for accurate communication with other mental health providers and third-party reimbursement managers (Stanton, Revenson, & Tennen, 2007). Each individual involved in the client's treatment should have the same basic understanding of what is going on with the client and how those problems are going to be addressed.

Case Conceptualization

Once counselors have gathered initial information and made a diagnostic decision about a client, they can begin working to understand or conceptualize the client. In many ways, case conceptualization is one of the most integral components of the counseling process. According to Sperry and Sperry (2012), **case conceptualization** can best be defined as "a method and clinical strategy for obtaining and organizing information about a client, understanding and explaining the client's situation and maladaptive patterns, guiding and focusing treatment, anticipating challenges, and roadblocks, and preparing for successful termination" (p. 4). Specifically, case conceptualization provides counselors with a framework by which they can observe, understand, and conceptually integrate client behaviors, thoughts, feelings, and physiology from a clinical perspective (Neukrug & Schwitzer, 2006). In addition to assisting counselors in organizing the information they gather, case conceptualization helps to facilitate the setting of treatment goals and selection of counseling interventions. As Sperry (2010) notes, having a conceptual frame is perhaps the most basic competency a counselor can possess. In this section we will examine how counselors establish a conceptualization of their clients and the presenting concerns of those clients. More important, we will look at the role that assessment plays in the development of a sound case conceptualization.

According to Sperry (2005, 2010), the case conceptualization process can be broken down into four distinct phases (see Table 6.2). The first phase is known as the *diagnostic formulation* phase. In the diagnostic formulation phase, the focus is on gathering as much information as possible about the client to accurately understand his or her presenting issues. During this exploratory phase, counselors use a variety of assessment activities. For example, counselors could have clients share with them their story through the use of open-ended questions. This allows the counselor to hear the problem in the client's own words as the client perceives it. Additional assessment interventions might include using questionnaires, checklists, rating scales, or even conducting observations of the client. Additionally, counselors may choose to obtain information from the client directly or from external sources such as spouses, family members, friends, teachers, coworkers, or employers. While the primary focus is on gathering information related to the presenting signs and symptoms of the client, effective counselors should assess beyond the presenting concerns or reasons for referral. Many times the issues that lead a client to seek counseling are not their true problems. Rather, they often are seen as manifestations of larger, more complex problems in the client's life. As a result, counselors should take care to assess the scope of the presenting issue and how it impacts the client in all aspects of the client's life. A wide range of assessment interventions can be used to accomplish this goal. Doing so helps ensure that the counselor has considered all possibilities in terms of what may be the root source of the client's current symptoms.

The second phase of the case conceptualization process is known as the *clinical formulation* phase. During the diagnostic phase a wealth of information is obtained about the client and his or her functioning, both past and present. In the clinical phase, counselors must now take this collection of information and begin the process of organizing it in a meaningful manner. Specifically, counselors look for patterns and themes to see how the issues clients are experiencing first developed, how they are maintained, and how pervasive they are in various parts of the client's life. Knowing how the individual pieces of a client's experience fit together helps complete the puzzle and allows the counselor to see what is really going on with that client. Whereas the diagnostic phase is more descriptive in nature, the clinical phase can be viewed as more explanatory and longitudinal in nature (Sperry, 2005). The goal of the counselor is to understand why a client is experiencing the symptoms he or she is reporting. Rather than identifying areas of concern, the counselor assesses to fill in the knowledge gaps, expand the picture, and learn why these areas of concern exist in the client's subjective world.

To aid in their understanding, counselors select a theoretical orientation to help explain what it is that the client is experiencing. This orientation serves as the lens through which the client's presenting issues are viewed and understood. A counselor operating from an Adlerian perspective would view the nature of a client's problem differently than a counselor who had adopted a cognitive-behavioral perspective. In addition to contextualizing the client's problem, the theoretical orientation chosen by a counselor also helps identify potential treatment strategies. According to Paul (1967), the adherence to a particular theoretical orientation assists counselors in determining "what treatment, by whom, is most effective for this individual with that specific problem, and under which set of circumstances" (p. 111). As a result, the ability to conceptualize a client's issues and concerns from a particular theoretical orientation allows the counselor to move more fluidly from the diagnostic phase to the treatment phase. By the end of the clinical phase, counselors should have a clear sense of what they believe to be the client's principle concerns, the factors involved in maintaining or perpetuating the problem for the client, and the approach they will take to address and treat these concerns. In Guided Practice Exercise 6.3, you are asked to think about your own theoretical orientation and how that might influence the way you assess your clients and their presenting problems.

GUIDED PRACTICE EXERCISE 6.3

What Is Your Personal Theoretical Orientation?

By now you have most likely been exposed to a number of counseling theories and approaches. Thinking about what you have learned, and what you know about yourself as a person, what would you say is your personal theoretical orientation? How does this perspective help shape the way you view clients and their presenting problems?

The third component is the *cultural formulation* phase. In this phase, counselors examine the role a client's cultural background plays in the problems he or she is experiencing. Counselors are cautioned to not view clients' problems in a vacuum. Instead they should consider the many unique characteristics of the clients and their backgrounds that make them who they are. This could include examining such factors as race, ethnicity, age, gender, religious or spiritual affiliation, sexual orientation and gender identity, socioeconomic status, and family background. In addition, counselors should assess the cultural identity of their clients and how they manage the acculturation process. Examining these aspects may help counselors uncover factors that maintain the existence of a problem and will need to be either addressed or resolved before treatment can progress.

In the cultural formulation phase counselors should use formal and informal assessments to better understand the role cultural factors may play in the client's life. Informally, counselors could engage their clients in a discussion of who they are and how they relate to the world in which they live. For first-generation or international clients, it would be important to talk about the challenges and cultural barriers they may perceive in terms of acculturating to the dominant culture. More formal assessments can be used to assess the client's sense of identity along a number of factors. Gender, racial, and cultural identity instruments exist, which the counselor can use in session with a client. These instruments may provide some insight into how the client views his or her own culture and how that can be used as an asset throughout the treatment process. As demonstrated in Case Illustration 6.3, they also can help explain how clients conceptualize the concepts of privilege and oppression and how these lived experiences shape who they are and influence the issues for which they are seeking treatment.

CASE ILLUSTRATION 6.3

A 15-year-old Hispanic boy is new to his school. After a few weeks, the boy's teacher refers him to the school counselor because he is having difficulty in class. In addition to struggling to learn the material, he is becoming a distraction to his fellow classmates. When given a reading assignment he usually begins acting out and preventing others from completing their work as well. The counselor agrees to meet with the boy. During their first meeting together, the counselor conducts an intake assessment to learn a little more about the boy as he is new to the school. As the counselor collects information, he makes sure to address the boy's culture and how it may relate to the presenting problem. He assesses what the boy's previous schooling was like, how education is viewed in his family, and what types of support are available at home. Through this assessment the counselor learns that the boy is a first-generation student in America and his parents have little formal education. He also learns that working to support the family was valued more than education growing up. By assessing the impact of cultural factors, the counselor can begin developing a treatment plan that meets the boy's needs and maximizes the chances for counseling success. What initially may have been seen as evidence of some type of learning disorder or attention deficit issue can now be conceptualized more accurately as an acculturation issue, and the correct interventions can be employed.

The fourth, and final, component of the case conceptualization process is the *treatment formulation* phase. Having already addressed the *what* and the *why* of the problem, counselors now turn their attention to addressing the *how* of the problem. Specifically, counselors look to determine how the problem will be treated through the counseling process. It is in the treatment phase that counselors put into action their plan for helping their clients. Establishing treatment goals, selecting interventions, monitoring treatment progress, and assessing outcomes are all activities that take place in the treatment phase. During this phase counselors are able to assess the accuracy of their initial conceptualization of the client's presenting problem. Revisions to the initial conceptualization may be needed as additional information is uncovered or clients' responses to treatment interventions are evaluated by the counselor.

While there is no singular way to complete a case conceptualization, the efficacy of these conceptualizations can be evaluated by how well they encapsulate all of the dynamics at work in a client's life that impact that client's subjective experience and relate to the current problems and issues reported. In evaluating the efficacy of a counselor's case conceptualization, Sperry and Sperry (2012) describe three levels of sufficiency: high, moderate, and low. Lower level case conceptualizations are characterized by their lack of detail and specificity. Information is gathered from a client without any contextual understanding. Furthermore, treatment plans are designed to address only symptoms currently experienced. There is no focus on addressing the source of the problem, nor are there any contingencies in place should unexpected obstacles manifest themselves. Using their full range of assessment skills, counselors can achieve higher level case conceptualizations by working to truly understand their clients, tailoring a treatment plan specific to the problems and needs of those clients, and evaluating the fit of the treatment plan continually throughout the counseling process.

Table 6.2   Four Components of a Case Conceptualization

Component	Description
Diagnostic formulation	Provides a description of the client's presenting situation and its perpetuants or triggering factors as well as the basic personality pattern; answers the what questions (e.g., "What happened?"); usually includes a DSM diagnosis.
Clinical formulation	Provides an explanation of the client's pattern. Answers the why question (e.g., "Why did it happen?"); the central component in a case conceptualization which links the diagnostic and treatment formulations.
Cultural formulation	Provides an analysis of social and cultural factors; answers the "What role does culture play?" question; specifies cultural identity, level of acculturation and stress, explanatory model, and mix of cultural dynamics and personality dynamics.
Treatment formulation	Provides an explicit blueprint for intervention planning; is a logistical extension of the diagnostic, clinical, and cultural formulations which answer the "How can it change?" question; contains treatment goals, focus, strategy, and specific interventions, anticipates challenges and obstacles in achieving those goals.

Source: Sperry & Sperry (2012, Table 1.2, p. 11).

On the opposite end of the spectrum, higher level case conceptualizations are characterized by their detail and scope. Information is collected from various sources and accounts for the social and cultural factors affecting the client. Treatment goals and interventions are clearly tied to the client's symptoms and presenting problems and align with an appropriate theoretical orientation. Additionally, higher level case conceptualizations are forward thinking and address contingency plans that can be used to address future challenges or obstacles that might arise. To increase the likelihood that they are creating high-level conceptualizations of their clients' presenting problems, counselors should ask themselves the following questions:

1. Have I used multiple methods of assessment to collect information?

2. Have I used alternative sources (parents, siblings, teachers, friends, coworkers, educational records, employment files) to validate the information obtained from the client directly?

3. Have I used standard (DSM) criteria to arrive at an initial diagnosis?

4. Have I ruled out potentially competing diagnoses?

5. Have I established a theoretical understanding of why my client is experiencing this problem at this time?

6. Have realistic, obtainable, and measureable goals been established?

7. Have evidence-based interventions been used to help the client achieve change?

8. Have appropriate strategies for evaluating treatment outcomes been identified?

The answers counselors provide to these questions will help them better understand where additional assessment efforts may be needed. The higher the conceptualization level, the more likely it will be that the counselor will be able to formulate an effective treatment plan that meets the specific needs of the client and that the client ultimately will experience positive treatment outcomes.

Developing Client Treatment Plans

Following case conceptualization, counselors must then build on the diagnostic impressions they have formulated by constructing treatment plans for their clients. According to Linda Seligman (1996), a **treatment plan** includes

> plotting out the counseling process so that both counselor and client have a road map that delineates how they will proceed from their point of origin (the client's presenting concerns and underlying difficulties) to their destination, alleviation of troubling and dysfunctional symptoms and patterns, and establishment of improved coping. (p. 157)

As you can see from this definition, treatment plans are an important part of the counseling process. They provide the roadmap which will be followed throughout the counseling process. As such, treatment plans represent a vital part of today's mental healthcare delivery system (L. Seligman & Reichenberg, 2012).

Counselors have many different approaches or strategies at their disposal that can be used to help a client work on established goals. Assessing where the client has been, where he or she is currently, and where he or she hopes to go in the future provides the counselor with the information needed to select the best-fitting approach for the client given his or her specific area of concern. As noted by Erford (2013), "treatment planning must flow logically from assessment results, fit the given environmental context of the client, and be individualized to mesh with the client's strengths and weaknesses" (p. 3).

When client-driven treatment plans are created, they not only increase client buy-in and engagement, they also give clients a sense of accomplishment when goals are successfully achieved. However, the value of treatment plans are not limited to the counselor and client alone. Several additional parties benefit from the use of detailed, written treatment plans, including treatment teams, managed care companies, and program administrators (Jongsma & Peterson, 2006). To help all of these invested parties remain on the same page, the treatment plan should contain several components. These components help document what will happen in counseling and who will be responsible for each individual aspect of treatment. In total, a basic treatment plan includes four primary components: operationally defining the problem, establishing treatment goals, selecting counseling interventions, and evaluating client progress (Neukrug & Schwitzer, 2006).

Operationally defining the problem. Throughout the assessment process, and on into case conceptualization, the counselor is gathering information about the client and his or her presenting problem. Much of what is shared with the counselor is in the form of symptoms experienced. Clients share how they physically feel, the emotions they are experiencing, and the thoughts they are having. For an effective treatment plan to be developed, the counselor needs to take all of this information, analyze it, and establish an operational definition of the target problem. For example, an individual may present for counseling with complaints of difficulty sleeping, changes in eating patterns, increased feelings of fatigue, thoughts of hopelessness, and a decreased interest in social interaction. The counselor assesses all of this information and comes up with an operational definition of the client's problem: depression. When counselors seek to operationally define the target problem to be addressed with clients, it is helpful to do so using a common language. The DSM-5 serves this purpose. Over 300 disorders and their diagnostic criteria are included in the DSM-5. As a professional counselor, a working knowledge of the DSM system will be important (see Case Illustration 6.4). To aid in your understanding of this important professional tool, a more in-depth discussion of the DSM-5 appears in Chapter 13.

CASE ILLUSTRATION   6.4

A counselor at a local mental health agency is working with a client who presents for an evaluation. The client is a 33-year-old Caucasian woman with a history of depression, multiple drug overdoses, and alcohol dependence. She presents for counseling complaining of depressed mood for the past month, including suicidal thoughts, severe insomnia, hyperactivity, racing thoughts, and impulsivity. She has never sought counseling before and reports that her current mood state is one that she has had in the past on several occasions. Taking all of the client's reported symptoms into account, the counselor uses the DSM-5 to determine possible disorders with which the client may be presenting. A differential diagnosis is used to assess the fit for all possible disorders. The counselor eventually determines that a diagnosis of bipolar disorder is most appropriate for this client based on her presenting symptoms.

As the counselor gathers information from the client and other available sources, it may become apparent that there are several issues that will need to be addressed. This is not unusual. Several disorders share common symptoms and often present together. In situations like this, the counselor needs to operationally define as many discrete problems as is warranted. Counselor and client then work together to try to prioritize these problems in terms of their severity and impact on the client's quality of life. The hierarchy created should take into account such factors as the current level of distress the client is experiencing, how motivated the client is to make a change at this time, what support systems are in place to assist the client in making the requisite changes needed, and any other real-world influences on the client's needs.

Although problem identification works best when it is a collaborative effort between counselor and client, there are some situations in which counselors will need to use their clinical judgment and prioritize problems for clients. Examples include situations in which clients may express thoughts of suicide, represent an imminent threat of harm to self or others, be using illicit drugs or alcohol, or be acutely decompensating in their daily functioning. Assessing for these situations requires counselors to have a well-established rapport with their clients and also to be mindful and observant of clues that might indicate trouble in some way.

Establishing treatment goals. Once the target problems have been operationally defined, goals can then be established related to the resolution of the target problem. When establishing treatment goals, there are guidelines that should be followed. The first is that a goal needs to be measureable. For a counselor or client to know when a goal has been met, there needs to be a way to quantifiably assess outcomes. A goal for a client to "feel better" would not be a very effective goal. How would goal attainment be assessed? What does "better" mean? The more specific you can get, the easier it will be to measure. When working with a client who suffers from panic attacks, a goal might be set that the client will report a reduction in the number of attacks each week. Setting goals of course requires the counselor to assess baseline performance and determine what would be a realistic goal for a client depending on his or her situation and unique characteristics. For a client who has been experiencing 8–10 panic attacks per week, a goal of reducing this number to 1–2 attacks after a week of counseling might be too ambitious. Knowing your client will allow you to set the right goals.

Goals need to be challenging yet attainable. For the client experiencing 8–10 panic attacks, reducing this number to 1 or less may be too challenging. Alternatively, reducing this number to 7–8 attacks might not be challenging enough. An effective goal should take clients out of their comfort zones and require them to exert effort to achieve. At the same time, goals should not be too challenging. When goals are too challenging, clients may become discouraged when results are not noticed and give up trying. Establishing the right amount of rigor in a goal is a challenge for counselors. Again, knowing your client is helpful. Counselors should use information gained from earlier assessments to identify the personal strengths and external resources available to the client that can help facilitate goal attainment.

Finally, a combination of process and outcome goals should be included. When change is broken down into smaller increments, it seems easier to accomplish. A goal of trying to lose 50 pounds in 4 months may sound overwhelming to a client, but a goal of losing 3 pounds each week for 16 weeks may seem more manageable. Depending on the issues being addressed, process goals may also be beneficial. Allowing the client to feel successful when progress is made toward a goal, although the end goal has not yet been met, can be a positive force in the counseling process. Process goals help clients remain motivated and invested in the process. They also help counselors convey to their clients that they recognize the challenges associated with making significant life changes and want to acknowledge and reward the effort clients are making. In Guided Practice Exercise 6.4, you are asked to select goals for a client that will be appropriate for his presenting problem.

Selecting counseling interventions. Once you have identified your client's presenting problem and collaborated on the establishment of treatment goals, you can then begin the process of selecting interventions to employ in order to help your client meet his or her goals. Regardless of the theoretical orientation you choose, there are numerous interventions available for you to use in your work with clients. Although your choices are plenty, intentionality in your selection process is important. Best practice guidelines specify that

---

GUIDED PRACTICE EXERCISE 6.4

Helping a Client Lose Weight

A client, Charles, comes to you looking for assistance in helping to lose weight. He states that he has tried numerous fad diets and commercial products with no success. He knows he needs to cut back but he cannot seem to stop himself once he begins eating. In working with Charles you have him complete a food diary for a week. In it he writes down everything he eats, including the time he ate each item and a brief description of why he ate it (hungry, bored, depressed, etc.). At the end of the week he brings his food diary to you and you see that he has several binge eating periods that seem to be emotionally based. Based on this information, construct an initial treatment plan for working with Charles. What goals would you set and what activities would you have Charles engage in to reach these goals? Keep in mind that successful goals are those for which achievement can be easily measured.

---

the interventions you choose to introduce into the counseling process should match the needs of the client and be evidence-based. When you follow these principles, you personalize the counseling process for the client. Treatment becomes a unique experience specific to the individual client and not simply a collection of known techniques and interventions made to fit the current situation.

Selecting appropriate interventions requires counselors to assess several aspects of the present situation. For example, did the client present for treatment voluntarily or was treatment mandated by family, employer, or court official? Knowing how clients come to treatment can help you gauge how participatory they will be and what interventions are likely to be successful. Counselors also should assess the resources currently available to the client. Does the client have supportive family members willing to participate in counseling? Does the client have reliable transportation? Does the client have financial resources? Is the client able to make substantive changes in living conditions (e.g., new social network, new job) if needed? The answers to these and other questions help counselors select interventions that can realistically be implemented and used in the counseling process. When interventions are chosen to match the needs of the client, evaluating client progress becomes a more straightforward endeavor.

Evaluating client progress. Although goals have been set and therapeutic work has begun, the assessment process does not conclude. Counselors must continually assess to determine whether the current treatment approach remains the best choice for the client. As new information is revealed, it may become evident that the counseling process must take a different direction. A new focus may emerge, or client strengths may be identified that affect what counselors and clients work on in session together. As Whiston (2009) notes, "because the matching of effective treatment to specific clients is not always a simple task, counselors must continually reassess the client and the efficacy of the counseling services they are providing" (p. 9).

Evaluating client progress can be accomplished in a number of ways. Counselors could opt to conduct either a formative or summative evaluation. In **formative evaluation**, counselors are interested in finding out whether a current approach is successful as it is unfolding. They conduct real-time assessments during the counseling process to determine the efficacy of a given treatment or intervention. As the process is unfolding, the client is asked to provide his or her feedback on whether therapy is working or beneficial. The benefit of using formative assessment is that it allows clients and counselors to change course or adjust their working hypotheses should it be noted that the current approach is not working nor producing the desired results.

On the other hand, **summative evaluations** occur at the end of the counseling process. They are designed to assess outcomes. A counselor might use a summative evaluation during the final session with a client to assess how the client is now functioning. The use of summative evaluations typically requires counselors to have baseline data on their clients so that current functioning can be compared to prior functioning to determine whether successful change occurred. Whereas counselors conducting a formative evaluation usually rely on qualitative self-report from the client, counselors conducting summative evaluations often use more formal measures such as standardized interviews or psychological tests in which a criterion score is used to measure a client's overall performance (Bernard & Goodyear, 2009). Instruments often used to assess client progress are the Symptom Checklist-90-Revised (Derogatis, 1994) and the Brief Symptom Inventory (Derogatis, 1993). When compared to the results obtained at intake or in the early stages of therapy, counselors can assess how clients have changed. These assessments can then be used to determine whether treatment approaches may need to be changed (used as a summative evaluation) or if treatment was effective overall (formative evaluation). An example of the application of formative and summative evaluation is presented in Case Illustration 6.5.

CASE ILLUSTRATION 6.5

A school counselor is working with a seventh-grade student who has been referred by his teacher for issues related to classroom behavior. In particular, the student is having difficulty remaining attentive throughout the class. His attention drifts and he becomes easily distracted. In counseling, the school counselor and student would work on addressing his inattentiveness in class. Formative assessment would take place on a weekly basis in the form of interviews, student self-report, and teachers completing a behavioral rating scale. The school counselor could see each week whether the current approach toward helping the student become more attentive is working. The student could be interviewed to determine how he sees his progress unfolding, and his teacher can be assessed to gather her input. The teacher's perceptions could be measured using a rating scale whereby she provides a subjective rating of how well the student performed on a number of behavioral indicators that week. Progress from the week prior would indicate that the current approach was working and should be continued. At the end of the semester, the school counselor could then use a summative assessment to determine how much progress the student has made. Current functioning could be compared to baseline data collected at the initial meeting to determine how successful the counseling process was for this student. The stages listed above are included as a guide for counselors to reference as they work with clients. They should not be interpreted as absolutes that must occur with each and every client. Counselors are encouraged to use their own clinical judgment to determine the best course of treatment for their client. It may be that these stages are followed or that they are supplemented with additional stages. The key is that assessment should remain a central activity the counselor performs throughout the counseling process. Constant assessment not only helps build rapport with clients, it also assists in ensuring that counselors are providing clinical services that are individual in nature and clinically appropriate.

WRITING EFFECTIVE ASSESSMENT REPORTS

An effective **assessment report** is a document that outlines the presenting problem that led the client to seek counseling, summarizes the services provided, and addresses the outcomes of those services that were provided. According to Sattler (2001), assessment reports—which you also may see referred to as psychological reports—have four primary objectives:

1. To provide accurate assessment-related aspects to the referral source and other concerned parties

2. To serve as a source of clinical hypotheses, appropriate interventions, and information for program evaluation and research

3. To furnish meaningful baseline information for evaluating (a) the examinee's progress after the interventions have been implemented or (b) changes that occur as a result of time alone

4. To serve as a legal document (p. 677)

Stylistically, assessment reports can be structured according to one of three different models. In the *test-oriented* model, results are discussed on a test-by-test basis. Separate sections are included for each test. Although results are presented for each test administered, the counselor makes no effort to connect or integrate the results into a holistic picture of client functioning. A second model counselors could use is the *domain-oriented* model. In this model results are grouped according to the client's abilities or functional domains. Examples of domains might include intellectual ability, motor functioning, interpersonal skills, and symptoms experienced. The final model is the *hypothesis-testing* model. Here counselors use their initial hypotheses or conceptualizations about a client's primary issue and arrange the data they have in a way that supports their diagnosis. Information that is consistent with their conceptualization of the client is included in the report. Information that does not support this conceptualization is omitted. There is utility in each approach, and counselors will need to consider the purpose of the report and the intended audience of the report when choosing a reporting model.

Regardless of the reporting model chosen, there are several basic parts to an assessment report that will need to be addressed: the client's reason for referral, a description of assessment procedures used, background information, behavioral observations, test results, interpretations and conclusions, and recommendations for the future. The manner in which counselors address these areas in their reports may vary; however, the essential information conveyed will be the same (Flanagan & Caltabiano, 2004). Each of these parts is described in further detail below.

Reason for referral. In this section, the counselor notes the reason why the client is presenting for counseling. Also noted is who presents with the client and if the presentation was voluntary or not. This information is helpful not only in assessing the motivation of the client and how engaged he or she will be in the process but also in identifying those individuals in the client's life who are supportive and possibly could play an important role in the treatment process.

Assessment procedures. Here is where counselors describe the various methods of assessment used to gather information about a client. Typically a list of the assessments administered is included along with a rationale for the selection of each. This list includes all formal and informal tests used, observations made, and interviews conducted. In addition to listing each of the assessments used, the counselor also notes the dates on which they were administered.

Background information. This section provides a brief history of the client in various domains. A summarized version of the intake interview is often included in this section. Counselors note the history and development of the current problem, the client's treatment history, cognitive development, medical history, and psychosocial stressors. The information included in this section provides context for the assessment results presented.

Behavioral observations. In addition to administering tests, counselors also might observe a client to gather additional information. Observations are frequently used in school counseling settings. The counselor notes any significant behaviors as well as the circumstances surrounding their occurrence, including any antecedents and consequences. If a counselor did not conduct a behavioral observation, he or she could include any observations made during the administration of a test, such as how the client performed on the test and whether there were any episodes that might affect the reliability of the results obtained.

Test results. This section includes the results of any and all tests administered. When reporting test results it is important to include several pieces of information to put those scores in proper context. When available, standard scores are preferred. Additionally, counselors should make note of the range of scores possible on each test, normative data reported for the test, and any measures of power or effect size that might further highlight clinical significance of the test results. For tests that produce multiple scores, only those subscale or factor scores that are found significant (based on scoring procedures outlined in the corresponding test manuals) need be included in the assessment report.

Interpretations and conclusions. This is the section where counselors begin to make sense of the results obtained. It includes an explanation of what the results indicate as well as an identification of any connections between results on individual tests. The purpose of this section is to summarize test results and help readers understand what these results say about the person from whom they were gathered. Providing a diagnosis or describing the problem would be appropriate information to include here.

Recommendations. This section describes the next steps to take. Based on the results gathered and what those results mean, what does the future hold for the client? Is additional counseling needed or are alternative means of help required? This section also allows a counselor to offer a prognosis for the client. Based on current level of functioning and what the counselor knows about the client, what are the chances the client is able to have a successful treatment outcome? Recommendations included in the assessment report should be specific rather than general. Should a counselor believe a client might benefit from psychopharmacological treatment, the recommendation should be that the client schedule an appointment to see a psychiatrist and discuss possible options for treating whatever diagnosis has been made. An example of an assessment report can be found in Figure 6.2.

Presenting Assessment Reports

When presenting an assessment report to a client, a counselor should always schedule time to go over it in detail. Assessment reports should not be delivered without an opportunity to debrief the client and explain the report. In this session clients are given an opportunity to ask any questions they might have about the results and their meaning. Counselors should report only the information that can be supported by the assessment results. Opinion or conjecture should not be presented as fact. When children are the clients, counselors should make sure that a parent or legal guardian is present and that person is briefed on what the purpose of the assessment report is and why counseling was being sought at this time. To facilitate the process, counselors should refrain from using technical jargon and present the results in a way that is easily understood and relatable to the client.

Figure 6.2 Sample Psychological Report Format

Psychological Assessment Report Template

The psychological assessment report is a detailed narrative of the appraisal and assessment made of your client. The content of your assessment should be based on the client information provided (background information and test scores) as well as your newfound knowledge of test interpretation and usage of results.

Include the following heading for your report:

PSYCHOLOGICAL REPORT: FOR PROFESSIONAL USE ONLY

For sections 3-5 you **must cite specific test data** to support the conclusions that you make about the client. Remember, the most valid conclusions are those that are supported by consistent patterns and findings from across the various tests you administer.

For section 7 (the recommendations), summarize and integrate your findings **without** referring specifically to the test data. Imagine you are writing this section for someone who is not

(Continued)

Figure 6.2 (Continued)

necessarily sophisticated about psychological tests. **Do not** be technical, but do accurately describe the psychological make-up of your client.

Make sure you provide a signature line at the end of the document and remember to **sign and date** the report.

1. Background Information:

Age, gender, occupation, living situation, educational background, and any other relevant information the person might have mentioned in session. Describe the reason why the client is being tested (was he/she referred to you by a boss, another psychologist, a doctor?; did he/she come to a psychological clinic or hospital and is being tested as part of an intake procedure; is he/she part of a research study?).

2. Tests Administered:

Lists of Tests Administered and Date of Administration
For each test:
  Name of test
  Purpose of test
  Test construction methodology (how was test developed conceptually?)
  Reliability and validity data (if available)
  Findings (focus in particular on very high and low scores)

3. Behavioral Observations:

How did the person act during the testing? How did he/she seem to feel about taking the tests? Did the client have any particular reaction to any particular part of the testing? Were there any interesting comments that he/she made?

4. Personality and Interpersonal Style:

Personality traits, salient needs and emotions, conflicts, personality strengths and weaknesses. How does the client interact with other people? What are his/her feelings about dealing with the people in his/her life (particularly family members and other close people)?

5. Diagnostic Assessment:

Any evidence of psychological or physiological abnormalities (significant organicity, depression, anxiety, thought disorder, etc.)? What are the client's most significant psychological conflicts and defense mechanisms? Describe what symptoms you observe in your client that may be the focus of future sessions.

6. Clinical Recommendations:

Summarize and integrate the above conclusions to present a "total picture" of the client. Use your conclusions to predict how the client may respond to a specific situation (a new job, entering school, dealing with other upcoming life situations). What recommendations can you make about the client? Respond to the referral question, if there is one.

7. Summary:

Ties all the findings together and offers a diagnostic picture of the client.

KEYSTONES

- Assessment plays an important role in many stages of the counseling process.
- An initial goal of the counselor is to triage the client and determine the appropriate steps to take based on the presenting issue or problem. This process is best accomplished by conducting an initial intake interview.
- The results of an initial intake are then used to make a diagnosis. The diagnostic decisions counselors make are related to the symptoms reported by the client and align with established criteria delineated in the DSM-5.
- Once a problem is diagnosed, a counselor can begin conceptualizing the problem. The conceptualization process involves considering all available information about a client and making informed decisions about how counseling should play out.
- Based on conceptualizations, counselors begin formulating treatment plans for their clients. These treatment plans should be individually designed for each client, taking into account the client's known strengths, weaknesses, available resources, cultural background, and any other environmental factors that might affect treatment outcomes.
- As part of the treatment planning process, goals will be set with the client. Goals should be measureable, challenging but attainable, and both process- and outcome-oriented.
- Evaluation is an important part of counseling. Counselors will need to be familiar with several ways to assess the outcome of counseling.
- The assessment report is an important artifact counselors may need to produce. It details the findings counselors obtain from various sources (interview, observation, self-report, and test results) and describes what will be done based on that information.

KEY TERMS

assessment report

case conceptualization

diagnosis

formative evaluation

intake interview

summative evaluations

treatment plan

ADDITIONAL RESOURCES

Counselors may find the following books helpful in learning more about clinical interviewing skills and assessment report writing strategies.

Goldfinger, K., & Pomerantz, A. M. (2014). *Psychological assessment and report writing* (2nd ed.). Thousand Oaks, CA: Sage.

Lichtenberger, E. O., Mather, N., Kaufman, N. L., & Kaufman, A. S. (2004). *Essentials of assessment report writing*. San Francisco, CA: Wiley.

Sommers-Flanagan, J., & Sommers-Flanagan, R. (2013). *Clinical interviewing*. San Francisco, CA: Wiley.

Student Study Site: Visit the Student Study Site at **www.sagepub.com/watson** to access additional study tools, including quizzes, web resources, and journal articles.

SECTION II
Overview of Assessment Areas

CHAPTER 7

Intelligence and General Ability Assessment

LEARNING OBJECTIVES

After reading this chapter, you will be able to

- Define intelligence
- Describe various models of intelligence
- Identify and describe various individual and group intelligence assessments
- Discuss issues in assessing intelligence
- Apply intelligence assessments to case examples

As a construct, intelligence has received a great deal of scrutiny. Since Francis Galton's first attempt in the 1800s, researchers have made efforts to define intelligence in a manner that would allow for it to be readily assessed. As a result of various researchers and the theoretical foundations of their research, numerous conceptualizations of intelligence have been developed with coinciding strategies to assess and measure the mental aptitudes related to intelligence definitions. From the publication of the first official intelligence test, the Binet-Simon Intelligence Test, in 1905 to the adaptations of tests used today, the history of intelligence tests has been marked by concerns regarding inequality.

Developed as a means to assess mental retardation from behavioral problems in children, the Binet-Simon consisted of 30 short tasks requiring basic reasoning or what was categorized as memory, attention, and verbal skills (Baron & Leonberger, 2012). This test was revised in 1916 and continued to be revised into what it has become known as today, the Stanford-Binet. We will focus more on this assessment later in the chapter. Following the establishment of the Stanford-Binet, intelligence tests were integrated in a variety of settings and were even utilized during World War I to assess what individuals were suited for roles in the war. Dissatisfied with the limitations of the Stanford-Binet, David Wechsler began developing intelligence tests of his own (Baron & Leonberger, 2012). Although Wechsler agreed with the general principles of the Stanford-Binet, he felt that various scales needed to be developed for use with various age groups and noted the need to incorporate nonverbal components of testing. Several of these scales developed by Wechsler will also be discussed in more depth throughout this chapter.

Despite the relative popularity of measures such as the Stanford-Binet and those scales developed by Wechsler, these approaches were questioned for their relative establishment of a single, general type of intelligence. Breaking away from a focus on singular, measurable measures of intelligence, Raymond Cattell proposed two distinct intelligences. Fluid intelligence, Cattell noted, was the type of intelligence needed for problem solving, while crystallized intelligence was identified as that which a person learns. Additional information regarding Cattell's theory is discussed later in the chapter.

The broadening of focus by Cattell was further widened in 1983 by Howard Gardner, who proposed seven independent intelligences. Although the evolvement of Gardner's theory of Multiple Intelligences will be discussed in detail later, it is relevant to note here that Gardner's model became the first to bring into question the accurate depiction of the widely used intelligence quotient (IQ). Questions regarding the use of this single quotient have surfaced quite a bit over the past decades, with various studies (e.g., Edwards, 2006; Furnham, Boo, & McClelland, 2012; Wicherts & Dolan, 2010) demonstrating bias against specific populations including minorities, resulting in the single IQ quotient being used to label individuals as intellectually deficient. These concerns eventually led the American Psychiatric Association (2013) to mandate the use of a functioning score in addition to the IQ score in diagnosing levels of cognitive functioning. Still, intelligence testing has continued to play an important role in society by shaping the way intelligence is viewed and directly impacting the lives of countless children and adults around the world (Anastasi & Urbina, 1997).

In this chapter, we will examine historical intelligence theories that have helped shape our current understanding of intelligence. In addition, we will introduce the intelligence assessment instruments you will most likely encounter in your work as a professional counselor. Although these instruments are of high quality and are supported by a substantial amount of research (see J. R. Graham & Naglieri, 2002), they also are the subject of considerable criticism from both the professional community and the general public. By the end of this chapter you should be able to identify the advantages and disadvantages of the various assessment instruments discussed and know how to effectively integrate them into your work with the clients you serve.

INTELLIGENCE DEFINED

When you hear the term *intelligence*, what comes to mind? A basic definition of **intelligence** is that it is a measure of your ability to acquire and apply knowledge. But what type of knowledge, and by what methods of acquisition? Is it an account of how much you have learned through your many years of schooling? Does it refer to your ability to function as a productive member of society? Or is it really an example of your ability to think abstractly? Depending on who you talk to, intelligence can be a measure of all of these characteristics. The construct of intelligence has been studied by researchers for over a hundred years. To date, there still is not a consensus understanding of what exactly is intelligence. A review of the professional literature reveals that there are numerous ways to describe intelligence. The volume of unique definitions of intelligence have led some to believe that the construct of intelligence is one that cannot be fully defined, and at best can only be approximated (Legg & Hutter, 2006).

This lack of consensus certainly proves challenging to those seeking to measure and assess this construct. Consequently, attempts to quantify and assess intelligence have resulted in a history of misunderstanding, controversy, and occasional misuse (Bartholomew, 2006; Groth-Marnat, 2009; Weinberg, 1989). Although there is no single definition of intelligence that is universally accepted, there are strong similarities among the many existing definitions (Legg & Hutter, 2006). According to Sax (1997), each of the various definitions of intelligence found in the professional literature include reference to at least one of three primary components: *origin*, whether intelligence is a trait that is inherited or learned; *structure*, whether intelligence is conceptualized as a singular or multidimensional construct; and *function*, how intelligence is used by an individual and the purpose it serves. Collectively, then, intelligence seems to be an inferred process that researchers use to explain the different degrees of adaptive success observed in an individual's behavior. As you begin learning about the different models of intelligence discussed in the following section, make note of how each theorist attended to these three components in building his theory of intelligence. Before we review the different theories of intelligence, see Case Illustration 7.1, and keep in mind the three friends that it describes.

CASE ILLUSTRATION 7.1

Think about the people in your life. Who would you classify as intelligent? When you think about the term *intelligence*, what comes to mind? Do you immediately think about people like Albert Einstein? Do you instantly think of someone who is categorized as a "genius"? What exactly is intelligence, and how do we define it?

Let's look at the case of three friends, all age 22, named Travis, Richard, and Xavier. All three boys have grown up together and have been friends since the third grade. Travis is socially shy. It is difficult for him to make friends or speak in public, and he always feels socially awkward. His only friends are Richard and Xavier, and he has only had three girlfriends thus far in his life. All three girls approached him. Travis graduated from high school with a 2.50 grade point average (GPA). However, Travis is very mechanically inclined. At age 15 he was able to take apart the entire engine of his car and rebuild it himself, with just the knowledge of one high school class in small engine repair and the Chilton's manual for his car. Travis can easily remember the order in which car parts go back on a car, without having to take pictures or write himself notes. He seems to have a great memory for visual

(Continued)

(Continued)

or mechanical information. Currently, Travis makes his living buying broken-down cars, repairing them, and then reselling them at a substantial profit.

Richard has no mechanical skills at all and cannot even do the simplest of repairs on his own car, despite how many times Travis has shown him what to do. Like Travis, Richard was also not very good at school. However, Richard has lots of friends and girlfriends. Richard has always been able to make friends easily. He is very charismatic and comfortable in social situations. Richard can easily connect with other people who seem drawn to him. People instantly trust Richard, and all of his friends' parents think of Richard as another son. Over time, Richard has come to know many influential people in the city where he grew up. Richard is always inviting Travis and Xavier to go to social events, but Travis nearly always declines. Xavier will sometimes go as long as it does not interfere with his academic life. Richard currently works at a local car dealership as a sales representative. He has many repeat customers, due to his ability to make others feel comfortable and respected. Richard has been contemplating running for public office in his city at the urging of a local politician who sees potential in Richard's ability to connect easily with others.

Last, we have Xavier. Xavier is also not very mechanically inclined and always pays Travis to do the routine maintenance on the car he bought from Richard. Xavier considers himself moderately social, and while he does not make friends as easily as Richard, he doesn't have as much difficulty making friends as Travis. Unlike Travis and Richard, Xavier did well in school. He graduated from high school with a 4.0 GPA and was the class valedictorian. Xavier is currently in college pursuing a degree in law. He still maintains a 4.0 GPA in college. Xavier has a large fund of knowledge and seems to easily apply what he has learned to many different situations. Richard and Travis call Xavier a "walking Wikipedia." Xavier always seems to remember facts, no matter how obscure. One of Xavier's favorite things to do is watch shows like "Who Wants to Be a Millionaire" or "Jeopardy." Richard and Travis are always encouraging Xavier to apply to be on one of those shows.

After having met these three friends, if you were asked to pick which of them best demonstrates the concept of intelligence, who would you pick? Many people would pick Xavier, because of his GPA, his ability to remember information, and the fact that he is doing well in college while working on a law degree. However, both Richard and Travis also demonstrate aspects of intelligence. At the end of this chapter, return to this case and revisit these three friends. After having read the chapter, what are your thoughts about how you would define these three friends in terms of their demonstrated intelligence?

OVERVIEW OF INTELLIGENCE MODELS

There is an enormous amount of literature on various ways that intelligence has been conceptualized. These definitions have led to the formation of theories, followed by the development of intelligence tests. Today, many of these assessments are used in schools but may also be applied in counseling settings to build a more comprehensive understanding of functioning processes, establish strengths that are important for treatment planning, and highlight the individuality of people in the therapeutic relationship. You will discover that some theories (e.g., Binet's, Wechsler's, Piaget's) are based on **interactionism,** which is a concept used to describe the interaction between one's heredity and environment and the influence this has on one's intelligence. Other theories are considered **factor-analytic theories,** in which factor analysis is used to determine the underlying relationship between a set of variables such as test scores. Finally, we briefly discuss **information-processing theories** that focus on how information is processed and the mental processes that make up intelligence. In the upcoming section, we provide a brief overview of the major theories of intelligence, including Spearman's *g* Factor Approach, Cattell's Fluid and Crystallized Intelligences, Thurstone's Primary Mental Abilities, Vernon's Hierarchical Model of Intelligence, Sternberg's Triarchic Theory, Piaget's Cognitive Development Model, Gardner's Multiple Intelligences, Emotional Intelligence, and the Information-Processing View. Before we get too far along in this chapter, take a moment to reflect on your own definition of intelligence with Guided Practice Exercise 7.1, and keep in mind the examples of the individuals from history with above-average intelligence by reading Case Illustration 7.2.

GUIDED PRACTICE EXERCISE 7.1

What is intelligence? In small groups or pairs, discuss and debate your own perceptions and understanding of intelligence. Take notes of your own and the group's ideas. We will refer back to them at the end of the chapter.

CASE ILLUSTRATION   7.2

When people are asked who has the highest IQ in the world, they often name Stephen Hawking. His IQ is 228. As you will learn in this chapter, an average intelligence quotient (IQ) is considered to be 100, with a range of 85–115. So Stephen Hawking is clearly at the far range of human intelligence. In comparison, Albert Einstein's IQ was said to be only 160 and Leonardo Da Vinci's was estimated at 190. All of these men did great things with their brain power. While Albert Einstein and Leonardo Da Vinci are no longer living, Stephen Hawking is still with us and is a theoretical physicist. He is a former professor at the University of Cambridge in England and is the current director of research at the Centre for Theoretical Cosmology at the same institution. Stephen Hawking is considered one of the most famous scientists of all time.

Sources: Most Extreme.Org (2012); *Stephen Hawking* (n.d.).

Spearman's *g* Theory

In 1904, Charles Spearman, a British psychologist, produced a manuscript applying factor analysis to study the construct of intelligence and found an individual's performance on a variety of tests was highly correlated. Spearman postulated that performance on intelligence tests is based on a **general ability factor** (g) and one or more specific factors (s). The **g factor** represented a measure of general intelligence that underlies performance on a wide variety of tasks, while s factors were specific learned skills which can influence intelligence performance. Thus, Spearman's model is sometimes referred to as a two-factor theory of intelligence. Spearman's theory served as an original theory of intelligence, and although theories of intelligence have evolved significantly in the past century, his works (including his statistical approach) have been a valuable tool for continued research into intelligence and its application in practice.

Cattell's Fluid and Crystallized Intelligence

Raymond Cattell (1963) suggested that Spearman's single unitary factor (g) could be divided into two components: **fluid intelligence** (known as gf) and **crystallized intelligence** (known as gc). Cattell viewed fluid intelligence as an inherited (innate) quality that refers to problem-solving and information-processing ability, uninfluenced by culture or education. According to Cattell, fluid intelligence increases from birth through adolescence, when it reaches its peak and then begins a slow decline during the adult lifespan. The use of abstract reasoning, memory span, and analogies are tasks used on standardized intelligence tests to measure fluid intelligence.

Crystallized intelligence refers to the skills and knowledge acquired over the course of one's lifetime based on formal learning and experiences, and therefore it does not decline. Cattell viewed crystallized intelligence as largely environmental. Crystallized abilities measured by standardized instruments include general knowledge and verbal comprehension.

Drawing on factor analytic studies, John Horn, a student of Cattell's, helped expand the *Gf-Gc* model of intelligence. By 1994, the **Cattell-Horn *Gf-Gc* model** included nine broad abilities: Crystallized Intelligence (Gc), Quantitative Knowledge (Gq), Reading/Writing (Grw), Fluid Intelligence (Gf), Visual-Spatial Thinking (Gv), Auditory Processing (Ga), Long-Term Retrieval (Glr), Short-Term Retrieval (Gsm), and Processing Speed (Gs).

Combining the elements of the g and *Gf-Gc* model, John Carroll developed the hierarchical **Three Stratum theory**. The top of the model is stratum III (general level), which consists of a single general ability, g. This is followed by stratum II (broad level), which includes eight factors similar to Horn's (Fluid Intelligence, Crystallized Intelligence, General Memory and Learning, Broad Visual Perception, Broad Auditory Perception, Broad Retrieval Ability, Broad Cognitive Speediness, and Processing Speed). This is followed by stratum I (specific level), which includes numerous skills and abilities depending on the second-level stratum to which they are linked (Carroll, 1997).

The **Cattell-Horn-Carroll (CHC) model** integrates the *Gf-Gc* theories of Cattell and Horn with Carroll's three-stratum theory. At the top of the model, Stratum III is general ability (g). Stratum II includes nine broad factors: Fluid Reasoning (Gf), Comprehensive-Knowledge (Gc), Short-Term Memory (Gsm), **Visual Processing (Gv)**, Auditory Processing (Ga), Long-Term Retrieval (Glr), Processing Speed (Gs), Decision/Reaction Time Speed (Gt), Reading and Writing (Grw), and Quantitative Knowledge (gq). The bottom Stratum I includes over 70 primary cognitive abilities (e.g., reading speed, memory span, mechanical knowledge).

Contributions by Cattell, Horn, and Carroll served not only to increase an understanding of the complexities of intelligence but also to enhance the use of research practice in order to investigate other aspects of human behaviors. When applied to the counseling relationship, these models provide an increased understanding of the client's ability to function, including an establishment of strengths and areas in which the client can be further educated.

Thurstone's Primary Mental Abilities

Louis L. Thurstone, a British psychologist who lived from 1887 to 1955, did not believe that *g* was the only factor that constitutes intelligence, nor did he support the idea that a single IQ fully and comprehensively assessed intelligence. In fact, his theory is often viewed as the opposite of Spearman's. Thurstone used factor analytic techniques to demonstrate that intelligence consisted of seven primary mental abilities, which are the skills that enable one to learn, think, and reason. The seven primary abilities are verbal comprehension (e.g., interpreting quotes or proverbs, generating antonyms, synonyms, analogies), numerical ability (e.g., mental manipulation of numbers, speed and accuracy of ability), memory (e.g., paired-association tasks), inductive reasoning (e.g., inference, extrapolation, interpolation), perceptual speed (e.g., grouping objects, rearranging disordered words into sentences), word fluency (e.g., anagrams), and spatial relations (e.g., spatial manipulation, imagining how visuals maybe rotated in other orientations; Thurstone & Thurstone, 1941). Thurstone believed it was more important to assess a person's pattern of mental abilities than to rely on an overall average score. Along with his wife, Thelma Thurstone, he developed the **Primary Mental Abilities Test (PMA)** to measure the seven primary mental abilities. As we discuss individual assessments, you will read about David Wechsler. You will find that his approach was similar to Thurstone's as he, too, defined and measured intelligence as a pattern of different abilities.

Thurstone's model recognizes differences in abilities as a result of experience. By evaluating an individual's patterns of mental abilities as opposed to a single identified factor, Thurstone demonstrated the potential for individuals to have differing areas of strength. Knowledge of these areas may be beneficial in the counseling relationship, including the impact that knowledge of strength areas may have on career decisions (as will be discussed in Chapter 12). Now that you have read a few theories of intelligence, consider Case Illustration 7.3.

CASE ILLUSTRATION   7.3

David is a 45-year-old Caucasian male with an intellectual disability. He was born with Down syndrome. When tested, David's IQ was assessed at 49. David also has some problems with adaptive functioning in his environment. For example, he has had difficulty learning social rules and has problems with some self-care practices such as shaving, fixing himself a meal, and doing some household chores. David lives in a group home, and his parents and siblings come to visit him regularly. David's intellectual disability is common for those who suffer from Down syndrome, and Down syndrome is an example of a genetic cause for having a low IQ. In his group home, David receives support in the manner of increased educational experiences, help with his self-care routine, and socialization with others in the home as well as outside volunteers. Counselors also work with David to help improve his social and living skills. These supports have substantially improved David's quality of life.

Vernon's Hierarchical Model of Intelligence

Phillip **Vernon's theory of intelligence** takes an intermediate position between Spearman's unitary g factor and Thurstone's multiple-factor theory. He believed intelligence was unitary, integrated, and comprising small and large abilities. Vernon is often credited with designing the first hierarchical model of intelligence. In hierarchical theories, abilities can be ordered in terms of levels from general to specific. Vernon, a colleague of Spearman, expanded on Spearman's model by further dividing g into two minor group factors primarily based on his review of many factor analytic studies. Vernon's (1984) model consists of four levels. At the top level of the model is a general cognitive factor (g) similar to Spearman's g. The next level includes two major group factors: verbal-educational (v:ed) and practical-mechanical (k:m). These two factors are further broken down into a number of minor group factors (verbal ability, numerical ability, mechanical ability, spatial ability, and practical ability), which are then broken down even further into a fourth level. This bottom level is composed of several specific factors of intelligence related to particular tests. Figure 7.1 represents Vernon's hierarchical model of intellectual abilities. Notice how the top of the model is broader and encompasses a wider range of factors. As you move down, the range becomes smaller and the abilities become more specific. The WISC-IV ability arrangement, which you will read about later in this chapter, can be categorized by Vernon's model.

Sternberg's Triarchic Theory of Intelligence

Robert Sternberg, a psychologist born in 1949, also believed that intelligence was made up of more than a single general factor. However, rather than focusing on different types of intelligence as Gardner did, Sternberg was interested in how different aspects of intelligence come together and interact with one another. In other words, he was interested in how intelligence operates as a system (Sternberg, 1988). Sternberg developed the **triarchic theory of intelligence**, which includes three types of reasoning processes that people use to solve problems: analytic (also referred to as componential), creative (also referred to as experiential), and practical (also referred to as contextual). **Analytic intelligence** includes executive processes such as analyzing, comparing, and evaluating. **Creative intelligence** involves creating, inventing, or designing new ways of solving problems when we are faced with an unfamiliar situation. **Practical intelligence** is applying and using what we know to everyday life, similar to common sense. According to the triarchic theory of intelligence, individuals can have strengths in one or all of the aspects of intelligence, and individuals with higher cognitive ability integrate all three of the aspects of intelligence daily.

Sternberg believed that the traditional definition of intelligence relies too heavily on cognitive ability and that intelligence cannot be assessed using a single measure. He was a proponent for intelligence testing to include more creative and practical measures. Sternberg created the **Sternberg Triarchic Abilities Test** (STAT)—a multiple-choice test which uses verbal, quantitative, and figural items—which measures the three aspects of intelligence on different scales (Sternberg & Grigorenko, 2000–2001). Unlike the models we previously discussed, which used factor analysis to develop intelligence theories, Sternberg developed a measure based on a theory. Thus, one of the limitations to Sternberg's theory is the lack of empirical evidence. Furthermore, because the STAT measures aspects of intelligence that differ from those

Figure 7.1 Vernon's Hierarchical Model

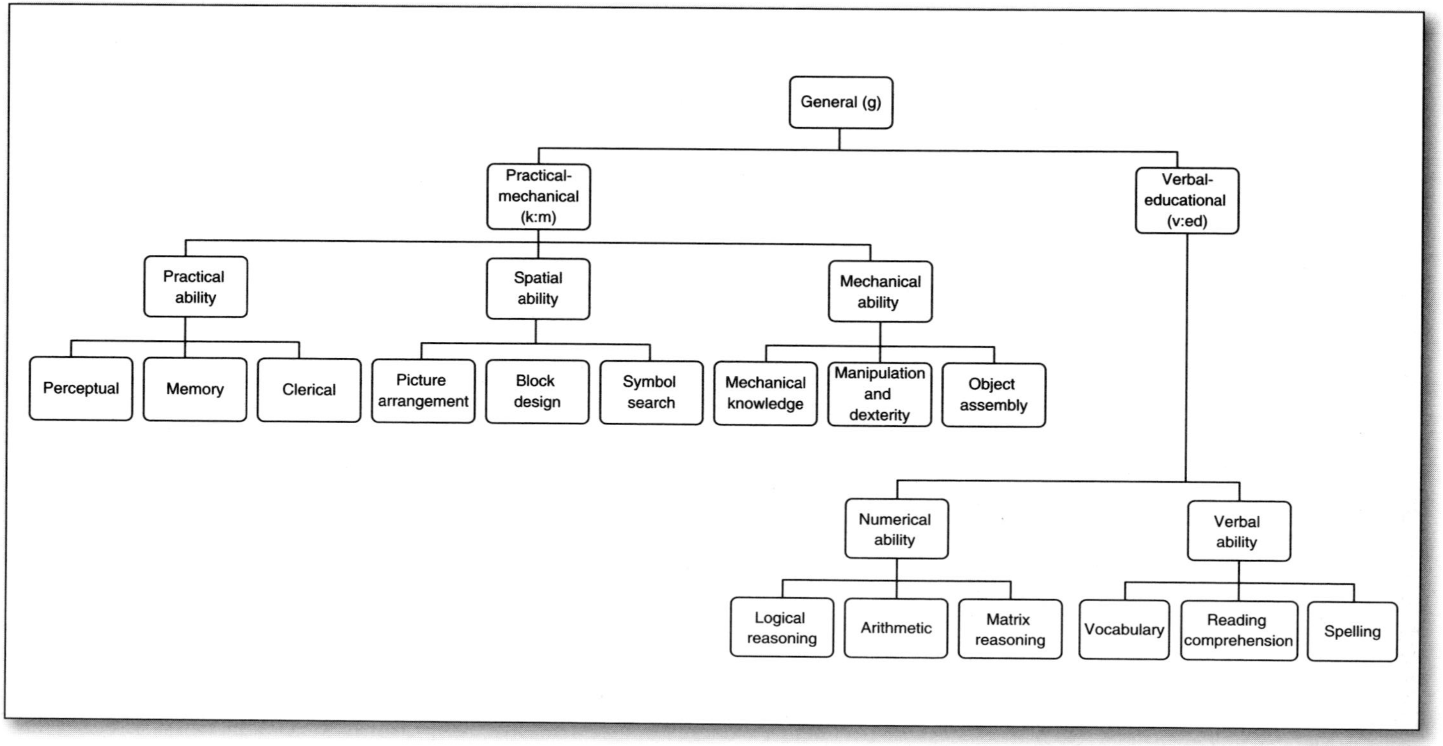

measured by traditional intelligence tests, there is limited information on the STAT's ability to predict academic achievement (see Chapter 8). Nonetheless, Sternberg's shift from previous theory to better understand the cognitive processes of intelligence has had a wide impact on curriculum as many schools are now striving to include instruction that reflects analytical, practical, and creative abilities.

Sternberg's theory of processing is important in developing person-centered treatment plans. For example, an individual who possesses high levels of creative abilities and low levels of analytic abilities may benefit more from a creative approach as opposed to an approach which requires the client to analyze his or her behaviors. Understanding the ways that individuals process information is important in assessing the most appropriate approaches.

Piaget's Cognitive Development Theory

Jean Piaget, a Swiss developmental psychologist, studied cognitive development (intelligence) in children from a constructivist approach. He was interested in discovering how children think, understand the world around them, and solve problems. Piaget (1954) used the term **schema** to describe a cognitive structure that grows with life experiences, helps people understand, and leads to knowledge. As children adapt to new challenges and demands, schemas change. Piaget believed we inherit two tendencies: **organization** (how we organize mental processes) and **adaptation** (how we adjust to the environment). Two processes within adaptation are assimilation and accommodation. Piaget believed learning occurred through assimilation (the process of incorporating new objects into present schema) and accommodation (the processes of modifying existing schemas or creating new ones to deal with new information). I'll never forget the day my daughter and I were swimming and she shouted, "Whale! Whale!" I think that is the fastest I ran out of the water! As it turns out, my daughter was referring to a baby minnow. What does this have to do with Piaget? Well, my daughter seeing a fish and calling it a whale means she had processed her new experience using an already existing structure (e.g., assimilation). Once she was able to separate the concept of fish from whale, accommodation took place, and she was able to understand a new idea.

Piaget identified four stages of cognitive development that children move through as a result of the interaction of biological factors and learning. Although age ranges at which children move through the stages are associated with each stage, Piaget noted that children pass through the stages at varying rates but in an invariant sequence (i.e., in the same order). Table 7.1 highlights Piaget's stages of development.

Piaget's stage theory has greatly influenced teaching pedagogy, cognitive assessment, and even therapeutic approaches. He was an advocate of **activity-based learning** and claimed children gain knowledge through their experiences and the process of constructing and reconstructing knowledge. Teachers have used his theory to design age-appropriate curriculum. In addition, Piaget's ground-breaking work significantly impacted the intelligence assessment field. He pioneered concepts of **constructivist learning** and **contextual perception**, which provided the foundation for more accurate testing instruments. Finally, Piaget's establishment of age-appropriateness provides a foundation for working with various generations of populations. After all, you would not approach a toddler client in the same way you would approach an adult client.

Table 7.1   Piaget's Stages of Cognitive Development

Stage	Age	Characteristics of Thought
Sensorimotor period	Birth–2 years of age	Differentiates self from objects, object permanence, centered on immediate physical environment (grabbing, touching, smelling, eating); reflexes important
Preoperational period	2–6 years of age	Language development, egocentric thought (difficulty taking other's point of view, e.g., "The rain is following me"), animism in play (nonliving objects have lifelike capabilities); centration (focusing on key feature of object and not noticing the rest)
Concrete operation period	7–12 years of age	Performs logical operations (adding, subtracting, ordering); can order objects (e.g., small to large), can count mentally, understands reversibility and conservation (e.g., substance's weight, mass, volume remain the same even when shape changes)
Formal operations period	12 years+	Increased ability for abstract thinking; can generate hypotheses and test them; evaluates own thought

Gardner's Multiple Intelligences

Howard Gardner, a psychologist at Harvard, was dissatisfied with the concept of IQ, and like Spearman he did not view intelligence as unitary. In the early 1970s, Gardner conducted research in developmental psychology and neuropsychology with veterans at the Boston VA Medical Center and with Project Zero at Harvard's Graduate School of Education. His work led him to develop his **theory of Multiple Intelligences** (MI; Gardner, 2011), in which he hypothesized that there are seven intelligences: linguistic, musical, logical-mathematical, spatial, bodily-kinesthetic, interpersonal, and intrapersonal. Although his theory included traditional and accepted competencies assessed by IQ tests at the time (verbal and mathematical), Gardner's theory was unique in that he believed intelligence encompassed musical, kinesthetic, and interpersonal intelligence. Case Illustration 7.4 highlights Gardner's intelligences (or competencies) which relate to a client's unique aptitude set of capabilities. Gardner (1999) defined intelligence as "a biopsychological potential to process information that can be activated in a cultural setting to solve problems or create products that are of value in a culture" (pp. 33–34). Gardner also valued naturalistic inquiry and questioned the validity of determining intelligence when individuals are removed from their naturalistic environment. This led Gardner to add an eighth intelligence (naturalistic) to his theory. Today, as Gardner's (2011) theory of Multiple Intelligences has evolved, a range of abilities are grouped into nine comprehensive categories, with existential intelligence being the most recently added. Gardner also proposed that spiritual intelligence be added. Table 7.2 briefly summarizes the current nine intelligences.

Table 7.2 Gardner's Multiple Intelligences

Identified Intelligences	Description
Spatial-visual	Ability to think in images and pictures, create and manipulate mental images, and visualize abstractly and accurately
Linguistic-verbal	Ability to use words effectively both orally and in writing (e.g., use of rhetoric, mnemonics, explanation, metalanguage)
Logical-mathematical	Ability to use numbers effectively, think abstractly, and apply logic, including recognizing numerical patterns and relationships and propositions (e.g., cause-effect)
Musical	Ability to perceive, comprehend, and produce musical forms; includes sensitivity to and appreciation of rhythm, pitch or melody, and timbre
Bodily-kinesthetic	Ability to control and use one's bodily movements, including balance, flexibility, speed, coordination, and dexterity
Intrapersonal	Self-awareness of one's strengths, limitations, moods, motivations, values, and beliefs as well as capacity for self-esteem and self-discipline
Interpersonal	Ability to perceive and respond appropriately to the moods, intentions, motivations, feelings, desires, and goals of others
Naturalistic	Ability to recognize and categorize species, including plants, animals, and other inanimate objects in nature
Existential	Concern with life issues and ability to answer deep questions (e.g., What is the meaning of life?)

Source: Gardner (2011).

CASE ILLUSTRATION 7.4

News reports have recently told a story about Carson Huey-You, an 11-year-old boy from Texas who is starting his freshman year of college at Texas Christian University (TCU). Carson is 4'7" and weighs only 75 pounds. He is the youngest student ever on record at TCU. Carson is majoring in quantum physics and is currently enrolled in calculus, physics, history, and religion.

Carson was homeschooled by his mother until he was 5. He was reading chapter books and could add, subtract, multiply, and divide at the age of 2. Carson was also writing with good penmanship by the age of 3. At age 5 he could do algebra and he was placed into the eighth grade at a private school. At age 10, Carson graduated from high school and was the co-valedictorian. He scored 1770 on his SATs. Carson also is an excellent pianist and speaks multiple languages.

Carson reported that he is a little awed and overwhelmed to be going to college at age 11, but he is also excited and the other students have been kind to him. Carson's mother reported that aside from Carson's intellectual abilities, he is just a normal 11-year-old kid who likes to do things any other kid his age would, such as playing video games, hanging out, and wrestling. Being so gifted at a young age, perhaps young Carson will give Stephen Hawking a run for his money in the field of physics! Keep young Carson in mind as you read about Gardner's Multiple Intelligences.

Source: Dechant (2013).

Gardner's theory recognizes individual strengths. For example, a client who may achieve a low score on an IQ test but is a successful college swimmer may still be considered intelligent according to Gardner's theory. Gardner (2006) notes,

> It is of utmost importance that we recognize and nurture all of the varied human intelligences and all of the combinations of intelligences. We are all so different largely because we have different combinations of intelligences. If we recognize this, I think we will have at least a better chance of dealing appropriately with the many problems we face in the world. (p. 36)

Guided Practice Exercise 7.2 asks you to consider your views on Howard Gardner's theory of Multiple Intelligences.

GUIDED PRACTICE EXERCISE 7.2

With a partner or in small groups, discuss Howard Gardner's theory of Multiple Intelligences. What are your views on this theory? Of the seven original intelligences (linguistic, musical, logical-mathematical, spatial, bodily-kinesthetic, interpersonal, and intrapersonal), in which areas do you feel strong? Why? In which areas do you feel not as apt? Why? How do you differ from the people with whom you are discussing this theory? Think back to young Carson Huey-You, the 11-year-old boy from Texas who is starting his freshman year of college at Texas Christian University. Carson seems to excel in many different areas. In which areas of Gardner's Multiple Intelligences does Carson seem to have strengths?

Gardner's establishment of appreciation for unique strengths and abilities may actually serve as a predecessor of multicultural theory, largely in part due to his emphasis on diversity. Furthermore, Gardner's emphasis on strengths as opposed to limitations shares a foundation with strength-focused therapy. Although Gardner focused on issues of intelligence, his contributions can still be felt today in other areas of counseling.

Emotional Intelligence

Gardner's shift away from traditional theories that viewed intelligence as a single general factor to a theory that focused on a broad array of mental abilities, including both

interpersonal and **intrapersonal intelligences**, helped lead to the outgrowth of **emotional intelligence**. Salovey and Mayer (1990) first defined emotional intelligence (EI) as "the ability to monitor one's own and other's feeling and emotions, to discriminate among them and to use this information to guide one's thinking and actions" (p. 189). However, after additional research, they came to realize that their original definition for EI was vague and omitted thinking about feelings. As a result, Mayer and Salovey (1997) revised their original definition of EI and concluded that

> emotional intelligence involves the ability to perceive accurately, appraise, and express emotion; the ability to access and generate feelings when they facilitate thought; the ability to understand emotion and emotional knowledge; and the ability to regulate emotions to promote emotional and intellectual growth. (p. 10)

Based on their definition that EI is an intelligence defined and measured by the aforementioned abilities, the four-branch model emerged. Today the four-branch model is known as the **mental ability model** and includes perceiving emotions, using emotions to facilitate thought, understanding emotions, and managing emotions.

However, it was not until Daniel Goleman (1995) published his book *Emotional Intelligence: Why It Can Matter More Than IQ* that EI gained research and media attention. Goleman's model included five dimensions of emotional intelligence and 25 emotional competencies. According to Goleman (1998),

> our emotional intelligence determines our potential for learning the practical skills that are based on its five elements: self-awareness, motivation, self-regulation, empathy, and adeptness in relationships. Our emotional competence shows how much of that potential we have translated into on-the-job capabilities. (pp. 24–25)

Goleman's five main EI constructs led to the development of the **mixed ability model,** which focuses on the competencies and skills that influence leadership performance. In addition to the mental ability model and mixed ability model, several additional EI models exist, including the **trait model of emotional social intelligence** and the **bar-on model of emotional social intelligence**. Today there are a number of published instruments that assess EI based on specific models of EI: the Mayer-Salovey-Caruso Emotional Intelligence Test (MSCEIT), which is based on the four branch model; the Emotional Competence Inventory (ECI) and the Emotional Intelligence Appraisal, based on the mixed ability model; and the Emotional Quotient Inventory (EQ-i), a self-report measure based on trait emotional intelligence.

The concept of emotional intelligence is fairly new and as a result has only limited empirical support. Relatively few studies have been conducted that examine the impact of emotional intelligence on learning, decision making, or relationships, and even fewer that consider the relevance of these impacts. Critics of this model assert that EI expands concepts of intelligence too far and is little more than an integration of individual personality influences and cognitive assessment (Schulte, Ree, & Carretta, 2004; Waterhouse, 2006). However, interest in this model and its place in education, occupational, and medical environments continues to grow (Van Rooy & Viswesvaran, 2004). Contemporary research has found correlations between EI and constructs of decision making, learning, and identity development (Fernandez-Berrocal & Ruiz, 2008; Martínez Pons, 1997; Trinidad, Unger, Chou, & Johnson, 2004). Still, a significant challenge to identifying the validity of EI instruments lies in the variations of culture, experiences, and interpretations—noteworthy criticisms of this model.

INFORMATION-PROCESSING VIEW

Aleksandr Luria (born in 1902), a Russian neuropsychologist, is considered to have founded the field of **neuropsychology**. Luria's (1966) conception of intelligence focused on how information is processed in two ways: **simultaneous processing** (simultaneous integration of information all at one time) and **successive processing** (information is processed in sequential or serial order). Simultaneous processing is often referred to as parallel processing, and successive processing is also known as sequential processing. An example of successive processing would be arranging stimuli in sequential order or memorizing a telephone number. An example of simultaneous processing is solving abstract analogies or recognizing figures such as a square placed inside a circle.

Later in the chapter, you will read about the Kaufman Assessment Battery for Children, Second Edition (KABC-II), which relies on successive and simultaneous information processing.

Luria's clinical procedures and writings also inspired the development of a comprehensive standardized assessment that measures neuropsychological functioning called the **Luria-Nebraska Neuropsychological Battery** (LNNM). The LNNM is used by clinicians as a screening tool to determine if significant brain injury or psychological impairments are present and to distinguish between brain damage and mental health disorders such as schizophrenia.

Guided Practice Exercise 7.3 is meant to help you consider which intelligence theory best fits your own ideas and perceptions. Now that we have discussed various models of intelligence, let's look at popular individual and group assessments used to measure intelligence.

GUIDED PRACTICE EXERCISE 7.3

By now you have been exposed to many different theories related to intelligence. Take a moment to reflect on what you've learned. Which theorist best captured your own ideas or perceptions of intelligence from your discussion earlier in this chapter in Guided Practice Exercise 7.1? Discuss your thoughts with a partner. Which theory best captured your partner's perception of intelligence? How has your perception changed or stayed the same from when you discussed this earlier in Guided Practice Exercise 7.1?

Individual Assessment

There are a number of individual intelligence tests available today. Three of the most common and widely used tests are the Stanford-Binet Intelligence Scales, 5th edition, the Wechsler Scales, and the Kaufman Brief Intelligence Test, Second Edition (KBIT-2). Before we dive into discussing each of these instruments, it is important to reflect on what we learned in the previous chapters (e.g., standard scores, percentiles, standard error of measurement). Although intelligence testing is useful and helpful, many intelligence assessments require advanced training and supervision beyond a master's level education. However, even if you do not plan to administer these tests in the future, you must still understand the fundamental principles of assessment to avoid misinterpretation of intelligence scores and/or mislabeling individuals with learning disabilities. Furthermore, how one communicates the results to the client is vital.

As you read about the different intelligence assessments, you will find that each assessment is divided into sections containing a number of subtests. Once these subtests are complete, a composite score, which takes into account all the sections, is computed to identify a full (overall) scale IQ (FSIQ). If you recall from Chapter 2, raw scores can be converted into standard scores. For intelligence tests, converted scores typically have a floor of 40 and a ceiling of 160 using a mean of 100 and standard deviation of 15. You might be asking yourself, why is the author talking about floors and ceilings in an assessment chapter. The **intelligence floor** of a test simply means the lowest level of intelligence the instrument measures, while the **intelligence ceiling** of a test refers to the highest level of intelligence the instrument reportedly measures. For example, the Wechsler Adult Intelligence Scale-Fourth Edition (WAIS-IV) has a full scale IQ floor of 40 and a full scale IQ ceiling of 160. The below assessments have a 4–5 standard error of measurement (SEM). In Chapter 3, you learned that the SEM provides an estimation of the range of scores that would be obtained if someone were to take the instrument over again. Why might the role of SEM be important in this chapter? Take a look at Table 7.3, which shows the classification of intelligence scores used in score interpretation. Please note that other assessments may have different ranges, and thus you should always consult the manual to ensure your accurate interpretation of results. For example, the previous version of the WAIS-IV, the WAIS-III, has a full scale IQ floor of 45 and a full scale IQ ceiling of 155.

Imagine you have a client whose obtained FSIQ score on a **norm-referenced test** is 70. The test manual reports that the SEM is 5. Given the client's obtained score of 70, you are 68% confident that his or her "true" score is somewhere between 65 and 75. Given the client's obtained score of 70, you are also 95% confident that his or her true score is somewhere between 60 and 80. If a counselor simply looked at the score of 70, he or she might believe that the client is only 1 point off from being diagnosed with a developmental disorder; however, knowing the standard score along with the SEM demonstrates the need for further assessment before making this conclusion.

In addition to looking at the full scale IQ, one can make comparisons between the different subtests. For example, the test scores for the Wechsler Intelligence Scale for Children are reported in terms of verbal scale IQ, performance scale IQ, and full scale IQ. Thus, as you read about each intelligence assessment, it is important to understand the different

Table 7.3   Nominal Categories for SB5 IQ Scores

Range of Measured IQ	Category
145–160	Very gifted or highly advanced
130–144	Gifted or very advanced
120–129	Superior
110–119	High average
90–109	Average
80–89	Low average
70–79	Borderline impaired or delayed
55–69	Mildly impaired or delayed
40–54	Moderately impaired or delayed

domains that each test measures. Guided Practice Exercise 7.4 asks you to consider the reliability and validity of the results of an IQ test. As noted in Chapter 5, a comprehensive assessment is essential to provide a diagnosis. Furthermore, a score is simply a snapshot of how a client thinks, feels, acts, or performs in a given moment in time. It is by no means a definitive statement of who a client is as a person. As a result, it is important to give context when sharing test scores with a client. Let's take a look at some of the more popular intelligence tests.

GUIDED PRACTICE EXERCISE 7.4

Before class, and prior to reading about the various intelligence assessments, go to the website www.free-iqtest.net. Take the IQ test. There are only 20 questions. After you complete the test, click on the icon to get your results. What were your perceptions of this IQ test? Do you think your results are accurate? Why or why not? Remember what you learned about reliability and validity. Do you have any concerns about the validity or reliability of your results? Why or why not? Did your results surprise you?

Some IQ tests have components similar to the one you just took. Do you think answering these types of questions can accurately assess your intelligence? Why or why not? What aspects of intelligence do you think this type of assessment evaluates (e.g., crystallized or fluid, verbal comprehension, numerical ability, memory, inductive reasoning, perceptual speed, word fluency, spatial relations, linguistic, musical, logical-mathematical, spatial, bodily kinesthetic, interpersonal, intrapersonal). Why? Hint: Remember or review the theories you just read.

STANFORD-BINET

In 1904, Alfred Binet was appointed by the French government to develop a test that would screen for developmentally disabled children in Paris schools. In 1905, Binet collaborated with Theodore Simon and created the first formal intelligence test, consisting of 30 questions pertaining to school-related items, each with increasing difficulty. In 1908, the original Binet-Simon Scale started to be used in the United States. By 1916, Lewis Madison Terman at Stanford University tested over 3,000 children in the United States. After years of research that included a normative sample, Terman published an American version of the Binet, which included new items; today we know this as the **Stanford-Binet Intelligence Scale**. So the current name for this test comes from Lewis Terman's affiliation with Stanford and from Alfred Binet, the original developer. Terman continued to work on the instrument and published several editions.

Wilhelm Stern produced a **ratio IQ** based on mental age, which is the age at which the individual appears to be functioning intellectually. Taking the mental age divided by the chronological age and multiplying by 100 computes the ratio IQ.

$$\text{Ratio IQ} = \text{mental age/chronological age} \times 100$$

One of the major revisions of the third edition of the Stanford-Binet was the use of the deviation IQ instead of the ratio IQ. For the **deviation IQ**, an individual's performance is compared to other individuals in his or her age group in the standardized sample. The deviation IQ represents deviation from the norm. An individual's raw score is converted into a standard score, with a mean of 100 and standard deviation of 16. Thus, if an individual obtained a 100, he or she is considered to be performing at a level equal to the average person in his or her same age group.

The current version, the Stanford-Binet Intelligence Scale-Fifth Edition (SB5), assesses verbal and nonverbal intelligence across five domains among individuals as young as 2, through 85 years and older, with a comprehensive set of 10 subtests. The current version yields a **full scale IQ**, a **verbal IQ**, and a **nonverbal IQ**, with a mean of 100 and standard deviation of 15. The SB5 continues to be one of the most popular and widely used intelligence tests to identify students with intellectual giftedness and students who quality for special education or have a learning disability, assess intellectual disability, and provide considerations for worker's compensation. The nonverbal sections are useful for professionals who evaluate clients with communication disorders, deafness or hard of hearing, a non-English background, and preschool learning difficulties.

The SB5 is based on the Cattell-Horn-Carroll (CHC) theoretical model. If you recall from our earlier discussion, this model views intelligence as a multifaceted array of cognitive abilities. There is a general (*g*) overarching ability, which consists of several dimensions: fluid intelligence, crystallized knowledge, quantitative knowledge, visual processing, and short-term memory. Through the use of different types of tasks and subtests at different levels, the SB5 measures the five CHC factors. However, the SB5 factors are referred to as fluid reasoning, knowledge, quantitative reasoning, visual-spatial processing, and working memory. The SB5 is unique in that it is the first intelligence assessment to measure the five cognitive factors in both the nonverbal and verbal domains. The five cognitive factors are assessed by one verbal and one nonverbal subtest each. Thus, 2 domains × 5 factors = 10 subtests. Figure 7.2 illustrates the hierarchical structure of the SB5 scoring system. Examples of the type of tests given under each domain are listed as well.

Another distinctive feature of the assessment is the use of a **routing test** to save test administrator time, as well as the use of **basal levels** and ceiling levels to help the test

Figure 7.2   Hierarchical Structure of SB5 Scoring System

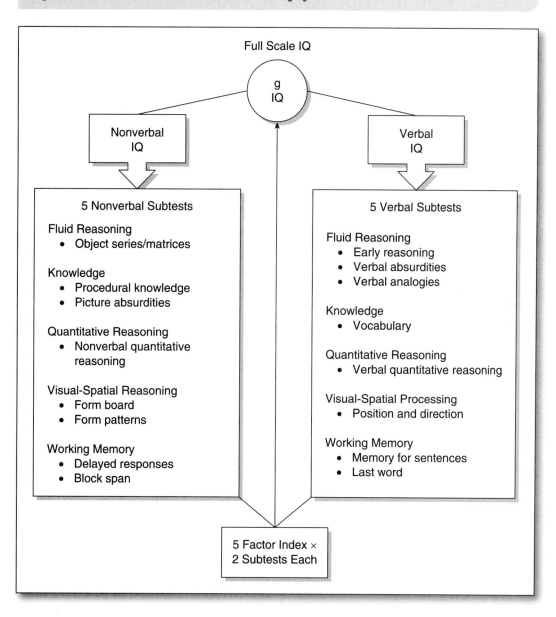

administrator determine starting and stopping points. You can think of the routing test as a pretest, a basal score as the entry level, and the ceiling score as the test terminating score. For example, in the Nonverbal domain an Objects Series/Matrices routing subtest is given to the examiner to determine the age level at which the test should begin. Then the examiner determines the basal level, which is where the examinee answers all the questions correctly on two consecutive age levels. Once the basal level is established, the prior items are considered correct and the examiner moves forward until reaching the ceiling level. The ceiling level on the SB5 is the highest level of test items administered and the point at which the examinee answered 75% of the items incorrectly on two consecutive age levels.

The five subtests under the verbal domain and the nonverbal domain yield a nonverbal IQ and a verbal IQ. The five factor indexes yield an FSIQ. The raw scores on the nonverbal IQ, verbal IQ, and FSIQ are converted to standard scores with a mean of 100 and standard deviation of 15. Table 7.4 lists the nominal categories that have been created as a quick reference to certain cutoff scores.

The SB5 record form includes a checklist, which gives the examiner the opportunity to observe the examinee's behavior and note the examinee's physical appearance, mood, activity level, and medications. All of these factors provide useful information that will be considered in reporting formal scores. As discussed in Chapter 6, when reporting results, you want to stay away from labeling your client. Rather than labeling your client as "superior," you would highlight his or her skills and abilities. Remember, the SB5 is regarded as a Class C instrument and requires extensive training.

The SB5 reports high reliability and strong validity. Average internal consistency composite reliability for the FSIQ, nonverbal IQ, and verbal IQ are reported to range from .95

Table 7.4 Nominal Categories for SB5 IQ Scores

Range of Measured IQ	Category
145–160	Very gifted or highly advanced
130–144	Gifted or very advanced
120–129	Superior
110–119	High average
90–109	Average
80–89	Low average
70–79	Borderline impaired or delayed
55–69	Mildly impaired or delayed
40–54	Moderately impaired or delayed

to .98. The FSIQ SEM = 2.30, nonverbal IQ SEM = 3.26, and verbal IQ SEM = 3.05. Normative data is based on 4,800 individuals between the ages of 2 and 85 years and older stratified by age, gender, race, ethnicity, geographical region, and educational attainment. Content, criterion-related, and predictive validity are thoroughly discussed in the manual.

WECHSLER SCALES

During the 1930s, David Wechsler was working at Bellevue Hospital in New York City. Many of his clients were multilingual and multicultural. He did not believe that the most popular individually administered intelligence test at that time, the Stanford-Binet, met his clients' testing needs. Dissatisfied with the Stanford-Binet and the emphasis that it placed on language and verbal skills, Wechsler wanted to develop an intelligence test that included nonverbal intelligence. Thus, in 1939, the **Wechsler Bellevue Intelligence Scale** (WB-I) was developed. Unlike the Stanford-Binet, which was a chronological scale and classified items by age, the WB-I was a point scale, which classified items by subtests. The test included six verbal subtests and five performance subtests with items becoming progressively more difficult.

Over the years, David Wechsler designed a series of individually administered intelligence tests to measure intellectual abilities from preschool to adulthood, with the most common and currently used being Wechsler Adult Intelligence Scale-Fourth Edition (WAIS-IV) for ages 16 to 90 years and 11 months; the Wechsler Intelligence Scale for Children-Fourth Edition (WISC-IV) for ages 6 years through 16 years and 11 months; and the Wechsler Preschool and Primary Scale of Intelligence-Fourth Edition (WPPSI-IV) for ages 2 years and 6 months to 7 years and 7 months. The Wechsler tests are based on the g factor of intelligence and consist of subtests representing fluid and crystallized intelligence. As you read about these assessments, you will notice several commonalities. All the Wechsler assessments yield IQs with a mean of 100 and standard deviation of 15, and the examinees' scores are compared to others in the same age group. The assessments include a full scale IQ used to measure general intelligence, a verbal IQ calculated from scores on subtest categorized as verbal, and a performance IQ calculated from scores on subtest categorized as nonverbal. However, the exception is the WISC-IV, which does not yield separate verbal and performance IQs, discussed below.

Other terms you will want to be familiar with include core and supplemental subtests. **Core subtests** are used to obtain a composite score, while **supplemental subtests** are optional tests. Supplemental subtests are used to help gather and provide additional clinical information and sometimes are used in place of core subtests. Why might supplemental subtests be used in place of core subtests? A supplemental subtest is often substituted for a core subtest when the examinee's physical limitation may prevent him or her from completing a certain subtest or when the examinee may have been exposed to previous items. Supplemental subtests can also be substituted for core subtests when the examiner administers core subtests incorrectly. As we now turn our attention to discussing the three common Wechsler tests, please keep in mind that these instruments are regarded as C qualification level. The use of the WISC-IV in a counseling situation is described in Case Illustration 7.5.

CASE ILLUSTRATION 7.5

Jesus is a 10-year-old fifth grader. He has been an excellent student and has received scores of 90%–100% on all of his assignments up until this year. However, this year things have changed. Jesus now rarely turns in his work and he has started having behavioral problems, such as talking in class or reading outside materials during instruction time. Jesus has also started skipping school.

A hypothesis of Jesus's parents is that Jesus is bored, because the work he is doing is too simple for him. His parents believe that he is very smart. They state that Jesus has always complained that his schoolwork was too easy for him. However, Jesus's teacher and the school disagree. While they agree that Jesus is smart, they maintain that he is sufficiently challenged academically in the classroom. The school maintains that the issues with Jesus are related to a behavioral issue and lack of respect for his teacher.

Jesus's parents decide to take him to counseling. Through the counseling process, the counselor suggests that his parents have his intelligence tested. The counselor states that if Jesus tests high enough, this could support their argument with the school that Jesus's learning capacity is greater than his current grade level.

Jesus is referred to a psychologist who administers the Wechsler Intelligence Scale for Children-Fourth Edition (WISC-IV). Jesus was given the WISC-IV because it can provide information to help in diagnoses and treatment planning. Besides giving information about intellectual capability, the WISC-IV can also help distinguish learning and intellectual disabilities.

Jesus's scores clearly demonstrate he has a higher IQ than peers in his age group. Whereas average intelligence scores on the WISC-IV range from 85 to 115, Jesus's full scale IQ measured at 125. However, it is determined through the administration of the WISC-IV that Jesus has some problems with processing information, which would lead to frustration for him. When frustrated, Jesus tries to disengage from the task. When challenged to return to the task, his frustration causes him to act out behaviorally.

During the clinical interview conducted by the psychologist prior to administering the exam, it was noted that Jesus had been in a car accident during the summer prior to the current academic year and had sustained a concussion for which he was treated. Given that Jesus had not previously sustained the level of difficulty in his schoolwork, nor had acted out behaviorally prior to the accident, the psychologist recommends that Jesus undergo further cognitive testing to evaluate whether he sustained a brain injury that has caused him problems with information processing.

Source: Callahan & Eichner (2008).

Wechsler Adult Intelligence Scale-Fourth Edition (WAIS-IV)

The **Wechsler Adult Intelligence Scale-Fourth Edition (WAIS-IV)**, published in 2008, is the most recent Wechsler instrument used to measure intelligence in people from 16 to 90 years and 11 months. The assessment is composed of the following 10 core subtests, which take approximately 60–90 minutes to complete: Block Design, Similarities, Digit Span, Matrix Reasoning, Vocabulary, Arithmetic, Symbol Search, Visual Puzzles, Information, and Coding. There are also five supplemental subtests available: Letter-Number Sequencing,

Figure Weights, Comprehension, Cancellation, and Picture Completion. These subtests yield four index scores: Verbal Comprehension, Perceptual Reasoning, Working Memory, and Processing Speed. Each of these index scores has a mean of 100 and standard deviation of 15. The four indices compose the FSIQ. If you recall from earlier, we stated that the WAIS-IV has a floor of 40 (very low) and ceiling of 160 (very high). Table 7.5 lists the WAIS-IV subtests grouped according to indices and provides a brief description of the core and supplemental subtests. Although not listed, there is a fifth index score, **General Ability Index** (GAI), that is calculated using the verbal comprehension and perceptual reasoning indexes.

Table 7.5   Brief Description of WAIS-IV Subtests Grouped According to Indexes

Verbal Comprehension Scale	
Similarities	Pair of words are presented and the examinee explains how two objects are alike; assesses examinee's ability to analyze relationships and abstract thinking
Vocabulary	The task is to define words that increase in difficulty; correlates highly with FSIQ; thought to be a good measure of intelligence
Information	Includes wide-ranging questions that one would be expected to know in formal education, everyday living, and cultural interactions
Comprehension*	Assesses the examinee's ability to organize and apply knowledge by asking open-ended questions that require an explanation of why certain procedures are followed, understanding of verbal abstraction, often referred to as common sense
Perceptual Reasoning Scale	
Block Design	Requires visual motor coordination; examinee is presented with a design consisting of colored blocks; the examinee assembles up to nine blocks to match the design on a card
Matrix Reasoning	Nonverbal analogy tasks that measure visual information-processing and abstract-reasoning skills with which the examinee identifies patterns and uses spatial reasoning
Visual Puzzles	A puzzle picture is presented and examinee chooses from a list the correct pieces of a puzzle that, when placed together, would reconstruct the puzzle in the picture
Picture Completion*	Colored cards with a picture are shown to the examinee, the picture is missing a colored piece and the examinee identifies the missing part
Figure Weights*	Examinee looks at a scale with missing weights and then chooses the weights needed to balance the scale (ages 16–69)
Working Memory Scale	
Digit Span	Measures concentration, attention, and short-term memory; three sets of digits are read by the administrator, and the examinee repeats the numbers back to the administrator in order, backward, or in ascending order

(Continued)

Table 7.5 (Continued)

Working Memory Scale (continued)	
Arithmetic	Measures learning of arithmetic, concentration, and short-term auditory memory; must be solved verbally with no pencil or paper
Letter-Number Sequencing *	Examiner reads a combination of numbers and letters in a mixed-up order and the examinee has to recall the numbers in ascending order and the letters in alphabetical order (ages 16–69)
Processing Speed Scale	
Symbol Search	Measures cognitive processing speed, motor speed, and visual perception; examinee scans two groups of symbols (search group and target group) and indicates whether a stimulus/target symbol appears in the search group
Coding	Examinee receives a code from a printed key and a piece of paper with blanks under a series of numbers, then fills in the blanks using the key
Cancellation*	Examinee scans a list of structured or unstructured colored shapes and marks targeted shapes within a specified time limit (ages 16–69)

Note: * indicates supplemental subtests.

The WAIS-IV has strong psychometric soundness. The normative sample consisted of 2,200 individuals between the ages of 16 and 90 years stratified by age, gender, race, ethnicity, geographical region, and educational level. High internal consistency reliability estimates on all subtests and composite scores as well as strong content, construct, and criterion-related validity were reported in the manual. The numerous validity studies also include clinical samples. Although the WAIS-IV is regarded as a highly valuable instrument, there are a couple items worth mentioning. If you recall, the Processing Speed Index is composed of subtests that require motor control. Some clients may not have the motor ability to complete these tests; therefore, one must consider how this might impact scoring. For example, an individual's color vision as well as frustration level could influence performance on the Block Design subtest. Using the FSIQ can be misleading and even invalid if a client has large discrepancies between index scores. Instead, the strengths and weaknesses in the client's profile should be discussed, and the FSIQ should be de-emphasized. Scoring of items on Comprehension, Similarities, and Vocabulary subtests appears less clear compared to the other subtests and is subjective. An examinee might have a lower score on these sections depending on the administrator's interpretations. Now that we have discussed one of the most popular intelligence assessments for adults, let's review an intelligence assessment for children.

Wechsler Intelligence Scale for Children (WISC-IV)

The Wechsler Intelligence Scale for Children (WISC) was first published in 1949 as an extension of the Wechsler Bellevue Intelligence Scale to be used with children. Today, the recent version published in 2003 is known as the **Wechsler Intelligence Scale for**

Children-Fourth Edition (WISC-IV) and is used to assess children's intellectual ability in children ages 6 years to 16 years and 11 months. The instrument yields an FSIQ and four index scores: Verbal Comprehension Index, Perceptual Reasoning Index, Working Memory Index, and Processing Speed Index. Sound confusing? The index scores are calculated based on the scores the examinee obtains on the three to five subtests. The scores on the index combine to yield the FSIQ. It is important to note that there are 10 core subtests and 5 supplemental subtests on the WISC-IV, and only the core subtests for each of the indexes are used to yield the FSIQ.

The WISC-IV and the SB5 are similar in many respects, including that they (a) were published in 2003, (b) are individually administered assessments with a test time of approximately an hour, (c) yield FSIQ cores, and (d) were normed on 2,200 test takers between the ages of 6 and 16. There are differences based on exclusionary criteria, cognitive and nonverbal factors measured, and populations used for validity studies. For example, the WISC-IV contains five supplemental tests and the SB5 does not. The cognitive factors included on the WISC-IV are Working Memory, Processing Speed, Verbal Comprehension, and Perceptual Reasoning, while the cognitive factors on the SB5 are Working Memory, Visual-Spatial Processing, Knowledge, Fluid Reasoning, and Quantitative Reasoning. The nonverbal factors on the WISC-IV are Working Memory, Processing Speed, and Perceptual Reasoning, while the nonverbal factors on the SB5 consist of Working Memory, Visual Spatial Processing, Fluid Reasoning, Quantitative Reasoning, and Knowledge. Unlike the SB5, which has an Abbreviated Battery IQ, there is no current short form for the WISC-IV.

Today the WISC-IV is used for more than measuring a child's intellectual ability. It is often used to aid in diagnosing learning and intellectual disabilities. If the examinee's processing problems are affecting the results on the WISC-IV, 16 of the optional subtests can be given. These 16 optional subtests are available on the WISC-IV Integrated. The WISC-IV Integrated helps obtain a more comprehensive measure of cognitive ability to assist in intervention planning. Many validity studies are available in the manual that describe the use of the WISC-IV with people diagnosed with ADHD, learning disabilities, traumatic brain injury, and Autism Spectrum Disorders.

Wechsler Preschool and Primary Scale of Intelligence (WPPSI-IV)

Prior to 1967, the Stanford-Binet was the test of choice to be used to measure intelligence in preschool children. Wechsler (1967) believed a test should be developed and re-standardized for children under 6 years of age, thus the original Wechsler Preschool and Primary Scale of Intelligence (WPPSI) was developed. According to Zimmerman and Woo-Sam (1978), the WPPSI was the first intelligence test that "adequately sampled the total population in the United States, including racial minorities" (p. 10). The original WPPSI has undergone several revisions, with the addition of some subtests and the deletion of others. The most current version was published in 2012 and is the **Wechsler Preschool and Primary Scale of Intelligence (WPPSI-IV)**.

The WPPSI-IV is a comprehensive, standardized intelligence test for ages 2 years and 6 months to 7 years and 7 months. The newest version includes new processing speed tasks, working memory subtests, and visual spatial and fluid reasoning composites for children ages 4 years to 7 years and 7 months. The WPPSI-IV is divided into two age bands. The first age band is for 2 years and 6 month to 3 years and 11 months. The second age band is for 4 years to 7 years and 7 months. Each age band yields an FSIQ, a Primary Index Scale, and Ancillary Index Skill levels. In order to obtain an FSIQ for the youngest age band, five core subtests are administered: Receptive Vocabulary, Information, Block Design, Object Assembly, and Picture Memory. You can see in Figure 7.3, which shows the test framework for each age band, that Picture Naming is under Verbal Comprehension and Zoo Locations is under Working Memory. These tests are not required to obtain an FSIQ but are available and used to detect emerging working memory difficulties. To obtain an FSIQ for ages 4 years to 7 years and 7 months, six subtests are administered: Information, Similarities, Block Design, Matrix Reasoning, Picture Memory, and Bug Search.

The WPPSI-IV is useful to clinical and school psychologists in identifying students who may be eligible for gifted classes as well as those who may have cognitive delays and intellectual disabilities, and may qualify for special services. The WPPSI-IV is often used by neuropsychologists to determine the impact of traumatic brain injury on cognitive ability and functioning among children.

Wechsler Abbreviated Scale of Intelligence (WASI)

The **Wechsler Abbreviated Scale of Intelligence** is a standardized, brief measure of intelligence for ages 6 to 89 years of age. The instrument is administered by paper-and-pencil and is hand-scored. The assessment is regarded as a Class C instrument. The WASI comes in two forms: the four-subtest form which takes approximately 30 minutes or the two-subtest form which takes approximately 15 minutes. The four-subtest form consists of Vocabulary, Similarities, Block Design, and Matrix Reasoning and yields a verbal IQ score, a performance IQ score, and an FSIQ. The two-subtest form includes Vocabulary and Matrix Reasoning and yields only an FSIQ. Although the WASI has multiple uses (such as measuring a person's verbal, nonverbal, and general cognitive functioning quickly and screening for gifted programs or intellectual disability), one should note that the WASI is not meant to be a substitute for the WISC-IV and the WAIS-IV. Let's now discuss a Class B instrument.

KAUFMAN BATTERIES

Kaufman Brief Intelligence Test, Second Edition (KBIT-2)

Alan S. Kaufman and Nadeen L. Kaufman have developed a variety of intellectual and educational assessments. Alan Kaufman was a student of Robert Thorndike and completed a clinical apprenticeship with David Wechsler. We will highlight a few of their intelligence tests, beginning with the **Kaufman Brief Intelligence Test, Second Edition (KBIT-2)**. If you recall, the previous complex intelligence tests we discussed are Class C instruments. Unlike the SB5 and the Wechsler scales, the KBIT-2 is regarded as a Class B instrument and has a shorter administration time (approximately 20 minutes). The KBIT-2 provides a verbal score, nonverbal score, and composite IQ.

Counselors may find the KBIT-2 helpful in obtaining a quick estimate of intelligence in people from 4 to 90 years of age. For example, a counselor may need to reevaluate children

Figure 7.3   WPSSI Framework

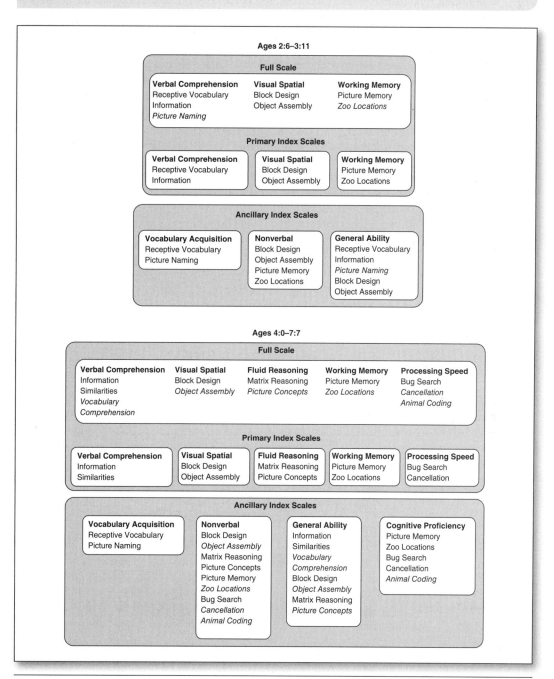

Source: WPPSI-IV Framework.

and adults who received cognitive assessments in the past in order to obtain a more current assessment. The KBIT-2 is also used to screen students who may be eligible for gifted programs. Some schools administer the KBIT-2 for entrance into a gifted program, while other schools require students to score well on the KBIT-2 before receiving further testing to gain entrance into gifted programs. In addition, to screen children for gifted programs, the KBIT-2 is often used to identify students who may be at risk and require more formal testing. For example, you might have concerns about your client's intellectual functioning. The KBIT-2 allows you to obtain a quick estimate, identify any cognitive deficits, and discover if a more comprehensive evaluation is warranted. Although the KBIT-2 has many benefits, counselors should be aware that this instrument is not a comprehensive intelligence test compared to the previously discussed intelligence tests. Let's take a look at the instrument.

The KBIT-2 measures crystallized and fluid ability through two domains: verbal and nonverbal. If you recall, crystallized ability is measured through verbal subtests while nonverbal subtests measure fluid ability. The Crystallized (Verbal) Scale includes two types of items: Verbal Knowledge and Riddles. These items are designed to measure vocabulary, general information, and reasoning ability. Sound familiar? Remember in the Cattell-Horn-Carroll theory that general information and vocabulary were the two ways to measure crystallized ability (gc; Kaufman & Kaufman, 2004). In Verbal Knowledge, the administrator shows the examinee several pictures and the examinee is then asked to point to the picture that best represents the word mentioned. For example, the examinee may be shown six pictures on one sheet of paper and the examiner says "molding." The child would then point to the picture that contains molding. Figure 7.4 is an example of pictures that would accompany a Verbal Knowledge item. The Riddles subtest evaluates knowledge of information

Figure 7.4   Verbal Knowledge Test Picture

Source: Kaufman & Kaufman (2004).

and vocabulary, but also measures logic. During the Riddles subtest, the examiner asks a question and the examinee responds by giving a one-word answer that solves the riddle. With children ages 4 to 6 years of age, pictures are used instead and the child would point to the picture that shows the answer.

The Fluid (Nonverbal) Scale includes only one subtest, Matrices, which assesses fluid thinking skills or ability to solve new problems by perceiving relationships between shapes and figures and completing analogies without testing vocabulary or language skills. The Matrices subtest measures Fluid Reasoning (Gf) and Visual Processing (Gv). For example, the examinee is shown designs that follow a pattern but are missing an element. The examinee is asked to point to the picture that would complete the pattern. The examinee decides which figure will go into the empty box that will create the same relationship between the two figures on the bottom. An example of the use of the KBIT-2 in counseling is presented in Case Illustration 7.6.

CASE ILLUSTRATION 7.6

Ronald McNair is a combat Marine who was stationed in Afghanistan. In 2012, he became a victim of an improvised explosive device (IED), or a homemade bomb, which are popular among terrorist and guerilla groups in various countries around the world. The Humvee vehicle in which Ronald's team was traveling while on patrol ran over the device. As a result of the explosion, everyone in the vehicle except for Ronald was killed; he suffered extensive head injuries. After months of surgeries, treatment, and rehabilitation, it is suspected that Ronald sustained permanent brain damage that has impacted his intellectual and cognitive functioning. Therefore, his doctors requested that Ronald be tested to determine his current level of functioning.

In order to facilitate that goal, Ronald was given the Kaufman Brief Intelligence Test (KBIT-2). The KBIT-2 was chosen for Ronald because it has a brief administration time. As a result of Ronald's head injury, he quickly gets frustrated and agitated if a task takes too long to complete. The KBIT-2 takes only about 15–30 minutes to administer and therefore fits inside Ronald's window of sustained mental activity. In addition, with the KBIT-2, Ronald can give his responses to the prompts simply by pointing at the test booklet or giving one-word answers. This will also help minimize Ronald's frustration during the assessment period. The KBIT-2 was chosen also because it provides a verbal and a nonverbal score in addition to a composite IQ score and it measures both crystallized and fluid ability.

The results from this assessment will allow Ronald's doctors to evaluate his scores to determine where Ronald might be having difficulties. They will also be able to gain a clearer understanding of what other testing may be required. The results will help his treatment team further refine his treatment plan.

Kaufman Assessment Battery for Children, Second Edition (KABC-II)

Additional assessments developed by the Kaufmans include the **Kaufman Assessment Battery for Children, Second Edition (KABC-II)** and the **Kaufman Adolescent and Adult Intelligence Test (KAIT)**. The KABC-II assesses cognitive ability in children 3 to 18 years of age. A unique aspect of this assessment is that it is based on a dual theoretical foundation and uses the Luria neuropsychological model or the Cattell-Horn-Carroll (CHC) approach, providing the administrator with options for children who may not be mainstreamed in the culture or language (Kaufman & Kaufman, 2004). The test administrator chooses between using the CHC or Luria model. If you recall, the CHC model is based on fluid and crystallized intelligence. When selecting the CHC model on the KBIT-2, five scales are produced: Short-Term Memory, Visual Processing, Long-Term Storage and Retrieval, Fluid Reasoning, and Crystallized Abilities, yielding a Fluid-Crystallized Index. This model would be appropriate for children who are mainstreamed with the societal culture and language. If it would be unfair to measure the examinee's crystallized ability due to deficiencies, the Luria model can be chosen. The Luria model scales are Sequential Processing, Simultaneous Processing, Learning Ability, and Planning Ability, yielding a Mental Processing Index. In addition, the test items contain minimal cultural content, reduced verbal instructions, and shortened responses, allowing children of diverse backgrounds to be assessed more accurately and decreasing the impact of ethnic differences on scores. The KABC-II includes 18 subtests. The examinee's age range and the model chosen determine how many subtests are given. The maximum number of subtests given is 10, with the total test time ranging from 25 to 70 minutes. One should note that unlike the KBIT, the KABC-II is considered a Class C instrument.

Kaufman Adolescent and Adult Intelligence Test (KAIT)

The KAIT is an individually administered test that measures both fluid and crystallized intelligence for individuals from 11 to 85 years of age. The KAIT includes a Core Battery and an Expanded Battery. The Core Battery takes 65 minutes to complete and is made up of six subtests (three crystallized and three fluid) yielding three intelligence scales: Fluid (Gf), Crystallized (Gc), and Composite Intelligence. Some items on the battery measuring fluid intelligence include logical steps, mystery codes, and a test of long-term memory. Some items measuring crystallized intelligence are definitions, double meanings, auditory comprehension, and test of listening ability. The three IQ scores have a mean of 100 and standard deviation of 15. The Expanded Battery includes the same core battery elements as well as four additional subtests and takes 90 minutes to complete. A distinctive aspect of the KAIT is that the subtests are presented in both visual and auditory formats, allowing for a broader measurement of intelligence.

OTHER INTELLIGENCE TESTS

Universal Nonverbal Intelligence Test (UNIT)

The **Universal Nonverbal Intelligence Test (UNIT)** is a standardized and norm-referenced assessment that assesses general intelligence in people 5 to 17 years of age using nonverbal test administration and item response. The test administrator uses eight universal hand/body gestures to explain the task to the test taker. Multiple response modes are used on the UNIT subtests, including manipulative, paper-and-pencil completion, and pointing. The instrument requires a qualification level B and comes in three testing options: Abbreviated (10–15 minutes), Standard (30 minutes), and Extended batteries (45 minutes). The extended version is composed of six subtests: Symbolic Memory, Cube Design, Spatial Memory, Analogic Reasoning, Object Memory, and Mazes (Bracken & McCallum, 1998).

The instrument is ideal for children and adolescents who are verbally uncommunicative; have speech, language, or hearing impairments; and/or have different language backgrounds. The instrument is culturally and ethnically sensitive and was normed on a comprehensive national sample of 2,100 children and adolescents with respect to gender, race, Hispanic origin, region, community setting, level of parental educational attainment, classroom placement (full-time regular classroom, full-time self-contained classroom, part-time special education resource), and special educational services. The manual contains detailed information about use of the UNIT across ethnicities including African Americans, Asians, Hispanic, Native Americans as well as those who may be hearing impaired and have limited English ability.

Reliability coefficients for the UNIT are high and demonstrate strong concurrent and discriminate validity.

Comprehensive Test of Nonverbal Intelligence (CTONI-2)

The **Comprehensive Test of Nonverbal Intelligence, Second Edition (CTONI-2)** is another popular nonverbal, norm-referenced intelligence instrument that is ideal for those with language or motor ability impairments. Unlike the UNIT, which is appropriate for children and adolescents, the CTONI-2 is designed for both children and adults and assesses intellectual ability for ages 6 to 89 years old. The CTONI-2 measures analogical reasoning, categorical classification, and sequential reasoning. Two types of stimuli are used: pictures of familiar objects (e.g., animals, people, toys) followed by geometric designs (e.g., unfamiliar sketches, drawings). The CTONI-2 includes six subtests: Pictorial Analogies, Geometric Analogies, Pictorial Categories, Geometric Categories, Pictorial Sequences, and Geometric Sequences. The CTONI-2 does not require oral responses, reading, writing, or object manipulation; the test taker simply points to the selected responses. There are six subtest scores and three composite scores: Global Nonverbal IQ, Pictorial Nonverbal IQ, and Geometric Nonverbal IQ (Hammill, Pearson, & Wiederholt, 2009). A shorter nonverbal intelligence test is the **Test of Nonverbal Intelligence, Fourth Edition (TONI-4).** The TONI-4 is appropriate for ages 6 through 89 years old and measures intelligence, aptitude, abstract reasoning, and problem solving in approximately 15–20 minutes. The TONI-4 was standardized on a national sample of 2,272 people stratified against age, gender, race, ethnicity, geographic location, community size, language spoken in the home, family income, and educational attainment (Brown, Sherbenou, & Johnsen, 2010).

Slosson Intelligence Test-Revised Third Edition (SIT-R3)

The **Slosson Intelligence Test-Revised Third Edition (SIT-R3)** is often used in schools and clinics to assess verbal intellectual ability in children and adults from 4 to 65 years of age. The SIT-R3 includes six verbal cognitive subtests: General Information, Comprehension, Quantitative, Similarities and Differences, Vocabulary, and Auditory Memory. These subtests include items similar to those found on the Wechsler verbal subtests. A distinctive aspect of this instrument is that the subtests are simultaneously administered and scored, thus allowing the instrument to be given in approximately 10–20 minutes. One should note that, according to the manual, the test cannot be administered to groups. The SIT-R3 overall score yields a Totals Standard Score (TSS) with a mean of 100 and standard deviation of 16. Percentile ranks, mean age equivalents, T-scores, normal curve equivalents (NCEs), and stanines can be used to interpret results and make comparisons to other tests that have standard scores on the verbal side. The **Slosson Intelligence Test-Primary (SIT-P)** is an additional brief, standardized instrument available to screen and provide quick estimates of a child's intelligence and identify children who may need further testing. The instrument includes both verbal items of the crystallized ability (vocabulary, similarities and differences, digit sequence, sentence memory, and quantitative skills) and fluid performance items of nonverbal abilities (e.g., block design, visual-motor integration, fine motor, gross motor). The SIT-P yields Verbal and Performance subscales, a TSS, and a deviation IQ with a mean of 100 and standard deviation of 15. The instrument was normed on 825 children, reports high reliabilities (.90+ on full scale scores), and shows concurrent validity with other instruments such as the WISC III and SIT-R (Erford, Vitali, & Slosson, 1999).

Group Assessment

As you learned in Chapter 1, the group intelligence movement began during World War I with over 2 million men being tested using the Army Alpha and Army Beta. The Otis Mental Ability test, today called the Otis-Lennon School Ability Test, Eighth Edition (OLSAT 8), was the first group intelligence test to be used in schools.

Today, popular **group intelligence tests**—also known as **school ability tests**—include the Cognitive Abilities Test, Form 7 (CogAT-7), InView, California Test of Mental Maturity, and Henmon-Nelson Tests of Mental Ability. In addition to schools, group intelligence tests such as the Wonderlic Personnel Test, Shipley Institute of Living Scale, and Multidimensional Aptitude Battery are used in a wide range of other settings.

Group intelligence tests can be useful when having to evaluate a large number of test takers at one time or within a limited amount time. In addition to offering efficient use of time, group testing is often less expensive than individual testing. Typically, the test administrators do not need to be as highly trained as those who give individual tests, and items are easily scored on a computer. Furthermore, the administrator of the group test may have less influence or effect on the examinee's score compared to an individually administered test. For the purposes of this chapter, we will further discuss the CogAT-7, Test of Cognitive Skills, InView, and Wonderlic Personnel Test.

Cognitive Abilities Test, Form 7 (CogAT-7)

The **Cognitive Abilities Test, Form 7 (CogAT-7)**, previously known as the CogAT-6, has recently been renormed (Lohman, 2011). The CogAT-7 is a group-administered ability test for students in kindergarten through Grade 12 that is used to assess students' general and specific abilities in reasoning and problem solving through verbal, nonverbal, and quantitative batteries. Each battery includes subtest that use three different tests. The CogAT-7 includes a Primary Battery containing Levels K, 1, and 2 used from kindergarten to Grade 2 and a Multilevel Battery containing Levels A through H to be administered to students in Grades 3 through 12. In other words, test levels are designated by age and all levels have three independent batteries (verbal, quantitative, and nonverbal). A score is provided for each battery along with a **standard age score**, percentile ranks by age and grade, and stanines by age and by grade. Age norms can be used to compare a student to other students in the same age group, while grade norms allow a student's performance to be compared to other students in the same grade. In addition, a composite or total score for all three batteries is provided. Figure 7.5 shows the three batteries and the items under each battery based on the level of the instrument.

According to the test creators, the primary uses of the CogAT scores are to develop instruction based on the abilities of students, provide an alternative measure of cognitive development, and aid in identifying students whose levels of achievement are vastly different from predicted levels of achievement (Riverside, 2002). The CogAT is normed with the **Iowa Test**. When given with one of the Iowa Tests, the CogAT can be used to determine predictive achievement as well as whether there are any discrepancies between achievement (see Chapter 8) and ability. Discrepancies may warrant further testing to rule out a learning disability. The CogAT is widely used to identify academically talented students because the instrument assesses student cognitive development, which may not be captured by grades or academic achievement alone. A short **Cognitive Abilities Test (CogAT-7) Screening Form** is also available to screen for students being considered for academically talented programs when schools cannot administer the complete CogAT. The CogAT-7 Screening Form includes one subtest from each of the three batteries.

Test of Cognitive Skills (TCS/2)

The **Test of Cognitive Skills, Second Edition (TCS/2)** is a group-administered test of cognitive abilities that was originally designed to be an equivalent to the Stanford-Binet. The instrument is standardized with the **California Achievement Tests** (CAT/5) and the Terra Nova (a group grade-level achievement test). The concept of achievement, as well as the TerraNova, is discussed in more detail in Chapter 8. This instrument can be used with students in Grades 2 through 12 to measure skills and abilities that are important to academic success. A distinctive aspect of this assessment is that it is one of the few academic ability tests that measures **short-term memory**. In addition, the instrument has six test levels, and each level includes four subtests: sequences, analogies, memory, and verbal reasoning. The instrument yields scores for three cognitive factors—verbal, nonverbal, and memory—and a Cognitive Skills Index (CSI), which provides a deviation IQ score. Although this test alone does not typically meet state achievement test requirements, the TCS/2 is often used with a group test to identify children for gifted and talented programs.

InView

InView is another group intelligence test that assesses cognitive abilities in students in Grades 2 through 12. The instrument includes verbal reasoning (words and context), sequences, analogies, and quantitative reasoning. InView is standardized with the TerraNova

Figure 7.5 Three Batteries on CogAT-7

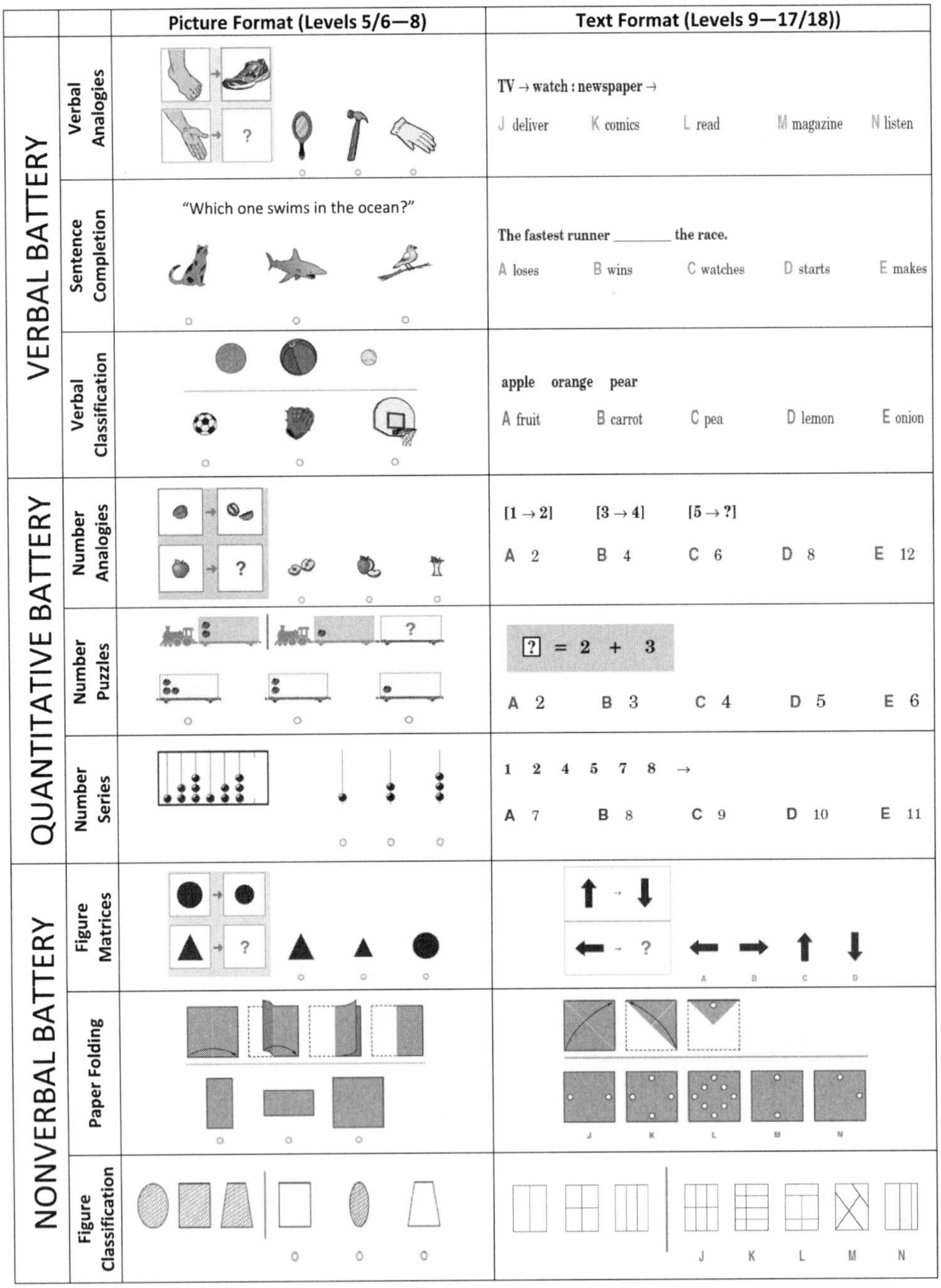

Source: Riverside (n.d.).

Third Edition to provide anticipated-achievement scores. When used with the TerraNova, one can evaluate whether students are achieving their full potential. The results from InView can help guide instruction, plan activities, highlight students' needs and strengths, and provide teachers with valuable and helpful information for parent-teacher conferences.

Wonderlic Personnel Test

The **Wonderlic Personnel Test** is often given by human resources professionals, especially in business during the hiring process to measure a potential employee's cognitive ability. The U.S. Department of Labor collaborated with the inventors of the Wonderlic to determine the cognitive ability that is needed for each occupation. A key goal of this effort was to match a potential employee with an occupation that suits his or her abilities. Thus, this instrument is not used to measure one's definitive intelligence, but instead to match the examinee with jobs that are consistent with his or her ability. The instrument is a 12-minute speed test of mental ability that includes 50 items on vocabulary, visual identification, math word problems, and brief logic statements. While the Wonderlic Personnel Test may still be given in many industrial settings, the most current version is the **Wonderlic Cognitive Ability Test**. The instrument is available in three versions: Wonderlic Cognitive Ability Pretest, Wonderlic Contemporary Cognitive Ability Test, and Wonderlic Classic Cognitive Ability Test. Guided Practice Exercise 7.5 is meant to help you further conceptualize your thoughts and perceptions of intelligence.

GUIDED PRACTICE EXERCISE 7.5

Now that we are at the end of the chapter, get out your notes that you made earlier regarding your thoughts and perceptions regarding intelligence. Get into the same small group or pair in which you had your original discussion. Now discuss your perception of intelligence once again. Did your perception of intelligence change after reading this chapter? If so, how did it change?

Current Issues and Trends in Intelligence Assessment

Since the development of the Stanford-Binet test in 1905, the assessment of intelligence has been a controversial practice. The variety of models and overall lack of consistency in describing the factors that make up the construct have complicated attempts to accurately assess intelligence. Despite these controversies, the practice of assessing intelligence remains quite popular. In this section we briefly highlight some of the current issues and trends in intelligence assessment and discuss how they may impact your future work with clients.

Defining the Target Construct

Recent researchers of intelligence assessment have noted that the contemporary methods of assessing intelligence have been found to overlap considerably with **achievement tests** (Naglieri & Goldstein, 2009). In fact, the strong correlations found between the scores on both intelligence and achievement tests appear to suggest that the two test types may in fact be measuring the same latent ability (Rindermann, 2007). This overlap, coupled with the negative perceptions of the term *intelligence* that many people have, has led to a paradigm shift in which the construct of intelligence is being redefined. In the place of the term *intelligence* you may often see the term **cognitive ability** used. This term refers to the brain-based skills and mental processes needed to carry out any task and has more to do with the mechanisms of how you learn, remember, and pay attention rather than any actual knowledge you have learned (Latham, 2006).

Theory-Based Assessment

Unlike the industry standard instruments like the Stanford-Binet and the Wechsler scales, which are **empirically based assessments,** the new generation of assessments designed to measure intelligence and cognition are based on psychological theory (Sparrow & Davis, 2000). Examples of **theory-based assessments** include the Kaufman Assessment Battery for Children (K-ABC), the KAIT, and Naglieri's Cognitive Assessment System (CAS). Assessments such as these are moving away from focusing on producing a single IQ score. Instead, these new theory-based tests, often called **neuropsychological assessments,** emphasize the existence of multiple intelligences.

The mainstream acceptance of these instruments faces many challenges. Many practitioners and researchers believe that theories that seem to be well written and show promise in controlled settings may not hold up in actual clinical or classroom environments (Benson, 2003). In addition, many of these theoretical models have yet to fully establish operational definitions of their constructs. Despite these challenges that must be overcome, these relatively new instruments show promise and should become valuable tools counselors can use in assessing intelligence either on their own or as supplemental measures to use in conjunction with more empirically supported instruments such as the Wechsler scales.

Assessing Low-Functioning Populations

Assessing clients with intellectual disabilities (previously referred to as **mental retardation** in earlier versions of the *Diagnostic and Statistical Manual*) is a challenge for counselors using currently available assessment instruments. According to Sparrow and Davis (2000) there is a growing need for instruments capable of effectively assessing these individuals in many psychological and school-based settings. As the trend toward offering services and interventions to younger populations and those with greater needs grows, the development of instruments that can attain accurate measures of intelligence and cognitive functioning of individuals with diminished abilities will become more important. Though still a relatively new instrument, the Universal Nonverbal Intelligence Test (UNIT; Bracken & McCallum, 1998) shows promise in this area. The UNIT is a nonverbal instrument that requires no language on the part of the counselor or the client. Researchers are hopeful that nonverbal tests such as the UNIT will fill an important void in the delivery of services to lower functioning individuals (Lopez, 1997; McCallum & Bracken, 1997).

Group-Administered Tests

As the amount of time counselors have to work with clients continues to decrease, the use of group-administered tests increases. Across clinical and school-based settings alike, counselors are being asked to do more with less. **Managed care companies** are reducing the number of sessions clients receive and limiting reimbursement for many testing-related activities. In schools, counselors have multiple demands on their time that make the traditional evaluation of intelligence impractical. In response to these time constraints, group-administered intelligence tests might play an important role. While these tests are an attractive alternative, counselors should be cautioned that the evidence supporting the viability of group-administered intelligence tests is still weak. Many of the group-administered tests now available do not meet the psychometric rigors of standardization and validation of individually administered intelligence tests (Sparrow & Davis, 2000). The use of these instruments is questionable, and they should never be used as the lone measure of intelligence collected. Despite the inadequacy of current instruments, the need for quicker, more efficiently administered tests will only increase and the appeal of a viable group-administered test will continue to drive research and development in this area.

KEYSTONES

- Major theories of intelligence include Spearman's *g* Factor Approach, Cattell's Fluid and Crystallized Intelligences, Cattell-Horn-Carroll Theory, Thurstone's Primary Mental Abilities, Vernon's Hierarchical Model of Intelligence, Sternberg's Triarchic Theory, Piaget's Cognitive Development Model, Gardner's Multiple Intelligences, Emotional Intelligence, and the Information-Processing View.
- The floor of an intelligence test is the lowest level of intelligence the instrument measures, while the ceiling of an intelligence test is the highest level of intelligence the instrument measures.
- A full (overall) scale IQ is a composite score of the subtests used to define overall intelligence. Raw scores are transformed to standard scores, with most intelligence tests having a floor of 40 and a ceiling of 160 (i.e., a range of 40 to 160), a mean of 100, and a standard deviation of 15.
- Commonly used individual, standardized intelligence tests are the Stanford-Binet Intelligence Scales, 5th edition, the Wechsler Scales (WAIS-IV, WISC-IV, and WPPSI-IV), and the Kaufman Brief Intelligence Test-2nd Edition (KBIT-2).
- Two commonly normed referenced intelligence instruments that are ideal for those with language or motor ability impairments are the Universal Nonverbal Intelligence Test (UNIT) and Comprehensive Test of Nonverbal Intelligence, 2nd Edition (CTONI-2).
- Widely used group intelligence tests include the Cognitive Abilities Test, Form 7 (CogAT-7), Test of Cognitive Skills, InView, and Wonderlic Personnel Test.

KEY TERMS

achievement tests

activity-based learning

adaptation

analytic intelligence

bar-on model of emotional social intelligence

basal levels

California Achievement Tests

Cattell-Horn-Carroll (CHC) model

Cattell-Horn *Gf-Gc* model

Cognitive Abilities Test, Form 7 (CogAT-7)

Cognitive Abilities Test (CogAT-7) Screening Form

cognitive ability

Cognitive Development theory

Comprehensive Test of Nonverbal Intelligence, Second Edition (CTONI-2)

constructivist learning

contextual perception

core subtests

creative intelligence

crystallized intelligence

deviation IQ

emotional intelligence

empirically based assessments

factor-analytic theories

fluid intelligence

full scale IQ

g factor

general ability factor

General Ability Index

group intelligence tests

information-processing theories

intelligence

intelligence ceiling

intelligence floor

interactionism

interpersonal intelligence

intrapersonal intelligences

InView

Iowa Test

Kaufman Adolescent and Adult Intelligence Test (KAIT)

Kaufman Assessment Battery for Children, Second Edition (KABC-II)

Kaufman Brief Intelligence Test, Second Edition (KBIT-2)

Luria-Nebraska Neuropsychological Battery

managed care companies

mental ability model

mental retardation

mixed ability model

neuropsychological assessments

neuropsychology

nonverbal IQ

norm-referenced test

organization

practical intelligence

Primary Mental Abilities Test (PMA)

ratio IQ

routing test

schema

school ability tests

short-term memory

simultaneous processing

Slosson Intelligence Test-Primary (SIT-P)

Slosson Intelligence Test-Revised Third Edition (SIT-R3)

standard age score

Stanford-Binet Intelligence Scale

Sternberg Triarchic Abilities Test (STAT)

successive processing

supplemental subtests

Test of Cognitive Skills, Second Edition (TCS/2)

Test of Nonverbal Intelligence, Fourth Edition (TONI-4)

theory of Multiple Intelligences

theory-based assessments

Three Stratum theory

trait model of emotional social intelligence

triarchic theory of intelligence

Universal Nonverbal Intelligence Test (UNIT)

verbal IQ

Vernon's theory of intelligence

Visual Processing (Gv)

Wechsler Abbreviated Scale of Intelligence

Wechsler Adult Intelligence Scale-Fourth Edition (WAIS-IV)

Wechsler Bellevue Intelligence Scale

Wechsler Intelligence Scale for Children-Fourth Edition (WISC-IV)

Wechsler Preschool and Primary Scale of Intelligence (WPPSI-IV)

Wonderlic Cognitive Ability Test

Wonderlic Personnel Test

ADDITIONAL RESOURCES

- Discovering Psychology: Testing and Intelligence

  http://www.learner.org/series/discoveringpsychology/16/e16expand.html

This website has a 27-minute video discussing the history of intelligence testing. In particular, it discusses the work of Alfred Binet and talks about the issue of bias in testing and the influence of culture. The text of the site contains an interview with Dr. Howard Gardner.

- *Ivey Business Journal.*

  http://www.iveybusinessjournal.com/topics/leadership/the-effective-leader-understanding-and-applying-emotional-intelligence#.UiKHKCqF-Y0

The *Ivey Business Journal* website has articles on other areas of psychology as it relates to succeeding in business, such as "Neuroscience and Leadership: The Promise of Insights."

- Mensa International

  http://www.mensa.org

Mensa International is an organization for people who are intellectually gifted and have high IQs. Mensa has an Education and Research Foundation and raises funds to provide scholarships to students. Mensa also has a research journal that publishes on issues related to intelligence.

- Neag Center for Gifted Education and Talent Development

  http://www.gifted.uconn.edu/nrcgt/ford5.html

This website discusses the cautions, concerns, and considerations of testing intelligence with diverse populations. It also provides resources for working with gifted and talented kids and young adults.

- Kaufman, S. B. (2009, October 25). Intelligent testing: The evolving landscape of IQ testing. *Psychology Today*.

  http://www.psychologytoday.com/blog/beautiful-minds/200910/intelligent-testing

This article discusses some criticisms and concerns of IQ testing and how the field has evolved.

- Role of Intelligence Testing in Society

  http://sitemaker.umich.edu/356.loh/modern_intelligence_testing

This website discusses modern intelligence testing but also has links to biographies of the more famous intelligence theorists such as Alfred Binet, Lewis Terman, Charles Spearman, and Howard Gardner. In addition, there are links to a discussion of intelligence testing in the past and the future as well as a link to harmful aspects of intelligence testing.

- The Performance Improvement Blog

  http://stephenjgill.typepad.com/performance_improvement_b/2007/12/un-intelligence.html

This is a blog that explores the use of intelligence testing. Join an international debate on the use of intelligence testing.

Student Study Site: Visit the Student Study Site at **www.sagepub.com/watson** to access additional study tools, including quizzes, web resources, and journal articles.

Achievement and Aptitude Assessment

After reading this chapter, you will be able to

- Distinguish between achievement testing and aptitude testing
- Describe the purpose and characteristics of achievement tests
- Identify and describe various survey battery, diagnostic, and readiness standardized achievement tests
- Describe the purpose and characteristics of aptitude tests
- Discuss tests of general and specific aptitude
- Discuss tests that are typically used for admission into college, graduate school, and professional training
- Explain factors affecting achievement and aptitude testing

By the time you entered your master's program, you had probably taken hundreds of achievement tests and several aptitude tests to get to where you are today. Some of you might even be preparing for your comprehensive exams and upcoming licensure board exams. In this chapter, we focus on ability testing. Assessment of ability measures what one can do, and it can be broken down into two broad categories: (a) achievement testing which measures what one has mastered or learned and (b) aptitude testing which predicts future behavior and measures what one is capable of learning. We begin the chapter by discussing the purpose of achievement measures and each of the categories of achievement testing: (a) multilevel survey battery tests, (b) diagnostic tests, and (c) readiness tests. We then turn our focus to aptitude testing and briefly discuss four of the main categories of aptitude testing: (a) cognitive ability, (b) intellectual and cognitive functioning, (c) special aptitude, and (d) multiple aptitude. Because many of the aptitude tests will be covered in upcoming chapters, we focus on scholastic aptitude tests that are often used to predict performance in college or graduate school. We conclude the chapter by reviewing factors that can affect achievement and aptitude assessments.

As you read the chapter, you may find it easy to confuse the terms *ability, achievement*, and *aptitude*. Many of these tests have similar items and types of questions. For example, the ACT, which is an admissions test for entrance into many undergraduate colleges, consists of achievement-like items, yet it is often used to predict how students will do during college. Thus, as you read through the chapter, expect some overlap in terms of what the test is measuring. As you ask yourself, "What type of test is this?" remember the difference between achievement tests and aptitude tests often comes down to "What is the test used for?"

ASSESSING ACHIEVEMENT

Achievement tests are designed to measure how much someone has learned or mastered in a given context. They serve additional purposes such as helping teachers assess specific areas of importance, determining whether the necessary knowledge has been met to progress to the next step, grouping individuals into skill areas, and measuring the success of a program by showing that a representative group of children from the program improved. They can be used as formative tests to evaluate a person's progress or summative tests to measure what a person learned. Achievement tests can also be used diagnostically to identify problem areas of learning and address weaknesses. Although several of the tests described in this chapter are utilized in an educational setting, a clear understanding of their format, purpose, and the ways in which results are used is necessary as a counselor. You may even find yourself administering some of these tests to clients to gain a better understanding of your client's knowledge to help him or her develop plans for his or her future or problem solve around barriers he or she may be experiencing.

There are several achievement tests. For the purposes of this chapter, we organized the test into three broad categories: multilevel survey achievement battery tests, diagnostic achievement tests, and readiness tests. Table 8.1 highlights the most commonly used tests in these categories that we will discuss throughout this chapter.

Multilevel survey achievement batteries have a number of subtests to measure achievement in certain areas at once. Some may consist of a few subtests, such as reading, spelling, and arithmetic, while others are more comprehensive and include areas in reading, vocabulary, mathematics, writing skills, language arts, science, and social studies. These test are often administered in schools and are used to measure academic progress. Testing for the purpose of measuring how much progress each child is making in core areas of learning began in the 1990s, but became mandatory in 2002. According to the No Child Left Behind Act (NCLB) of 2001, all public schools that receive public funding must give a statewide standardized test each year to all students (see Case Illustration 8.1). All 50 states must specify what children are expected to learn per grade level in core subjects and develop achievement tests to assess these areas.

Table 8.1   Common Standardized Achievement Tests

Multilevel Survey Achievement Battery Tests

Iowa Test of Basic Skills (ITBS) and Iowa Test of Educational Development (ITED)

Stanford Achievement Test Series, Tenth Edition (Stanford 10)

TerraNova, Third Edition Tests (TN3)

Diagnostic Achievement Tests

Wechsler Individual Achievement Test (WIAT)

Woodcock-Johnson Tests of Achievement (WJ III ACH)

Kaufman Test of Educational Achievement (KTEA-II)

Wide Range Achievement Test 4 (WRAT4)

Peabody Individual Achievement Test-Revised/Normative Update (PIAT-R/NU)

KeyMath 3 Diagnostic Arithmetic Test

Readiness Tests

Boehm Test of Basic Concepts-3 (Boehm-3) and Boehm Test of Basic Concepts-3 Preschool (Boehm-3 Preschool)

Metropolitan Readiness Tests, Sixth Edition (MRT)

Kindergarten Readiness Test (KRT)

Gesell Developmental Observation-Revised (GDO-R)

CASE ILLUSTRATION   8.1

In many states, such as Texas, students are assessed each year for learning competencies at grade level. Stephanie Rose is a senior in high school in a small Texas town and is worried, because even though she passed all of her classes, she failed the State of Texas Assessments of Academic Readiness (STAARS) exam. Stephanie cannot graduate without passing that exam. She did not meet the cumulative score for math at the senior grade level. Fortunately, she will be able to retest and try again to pass it. Stephanie Rose has formed a group with other students who have failed the math portion of the STARRS exam, and they are studying together in an effort to pass it. Stephanie is hopeful that she will pass it this next time, because she admits she didn't really study as she should have the first time around.

Source: Texas Education Agency (2013).

Furthermore, since the creation and widespread adoption of the **Common Core State Standards**, a significant development in testing occurred. The National Governors Association and the Council of Chief State School Officers pioneered the development of the

Common Core State Standards. Teachers, school administrators, and experts collaborated to form the standards, which include the expectations that students in kindergarten through Grade 12 must achieve in English language arts and mathematics in order to be prepared for success in college or workforce training programs. Beginning in 2010, each state made the decision about whether to adopt the Common Core Standards. States that chose to adopt these standards needed to adopt a national achievement test to measure the standards. The U.S. Department of Education created consortiums that are currently working on the development of a set of common assessments. In the spring of 2015, these common assessments will replace the end-of-the-year state assessments. Currently, the **Smarter Balanced Assessment Consortium** specifies guidelines for assessments measuring the Common Core. These assessments must include certain items: short constructed responses, extended constructed responses, and performance types. The assessments must have state-to-state comparability, and data should include current achievement and growth. Below we discuss some of the major achievement batteries used in public schools. Guided Practice Exercise 8.1 helps to familiarize you with a common multilevel achievement battery used in Tennessee.

GUIDED PRACTICE EXERCISE 8.1

Prior to class, go to the Tennessee Department of Education website: www.tn.gov/education/assessment/ach_samplers.shtml. This website provides samples of achievement test items and practice tests for Grades 3–8 used for the Tennessee Comprehensive Assessment Program (TCAP) achievement testing in schools. The TCAP is a good example of a multilevel survey achievement battery as discussed in this chapter.

Pick a practice exam or an item sampler for any grade. Complete the first five questions under each of the areas being tested in reading/language arts, mathematics, science, and social studies. Scroll down and read the test items representative of this exam. What are your thoughts about how accurately this test would measure the achievement of a child taking the exam for the grade you chose? What are your thoughts and feelings regarding your participation in this exam? Be prepared to discuss your results and experiences in small groups or with the entire class.

Diagnostic achievement tests in conjunction with intelligence tests are often used to diagnosis a learning disability and assess learning difficulties. Achievement test scores are compared to intelligence scores, and when there are severe differences in ability, this could indicate the presence of a learning disability. In 1975, the **Education for All Handicapped Children Act** (Public Law 94-142) required that all public schools that receive federal funds provide handicapped children and adults ages 3–21 with an education in the "least restrictive environment," meaning that, as much as possible, they must be educated with other children who are not handicapped. The act has been revised and renamed the **Individuals with Disabilities Education Improvement Act (IDEIA)**. According to this law, if a child is suspected of having a learning disability, he or she has the right to be tested at the school's expense.

Before a child becomes eligible for special education programs, an extensive evaluation must take place and certain criteria must be determined. Some of the criteria include determining whether a child has a physical or mental disability that substantially limits learning, the possible causes of the child's disability, and the educational diagnosis category that best describes a child's disability ("Regulation Implementing," 1977). IDEIA further specifies that the evaluation team must find that a child has a severe discrepancy between achievement and intellectual ability in one or more of the following areas: oral expression, listening comprehension, written expression, word reading skill, reading comprehension, mathematics calculation, and math reasoning. The school's diagnostician or school psychologist administers diagnostic testing. Once a child's evaluation is complete and the child is eligible for special education, an interdisciplinary team is formed consisting of a local representative of the school district, the child's teachers, and the child's parents. The team creates an Individualized Education Plan (IEP) to meet the needs of the child (see Case Illustration 8.2).

CASE ILLUSTRATION   8.2

Lamar is a first grader who is struggling in his classwork due to poor reading skills. His teacher, Mrs. Washington, suspected he may have a learning disability because Lamar was not making effective progress and was underachieving as compared to his classmates. Mrs. Washington did not see lack of effort on Lamar's part as a potential factor, because she could see that Lamar tried really hard to complete his coursework and that he got frustrated when he failed.

Following the Individuals with Disabilities Education Act, Mrs. Washington began some interventions with Lamar called Response to Intervention (RTI). She met with Lamar's parents, began working with the family, and made suggestions on how the parents could reinforce what Mrs. Washington was doing in the classroom. However, Lamar still was not progressing. Mrs. Washington then initiated the Individualized Education Plan (IEP) team to begin to discuss whether Lamar needed a formal evaluation for a learning disability.

Mrs. Washington and the IEP team made a referral to the school psychologist, who, after a preliminary assessment, agreed that Lamar should be tested. First the school psychologist gave Lamar's parents a medical referral to rule out any medical reason, developmental delay, or psychological issue that might be causing Lamar's difficulty. When Lamar's medical exam came back negative for any medical or psychological factors, the school psychologist approved formal testing for Lamar. Under state and federal law, Lamar must be tested before he can be considered for support through special education services.

Readiness assessments, which measure one's readiness for moving forward, can include a range of evaluations, such as evaluation of a child, teacher, program, or school. Schools often use readiness tests to assess whether a child is "ready" to enter kindergarten or first grade. Readiness tests are also used frequently to help teachers modify classroom instruction and improve learning by identifying children's strengths and weaknesses. Because readiness tests include general developmental milestones in multiple areas, the assessments can be used to help identify children with special needs.

Achievement tests can also vary widely from one another and in terms of their psychometric properties. For example, there are standardized versus teacher-made tests, group versus individual achievement test, and criterion- versus norm-referenced tests. We will focus on standardized achievement tests. Although we will discuss several different standardized achievement tests, they all have certain characteristics. If you recall from Chapter 5, standardized tests are normed on a sample for which the test was designed, include specific instructions for administering and scoring, describe the development of reliability and validity data, and include fixed items used to measure the specific domain (e.g., achievement). We will now discuss some of the most popular achievement tests.

STANDARDIZED ACHIEVEMENT TESTS

Multilevel Survey Achievement Battery Tests

Iowa Test of Basic Skills (ITBS) and
Iowa Test of Educational Development (ITED)

The **Iowa Test of Basic Skills (ITBS)** has been in existence for over 80 years and is the most widely used comprehensive achievement battery. The instrument includes assessments in vocabulary, word analysis, listening, reading comprehension, language, math, social studies, and science. There are 10 levels (Level 5–14) appropriate for kindergarten to eighth grade, and three forms: Form A (2001), Form B (2003), and Form C (2007). Each level corresponds to the approximate age. Depending on one's level, the number of subtests administered will vary.

Achievement as measured by the ITBS allows for student comparison to national, local, or specific norm groups (e.g., Catholic/private schools, large city schools, high-/low-socio-economic-status groups) and provides criterion-referenced interpretations based on content standards. While reliability coefficient estimates were high and around .90 for middle and upper elementary school grades, only moderate levels of reliability as demonstrated by coefficients around .80 were found among kindergartners and first graders. The ITBS content, construct, and criterion validity is sound.

The **Iowa Test of Educational Development (ITED)** is a high school achievement battery for Grades 9–12 with Levels 15, 16, and 17/18. If you notice, these levels are continuous from the levels of the ITBS and provide a continuous scale of achievement from kindergarten through Grade 12. If you recall from Chapter 7, you learned about the Cognitive Abilities Test (CogAT). The ITBS or ITED is compared to the CogAT to determine if there are any discrepancies between achievement and ability. If there are significant differences, then further testing is needed to rule out a potential learning disability.

Stanford Achievement Test Series, Tenth Edition (Stanford 10)

The Stanford Achievement test has also existed for over 80 years and has gone through numerous revisions. The latest edition, published in 2003 and known as the **Stanford Achievement Test Series, Tenth Edition (Stanford 10)**, is appropriate for students in kindergarten through 12th grade. The Stanford 10 overall comprises 17 subtests over 13 levels; however, most batteries include 8–10 subtests. Content areas include reading, mathematics, language, spelling, listening comprehension, science, and social science. Rather than presenting items from an easy to difficult format, the multiple-choice items are varied in terms of difficulty, which is thought to help decrease frustration and allow students to stay focused throughout the test. The Stanford 10 test items align with the Common Core State Standards and meet federal requirements for accountability under NCLB.

A variety of scores are available. Norm-referenced scores such as national and local percentile ranks, stanines, and grade equivalents are provided. Performance standards scored as Below Basic, Basic, Proficient, and Advanced are also available as well as Individual Profile Sheets, Class Grouping Sheets, and Grade Group Sheets. The test was normed in the spring and fall of 2002 at the same time as the **Otis-Lennon School Ability Test, Eighth Edition (OLSAT 8)**. The OLSAT 8 is a cognitive ability test that assesses a student's verbal, nonverbal, and quantitative ability. Reliability consists of KR-20 internal coefficient estimates and ranged from the mid .80s to low .90s for most of the subtests. Content validity was established by analyzing current curricula and instructional standards, reviewing recent editions of textbooks, and consulting experts.

A unique feature of this test, compared to other achievement tests, is that it is untimed and has flexible guidelines. However, the manual does provide recommendations for allotted times to aid in scheduling and planning. The decision to make this instrument untimed was highly influenced by trying to provide the most appropriate accommodations for students with a disability and to provide states that participate in high-stakes testing with an assessment that parallels other states that use untimed achievement tests.

TerraNova Tests (TN3)

The **TerraNova, Third Edition Tests (TN3)**, once known as the California Achievement Test (CAT-6), is a series of standardized achievements tests designed to assess student achievement in reading, language arts, mathematics, science, social studies, vocabulary, spelling, and other areas for students in Grades K–12. The TerraNova content is aligned to the Common Core and is often used by schools to compare students nationally on Common Core State Standards across grades and ability levels and to measure student progress. The instrument includes 12 overlapping levels. For example, Level 10 is grade range K.6-1.6 and Level 11 is grade range 1.6-2.6. There are different versions available, including the TerraNova (a) Common Core, (b) Multiple Assessments, (c) Complete Battery, (d) Survey (abbreviated version of the Complete Battery), and (e) Plus Tests. The tests can be administered in English, Spanish, or Braille. The tests include multiple response formats, such as selected, constructed, and extended responses. Depending on the grade level and version of the instrument, test time can range from 15 minutes for a subtest to almost six hours.

The TN3 provides multiple scores, including norm- and criterion-referenced scores as well as language, reading, mathematics, and total composite scores. Figure 8.1 illustrates individual profile reports for the TN3. Because there are different levels, the TN3 allows for a standard-referenced approach. In other words, we can analyze specific performance levels and identify how many students progress through these levels. These levels can then be used as cutoff scores. The Third Edition is based on a 2007 normative sample of over 210,000 students to reflect ethnic, racial, gender, regional, age, and special student groups and public, private, and parochial schools. Internal consistency coefficient

Figure 8.1   Individual Profile Report 1 and 2

Individual Profile Report, Page 1

The Individual Profile Report is one of many assessment reports that CTB offers.

The report helps you identify a student's strengths and weaknesses in both norm- and criterion-referenced terms. Data are presented in an attractive, understandable format of numeric, graphic, and narrative elements that describe student performance on each content area and objective. The Individual Profile Report is a valuable tool for parent-teacher conferences.

The primary audiences for the Individual Profile Report are teachers and counselors, followed by parents or guardians and principals.

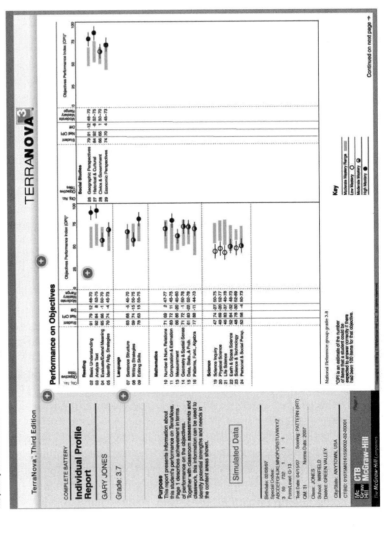

Individual Profile Report, Page 2

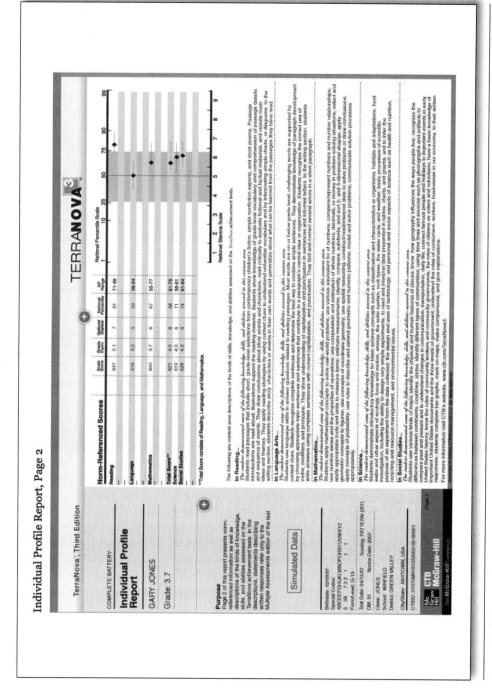

Source: CTB/McGraw-Hill (2014). CTB/McGraw-Hill LLC, TerraNova, The Third Edition Individual Profile Report. Reproduced with permission of CTB/McGraw-Hill LLC. TerraNova3 and TerraNova are registered trademarks of McGraw-Hill Education.

estimates range from .80 to .92 for complete battery subtests and .84 to .93 for multiple assessment subtests for the fall standardization period. Content, construct, and criterion-related validity are sound.

Diagnostic Achievement Tests

Guided Practice Exercise 8.2 encourages you to consider the benefits and limitations of various diagnostic achievement tests and select the most appropriate one for evaluating a specific client.

GUIDED PRACTICE EXERCISE 8.2

As you read about the various diagnostic achievement tests, think back to the case of Lamar that you encountered earlier. Which of the following diagnostic achievement tests would be appropriate as a tool for evaluating him? There is no one right answer, but be prepared to discuss your suggestions with the class.

Wechsler Individual Achievement Test (WIAT-II)

The **Wechsler Individual Achievement Test, Second Edition (WIAT-II)**, is an individually administered measurement tool used for achievement assessment, learning disability diagnosis, and special education placement for ages 4 to 85 and grades prekindergarten through 16 (Pearson, 2012e). The use of the WIAT-II is helpful for counselors as it assists with forming and guiding IEPs and determining effective accommodations for students with learning difficulties. The test includes nine subtests in four content areas: reading, mathematics, written language, and oral language. The test time ranges from 45 minutes to 120 minutes depending on grade level. The WIAT-II was nationally standardized with an age-based sample of 2,950 and a grade-based sample of 3,600. The assessment yields age-based standard scores, grade-based standard scores, percentiles, stanines, normal curve equivalent, and age and grade equivalents for each of the nine subtests. If you recall from our discussion above, IDEIA specifies that the multidisciplinary IEP team must find that a child has a severe discrepancy between achievement and intellectual ability in one or more certain areas. The WIAT-II is connected to many of the intelligence tests we discussed in Chapter 7, including the WISC-IV, WPPSI-III, and WAIS-III, thus the WIAT-II is helpful in determining discrepancies and making comparisons between achievement and intelligence.

Woodcock-Johnson III Normative Update (NU) Complete

Another measurement tool counselors use to aid in diagnosing learning disabilities, plan IEPs, and determine discrepancies between achievement and ability testing is the

Woodcock-Johnson III Normative Update (WJ III NU) Complete. The Woodcock-Johnson III NU contains two batteries: the WJ III NU Tests of Achievement and the WJ III NU Tests of Cognitive Abilities. Together these batteries provide a comprehensive assessment of general intellectual ability (g), specific cognitive abilities, scholastic aptitude, oral language, and achievement. Furthermore, the combined assessments yield three types of ability/achievement discrepancies: general intellectual ability to achievement, predicted achievement to achievement, and oral language to achievement. Although both assessments are appropriate for ages 2 to 90+ years, they are primarily used for school-aged populations. Both forms come in the standard or extended versions (Schrank, Miller, Wendling, & Woodcock, 2010).

Because we are focusing on achievement tests in this chapter, let's briefly discuss the components of the **Woodcock-Johnson III Tests of Achievement (WJ III ACH)**. The WJ III ACH measures academic achievement and is composed of 22 tests in five clusters: reading, oral language, math, written language, and academic knowledge. These five clusters parallel the areas in IDEIA. Many counselors find this test useful to determine whether students are eligible for accommodations because the ability/achievement discrepancy required by IDEIA can be calculated using only the achievement battery. The oral language cluster is used as the ability score and is compared to the subject's achievement score.

Normative data are based on more than 8,800 subjects, with the majority of the WJ III NU tests reporting strong reliabilities of .80 or higher. The coefficient alphas for the WJ III ACH standard battery ranged from .81 to .94 and .76 to .91 on the extended battery. Validity evidence is adequately reported in the manual. Evidence of construct and criterion validity shows moderate correlations with the Wechsler Individual Achievement Test (.65) and the Kaufman Test of Education Achievement (.79).

Kaufman Test of Educational Achievement, Second Edition (KTEA-II)

The **Kaufman Test of Educational Achievement, Second Edition (KTEA-II)**, is an individually administered academic achievement test that measures reading, math, written language, and oral language. The test exists in two forms: the Comprehensive Form appropriate for ages 4 years, 6 months through 25 and the Brief Form appropriate for ages 4 years, 6 months through 90+. An overall Comprehensive Achievement Composite is computed. In addition, a Reading, Math, Written Language, and Oral Language Composite score is estimated based on results from two individual subtests. Raw scores are computed to age- and grade-based standard scores, age and grade equivalents, percentile ranks, normal curve equivalents, and stanines. Internal consistency estimates were high, with composite scores for Reading and Math ranging from .93 to .97. The Oral Language reliability was the lowest compared to the other tests, with a correlation of .78. Evidence of validity was established through factor analysis for subtests and composites and correlations with other achievement tests, such as the WJ III, WAIT-II, and original KTEA (AGS, 2004).

The KTEA-II is similar to the WIAT-II and the WJ III in that all seven areas of learning disability defined by IDEIA are assessed. However, the difference between the assessments is that the KTEA-II includes seven subtests to assess early and developing reading skills, while the WJ III includes four and the WIAT-II offers two. Table 8.2 lists the KTEA-II composite scores and subtests.

Table 8.2 KTEA-II Composite Scores and Subtests

Reading Composite	Math Composite
Letter and Word Recognition	Math Concepts and Application
Reading Comprehension	Math Computation
Reading-Related Subtests	Written Language Composite
Phonological Awareness	Written Expression
Nonsense Word Decoding	Spelling
Word Recognition Fluency	Oral Language Composite
Decoding Fluency	Listening Comprehension
Associational Fluency	Oral Expression
Naming Facility	Comprehensive Achievement Composite

Source: Pearson (2012c).

Wide Range Achievement Test 4 (WRAT4)

The **Wide Range Achievement Test 4 (WRAT4)** measures basic academic skills in reading, sentence comprehension, spelling, and math computation. Although the test can be used to assess learning ability, help design remedial plans, and compare achievement of one person to another, it is often used to assess a potential learning disability. The exam is designed to test individuals from 5 to 94 years of age. The instrument is administered individually but some specific subtests can be administered in groups. The WRAT4 takes approximately 15–25 minutes for younger children and 35–45 minutes for individuals ages 8 and older.

Scores are derived from four subtests: Word Reading, Sentence Completion, Spelling, and Math Computation. The Reading Composite score is computed by summing the Word Reading and Sentence Completion standard scores. Raw scores are converted into standard scores, percentile ranks, stanines, normal curve equivalents, and age and grade equivalents. The WRAT4 also uses a deviation IQ (DIQ). If you recall from Chapter 7, a DIQ is an age-based index of general mental ability, which has a mean of 100 and standard deviation of 15. So why is a DIQ important? As counselors, we are looking to see if there are significant differences between the WRAT4 and intelligence that could possibly indicate a learning disability. For example, if we were working with a child, we could use the DIQ scores to compare the WRAT4 with the WISC-III to see if there is a severe difference in ability and performance.

The WRAT4 was normed on a sample of over 3,000 individuals ages 5 to 94 years. Reliability is sound, with internal consistency reliability estimates reported mostly in the .90s and test-retest reliability coefficients ranging from .78 to .89 for age-based samples and from .86 to .90 for grade-based samples (Psychological Assessment Resources, 2012). Evidence of validity is demonstrated with moderate to high correlations with other popular achievement and ability tests we discussed, including the WRAT-expanded, KTEA-II, WIAT-II, WJ III, and WASI-III.

Peabody Individual Achievement Test-Revised/Normative Update (PIAT-R/NU)

The **Peabody Individual Achievement Test-Revised/Normative Update (PIAT-R/NU)** is an individually administered achievement test that was designed to evaluate students referred for special education. The PIAT-R/NU is also used to help identify specific learning disabilities and assist schools in instructional program planning. The instrument is appropriate for ages 5 to 22 and in kindergarten through Grade 12 and takes 60 minutes to complete. The instrument consists of six content areas: General Information, Reading Recognition, Reading Comprehension, Mathematics, Spelling, and Written Expression. Standard scores, percentiles, stanines, age and grade equivalents, and norm curve equivalents (NCEs) accompany the composite scores. A distinctive feature of the report is that confidence intervals are provided for both age and grade equivalents. In addition, a deviation IQ can be calculated using the PIAT-R/NU. Figure 8.2 shows a PIAT-R/NU sample report. Note that the Total Reading Composite Score is calculated by summing the Reading Recognition and Reading Comprehension subtest raw scores. The Total Test composite score is calculated by adding the General Information, Reading Recognition, Reading Comprehension, Mathematics, and Spelling subtest raw scores.

The PIAT-R/NU contains different response formats, such as oral, multiple choice (pointing or oral response), copying, and writing, free response. The different response formats is a distinctive feature of this instrument that can be useful when assessing lower functioning individuals.

The PIAT-R/NU normative sample consisted of 3,429 for the age-norm sample and 3,184 for the grade-norm sample. The sample was representative of age, gender, race, geographic region, and socioeconomic status. Special education students were also included in representative populations (Pearson, 2012d). Split-half reliability coefficients were in the low to mid .90s for the subtests and upper .90s for the composite scores. While test-retest by age norms was reported in the low to mid .90s, test-retest by grade norms was given in 2- to 4-week intervals and correlations were in the high .80s to mid .90s. Using expert curriculum consults and drawing item content from grade-appropriate textbooks established content validity. Evidence for construct validity was established by comparing scores with other achievement measures. Predictive validity was not reported.

KeyMath 3 Diagnostic Assessment

The **KeyMath 3 Diagnostic Assessment** is an individually administered achievement test used to assess mathematics concepts and skills. The instrument helps identify those who are struggling in math and is often used as a follow-up for those suspected of having a mathematics disorder. The instrument tests math concepts from kindergarten through eighth or ninth grade and thus is appropriate for children in kindergarten through Grade

Figure 8.2 PIAT-R/NU Sample Report

```
04/05/2001    Peabody Individual Achievement Test - Revised/NU

Examinee: Obatu, Kieta                    Sex: Female
School/Agency: North Community School     Grade: 2
Teacher/Counselor: Karla Liebowitz        Examiner: Emilio Juarez
                                   Reasons for testing
Test Date:  01/04/2001       -----------------------------------------------
Birth Date: 05/19/1992       Experiencing difficulties in reading
Age: 8-7


                              SCORE SUMMARY
===============================================================================
Standard scores were derived from Age norm tables.
-------------------------------------------------------------------------------
Subtest or        68%        Raw    Grade    Age    Standard   %ile
Composite     Conf. Level    Score  Equiv.   Equiv.  Score     Rank    NCE
-------------------------------------------------------------------------------
General       +1.00 SEM       33             7-9      90        25      36
Information   Obtained Score  30     2.0     7-5      86        18      30
Subtest       -1.00 SEM       27             7-1      82        12      25

Reading       +1.00 SEM       25             7-2      82        12      25
Recognition   Obtained Score  23     1.5     6-11     80         9      22
Subtest       -1.00 SEM       21             6-8      78         7      19

Reading       +1.00 SEM       23             6-10     81        10      23
Comprehension Obtained Score  20     1.2     6-7      77         6      18
Subtest       -1.00 SEM       17             6-4      73         4      12
-------------------------------------------------------------------------------
              +1.00 SEM       47             6-11     79         8      21
TOTAL         Obtained Score  43     1.3     6-9      77         6      18
READING       -1.00 SEM       39             6-6      75         5      15
-------------------------------------------------------------------------------
              +1.00 SEM       31             8-5      99        47      49
Mathematics   Obtained Score  29     2.6     8-1      95        37      43
Subtest       -1.00 SEM       27             7-10     91        27      37

              +1.00 SEM       24             6-7      80         9      22
Spelling      Obtained Score  22     1.0     6-5      77         6      18
Subtest       -1.00 SEM       20             6-2      74         4      13
-------------------------------------------------------------------------------
              +1.00 SEM      130             7-1      79         8      21
TOTAL         Obtained Score 124     1.5     7-0      77         6      18
TEST          -1.00 SEM      118             6-11     75         5      15
===============================================================================
Written Expression II (Prompt A)
   Raw Score = 17  Developmental Scaled Score = 2  Grade-based Stanine = 2
-------------------------------------------------------------------------------
WRITTEN LANGUAGE        Scaled Score Sum = 2 + 2 = 4
   Age Standard Score = 74 +/- 4  %ile Rank = 4  %ile Range = 2 - 7
======================= APTITUDE ACHIEVEMENT =========================
Aptitude Test: K-ABC MPC
Aptitude Standard Score: 94       Aptitude Ach. Correlation: .65

Expected TOTAL READING Standard Score: 96
Standard Score Discrepancy: 19     Frequency of Occurrence: 5%

COPYRIGHT 1998, AMERICAN GUIDANCE SERVICE, INC., CIRCLE PINES, MN 55014-1796
```

```
04/05/2001     Peabody Individual Achievement Test - Revised/NU        Page 2

EXAMINEE:Obatu, Kieta

                        DEVELOPMENTAL SCORE PROFILES
                           68% Confidence Level

                        Age Equivalent Profile
         Age         !
Equivalent Range! 4   5   6   7   8   9  10  11  12  13  14  15  16  17  18  19
================!-+---+---+---+---+---+---+---+---+---+---+---+---+---+---+---+
General Info.   !            ****
    7-1 to 7-9  !              A
----------------!-+---+---+---+---+---+---+---+---+---+---+---+---+---+---+---+
Reading Recog.  !          ***
    6-8 to 7-2  !              A
----------------!-+---+---+---+---+---+---+---+---+---+---+---+---+---+---+---+
Reading Comp.   !          ***
    6-4 to 6-10 !               A
================!-+---+---+---+---+---+---+---+---+---+---+---+---+---+---+---+
TOTAL READING   !          **
    6-6 to 6-11 !               A
================!-+---+---+---+---+---+---+---+---+---+---+---+---+---+---+---+
Mathematics     !            ***
    7-10 to 8-5 !               A
----------------!-+---+---+---+---+---+---+---+---+---+---+---+---+---+---+---+
Spelling        !          ***
    6-2 to 6-7  !               A
----------------!-+---+---+---+---+---+---+---+---+---+---+---+---+---+---+---+
TOTAL TEST      !           **
    6-11 to 7-1 !               A
================!-+---+---+---+---+---+---+---+---+---+---+---+---+---+---+---+
```

(Continued)

Figure 8.2   (Continued)

```
04/05/2001    Peabody Individual Achievement Test - Revised/NU         Page 3

EXAMINEE:Obatu, Kieta

                         STANDARD SCORE PROFILE
                         68% Confidence Level


     Age Based         !-------- STANDARD SCORE (Mean=100, SD=15) --------!
  Standard Score Range !  60   70   80   90  100  110  120  130  140   !
======================!+----+----+----+----+----+----+----+----+----+----+
General Information    !                   *****
    82 to 90           !
----------------------!+----+----+----+----+----+----+----+----+----+----+
Reading Recognition    !               ***
    78 to 82           !
----------------------!+----+----+----+----+----+----+----+----+----+----+
Reading Comprehension  !            *****
    73 to 81           !
======================!+----+----+----+----+----+----+----+----+----+----+
TOTAL READING          !             ***
    75 to 79           !
======================!+----+----+----+----+----+----+----+----+----+----+
Mathematics            !                    *****
    91 to 99           !
----------------------!+----+----+----+----+----+----+----+----+----+----+
Spelling               !             ****
    74 to 80           !
======================!+----+----+----+----+----+----+----+----+----+----+
TOTAL TEST             !             ***
    75 to 79           !
======================!+----+----+----+----+----+----+----+----+----+----+
WRITTEN LANGUAGE       !            *****
    70 to 78           !
======================!+----+-%--+--%-+----+-%---%----%----+-%--+-%-+----+
  Standard Score Range !    1    5   25   50   75   95   99        !
                       !---------------- PERCENTILE RANK ----------------!
```

```
04/05/2001    Peabody Individual Achievement Test - Revised/NU     Page 4

EXAMINEE:Obatu, Kieta


                         SUBTEST COMPARISONS

                            Age Based
                            Standard   Standard Score  Significance
    Pairwise Comparisons      Scores     Difference      Level
    ---------------------------------  ---------  ------------  ---------
    General Info.  vs.  Reading Recog.  86 > 80         6            NS
    General Info.  vs.  Reading Comp.   86 > 77         9            NS
    General Info.  vs.  Mathematics     86 < 95         9            NS
    General Info.  vs.  Spelling        86 > 77         9            NS
    Reading Recog. vs.  Reading Comp.   80 > 77         3            NS
    Reading Recog. vs.  Mathematics     80 < 95        15           .01
    Reading Recog. vs.  Spelling        80 > 77         3            NS
    Reading Comp.  vs.  Mathematics     77 < 95        18           .01
    Reading Comp.  vs.  Spelling        77 = 77         0            NS
    Mathematics    vs.  Spelling        95 > 77        18           .01


    A comparison of Kieta's subtest scores on Reading Recognition and
    Mathematics reveals that her Reading Recognition subtest standard score of
    80 was significantly less than her Mathematics subtest standard score of 95
    at the .01 level of significance.

    A comparison of Kieta's subtest scores on Reading Comprehension and
    Mathematics reveals that her Reading Comprehension subtest standard score
    of 77 was significantly less than her Mathematics subtest standard score of
    95 at the .01 level of significance.

    A comparison of Kieta's subtest scores on Mathematics and Spelling reveals
    that her Mathematics subtest standard score of 95 was significantly greater
    than her Spelling subtest standard score of 77 at the .01 level of
    significance.
```

Table 8.3   KeyMath 3 Subtests and Items

Area and Subtest	Number of Items
Basic Concepts	
Numeration	49
Algebra	39
Geometry	36
Measurement	40
Data Analysis and Probability	40
Operations	
Mental Computation and Estimation	40
Written Computation: Addition and Subtraction	35
Written Computation: Multiplication and Division	31
Applications	
Foundations of Problem Solving	27
Applied Problem Solving	35

Source: Connolly (2012).

12 or ages 4 to 21 years old who are functioning at these levels. The test takes approximately 30–90 minutes to complete. The KeyMath 3 items are grouped into three broad general math content areas: Basic Concepts (conceptual knowledge), Operations (computational skills), and Applications (problem solving). These three content areas are divided into 10 total subtests. Table 8.3 lists the subtests of the KeyMath 3 and the number of items for each subtest.

KeyMath 3 aligns with the National Council of Teachers of Mathematics (NCTM) standards and most state standards, and it is used in a broad range of classroom settings. KeyMath 3 is also used extensively in special education classrooms and can be used to customize individual lessons. The KeyMath 3 has two parallel forms (Form A and Form B), growth scale values, and normed scores, such as scale and standard scores, percentiles, age and grade equivalents are provided. The test can be administered every 3 months to measure progress across the math concepts and skills and to compare the student's growth rate with the average growth rate (Connolly, 2012).

The normative sample consisted of approximately 4,000 children ranging in age from 4 years 5 months to 21 years 11 months with respect to demographics by sex, race, socioeconomic status, region, and disability condition in the United States. The majority of the reported internal consistency and alternate form reliability estimates were in the mid .90s. Both content and concurrent validity were reported in the manual. Content validity was established by surveying the NCTM standards and state standards. The five basic content skills were designed to parallel the five content standards of the NCTM. Concurrently, validity was established by demonstrating that the KeyMath 3 correlated well with the Kaufman Test of Educational Achievement and the Iowa Test of Basic Skills.

Readiness Tests

Boehm Test of Basic Concepts-3 (Boehm-3) and
Boehm Test of Basic Concepts-3 Preschool (Boehm-3 Preschool)

The Boehm-3 and Boehm-3 Preschool are standardized assessments that measure children's understanding of basic relational concepts (e.g., space, quantity, time) that are important for language and cognitive development. Both of these tests are often used to measure how a child performs overall in relation to age and/or grade level. The results of the assessment can be used to identify concepts the child finds difficult, explore possible reasons for difficulty, raise hypotheses, set learning goals, and help establish teaching and intervention plans. The results are often used to provide support for state benchmarks and/or core standards (see Case Illustration 8.3).

The **Boehm Test of Basic Concepts-3 (Boehm-3)** contains 50 concepts and is appropriate for kindergarten through second-grade students. The test takes approximately 30–45 minutes to complete and is usually group-administered in the fall and spring; however, it can be individually administered with older children who may have special needs. There is also a parallel form available in Spanish. The assessment includes separate norms for the fall and spring testing and English and Spanish versions. Four measures are provided: raw scores, percent correct, performance range, and percentile. The Boehm-3 includes a Testing Summary and Ongoing Observation and Intervention Planning Form, which provide a summary of the child's results by concepts. The Boehm-3 also includes a Parent Report Form that summarizes the concepts covered in the assessment and provides suggestions on how the parents can assist their child to learn basic concepts at home.

The **Boehm Test of Basic Concepts-3 Preschool (Boehm-3 Preschool)** is an extension of the Boehm-3 and contains 26 concepts (e.g., size, directions, position in space, time, quantity, classification), which is appropriate for children ages 3 years to 5 years 11 months and takes approximately 20–30 minutes to administer. Each concept is tested twice, which helps the examinee identify the mastered, emerging, and challenging concepts. The child responds by pointing to one of the four options in the colored pictures. The test also comes in a Spanish version. Similar to the Boehm-3, the Boehm-3 Preschool provides four measures: raw scores, percent correct, performance range, and percentile.

The test was normed on 660 children ages 3 years to 5 years 11 months with respect to equal gender and age groups. The sample also replicated the U.S. population by age, gender, race/ethnicity, parent education level (socioeconomic status), and geographic region

(Boehm, 2008). The test was revised to address gender and ethnic biases. The pictures include more illustrations of diverse racial groups and individuals in nonstereotypical roles. Internal reliability estimates across individual age bands ranged from .85 to .92. Test-retest reliability coefficients for children ages 4 years to 5 years 11 months with a retest period of 1 week ranged from .90 to .94. No test-retest reliability was reported for children younger than 4. Concurrent validity was established with correlations between the Boehm-3 Preschool and a previous version (Boehm-Preschool) reported at .84. The Boehm-3 Preschool was compared with the Bracken Basic Concept Scale-Revised, which also tests basic concepts, and there was a correlation of .80 for 3-year-olds and .73 for 5-year-olds, which demonstrates that each test measures the same concepts.

CASE ILLUSTRATION 8.3

Mr. Franco works with kids at the prekindergarten and kindergarten levels. Each year his classes undergo readiness testing. The school district in which Mr. Franco works is proactive in trying to meet the needs of its students and regularly obtains grant funding to provide testing and follow up services. These assessments help determine students' strengths and needs so that students who are struggling can receive early support. In addition, student strengths can be utilized most effectively in helping students advance. While decisions for each student are made based on multiple sources of information, the testing and assessments' quantitative scores support positive outcomes, which helps the district obtain additional grant funding for its schools.

Source: Council of Chief State School Officers (2011).

Metropolitan Readiness Tests, Sixth Edition (MRT)

The **Metropolitan Readiness Tests, Sixth Edition (MRT)**, was created to assess beginning reading, story comprehension, and quantitative concepts and reasoning in preschoolers, kindergarteners, and first graders. The MRT 6 Level 1 is individually administered and assesses skills needed before and during kindergarten, and the MRT6 Level 2 is group-administered and assesses skills needed from mid-kindergarten through the start of first grade. The results of both Level 1 and Level 2 evaluate not only where the child is relative to the expected competencies but provide valuable information for parents and teachers to develop comprehensive tools to support individuals who may not possess the skills needed (e.g., extra tutoring, extra evaluation). Level 1 measures literacy development in prekindergarten and beginning kindergarten children and takes approximately 85 minutes in four settings. Level 2 measures beginning reading and mathematics development and takes 100 minutes in four settings.

The Beginning Reading composite consists of three subtests (visual discrimination-Level I, beginning consonants-Level I and II, sound-letter correspondence-Level I and II, Aural Cloze-Level II), and the Story Comprehension and Quantitative Concepts and Reasoning is made of one subtest each (Story Comprehension-Level I and II, Quantitative Concepts and

Reasoning-Level I and II). The Beginning Reading Composite score is calculated by summing the raw scores for Visual Discrimination, Beginning Consonants, and Sound-Letter Correspondence. The Prereading composite score is calculated by summing the Beginning Reading composite and the Story Comprehension score. All raw scores are then summed for a Total Test Composite, which is converted to percentiles, stanines, scaled scores, and normal curve equivalents based on percentile ranks. A performance rating indicates whether the student has learned enough of the skills to be judged proficient, is in the process of learning the skills, or needs instruction in the skills.

The majority of the internal consistency estimates for the Total Composite score exceeded .90 and the test-retest reliability for the Total Test composite was greater than .90. However, it should be noted that the test-retest reliabilities for two subtests were less than .80. While the Total Composite score appears high enough for making decisions for students, the other scores should be used with caution for that purpose. Evidence of validity is inadequate for the MRT6 as there is no evidence for content validity and construct validity. Predictive validity was presented only for Level II, not Level I. Criterion-related validity was suggested through comparing the MRT6 with the Metropolitan Achievement Tests, Seventh Edition and the Stanford Achievement Test, Ninth Edition.

Kindergarten Readiness Test (KRT)

The **Kindergarten Readiness Test (KRT)** assesses the levels of maturity and development of children ages 4 to 6 to determine if they are developmentally ready to begin kindergarten. Results are shared with both parents and educators to develop plans to support individuals with noted deficiencies. The KRT takes approximately 15–20 minutes and assesses five skills: (a) understanding, awareness, and interaction with one's environment; (b) judgment and reasoning in problem solving; (c) numerical awareness; (d) visual and fine-motor coordination; and (e) auditory attention span and concentration. The KRT is sensitive to identifying possible handicap conditions at an early age and identifying children who should be referred for further evaluations. The KRT test booklet comes with two scoring interpretation sheets (one for the parents/guardians and one for the school), a letter to the parent, and a General Performance Grid that graphically represents a child's strengths and weaknesses. The Score Interpretation sheet includes four ranges of performance: Above Average (100%–92%), Average (90%–78%), Lower Average (76%–63%), and Below Average/Questionable Readiness (61%–45% and below; S. L. Larson & Vitali, 1988).

Although the KRT is widely used as a screening device for kindergarten readiness, the instrument has limitations that should be considered. The KRT was normed on 1,015 children from Midwestern schools; the representative sample consisted of only 5% minority children, far from a representation of students nationwide. As a result, it is highly probably that administration of this test to culturally diverse students will result in cultural biases. (In-depth examination of the importance of cultural considerations in administering assessments will be targeted in Chapter 15.) Another concern related to the development of the KRT is the focus that the authors placed on measures of intelligence. Because the purpose of the instrument is to measure children's readiness to attend kindergarten, which is a measure of maturation, and the foundation of the test appears to focus more on measures of intelligence, the absence of any discrimination between the two measures is concerning. These concerns are further increased by the lack of data relative to the accuracy of the test to measure educational success, issues in the methods with which inter-rater reliability was reported (i.e., due to multiple raters rating multiple participants as opposed to a single participant), and questionability regarding validity and reliability information, which does not appear to have been updated since 1988. Furthermore, despite mandates in numerous states regarding the use of readiness measures, there is an absence of studies to provide empirical evidence of effectiveness. Because of this, the KRT may serve better as a tool in evaluation as opposed to the determining factor.

Gesell Developmental Observation-Revised (GDO-R)

If you recall, many of the tests we discussed in this chapter and in the previous chapter assessed and quantified IQ or specific academic performance skills; however, the **Gesell Developmental Observation-Revised (GDO-R)** is a criterion-referenced test that measures a child's behavior through direct observation and through surveying parents and teachers. Unlike the previous readiness tests, which are ability readiness tests, the GDO-R is considered a developmental readiness test. Gesell is a pioneer in the field of growth and development; the first GDO was published in 1925 and it was updated several times, with its most recent update in 2011.

The purpose of the GDO-R is to "observe a child's overall performance on developmental tasks and determine where a child's behaviors fit on a development scale" (Gesell Institute of Child Development, 2013, p. 2). The GDO-R is appropriate for children ages 2 years six months to 9 years of age and takes 25–45 minutes to administer. In order to administer the GDO-R, counselors must attend a comprehensive 3-day workshop offered by the Gesell Institute. The GDO-R includes an Examiner's Manual, a standardized Examiner's script, a Child Recording Form, and a Teacher and Parent/Guardian Questionnaire.

GDO-R tasks are divided into five strands, which consist of sets of related tasks. Figure 8.3 provides a description of the following strands and tasks measured. Direct observations are used to evaluate a child's cognitive, language, motor, and social emotional development in five strands: Developmental (Strand A), Letter/Numbers (Strand B), Language/Comprehension (Strand C), Visual/Spatial Discrimination (Strand D), and Social Behavior/Emotional Development and Adaptive Skills (Strand E). The GDO-R Child Recording Form includes a checklist on the inside cover and blank spaces for notes. Not only is the counselor concerned about direct responses to the various tasks, the counselor is also paying close attention to the child's process, organization, overt behavior, and verbalizations. A **Developmental Age Score** (Strand A) based on a strand of developmental tasks and child processes is calculated relative to chronological age. The Developmental Age Score informs parents and educators about a child's individual developmental and associated abilities in relation to typical growth patterns. A child's performance on each of the five strands yields the following Performance Level Rating: Age Appropriate (solid or qualified expectation responses for all or most of the tasks in the strand), Emerging (solid or qualified expectation responses for most or only some tasks in the strand), or Concern (atypical responses for most tasks in the strand). This allows for an Overall Performance Level rating. These scores can be used to provide developmental levels and abilities for

Figure 8.3 GDO-R Tasks and Strands

GDO-R Strands and Task Measured		
Strand A Developmental • Hand-eye coordination • Visual tracking and integration • Fine motor skills • Large motor skills • Overt behavior	**Strand B Letters/Numbers**	• Visual perception • Writing name, numbers • Familiarity with letters and numbers
Strand C Language/Comprehension • Sentence structure • Semantics • Vocabulary • Ability to express self verbally • Verbal classification skills • Ability to understand what is said	**Strand D Visual/Spatial Discrimination**	• Depth perception • Visual discrimination • Visual motor integration
	Strand E Social Behavior–Emotional Development and Adaptive Skills	• Social interaction with peers/adults • Self-regulation • Self-help skills

Source: Gesell Institute of Child Development (2013).

children; to identify children who are at risk for developmental, social-emotional, or academic abilities and may need further testing; and as a tool for teachers to customize learning and strategize for curriculum planning. In counseling, this tool may also offer support in informing clients of developmental expectations of their children and supporting them in advocating for individual needs.

A nationwide study of 3- to 6-year-old children from 2008 to 2010 was conducted to provide reliability and validity evidence for 17 of the 19 tasks on the 2007 GDO. The study also examined whether the Developmental Age Score that was assigned by trainers was reliable. Inter-rater reliability correlations were strong among trainers, with a range of .91 to .93, which provides evidence to the qualitative training piece in that developmental age can be reliably assigned by trained raters using the GDO-R (Gesell Institute of Child Development, 2013).

The **Gesell Early Screener (GES),** published in 2011, for children ages 3 to 6 provides a quick evaluation of the child's developmental capacities. The GES consists of selected items from the GDO-R and takes less than 15 minutes to complete. In addition to providing information on whether children meet expectations for their age, the three-tiered scoring rubric identifies children who may be in need of further assessment to determine remediation in specific areas of development. The GES does not require training through the 3-day workshop, though it is recommended.

ASSESSING APTITUDE

We have reviewed popular achievement tests that assess a person's knowledge and previous learning. Now, we will focus on popular aptitude tests. If you recall, aptitude tests measure the potential to learn or acquire a new skill. While achievement tests reflect a person's current level of performance, an aptitude test evaluates an individual's potential for future performance. For example, an aptitude test can be used to determine how well a person might do at a particular employment position, predict the likelihood of success in college or graduate school, or quantify how prepared someone is for the future. Aptitude tests are common in places of employment to gain a deeper understanding of their employees and predict future performance. The term *aptitude* includes many tests used to measure what one is capable of learning, thus it is often easier to break down the tests into categories based on what each test focuses on. As we conceptualize different aptitude tests, we find it easiest to put them in the following four categories: cognitive ability tests, intellectual and cognitive functioning tests, specific aptitude tests, and multiaptitude tests. We will briefly discuss each category below.

Tests of General and Specific Aptitude

Cognitive ability tests measure cognitive ability and focus on cognitive skills, such as reading and mathematics. The Otis-Lennon School Ability Test and the Cognitive Ability Test are two popular aptitude tests used to assess a student's potential to succeed in kindergarten through 12th grade. Cognitive ability tests are also often used to assess the likelihood of success in college and graduate degree programs. Such tests include the SAT and Graduate Record Examination (GRE) revised General Test.

Another domain of aptitude testing includes **intellectual and cognitive functioning tests**. As we discussed in Chapter 7, these tests measure intelligence and changes in cognitive functioning. Popular intelligence tests include the Stanford-Binet, Fifth Edition, the Wechsler tests, and the Kaufman Assessment Battery for Children. Common tests that measure changes in cognitive functioning include the Halsted-Reitan Battery and the Luria-Nebraska Neuropsychological Battery.

Specific aptitude tests focus on one aspect of ability. These tests are often used in determining how well a person might perform in a particular employment profession or the likelihood of success in a specific vocation. Educational institutions as well as human resources departments use these tests as a screening process. For example, there are mechanical aptitude tests, artistic aptitude tests, and clerical aptitude tests. **Mechanical aptitude tests** measure the ability to learn mechanical principles and use reasoning skills to solve mechanical-type problems. Such tests include the Bennet Mechanical Comprehension Test, the Mechanical Aptitude Test (MAT-3C) and the Wiesen Test of Mechanical Aptitude (WTMA). Artistic aptitude tests evaluate artistic talent (e.g., musical ability, drawing, creative expression); these tests include the Primary Measures of Music Auditions and the Intermediate Measures of Music Auditions. Clerical aptitude tests are frequently used to screen job applicants for clerical jobs. Two popular clerical assessments include the Minnesota Clerical Test (MCT) and the Clerical Test Battery (CTB2). In Guided Practice Exercise 8.3 you will practice taking an aptitude test and reflect on your experience.

GUIDED PRACTICE EXERCISE 8.3

Prior to class, go to the Free Aptitude Tests Online website www.aptitude-test.com. This website provides a series of aptitude tests in the categories of General Aptitude, Numerical Aptitude, Verbal Aptitude, and Non-Verbal Aptitude.

Choose a category and click on the link for the aptitude test you want to take. Each test takes 10–20 minutes. Some tests are free, while others require you to be a member to take the test. You do not need to become a member to participate in this exercise. Just choose a test that does not require membership. The purpose of this exercise is to give you an experience of what taking an aptitude test might be like. We cannot verify the accuracy, validity, or reliability of these assessments, so we caution you not to read too much into your individual test results. What were your thoughts and feelings when you received the results of your test? Did you feel the test accurately and fairly captured your aptitude for the area in which you selected? Why or why not? You will have received a score from this assessment. What did this score tell you? Hint: Review Chapter 2 for information regarding how to interpret your score. Be prepared to discuss your results and experiences in small groups or with the entire class.

Multiaptitude tests measure several aspects of ability. Rather than determining the likelihood of success in a vocation, multiaptitude tests provide information on the likelihood of success in several vocations. Some of the most popular multiaptitude batteries include the Armed Services Vocational Assessment Battery (ASVAB) and the O*Net Ability Profiler. The ASVAB is primarily used for testing the potential of armed services enlistees but is frequently used as an educational and vocational counseling tool to help students in 10th grade and above explore job opportunities and training in civilian and armed services careers. The O*Net Ability Profiler is also used in vocational guidance and helps clients identify occupations that fit their strengths and plan their work lives.

Because we already discussed aptitude tests that cover intellectual and cognitive functioning in Chapter 7 and will discuss specific aptitude tests and multiple aptitude tests when we discuss career and vocational assessment in Chapter 12, the remainder of this chapter will focus on cognitive ability tests, specifically **scholastic aptitude tests**.

SCHOLASTIC APTITUDE TESTS

SAT and ACT scores aid universities in making decisions about admission, course placement, scholarship offers, and placing students in appropriate courses of study at the undergraduate level. In addition, there are tests, such as the GRE revised General Test and the Miller Analogies Test, designed to predict performance in graduate school. Throughout this section, you will see the term *predictive validity*, which is simply the power to accurately describe future behavior or events. In this section, we will discuss aptitude tests given at the high school level to predict undergraduate performance and aptitude tests given at the undergraduate level to predict graduate school performance.

High School Level

Preliminary Scholastic Aptitude Test/National Merit Scholarship Qualifying Test (PSAT/NMSQT)

The **Preliminary Scholastic Aptitude Test/National Merit Scholarship Qualifying Test (PSAT/NMSQT)** is a standardized test many students take as practice for the SAT in their sophomore or junior year of high school. The most common reasons for taking the test include preparation for the SAT, to enter the National Merit Scholarship program (11th grade), to discover strengths and weaknesses on skills necessary for college study, and to compare one's performance to others applying for college (College Board, 2013).

The test is composed of five sections: two 25-minute Critical Reading sections, two 25-minute Mathematics sections, and one 30-minute Writing Skills section. Scores are reported on a scale of 20 to 80. In 2012, the average scores for 10th graders was 43 in Critical Reading, 44 in Mathematics, and 42 in Writing Skills; for 11th graders, 48 in Critical Reading, 49 in Mathematics, and 47 in Writing Skills (College Board, 2013). Score reports include national percentiles based on 10th or 11th grade. For example, a student who is a sophomore will receive a percentile ranking which compares him or her to all other sophomores taking the test. The score report also contains the Selection Index, which sums the three scores in each section (Critical Reading, Mathematics, and Writing) in order to determine eligibility for National Merit Scholarship programs. Scores range from 60 to 240, with the average Selection Index of 144 for 11th graders. Approximately 16,000 high-scoring participants qualify as semifinalists on state representational basis. Semifinalists must then meet additional requirements to be considered as finalists for National Merit Scholarships. Approximately 8,300 awards are offered annually.

SAT

If I were to ask you to name an aptitude test you took in high school, I would not be surprised if your response was the SAT since the test has been around since 1926. The SAT is one of the most common aptitude tests given at the secondary level and is usually taken in the spring of junior year or fall of senior year in high school (see Case Illustration 8.4). The SAT, previously known as the Scholastic Aptitude Test until 1993, was renamed the **Scholastic Assessment Test-I (SAT-I)**, and since 2005 is referred to as the New SAT or SAT Reasoning Test. However, you typically hear people refer to the "SATs" collectively. The SATs are made up of the **New SAT** (also called the **SAT Reasoning Test)** and the **SAT Subject Tests.**

The SAT Reasoning Test includes three main sections: (a) critical reading (reading passages and sentence completions), (b) writing (short essay and multiple-choice questions on improving grammar and identifying errors), and (c) mathematics (arithmetic operations, algebra, geometry, statistics, and probability). The SAT is made up of 10 sections with a total test time of 3 hours and 45 minutes. The first test administered is a 25-minute essay, followed by six 25-minute sections, two 20-minute sections, and ending with a 10-minute multiple-choice writing section. The six 25-minute and two 20-minute sections, which contain mathematics, critical reading, and writing, are varied to ensure that no two test takers are taking the same test while sitting next to each other. Each of the three main sections (critical reading, mathematics, and writing) is scored on a 200- to 800-point scale for a possible total score of 2400. A percentile score is given for each of the three main sections in which a student's performance is compared to those who have already taken the test. In addition, the writing section includes two subscores: an essay score from 2 to 12 and a multiple-choice score from 20 to 80. Each SAT includes a 25-minute section (critical reading, mathematics, or writing multiple choice) used for experimental testing to develop future exams. This section is unscored and does not count toward the total score.

CASE ILLUSTRATION 8.4

Do you remember Stephanie Rose from the beginning of this chapter? The good news is that Stephanie passed her STAARS exam and can now graduate from high school in Texas. While she is thrilled that she will get to walk across the graduation stage with her friends, she is now also stressed and anxious, because her parents are insisting that she go to college. Therefore, Stephanie must now study for the SAT exam. Her ability to score well on that exam will determine two issues that are important to her: how much debt she will incur for school (will she have any scholarship opportunities?) and whether she will have to take a remedial math class (remember, math was not her favorite subject per the STAARS assessment). Stephanie has learned her lesson from the STAARS exam and she is studying hard for her SAT exam. She has joined a study group and has ordered study materials online. She wants to refresh herself on some of the areas she feels she may have forgotten from her course work. Let's wish Stephanie well on her exam!

The SAT includes 20 Subject Tests, which are divided into five broad categories: English, history, mathematics, science, and languages. Some colleges may require students to take subject tests in addition to the SAT for admissions, for course placement, or to advise students about future course selection. Each test is 1 hour, and examinees can take up to three in one sitting.

Internal consistency and alternate-form reliability estimates are notably lower for writing compared to critical reading or mathematics. If you recall from Chapter 3, acceptable internal consistency usually are above .85. Internal consistency estimates were reported at .93 for critical reading, .92 for mathematics, and .83 for writing; alternate-form reliability estimates were reported at .88 for critical reading, .91 for mathematics, and .80 for writing.

Although the SAT was not originally designed as a predictive placement test, researchers indicate that SAT section scores along with high school GPA (HSGPA) predicts performance in undergraduate studies. In a recent report by the College Board (2013), 160 institutions provided data on 287,881 students, including their HSGPA; SAT critical reading, mathematics, and writing scores; and first-year GPA (FYGPA). The correlation between HSGPA and

FYGPA was reported at .54; however, the combination of SAT section scores and HSGPA had the highest/strongest correlation with FYGPA ($r = .63$). Correlation of SAT scores and HSGPA with FYGPA showed cultural differences; correlations with FYGPA were reported higher for White and Asian students than for African American and Hispanic students and were higher for female than for male students (Patterson & Mattern, 2013).

ACT

Similar to the SAT, the **ACT** is a widely used entrance exam for undergraduate studies. However, unlike the SAT, which measures general verbal and quantitative reasoning and is considered an aptitude test, the ACT is considered an achievement test measuring skills and knowledge taught in high school. The ACT assessment includes four academic achievement tests, an optional writing component, an interest inventory, and a question-naire. The four subject areas assessed are English (75 questions, 45 minutes), Mathematics (60 questions, 60 minutes), Reading (40 questions, 35 minutes), and Science (40 questions, 35 minutes). The ACT content is similar to the Iowa Test of Educational Development that we discussed previously. The test consists of 215 multiple-choice questions and takes approximately 3 hours and 30 minutes to complete. A test score for each of the four subject areas ranging from 1 (low) to 36 (high) is given along with a composite score (1 to 36), which is the average of the four test scores. The optional ACT Writing Test is a 30-minute essay. Two readers score the responses on a scale of 1 to 6; scores are added together, resulting in a score of 2 (low) to 12 (high). Figure 8.4 shows the mean and standard deviation for each subject area and composite score. The composite score mean is 21.1 with standard deviation of 5.2 and SEM of 1. In the ACT (2007) *Technical Manual,* reliability coefficients for the four subject areas ranged from .85 to .91 and the composite score was reported at .96. Researchers investigated predictive validity by analyzing the correlation between HSGPA and ACT scores as well as ACT scores and FYGPA; they found adequate correlations. HSGPA and ACT scores had a median of .42, and a median of .53 for ACT scores and FYGPA was found.

College Level

Graduate Record Examination (GRE) Revised General Test

The **GRE revised General Test**, often referred to as the GRE, is a widely used scholastic aptitude test used for graduate admissions. The test was revised in August 2011 and measures verbal reasoning, quantitative reasoning, critical thinking, and analytical writing skills. Table 8.4 provides a brief summary of the test content and structure of items. The test is available by computer or paper-and-pencil for countries that do not have access to computers. The computer-based test takes approximately 3 hours and 45 minutes and consists of (a) analytical writing (one section with two timed tasks), (b) verbal reasoning (two sections with 20 questions per section), (c) quantitative reasoning (two sections, 20 questions per section), (d) an unscored section, and (e) a research section. The paper-based test is approximately 3 hours and 30 minutes and consists of (a) analytical writing (two sections: analyze an issue task and an argument task), (b) verbal reasoning (two sections, 25 questions per section), and (c) quantitative reasoning (two sections, 25 questions per section).

Figure 8.4   ACT Mean in Deviation Subject Area and Composite Score

National Distributions of Cumulative Percents for ACT Test Scores
ACT-Tested High School Graduates From 2009, 2010, and 2011

Score	ENGLISH	Usage/ Mechanics	Rhetorical Skills	MATHEMATICS	Pre-Algebra/ Elem. Alg.	Alg./Coord. Geometry	Plane Geometry/Trig.	READING	Soc. Studies/ Sciences	Arts/Literature	SCIENCE	COMPOSITE	Score
36	99			99				99			99	99	36
35	99			99				99			99	99	35
34	99			99				99			99	99	34
33	97			98				97			99	99	33
32	96			97				95			98	98	32
31	94			96				93			98	97	31
30	93			94				91			96	95	30
29	91			93				87			95	93	29
28	88			91				85			93	91	28
27	85			88				82			91	87	27
26	82			84				78			88	84	26
25	78			79				75			84	79	25
24	73			74				71			77	74	24
23	68			67				66			71	68	23
22	63			61				60			63	62	22
21	57			57				54			56	55	21
20	50			52				48			47	48	20
19	43			47				42			38	41	19
18	38	99	99	41	99	99	99	35	99	99	31	34	18
17	33	96	99	34	96	99	99	30	97	97	24	28	17
16	29	92	98	26	91	98	98	25	94	91	19	21	16
15	24	88	92	14	87	95	95	19	88	85	14	16	15
14	18	83	86	06	81	92	90	15	82	77	11	11	14
13	14	78	79	02	74	83	82	10	76	71	08	06	13
12	11	71	71	01	66	74	72	06	69	65	05	03	12
11	09	64	60	01	58	64	63	03	59	57	03	01	11
10	06	56	49	01	48	51	52	01	50	47	02	01	10
09	04	44	38	01	40	36	38	01	40	39	01	01	09
08	02	35	27	01	32	22	25	01	29	31	01	01	08
07	01	27	19	01	20	13	15	01	18	23	01	01	07
06	01	19	12	01	09	07	09	01	10	16	01	01	06
05	01	13	08	01	03	04	06	01	05	09	01	01	05
04	01	07	04	01	01	02	03	01	02	04	01	01	04
03	01	03	02	01	01	01	02	01	01	01	01	01	03
02	01	01	01	01	01	01	01	01	01	01	01	01	02
01	01	01	01	01	01	01	01	01	01	01	01	01	01
Mean	20.6	10.2	10.6	21.0	10.9	10.6	10.5	21.3	10.8	10.9	20.9	21.1	
S.D.	6.4	3.9	3.4	5.3	3.6	2.9	3.1	6.2	3.5	3.9	5.1	5.2	

Source: ACT (2007).

Note: These norms are the source of national norms, for multiple-choice tests, printed on ACT score reports during the 2011–2012 testing year. Sample size: 4,665,862.

Table 8.4 GRE Revised General Test Content and Structure

Test Content	Structure
Verbal Reasoning	
Analyze and draw conclusions from discourse; reason	Reading Comprehension
Incomplete data; identify author assumptions	Text Completion
Select important points; summarize text; understand meaning of words, sentence, and entire texts	Sentence Equivalence
Quantitative Reasoning	
Understand, interpret, and analyze quantitative information	Multiple-choice, select one answer
Use mathematical models to solve problems	One or more answers
Apply arithmetic, algebra, geometry, probability of statistics	Numeric entry questions, quantitative comparison
Analytical Writing	
Articulate complex ideas clearly and effectively	Analyze and Issue Task
Support ideas with reasons and examples; provide well-focused coherent discussion	Analyze and Argument Task

Source: Educational Testing Service (2013).

Scores are reported on a scale of 130–170 in 1-point increments for both the Verbal and Quantitative Reasoning, and 0–6 in half-point increments for Analytical Writing. The mean for Verbal Reasoning was reported at 150.8 with standard deviation of 8.5, Quantitative Reasoning at 151.3 with standard deviation of 8.7, and Analytical Writing at 3.7 with standard deviation of 0.9. This information was based on the performance of all examinees who tested between August 1, 2011, and April 30, 2012 (Educational Testing Service, 2013). Because many people might have taken the previous GRE, which was scored from 200 to 800 on the Verbal and Quantitative Reasoning, new charts comparing the prior scale to the new Verbal and Quantitative scale (130–170) and providing a percentile ranking are available. In the GRE guide, score users are advised to, "use special care in evaluating test takers who received a Quantitative (or Verbal) Reasoning score at the top end of the prior 200-800 score scale" (Educational Testing Service, 2012, p. 25). This information is important for counselors as well as examinees since the new scale provides more differentiation for higher ability test takers. For example, a prior score of 800 corresponds to a new scale score of 166 and a percentile rank of 94%.

The reliability estimates for the GRE revised General Test were reported at .93 for Verbal Reasoning, .94 for Quantitative Reasoning, and 0.79 for Analytical Writing (Educational Testing Service, 2013). Since the test was recently revised, no information in terms of correlations for the GRE test with first-year undergraduate grades was reported in the new scoring handbook. However, in the past, the correlation of GRE scores and first-year graduate grades was reported around .3, which is weak. If you recall from Chapter 3, .3 correlation translates to 9% of variance, meaning the exam accounts for only a mere 9% of the difference among students' first-year grades (Bridgeman, Burton, & Cline, 2008).

The Miller Analogies Test (MAT)

Many graduate schools accept **Miller Analogies Test (MAT)** scores for admission. The MAT is a norm-referenced standardized test that measures analytical ability and content by requiring examinees to solve problems stated as analogies. Each analogy addresses a relation type (e.g., semantic, classification, association, logical/mathematical) and a content area (e.g., general, humanities, mathematics, language, natural sciences, social sciences). Analogy items are written as A : B :: C: D. This can be read as either "A is related to B in the same way that C is related to D" or "A is related to C in the same way as B is related to D" (Pearson, 2013). For example, (a. radius, b. diameter, c. area, d. circumference): Perimeter :: Circle : Square. (answer d. circumference).

Scores are based on the number of items answered correctly, and raw scores are computed into scaled score and percentile ranks. The MAT is a 60-minute test that contains 120 items; 100 items count toward a score while the other 20 are experimental items and do not affect the examinee's score. Scaled scores currently range from 200 to 600 with a mean of approximately 400. The norm group was based on examinees who took the MAT from January 1, 2008, to December 31, 2011. In 2013, Pearson introduced new norms, which will update the MAT percentile ranks to represent the current candidate population; however, the 200–600 score range will remain the same.

Adequate reliability and validity were reported. The internal consistency of all MAT test forms administered during the 2008–2011 normative sample period had a total group reliability of .91 and SEM of 7.46. For example, if you score a 500 on the MAT, you could be 68% confident if you took the test again that you would score between 492.5 and 507.5 and 95% confident of a score between 485.4 and 514.6. In terms of construct validity, evidence from a meta-analysis of 127 studies found that the MAT measures abilities that other cognitive ability instruments measure and the principles of cognition are used with analogical reasoning (Kuncel, Hezlett, & Ones, 2004). Predictive validity studies showed a positive correlation between MAT scores and success in graduate programs. Furthermore, in a meta-analysis Kuncel and Hezlett (2007) found MAT scores to correlate slightly higher with graduate GPA than with GRE Total scores or GMAT scores.

Table 8.5 briefly describes additional widely used aptitude tests used to assess academic or professional aptitude for entry into graduate school programs. Guided Practice Exercise 8.4 asks you to choose an assessment for a potentially gifted student.

Table 8.5   Some Entrance Examinations for Graduate School Training

Examinations	Brief Description
Medical College Admission Test (MCAT)	Assesses problem solving, critical thinking, and knowledge of science concepts and principles perquisite to the study of medicine; consists of four sections: Physical Sciences, Verbal Reasoning, Biological Sciences, and an optional Trial Section; writing section removed in 2013 and replaced with Trial Section; takes approximately 5 hours and 10 minutes; each section except the Trial Section is scored from 1 (low) to 15 (high); total score is sum of three individual section scores; score sheet provides the mean, SD, and percentile ranking; in 2015, a new MCAT will be released and consist of four sections: (a) biological and biochemical foundations of living systems, (b) chemical and physical foundations, (c) psychological, social, and biological foundations of behavior, and (d) critical analysis and reasoning skills
Law School Admission Test (LSAT)	Provides a standard measure of acquired reasoning and reading skills; consists of 100–102 questions and is 3 hours and 30 minutes long; format consists of (a) four scored multiple-choice sections measuring reading comprehension, analytical reasoning, and logical reasoning, (b) one unscored multiple-choice section, and (c) one unscored writing sample; scores range from 120 to 180 with approximately 150 average score with SD of 10; median correlation between LSAT scores and first-year law school grades was .36, but median correlation between LSAT scores combined with undergraduate GPA and first-year law school was .48 (Law School Admission Council, 2013)
Dental Admission Test (DAT)	Designed to measure general academic ability, comprehension of scientific information, and perceptual ability; consists of a battery of four tests: (a) survey of natural sciences, (b) perceptual ability test, (c) reading comprehension test, and (d) quantitative reasoning test; results reported as scale scores, which are neither raw scores nor percentiles; scores range from 1 to 30 with a scale score of 17 typically signifying average performance on a national level (American Dental Association, 2012); validity studies show that pre-dental GPA, science GPA, DAT academic average score, and quantitative reasoning score were the strongest predictors of first-year GPA (Dental Admission Testing Program, 2012)
Graduate Management Admission Test (GMAT)	Measures verbal, mathematical, integrated reasoning, and analytical writing skills developed in education and work; consists of four sections: (a) analytical writing assessment, (b) integrated reasoning, (c) quantitative, and (d) verbal; total exam time is 3 hours and 30 minutes; total GMAT scores range from 200 to 800 with two-thirds scoring between 400 and 600; quantitative and verbal sections are scored 0–60, integrated reasoning 1–8, and analytical writing assessment 0–6; median correlation between undergraduate GPA and first-year grades was .28, but median correlation of .51 was reported when predicting first-year grades from total GMAT score and undergraduate GPA; integrated reasoning section is a newer section and researchers believe the addition will increase correlation to .59 or better (Rudner, 2013)

GUIDED PRACTICE EXERCISE 8.4

Latecia is in the fourth grade in Georgia and has stood out in her classroom in terms of academics. Since kindergarten, she has been at the top of her class. It is suspected that she could qualify for the gifted and talented program at her school. Her teacher brought up this idea to Latecia's parents at a parent-teacher conference. Her parents readily sign the Gifted Referral and Parental Permission Form required in the Atlanta Public School system. In order to qualify for the gifted and talented program, Latecia must be tested with a nationally normed test and with a criterion-referenced competency test. She must also undergo observation, or a classroom screening, to be evaluated for traits, abilities, and behaviors (or a TABS assessment) per Georgia state law. Given what you have learned thus far in this chapter, what assessments would you recommend for Latecia? Why? There is no one right answer, but be prepared to discuss your answer in class.

Source: Atlanta Public Schools (n.d.).

CONTROVERSIAL ISSUES IN APTITUDE AND ACHIEVEMENT TESTING

The use of aptitude and achievement tests has drawn plenty of criticism in recent years. The high-stakes testing movement has influenced increased focus on the shortcomings of aptitude and achievement tests. **High-stakes testing** is a term used to describe a situation in which the results of a single assessment, usually a standardized test, are used to make an important decision. According to the *Standards for Educational and Psychological Testing*, when used properly, tests results are among the most sound and objective ways to measure student performance (American Educational Research Association, American Psychological Association, and National Council on Measurement in Education, 1999). However, when test results are used inappropriately or as a single measure of performance, they can have unintended adverse consequences. In this section, we will explore some of the ways in which aptitude and achievement test results are used inappropriately.

Achievement tests have been a staple of the educational system for years. While they represent the industry standard for assessing student comprehension, our understanding of how students perform and the result this has on their test-taking ability draws attention to the validity of still using these tests to make high-stakes decisions. Achievement tests are valid only when they assess a knowledge set that those taking the test have been exposed to in their schooling. When students have not learned the material, their scores on standardized tests undoubtedly suffer. As a result, one of the challenges of most large-scale, national standardized tests is including items to assess a knowledge domain familiar to all students without a universal national curriculum. Because different schools and teachers may focus on different content, a single national examination that addresses the content all students learned would be nearly impossible to construct. Attempts to address this issue are behind recent legislation like No Child Left Behind and the development of the Common Core State Standards to universalize the educational curriculum for students.

Like achievement tests, aptitude tests also have come under scrutiny recently. Traditionally, aptitude tests have been used to assist in making admission and candidate selection decisions. The most common aptitude tests are those used to make college admission decisions (ACT, SAT, GRE). There are many arguments that these standardized tests have become antiquated and should no longer factor into the student admission process. The arguments against tests like the ACT, SAT, and GRE include the following:

- They are culturally biased and favor affluent European American test takers.
- They assess more global knowledge and do not take into account an individual's ability to succeed at more discipline-specific information.
- They are designed to provide an advantage to students who are naturally good standardized test takers.
- They do not account for individual factors and personal motivation that may allow an individual to succeed once admitted into an undergraduate or graduate program of study.

Guided Practice Exercise 8.5 helps you further explore your position regarding controversial issues in aptitude and achievement testing.

GUIDED PRACTICE EXERCISE 8.5

Prior to class, read the article "Cultural Bias in Testing" at www.education.com/reference/article/cultural-bias-in-testing. Reflect on your experiences as a test taker over the course of your life. What are your thoughts about achievement, aptitude, or intelligence testing? Are these measures of ability and intelligence culturally fair? Which argument do you endorse: (1) that intelligence tests are biased or (2) that intelligence tests are not biased? Why? Be prepared to discuss your results and experiences in small groups or with the entire class.

As a result of these criticisms, several universities have begun reexamining their policies on including these tests as part of their admission process. According to Fair-Test (2013), in 2013 more than 850 colleges and universities throughout the United States did not require potential applicants to submit either an ACT or SAT score. Although drawbacks to these types of tests exist, they still appear to play an important role in the selection process. The key to remember, as indicated in the *Standards for Educational and Psychological Testing,* is that test results should be interpreted in concert with other available information about the applicant to ensure that decisions made based on the available information are informed and reliable. Guided Practice Exercise 8.6 asks you to reflect on your thoughts about using aptitude tests as part of the admissions process.

GUIDED PRACTICE EXERCISE 8.6

As noted in this chapter, many professionals consider aptitude tests to be outdated and insufficient in predicting student aptitude or a student's future success in college. Think back to your own educational experiences. Did you have to take an aptitude test to get into college? Prior to class, go to the websites of five universities or colleges and look at their admission criteria for undergraduate and graduate students. How many of the five require an aptitude test to gain admittance? For those schools that require an aptitude test, how heavily are these tests weighted in terms of granting a student admission? Given what you've read so far in this book, what are your thoughts about the use of aptitude tests as a part of admission into educational programs? This exercise could be conducted as a group discussion in the classroom by having students compare their findings and then discuss the pros and cons of using aptitude tests for admission into educational programs.

KEYSTONES

- Assessment of ability includes achievement testing which measures what one learned and aptitude testing which predicts future behavior and measures what one is capable of learning.
- There has been a significant development in achievement testing since passage of the Individuals with Disabilities Education Act and the No Child Left Behind Act and creation and widespread adoption of the Common Core State Standards.
- There are several kinds of achievement tests, including multilevel survey achievement battery tests, diagnostic achievement tests, and readiness tests.
- Achievement tests are often used to measure academic progress, diagnosis a learning disability or learning difficulties, and measure one's readiness for moving forward. Achievement tests can be used as formative tests to evaluate a person's progress or summative tests to measure what a person learned.
- Popular achievement tests include ITBS, Stanford 10, MAT 8, KTEA-II, WIAT, WJ III, ACH, Boehm-3, and Metropolitan Readiness Tests, Sixth Edition.
- There are several types of aptitude tests, including cognitive ability tests, intellectual and cognitive functioning tests, specific aptitude tests, and multiaptitude tests.
- Popular cognitive ability tests that measure scholastic aptitude and are often used for college admissions include the PSAT/NMSQT, SAT, and ACT. Popular aptitude tests used for graduate and professional school admission include the GRE revised General Test, MAT, MCAT, DAT, LSAT, and GMAT.
- Counselors should be aware of high-stakes testing and ensure that test results are interpreted in concert with other available information about the applicant.

KEY TERMS

ACT

Boehm Test of Basic Concepts-3 (Boehm-3)

Boehm Test of Basic Concepts-3 Preschool (Boehm-3 Preschool)

cognitive ability tests

Common Core State Standards

Developmental Age Score

diagnostic achievement tests

Education for All Handicapped Children Act

Gesell Developmental Observation-Revised (GDO-R)

Gesell Early Screener (GES)

GRE revised General Test

high-stakes testing

Individuals with Disabilities Education Improvement Act (IDEIA)

intellectual and cognitive functioning tests

Iowa Test of Basic Skills (ITBS)

Iowa Test of Educational Development (ITED)

Kaufman Test of Educational Achievement, Second Edition (KTEA-II)

KeyMath 3 Diagnostic Assessment

Kindergarten Readiness Test (KRT)

mechanical aptitude tests

Metropolitan Readiness Tests, Sixth Edition

Miller Analogies Test (MAT)

multiaptitude tests

multilevel survey achievement batteries

New SAT

Otis-Lennon School Ability Test, Eighth Edition (OLSAT 8)

Peabody Individual Achievement Test-Revised/ Normative Update (PIAT-R/NU)

Preliminary Scholastic Aptitude Test/National Merit Scholarship Qualifying Test (PSAT/NMSQT)

readiness assessments

SAT Reasoning Test

SAT Subject Tests

scholastic aptitude tests

Scholastic Assessment Test-I (SAT-I)

Smarter Balanced Assessment Consortium

specific aptitude tests

Stanford Achievement Test Series, Tenth Edition (Stanford 10)

TerraNova, Third Edition Tests (TN3)

Wechsler Individual Achievement Test, Second Edition (WIAT-II)

Wide Range Achievement Test 4 (WRAT 4)

Woodcock-Johnson III Normative Update (WJ III NU) Complete

Woodcock-Johnson III Tests of Achievement (WJ III ACH)

ADDITIONAL RESOURCES

- Advantages and Disadvantages (of Standards-Based Education)

  http://www.stanford.edu/ ~ hakuta/www/archives/syllabi/CalTex_SBR/procon.html

This website discusses the advantages and disadvantages of using standardized testing in education.

- Family Education: Testing

  http://school.familyeducation.com/educational-testing/study-skills/34555.html

This website provides a series of articles related to aptitude and achievement testing in K–12 schools.

- *Practical Assessment, Research, and Evaluation*

  http://pareonline.net/getvn.asp?v=2&n=5

This website provides free articles on assessment that can help develop your knowledge about the assessment process for aptitude and achievement testing.

- Carnegie Foundation for the Advancement of Teaching: Aptitude, Ability, and Achievement

  http://bondessays.carnegiefoundation.org/?p=6

This blog allows you to join the national debate about assessing aptitude, ability, and achievement testing.

- *Frontline*: Testing Our Schools

  http://www.pbs.org/wgbh/pages/frontline/shows/schools/etc/guide.html

This website provides definitions of common terms in testing in K–12 schools and a synopsis of the national debate regarding the pros and cons of continuing such testing.

Student Study Site: Visit the Student Study Site at **www.sagepub.com/watson** to access additional study tools, including quizzes, web resources, and journal articles.

CHAPTER 9

Standardized Methods of Personality Assessment

LEARNING OBJECTIVES

After reading this chapter, you will be able to

- Define personality
- Explain the difference between informal and formal assessment tools in the area of personality assessment
- Explain the purpose for assessing personality
- Describe and apply popular structured personality assessments used in a variety of settings

The word *personality* seems to appear in everyday conversation. I was sitting in a coffee shop the other day, and I overheard a lady describe her first date with a friend. She said, "He has a great personality." Her friend said, "Well, that is better than no personality." Numerous musicians sing about and describe personality in several ways. In Nat King Cole's popular song "You're My Everything" he sings, "You're my everything underneath the sun, You're my everything rolled up into one, You're my only dream, my only reality, You're my idea of a perfect personality." And Pink in her song "Split Personality" sings, "Tell me what do they see, When they look at me, Do they see my many personalities, oh no?" The band Hogni even has a song called "Big Personality" with the lyrics "I know that I got a big personality, And a strong magnetism too, But it often seems to keep good people away from me, I don't know why that is." But how do we as counselors define personality and why might we be interested in learning about a client's personality?

In this chapter, we first define personality and then discuss the purpose of personality assessment. There are many tools counselors can use to explore various aspects of one's personality. We have divided the personality assessment into two chapters. This chapter

235

discusses a variety of methods for assessing personality, including interviews, observations, and different structured tests. In the next chapter, we will highlight projective tests and conclude the chapter with a discussion on the strengths and limitations of structured and projective assessments.

PERSONALITY DEFINED

Introduced as early as the fourth century BCE, the concept of personality and the factors which influence it have been the focus of numerous theorists and researchers. Hippocrates, an early philosopher, served as one of the earliest theorists to address issues of personality in which he proposed the four humors of temperament, attributing imbalances in these temperaments to be responsible for differences in personality. Largely due to the fact that other philosophers at the time, including Aristotle and Plato, shared similar views of personality formation, studies in personality remained unchanged for several centuries.

Revived in the 19th century, researchers again began to examine personality, turning their attention to the brain. One of the most notable studies of the time which involved evaluation of the brain was the case of Phineas Gage. In this case, a rod went through Gage's face to the top of his skull. The resulting brain damage was accompanied by changes in personality, providing a link between specific areas of the brain and personality development.

Whereas the 19th century served as a revival of personality theory and investigation, the 20th century provided many of the foundations for personality theory today. Sigmund Freud's concepts of the id, ego, and superego, for example, identified both conscious and unconscious elements of personality, while Carl Jung's establishment of dynamics such as extraversion and introversion are used in personality theory today. Works of Abraham Maslow and Carl Rogers can also be seen as important in the development of personality theory.

Despite a long and rich development and investigation of personality, several different definitions of personality continue to exist in the counseling literature. In fact, there is no consensus within the literature in terms of an all-encompassing definition. A basic general definition of **personality** is that it is the psychological characteristics or blend of characteristics that make a person unique. These characteristics might include attitudes, values, interests, motives, and behavioral or cognitive styles that are shaped by genetic, biological, and social influences. These cultural factors result in diverse, complex personalities which are theoretically approached in various ways. For example, an individual who grows up in a close-knit family in which all individuals contribute equally to the family responsibilities may develop a personality that values togetherness and equality. He or she may be described as cooperative, genuine, and respectful. The different experiences of each individual outside of the home may shape these personality characteristics. For example, a female member of the family who has been physically assaulted by her boyfriend may develop distrust of men and be viewed as distrustful, angry, and reserved.

One way to conceptualize personality is to think of a personality pyramid where you have *psychological core* at the bottom, *typical responses* in the middle, and *role-related behavior* on top. The psychological core is where a person's deepest and most basic attitudes, values, interests, motives, and self-worth are. The **psychological core** is the representation of the "real" person. The content of our psychological core typically develops in early childhood and comes from our parents, teachers, and caregivers. An example of the psychological core would be your individual religious values and beliefs. **Typical responses** represent the way individuals usually adjust or respond to the demands of their environment. An example would be a person who is happy, cheerful, and upbeat. **Role-related behavior** is how an individual acts in a particular situation that is usually gained through modeling and social learning experiences. These behaviors typically have an adaptive function as they help us function effectively in different environments. Examples include our behavior as students, employees, parents, children, and friends.

Another way to conceptualize personality is to view it as a combination of trait and state characteristics measured on a continuum. **Trait characteristics** are the enduring components of personality and can be represented as attitudes, behaviors, or dispositions. They represent our general presentation the majority of the time. For people who seem to always find the positive in any situation, optimism may be one of their personality traits. These traits can be grouped together to form what is known as a type. A **type** is a collection of traits. Someone who has the traits of being outgoing, friendly, and compassionate might have a personality type defined as being "likable." Opposite of traits are states. A **state** is a more temporary expression of a personality characteristic. It is typically exhibited in response to some environmental trigger. Recall that optimistic person we mentioned earlier. Now, imagine that this same person just had a week during which she forgot about an exam and did poorly, received a speeding ticket, and found out she was coming down with a fever. The collection of negative events in such a short period of time may cause her to temporarily become more pessimistic and wonder why everything is going wrong. This is not her normal personality presentation, but a more accurate representation of how she feels at this particular state in her life. Once the immediate stressors resolve themselves, she most likely will revert back to her typical optimistic self. Guided Practice Exercise 9.1 helps you reflect on the differences between traits and states.

GUIDED PRACTICE EXERCISE 9.1

Given what you have just read about personality traits, what do you think your predominant traits are? Together with a partner, discuss your traits. In addition, describe a time when you were under the influence of an environmental stressor and reacted in a way that went against your usual personality type. What was that like for you? How did those around you who know you react?

As you can see, personality comprises several components that are shaped by various factors, including biological and social influences, all of which need to be considered when conceptualizing a client. Thus, **personality assessment** may be defined as the measurement and evaluation of psychological traits, states, values, interests, motives, individual religious values and beliefs, and cognitive and behavioral styles.

PURPOSE OF PERSONALITY ASSESSMENT

Why might we assess personality? Personality assessments help the counselor and client understand the client's attitudes, character traits, interpersonal needs, and/or intrinsic motivation. Personality assessments have been used to identify psychopathology as well as strengths and weaknesses in occupational decisions. These assessments can be used to aid in making clinical diagnoses, case conceptualization, and treatment planning. Personality assessments can help provide a realistic picture of the client and assist clinicians in forming or disregarding hypotheses as they proceed throughout the counseling process.

There are several different methods used to assess personality. Personality can be assessed through observation, face-to-face interviews, paper-and-pencil tests, and computer-generated tests. Personality assessments are often grouped into objective and projective measures. **Objective assessments** are **structured assessments**, meaning clients respond to a fixed set of questions or items typically in a forced-choice format, such as true/false, yes/no, or multiple choice. Objective personality assessments often consist of questionnaires, self-report inventories, or rating scales. **Projective assessments** are considered **unstructured assessments** in that stimuli presented are ambiguous or incomplete and a person's responses to the stimuli are not limited to true, false, or a variety of specific given response choices. We cover projective assessments in more detail in the Chapter 10.

In assessment, we often use **informal techniques** and **formal techniques** as ways to measure personality. As discussed in Chapter 6, clinicians use a variety of informal techniques, including observations, interviews, self-reports, case notes, and checklists. Formal techniques consist of structured personality instruments and projective techniques. Interviews and observations are considered the central part of assessment as they attempt to determine a person's beliefs, attitudes, or concerns and help counselors formulate hypotheses. Coupled with an understanding of the test strengths, limitations, and population to which it can be applied, a counselor can then select a test to measure specific personality characteristics. For the purposes of this chapter, we will briefly describe informal techniques but focus more on specific formal personality assessments.

INFORMAL PERSONALITY ASSESSMENT: OBSERVATIONS AND INTERVIEWING

The addition of informal assessments such as observation and interviews in the here-and-now can increase our ability to understand a client's personality. **Observation** is the most common assessment tool a counselor has available to directly assess a client's personality. Throughout your counseling program, you will be trained on becoming a skilled observer. By the time you reach practicum, you will have learned about the importance of attending to nonverbal behavior, verbal behavior, and conflict or discrepancies. Because observation is based on the individual counselor's judgment, one can imagine how a major limitation might include making inferences or misinterpreting behaviors. As you assess personality, it is important for you to have an understanding of individual and cultural differences that may arise in verbal and nonverbal behavior as well as to reflect on any biases you may possess. Without this understanding and self-awareness, you may risk making an inaccurate or biased assessment (see Case Illustration 9.1).

CASE ILLUSTRATION   9.1

Sani is a 24-year-old Native American man from the Navajo tribe. He was born and raised on the reservation, but recently he won an academic scholarship and is now enrolled in a prestigious university in a primarily Caucasian community. Sani is having difficulty integrating into his new environment, because his cultural traditions are often misunderstood. For example, some of the feedback he has gotten from one of his roommates was that Sani is not realistic, he does not properly prepare for misfortune, and he is overly optimistic. Sani was told this because he never saved money in case of an emergency. Sani's cultural tradition is that if one plans for misfortune, then he will cause the misfortune. It is the Navajo tradition to keep thoughts positive and not to stockpile resources so that one does not bring misfortune on the tribe. It has also been noted that Sani becomes quiet during class discussions. This is a cultural sign of respect, but Sani loses points from his professor for not being active enough in class. Due to these factors, Sani has been characterized in a certain way and people ascribe certain personality traits to him (e.g., quiet, shy, unrealistically optimistic). However, these features are less a personality trait for Sani than aspects of a cultural tradition of his tribe.

Sources: Dykeman & Roebuck (2008); Fiske (1978).

In addition to observation, personality may be assessed by means of a **structured interview, semistructured interview,** or **unstructured interview**. If you recall from Chapter 6, interviewing is one of the most basic information gathering tools; it usually involves a face-to-face verbal exchange and interaction between the client and the counselor in which the counselor gathers various information about the client. In a structured interview the counselor follows a predetermined set of questions; whereas in an unstructured interview the counselor begins with general statements, but the questions are not predetermined. Ratings scales can also be employed to enhance reliability and objectivity of the assessment interview. In counseling, we often refer to structured interviews as being either diagnostic assessments or descriptive assessments. With diagnostic assessments, we are looking for specific criteria related to the *Diagnostic and Statistical Manual* in order to identify disorders. With descriptive assessments, we are not looking for a diagnosis but rather for descriptive client aspects. For example, we might be interested in looking at personality functioning in order to provide direction in the counseling session.

In terms of using interviews for gathering information about personality, you will most likely use a descriptive assessment to describe some aspect of the client's personality. As discussed in Chapter 6, the quality of the interview will depend on both your skills as an interviewer, including your ability to establish rapport, and the value of your questions. Whether you use a simple set of questions or a more detailed and extended format to gain information about a client's personality, the questions should directly assess personality. Because personality comprises several components, all of which need to be considered when conceptualizing a client, it is important that you have a thorough understanding of the personality characteristics you are trying to assess as you gather information.

FORMAL PERSONALITY ASSESSMENT: STRUCTURED PERSONALITY ASSESSMENT

As mentioned previously, objective personality assessments are often referred to as structured personality assessments, meaning clients respond to a fixed set of questions or items typically in a forced-choice format, such as true/false, yes/no, or multiple choice. Structured instruments are the most popular and widely used technique to assess personality and are preferred because of the ease in scoring and interpretation. These instruments can be administered as individual or group tests. There are a large number of structured personality assessments, the most popular of which are the Minnesota Multiphasic Personality Inventory (MMPI-2), California Psychological Inventory (CPI), Sixteen Personality Factor Questionnaire (16PF), and Myers-Briggs Type Indicator (MBTI). There are four main approaches to the development of objective measures of personality. Please refer to Table 9.1 for a brief summary of each method and examples of each approach. Note that the Criterion Group Method and Factor-Analytic Method are considered empirical approaches. In these two approaches, the only items that are retained are those that demonstrate an actual relationship between the trait measured and test items. In the next section, we will focus primarily on the most widely used structured personality assessment instruments.

Myers-Briggs Type Indicator (MBTI)

The **Myers-Briggs Type Indicator (MBTI)**, based on Jungian theory, is the most popular and widely used personality assessment around the world for normal functioning individuals. The MBTI is based on Carl Jung's typological theories published in his 1921 book *Psychological Types*. Jung theorized that individuals use four mental functions or processes to become aware and make conclusions about the world around them: sensing, intuition, thinking, and feeling. Jung also theorized that people have attitudes and interaction preferences for engaging with and seeing the world. He called these attitudes extraversion and introversion (Jung, 1921/1964). Katharine Briggs and her daughter Isabel Myers studied Jung's theory extensively. At this time, during World War II, women were entering the industrial workforce for the first time. Briggs and Myers began working on developing the MBTI as an assessment that could help women identify jobs where they might feel comfortable and effective. In addition to Jung's four functions and two attitudes, Briggs and Myers added two lifestyle preferences: judging and perceiving. The original MBTI was published in 1962. The functions, attitudes, and lifestyle are sorted into four opposite pairs, which we call dichotomies. There are two preferences for each of the four dichotomies; next we will briefly discuss each of the four dichotomies.

Table 9.1   Approaches to the Development of Objective Measures of Personality

Approach	Example
1. Logical or Content Method • Items are developed based on those that logically or intuitively would represent the personality characteristic we are trying to measure.	Minnesota Multiphasic Personality Inventory (MMPI-2) content scales Personality Assessment Inventory Coopersmith Self-Esteem Inventory
2. Theoretical Method • Items are based on a particular personality theory and are designed to measure traits and states based on the theory.	Myers-Briggs Type Indicator

3. Criterion Group Method
 	
  • Test items are administered to two groups: criterion group (possess the trait) and control group (does not possess trait).
  • Retain items that discriminate between the two groups, disregard items that do not discriminate.
  • Each item is thus keyed/related to a criterion.
	MMPI-2 clinical scales
	
	Minnesota Multiphasic Personality Inventory-Adolescent
	
	California Psychological Inventory (majority of scales)

4. Factor-Analytic Method
 	
  • This is the most common method.
  • Data reduction is a statistical method that is used to discover in a large set of variables a smaller subset of variables that explains the entire domain.
  • Statistically significant items are clustered, which shows the correlation among items, and items that are strongly correlated are grouped to see what they are measuring.
  • This method identifies significant dimensions.
	Sixteen Personality Factor Questionnaire
	
	NEO Inventories
	
	Piers-Harris Children's Self-Concept Scale-2

The first dichotomy describes complementary attitudes and interactions, which function on a continuum known as extraversion (E) and introversion (I). These two attitudes describe how one prefers to interact with and sees the world. **Extraversion** does not mean someone is loud or extremely talkative. Instead most people who prefer extraversion direct more energy outward and less energy toward inner activity. Verbal and physical activity are important. For example, they prefer thinking by talking to others, enjoy variety and action, like to see how other people do a job, and prefer to work in a team rather than alone. In terms of the MBTI, introversion does not mean shy. Most people who prefer **introversion** direct more energy inward and less energy toward outward activity. For example, they often prefer thinking privately before talking to others or take time to consider before acting. They enjoy thinking and reflecting and may be considered more quiet, not because they are shy, but because they are taking time to process the information. They often prefer to work alone without interruptions.

The next dichotomy describes the ways of becoming aware of the world. The two ways of perceiving are sensing (S) and intuition (N). People who prefer **sensing** observe through the physical senses: smell, taste, touch, sight, and hearing. They focus on what is real and actual, and they value practical application. They are factual and concrete, have a good memory for detail, and are considered practical and present-focused. People who prefer **intuition**, use their insight. They trust insight and minimize the value of experience. For example, you have probably heard someone say, "It's just a feeling I have," as they made a decision. They find meaning in events, focus on the future, and value imagination.

The third dichotomy describes the ways of coming to conclusions about the world. The two ways of judging are thinking (T) and feeling (F). Most people who prefer **thinking** analyze readily, are considered objective rational, and focus on logical problem solving. They value fairness, and justice means everyone is treated the same. Most people who prefer **feeling** are concerned with the impact of judgment and are concerned for others' well-being. Rather than focusing on logical problem solving, they focus on the impact on people and assess decisions according to their personal values. They are compassionate, and justice means everyone is treated according to his or her needs.

The last dichotomy describes lifestyle preference. The two preferences for dealing with the outer world are judging (J) and perceiving (P). Most people who prefer **judging** like to make a plan and stick to the plan, finish one project before beginning another, and follow rules and schedules. They often want to be right and may decide things too quickly. Most people who prefer **perceiving** like to stay flexible rather than having fixed plans. They often start many projects and have trouble finishing them and may decide things too slowly. Rather than living by rules and schedules, they live by dealing with and adjusting to problems when they arise.

Because there are four pairs of dichotomies, the MBTI categorizes individuals into 16 psychological types. For example, ENFJ is one out of the 16 psychological types and consists of the four preferences E, N, F, and J. An ENFJ personality type is described as warm and responsible, in tune with the emotions and needs of others, and provides inspiring leadership. Individuals with this personality type are likely to be givers, focused on the needs of others, and harder on their selves than they are on others. As a result, ENFJ personality types should avoid more stressful jobs in which criticism is a significant factor (e.g., corporate management) and should instead focus on careers which allow them to interact with and help other people. In relationships, individuals with an ENFJ personality type are more likely to define themselves less as individuals and more based on the quality of their relationship. As a result, they may present as more insecure and require that their partner demonstrate the same investment in their relationship as they do. For a listing of all 16 types, see Figure 9.1, which shows MBTI Form M, Characteristics Frequently Associated With Each Type.

The MBTI is available in Form M or Form Q, both of which use Item Response Theory (IRT). IRT is used to develop a test in which the association between the individual items on the test and the latent variable (construct) of interest can be measured. Internal reliability of the facets measured by Form Q was examined across many samples based on common demographics, employment status, ethnicity, age, and country of origin. Most of the facets had adequate reliability, similar to those reported for the Revised NEO Personality Inventory, ranging from .56 to .81. Test-retest reliability indicated good reliability for most

Figure 9.1 MBTI Form M

STEP **I** / REPORT FORM **FORM M**

mbti

Name _____ Date _____

The MBTI® instrument reports your preferences on four dichotomies.
There are two opposite preferences on each dichotomy, as shown below.

E–I Dichotomy Where you like to focus your attention	**E Extraversion** You prefer to focus on the outer world of people and things	**I Introversion** You prefer to focus on the inner world of ideas and impressions
S–N Dichotomy The way you like to look at things	**S Sensing** You tend to focus on the present and on concrete information gained from your senses	**N Intuition** You tend to focus on the future, with a view toward patterns and possibilities
T–F Dichotomy The way you like to go about deciding things	**T Thinking** You tend to base your decisions primarily on logic and on objective analysis of cause and effect	**F Feeling** You tend to base your decisions primarily on values and on subjective evaluation of person-centered concerns
J–P Dichotomy How you deal with the outer world	**J Judging** You like a planned and organized approach to life and prefer to have things settled	**P Perceiving** You like a flexible and spontaneous approach to life and prefer to keep your options open

YOUR REPORTED TYPE AND PREFERENCE CLARITY CATEGORY

Your reported type comprises four letters representing the four preferences you chose. Your preference clarity category (pcc) shows how consistently you chose one preference over the other. High points indicate a clear preference; note, however, that the pcc does not measure abilities or development. To determine your pcc, follow these steps:

1. Refer to the "Points" chart on page two of the answer sheet. For each dichotomy, identify the preference with

the greater number of points, and record that letter and number in the "Your Reported Type" column.

2. For each dichotomy, circle in the chart below the range that includes the number next to your preference.

3. Identify the preference clarity category ("slight," "moderate," etc.) shown above each circled range and record it below. If you did not answer all of the items, your points may be lower than the lowest range of numbers on the chart. If so, use "slight" as your pcc.

PREFERENCE CLARITY CATEGORY

YOUR REPORTED TYPE	DICHOTOMY		Slight	Moderate	Clear	Very Clear	YOUR PREFERENCE CLARITY CATEGORY
		E–I	11–13	14–16	17–19	20–21	_____
		S–N	13–15	16–20	21–24	25–26	_____
		T–F	12–14	15–18	19–22	23–24	_____
		J–P	11–13	14–16	17–20	21–22	_____

Each type, or combination of preferences, tends to be characterized by its own interests, values, and unique gifts. On the back of this page is a brief description of each of the sixteen types. Find your reported type and see whether the description fits you. If not, the person who administered the MBTI® instrument to you can help you identify

a better-fitting type. Whatever your preferences, you may still use some behaviors that are characteristic of contrasting preferences. For a more complete discussion of the sixteen types and applications, see *Introduction to Type®*, 6th ed. (Myers, I. B., 1998, CPP, Inc.) or *Gifts Differing* (Myers, I. B., with Myers, P. B., 1995, Davies-Black® Publishing).

cpp 3803 East Bayshore Road · Palo Alto, California 94303 · 800-624-1765 · www.cpp.com   6134

(Continued)

Figure 9.1 (Continued)

mbti STEP I / REPORT FORM **FORM M**

CHARACTERISTICS FREQUENTLY ASSOCIATED WITH EACH TYPE

	Sensing Types		Intuitive Types	
Introverts	**ISTJ** Quiet, serious, earn success by thoroughness and dependability. Practical, matter-of-fact, realistic, and responsible. Decide logically what should be done and work toward it steadily, regardless of distractions. Take pleasure in making everything orderly and organized—their work, their home, their life. Value traditions and loyalty.	**ISFJ** Quiet, friendly, responsible, and conscientious. Committed and steady in meeting their obligations. Thorough, painstaking, and accurate. Loyal, considerate, notice and remember specifics about people who are important to them, concerned with how others feel. Strive to create an orderly and harmonious environment at work and at home.	**INFJ** Seek meaning and connection in ideas and relationships, and material possessions. Want to understand what motivates people and are insightful about others. Conscientious and committed to their firm values. Develop a clear vision about how best to serve the common good. Organized and decisive in implementing their vision.	**INTJ** Have original minds and great drive for implementing their ideas and achieving their goals. Quickly see patterns in external events and develop long-range explanatory perspectives. When committed, organize a job and carry it through. Skeptical and independent, have high standards of competence and performance for themselves and others.
Introverts	**ISTP** Tolerant and flexible, quiet observers until a problem appears, then act quickly to find workable solutions. Analyze what makes things work and readily get through large amounts of data to isolate the core of practical problems. Interested in cause and effect, organize facts using logical principles, value efficiency.	**ISFP** Quiet, friendly, sensitive, and kind. Enjoy the present moment, what's going on around them. Like to have their own space and to work within their own time frame. Loyal and committed to their values and to people who are important to them. Dislike disagreements and conflicts, do not force their opinions or values on others.	**INFP** Idealistic, loyal to their values and to people who are important to them. Want an external life that is congruent with their values. Curious, quick to see possibilities, can be catalysts for implementing ideas. Seek to understand people and to help them fulfill their potential. Adaptable, flexible, and accepting unless a value is threatened.	**INTP** Seek to develop logical explanations for everything that interests them. Theoretical and abstract, interested more in ideas than in social interaction. Quiet, contained, flexible, and adaptable. Have unusual ability to focus in depth to solve problems in their area of interest. Skeptical, sometimes critical, always analytical.
Extraverts	**ESTP** Flexible and tolerant, they take a pragmatic approach focused on immediate results. Theories and conceptual explanations bore them—they want to act energetically to solve the problem. Focus on the here-and-now, spontaneous, enjoy each moment that they can be active with others. Enjoy material comforts and style. Learn best through doing.	**ESFP** Outgoing, friendly, and accepting. Exuberant lovers of life, people, and material comforts. Enjoy working with others to make things happen. Bring common sense and a realistic approach to work, and make work fun. Flexible and spontaneous, adapt readily to new people and environments. Learn best by trying a new skill with other people.	**ENFP** Warmly enthusiastic and imaginative. See life as full of possibilities. Make connections between events and information very quickly, and confidently proceed based on the patterns they see. Want a lot of affirmation from others, and readily give appreciation and support. Spontaneous and flexible, often rely on their ability to improvise and their verbal fluency.	**ENTP** Quick, ingenious, stimulating, alert, and outspoken. Resourceful in solving new and challenging problems. Adept at generating conceptual possibilities and then analyzing them strategically. Good at reading other people. Bored by routine, will seldom do the same thing the same way, apt to turn to one new interest after another.
Extraverts	**ESTJ** Practical, realistic, matter-of-fact. Decisive, quickly move to implement decisions. Organize projects and people to get things done, focus on getting results in the most efficient way possible. Take care of routine details. Have a clear set of logical standards, systematically follow them and want others to also. Forceful in implementing their plans.	**ESFJ** Warmhearted, conscientious, and cooperative. Want harmony in their environment, work with determination to establish it. Like to work with others to complete tasks accurately and on time. Loyal, follow through even in small matters. Notice what others need in their day-to-day lives and try to provide it. Want to be appreciated for who they are and for what they contribute.	**ENFJ** Warm, empathetic, responsive, and responsible. Highly attuned to the emotions, needs, and motivations of others. Find potential in everyone, want to help others fulfill their potential. May act as catalysts for individual and group growth. Loyal, responsive to praise and criticism. Sociable, facilitate others in a group, and provide inspiring leadership.	**ENTJ** Frank, decisive, assume leadership readily. Quickly see illogical and inefficient procedures and policies, develop and implement comprehensive systems to solve organizational problems. Enjoy long-term planning and goal setting. Usually well informed, well read, enjoy expanding their knowledge and passing it on to others. Forceful in presenting their ideas.

07 06 05 04 15 14 13 12 11 10

Source: Myers-Briggs Type Indicator Report Form-Form M by Isabel Briggs Myers. Copyright 1998 by Peter B. Myers and Katharine D. Myers. All rights reserved.

Table 9.2 MBTI Form M and Form Q

	Form M	Form Q
Released	1998	2001
Items	93 forced-choice questions; includes Item Response Theory (IRT)	144 forced-choice questions; includes IRT
Duration	15–25 minutes	25–30 minutes
Age-appropriate	14 and older, seventh-grade reading level	18 and older

of the facets over a long period of time, ranging from .44 (Questioning-Accommodating, > 1-year interval) to .88 (Expressive-Contained, > 1-year interval). *Note*: Questioning-Accommodating falls under the T-F facet scale while Expressive-Contained falls under the E-I facet scales. The test-retest reliabilities were also compared to other tests, including the 16PF and showed that the internal consistency was comparable to other personality assessments. Construct validity was reported in detail by comparing the assessment with seven other assessments, which showed expected relationships with other instruments (Schaubhut & Thompson, 2011). Table 9.2 highlights the similarities and differences between the two forms.

The MBTI provides assessment of an individual's personality type and preference and does not measure pathology. No type or individual preferences should be considered "good" or "bad" or "correct" or "incorrect." Instead, the individual preferences and types highlight differences and provide insight into individuals' learning styles (Bolliger & Erichsen, 2013), occupational matches (Bradley-Geist & Landis, 2012), and leadership style (Bahreinian, Ahi, & Soltani, 2012), among other factors. Consequently, this insight can be useful in various settings, including by couples counselors in evaluating compatibility and developing necessary strategies of compromise, individual counselors in gaining insight into the potential drivers for perceived issues, career counselors in evaluating appropriate job fits, and corporate consultants in determining the most effective leaders.

With high reliability estimates across facets, a relatively short time to administer, and the ability for counselors with a minimum of a master's degree in counseling or a related field to administer it, the MBTI is an appealing choice for many practitioners. Optimally, it should be utilized to support individuals in better understanding their behaviors as well as the behaviors of others. As a result of this knowledge, individuals are able to establish strategies to effectively work with others. As with any instrument, however, the MBTI should not be used in isolation to make any substantial decisions and should instead serve as a tool to guide and inform decisions. In Guided Practice Exercise 9.2 you are given the opportunity to take an assessment based on the Myers Briggs Type Indicator and to process your report.

GUIDED PRACTICE EXERCISE 9.2

Prior to class, go to the HumanMetrics website www.humanmetrics.com/cgi-win/jtypes2.asp. It contains a free personality assessment based on the Myers Briggs Type Indicator. It contains 72 forced-choice yes/no questions. When you click "submit," the assessment will give you a four-letter type, similar to that of the Myers Briggs assessment. The website will also give you a report of your strengths and preferences and a description of your basic personality traits. As an added bonus, this version also will give you career ideas based on your personality type. After you take the assessment, review your results. Did your results surprise you? Why or why not? Were any of the suggested career paths some that you had considered previously? Be prepared to discuss your results and experiences in small groups or with the entire class.

Sixteen Personality Factor (16PF)

The **Sixteen Personality Factor (16PF), Fifth Edition,** developed through factor analysis by Raymond B. Cattell and his colleagues, is widely used to measure normal adult personality. The first edition was published in 1949 and since then has undergone four revisions; the most recent revision, the fifth, occurred in 1993. Over 45 years ago, Cattell and his colleagues measured personality by creating an extensive list of adjectives commonly used to describe people. They then asked participants to rate others close to them based on this list. Through factor analysis, Cattell discovered 16 factors that he considered to be the basic elements of personality. If you recall from Chapter 4, factor analysis is a statistical method that is used to discover in a large set of variables a smaller subset of variables that explains the entire domain. These primary factors which correspond to letters A–O and Q1–Q4 on the individual record form are warmth, reasoning, emotional stability, dominance, liveliness, rule-consciousness, social boldness, sensitivity, vigilance, abstractedness, privateness, apprehension, openness to change, self-reliance, perfectionism, and tension. In addition, Cattell factor analyzed the 16 personality factors and discovered four global factors: extraversion, anxiety, tough-mindedness, independence, and self-control. For example, if you look at the global factor Independence on the Record Form (Figure 9.2) and follow the column up, you will notice it is composed of the following primary factors: E: Dominance, H: Social Boldness, L: Vigilance, Q1: Openness to Change. Global factors can be used to describe personality on a broader level compared to the primary factors. See Table 9.3 for the primary factors that make up the global factors. *Note:* The negative sign (-) means scoring low, and the plus sign (+) means scoring high. For example, scoring high (+) on dominance (factor E) contributes to the Independence Global Factor Score, while scoring low (-) on emotional stability contributes to the Anxiety Global Score.

The 16PF assessment is composed of 185 items and is appropriate for ages 16 and older. There are approximately 10–15 questions per factor. Test questions 1–170 have a three-choice response with the middle question always as a question mark (?). For example, "I tend to be too sensitive and worry too much about something I've done": a. hardly ever, b. ?, and c. often. The remaining questions (171–185), referring to Factor B: Reason, have all three

Figure 9.2 16PF Score Report

IPAT

16PF® Fifth Edition Individual Record Form
Profile Sheet

Name

Date

Instructions: Write the sten score for each factor in the second column. Starting with Factor A, place a mark over the spot representing the appropriate sten score. Repeat for each factor. Connect the marks with straight lines.

PRIMARY FACTORS

Factor	Sten	Left Meaning	Standard Ten Score (STEN) 1 2 3 4 5 6 7 8 9 10 (Average 4–7)	Right Meaning
A: Warmth	6	Reserved, Impersonal, Distant		Warm, Outgoing, Attentive to Others
B: Reasoning	6	Concrete		Abstract
C: Emotional Stability	8	Reactive, Emotionally Changeable		Emotionally Stable, Adaptive, Mature
E: Dominance	3	Deferential, Cooperative, Avoids Conflict		Dominant, Forceful, Assertive
F: Liveliness	5	Serious, Restrained, Careful		Lively, Animated, Spontaneous
G: Rule-Consciousness	6	Expedient, Nonconforming		Rule-Conscious, Dutiful
H: Social Boldness	6	Shy, Threat-Sensitive, Timid		Socially Bold, Venturesome, Thick-Skinned
I: Sensitivity	6	Utilitarian, Objective, Unsentimental		Sensitive, Aesthetic, Sentimental
L: Vigilance	5	Trusting, Unsuspecting, Accepting		Vigilant, Suspicious, Skeptical, Wary
M: Abstractedness	4	Grounded, Practical, Solution-Oriented		Abstracted, Imaginative, Idea-Oriented
N: Privateness	4	Forthright, Genuine, Artless		Private, Discreet, Non-Disclosing
O: Apprehension	6	Self-Assured, Unworried, Complacent		Apprehensive, Self-Doubting, Worried
Q_1: Openness to Change	7	Traditional, Attached to Familiar		Open to Change, Experimenting
Q_2: Self-Reliance	7	Group-Oriented, Affiliative		Self-Reliant, Solitary, Individualistic
Q_3: Perfectionism	5	Tolerates Disorder, Unexacting, Flexible		Perfectionistic, Organized, Self-Disciplined
Q_4: Tension	5	Relaxed, Placid, Patient		Tense, High Energy, Impatient, Driven

GLOBAL FACTORS

Factor	Sten	Left Meaning	1 2 3 4 5 6 7 8 9 10 (Average 4–7)	Right Meaning
EX: Extraversion	6	Introverted, Socially Inhibited		Extraverted, Socially Participating
AX: Anxiety	4	Low Anxiety, Unperturbed		High Anxiety, Perturbable
TM: Tough-Mindedness	5	Receptive, Open-Minded, Intuitive		Tough-Minded, Resolute, Unempathic
IN: Independence	5	Accommodating, Agreeable, Selfless		Independent, Persuasive, Willful
SC: Self-Control	6	Unrestrained, Follows Urges		Self-Controlled, Inhibits Urges

Source: Copyright 1993 by the Institute for Personality and Ability Testing.

Table 9.3 16PF Global Factors and Contributing Primary Factors

Extraversion	A: Warmth
	B: Liveliness
	H: Social Boldness
	N: Privateness (-)
	Q2: Self-reliance (-)
Independence	E: Dominance
	H: Social Boldness
	L: Vigilance
	Q1: Openness to Change
Tough-mindedness	A: Warmth (-)
	I: Sensitivity (-)
	M: Abstractedness (-)
	Q1: Openness to Change (-)
Self-control	F: Liveliness (-)
	G: Rule-Consciousness
	M: Abstractedness (-)
	Q3: Perfectionism
Anxiety	C: Emotional Stability (-)
	L: Vigilance
	O: Apprehension
	Q4: Tension

choices and no ? option. The test is untimed but on average takes 35–50 minutes by pencil and 25–35 minutes by computer and can be administered individually or in a group.

Now take a look at the 16PF Fifth Edition Individual Record Form (Figure 9.2). You will notice that the 16 primary factors and 5 global factors fall on a bipolar continuum (left meaning and right meaning) with Standard Ten Scores (sten) ranging from 1 to 10. Sten scores have a mean of 5.5 and standard deviation of 2. Stens of 4–7 are considered within the average range, stens of 1–3 in low range, and stens of 8–10 in high range. Recall from Chapter 2 that plus or minus one standard deviation is equal to 68% of the population. Thus, it is expected that 68% of the population falls between 3.5 and 7.5 sten.

To score the 16PF, you convert the 16 raw primary personality factors into sten scores and the Impression Management (IM) index into a percentile. Next, you calculate the

5 global factor sten scores. Finally, you profile the sten scores for both the primary factors and global factors. The manual suggests interpreting the results in the following order: Evaluate response style indices to check for atypical test response styles, examine global factor scales to obtain a broad picture, and evaluate the primary scales to gain details of the personality (Russell & Karol, 2002).

The results of the 16PF are compared to a large group that completed the survey and describes the examinee's likely style. One should note that there is no "bad" or "good" or "right" or "wrong" in personality. The results of the 16PF can serve as a good predictor of how people will act or behave in a variety of sessions. It is important to understand that the results are based on the examinees' description of their own personality, thus the accuracy is dependent on the examinees' self-awareness.

Gracie, a 33-year-old female, recently applied and was accepted for a new position at work. As part of the selection and assessment process, she was asked to complete the 16PF. The 16PF is useful to managers in developing and motivating people and can help Gracie achieve personal insight into her strengths, potential, and career fit. Look at Figure 9.2, Gracie's score report on the 16PF. First, looking at the global factors, we can see Gracie scored within average for all 5 global factors (Extraversion: 6, Self-Control: 6, Tough-Mindedness: 5, Independence: 5, Anxiety: 4). The first profile for an examinee's scores usually consists of his or her most extreme global factor along with primary traits. Notice how Gracie obtained a low average score for the global factor Anxiety. For the 16PF Anxiety is defined as emotional adjustment, and the types and intensity of emotions experienced. Let's take a look at Table 9.4, Gracie's scores on the primary factors that contribute to Anxiety.

At the present time, Gracie describes herself as being less anxious than most people. This could reflect a characteristic of a calm style or it could reflect the behavior in the absence of significant pressures. It appears Gracie meets challenges with inner strength and feels in control of life's current demands. She generally trusts other people unless she sees a reason not to. Reflecting on her Apprehension sten score, she is more likely to doubt herself or be self-critical than most people. She generally appears composed, but demonstrates enough sense of urgency to be able to meet demands placed on her.

If we now look at individual primary factors, we notice that Gracie's Emotional Stability (C) sten score was reported at an 8. Emotional Stability refers to feelings about coping with

Table 9.4   Primary Contributing Factors of Global Factor: Anxiety

Primary Contributing Factor	Sten Score
Emotional Stability (C)	8
Vigilance (L)	5
Apprehension (O)	6
Tension (Q4)	5

day-to-day life, with high scores taking life in stride. According to Russell and Karol (2002), an "extremely high score on this scale can indicate that an examinee may be strongly disinclined to report, or even to experience, so-called negative feelings" (p. 44). Presenting ourselves as able to cope is considered socially desirable, thus in a future session the counselor may want to address whether the examinee denied any problems in order to present favorably.

Gracie's lowest sten score was for the primary factor Dominance (E = 3). Her score reflects Deference (accommodating others' wishes) rather than Dominance (exerting one's will over others). Low scores tend to mean people avoid conflict, set aside their wishes and feelings, and are more cooperative than assertive (Russell & Karol, 2002). If you recall, the contributing factors for the global factor Independence are Dominance (E+), Social Boldness (H+), Vigilance (L+), and Openness to Change (Q1+), with Dominance (E+) being the strongest contributor to the Independence Scale.

Scores on the 16PF can also provide valuable predictions on self-esteem and adjustment, social skills, and leadership and creativity. These fall under the Criterion Scores section of the manual in which interpretive comments are generated from prediction equations of criterion scores. For example, Leadership Potential is characterized by extraversion and low anxiety and is predicted by the factors Reasoning (B+), Emotional Stability (C+), Dominance (E+), Liveliness (F+), Social Boldness (H+), low Sensitivity (I-), low Abstractedness (M-), low Self-Reliance (Q2-), Perfectionism (Q3+), and low Tension (Q4-). Table 9.5 presents Gracie's calculated criterion scores. Her Emotional Sensitivity (ES) score was high average, which is predicted by the 16PF factors of Warmth (A+) and Openness to Change (Q1+). According to Russell and Karol (2002), "high (ES) scores are skilled in receiving nonverbal communications. They excel at interpreting emotional cues as they continually analyze other people's gestures, feelings, and interactions" (p. 111).

Table 9.5 Gracie's Criterion Score on 16PF

Self-Esteem and Adjustment

- Self-Esteem is average (6)
- Emotional Adjustment is average (6)
- Social Adjustment is average (6)

Social Skills

- Emotional Expressivity is average (5)
- Emotional Sensitivity is high average (7)
- Emotional Control is average (5)

- Social Expressivity is average (6)
- Social Sensitivity is average (6)
- Social Control is average (5)
- Empathy is average (6)

Leadership and Creativity

- Leadership Potential is average (6)
- Creative Potential is average (5)
- Creative Achievement is average (5)

The norm group for the 16PF consisted of a sample size of 10,261 (5,124 males and 5,137 females) ranging in age from 16 to 82, with a mean of 32.7 years (Russell & Karol, 2002). Internal consistency coefficient alpha reliabilities were reported as .76 (average), with a range of .68 to .87. Test-retest reliability after 2 weeks was reported as an average of .80. The manual thoroughly discusses construct, criterion, and convergent validity.

Case Illustration 9.2 shows how a counselor can incorporate the results of the 16PF to help a couple achieve their goal of determining areas of compatibility and potential conflict in order to give them the most positive start to their upcoming marriage.

CASE ILLUSTRATION 9.2

Donovan is a marriage, couples, and family counselor. One of the couples he counsels, Li Mei and Cheng, are being proactive in their relationship and have come to him for premarital counseling. Li Mei and Cheng want to identify potential differences in values, beliefs, and personality that might present a challenge to a successful marriage. They want to work on these issues prior to getting married. To facilitate this goal, Donovan administers the 16PF to them. Donovan chose this particular assessment because it takes only 35–50 minutes to administer and provides a Couples Counseling Report as an option that he can easily share with Li Mei and Cheng. The 16PF was also written at the fifth-grade level, which makes it easier for individuals for whom English is a second language. While Li Mei was born as a U.S. citizen and has lived in the United States for a long time, Cheng has recently immigrated to the United States and he is still working on his English language skills. If needed, Donovan can also obtain the version of the 16PF that has been translated into Chinese. The 16PF will easily identify areas of compatibility, areas of strengths for each person, and areas where potential conflict might originate. For example, Cheng scored high in Dominance, indicating he might be more dominant, forceful, and assertive than Li Mei, who scored low on this scale. However, because Li Mei scored low, it is more likely that she will be deferential and cooperative, and will avoid conflict with Cheng. She will likely not mind Cheng's leadership as compared to someone who also scored high on Dominance. On the other hand, Li Mei scored high in Sensitivity and Cheng scored low. So while Li Mei is likely to be sensitive, sentimental, and tender-minded, Cheng is more apt to be tough-minded and take a no-nonsense stance. This could pose a potential conflict for the couple that could be highlighted once they begin living together after getting married. Donovan will use the results of the 16PF to help this couple achieve their goal of determining areas of compatibility and potential conflict in order to give them the most positive start to their impending marriage.

Although administration of both the MBTI and 16PF would be ideal to provide the most comprehensive establishment of personality, the opportunity to administer both may not be available. Decisions regarding the administration of the 16PF over the MBTI include the 16PF's applicability to a population with lower reading levels (i.e., fifth grade as opposed to seventh grade), multitiered investigation of personality, translation into 20 languages, and availability of separate reports (e.g., client, practitioner, employer). Still, the MBTI is often chosen due to the simplified grouping of individuals into 16 categories. Guided Practice Exercise 9.3 allows you to reflect on and compare your results from two different personality assessments based on the Big Five personality factors.

GUIDED PRACTICE EXERCISE 9.3

Prior to class, go to this website that offers the Big Five Personality Test: www.outofservice.com/bigfive. This is another free personality assessment, based on the Big Five personality factors. When you get your results, compare them to your results from the Myers Briggs assessment you did earlier. What did you learn from this assessment that was new or different from what you learned from the previous one? Did any of the results surprise you? Why or why not? Do you disagree with anything you learned from this assessment? What were the benefits of taking both assessments? Be prepared to discuss your results and experiences in small groups or with the entire class.

The NEO Inventories

Over the years, researchers using factor analysis have found that personality can be described by five factors. The **NEO inventories** are based on the five-factor model of personality known as the **Big Five**. The five factors or domains are neuroticism, extraversion, openness, agreeableness, and conscientiousness. Each factor includes six subscales known as facets (30 facets total), which provide a comprehensive assessment of adolescent and adult personality. In Figure 9.3 you will notice the five domains listed on the left. Each domain is then broken down into facets on the right. For example, Neuroticism is composed of the following facets: Anxiety, Angry Hostility, Depression, Self-Consciousness, Impulsiveness, and Vulnerability. Table 9.6 provides a brief summary of the five domains. The manual provides detailed information for the facet scores, which is useful for interpreting constructs and formulating theories.

The current versions of the NEO Inventories are the **NEO Personality Inventory-3 (NEO-PI-3)**, the **Revised NEO Personality Inventory (NEO PI-R)**, and the short version, the **NEO Five-Factor Inventory-3 (NEO-FFI-3)**. All NEO inventories consist of two versions: Form S (self-report item booklet) and Form R (observer rating booklet). Form S is answered by the examinee while Form R is the companion instrument with items written in third person for peer, spouse, or expert ratings (McCrae & Costa, 2010). Both the NEO-PI-3 and NEO PI-R contain 240 statements based on a 5-point Likert Scale from *strongly disagree* to *strongly agree*. The NEO-PI-3 is a modification of the NEO PI-R in which 37 of the 240 items have been replaced to improve psychometric properties. The assessment is appropriate for ages 12 years and older. The assessment can be individually or group-administered and takes approximately 30–40 minutes to complete. Raw scores can easily be converted to T scores for each domain and facet on the profile forms (see Figure 9.3). T scores have a mean of 50 and standard deviation of 10. A one-sheet NEO Summary Form (see Figure 9.4) can be used to report the results of the NEO-PI-3,

Table 9.6   NEO Five Domains

Domain	Basic Definitions
Neuroticism (N)	General tendency to experience fear, sadness, embarrassment, anger, and disgust; high scores indicate being prone to irrational ideas, being unable to control impulses, coping poorly with stress; low scorers indicate calm, relaxed, emotionally stable
Extraversion (E)	Sociable, prefers large groups, active, talkative
Openness to Experience (O)	Attends to inner feelings, intellectually curious, prefers variety, entertains novel ideas and unconventional values; low scores indicate often being conventional in behavior and conservative in outlook
Agreeableness (A)	Altruistic, sympathetic to others, eager to help; low scorers indicate being disagreeable, egocentric, questioning intention, competitive
Conscientiousness (C)	Purposeful, determined, strong-willed; high scores indicate being punctual and reliable, associated with academic and occupational achievement

NEO PI-R, or NEO-FFI-3 to the examinee in understandable terms. Case Illustration 9.3 provides a description of the NEO-PI-3, Form R and the NEO Summary sheet.

The NEO-FFI-3 is a shorter version consisting of 60 items (five 12-item scales that measure each domain) appropriate for age 12 years and older. McCrae and Costa (2010) note that the NEO-FFI-3 scales are less reliable and valid compared to the NEO-PI-3 scales.

The manual reported to evaluate reliability by using internal consistency. Internal consistency for NEO-PI-3 Form S ranged from .89 to .93 for the five domains and .54 to .83 for the 30 facets. Due to the recent revisions, no test-retest reliability and direct evidence of construct validity was reported in the NEO-PI-3 manual. However, it should be noted that adequate construct validity evidence (both convergent and discriminant) is reported in the NEO PI-R manual, and the NEO-PI-3 maintains the validity of the NEO PI-R.

According to Rossier, Meyer de Stadelhofen, and Berthoud (2004), both the 16PF and NEO inventories measure similar components of personality, noting that the only significant difference was that Agreeable was not represented in the 16PF. Consequently, the major difference between the 16PF and NEO inventories lies in whether the counselor or administrator wishes to take the top-down approach of the NEO or the bottom-up approach of the 16PF. Despite the potential usefulness of the NEO, there is a limited normative data across populations, making the results too general and less applicable to its intended purposes (Lahti et al., 2013). Categorical labels such as *depression* have also been established as potentially problematic as they may be inappropriately related to clinical diagnosis. As a result, administrators must evaluate the strengths and limitations of using each test with their targeted population in order to make an informed decision. Administration of both measures, however, will provide the most comprehensive picture of the client's personality.

Figure 9.3 NEO-PI-3 Score Report

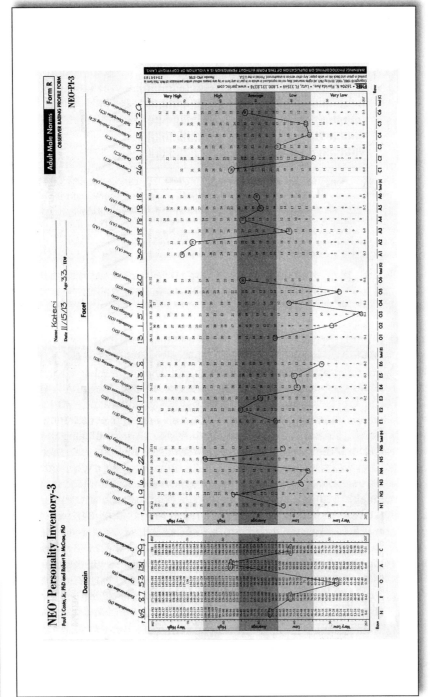

Source: Reproduced by special permission of the Publisher, Psychological Assessment Resources, Inc., 16204 North Florida Avenue, Lutz, Florida 33549, from the NEOTM by Paul T. Costa Jr., PhD and Robert R. McCrae, PhD, Copyright 1987, 1989, 1991, 2010 by Psychological Assessment Resources, Inc. (PAR). Further reproduction is prohibited without permission of PAR.

Figure 9.4 NEO-PI-3 Figure

Your NEO™ Summary

Paul T. Costa, Jr., PhD and Robert R. McCrae, PhD

The NEO Inventory measures five broad domains, or dimensions, of personality. Responses describing your thoughts, feelings, and goals can be compared with those describing others' to portray your personality.

This summary is intended to give you a general idea of what your personality is like. It is not a detailed report. If you completed the inventory again, or if someone else described you, you might score somewhat differently.

The NEO Inventory measures differences among people in general. It is not a test of intelligence or ability, and it is not intended to diagnose problems of mental health or adjustment. It does, however, give you some idea of what makes you unique in your ways of thinking, feeling, and interacting with others.

Compared with the responses of other people, your responses suggest that you can be described as:

☐ Sensitive, emotional, and prone to experience feelings that are upsetting.	☑ Generally calm and able to deal with stress, but you sometimes experience feelings of guilt, anger, or sadness.	☐ Secure, hardy, and generally relaxed, even under stressful conditions.
☐ Extraverted, outgoing, active, and high-spirited. You prefer to be around people most of the time.	☐ Moderate in activity and enthusiasm. You enjoy the company of others, but you also value privacy.	☑ Introverted, reserved, and serious. You prefer to be alone or with a few close friends.
☐ Open to new experiences. You have broad interests and are very imaginative.	☐ Practical, but willing to consider new ways of doing things. You seek a balance between the old and the new.	☑ Down-to-earth, practical, traditional, and pretty much set in your ways.
☑ Compassionate, good-natured, and eager to cooperate and avoid conflict.	☐ Generally warm, trusting, and agreeable, but you can sometimes be stubborn and competitive.	☐ Hardheaded, skeptical, proud, and competitive. You tend to express your anger directly.
☐ Conscientious and well-organized. You have high standards and always strive to achieve your goals.	☐ Dependable and moderately well-organized. You generally have clear goals, but are able to set your work aside.	☑ Easygoing, not very well-organized, and sometimes careless. You prefer not to make plans.

PAR • 16204 N. Florida Ave. • Lutz, FL 33549 • 1.800.331.8378 • www.parinc.com

Source: Reproduced by special permission of the Publisher, Psychological Assessment Resources, Inc., 16204 North Florida Avenue, Lutz, Florida 33549, from the NEOTM by Paul T. Costa Jr., PhD and Robert R. McCrae, PhD, Copyright 1987, 1989, 1991, 2010 by Psychological Assessment Resources, Inc. (PAR). Further reproduction is prohibited without permission of PAR.

CASE ILLUSTRATION   9.3

Kateri is a 33-year-old Native American woman from the Mohawk tribe who had lived on the Saint Regis Mohawk Reservation in New York for 29 of her 33 years. Four years ago while working at the tribe's Akwesasne Mohawk Casino, Kateri met Juan. It was "love at first sight" for both of them. Juan was 43, worked as a general contractor, and self-identified as Mexican and "staunchly Catholic." The couple began dating and a year later on the anniversary of the day they met, they married.

The first 3 years of their marriage was "blissful" according to Kateri, but then the couple began to have some difficulty bridging their two cultures. Kateri was still very active on her reservation and maintained many of her ancestors' spiritual and cultural beliefs. Initially, Juan was fascinated by Kateri's culture, but when Kateri gave birth to their first child, it became evident to both of them that their beliefs and values about raising children were very different.

This clash became very evident when it was time to baptize the baby in Juan's Catholic cultural tradition, but the timing fell during the Mohawk winter ceremony. Kateri was expected by her family to be on the reservation for the full 5 days of the ceremony as she always had been. In the Mohawk culture, the birth of children and their subsequent birthdays are not celebrated; however, the Mohawk do celebrate the changing of the seasons.

Juan could not understand how celebrating the changing of the seasons could be more important than the baptism of their child. Another important conflict between Kateri and Juan was the role of "head of household." Mexican culture is patrilineal and the male is the head of household, but in Mohawk culture the female leads the household and the Mohawk is a matrilineal society. Becoming new parents brought out important cultural and religious preferences that neither had discussed before, and as each clung to his or her ways of doing things, communication began to break down between them.

Kateri became very distressed at this time and felt a lot of pressure trying to bridge the cultural divide between her family and their traditions and Juan's family and their expectations. The fourth year of their marriage produced a great deal of discord between the couple. Kateri tried to find compromises that would work for her family, but she perceived Juan as being stubborn and felt he was not accepting of any of her "Mohawk ways."

When talking to a co-worker who was neither Mohawk nor Mexican, the co-worker suggested that Kateri and Juan go to couples counseling to try to sort out these differences. When Kateri suggested it to Juan, he refused. However, when Kateri investigated couples counseling on the Internet, it was suggested that if both parties could not go, it would still be beneficial to the relationship for one person to go. So Kateri made an appointment for herself.

During the course of counseling, Kateri learned that if she changed the way she approached conflict resolution, communication, and the relationship, it would also impact the way that Juan approached the same issues. Kateri felt empowered by that opportunity. Her counselor suggested that Kateri take the NEO-PI-3, which could help Kateri gain some needed insights into Juan's personality and preferred way of dealing with the world. The counselor picked the NEO-PI-3, Form R, because Kateri could fill out the assessment based on her observations of Juan (see Figure 9.3). Therefore, Juan did not need to come to counseling. The NEO also provided a summary sheet (see Figure 9.4) that made it very easy for Kateri to understand the results.

The NEO-PI-3 measures the Big Five major domains of personality: neuroticism, extraversion, openness to experience, agreeableness, and conscientiousness. Each domain is composed of six facets.

Neuroticism	Extraversion	Openness	Agreeableness	Conscientiousness
Anxiety	Warmth	Fantasy	Trust	Competence
Anger Hostility	Gregariousness	Aesthetics	Straightforwardness	Order
Depression	Assertiveness	Feelings	Altruism	Dutifulness
Self-consciousness	Activity	Actions	Compliance	Achievement Striving
Impulsiveness	Excitement Seeking	Ideas	Modesty	Self-discipline
Vulnerability	Positive Emotions	Values	Tender-mindedness	Deliberation

The NEO-PI-3 compares the answers of the individual taking the assessment to the answers of the participants upon which it was normed. Compared to the norming group, the observations Kateri made for Juan could then fall into the average range, the low to very low range, or the high to very high range. Based on Kateri's observations, Juan scored high on the domain of Agreeableness, low on Extraversion and Conscientiousness, very low on Openness, and he scored in the average range for Neuroticism.

When looking at the facets that make up the domain of Neuroticism, Juan scored high for Anger Hostility and Impulsiveness. He also scored low in Anxiety, Depression, Self-consciousness, and Vulnerability. All other facets in this domain were in the average range for Juan. Under the domain of Extraversion, he scored low for the facets of Activity, Excitement Seeking, and Positive Emotions. All other facets in this domain were in the average range. For the domain of Openness, Juan scored very low in Aesthetics, Feelings, and Ideas. He scored low in Actions, and all the rest of the facets fell within the average range. For the domain of Agreeableness Juan had very high scores in Trust and Straightforwardness and a low score in Altruism, with all other facets falling in the average range. Finally, for the domain of Conscientiousness, Juan scored high in Competence and low in Dutifulness, Achievement Striving, and Self-discipline. He also scored very low in Order and average in Deliberation (see Figure 9.3).

When evaluating Juan's responses on each of the five domains and 30 facets, compared to other people who have taken the NEO-PI-3 and per Kateri's observations, he is typically a calm person who can easily handle stress, but in certain circumstances, possibly when in conflict with Kateri, Juan can experience feelings of guilt, anger, and sadness (see Figure 9.4). Also compared to others, Juan is more likely to prefer quiet social situations composed of just a few people and may prefer to spend a significant amount of time by himself. He is also most likely to be rigid and would prefer to stick to his own cultural traditions rather than try new things. Also compared to others, Juan is mostly likely to want to avoid conflict and may prefer to project himself as good-natured and compassionate. Finally, Juan may be perceived as someone who is too casual and spontaneous, rather than planful or organized.

Kateri felt from her perspective that the results of the NEO-PI-3 were accurate and Juan's profile resonated with her and potentially explained why he did not like to join her for her family and tribal celebrations or events. Perhaps there were too many people present that Juan did not know. It might

(Continued)

(Continued)

better suit Juan to bring him to smaller immediate family gatherings where he would feel more comfortable and be more likely to engage.

Kateri also gained insight that Juan really did not want to have conflict with her, but if he felt pushed, he would cling rigidly to his cultural traditions and be less open to compromise. A better approach to take with Juan might be to explore common ground between the two cultures to which they both could agree, and then wait for opportunities to approach Juan with other compromises when he was relaxed and more open to discussion. Kateri realized that she often approached Juan when he was tired from work or when a tribal event was imminent, rather than approaching him several weeks in advance. She realized that her timing for discussion did not allow Juan time to process what she was asking, therefore he felt pressured and then would cling to his traditions instead of being open to exploring hers. She also realized that she was not giving his culture enough serious consideration either and that compromise needed to happen on both sides. The last insight Kateri gleaned from this assessment was that Juan was spontaneous when he felt comfortable, such as with his culture and family, but for activities for which he was less familiar, such as her family and her culture, he would probably like more notice.

California Psychological Inventory (CPI) and California Psychological Inventory 260

Originally published in 1956, The **California Psychological Inventory**, now in its third edition, was constructed by the criterion method and half of the items were drawn or revised from the MMPI (Gough & Bradley, 2002). The developer, Harrison Gough, constructed the CPI for assessing "normal" individuals and wanted to measure what he referred to as "folk concepts" which are defined as "the kind of everyday variables that ordinary people use in their daily lives to understand, classify, and predict their own behavior and that of others" (Gough, 1987, p. 1).

The objective was to diagnose and better understand interpersonal behavior (e.g., self-control, independence) in the general population. In comparison to the MMPI, which assesses maladjustment and clinical diagnosis, the scales on the CPI are designed to measure more normal characteristics of personality and emphasize positive aspects of personality in ages 13 and older. The CPI continues to be widely used among adolescents and adults and is successful in predicting behavior, success, and social reputation.

The CPI consists of 434 true/false items and measures 20 Folk Scales. These subscales are grouped into four independent themes referred to as clusters/classes: (a) poise and self-assurance, (b) normative orientation and values, (c) cognitive and intellectual functioning, and (d) role and personal style. See Table 9.7 for a description of what each class was designed to measure and Folk Scales that fall under each class. T scores are reported at a mean of 50 and standard deviation of 10. Scores of 60 or more indicate psychological health and scores of 40 and below refer to psychological inadequacy.

Gough created three vectors based on factor analysis: Vector 1: internality versus externality, Vector 2: norm favoring versus norm questioning, and Vector 3: self-realization

Table 9.7 California Psychological Inventory Clusters

Class	Folk Scales
Class I: Poise and self-assurance	Dominance (Do) Capacity for Status (Cs) Sociability (Sy) Social Presence (Sp) Self-acceptance (Sa) Independence (In) Empathy (Em)
Class II: Normative orientation and values	Responsibility (Re) Socialization (So) Self-control (Sc) Good Impression (Gi) Communality (Cm) Well-being (Wb) Tolerance (To)
Class III: Cognitive and intellectual functioning	Achievement via Conformance (Ac) Achievement via Independence (Ai) Intellectual Efficiency (Ie)
Class IV: Role and personal style	Psychological Mindedness (Py) Flexibility (Fx) Femininity/Masculinity(F/M)

versus self-actualization. Vectors 1 and 2 assess personality type, and Vector 3 assesses personality adjustment. Once scores are computed for all the Folk Scales and the vectors, they are plotted on a grid to determine personality type. The grid consists of two axes: Vector 1 scale on the x axis is the degree to which an individual is internally or externally focused, and Vector 2 on the y axis is the degree to which the examinee favors or questions the norm. These two vectors form four quadrants, which describe a person's personality type: (a) Alphas (e.g., ambitious, outgoing), (b) Beta (e.g., cautious, conventional), (c) Gamma (e.g., adventurous, progressive), and (d) Delta (e.g., reflective, quiet, reserved). Vector 3 is used to assess the degree to which a person has developed an integrated sense of self-realization or authenticity. It is used to provide additional meaning to the personality types identified in Vectors 1 and 2 by describing how well the person has fully integrated these types and become a more self-realized and satisfied individual. In totality, these three vectors provide insight to the client and counselor on how a person thinks, feels, and behaves in a way he or she is comfortable with.

The CPI has been widely researched for over 50 years. It was normed on 6,000 males and 6,000 females. The alpha coefficients for the Folk Scales were reported at .73 for women and .72 for men. Test-retest reliability was reported to range from .51 to .84 after

1 year. Although the CPI continues to be widely used, it has been criticized for its high intercorrelations between the scales.

The **California Psychological Inventory 260** is a shorter version of the CPI that is often used in leadership development and management training programs. The assessment measures four ways of living and levels of satisfaction in each style: implementer lifestyle, supporter lifestyle, innovator lifestyle, and visualizer lifestyle. Scores on 26 measures are grouped into five broad categories: dealing with others, self-management, motivation and thinking style, personal characteristics, and work-related measures. For example, the broad category Dominance measures Dominance (Do), Capacity for Status (Cs), Sociability (Sy), Social Presence (Sp), Self-acceptance (Sa), Independence (In), and Empathy (Em). See Table 9.8 for the 26 characteristics measured across all of the categories.

Table 9.8 California Psychological Inventory 260 Categories and Characteristics Measured

Category	Characteristic Measuring
Dealing With Others	• Dominance (Do) • Capacity for Status (Cs) • Sociability (Sy) • Social Presence (Sp) • Self-acceptance (Sa) • Independence (In) • Empathy (Em)
Self-Management	• Responsibility (Re) • Social Conformity (So) • Self-control (Sc) • Good Impression (Gi) • Communality (Cm) • Tolerance (To)
Motivation and Thinking Style	• Achievement via Conformance (Ac) • Achievement via Independence (Ai) • Conceptual Fluency (Cf)
Personal Characteristics	• Insightfulness (Is) • Flexibility (Fx) • Sensitivity (Sn)
Work-Related Styles	• Managerial Potential (Mp) • Work Orientation (Wo) • Creative Temperament (Ct) • Leadership (Lp) • Amicability (Ami) • Law Enforcement Orientation (Leo)

These measures are reported in standardized scores, ranging from 0 to 100, with a mean of 50 and standard deviation of 10, with higher or lower scales signifying one's temperament and behavior.

Capacity for Status (Cs)

0—10—20—30—40—50—60—70—80—90—100

∧   ∧

For example, on the Cs scale from 0 to 100, those closer to 0 can be described as non-assertive, uncomfortable exerting authority, hesitant in making decisions, and unassuming behavior. In contrast, those closer to 100 like to be in charge and are self-confident, persuasive, and task-centered.

A Lifestyle Diagram is then created to provide information on how a person views himself or herself in each lifestyle and how others view that person. See Figure 9.5.

Overall the CPI 260 is a useful personality assessment in measuring clients' dealings with others, self-management, motivations and thinking styles, personal characteristics, and work-related characteristics. Similar to the aforementioned personality tests, the CPI is most appropriately used with normal functioning individuals and should be avoided as a measure of dysfunction. Administrators of personality tests are likely to choose the CPI due to its broad-ranging questions and ability to obtain a wide array of information. Despite this ability to address various aspects of everyday life, Soto and John (2009) note that research has uncovered the inability of the CPI to cover all of the five personality dimensions, noting that additional questions associated with these dimensions are necessary in addition to the already established questions. Furthermore, Soto and John caution that the presence of a true/false dichotomy reduces the variability which can be established within the dimensions. Evaluating the potential effects of these strengths and limitations is therefore necessary in deciding which one to administer.

Millon Index of Personality Styles Revised (MIPS Revised) and Millon Adolescent Personality Inventory (MAPI)

The **Millon Index of Personality Styles-Revised** (MIPS Revised) is used with individuals 18 and older to assess different personality styles among normal functioning adults who may experience difficulties in work, family, or social relationships (Millon, 2003). Originally designed in 1994 and then revised in 2003, the MIPS Revised has been used in a variety of settings, such as career planning, marriage counseling, individual counseling, and leadership development programs. The test is grounded in evolution and psychoanalytic, Jungian, and interpersonal and social theories. The MIPS Revised correlates with previously discussed personality assessments, including the 16PF, CPI, NEO-PI, and MMPI-2. Moderate internal consistency, high alpha coefficient ratings ($r = .82$ adults, $r = .77$ students), and test-retest reliability at .85 for adults and .84 for students were reported (Millon, 2003).

The instrument has 180 true/false items and takes 25–30 minutes to complete. The three key dimensions of normal personality measured are motivating styles, thinking styles, and behaving styles. The assessment includes validity indices as well as a clinical index to screen

Figure 9.5 Lifestyle Diagram

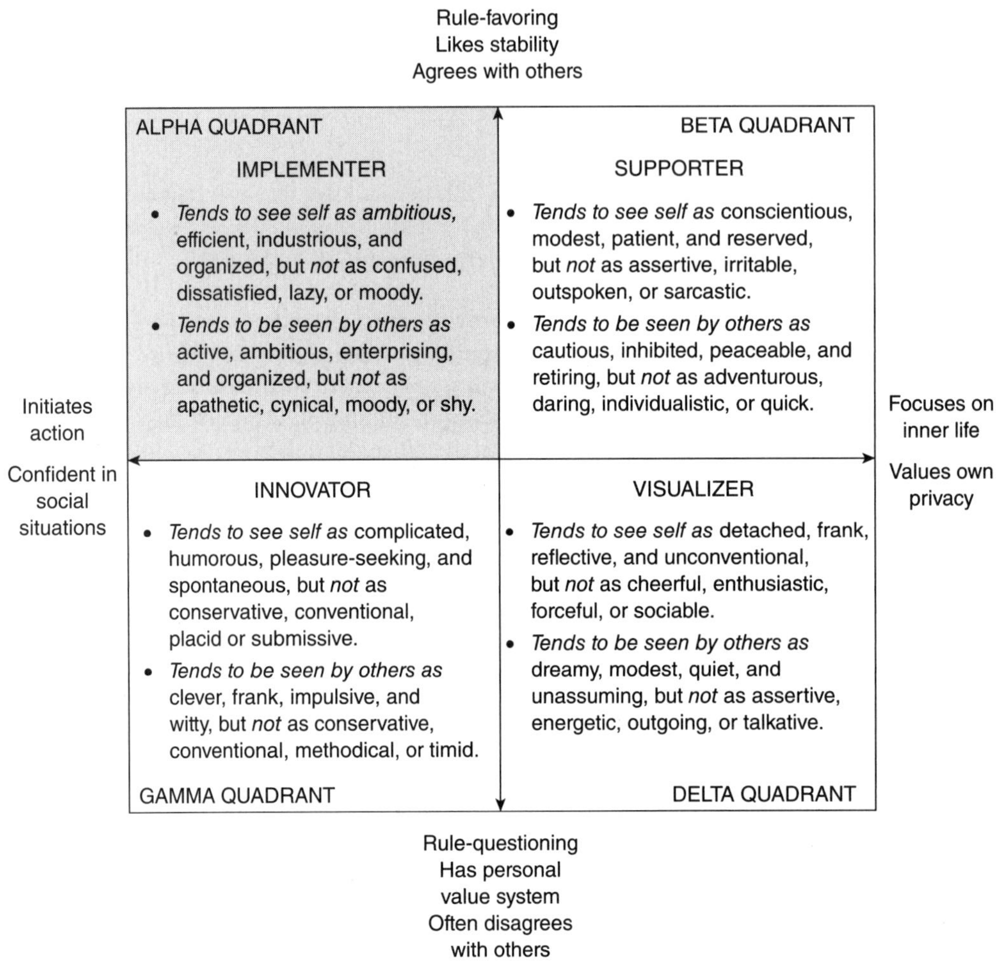

Rule-favoring
Likes stability
Agrees with others

ALPHA QUADRANT	BETA QUADRANT
IMPLEMENTER	SUPPORTER
• *Tends to see self as ambitious,* efficient, industrious, and organized, but *not* as confused, dissatisfied, lazy, or moody. • *Tends to be seen by others as* active, ambitious, enterprising, and organized, but *not* as apathetic, cynical, moody, or shy.	• *Tends to see self as* conscientious, modest, patient, and reserved, but *not* as assertive, irritable, outspoken, or sarcastic. • *Tends to be seen by others as* cautious, inhibited, peaceable, and retiring, but *not* as adventurous, daring, individualistic, or quick.
INNOVATOR	VISUALIZER
• *Tends to see self as* complicated, humorous, pleasure-seeking, and spontaneous, but *not* as conservative, conventional, placid or submissive. • *Tends to be seen by others as* clever, frank, impulsive, and witty, but *not* as conservative, conventional, methodical, or timid.	• *Tends to see self as* detached, frank, reflective, and unconventional, but *not* as cheerful, enthusiastic, forceful, or sociable. • *Tends to be seen by others as* dreamy, modest, quiet, and unassuming, but *not* as assertive, energetic, outgoing, or talkative.
GAMMA QUADRANT	DELTA QUADRANT

Initiates action
Confident in social situations

Focuses on inner life
Values own privacy

Rule-questioning
Has personal
value system
Often disagrees
with others

Source: Schaubhut & Thompson (2011).

for the presence of a mental disorder. Table 9.9 summarizes the personality styles assessed, the specific scales that fall under each style, and the theory each scale is anchored in. The MIPS Revised prevalence score (PS) ranges from 0 to 100; PS = 50 corresponds to the prevalence rate in the general population. Furthermore, an examinee who obtains a PS of 50 or above on any scale is considered a member of that trait group. For example, a person scoring above 50 on the Self-Indulging Scale is oriented to actualizing his or her own wishes and needs, and or a person who scores a 50 on the Other Nurturing Scale is motivated to meet the needs of others first. After assessing the amount of the trait the person possesses, the examiner can look at the examinee's position relative to others on the dimension. For

Table 9.9   Millon Index of Personality Styles Revised

Scales	Assesses	Theory
Motivating Styles Pleasure-Enhancing Pain-Avoiding Actively Modifying Passively Accommodating Self-Indulging Other-Nurturing	Emotional style to environment	Evolution and psychoanalytic
Thinking Styles Externally Focused Internally Focused Realistic/Sensing Imaginative/Intuiting Thought-Guided Feeling-Guided Conservation Seeking Innovation Seeking	Cognitive processing	Jungian
Behaving Styles Asocial/Withdrawing Gregarious/Outgoing Anxious/Hesitating Confident/Asserting Unconventional/Dissenting Dutiful/Conforming Submissive/Yielding Dominant/Controlling Dissatisfied/Complaining Cooperative/Agreeing	Way of working with others	Interpersonal and social theories

example, client A scores a PS of 50 on the Nurturing Scale while client B scores a PS of 90 on the Nurturing Scale. Clients A and B are both categorized as nurturing compared to self-indulging. However, Client B is more likely to possess the Nurturing trait to a greater degree and demonstrate the trait with greater frequency than Client A.

The **Millon Adolescent Personality Inventory (MAPI)** is a widely used personality assessment appropriate for ages 13–18 years old with at least a sixth-grade reading level. The MAPI is composed of three scale dimensions—personality styles (introversion, inhibited, cooperative, sociable, confident, forceful, respectful, and sensitive), expressed concerns (self-concept, personal esteem, body comfort, sexual acceptance, peer security, social tolerance, family rapport, and academic confidence), and behavioral patterns (impulse control, social conformity, scholastic achievement, and attendance consistency)—as well as two validity indices. The test is composed of 150 true/false items and takes approximately 20–30 minutes to complete. Computer software is available for scoring and comes with a narrative report of the scores and highlights areas of concern.

The correlation between the MIPS Revised and other previously discussed tests makes it a viable option to be administered by individuals with a Level B qualification (Millon, 2003). The MAPI, on the other hand, requires an individual with a Level C qualification (Millon, 2003), reducing the number of individuals who can administer the test. As with the CPI, the true/false structure of the questions may prevent the administrator from fully understanding the variability in individual responses. Because results can be scored either through a computer-based program or by hand, both the MAPI and MIPS Revised provide the administrator with scoring support.

Minnesota Multiphasic Personality Inventory (MMPI)

The **Minnesota Multiphasic Personality Inventory (MMPI)**, originally developed in 1942 at the University of Minnesota Hospital by Hathaway and McKinley, was created to assist in the diagnosis of psychological disorders (Butcher, 2005). The test was developed using empirical criterion keying and is not based on personality theory. The original MMPI was replaced by the **Minnesota Multiphasic Personality Inventory-2 (MMPI-2)** in 1989 and since then was revised in 2001 and updated in 2003 and again in 2009. The MMPI-2 continues to be the most widely used and researched diagnostic personality test.

The first revisions in 1989 consisted of several changes including language, newly added items, modified and rewritten items, and, most important, a different standardized sample. Sixty-six items were rewritten and the language was changed to be more readable and contemporary. Also, 107 new items were added and addressed topics such as suicide potential, drug abuse, marital adjustment, and Type A behavior patterns. Although the clinical scales were retained, the MMPI-2 added a new set of content scales. A total of seven validity scales were included compared to the four validity scales on the original MMPI. However, the most important reason for revising the MMPI is because the original version was standardized on 724 White individuals from Minnesota. The MMPI-2 is standardized on 2,600 individuals (1,462 females and 1,138 males). The sample was matched to the 1980 U.S. Census data in terms of gender, age, minority status, and education.

The MMPI-2 is a standardized personality test designed for people 18 years old and over; consists of 567 items in which the examinee reads statements and selects *true, false,* or *cannot say*; and takes approximately 60–90 minutes to complete. There are 7 validity scales, 10 clinical scales, and 15 content scales. A variety of supplemental scores were also developed. In analyzing the client's results, the clinician first evaluates how long the client took to complete the test, plots the clinical scores, evaluates the validity scales, and finally, reviews the content and additional supplementary scales. It is important to note that the MMPI Inventories require extensive training and a Level C qualification to administer. Thus, rather than going into detail on how to interpret the assessment, a brief summary of the validity, content, and clinical scales is provided in Table 9.10.

Validity scales detect the degree to which the examinee answered the questions in an honest manner. The 10 clinical scale scores measure the client's tendency to respond in psychologically deviant ways and are useful for diagnosis and treatment planning. The client's raw score for each clinical scale is plotted on the MMPI-2 profile form and a line is drawn to connect the raw scores. If you look at the MMPI-2 profile (Figure 9.6), you will notice T scores

Table 9.10 Validity, Clinical, and Content Scales of the MMPI-2

Validity Scales	Characteristics Associated With High Scores on Scale	
?	Cannot say score	Measures items unanswered
VRIN Scale	Variable response inconsistency	Measures total item pairs answered inconsistently
TRIN Scale	True response inconsistency	Measures tendency to inconsistently respond true or false to items (e.g., marking all true for opposite pairs)
F Scale	Infrequency	Measures exaggerated pattern of symptom checking in first part of booklet (e.g., individual presenting himself as more disturbed than he actually is)
F_B	Back F	Measures falsely responding to items toward back of booklet
F_P	Infrequency psychopathology	Measures unlikely symptoms that are not even endorsed by severe psychiatric patients
L Scale	Lie	Measures tendency to present in overly positive light, unrealistic view
K Scale	Correction	Measures willingness to disclose and discuss problems
S Scale	Superlative self-presentation	Measures tendency to display oneself in superlative manner
Clinical Scales	Characteristics Associated With High Scores on Scale	
Hs-1	Hypochondriasis	Numerous physical and somatic problems, generally unhappy, self-centered, demand attention
D-2	Depression	Depressed mood, low self-esteem, described as moody, overcontrolled, pessimistic, lethargic, or high-strung
Hy-3	Hysteria	Use denial and repression to cope with stress, described as dependent, narcissistic, little insight into problem, disrupted relationships
Pd-4	Psychopathic deviate	Antisocial behavior; impulsive, disrupted family relationships, hostile, aggressive
Mf-5	Masculinity-femininity	Gender-role reversal (e.g., high-scoring males have stereotypical female interest; opposite for females)
Pa-6	Paranoia	Worried, suspicious, aloof, typically hostile and argumentative
Pt-7	Psychasthenia	Tense, preoccupied, anxious, often feel inferior and is self-condemning

(Continued)

Table 9.10 (Continued)

Clinical Scales	Characteristics Associated With High Scores on Scale	
Sc-8	Schizophrenia	Very high scores: poor judgment and reality contact, delusions, hallucinations
Ma-9	Hypomania	Very high scores: impulsive and bizarre behavior, erratic moods, delusions
Si-0	Social introversion	Shy, withdrawn, tense, guilt-prone
Content Scales	Characteristics Associated With High Scores on Scale	
ANX	Anxiety	Tension, sleep difficulties, poor concentration, somatic problems (e.g., shortness of breath)
FRS	Fears	Many specific fears (e.g., high places, blood, natural disasters)
OBS	Obsessiveness	Difficulty making decisions, excessive worrier, may have compulsive behavior
DEP	Depression	Significant depressive thoughts, uncertain about future, uninterested in life
HEA	Health concerns	Several physical symptoms (e.g., gastrointestinal, neurological, sensory, cardiovascular), feel sicker and worry about health more than average person
BIZ	Bizarre mentation	Psychotic thought processes, paranoid ideation, may indicate hallucinations
ANG	Anger	Anger-control problems, irritable, grouchy, annoyed, stubborn
CYN	Cynicism	Misanthropic beliefs, suspect hidden motives of others
ASP	Antisocial practices	Misanthropic attitudes, problem behavior during school years, antisocial practices (e.g., stealing, shoplifting)
TPA	Type A	Hard-driving, work-oriented, frequently annoyed or irritable, direct, overbearing
LSE	Low self-esteem	Negative attitude about oneself, lacks self-confidence, hard to accept compliments
SOD	Social discomfort	Uneasy around others, views oneself as shy and prefers to be by oneself than in social groups
FAM	Family problems	Family discord, quarrelsome, unpleasant, marriages lacking in affection and unhappy
WRK	Work influence	Encompass behaviors that contribute to poor work performance (e.g., concentration difficulties, low self-confidence, obsessiveness)
TRT	Negative treatment indicators	Negative attitude to medical doctors and mental health professionals, does not believe anyone can help

Figure 9.6　MMPI-2

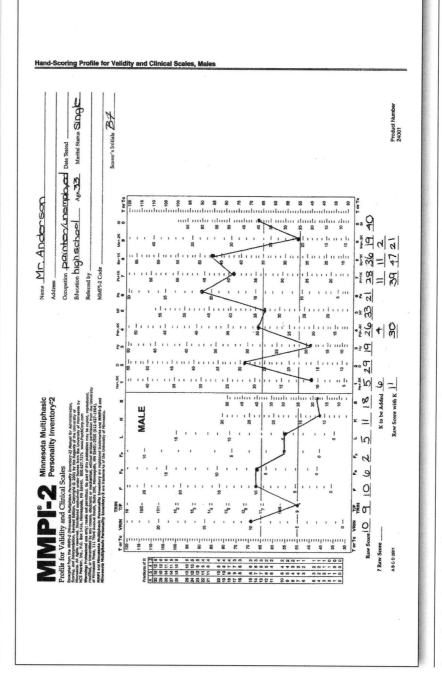

Source: Butcher (2005). Used by permission of the University of Minnesota Press. All rights reserved. "MMPI" and "Minnesota Multiphasic Personality Inventory" are trademarks owned by the Regents of the University of Minnesota.

on the left. Raw scores are converted into T scores with a mean of 50 and standard deviation of 10. T scores of 65 or higher are considered clinically significant and are suggestive of pathology. It is important to understand that those who score high on certain scales does not warrant a diagnosis, but instead they typically show characteristics of that population. For example, imagine your client scores high on the Schizophrenia (Sc-8) clinical scale. This particular scale consists of items that those diagnosed with schizophrenia answered in a particular way compared to the normal population. If your client scores high in this area, it does not mean he or she is schizophrenic, but instead your client typically shows characteristics of those diagnosed with schizophrenia. These characteristics might include a wide range of strange beliefs, unusual experiences, and special sensitivities, and the client may be socially or emotionally withdrawn. If you recall, the content scales were developed after the original MMPI. The content items were developed based on item content unlike the clinical scales that were developed based on criterion keying. The content items which contain 15 traits are useful in predicting client behavior and providing a detailed perspective of the client. As previously mentioned, there are a variety of supplemental scales. For example, the MacAndrew Alcoholism Scale (MAC-R) and the Marital Distress Scale (MDS) are useful in providing clues to addiction problems and marital distress, respectively. Again, rather than interpreting each scale in isolation, the entire profile is analyzed as a whole.

Adequate test-retest reliability estimates were reported for the majority of the content, clinical, and supplementary scales, with scores ranging from .54 to .92 for females and .63 to .93 for males. Internal consistency for the clinical scales appears low, ranging from .34 to .85 for males and .37 to .87 for females. Discriminant validity was reported, but criterion and construct validity were lacking.

A shorter version of the MMPI, known as the **Minnesota Multiphasic Personality Inventory-2 Restructured Form (MMPI-2-RF),** was published in 2008. The test consists of 338 items and takes approximately 35–50 minutes to complete by pencil and paper and 25–35 minutes on the computer. Although the 338 items are taken from the MMPI's 567 items, new validity scales (e.g., Symptom Validity) and additional High-Order scales were added.

CASE ILLUSTRATION 9.4

Roberta is a mental health counselor who works in a correctional facility. She works with inmates that have mental health disorders and are housed in the "mental health dorm." She has one patient that has symptoms congruent with paranoid schizophrenia and antisocial personality disorder. However, Roberta knows that this inmate has a history of heavy methamphetamine use and was using daily until he was incarcerated last week. She knows that methamphetamine can create similar symptoms as these two disorders, and she needs to sort out whether her patient's symptoms are a manifestation of his drug use or are indeed caused by these two disorders. She decides to administer the MMPI-2 to help her with this differential diagnosis. She chose the MMPI-2 because it has scales that will assess for antisocial personality disorder and schizophrenia, and it has subscales related to substance abuse. She also likes the MMPI-2 because it can be scored by computer. Hand-scoring the MMPI-2 is very time-consuming and tedious. The MMPI-2 also has validity scales that will indicate whether the person taking the assessment has tried to "fake good" or "fake bad," whether he or she answered test items in a truthful manner, and whether the individual was defensive when taking the assessment.

As demonstrated in Case Illustration 9.4, the MMPI-2 provides extensive information on variables not collected through other personality tests, including information relative to substance abuse. Because the test incorporates evaluation of normal behaviors with evaluation of abnormal behaviors, the MMPI-2 presents as one of the most comprehensive of the personality tests. Length of time required for completion and scoring, however, may result in an administrator choosing another test.

Minnesota Multiphasic Personality Inventory-Adolescent (MMPI-A)

Originally, the MMPI was widely used to study psychopathology in adolescents as well as adults. In 1992, the **Minnesota Multiphasic Personality Inventory-Adolescent (MMPI-A)** was introduced as an alternative to the MMPI-2 for measuring psychopathology in adolescents 14–18 years old. The test consists of 478 true/false items and takes approximately 60 minutes to complete. The MMPI-A retains the clinical scales of the MMPI-2, but Table 9.11 highlights some of the noteworthy differences in the MMPI-A. Adequate internal consistency and test-retest reliability are reported for both content and clinical scales.

Similar to the MMPI-2, the number of questions presented in the MMPI-A is likely to result in decreased use. This is offset by the fact that the MMPI-A provides the most comprehensive illustration of both normal and abnormal aspects of personality in adolescents. Using this test, therefore, requires an evaluation of what information is desired and the ability of the individual to complete a lengthy test.

Table 9.11 Differences in the MMPI-A compared to MMPI-2

Norms	• Normed on 1,620 adolescents (805 boys and 815 girls) 14–18 years old
New content scales and revised content scales	• Fears (FRS), Antisocial Practices (ASP), Type A Personality (TPA), and Work Interference (WRK) on MMPI-2 replaced with Conduct Disorder (A-con), Alienation (A-aln), School Problems (A-sch), and Low Aspiration (A-las) on MMPI-A • Family Problems Scale (A-fam) added adolescent-specific content • Alcohol-Drug Proneness (PRO) and Alcohol-Drug Problem Acknowledgement (ACK) developed to describe adolescent drug and alcohol use
Supplementary scales	• Immaturity (IMM) added
Items	• Has 478 items; 89 fewer than MMPI-2 • Items previously worded in past tense for youthful behaviors changed to present tense on MMPI-A
Cut-off scores for interpretation	• 60–64 T score range compared to T score of 65 for MMPI-2

Personality Assessment Inventory (PAI) and Personality Assessment Screener (PAS)

The **Personality Assessment Inventory (PAI)** is a widely used self-report, objective inventory used to assess psychopathology, some personality disorders, and interpersonal traits in adults 18 years and older (Morey, 2007). The assessment is helpful in providing diagnosis information relevant to treatment planning. The assessment takes approximately 50 minutes to complete, is written at a fourth-grade reading level, and consists of 344 items with the following four item responses: false—not at all true, slightly true, mainly true, or very true. The PAI comprises 22 non-overlapping full scales: 4 validity scales, 11 clinical scales, 5 treatment consideration scales, and 2 interpersonal scales. The 11 clinical scales are organized into three categories: neurotic spectrum, psychotic spectrum, and behavior disorder. The 11 clinical scales contain subscales as well. The PAI also includes 27 critical items, which serve as indicators of a possible crisis situation. You can think of the critical items as red flags that indicate the clinician would need to facilitate follow-up questioning. Table 9.12 contains the 22 non-overlapping full scales for the PAI. Table 9.13 represents the PAI Clinical Report Subscale Profile, which includes nine clinical scales (Somatic Complaints, Anxiety, Anxiety-Related Disorders, Depression, Mania, Paranoia, Schizophrenia, Borderline Features, and Antisocial Features) and one treatment consideration scale with the respective subscales (Aggression). See Figure 9.7 for the Full Scale Profile and Figure 9.8 for the Subscale Profile.

Table 9.12 Personality Assessment Inventory Full Scale

Validity Scale	Clinical Scale	Treatment Consideration Scale	Interpersonal Scale
Inconsistency (ICN)	**A. Neurotic Spectrum Scales**	Aggression (AGG)	Dominance (DOM)
Infrequency (INF)	Somatic Complaints (SOM)	Suicidal Ideation (SUI)	Warmth (WRM)
Negative Impression (NIM)	Anxiety (ANX)	Stress (STR)	
Positive Impression (PIM)	Anxiety-Related Disorders (ARD)	Nonsupport (NON)	
	Depression (DEP)	Treatment Rejection (RXR)	
	B. Psychotic Spectrum Scales		
	Mania (MAN)		
	Paranoia (PAR)		
	Schizophrenia (SCZ)		
	C. Behavior Disorder Scales		
	Borderline Features (BOR)		
	Antisocial Features (ANT)		
	Alcohol Problems (ALC)		
	Drug Problems (DRG)		

Table 9.13   Personality Assessment Inventory Subscales for Clinical Scale

Somatic Complaints (SOM)

Conversion (SOM-C)

Somatization (SOM-S)

Health Concerns (SOM-H)

Anxiety (ANX)

Cognitive (ANX-C)

Affective (ANX-A)

Physiological (ANX-P)

Anxiety-Related Disorder (ARD)

Obsessive-Compulsive (ARD-O)

Phobias (ARD-P)

Traumatic Stress (ARD-T)

Depression (DEP)

Cognitive (DEP-C)

Affective (DEP-A)

Physiological (DEP-P)

Mania (MAN)

Activity Level (MAN-A)

Grandiosity (MAN-G)

Irritability (MAN-I)

Paranoia (PAR)

Hypervigilance (PAR-H)

Persecution (PAR-P)

Resentment (PAR-R)

Schizophrenia (SCZ)

Psychotic Experiences (SCZ-P)

Social Detachment (SCZ-S)

Thought Disorder (SCZ-Y)

Borderline Features (BOR)

Affective Instability (BOR-A)

Identity Problems (BOR-I)

Negative Relationships (BOR-N)

Self-harm (BOR-S)

Antisocial Features (ANT)

Antisocial Behaviors (ANT-A)

Egocentricity (ANT-E)

Stimulus-Seeking (ANT-S)

Aggression (AGG)

Aggressive Attitude (AGG-A)

Verbal Aggression (AGG-V)

Physical Aggression (AGG-P)

Raw scores from both the full scales and subscales are converted into T scores and plotted on a PAI profile form. The assessment can be hand-scored, or computer PAI-SP software is available. Clinical reports include both the PAI full scale and subscale profiles.

The development of the PAI is based on the construct validation method. After reviewing Table 9.12 you probably noticed that many of the clinical scales are very similar to the scales on the MMPI-2. The difference between the scales on the PAI and the MMIP-2 is that the PAI scales are non-overlapping. The sample was standardized in clinical and community settings, including 1,000 adults in community dwellings, 1,265 patients at clinical sites, and 1,051 college students over the age of 18. Adequate internal consistency and test-retest reliability as well as convergent and discriminated validity are reported. Internal consistency alphas across the full scales were reported at .81 (normative sample), .82 (college sample), and .86 (clinical sample), and median test-retest reliability was .83 for all three samples (Morey, 2007). The four Validity Scales

Figure 9.7 Personality Assessment Inventory Full Scale Profile

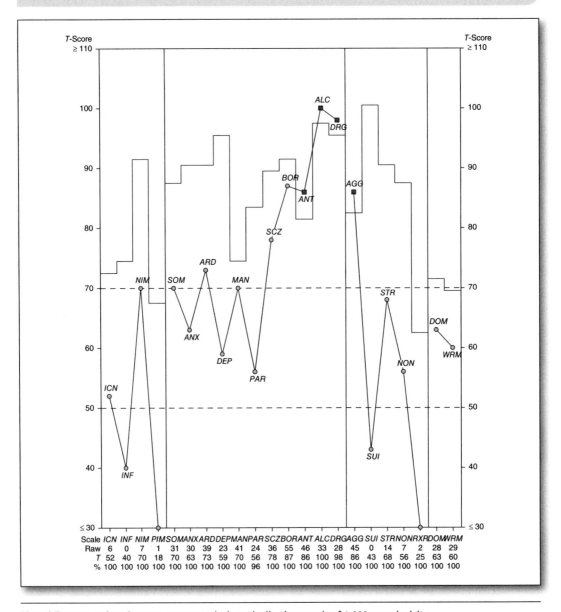

Plotted *T* scores are based upon a census matched standardization sample of 1,000 normal adults.

■ indicates that the score is more than two standard deviations above the mean for a sample of 1,246 clinical patients.

◆ indicates that the scale has more than 20% missing items.

Source: Psychological Assessment Resources, Inc. (2000). PAI Clinical Interpretive Report. Reproduced by special permission of the Publisher, Psychological Assessment Resources, Inc., 16204 North Florida Avenue, Lutz, Florida 33549 from the Personality Assessment Inventory Software Portfolio (PAI-SP) by Leslie C. Morey, Ph.D. and PAR Staff, Copyright 1992, 1998, 2000, 2005, 2008. Further reproduction is prohibited without permission of PAR.

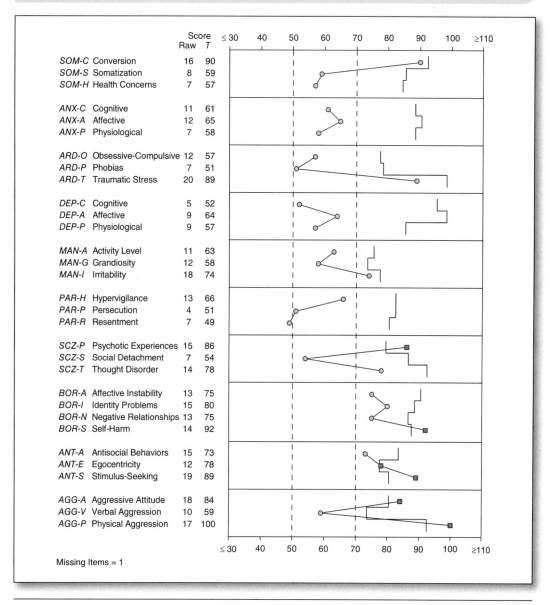

Figure 9.8   Personality Assessment Inventory Subscale Profile

Plotted *T* scores are based upon a census matched standardization sample of 1,000 normal adults.
■ indicates that the score is more than two standard deviations above the mean for a sample of 1,246 clinical patients.
◆ indicates that the scale has more than 20% missing items.

Source: Psychological Assessment Resources, Inc. (2000). PAI Clinical Interpretive Report. Reproduced by special permission of the Publisher, Psychological Assessment Resources, Inc., 16204 North Florida Avenue, Lutz, Florida 33549 from the Personality Assessment Inventory Software Portfolio (PAI-SP) by Leslie C. Morey, Ph.D. and PAR Staff, Copyright 1992, 1998, 2000, 2005, 2008. Further reproduction is prohibited without permission of PAR.

were correlated with other psychological assessment scales, including the MMPI Scales: L, F, and K that you recently read about.

The **Personality Assessment Screener (PAS)** includes 22 items from the PAI and is suitable for adults 18 and older. The PAI is often used in triage settings and college health settings as a quick personality screen to assess potential behavioral or emotional problems that might require follow-up testing and evaluation. Clinicians who suspect that potential crisis situations or resistance may occur with the client, including suicidal ideation, aggression, or treatment rejection, should use this measure to gain a preliminary understanding of how to approach the client. Guided Practice Exercise 9.4 helps you further your understanding of which personality assessments you might consider using to help you determine a client's diagnosis.

GUIDED PRACTICE EXERCISE 9.4

You are a mental health counselor working in a psychiatric facility. You have an 18-year-old female client, Myra, who has been referred to you for engaging in bizarre behavior. Myra frequently talks to someone who is not physically present in the room with her. Myra seems to be able to see this person, but no one else can. Myra has frequent anger outbursts and gets violent if anyone tries to reason with her regarding her "invisible" friend. Myra also reports tactile and olfactory hallucinations. She often reports that bugs are crawling on her when there are not any, and she also reports strange smells that no else can smell. You need to use an assessment to help determine what her diagnosis might be. Based on what you have learned in this chapter, what assessment would you recommend? Why? There is no one right answer, but be prepared to discuss your choice in class.

Coopersmith Self-Esteem Inventory (SEI)

Stanley Coopersmith (2002) developed the **Coopersmith Self-Esteem Inventory (SEI)** based on his extensive work on self-esteem with children. The SEI measures attitudes toward the self in social, academic, family, and personal areas of experience. In reference to the SEI, self-esteem is defined as "the evaluation a person makes, and customarily maintains, of him- or herself; that is, overall self-esteem is an expression of approval or disapproval, indicating the extent to which a person believes him- or herself competent, successful, significant, and worthy" (Coppersmith, 2002, p. 5). The SEI comprises three forms: School Form, School Short Form, and Adult Form. All forms consist of short statements, such as "Things usually don't bother me," in which the examinee selects *like me* or *unlike me*. The School Form is the longest form, consisting of 58 items (50 self-esteem items and 8 Lie Scale items used to measure a student's defensiveness), which yields a total score. In order to gain insight on how self-esteem may vary in different settings, one can calculate scores on the four subcategories of self-esteem: General Self, Social Self-Peers, Home-Parents, and School-Academics. Higher scores reflect higher self-esteem. The School Short Form consists of the first 25 items on the School Form but does not include the Lie Scale items. Only a total score is calculated. The Adult Form for ages 16 and older has 25 items adopted from the School Short Form and yields a total score and no subscale scores. Table 9.14 provides a summary of the different SEI forms.

Table 9.14   Coopersmith Self-Esteem Inventory

	Age	Number of Items	Scores Calculated
School Form	8–15	58 (50 self-esteem, 8 lie)	Total Self Score
			Lie Scale Score
			Four subscale scores: General-Self
			Social Self-Peers
			Home-Parents
			School-Academics
School Short Form	8–15	25 (no lie items)	Total Self Score
Adult Form	16+	25 (no lie items)	Total Self Score

The SEI remains a popular inventory and has been used in a number of studies, including those concerned with personality, psychiatric disorders, separation from parents, and friendship quality (Ponsoda, Abad, Francis, & Hills, 2008). The manual reports both validity and reliability and includes a chapter on building self-esteem in the classroom.

Because the SEI focuses specifically on self-esteem, an element of overall personality, this test is used when counselors wish to establish more detailed information about an individual's self-concept as opposed to when they wish to gain a broader prospective on the individual. Consequently, the SEI is likely to be used to gain insight into other aspects of personality. For example, administration of the MMPI-A to a 14-year-old female may reveal heightened scores on the depression index. The SEI may then be utilized to establish the client's level of self-esteem to determine whether a correlation exists. Guided Practice Exercise 9.5 helps you gain experience taking the Coopersmith Self-Inventory designed for school-aged children.

GUIDED PRACTICE EXERCISE 9.5

Prior to class, download and print out the document found at http://www.fetzer.org/sites/default/files/images/stories/pdf/selfmeasures/Self_Measures_for_Self-Esteem_COOPERSMITH_SELF-ESTEEM_INVENTORY.pdf. This is a copy of the Coopersmith Self-Esteem

(Continued)

(Continued)

Inventory. This form is designed for school-aged children. However, for the purposes of this class, you will take this assessment to get experience in administration and scoring and to see an example of a self-esteem assessment. In pairs, take the inventory and then exchange assessments with your partner and score each other's assessment. Discuss your perception of the results with your partner. Did anything surprise you from your results? If so, why? Do you disagree with the results? Why or why not? What was the experience of taking this assessment like for you? Would you use this assessment with a future client? Why or why not?

Tennessee Self-Concept Scale (TSCS:2)

Normed on a sample of more than 3,000 individuals between the ages of 7 and 90, the **Tennessee Self-Concept Scale, 2nd edition (TSCS:2)** is one of the most famous measures of self-concept in children, adolescents, and adults (Fitts & Warren, 1997). The test provides 15 scores: 6 Self-Concept scores (Physical, Moral, Personal, Family, Social, Academic/Work), 3 Supplementary scores (Identity, Satisfaction, Behavior), 4 Validity scores (Inconsistency, Self-Criticism, Faking Good, Response Distribution), and 2 Summary scores (Total Self-Concept, Conflict). The six Self-Concept scores evaluate the self-view a client brings to specific areas of experience. The **Total Self-Concept (TOT)** Score is considered the most important score as it indicates whether the client typically has positive and consistent or negative and variable self-view (Fitts & Warren, 1997). There is an adult form for ages 13 years and older (82 items) and a child form for ages 7–14 years (76 items), with each item rated on a scale of 1 (*always false*) to 5 (*always true*). An example item is "I am too sensitive about the things people in my family say." The first 20 items on both the adult and child form can serve as a short form. A manual accompanies the assessment, which can be hand-scored or computer-scored. Raw scores are transformed into T scores and percentile rank.

CASE ILLUSTRATION 9.5

Janessa works at a community mental health center. Her client Bianca is a 15-year-old female who is sexually promiscuous. Bianca has already had two abortions and three sexually transmitted diseases. In the course of their sessions, Bianca has expressed that she feels loved and appreciated only when she is having sex and when she has multiple partners. Janessa feels certain that Bianca is suffering from low self-esteem, but wants to give her an assessment to help with treatment planning. Janessa decides to give Bianca the Tennessee Self-Concept Scale, because it is a well-known assessment and includes areas Janessa feels might yield important information in terms of treatment planning for Bianca, such as moral, personal, family, identity, and behavior. Janessa feels it will give her a good picture of how Bianca sees herself in specific areas of her experience.

As you can see in Case Illustration 9.5, the counselor seeks to gain additional information as opposed to the blanketed category of self-esteem and instead seeks to gain details about specific elements of Janessa's self-concept which are affecting her behaviors. As a result, the TSCS:2 is more likely to be chosen when more detailed information regarding self-concept is valuable as a means of developing areas to target in treatment.

Piers-Harris Children's Self Concept Scale

The **Piers-Harris Children's Self Concept Scale (2nd Edition)**, another popular measure of self-concept for children and adolescents ages 7 to 18, is a 60-item instrument covering six subscales: Physical Appearance and Attributes, Intellectual and School Status, Happiness and Satisfaction, Freedom From Anxiety, Behavioral Adjustment, and Popularity. Children answer either yes or no to items presented in first person (e.g., "My classmates make fun of me," "I am a happy person"). Various methods for scoring exist, including computer-generated reports. Originally published in 1963, the current instrument, published in 2002, was normed on 1,387 students between the ages of 7 and 18 from schools throughout the United States. Reliability and validity were reported from moderate to high in several studies (Butler & Gasson, 2005).

Now that you have read about various personality assessments, Guided Practice Exercise 9.6 will help you reflect on the similarities and differences of these assessments.

GUIDED PRACTICE EXERCISE 9.6

In small groups, or as an entire class, discuss the similarities and differences you found between and among the various personality assessments you have read about. Which of the assessments are more appealing to you as a future/current counselor? If you were asked to take one of these assessments, which one would appeal to you? Why?

KEYSTONES

- A basic general definition of personality is that it consists of the psychological characteristics or blend of characteristics that make a person unique.
- Objective assessments are structured personality assessments, meaning clients respond to a fixed set of questions or items.
- Projective assessments are considered unstructured in that stimuli presented are ambiguous or incomplete and a person's response to the stimuli are not limited to *true, false,* or a variety of specific given response choices.
- Personality assessments include both informal (observations and interviews) and formal methods (structured instruments and projective techniques).

- Four methods used to develop construct objective personality inventories are logical or content method, theoretical method, criterion group method, and factor-analytic method.
- Popular structured personality assessments to measure personality discussed include the MBTI, MMPI, 16PF, NEO-PI-3, CPI, PAI, and MIPS Revised.
- Popular structured personality assessments used to describe self-concept include the Coopersmith Self-Esteem Inventory (SEI), Tennessee Self-Concept Scale (TSCS:2), and Piers-Harris Children's Self Concept Scale (2nd edition).

KEY TERMS

Big Five

California Psychological Inventory

California Psychological Inventory 260

Coopersmith Self-Esteem Inventory (SEI)

extraversion

feeling

formal techniques

informal techniques

introversion

intuition

judging

Millon Adolescent Personality Inventory (MAPI)

Millon Index of Personality Styles-Revised (MIPS Revised)

Minnesota Multiphasic Personality Inventory (MMPI)

Minnesota Multiphasic Personality Inventory-2 (MMPI-2)

Minnesota Multiphasic Personality Inventory-2 Restructured Form (MMPI-2-RF)

Minnesota Multiphasic Personality Inventory-Adolescent (MMPI-A)

Myers-Briggs Type Indicator (MBTI)

NEO Five-Factor Inventory-3 (NEO-FFI-3)

NEO inventories

NEO Personality Inventory-3 (NEO-PI-3)

objective assessments

observation

perceiving

personality

personality assessment

Personality Assessment Inventory (PAI)

Personality Assessment Screener (PAS)

Piers-Harris Children's Self Concept Scale (2nd Edition)

projective assessments

psychological core

Revised NEO Personality Inventory (NEO PI-R)

role-related behavior

semistructured interview

sensing

Sixteen Personality Factor (16PF), Fifth Edition

state

structured assessments

structured interview

Tennessee Self-Concept Scale, 2nd edition (TSCS:2)

thinking

Total Self-Concept (TOT) Score

trait characteristics

type

typical responses

unstructured assessments

unstructured interview

ADDITIONAL RESOURCES

- *Journal of Personality Assessment*

  http://www.tandfonline.com/toc/hjpa20/current#.Uh14KSqF-Y0

This is the website for the journal where you can go to find articles about personality assessment. Investigate whether this journal is in your university or college library database. If so, you can access these articles for free.

- Personality Pathways

  http://www.personalitypathways.com/type_inventory2.html

This website gives additional information in understanding your Myers Briggs Type Indicator and 16PF results. It also provides additional readings and resources related to personality assessment.

- Personality Test Site

  http://similarminds.com

This website is a clearinghouse for information about various personality assessments such as the MBTI, 16PF, and those based on the Big Five personality traits. It also gives the type descriptions that go along with the personality assessments. There is a tab dedicated to current research on personality as well as a tab for more information or articles for further information.

- Society for Personality Assessment

  http://www.personality.org

This international professional organization is dedicated to the discussion and development of personality assessment. The website has links to its publication, the *Journal of Personality Assessment*, and to its newsletters. It also offers a plethora of resources and conference information.

- The Myers & Briggs Foundation

  http://www.myersbriggs.org

This website is dedicated to the Myers Briggs Type Indicator and gives additional information on personality type, uses of the MBTI, and a page of frequently asked questions about the MBTI.

Student Study Site: Visit the Student Study Site at **www.sagepub.com/watson** to access additional study tools, including quizzes, web resources, and journal articles.

CHAPTER 10

Projective Methods of Personality Assessment

LEARNING OBJECTIVES

After reading this chapter, you will be able to

- Describe the difference between the two major categories of formal assessment: popular structured personality instruments and projective techniques
- Describe popular projective personality assessments used in a variety of settings
- Discuss strengths and limitations of structured and projective personality assessments

As discussed in the last chapter, objective techniques are important tools counselors can use to measure various aspects of one's personality. While some of the assessments discussed in the previous chapter may have been new to you, there is little doubt that many of them you had heard of before. Perhaps you wondered why some personality tests were not discussed in the previous chapter. The reason these personality tests may have been missing from discussion is the large number of personality tests which exists for counselors. In fact, it would be impossible to do the subject of personality tests justice if not for making an important distinction between the objective personality tests discussed in the last chapter and those more subjective, projective personality tests which will be discussed in this chapter. If you recall, last chapter we discussed a series of tests which possess a structured set of items and methods of interpreting responses to those items. In this chapter, we will shift focus to those personality tests which can provide extremely valuable information but require more interpretation to transform responses into meaning. In this chapter, we will review what makes these projective measures distinct from the objective personality assessments, discuss some popular projective techniques, and evaluate the strengths and limitations of their application in practice.

PROJECTIVE PERSONALITY ASSESSMENTS

As previously mentioned, there are both informal and formal personality assessments, and formal personality assessments can be categorized into either standardized or projective assessments. Unlike structured standardized assessments, projective personality assessments are considered unstructured.

Projective assessments are considered unstructured because stimuli presented are ambiguous or incomplete and a person's responses to the stimuli are not limited to *true, false,* or a variety of specific given response choices. People "project" themselves onto the unstructured stimuli (such as an inkblot), which is thought to be consistent with a person's subconscious or conscious desires, needs, wishes, fears, and so on (Frank, 1948). If you remember from the last chapter, structured assessments allow for easy interpretation of results. The projective nature of the instruments which will be discussed in this chapter and the potential responses make scoring and interpreting these tests more difficult. Still, these tests are important tools in assessing personality. Compared to the structured instruments previously discussed, projective techniques make it somewhat more difficult for clients to "fake" adjustment or pathology. Unlike with structured instruments that provide face-validity, the examinees do not know what projective tests are measuring (see Guided Practice Exercise 10.1).

GUIDED PRACTICE EXERCISE 10.1

Review the above image. This is an example of a projective test that is similar to what you would find in a Rorschach inkblot. What do you see? Write down your top five answers as to what you think this image depicts. Then in pairs or small groups, discuss your answers with your classmates. How many of you saw similar things in the image? How many of you saw different things? Discuss what this experience was like for you and why you think you saw similar or different things. What insights did you obtain from this experience?

The concept of projection can be traced back to Freud (1911). Projection was considered a defense mechanism in which an individual subconsciously attributes his or her unacceptable motives or characteristics onto others. Many of the projective personality assessments originated in hospital settings; however, assessments such as the Rorschach Inkblot Test, Thematic Apperception Test, and human figure drawings, which are among the most frequent projective assessments, are still used today in clinical settings. The use of projective personality assessments can be helpful for gaining insight into a client's conflicts, motives, and personality; however, these assessments should be used in conjunction with other formal and informal assessments.

Projective techniques are subjective in nature. Because of their subjectivity, many projective assessments require additional clinical training to administer and interpret. For example, test developers responsible for distribution of the Rorschach Inkblot Test require that users of this test possess Level C qualifications. In addition to qualifications set forth by the test administrators, state laws vary in terms of which professionals are allowed to administer projective assessments, and many of these assessments require extensive training. Make sure to check with your state laws before administering any type of projective test, and always practice within the scope of your training.

Despite the increased training requirements necessary to interpret the subjectivity of projective techniques and the availability of scoring manuals, issues of the reliability and validity of these assessments are highly questioned. According to Lilienfeld, Wood, and Garb (2000), validity estimates of individual projective tests vary, but these tests often lack the empirical evidence associated with more structured approaches. Furthermore, reliability estimates are also significantly varied, including variability reported within tests. Ultimately, Garb, Lilienfeld, Nezworski, Wood, and O'Donohue (2009) conclude that despite their widespread use, projective assessments may lack the minimum standards of reliability and validity associated with other assessments. Still, these assessments are important to understand as they are used substantially in the counseling field.

Further differentiating projective techniques from more objective techniques includes paying attention to the type of response patterns analyzed. Lindzey (1959) provided a classification of projective tests and divided projective techniques into five categories: association (e.g., inkblot and word association techniques), construction (e.g., story creations and human figure drawing such as the Thematic Apperception Test), completion (e.g., sentence completion tests such as the Washington University Sentence Completion Test (WUSCT), arrangement/selection (e.g., Szondi Test), and expression (e.g., Draw-A-Person). Table 10.1 presents a list of the popular projective assessments discussed in this chapter.

ASSOCIATION TECHNIQUES

With **association techniques**, respondents are presented with visual or auditory stimuli and asked to respond with the first association that comes to mind. Some association techniques include inkblots (e.g., Rorschach) or word association tests. The Rorschach Inkblot Test (Rorschach, 1921) is an unstructured projective personality assessment in which examinees are shown symmetrical inkblots and asked to respond with what each inkblot looks like. You

Table 10.1 Subtypes of Projective Tests

Association

Rorschach Inkblot Test (Rorschach, 1921)

Word Association Test (WAT)

Construction

Thematic Apperception Test (TAT; Morgan & Murray, 1938)

TEMAS

Children's Apperceptions Test (CAT; Bellak, 1975)

Roberts Apperception Test for Children: 2 (Roberts-2)

Expression

Draw-A-Man

Goodenough Harris's Draw-A-Person Test (GHDAP)

Machover's Draw-A-Person Test

House-Tree-Person Test (HTP)

Kinetic-House-Tree-Person Test (KHTP)

Kinetic Family Drawing (KFD)

Kinetic School Drawing (KSD)

Kinetic Drawing System for Family and School (KDS)

Completion

Rotter Incomplete Sentence Blank, Second Edition

Washington University Sentence Completion Test (WUSCT; Loevinger, 1976)

SCT-Y

EPS Sentence Completion Test

Mayers's Gravely Disabled Sentence Completion Task

Arrangement/Selection

Szondi Test (Szondi, 1947)

may have actually seen satirical imitations of characters conducting this assessment. Word association tests are verbal association projective personality techniques that are considered semistructured. These tests are referred to as semistructured because they have a basic framework while allowing for a variety of responses. With word association tests, examinees are asked to respond to a series of words with the first word that comes to mind after hearing each word. Responses can be oral or written.

Rorschach Inkblot Test

Developed by Swiss psychiatrist Hermann Rorschach, the **Rorschach Inkblot Test** was published in 1921. Although considered the most widely used projective personality assessment, the Rorschach "has the dubious distinction of being, simultaneously, the most cherished and the most reviled of all psychological instruments" (Hunsley & Bailey, 1999, p. 266). The test consists of 10 bilaterally symmetrical inkblots (5 black and white; 2 black, white, and red; and 3 multicolored). The client is handed each card one at a time while the examiner states, "People may see many different things in these inkblot pictures; now tell me what you see, what it makes you think of, what it means to you" (Exner, 1993, p. 5). In order to allow the examinee to project freely, the examiner does not engage in conversation during the administration of the cards.

Originally, there was no test manual or score interpretation, thus several test manuals along with scoring and interpretation systems emerged. Exner's (1993, 2001) **Comprehensive System (CS)** is the most commonly used Rorschach scoring system. Responses are scored based on over 100 characteristics in three categories: content, location, and determinants (e.g., Did the client report movement or shading?). The test usually takes 45 minutes to administer. However, a considerable amount of time is needed to score and interpret (1.5 to 2 hours; see Case Illustration 10.1). The CS is praised for its standardized administration, reliable scoring (Weiner, 1998), and impressive test-retest reliability (Wood & Lilienfeld, 1999). However, the CS is criticized for lack of appropriate normative data, which could be problematic for American minorities and non-Americans (Dana, 2000), and having shown to overpathologize individuals (e.g., randomly normal person displayed psychopathology; Wood, Lilienfeld, & Nezworski, 2010).

CASE ILLUSTRATION   10.1

Doctoral students in counseling psychology often have to practice giving assessments to each other in order to gain practice and experience in administration and scoring. These practice sessions also include administering and scoring the Rorschach. Two students who were paired together to practice wanted to be really helpful to each other, and each came up with multiple things that they saw in the Rorschach inkblots. They were really happy that each was so supportive of the other and that they worked so well together as a team. However, these two students came up with this plan before looking at how to score the Rorschach responses. As your textbook indicates, a normal administration of the Rorschach takes about 45 minutes, while scoring and interpreting can take up to 2 hours. These figures are based on a participant giving one or two responses to each inkblot. However, these two doctoral students had each given between five and ten responses to each inkblot. Hours later these two students finished their scoring and interpretations. The students got a lot of practice scoring and interpreting their Rorschach administration.

Word Association Test (WAT)

Word association was first introduced by Francis Galton (1879) when he presented examinees with a series of unrelated words and asked them to respond with the first thing that came to mind. To illustrate this type of assessment, think about how you may interpret two different responses to a word association assessment in which individuals are provided with the word *nothing*. The first individual responds, "Nothing is worth it," while the second responds, "She wants for nothing." Cattell and Bryant (1889) further developed the use of word association techniques by using cards with stimulus words printed on them for the first time. Jung (1907) was the first to study changes in both skin conductance and breadth frequency with word associations, and he focused on emotional reactions. Jung's (1910) **Word Association Test (WAT)** consisted of 100 words from a standardized list in which examinees were asked to say the first thing that came to mind after hearing the word. Jung's Word Association Test, developed by Rapaport, Gill, and Schafer (1945–1946) was influenced by Jung's (1910) previous findings. The test consists of 60 neutral and traumatic words and is administered in three sections. First, the examinee responds to the first word that comes to mind. Then, the examinee is presented with the same word in the second section but asked to recall the first word that originally came to mind in the first section. In the third section, the clinician asks for clarification of responses. The results are then interpreted based on reaction time, content, and test-retest responses.

STORY CONSTRUCTION TECHNIQUES

Pictures can be used as projective stimuli. A **story construction test** is a projective assessment in which the client constructs a story based on a picture (the stimulus) shown by the examinee. Examinees are typically shown a variety of ambiguous characters, scenes, or situations often with animals, real people, or objects. As you can imagine, the stories which individuals develop are likely to be different based on their individual personalities. The Thematic Apperception Test is the most widely used of all the story construction projective tests.

Thematic Apperception Test and TEMAS

In the 1930s, Christiana D. Morgan and Henry A. Murray developed the **Thematic Apperception Test (TAT)** at the Harvard Psychological Clinic. The TAT was based on Murray's (1943) theory of human needs and environmental pressures. The verb **apperceive** is defined as to perceive in terms of past events. Murray believed that when people were shown ambiguous situations they would interpret these based on past events or current motivations. Thus, the pictures are used to gather information about the examinees' drives, emotions, conflicts, and complexity of personality. The stimulus material, designed for children and adults, consists of 31 cards; 30 are black-and-white picture cards, and 1 card is blank. Murray recommended using 20 cards over two separate 1-hour sessions; however, today clinicians rarely use all 20 cards in one session. The pictures are kept face down, and the examiner hands the examinee one picture at a time. The examiner informs the examinee that this is a test of imagination and his or her task is to tell a story about each picture, which includes a description of (a) the events in the picture, (b) developments that led to the event, (c) feelings and thoughts of the people in the picture, and (d) the outcome of the story. If the blank card appears, the examinee is asked to imagine a picture on the card and then tell a story about the picture. A number of different systems for analyzing and interpreting the story exist. All counselors who wish to administer the TAT should be trained in interpreting the stories. Guided Practice Exercise 10.2 introduces you to an experiential example of the TAT and encourages you to process your experience taking the assessment.

GUIDED PRACTICE EXERCISE 10.2

Prior to coming to class, go to the website www.utpsyc.org/TATintro. This site gives you an example of the Thematic Apperception Test (TAT). Take the test. You will be shown a picture and will be asked to write a story about that picture for 10 minutes. After you have written your story, click "Finish." You will then get your responses evaluated for common themes, and your responses will be compared with the average responses of both males and females who have taken the assessment. The purpose of this exercise is just to give you an experiential example of the TAT. Of course, the actual TAT is much longer and comprehensive. In pairs or small groups, discuss your experience taking this sample TAT. What was it like to take the assessment? Did your results surprise you? Why or why not? Did you find your results accurate? Why or why not?

The **TEMAS**, an acronym for Tell-Me-A-Story and also Spanish and Italian for "theme," was designed to reformulate the TAT and Rorschach Comprehensive System for use with minority and nonminority children and adolescents ages 5–18 (Costantino, Malgady, & Rogler, 1988). The TEMAS was normed on a sample of 642 children ages 5–13 years old from the New York City area representing four ethic groups: Puerto Ricans, other Hispanics, Blacks, and Whites. The test consists of two parallel versions: a minority version for Blacks and Hispanics/Latinos/as and a nonminority version. Each version has a short (9 cards) and long (23 cards) form. Card 1 is always shown first and the remaining cards are administered in a random order, unlike the TAT and Rorschach. The picture stimuli depict a range of psychosocial situations, including family scenes at home, street scenes, and inner-city environments. Examinees are asked to tell a complete story about the pictures with a beginning and an end; describe what is currently happening in the pictures, what happened before, and what will happen in the future; and describe what the main character is thinking and feeling upon solving the problem. The test should be given in the examinee's primary language. The TEMAS has an objective scoring system that measures 10 personality functions (e.g., aggression, anxiety/depression, sexual identity, achievement motivation), 7 affective functions (e.g., happy, sad, inappropriate affect), and 18 cognitive functions (e.g., reaction time, omissions, imagination, relationships). Case Illustration 10.2 discusses the results of the TEMAS and other assessments as well as observations about a client to provide the counselor with important information and a more accurate treatment plan.

CASE ILLUSTRATION　10.2

Jorge Martinez is a 14-year-old freshman who just moved to a new high school. The family moved when Jorge's father got a better job in a new city. Jorge's parents have expressed concern to the school counselor because they have found that Jorge is having difficulty making friends and has become withdrawn. His parents have become worried about him and are feeling a lot of guilt for taking him out of the school district where he had spent all of his childhood. There Jorge had friends and was more social. Now all he does is go to class, where he remains quiet and doesn't interact with any of his classmates. When Jorge comes home from school, he goes to his room until it is time to eat dinner. At the dinner table, he responds in one-word answers to his parents' attempts to interact with him.

His parents have noted that Jorge has always been a quiet and shy kid, but it seems like he has given up on making any new friends. He is referred to a local psychologist, Ms. Sanchez. After she forms a relationship with Jorge based on trust and rapport, Ms. Sanchez decides to administer some assessments in order to get additional information to more accurately help him. One assessment that Ms. Sanchez administers is the Tell-Me-A-Story (TEMAS). She chose the TEMAS because it has a version that was developed and adapted to be used specifically with Latinos and has normative data for Latinos. Therefore, the TEMAS is a culturally relevant assessment for Jorge. Ms. Sanchez administers the TEMAS in Spanish because it is Jorge's first language. One thing that Ms. Sanchez observes is that Jorge is more verbally expressive when he talks in Spanish than in English. The themes that emerge after scoring Jorge's assessment are related to depression, anxiety, interpersonal relations, and self-concept.

The results of the TEMAS and other assessments, along with her observations of Jorge, give Ms. Sanchez important information and provide for a more accurate treatment plan. She is able to help Jorge work through his feelings of anger about being moved to a new school district, build his self-esteem, and find school environments where he feels accepted. One activity that Jorge begins is to tutor students who are struggling in Spanish class. This activity gives him confidence and a sense of worth and contribution. It also helps Jorge focus on activities outside of himself and gives him success in helping others. Slowly, Jorge adapts to his new environment and makes friends.

Children's Apperception Test and Roberts Apperception Test for Children: 2

The **Children's Apperception Test (CAT)** is useful for describing personality or emotional disturbance in children ages 3 to 10 years (Bellak, 1975). The test consists of 10 animal pictures in social context (e.g., conflict, roles, family structures) rather than human figures as in the TAT. This allows children to project their feelings on objects which are safer than if they were to do it on individuals. As you may have learned in discussions about culturally appropriate techniques with children, the use of animals or other objects is often substituted to reduce children's apprehensions. A supplemental form was created called the **Children's Apperception Test-Supplemental Form (CAT-S)**, which contains pictures of family situations (e.g., separation of parents, mother's pregnancy). Also available is the **Children's Apperception Test-Human Form (CAT-H),** which contains humans rather than animals.

The **Roberts Apperception Test for Children: 2 (Roberts-2)** for ages 6–18, uses free narrative to evaluate a child's social understanding. This test is often used with children who have been referred for emotional or social adjustment problems (Roberts & Gruber, 2005). The child is shown 16 test pictures depicting children's and adolescents' everyday experience and is asked to complete a story based on what he or she perceives. There are three versions of the test pictures—Caucasian, African American, and Hispanic children— which allow the test to be customized for different ethnic groups. Through the narratives, valuable information including the child's ability to read social cues, recognize and solve interpersonal problems, cope with difficulties, identify sources of support, and use problem-solving skills can be assessed. The Roberts-2 is accompanied by a manual providing a comprehensive scoring system that is applied to the story, which produces a series of scales. The test is composed of two scales, Developmental/Adaptive and Clinical, which are made up of seven sets of subscales: two Theme Overview scales, six Available Resources scales, five Problem Identification scales, five Resolution scales, four Emotion scales, four Outcome scales, and two Unusual or Atypical Responses scales. Subscale raw scores are converted to T scores. A computer-scoring program is also available. Roberts-2 was normed on a sample of 1,000 children and adolescents and has been shown to be representative by gender, ethnicity, and parental education.

EXPRESSIVE TECHNIQUE/FIGURE DRAWING TECHNIQUES

A **Figure-Drawing Test** is a projective assessment in which the client produces a drawing. This drawing is then analyzed according to its contents and other related variables. It is important to note that although these assessments require individuals to draw, they are not a measure of artistic ability and instead an approach to understanding individuals. Use of a figure-drawing test to understand people surfaced in the late 19th century. Goodenough (1926) developed the Draw-A-Man task, which was further developed by Harris (1963) into the Goodenough-Harris Draw-A-Person Test. Buck (1948) and Buck and Hammer (1969) first introduced and evaluated the House-Tree-Person drawing test. Twenty years later, Burns (1987) developed the Kinetic House-Tree-Person (KHTP) test. As you read about the different drawing tests, it is important to note that they should not be a substitute for a comprehensive evaluation. In addition, it is extremely important to practice within your scope. If you enjoy reading about some of the figure-drawing tests below, please remember the importance of gaining adequate training before interpreting any drawings.

Draw-A-Man and Goodenough-Harris Draw-A-Person Test

Goodenough (1926) developed the **Draw-A-Man task,** which is a brief test widely used to assess intelligence maturation in children (Jolly, 2010) when she wanted to find a way to supplement the Stanford-Binet intelligence test with nonverbal measures. Researchers have found a close relationship between general intelligence and concept development in children. When a child draws, it is a form of expression and he or she draws what he or she knows rather than what he or she sees. Goodenough's (1926) test relies on the idea that a child's intellectual development will determine the content and nature of the drawings. The Draw-A-Man test has also been used to elicit personality type and unconscious material (Buck, 1948; Machover, 1949). The scale has 51 items for judging two classes—Class A: the drawing cannot be recognized as a human figure, and Class B: the drawing can be recognized as the human form. The test is based on the accuracy of the elements drawn and how many elements are included.

Harris (1963) extended Goodenough's (1926) scale to include adolescent years with a scale range from 3 to 15 years old. The test became known as the **Goodenough-Harris Draw-A-Person Test (GHDAP)**. Harris also added new items to follow the Draw-A-Man test, which included Draw-A-Woman and Draw-A-Self. Clients are instructed to draw three figures: a man, a woman, and a self-portrait in complete form and not as a stick figure. Compared to Goodenough's scale, Harris's scale included 73 elements based on age differentiation, relation to total score on test, and relation to group intelligence scores. The test is untimed and takes about 15 minutes. If the child's drawing appears as scribbles, he or she is given zero credit, which equals 3 years on the scoring system. If the child's drawing appears to have direction, he or she earns one credit, which is equal to 3 years and 3 months. Each following credit adds 3 months. Subsequent credit is given by looking at the overall picture and assessing whether (a) body segments are included; (b) arms and legs are attached properly; (c) eyes, ears, hair, and mouth are present; (d) fingers are detailed; and (e) proportions are accurate. The manual provides tables, which convert raw scores for the Draw-A-Man and Draw-A-Woman test into standard scores and percentile ranks (Harris, 1963).

The test has been shown to have good test-retest reliability and internal consistency, and it differentiates between age groups successfully (Evans, Ferguson, Davies, & Williams, 1975). Harris's (1963) test continues to be used by mental health professionals to quickly detect intellectual development. In addition, the drawing test is often used to evaluate learning differences and personality differences in children and adolescents. Furthermore, it is used to assess children with auditory handicaps, adjustment problems, and neurological weaknesses (Oster & Crone, 2004).

Machover's Draw-A-Person Test

Although Goodenough's (1926) Draw-A-Man test was originally designed to assess intelligence, Karen Machover (1949) hypothesized in her well-known book *Personality Projection in the Drawing of the Human Figure* that certain contents of the drawing reflected specific personality characteristics. Machover believed that these traits reflected the person's self-concept as well as unconscious conflict. For **Machover's Draw-A-Person Test,** the examinee is given a blank 8½ × 11 sheet of paper and is instructed to "Draw a person." When examinees inquire about how the picture should be drawn, responses such as "Just do your best" or "Make the drawing the way you think it should be" are sufficient. Once the examinee completes the drawing, he or she is handed a second sheet of paper and is asked to draw a person of the opposite gender. Many clinicians will often ask the client to make up a story (e.g., "Tell me a story about that figure") or ask questions (e.g., "What is that figure doing? How does he or she feel?") about the figures to help formulate hypotheses about personality functioning. Common characteristics of the drawing that clinicians often analyze include placement of the figures relative to the paper, size of the figures, facial expressions, line quality (including pencil pressure used), and individual characteristics of the figures (e.g., large eyes, ears, breasts). For example, placement of the figure often symbolizes how the client functions within his or her environment. Drawing mostly on the right side of the paper suggests looking more to the future, while drawing on the left side often signifies someone who is orientated to the past (Buck, 1948).

House-Tree-Person Test (HTP) and Kinetic House-Tree-Person Test (KHTP)

Drawings of houses, trees, and persons have long been widely used, valuable projective techniques that yield client information. Buck (1948) and Buck and Hammer (1969) first introduced and evaluated the **House-Tree-Person drawing test**. The client was given three sheets of paper: one horizontal sheet for the house and two vertical sheets for the tree and person. The client was usually instructed as follows: "I would like you to draw a house, I would like you to draw a tree, and I would like you to draw a whole person." Although widely used and respected among clinicians, the instructions, interpretation, and standardization of the HTP has limited use in some clinical settings. In terms of instructions, the house, tree, and person were each drawn on separate sheets of paper; clinicians were unable to see an inter-action or action between the three (see Guided Practice Exercise 10.3). The interpretation is based on a Freudian matrix in which all symbols fit within the matrix. And the HTP was both developed and standardized with "abnormal patients" in psychiatric settings (Burns, 1987).

GUIDED PRACTICE EXERCISE 10.3

Prior to class, take three blank 8.5 × 11 pieces of paper. On the first paper draw a house, on the second paper draw a tree, and on the third paper draw a person. Then visit the following websites that describe how to interpret the House-Tree-Person (HTP) projective assessment.

www.intelligentietesten.com/house_tree_person_drawings.htm
www.ehow.com/how_8631546_interpret-housetreeperson-test.html

Keep in mind that these websites are .com sites and are not necessarily accurate in their discussions. The purpose of this exercise is just to give you an experiential sample of the HTP assessment. Your interpretations may not be accurate due to the questionable accuracy of the websites and your level of experience with projective assessments. But this gives you the experience of taking the assessment and going through a process related to interpretation.

However, please remember the caution we have given you. In order to accurately administer, score, and interpret projective assessments, you must receive training and supervised practice until you reach competence. In addition, the projective assessment should not be the only tool that is used to assess a client. Multiple sources of information should be used to formulate a treatment plan.

During class, get into pairs or small groups and discuss your experience. What did you learn from taking the HTP assessment? What did it feel like to take it? Based on the information from the websites, did your results surprise you? Why or why not? What was the experience like regarding interpreting your drawings? What concerns do you have about interpreting a projective assessment without being trained or having experience?

Twenty years later, Burns (1987) developed the **Kinetic House-Tree-Person (KHTP)** test. The KHTP varies slightly from the original HTP in that the client is given one horizontal sheet of 8½ × 11 paper and asked to draw the house, tree, and person all on that one sheet of paper. The client is instructed as follows: "Draw a house, a tree, and a whole person on this piece of paper *with some kind of action.* Try to draw a whole person, not a cartoon or a stick person." Notice that the client is asked to draw "with some kind of action," hence the word *kinetic* added to the title. According to Burns,

> In drawing the tree, the drawer reflects his or her individual transformation process. In creating a person, the drawer reflects the self or ego functions interacting with the tree to create a larger metaphor. The house reflects the physical aspects of the drama. (p. 3)

In other words, the house often represents the intrafamilial relationships, the tree represents the experience of one's environment, and the person symbolizes the interpersonal relationships. After the client completes the drawing, he or she is asked to describe and interpret it. In the KHTP manual Burns offers questions to examine possible experiences while analyzing the KHTP (e.g., What story does the picture tell? What is your first impression? Whom and what do you see? What is happening? How do you feel about what is happening? What styles are present?). In addition, the manual provides interpretations of general characteristics of the drawing. Please see Table 10.2 for a sample of KHTP interpretations.

Kinetic Family Drawing (KFD) and Kinetic School Drawing (KSD)

Hulse (1951) studied drawings of families and his technique became known as **Draw-A-Family (D-A-F)**. Although the instructions to "draw your family" provided counselors with valuable material, the drawings often appeared as a noninteracting portrait of the family. You will often hear clinicians state the D-A-F produced "stiff" drawings. In order to address the issue of portraits looking stiff and noninteractive, Burns and Kaufman (1970, 1972) designed a test, known as the **Kinetic Family Drawing (KFD)** test, in which clients were asked to draw their family doing something, hence the word *kinetic* in the title. The KFD, derived from Hulse's (1951, 1952) Family Drawing Test, is valuable to clinicians when attempting to learn about the client's relation to his or her family. The client is presented with an 8½ × 11 sheet of paper and a pencil with an eraser. The client is instructed by the counselor, "Draw a picture of everyone in your family, including you, DOING something. Try to draw whole people, not cartoons or stick people. Remember, make everyone DOING something—some kind of actions" (Burns & Kaufman, 1972, p. 5). After the client completes the task, the counselor asks the client to identify each figure, describe his or her relationship with the figure, explain what the figure is doing and why. The **Kinetic School Drawing (KSD)** is an adaptation of the KFD. With the KSD, the client is asked to draw a picture of himself or herself interacting with relevant school figures. Instructions include the following:

> I'd like you to draw a school picture. Put yourself, your teacher, and a friend or two in the picture. Make everyone doing something. Try to draw whole people and make the best drawing you can. Remember, draw yourself, your teacher, and a friend or two, and make everyone doing something. (Knoff & Prout, 1985, p. 4)

Table 10.2   Sample of Suggested Kinetic House Tree Person Interpretations

Characteristics	Interpretations
House	
Many windows	Openness and desire for environmental contact
Thin walls	Weak or vulnerable self
Shrubs/flowers	May represent people
No door	Isolation, possible psychosis
Tree	
Emphasis on roots	Unsettled business, people unsure of themselves
Upward branches	Reaching for opportunities
Downward branches	To "be sorry," thoughts moving into the past
Tree house	Attempts to find protection from threatening environment
Person	
Cutting off the head	Concerns dealing with issues of control
Very short arms	Lack of ambition, feelings of inadequacy
Large shoes	Need for stability
Mouth missing	Asthmatic conditions, depressive conditions, not wanting to communicate with others

Source: Burns (1987).

Kinetic Drawing System for Family and School (KDS)

The **Kinetic Drawing System for Family and School (KDS)**, used to evaluate children and adolescents, is useful with clients who have difficulty in verbal communication. As a projective technique the test can be used to explore a client's personality and attitudes and to assess a child's perception of relationships (e.g., peers, family, school). As stated in the manual,

> Its use should be restricted to individuals at or beyond the graduate level who are familiar with psychological assessment and visual-motor development in children of various ages. Accurate interpretation of children's drawings requires knowledge of normal conceptual, perceptual, and emotional development. (Knoff & Prout, 1985, p. 2)

The assessment combines two of the previous projective techniques described: Kinetic Family Drawing and Kinetic School Drawing. The Kinetic Drawing System for Family and School addresses both family and school settings and is approximately 20 minutes long. The family drawing is given first (see Figure 10.1), followed by the school drawing (see Figure 10.2). After the client completes the drawings, he or she is asked a series of guided questions contained in the manual. Some typical questions include "What is this person doing? What will happen to this person immediately after this picture? What does this drawing make you think of? If you could change anything at all about this family/school picture, what would it be?" (Knoff & Prout, 1985, p. 5).

The counselor then analyzes each drawing for the presence and absence of specific characteristics, which are all defined in the manual. A scoring booklet for the examiner is provided with the assessment and gives a list of the five categories used for interpretation: actions of and between figures; figure characteristics; position, distance, and barriers; style; and symbols. The drawing is then scored and interpreted according to the interpretive hypotheses located in the manual. Table 10.3 provides examples of a few interpretive suggestions.

The median inter-rater reliability among five independent judges was reported at .87; however, test-retest reliability appears unstable. Concurrent and construct validity was reported.

Figure 10.1 Family Baseball Picture

Source: Used by permission of Laura Haddock.

Figure 10.2   School Drawing

Source: Used by permission of Laura Haddock.

Table 10.3   Sample of Kinetic Drawing System for Family and School

Characteristic	Interpretation
Kinetic Family Drawing	
Family playing ball	Child willing to engage in constructive, competitive activities
Similarity between self drawing and others (e.g., clothing, facial expressions)	Feelings of admiration, identifies with other individual
Field of force (e.g., throwing a ball)	Rivalry between members involved
Kinetic School Drawing	
Back views of people	More common in KSDs, children often draw where they are seated looking toward the teacher and blackboard
Large teacher drawing	Positive academic achievement
Chalkboard	Writings may resemble feelings toward academic achievement and self-adequacy in school
Drawing self next to significant other	May resemble the child liking the individual (e.g., teacher in the drawing), wanting more attention or to be closer to person

Source: Knoff & Prout (1985).

COMPLETION TECHNIQUES

Sentence Completion Test

Sentence completion tests, like word association tests, are verbal completion projective personality techniques that are considered semistructured. These tests are referred to as semistructured because they have a basic framework yet allow for a variety of responses. Sentence completion tests require the client to finish a sentence for which the first word or words are provided; these words are often referred to as *stems*. Even though the initial part of the sentences is provided, you probably can imagine the diverse number of responses that individuals may provide to complete the sentence. Over the years, many different sentence completion tests have been developed to assess the need for achievement, emotional problems, learning problems, and locus of control. Some sentence completion tests are linked to theory while others are atheoretical. It is assumed that the client makes sentences that reflect his or her desires, wishes, or fears (see Case Illustration 10.3).

How might you complete the following sentences to express your real feelings?

I like _____.

I regret _____.

I can _____.

Sometimes I _____.

Marriage is _____.

I am best when _____.

I am most frightened when _____.

The future seems _____.

CASE ILLUSTRATION   10.3

Keesha is a 13-year-old African American girl who was referred to the school counselor because she was drawing disturbing pictures in class. The scenes Keesha was depicting were violent and bloody. Despite the disturbing nature of her drawings, Keesha was a friendly, outgoing, and engaged student. The dichotomy between her outward expression and her drawings disturbed Keesha's teachers. It was suggested she see the school counselor. The school counselor then referred her to a community counseling center for assessment and therapy. In the course of evaluating Keesha, her counselor administered a sentence completion test. Keesha's answers were as follows:

I like death.

I regret being born.

I can decide to live or die or kill or be killed.

Sometimes I don't understand why I feel so angry.

Marriage is a sham.

I am best when I am away from home.

I am most frightened when my mom is away from home on a business trip.

The future seems dark and hopeless.

Imagine you are Keesha's counselor. The sentence completion test is believed to provide insight into a person in terms of his or her attitudes, emotions, motivations, values, and beliefs. What information do you glean from Keesha's answers? What concerns you about her answers? Would it surprise you to learn that after spending time in counseling, Keesha told her counselor that her father was sexually abusing her?

Rotter Incomplete Sentence Blank, Second Edition

The **Rotter Incomplete Sentence Blank, Second Edition** (RISB-2; Rotter, Lah, & Rafferty, 1992; Rotter & Rafferty, 1950) is one of the most popular standardized sentence completion tests available for clinicians and has been used in college and university settings as well as medical, military, education, and research settings. According to Weis, Toolis, and Cerankosky (2008), 32% of clinicians use the RISB with referred adolescents, 18% use it with children, and 61% of school psychologists reported using the RISB to assess both children and adolescents (Hojnoski, Morrison, Brown, & Matthews, 2006). The RISB-2 was designed to assess overall adjustment in adolescents and adults and can be individually or group-administered. The forms include three levels: high school, college, and adults. The test consists of 40 sentence stems, with 15 items on the front and 25 items on the back. The test consists of a combination of numerical stems. For example, some stems on the college form consist of single-word (e.g., Boys . . .), two-word (e.g., Marriage is . . .), three-word (e.g., What pains me . . .), and four- and five-word stems (e.g., My greatest worry is . . .). Responses are scored using a manual on a 6 to 0 continuum to produce one overall adjustment score. High scores reflect "the presence of prolonged/unhappy/dysphoric states, difficulty in coping with frustration, a lack of constructive anxiety, interference in initiating or maintaining activity, or the inability to establish and maintain satisfying interpersonal relationships" (Rotter et al., 1992, p. 5); while low scores reflect psychosocial adjustment and competence.

Washington University Sentence Completion Test (WUSCT) and SCT-Y

The **Washington University Sentence Completion Test (WUSCT)**, developed by Loevinger and Wessler (1970), is one of the most validated sentence completion forms available to date, with excellent reliability and construct validity. Inter-rater reliability is estimated from .74 to .88, test-retest reliability from .67 to .76, and internal consistency in the high .80s

(Lilienfeld et al., 2000; Weiss, Zilberg, & Genevro, 1989). The WUSCT was originally published in 1970 and developed to assess one's self-concept based on Loevinger's (1998) theory of ego development. The most recent version, Form 81, is recommended for adults and consists of 36 sentence stems. The youth version of the WUSCT, for children and adolescents ages 8–18, is the SCT-Y, which consists of 32 items (see Table 10.4). The WUSCT and SCT-Y sentence stems address how examinees respond to personal relationships, responsibility, authority, frustration, and other responsibilities. Both instruments are scored using a detailed manual. A single total protocol rating is computed to assess the examinee's core level of psychosocial maturity (Hy & Loevinger, 1996).

Table 10.4 Sentence Completion Test for Children (SCT-Y)

First page

1. When a child will not join in group activities _____.
2. Raising children _____.
3. When I am criticized _____.
4. If I were in charge _____.
5. Being with other people _____.
6. The thing I like about myself is _____.
7. My mother and I _____.
8. What gets me into trouble is _____.
9. Education _____.
10. When people are helpless _____.
11. When I am afraid _____.
12. A good father _____.
13. My biggest fear _____.
14. I feel sorry _____.
15. When they avoid me _____.
16. Rules are _____.

Second page

17. Crime and delinquency could be halted if _____.
18. Women (Men) are lucky because _____.
19. I just can't stand people who _____.
20. At times I worry about _____.

21. I am _____.

22. A boy (girl) feels good when _____.

23. My main problem is _____.

24. Good friends _____.

25. The worst thing about being a man (woman) _____.

26. A good mother _____.

27. When I am with a girl (boy) _____.

28. Sometimes I wish that _____.

29. My father _____.

30. If I can't get what I want _____.

31. My conscience bothers me if _____ _____.

32. I felt proud that I _____.

Mayers's Gravely Disabled Sentence Completion Task

The **Mayers's Gravely Disabled Sentence Completion Task** (Mayers, 1991) was developed to identify clients with severely impaired mental status. The test consists of 21 items and is typically used on clients who are unable to complete a standard battery due to the extent of their mental impairment. No psychometric properties are reported; however, the test meets forensic standards of evidence during civil court hearings (Holaday, Smith, & Sherry, 2000). If you are working in forensic settings, you will likely encounter this task at some point in your career.

ARRANGEMENT/SELECTION TECHNIQUES

With **projective arrangement** or selection techniques, examinees either arrange or select certain presented visual stimuli. For example, assessment might involve showing various visual stimuli and asking the examinee to rank these stimuli based on preference or select the stimuli they least or most prefer.

Szondi Test

The **Szondi Test,** created by Léopold Szondi (1947), is a projective personality technique similar to the Rorschach but utilizes the selection technique. The assessment consists of 48 facial photos of various mental patients. The cards are divided into six piles, and each pile contains eight diagnostic categories. The examinee is instructed to choose two photographs he or she least likes and two photographs he or she most likes from each of the six sets. Each photograph contains a code on the back, which is then transcribed onto a grid called a Psychogram; the grid shows the quantitative distribution of the examinees choices. According to Szondi,

> The eight types of mental and emotional diseases represented . . . have to be thought of as expressing certain psychological mechanisms in extreme form, which to some degree exist in everybody. . . . Depending on the degree of . . . the state of tension in each of the eight need systems, the pictures representing the corresponding needs will assume valence character in various proportions. (p. 26)

The rationale was that people have unconscious motivations and responses, which they express through a series of choice (selection) reactions.

Although the Szondi Test is historically well known, it is rarely used due to its weak psychometric properties. Burley (1957) provided some of the most significant questions on which reports of psychometric properties were identified, noting that previous studies failed to provide necessary information regarding the procedures used to validate the test's applicability. Still, Rotarescu and Ciurea (2010) argue that the test's theoretical basis, founded on a belief in the impact of the unconscious on pathology, has been demonstrated to correlate with medical findings regarding lesions on the brain. Unfortunately, the study's findings fail to demonstrate application to the counseling field.

STRENGTHS AND LIMITATIONS

Since we discussed several structured personality instruments in Chapter 9 and projective techniques in this chapter, let's focus on the characteristic strengths and limitations of these formal techniques.

Self-report inventories, such as the MBTI or the NEO-PI-3, have several advantages compared to other personality tests. If you recall, a standardized instrument is one that has uniform administration and scoring procedures. The standardized nature of these tests makes them easy to administer, score, and interpret. Because these tests are objective, they provide precise estimates of aspects of the personality by minimizing subjective interpretation on the part of those scoring the tests. In other words, everyone taking the test is treated the same and given the same instructions. Many of these tests are highly reliable and there is a significant amount of empirical evidence to support their use.

A number of general drawbacks have been reported regarding the use of self-report inventories. Some clinicians view the standardization of procedures as too mechanistic and, thus, restricting the freedom of response. Furthermore, clinicians do not always assess the reasons behind the statements on the test. Self-report inventories require the cooperation of the client and for the client to know himself or herself. Keeping this in mind, the potential for social desirability bias and client deception is possible. A person might want to portray himself or herself in a certain way and distort his or her image. While some assessments, such as the MMPI-2, use validity scales to deal with this, not all self-report inventories include such scales. In addition, self-report inventories often have low predictive validity, meaning the test's ability to predict future behavior according to established criteria is low.

The highly ambiguous nature of stimuli used for projective testing offers several advantages. With projective tests, it is often difficult to "fake good" or "fake bad." Test takers do not know how the test provides information to the tester, thus the degree to which a test taker can answer in a socially desirable way is decreased. The flexibility in responses allows clients to respond in a less defensive manner as they do not feel they are being quizzed. This can help facilitate development of rapport. For example, the Kinetic Drawing System inventories can be used as an "ice-breaker" technique to examine a child's comfort and evaluate the rapport between the therapist and client.

Although the unstructured and ambiguous nature of the test stimuli can be beneficial, it introduces subjective interpretation. According to Schultz and Loving (2012), the subjectivity of these tests is often complicated by the readily available nature of projective measures of personality through sources which lack a scholarly basis. For example, many of the tests described in this chapter may have portions of the assessment made available through sources such as Wikipedia but also may provide inaccurate interpretations of responses. If the availability of inaccurate information and interpretation is not sufficient, as with other tests which have been described throughout this book, subjectivity of interpretation often is accompanied with concerns regarding empirical properties. Projective tests demonstrate poor reliability and validity, and responses are often difficult to interpret. As Forbey and Lee (2011) note, the lack of reliability and validity research on many of these assessments enhances the potential that interpretations will be biased.

Projective tests require advanced skills and extensive training beyond that offered in a graduate program. Not only are advanced skills needed to make interpretations, but these tests are often time-consuming. Although you may not administer these tests, it is important to know their functions as you will likely encounter reports containing these interpretations in the future.

Whether using a structured personality test, a projective technique, or a combination of both, it is important to remember that the value of the interpretations will depend on the counselor's skills. As stated in Chapter 5, always remember to practice within your scope of training. Always review the level of training needed to administer an assessment, and obtain the necessary training before administering any assessment.

KEYSTONES

- Projective techniques differ in the type of response patterns analyzed: association of ideas, construction of a story, completion, arrangement/selection, and expression in response to test stimuli.
- Popular projective techniques include the Rorschach Inkblot Test, WAT, TAT, TEMAS, CAT, Rotter Incomplete Sentence Blank, WUSCT, KHTP, GHDAP, KFD, and KDS.
- Strengths of projective tests include making it difficult to fake good or bad, facilitating development of rapport, and providing a high degree of response flexibility. Limitations include the

fact that responses are often difficult to interpret, interpretations are subjective, and there is poor reliability and validity.

- Strengths of structured personality tests include that they provide objective and precise estimates of personality, are easy to score and interpret, and are backed up by a significant amount of empirical support. Drawbacks include that they restrict freedom of response, have potential for a social desirability bias, and have low predictive validity,

KEY TERMS

apperceive

association techniques

Children's Apperception Test (CAT)

Children's Apperception Test-Human Form (CAT-H)

Children's Apperception Test-Supplemental Form (CAT-S)

Comprehensive System (CS)

Draw-A-Family

Draw-A-Man task

Figure-Drawing Test

Goodenough-Harris Draw-A-Person Test (GHDAP)

House-Tree-Person drawing test (HTP)

Kinetic Drawing System for Family and School (KDS)

Kinetic Family Drawing (KFD)

Kinetic House-Tree-Person (KHTP)

Kinetic School Drawing (KSD)

Machover's Draw-A-Person Test

Mayers's Gravely Disabled Sentence Completion Task

projective arrangement

projective techniques

Roberts Apperception Test for

Children: 2 (Roberts-2)

Rorschach Inkblot Test

Rotter Incomplete Sentence Blank, Second Edition (RISB-2)

sentence completion tests

story construction test

Szondi Test

Tell-Me-A-Story (TEMAS)

Thematic Apperception Test (TAT)

Washington University Sentence Completion Test (WUSCT)

Word Association Test (WAT)

ADDITIONAL RESOURCES

- AllPsych Online

  http://allpsych.com/personalitysynopsis/rorschach.html

This is a website of a virtual psychology classroom with links to journal articles, books, and other readings, which includes information on many projective personality assessments. The site also has biographies of many of the theorists whose work either created or inspired many of the assessments.

- Development of TEMAS as Multicultural Test

  http://www.hogg.utexas.edu/uploads/documents/rls14_GiuseppeCostantino.pdf

This is a presentation for the Hogg Foundation for Mental Health given in Houston, Texas, in 2006. It discusses the formation of the TEMAS and how it was constructed and validated for use with nonminority and minority children and adolescents. At the end of the presentation are the stimulus cards so students can see what they look like.

- Historical Overview of Projective Testing

  http://www.cohendelara.com/pdf/chapter_02.pdf

This is a book chapter on the history of projective testing.

- History of Projective Testing

  http://projectivetests.umwblogs.org/controversies

This website gives the history of some of the most well-known and frequently used projective tests and discusses the controversies surrounding them.

- Online Personality Tests

  http://personality-testing.info

This site offers sample personality tests that you can take online. It offers a brief overview of some of the more prominent personality tests such as those that are formed on the Big Five personality factors, the Jungian-based assessments, the Holland Code, the NEO, and the 16PF, among others.

- Serendip

  http://serendip.brynmawr.edu/sci_cult/mentalhealth/projective.html

This is an educational website focused on psychology that offers information about projective personality tests. It provides information on how to locate psychological tests as well as information regarding such topics as the rights and responsibilities of test takers.

- "The Scientific Status of Projective Tests"

  http://digitalcommons.utep.edu/cgi/viewcontent.cgi?article=1007&context=james_wood

This is an empirical article from the journal *Psychological Science in the Public Interest* that discusses the controversy of projective personality tests and provides a review of the literature.

Student Study Site: Visit the Student Study Site at **www.sagepub.com/watson** to access additional study tools, including quizzes, web resources, and journal articles.

CHAPTER 11

Behavioral Assessment

After reading this chapter, you will be able to

- Define the term *behavior* and describe the characteristics of behaviors
- Identify the components of a behavioral assessment
- Differentiate between direct and indirect forms of behavioral assessment
- Identify rating scales, checklists, and other instruments used to assess target behaviors
- List the advantages and disadvantages of behavioral assessment practices
- Describe the various sources of biases that can affect the validity of a behavioral assessment

In this chapter you will be introduced to the practice of behavioral assessment. Similar to the assessment of personality, intelligence, aptitude, and achievement covered in previous chapters, the assessment of behavior is an activity counselors engage in as part of their clinical practice. However, a major difference between behavioral assessment and these other types of assessment that counselors perform is in the utility and overall purpose of behavioral assessment. In addition to being a collection of assessment techniques and interventions, behavioral assessment also refers to a conceptual framework used to help counselors understand human behavior. Through assessment, counselors identify target behaviors and analyze the interrelatedness of the events or circumstances preceding the behavior, the components of the behavior itself, and the resulting consequences of the behavior occurring. As a result, behavioral assessment allows counselors to identify potential problem behaviors as well as treat and offer recommendations intended to help clients change unwanted behaviors. The following sections will describe the basic elements of behavioral assessment and will introduce you to common interventions and techniques used by counselors.

WHAT IS BEHAVIOR?

Before introducing you to behavioral assessment strategies and interventions, we felt that a good starting point would be to operationally define the term *behavior*. In simple terms, **behavior** refers to the range of actions exhibited by an individual. Our behaviors are observed in everything we do and all that we say. Think about all that you have done today from the moment you awoke until now. How many different behaviors have you exhibited? The number may shock you, as all of us engage in many different behaviors on a daily basis. Some of these may be quite brief and seem inconsequential, such as waving hello to someone or stretching our arms. Others may be more detailed and purpose-driven, such as driving a car or taking or studying for an upcoming exam. According to Miltenberger (2012), behaviors, regardless of their purpose or duration, share several characteristics. These characteristics are described below.

1. **Behavior refers to actions not dispositions**. When we consider an individual's behavior, we should focus exclusively on what that person does, not how that person acts. For example, you may think that your grumpy old professor who assigns too much homework and grades papers harshly is a "mean" teacher. In this example mean is not a behavior. Stating that the teacher is mean does not tell us anything about what it is that the teacher is doing. The behaviors assessed would be those specific actions the teacher does that collectively result in you considering this professor mean. When defining behaviors, keep in mind that they are temporary events and not static characteristics. Counselors engaged in behavior assessment should always have an operational definition of the behavior for which they are observing. This definition should identify the discrete action (including its beginning and resolution) that is being assessed. Using operational definitions facilitates the recognition of a target behavior by all observers.

2. **Behaviors are multidimensional in nature.** There are several dimensions of a behavior that can be assessed. Frequency, duration, intensity, and latency are a few of the dimensions that counselors may focus on in their assessment of a behavior. *Frequency* refers to how often the behavior occurs. How many times does a child make a disruptive remark in class? How often does a client mention his anger in session? In these situations, the counselor is assessing the frequency of the behavior by noting each individual occurrence and tallying a total at the end of the observation. *Duration* refers to how long the behavior lasts. Some behaviors can be instantaneous, such as a blink of an eye, whereas others can last considerably longer, such as a temper tantrum. Behaviors that are brief in duration may be easy to miss, so proper training is critical for those who will be conducting assessments. *Intensity* provides counselors with a measure of the magnitude of the behavior. Intensity is typically measured in quantitative terms. For example, a counselor may rate a client's behavior on a scale of 1–10, with 1 being minimally invasive and 10 being significant disruption. *Latency* refers to the amount of time it takes for a behavior to begin after an identified stimulus. The time it takes a

person to display an emotional reaction to bad news would be a measure of the latency of a behavior. Assessing the latency of behaviors offers some insight into the emotional connection a client may have to a particular event or stimulus.

3. **Behaviors are observable.** Behaviors are tangible actions that people perform or ways in which they conduct themselves. As such, behaviors can be directly witnessed and observed. For example, a counselor can observe a resistant client removing herself from the counseling session by avoiding eye contact and not responding to direct questions. The counselor is able to detect that there is a problem from the behaviors the client is exhibiting. The fact that behaviors are observable means they also can be measured and evaluated. There are numerous methods for recording behavioral observations, several of which are described later in this chapter.

4. **Behaviors are best understood in their native context.** Well-designed behavioral assessments are ecological in nature. To best understand a behavior, knowledge of the circumstances under which the behavior occurs is required. Behaviors may be readily observed in a particular environment but not appear in another. A client in an inpatient chemical dependency treatment center may abstain from drinking, but the same client may exhibit a different behavior when back home among friends in familiar surroundings and without clinical staff restricting access to alcohol. When examining context, counselors should take into account precipitating events, people involved, setting, situation, and consequences (Erford, 2013). Additionally, counselors should keep in mind the phenomenology of situations. Each person will have a different perspective and understanding of the situation, so we cannot assume that everyone involved will share the same experience. A recognition of diversity and the cultural lens through which individual clients view the world is important for counselors (see Chapter 15).

5. **A reciprocal relationship exists between behaviors and the environment.** As much as the environment influences human behavior, the behaviors we exhibit also have the power to evoke changes in the environment. In other words, every behavior elicits a response. Jumping into a swimming pool on a warm summer day will cause water displacement and create waves. Similarly, a student who raises his hand will catch the teacher's attention, causing her to acknowledge the student and entertain his question. This relationship between behaviors and their environment is cyclical and is often represented by the triadic reciprocality model (see Figure 11.1). In this model behaviors, cognitions, and environmental stimuli all operate as determinants of one another.

BEHAVIORAL ASSESSMENT

Now that you have learned what behaviors are, we can begin looking at how counselors assess behavior. **Behavioral assessment** can be defined as the identification and measurement of meaningful response units (including overt behavior, feelings, and cognitions) and

Figure 11.1   Triadic Reciprocality Model

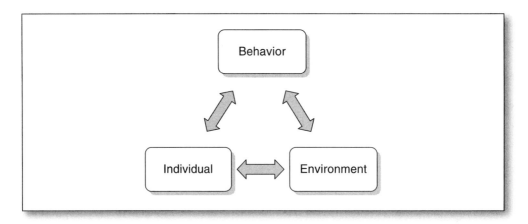

their controlling variables (both environmental and organismic) for the purposes of under-standing and altering human behavior (Nelson & Hayes, 1979). Rooted in social cognitive theory, behavioral assessments can easily be integrated with other forms of assessment to provide a deeper understanding of a client and the issues that led to that client participating in counseling. The benefit of behavioral assessment can be seen in many aspects of the counseling process, including screening, problem identification and analysis, intervention selection, evaluation, and follow-up. The practice of assessing behavior differs from other assessment activities like clinical interviewing and testing in three fundamental ways.

The first difference between behavioral assessment and traditional assessment is in the stated purpose of each. The purpose of a behavioral assessment is to observe and measure samples of behavior. These samples are then used to make hypotheses about how clients are likely to act in other situations. In traditional assessment, behaviors are seen as signs of some underlying internal process. Behaviors are merely symptoms of a larger issue that is troubling the client. The second difference is in the scope of the assessment. In traditional assessment, a target is identified and assessed individually. In a behavioral assessment, the context is expanded. Behavioral assessments include a much more functional analysis of exhibited behavior (see Guided Practice Exercise 11.1). Through behavioral assessment counselors seek to better understand behaviors (overt and covert), the antecedents (internal and external) preceding these behaviors, and the consequences (positive and negative) that follow the behavior. In a behavioral assessment attention is given to the contextual conditions surrounding the behavior as well. The third difference is in the importance assessment holds for the counselor. In behavioral assessment the counselor constantly assesses the client. Assessment becomes an ongo-ing process that factors into all phases of counseling treatment, whereas in traditional approaches assessment may be implemented only when the situation warrants its inclu-sion or the counselor is trying to validate a current conceptualization of the client's presenting concern.

GUIDED PRACTICE EXERCISE 11.1

Operationally Defining Target Behaviors

Think of an issue (depression, anxiety, stress, communication issues, relational problems, etc.) which you could see yourself addressing in your work as a counselor. Were you to conduct a behavioral assessment, what behaviors would you identify as being evidence that the client you were working with was having difficulty with this issue? Create a list of three to five behaviors that you believe would be exhibited by a client dealing with the issue you chose. How would you operationally define these behaviors? What dimensions (frequency, duration, intensity, latency) would you also need to assess? How would you account for environmental context in your assessment?

METHODS OF BEHAVIORAL ASSESSMENT

There are many methods counselors can use to assess behavior. The decision on which approach to use will vary depending on a number of factors, including who the client is, the problem to be assessed, the setting in which the problem is occurring, and the outcome expected from the assessment. Generally, behavioral assessments fall into one of two broad categories: clinical behavioral assessment and functional behavioral assessment. The difference between the two is in how assessment results will be used. Clinical assessments are primarily used to address problem behaviors noted across settings (home, school, or work), which results in the development of a clear treatment plan for counselors to follow. Functional assessments typically occur in schools and are used to help determine whether students exhibiting problem behaviors might meet criteria for a disability. As such, familiarity with several assessment methods is beneficial.

In this section we will introduce the more commonly used behavioral assessment methods in counseling practice. To facilitate our presentation, the interventions are presented in two sections representing direct and indirect methods. Direct methods are those in which behavior is assessed as it occurs. A behavior is produced and is then recorded and assessed. This assessment can be completed by a counselor, observer, or the client. Using indirect methods, assessment usually is completed by way of client self-report and is in reference to past behaviors. Individuals reflect on their behavior and report their perceptions to the observer. Each has its own inherent set of advantages and disadvantages. As a counselor it will be your responsibility to determine which approach would be most appropriate given your client, the current need for behavior to be assessed, and the setting where assessment will occur.

Direct Methods of Behavioral Assessment

Direct methods of assessing behavior are advantageous to counselors when they desire to better understand why behaviors are occurring. They allow for an objective recording of behaviors that includes both the events and triggers leading to a behavior as well as the results and consequences of the behavior being displayed. There are several advantages to the direct methods of behavioral assessment that make them popular assessment approaches. These advantages include (a) the ability to measure specific target behaviors, (b) the ability to use operational definitions of target behaviors that allow for observation with minimum interference, (c) the ability to employ standardized coding procedures, (d) the ability to provide quantitative scores that do not vary from one observer to another, and (e) the ability to be tested for reliability and validity across multiple observers, time periods, and environmental settings (Volpe & McConaughy, 2005). Examples of direct methods that a counselor may choose to implement in the counseling process include naturalistic observation, analogue observation, and self-monitoring.

Naturalistic Observation

In a **naturalistic observation** the counselor observes a client and records his or her behaviors as they occur without any manipulation of the environment by the observer. The goal of naturalistic observation is to analyze behaviors as they occur in their natural setting. The major advantage of this approach is that counselors are able to observe the genuine behaviors of their clients. In addition, using the natural setting allows the observing counselor to note the inherent restraints of the client's normal environment and account for them when setting goals with a client and treatment planning. There are several ways in which naturalistic observation can occur.

Naturalistic observations can be either overt or covert. In an overt observation, the subject of interest is aware that he or she is being observed. While overt observation increases the likelihood that the target behavior will be performed (i.e., clients know what the counselor is looking for and assessing), authenticity is sacrificed as the behavior may not be wholly representative of how the client would normally respond or act. Additionally, observer effect may occur and clients may perform differently if they know they are being observed. For example, a school counselor may tell a student that she plans to sit in on his class this afternoon and observe how he behaves. The student, knowing that the counselor is there to observe him, may curtail his behavior or perform in a manner that is uncharacteristic of his typical behavior. To ensure a more authentic demonstration of behavior, counselors may instead choose to conduct their observations covertly. Covert observations are made discreetly so subjects are not aware that they are being observed. Specifically, counselors should attempt to remain as unobtrusive as possible to ensure that the behaviors they observe are genuine. These observations can then be used to support a counselor's working conceptualization of the possible functions that particular behaviors serve.

Naturalistic observations also can be either structured or unstructured. A structured observation is one in which the counselor works from a pre-populated checklist of behaviors. The counselor observes only for those behaviors identified on the checklist and notes their occurrence. An unstructured observation is one in which the counselor does not have any identified behaviors to observe and simply records all behaviors that are observed. Although unstructured observations are designed to remove restrictions on what counselors observe, observer bias still is a concern. Counselors may be predisposed to note only those behaviors that match previous information they have about a client or that validate their conceptualization of the client and the client's problem behaviors.

To prevent such biases from occurring, these observations should occur on multiple occasions to obtain a more comprehensive understanding of the behavior being assessed. Multiple observations help prevent the chance that behaviors observed may be an artifact of the specific situation occurring that time (e.g., clients having a bad day). In addition, it is often a good idea to have more than one person complete the observation. At the end of the observation period, the different observers can compare their recordings and come to a general consensus regarding the behaviors that did and did not occur. Overall, the observation of behaviors in a natural setting is an activity that takes experience and practice (Martella, Nelson, Marchand-Martella, & O'Reilly, 2012). However, based on its utility, it is an approach that counselors may find quite useful in their work with clients. Case Illustration 11.1 presents a situation in which the naturalistic approach proved beneficial and increased the observers' understanding of the behaviors being exhibited.

CASE ILLUSTRATION 11.1

An example of naturalistic observation can be found in Kathryn Graham and Samantha Wells's (2001) study of late-night aggressive behavior. Over the course of 93 nights, Graham and Wells observed 117 incidents of aggressive behavior among bar patrons in a Canadian tavern. The observations were made on weekend nights between the hours of midnight and 2:30 a.m. without alerting the patrons that they were being observed. The researchers' observations allowed them to collect information on both the types of behaviors commonly occurring and the types of patrons most often involved in these incidents. Additionally, they were able to identify several triggers for aggression in bars, including problems with bar staff, rowdy behavior, and interpersonal relationship problems. Studies such as this might be helpful to bar managers who want to reduce aggressive incidents in their establishments.

Analogue Observation

Analogue observation is an alternative to the naturalistic approach. In an **analogue observation** the counselor creates a simulated environment (typically in an office or research laboratory) that replicates the client's natural surroundings and observes how the client behaves. Through the development of contrived situations and scenarios, counselors are able to develop working hypotheses about the factors that precipitated and maintain a client's problem behaviors. The goal of analogue behavioral observation, then, is to derive valid estimates of the client's behavior in a current or future natural environment (Haynes, 2001b). An example of an analogue observation would be observing how a client interacts with others in a group counseling session at a local mental health center. A counselor working on effective communication skills with the group members could observe how the members communicate with one another and assess how well they are able to apply the skills they have been learning.

A benefit of the analogue approach is that it gives the counselor a greater sense of control over the process. Using contrived settings, counselors are able to assess overt client behaviors in a setting designed to increase the chance that important behaviors and inter-actions will occur (Haynes, 2001a). An additional benefit of the analogue approach is that extraneous variables or uncontrolled stimuli that may detract from the target behavior can be reduced or eliminated (Whitcomb & Merrell, 2012). Using an analogue approach, a counselor could set up the group to ensure that the skills taught are displayed in a safe and structured environment. In addition, the counselor is afforded the opportunity to interrupt and interject with real-time suggestions and feedback to group members regarding their performance. While this approach provides counselors with a greater degree of control, this gain is offset by a loss of generalizability. The behaviors of the clients in the structured group session may not represent the behaviors that would have been noted had the coun-selor observed the clients in a more naturalistic setting. The decision as to which observa-tion technique to use will depend on the information needed to be gathered through observation. Guided Practice Exercise 11.2 asks you to consider the best observation tech-nique to use for a number of behaviors being assessed.

GUIDED PRACTICE EXERCISE 11.2

Selecting the Appropriate Observation Technique

For each of the following types of behavior, determine whether a naturalistic or analogue observa-tion would be the best assessment approach. Why do you believe your selection provides you with the most accurate and reliable data?

- inattentive behavior in a classroom
- anger outbursts
- lying
- bullying
- negative self-talk

Self-Monitoring

Self-monitoring is defined as the practice of observing and recording one's own behav-iors. Using this approach, counselors teach clients how to appropriately observe and record their behaviors. This instruction includes recognizing when a behavior occurs and how to note the circumstances surrounding the behavior, including who is involved, what events precipitated the behavior, and any consequences that occur as a result of the behavior (Vaughn, Bos, & Schumm, 2000). There are multiple advantages to the self-monitoring approach. In addition to being a low-cost and efficient approach, self-monitoring is an approach that can be used with clients of all ages (Whitcomb & Merrell, 2012). Counselors can use the data obtained from a client's self-report to better understand problem behaviors.

The practice of self-monitoring is not without its drawbacks. Specifically, the reliability and validity of observational data are questionable. Clients may not have been adequately trained in how to observe, so they may miss the occurrence of important target behaviors. Another issue is when clients underreport or exaggerate the occurrence of behaviors to present themselves in a more favorable light. Unaware of the true extent of the behavior and its occurrence, counselors may not be able to develop an accurate treatment plan. Because of these challenges, the data obtained from self-monitoring is best utilized as part of a multidimensional assessment plan (Whitcomb & Merrell, 2012).

Observational Recording Methods

Counselors conducting behavioral observations have at their disposal a number of different methods for evaluating the behaviors they observe. The aspect of the behavior that is of interest to the counselor (frequency, function, intensity, duration, latency, etc.) determines the approach that should be used. Among the methods counselors could use are continuous recording, interval recording, time sample recording, duration recording, and latency recording.

Continuous Recording

Continuous recording is an assessment process that involves documenting the number of times a specific behavior occurs over a defined period of time (Miltenberger, 2012). Once a target behavior has been operationally defined, the counselor observes the client and notes each time the behavior occurs. According to Merrell (2008), for continuous recording to be effective three criteria must be met:

1. Behaviors should have a clear beginning and end. The counselor conducting the observation should be able to correctly identify both the onset and conclusion of the target behavior.

2. Behaviors observed should generally be uniform in their duration. When there is considerable variance in the duration of a target behavior, it may signal that there is more to the behavior than originally thought and perhaps a different type of recording method may be needed.

3. Behaviors should not occur at a frequency that makes it difficult for them to be separated and assessed individually. For a counselor to be able to accurately observe and record the behaviors exhibited, they should not occur too frequently. The more frequent the behaviors, the greater the likelihood that occurrences may be missed and the more difficult it becomes to differentiate between the ending of one behavioral instance and the beginning of another.

To begin the continuous recording process, a counselor establishes a period of time in which to observe a client. This period could be an hour, a day, or even a week. The length of time set for observation will depend on a number of factors related to the client and the target behavior for which the client is currently seeking help. Once the observation period begins, the counselor documents each time the behavior occurs. This simple counting procedure continues for the duration of the observation period.

Other than assessing how frequently a behavior occurs, the data gathered using a continuous recording approach are limited in the information they provide. To increase our understanding of a client, we could include the A-B-C evaluation narrative into our assessment approach. The A-B-C evaluation narrative provides context to the behaviors observed by making note of the antecedents (A) and consequences (C) of the target behavior (B). In addition to noting when a behavior occurs, the counselor also records what happened directly prior to the occurrence and what happened directly after. The benefit of this approach is that it facilitates goal setting and treatment planning. Knowing what triggers a client has and how behaviors are reinforced will enable the counselor and client to work on changing the environment to help either increase or decrease the occurrence of a behavior depending on their intended goal. To record the information gathered using the A-B-C approach, a counselor would create a chart that includes three columns labeled *antecedents*, *behaviors*, and *consequences* (see Figure 11.2 for an example).

Figure 11.2 A-B-C Evaluation Narrative

A-B-C Evaluation Narrative

Subject Name: _____ Observer Name: _____

Behaviors Assessed: _____
(Behaviors should be defined in specific, observable, and measureable terms)

Date of Observation	Time of Observation	Behavioral Antecedent(s)	Behavior(s) Observed	Behavioral Consequence(s)	Possible Function of Behavior

Interval Recording

A second type of recording is known as interval recording. In the **interval recording** approach, the counselor establishes a period of time during which observations will occur (e.g., 10 minutes, 30 minutes) and divides that time period into a collection of equal intervals. For example, a 10-minute observation could be divided into 20 separate 30-second intervals. A chart is then created that includes 20 boxes, each representing one of the 30-second intervals, for each of the target behaviors being assessed. The counselor then records whether the target behaviors do or do not occur during each of the intervals. Typically, an X is used to note when a behavior occurs and an O when the behavior does not occur. As a general guideline, shorter time intervals are preferred and should be measured in terms of seconds rather than minutes (Bailey & Burch, 2002). Subsequently, the interval recording approach is best applied when target behaviors are noted to be occurring at a moderate but steady rate (Gast, 2009).

Within the interval recording approach there are multiple scoring methods that counselors can use. The first is the **whole interval recording method**. In this method, the counselor is interested whether the client exhibits target behaviors during the entire observation interval. A behavior is noted as occurring if the client performs the target behavior for the entire duration of the observation interval. The counselor would then mark an X on the chart to note that the behavior occurred during that time interval. This process continues throughout the entire observation period, with the counselor marking whether the behavior occurred during each of the specified time intervals. At the end of the observation period, the counselor tallies up the number of intervals in which the behavior was noted to occur and determines a percentage of target behavior occurrence. If the target behavior occurred during four out of ten 1-minute observation intervals, the counselor would report that the client engaged in the target behavior during 40% of the observation period. This approach is best applied when you are assessing behaviors that would be expected to continuously occur and span several time intervals (Shapiro & Skinner, 1990). An example of the whole interval recording method is presented in Case Illustration 11.2.

CASE ILLUSTRATION   11.2

An example of whole interval recording can be found in a study conducted by Graham-Day, Gardner, and Hsin (2010). These researchers examined the impact of a variety of intervention strategies on increasing the on-task behavior of high school students diagnosed with attention deficit hyperactivity disorder. Using a 10-second whole interval recording system during a high school study hall session, the researchers found that the use of audiotaped chimes and student checklists was effective in increasing on-task behavior of 3 students observed (out of a class of 13 students). On-task behavior was defined by the researchers as the student sitting with his or her body facing forward, both feet on the floor, eyes directed toward the academic discriminative stimulus; glancing (looking away from academic discriminative stimulus for 3 seconds or less and is still on task) only once (during a 10-second observation period); paying attention to the teacher; responding to teacher questions; discussing only the assigned task when asked to work in groups; complying with teacher requests; writing in response to academic instructional materials; asking academic questions; and ignoring distractions in the classroom. To improve reliability, two independent reviewers were used and their results were compared to determine the level of inter-observer agreement.

There are both advantages and disadvantages to using the whole interval recording method. The major advantage is that this method allows the counselor to more accurately observe how the target behavior occurs. Specifically, the counselor can note both the duration of the behavior and whether there are any lulls or sharp increases in the behavior. The disadvantage of this approach is that it requires the undivided attention of the observer for an extended period of time. Because the counselor is recording whether the behavior occurred for the duration of the time interval, any distraction that results in the counselor removing his or her focus from observing may result in an inaccurate recording. In addition, counselors using this approach are tasked with having to simultaneously observe a client and be aware of the time so that recordings are noted in the correct intervals. The use of a stopwatch or timer that has an alert function to note when each new observation interval begins is a helpful suggestion for counselors.

The second type of interval recording approach that a counselor could use is the **partial interval recording method**. This method is structured in much the same way as the whole interval recording method. The only difference is that in this method, the target behavior is recorded as occurring as long as it occurs for any portion of the time interval. An occurrence lasting for 10 seconds during a 1-minute observation interval would result in the counselor marking that the behavior occurred during that interval. Once a behavior is noted as occurring, it is no longer necessary to keep observing for that behavior until the next time interval begins (Merrell, 2008). The only caveat concerning duration is that the behavior must occur long enough to be witnessed by the observer. According to Shapiro and Skinner (1990), the partial interval approach is preferred when the identified target behaviors occur at lower frequencies and typically are expected to occur over a greater span of time. Examples of behaviors that could be assessed using the partial interval recording method include specific comments, gestures, or discrete behaviors (e.g., getting out of one's seat, interrupting when another client is speaking).

The advantage of the partial interval approach is that it allows counselors to record the occurrence of target behaviors that are brief and occur quite frequently. A counselor would be more successful observing a client's ability to maintain eye contact during a session using the partial interval recording approach because the target behavior occurs rapidly and would not be expected to ever last an entire observation interval. The disadvantage of this approach is that it has the potential to greatly underestimate the frequency with which a target behavior occurs. Because the counselor is looking for only a single occurrence of a behavior in each time interval, several exhibitions of that same behavior go unrecorded. A client may exhibit the target behavior 100 times in a 5-minute observation but would only be noted as exhibiting the behavior in ten of ten 30-second intervals.

According to Gast (2009), the decision whether to use the whole interval or partial interval recording method should be based on your answers to two primary questions. First, what is the dimension (rate, duration, latency, etc.) of interest for the target behavior? Counselors that are most interested in the frequency with which a behavior occurs should use the partial interval approach. When duration is the most important consideration, whole interval recording should be used. The second question asks, what is the research question guiding this observation? When interested in whether a client exhibits a particular target behavior, the partial interval approach would be appropriate. When the question focuses more on the preceding events and the subsequent consequences of the target behavior, the whole interval method is best. An example of an interval recording behavioral assessment chart is presented in Figure 11.3. Guided Practice Exercise 11.3 will help you gain experience recording your observational data.

Figure 11.3 Interval Recording Behavioral Assessment Chart

Interval Recording Observation Sheet

Client/student name: _____   **Date:** _____

Behavior being assessed *(stated in specific, observable, and measureable terms)*:_____

_____

_____

Total observation time:_____ Length of each time interval:_____

Recording method selected *(select one)*:

_____: Whole interval (behavior is observed continuously throughout the observation interval)

_____: Partial interval (behavior is observed at least once during the observation interval)

Date	Interval #										Total # of X
	1	2	3	4	5	6	7	8	9	10	
O or X											

Date	Interval #										Total # of X
	1	2	3	4	5	6	7	8	9	10	
O or X											

Date	Interval #										Total # of X
	1	2	3	4	5	6	7	8	9	10	
O or X											

Date	Interval #										Total # of X
	1	2	3	4	5	6	7	8	9	10	
O or X											

Date	Interval #										Total # of X
	1	2	3	4	5	6	7	8	9	10	
O or X											

Comments:_____

_____

GUIDED PRACTICE EXERCISE 11.3

Observation Recording

Identify a target behavior and observe a friend, family member, or classmate for two 15-minute sessions. During the first session use a whole interval recording approach. Use a partial interval recording approach for the second session. When you have completed both observations, compare your notes. Which approach was the more productive for you given the behavior for which you were observing and the data you collected?

Time Sample Recording

Also called momentary time sampling, time sample recording is very similar to the interval recording method (Bryan & Gast, 2000). In the **time sample recording** approach, an observation period is defined and that period is then divided into smaller intervals. The counselor observes the client to see whether the identified target behavior occurs. The time sample recording method differs from the interval recording method in that behaviors are observed only at the end of the preselected time intervals (Schilling & Schwartz, 2004). Unlike in the interval recording approach, the duration of the time intervals used do not have to be uniform. In fact, counselors can select to use either fixed or variable intervals.

A **fixed interval time sampling** approach is used when the observation period is divided into equal intervals (see Case Illustration 11.3). For example, a counselor could divide a 50-minute counseling session into five 10-minute intervals. Every 10 minutes the counselor would observe the client and record whether the target behavior was occurring. An X would be placed on the observation sheet if the behavior occurred during this brief observation period, and an O would be used if the behavior did not occur. Although a popular observation approach, the fixed interval time sample recording method is not without its problems. The most notable problem associated with this approach is that it inherently signals to the client when the recording of a behavioral observation will occur (Spriggs, Gast, & Ayres, 2007). This could cause the client to alter his or her behavior, knowing that it is being recorded. In our above example the client, knowing that the counselor is recording observations every 10 minutes, could act a particular way for 9 minutes and 30 seconds, behave differently for the next minute when observation will occur, then return to the original behavior until the next recording time nears. As a result, the counselor would most likely note that the target behavior did not occur.

CASE ILLUSTRATION   11.3

A school counselor is asked to assist an elementary teacher with one of her students who is having difficulty remaining on task during class assignments. They discuss what exactly is happening and identify the behaviors the teacher believes to be most problematic. The counselor decides to conduct a behavioral assessment to gain a better understanding of the problem. The counselor sits in on class one day for an hour. To record the student's behavior, the counselor decides to use a time sampling approach and record observations every 5 minutes. So as not to distract or influence the student being observed, the counselor focuses on the lesson the teacher is delivering. Five minutes into the observation, the silent alarm on the counselor's stopwatch goes off. The counselor then observes the student and records whether the target behaviors are occurring. After noting what was observed, the counselor resumes attending to the teacher. Five minutes later the alarm again goes off, and the counselor records what is happening with the student at the time. This process continues for the duration of the hour-long observation period. At the end of the observation the counselor notes the percentage of times the student was exhibiting the target behavior. Had the student exhibited the target behavior during 7 of the 12 observation periods, the counselor would document that the student exhibited the behavior during 58% of the observation times.

Variable interval time sampling addresses the inherent challenge in the fixed interval time sample method. Using the variable interval approach, counselors establish an unpredictable recoding schedule. This unpredictability prevents the inadvertent signaling of the beginning of the observation process that may cause clients to change their behaviors. When clients are unsure when the counselor will be observing their behavior, the chance of them exhibiting authentic behaviors increases greatly. To establish a variable interval schedule, the counselor divides the total observation period into a set number of observations, similar to the fixed interval method. These observations are then scheduled at varied times, producing an average time between observations. Rather than scheduling five observations 10 minutes apart, the counselor could schedule these five observations to occur at the 8-minute interval, 18-minute interval, 30-minute interval, 36-minute interval, and 50-minute interval. Although the length of time between these observations varies, the average time between observations is 10 minutes.

Collectively, the time sample recording approaches provide the counselor with the benefit of having to make far fewer observations than other methods require. Observations are made at specified times, eliminating the need for the counselor to remain focused on observing the client the entire time. Unfortunately, what makes this approach appealing also contributes to its shortcoming. Because observation is not a continuous process, significant behaviors may be missed or go unrecorded. This might cause the counselor to reach erroneous conclusions and significantly affect the way the counselor conceptualizes the client and the presenting issue. As counselors set up a time sample recording schedule, they should carefully consider the time scheduled between the observations. A general rule of thumb is that the longer the time interval used, the less accurate the data collected (Merrell, 2008). An example of a time sample recording sheet is shown in Figure 11.4. Now that you have been introduced to various observation techniques, see if you can match the appropriate technique with each of the identified target behaviors in Guided Practice Exercise 11.4.

Figure 11.4   Time Sampling Recording Sheet

Client/student name: _____   Date: _____

Behavior being assessed: _____

(Stated in specific, observable, and measureable terms)

Recording method: _____ Fixed Interval   _____ Variable Interval

Interval	+ / –

Interval	+ / –

Interval	+ / –

GUIDED PRACTICE EXERCISE 11.4

Matching Identified Target Behaviors and Observation Techniques

You are a counselor that will be working with a group of adults participating in an anger management support group. The group has been meeting for several weeks, and you are interested in assessing how well the members are assimilating the information and skills they are learning. You decide to observe each member of the group for a period of 15 minutes during one of the group sessions to see how they interact with other members. What types of target behaviors would you identify as being evidence that the members were in fact benefiting from the group and able to apply the skills they were being taught? Based on the target behaviors you identify, would you be better served using a fixed interval or variable interval recording approach?

Duration and Latency Recording

The previous recording methods all share a common characteristic: They all focus on assessing the frequency with which a behavior occurs. However, counselors sometimes are interested in more than just knowing how often a behavior occurs. Fortunately, there are methods for collecting data on the other temporal aspects of targeted behavior, namely duration recording and latency recording.

Duration recording involves collecting information on how long a behavior occurs. Here the focus is less on the number of times a behavior occurs and more on the length of time the behavior persists once it begins. Using this approach, a counselor would start a stopwatch or other timing device when the behavior begins and record how long it lasts. The counselor then restarts the clock and begins timing again when the behavior next occurs. At the end of the observation period, the counselor could then calculate a percentage of time spent engaged in the target behavior. The benefit of this approach is that it adds context to the behavior related to how problematic it might be. For instance, a client that briefly engages in negative self-talk once during a session would not be treated the same as a client who comes in and spends the entire session engaged in negative self-talk. If the frequency of the targeted behavior were all the information that was collected, both of these clients would be noted as exhibiting the behavior once. Clearly, however, the client who was engaged in this behavior for the entire session would be in need of an entirely different level of services.

When counselors wish to gather information related to both the frequency and duration of a behavior, they could apply a recording approach known as the *duration per occurrence* method. In this approach the counselor begins timing once the target behavior is first identified and continues timing until the behavior ends. Unlike before, the counselor now resets the timer and starts a new count for the next occurrence of the behavior. The exact length of time for each occurrence is recorded. This approach allows the counselor to record frequency and duration of the behavior as well as a number of descriptive statistics related to the behavior, including the mean, median, and range of time spent engaged in the behavior.

Opposite to duration recording is latency recording. Essentially, **latency recording** assesses the amount of time it takes a client to begin exhibiting a target behavior. For example, a counselor working with a resistant client may ask that client to share his or her expectations for their session that day. The counselor could then record how long it takes for the client to respond to the question and begin sharing his or her expectations. When using the latency recording method, it is important to have clearly defined cues or triggers. The connection between these triggers and the target behavior should be apparent to the client. Assessing the amount of time it takes a child to begin reading from a book would be meaningless if the antecedent of having the teacher ask the class to begin reading did not occur. This type of recording approach is helpful in gauging treatment progress. Changes in the amount of time it takes to engage in a behavior could reflect improvement and evidence client progress.

Indirect Methods of Behavioral Assessment

Indirect methods of behavioral assessment represent a less intrusive way of gathering data about the function of a problem behavior. Indirect methods often include the gathering of data from several sources such as parents, teachers, employers, family members, and even the client directly. Because information is gained from third-party report and not direct observation, it is highly subjective. These methods of data collection are often used to obtain information to add to what is gathered through more direct methods. They also can be used in situations in which direct observation is not practical due to either the infrequency of the target behavior or logistical concerns regarding how and when observation could occur. Common indirect methods used to assess behavior include interviews, rating scales, and checklists.

Behavioral Interviews

The **behavioral interview** is a structured interview that is used to collect information about past behavior. The behavioral interview is similar in format to the traditional interview. The difference between the two can be found in their focus. Behavioral interviews focus on target behaviors and are designed to help counselors gain a better understanding of a problem behavior and the variables that perpetuate that behavior. Information obtained during a behavioral interview should be viewed as a verbal representation of past or current events or of perceptions, motivations, or interpretations of these events (Lewis-Palmer, Reed-Schindler, & Ingram, 2005). Whereas traditional interview questions are more general and ambiguous (e.g., "Tell me about yourself?"), behavioral interview questions are more direct and probing. Because past performance has been shown to be a reliable predictor of future behavior, behavioral interviews include questions about past behavior in order to better understand future performance. Counselors conducting behavioral interviews are looking for as much information as they can obtain (see Guided Practice Exercise 11.5). As a result, follow-up questions designed to probe for additional material or evaluate the consistency of client responses are commonly included in behavioral interviews.

GUIDED PRACTICE EXERCISE 11.5
Behavioral Interviews

Imagine that you are a career counselor and you are working with a client to identify careers in which the client would likely find success. You decide to conduct an interview to gather data on past career-related behaviors. What types of questions would you include in your interview? Think of four to five questions you would ask. What is the intent of each question? How will the information obtained help you better understand the client and ultimately identify possible careers for which the client may be best suited?

Behavioral interviews can be designed to include structured, semistructured, or unstructured questions, or some combination of the three questions types. Most behavioral interviews used today are of the structured question variety. Structured interviews are more reliable, valid, and often carry a greater perception of fairness. In addition, they greatly enhance the quality and honesty of responses gathered. Structured interviews include an established set of questions that often may include multiple parts. These interviews can be used in a variety of settings and have been applied effectively in both school and career counseling practice settings.

Behavioral Rating Scales and Checklists

The previous assessment methods discussed would all be considered subjective or qualitative in nature. However, there may be times when a counselor may have an interest in gathering information that is more quantitative and objective. In other words, the counselor is interested in collecting data that describes the behavior as it actually occurs without any bias in reporting. To record data about a client's behavior in a more quantitative format, a counselor may opt to use a behavior rating scale. **Rating scales** are assessment techniques designed to quickly and effectively collect data about a client's presenting behaviors and their functionality across multiple settings using a standardized methodology. Although typically completed by a counselor, rating scales can also be completed by parents, teachers, family members, employers, or the client directly.

Rating scales are often created using a Likert-type response format. A Likert-type response format includes a series of options representing varying degrees of the criterion being assessed. For example, a question asking how well you understand the material being presented in this book could be followed with a series of possible responses such as *not very well*, *somewhat okay*, *pretty well*, or *I am now an expert in this field*. On behavioral rating scales, these types of questions typically address several characteristics of the behavior being observed, including the frequency with which it occurs, its duration, and its intensity. Numeric values can then be assigned to these ratings in order to produce item and scale scores that allow for comparisons to be made. These comparisons may be across settings or even among different individuals. Because these responses represent varying degrees of the criteria being observed, the data obtained from a rating scale are considered ordinal data.

Similar to rating scales are checklists. A **checklist** is a list of potential target behaviors that observers are asked to identify and note the number of times each behavior occurs during the course of an observation period. Checklists are additive in nature. This means that they simply provide frequency counts of behaviors. Their utility lies in the fact that they allow counselors to gain a better understanding of the severity of a problem. For instance, a couple may present for marital counseling with one partner reporting that the other is always dismissive of his or her feelings. The counselor could create a checklist that includes all of the behaviors the client identifies as making him or her feel dismissed. Equipped with this checklist, the counselor could then observe the couple during session and note the number of times these dismissive behaviors occur. At the end of the session, the counselor could then share the results with the couple and discuss the findings.

The efficiency and quality of existing rating scales and checklists have made their use in counseling quite appealing. As a result, several rating scales and checklists are available for counselors to use. Examples of popular rating scales and checklists include the Behavior Rating Profile-2nd Edition, Behavior Assessment System for Children-2nd Edition, Child Behavior Checklist System 6-18, and Conners Rating Scales-3rd Edition. A brief description of each of these instruments is provided below.

Behavior Rating Profile, 2nd Edition

The **Behavior Rating Profile, 2nd Edition** (BRP-2; Brown & Hammill, 1990) is designed as a norm-referenced, ecological, integrated behavior assessment system to be used with students between the ages of 6 years, 6 months and 18 years, 6 months. The system comprises six elements which, when used collectively, provide the counselor with a more ecological view of the individual's behavioral functioning. The student completes three of these elements directly in the form of the Student Rating Scales (SRS). A separate scale consisting of 20 true/false items exists to assess behaviors at home, at school, and among peers. According to the authors of the BRP-2, it is used most effectively to assess for emotional, behavioral, personal, or social adjustment problems students may be experiencing at home, at school, or in social-interpersonal settings (Brown & Hammill, 1990).

The fourth and fifth scales, the Teacher Rating Scale (TRS) and the Parent Rating Scale (PRS), are used to assess teacher and parent perceptions, respectively. The TRS consists of 30 items related to the student's behavior in the school setting. All of the statements are negatively oriented and rated on a 4-point Likert scale ranging from 1 (*very much like the student*) to 4 (*not at all like the student*). An example of an item from the TRS is "swears in class." The PRS also consists of 30 negatively worded items and uses the same item response set as the TRS. An example of an item on the PRS is "violates curfew."

The sixth element of the BRP-2 is a sociogram. The sociogram is less a rating scale and more a classroom-based peer nomination procedure used to understand how the student's classmates view him or her. In the sociogram, pairs of questions are asked and respondents are asked to nominate or rate three students in their class for each question. The questions asked in the sociogram will vary by student. Counselors have the option of choosing questions from a preset list included in the test manual or creating their own questions based on the unique situation of the student who it the target of the assessment. Examples of questions that could be included in a sociogram are "Who is the most popular child in class?" and "Who is the least popular child in class?" Students would then identify three of their peers who fit the description of each question. The counselor collects the results from each student and then rank-orders students based on their acceptance and rejection rates. Although a sociogram is usually a good starting point for other observations, there are some disadvantages to this assessment intervention. In addition to taking time to prepare and actually conduct an interview with a child, the results obtained from a sociogram are usually closed and completely dependent on the information that the child chooses to share.

Developed using norm samples that included 2,682 students, 1,948 parents, and 1,452 teachers, the BRP-2 appears to be a useful screening tool that has adequate psychometric properties. In terms of reliability, the BRP-2 test manual reports both internal consistency and test-retest data. Internal consistency estimates ranging between .74 and .98 were reported for each of the five rating scales across five grade levels, with the highest reliabilities being noted for the Teacher Rating Scale (Brown & Hammill, 1990). In a study of 198 students in Grades 1–12 that included ratings from 212 parents and 176 teachers, test-retest reliabilities ranging between .43 and .96 were calculated, with the lowest co-efficients being for students in Grades 1 and 2 (Ellers, Ellers, & Bradley-Johnson, 1989). In terms of validity, numerous studies representing both the test authors' own and independent researchers' work are reported in the manual. As noted in the manual, the results of these studies provide ample evidence to sufficiently demonstrate construct validity (Brown & Hammill, 1990).

BRP-2 scales can be administered individually or as a complete battery. Administration times for the individual scales vary between 20 and 30 minutes. When administered as a battery including the five rating scales and the sociogram, the total administration time should take approximately one hour (Reitman & Noell, 2003). Scoring for each of the scales is completed by hand. Although the authors of the instrument do not recommend using the BRP-2 in isolation (Brown & Hammill, 1990), it does represent a valuable tool when included as part of a multidimensional assessment of a student's behavior.

Behavior Assessment System for Children, 2nd Edition

The **Behavior Assessment System for Children, 2nd Edition** (BASC-2; C. R. Reynolds & Kamphaus, 2004) is a screening system designed to assess behavioral and emotional strengths and weaknesses in children and adolescents. Counselors use the BASC-2 to assist in diagnosing emotional and behavioral problems and designing treatment plans for individuals between the ages of 2 years and 21 years, 11 months. The BASC-2 includes five main components: structured developmental history, parent rating scale, teacher rating scale, self-report of personality, and student observation system. These components can be used either in isolation or in concert with one another to provide a more ecological view of the problem behavior. Data derived from the BASC-2 are then used to classify a child's performance as *normal*, *at risk*, or *clinically significant* on a number of maladaptive and adaptive behaviors (see Table 11.1). Separate scales are provided for use with preschool (2–5 years old), child (6–11 years old), or adolescent clients (12–21 years old).

Raters respond to the items on the Parent Rating Scale (PRS) and Teacher Rating Scale (TRS) using a 4-point response scale (N = *never*, S = *sometimes*, O = *often*, A = *almost always*). The number of items on each scale depends on the version of the scale (preschool, child, or adolescent) being used. The PRS can include 134–160 items and the TRS 100–139 items. For the Self-Report of Personality Scale (SRP), the same 4-point response set is used for older children and adolescents. However, for children ages 6–7 there is an SRP-Interview that can be used instead. All questions on the interview are answered using either yes or no responses. In total, scores are produced along 8 clinical scales, 7 optional "content" scales, and 5 composite scales. The exact number of scales produced depends on the form used and the age of the child being assessed. In total, scores are produced along 16 distinct clinical/adaptive scales, 7 optional "content" scales, and 5 composite scales. The exact number of scales produced depends on the form used and the age of the child being assessed (see Table 11.2). Hand, computer, or scanning scoring options are all available for the BASC-2. The optional content scales are available only when using computer scoring.

Table 11.1   BASC-2 TRS and PRS Content Scales

Scale	Description
Anger Control	The tendency to become irritated and/or anger quickly and impulsively, coupled with an inability to regulate affect and self-control.
Bullying	The tendency to be intrusive, cruel, threatening, or forceful to get what is wanted.
Developmental Social Disorders	The tendency to display behaviors characterized by deficits in social skills, communication, interests, and activities. Such behaviors may include self-stimulation, withdrawal, and inappropriate socializations.
Emotional Self-Control	The ability to regulate one's affect and emotions in response to environmental changes.
Executive Functioning	The ability to control behavior by planning, anticipating, inhibiting, maintaining goal-directed activity, and reacting appropriately to environmental feedback in a purposeful, meaningful way.
Negative Emotionality	The tendency to view everyday interactions or events in an overly negative or aversive way and to react negatively to any changes in plans or routines.
Resiliency	The ability to access support systems, both internal and external, to alleviate stress and overcome adversity or difficult circumstances.

Table 11.2   BASC-2 TRS and PRS Clinical Scales and Adaptive Scales

Scale	Teacher Rating Scales			Parent Rating Scales		
	Preschool	Child	Adolescent	Preschool	Child	Adolescent
Activities of Daily Living*				X	X	X
Adaptability*	X	X	X	X	X	X
Aggression	X	X	X	X	X	X
Anxiety	X	X	X	X	X	X
Attention Problems	X	X	X	X	X	X
Atypicality	X	X	X	X	X	X
Conduct Problems		X	X	X	X	X
Depression	X	X	X	X	X	X
Functional Communication*	X	X	X	X	X	X

Scale	Teacher Rating Scales			Parent Rating Scales		
	Preschool	Child	Adolescent	Preschool	Child	Adolescent
Hyperactivity	X	X	X	X	X	X
Leadership*		X	X		X	X
Learning Problems		X	X			
Social Skills*	X	X	X	X	X	X
Somatization	X	X	X	X	X	X
Study Skills*		X	X			
Withdrawal	X	X	X	X	X	X

Source: Pearson Education (2014a).

*Adaptive scales

According to the test manual, the BASC-2 has moderate to good reliability and validity (C. R. Reynolds & Kamphaus, 2004). High internal consistency and test-retest reliability estimates are noted for both the individual (.60s to .90s) and composite scales (.80s to .90s). In terms of validity, the test manual reports good evidence for construct validity through factor analysis and structural equation modeling, and concurrent validity with other behavioral rating systems such as the Achenbach and Conners instruments. In addition, the BASC-2 includes three scales to help control for threats to validity. The F index corrects for any potential bias that may result in raters excessively rating a child's behavior negatively. The L index is used to discern whether the child is attempting to portray an overly positive picture of self. Finally, the V index includes a set of statements that are deemed implausible. When two or more of these items are positively endorsed, it is an indication that the entire profile may be invalid.

Overall, the BASC-2 is a popular choice for counselors seeking to use a behavioral rating scale. A strong theoretical base and growing body of research supporting its efficacy add to its popularity. In addition, the inclusion of normative data for clinical samples in the manual is a plus; however, these clinical samples are based on *DSM-IV* diagnostic criteria and would need to be reevaluated with the recent release of the *DSM-5*. When used as part of a multi-method assessment approach, the BASC-2 provides useful information to help supplement the other more objective observations and perceptions counselors may make.

Child Behavior Checklist System 6-18

The **Child Behavior Checklist System 6-18** (CBCL 6-18; Achenbach, 2001) is a component of the Achenbach System of Empirically Based Assessment and is one of the most widely used standardized measures for evaluating both maladaptive behavioral and emotional problems. The current version of the questionnaire allows parents, teachers, or other individuals who know the child well to provide descriptive data on the competencies and problem behaviors of children and adolescents between the ages of 6 and 18 (previous versions were for ages 4–18). The CBCL 6-18 comprises two sections. The first section consists of 20 competence items covering the child's activities, social relations, and school performance. The second section consists of 118 items related to specific behavior or emotional problems the child has experienced during the past 6 months and two open-ended items for reporting additional problems. Respondents are asked to rate the child according to how true each item is using a scale from 0 (*not true*) to 2 (*very true or often true*). Similar questions are grouped into categories known as syndromes. The eight syndromes derived from the CBCL 6-18 are anxious/depressed, withdrawn/depressed, somatic complaints, social problems, thought problems, attention problems, rule-breaking behavior, and aggressive behavior.

The norm group for the CBCL 6-18 included 1,753 children and adolescents from 100 sites in 40 U.S. states. Both gender and cultural diversity are represented in the norm sample. In terms of psychometric properties, reported reliability estimates for the CBCL 6-18 full-scale score are quite high in terms of internal consistency (.78 to .97), test-retest reliability (.95 to 1.00), and inter-rater reliability (.93 to .96). In addition, criterion validity was assessed and found to be acceptable. The CBCL 6-18 is available in paper-and-pencil and computer-based formats. A scannable form also is available. In addition to the CBCL 6-18, two additional scales are available: the TRF-18 and YSR 11-18. Teachers and other school staff (e.g., administrators, coaches, counselors) who have known the student for at least 2 months complete the TRF-18, and the YSR 11-18 is a self-report completed by 11- to 18-year-olds to describe their perceptions of their own functioning. Each of these assessments can be administered in 15–20 minutes.

Conners Rating Scales, 3rd Edition

The **Conners Rating Scales, 3rd Edition (Conners-3**; Conners, 2008) is an integrated behavioral rating assessment system designed to assess for attention deficit hyperactivity disorder (ADHD) as well as other comorbid disorders such as Oppositional defiant disorder and conduct disorder in children ages 6 to 18 years, 11 months. The Conners-3 comprises three separate rating scales that can be administered in either a paper-and-pencil or computerized format. These scales include a rating scale for parents (Conners 3-P), teachers (Conners 3-T), and a self-report rating scale (Conners 3-R). In addition, two auxiliary scales also are included: the Conners 3 ADHD Index and Conners 3 Global Index. Responses to the test items are made using a 4-point response scale from 0 (*not at all true*) to 4 (*very much true*). A profile form can be used to convert raw scores to linear T scores. Guidelines for interpreting these standardized scores are provided in Table 11.3. In total, 13 different scales, including both content and clinical/diagnostic scales, can be derived from the Conners-3 (see Table 11.4).

Normative data were collected from a national sample of 3,400 cases. A stratified sampling approach was employed to target participants that would allow the sample to approximate the ethnic/racial distribution of the population according to available 2000 U.S. Census Bureau data (Frick, Barry, & Kamphaus, 2010). An equal number of boys and girls were included for each age group (separated by 1-year intervals). The resulting instrument

Table 11.3 Conners-3 T score Interpretation Guidelines

T score	Guideline
70 and above	Very elevated score (many more concerns than are typically reported)
60–69	Elevated score (more concerns than are typically reported)
40–59	Average score (typical levels of concern)
Below 40	Low score (fewer concerns than are typically reported)

Source: Multi-Health Systems (2009, Table 2, p. 3).

Table 11.4 Conners-3 Content and Clinical Scales

Content Scales	Clinical Scales
Inattention	ADHD Predominantly Inattentive Type
Hyperactivity/Impulsivity	ADHD Predominantly Hyperactive-Impulsive Type
Learning Problems	ADHD Combined Type
Executive Functioning	Conduct Disorder
Aggression	Oppositional Defiant Disorder
Peer Relations	
Family Relations	
General Psychopathology	

has demonstrated very good reliability and validity. Measures of internal consistency for the total sample range between .77 and .97, and test-retest coefficients at both 2- and 4-week intervals range between .71 and .98. Inter-rater reliability also was assessed, with alpha coefficients in the .52 to .94 range. Measures of the instrument's validity are also strong. In addition to the structure of the Conners-3 being supported by factorial validity studies, comparing the instrument to other available rating scales such as the BASC-2 and the Achenbach YSR assessed construct validity, and predictive validity was assessed by the instrument's ability to differentiate between youth with ADHD and those without a clinical diagnosis (Conners, 2008).

Full-length and short versions for each of these scales are available for use. Use of the full-length version is recommended when making initial assessments as it provides more detailed information about the frequency and intensity of symptoms included in the *DSM-IV* diagnostic criteria (Erford, 2013). The short version can be used as an alternative when performing follow-up testing or treatment monitoring. Administration times will vary depending on the scale and version being used, with a range of 5–10 minutes for the short forms and 10–20 minutes for the long forms. Although it is a relatively new revision, it does appear to build on previous versions of the instrument that were strongly supported in both research and counseling practice. As a result, the Conners-3 appears to be a reliable and dependable tool to assist in the assessment and diagnosis of ADHD and related behavioral disorders.

BIAS IN BEHAVIORAL ASSESSMENT

During the course of a behavioral assessment, it is possible that factors may arise that skew the conclusions reached following an observation period. These unintended factors are related to the human element associated with behavioral assessment. Although extensive training of observers is recommended before they are allowed to conduct observations, the reports of trained observers may still be unintentionally flawed. Among the various systematic errors in observations and reporting that can be noted are observer bias, observer drift, and observer fatigue.

Observer bias occurs when raters respond to an item due to extraneous factors unintended by the instrument (Haynes, Heiby, & Hersen, 2003). For example, a counselor may be tasked with observing for signs of disruptive behavior in class. That counselor may note an instance of disruptive behavior that was not one observers were trained to recognize, but one the counselor personally thought was a significant example. Because the behavior noted was based on the individual understanding of the observer, it is likely that the same behavior would not be noted by others who observe the child and follow the training protocol more closely.

A second type of systematic error is **observer drift**. Observer drift occurs when, during the observation process, the criteria by which the rater responds to each item changes. A counselor may start an observation recording every time a target behavior is exhibited. As the observation period progresses, the counselor begins to notice that the target behavior occurs infrequently. In an attempt to gather as much useful information as possible, the counselor changes methods and begins noting the duration of each episode of the target behavior. Because the observation method was switched midway through an observation, the results may be incomplete and may make meaningful interpretation a challenge.

The final type of systematic error we will discuss is **observer fatigue**, which is a common occurrence in behavioral assessment. When observation periods extend over a long period of time, the target behaviors are brief and infrequent, or the difference between a target behavior and normal behavior is small, fatigue may set in and cause the observer to miss noted behaviors. The observer becomes less sharp and his or her focus may not remain on targeted behaviors. Counselors can increase the value of the data they obtain by recognizing the potential for systematic error to enter into the assessment process and choosing their observation methods accordingly based on the needs and characteristics of the client being assessed.

KEYSTONES

- The operational defining of target behaviors is an important part of any behavioral assessment. Target behaviors should be specific, observable, and measureable.
- Behaviors are best understood in context. Consider the environment and circumstances surrounding behavior when attempting to determine its function.
- A reciprocal relationship exists between behaviors and their environment. Behaviors influence the surrounding environment as much as the environment acts to produce certain behaviors.
- Both direct and indirect methods of assessment are available for a counselor to use. Direct methods are used when the counselor collects information personally. Indirect methods are where information is gained through a third party or client self-report.
- When interpreting client behaviors it is important to take into account any biases, preexisting expectations, and outside influences that may skew your perspective.

KEY TERMS

analogue observation

behavior

Behavior Assessment System for Children, 2nd Edition (BASC-2)

Behavior Rating Profile, 2nd Edition (BRP-2)

behavioral assessment

behavioral interview

checklist

Child Behavior Checklist

System 6-18 (CBCL 6-18)

Conners Rating Scales, 3rd Edition (Conners-3)

continuous recording

duration recording

fixed interval time sampling

interval recording

latency recording

naturalistic observation

observer bias

observer drift

observer fatigue

partial interval recording method

rating scales

self-monitoring

time sample recording

variable interval time sampling

whole interval recording method

ADDITIONAL RESOURCES

- Functional Behavioral Assessment

  http://www.behavioradvisor.com/FBA.html

This website offers information on functional behavioral assessments and the role they serve for counselors and educators.

- Multimodal Functional Behavioral Assessment

  http://mfba.net

This website provides a number of free resources related to multimodal functional behavioral assessment that counselors can download and use in their practice.

- The IRIS Center

  http://iris.peabody.vanderbilt.edu/module/fba

This interactive website includes videos and learning modules that users can navigate and use to learn more about functional behavioral assessments and how to develop effective behavior plans.

Student Study Site: Visit the Student Study Site at **www.sagepub.com/watson** to access additional study tools, including quizzes, web resources, and journal articles.

CHAPTER 12

Career and Vocational Assessment

Last night at 3:00 a.m., my 4-year-old ran into my room and said, "Mommy, Mommy, wake up! I know what I want to be when I grow up." With excitement, Evelyn said, "I want to be a pirate and a pilot." Half asleep, I said, "Wow, that sounds exciting." She said, "I always knew I wanted to be a pilot so I can fly like Tinkerbell and Daddy, but now I can sail the sea like Captain Hook." Seems like only yesterday I was asked, "What do you want to be when you grow up?" I remember wanting to be Michael Jackson, an astronaut, and a medical doctor. But I also remember there were times I had no idea what I wanted to do in terms of a career, and I just needed a job. Remember the song "Get a Job" by The Silhouettes: "Every morning about this time she gets me out of my bed a-crying get a job. After breakfast every day she throws the want ads right my way And never fails to say, Get a job sha na na na, sha na na na na." And there were times in my life that mirrored the songs "9 to 5" by Dolly Parton, "Takin' Care of Business" by Bachman-Turner Overdrive, and not to mention "Take This Job and Shove It" by Johnny Paycheck. Songs about work, jobs, employment, and labor are popular in our culture because now more than ever people are switching jobs throughout their career.

As counselors, we may have clients who have established careers and are thinking of a career change, others may be trying to figure out what they might be successful at and enjoy, and some clients may be looking for a new vocation based on a certain lifestyle or benefits. Some of us might be in the school setting and work with students who, for the first time, are starting to examine their occupational likes and dislikes.

When it comes to assessment in terms of career development, we assess both the content (e.g., values, interests, aptitude) as well as the process (e.g., career readiness). In this chapter, we will first focus on popular interests and value assessments that can assist our clients in making career choices. If you recall from Chapter 8 when we discussed aptitude tests, we mentioned there are four main aptitude testing categories: cognitive ability, intellectual and cognitive functioning, specific aptitude, and multiaptitude. We will spend some time focusing on multiaptitude and specific aptitude tests that can assist clients regarding their abilities. After we explore the content of career development, we will focus on the process of career development as we talk about career readiness, which is often referred to as career maturity or career adaptability. We will conclude the chapter with a discussion on the role of counselors in career assessment.

CAREER ASSESSMENT

Career assessment is a multifaceted assessment process in which counselors assess an individual's aptitudes, achievements, interests, values, and personalities through testing and interviewing. As stated above, assessment in terms of career development examines both content and process. Career assessment is often traced back to Frank Parsons in 1909, when he described vocational guidance in his *Choosing a Vocation* (see Case Illustration 12.1). His views later developed into trait-and-factor theory. Implementing trait-and-factor theory consists of three elements: (1) knowledge of yourself (e.g., attitudes, abilities, interests, ambitions), (2) knowledge of jobs (e.g., advantages, disadvantages, opportunities, compensation), and (3) matching of these two. During this time, counselors relied more on interviews and observations; however, soon formal assessments were developed to support individuals in determining appropriate career goals.

CASE ILLUSTRATION 12.1

Frank Parsons (1854–1908) is known as the "father of vocational guidance." Though his first profession was as an engineer, he became very interested in the social movements that were occurring during his time. Parsons organized the Bureau of Vocational Guidance and trained men to become counselors. His ideas were incorporated by Harvard University, which offered the first counselor education program housed within a university. Parsons identified a three-step process to help individuals choose the right career path. Frank Parsons died shortly after he began working on vocational guidance and his book *Choosing a Vocation*, which was published in 1909 after he had died.

Although the foundations for career assessments are traced back to Frank Parsons in 1909, the development of the first noted career assessment did not occur until 1914. Created by Jesse Davis, an educator, the **Student Vocational Self Analysis** was intended for use with 10th-grade students in public schools as a means of establishing potential career paths (Harrington & Long, 2013). From its original roots in education, development of career assessments branched out to other professions, including weighted scored interest questions by psychologist James Minor in 1917 and the Carnegie Interest Inventory in 1920 by personnel from the Carnegie Institute of Technology.

The Carnegie Interest Inventory spearheaded an onslaught of additional assessment tools, including Storm's development of the Storm Vocational Interest Blank, which lay the foundation for current assessment measures. Building on these foundations, the first career assessment which integrated elements of psychological theory, L. L. Thurstone's An Interest Schedule, was developed in 1947 (Harrington & Long, 2013). As development of new interest inventories increased, so, too, did the support from both educational and business settings. As these assessments gained in popularity, their application in numerous fields also flourished. In fact, counselors today often use career assessments as an additional tool to support their clients.

Career assessments serve as valuable tools to support individuals in exploring careers, assisting in making effective career decisions, and helping to develop a career identity. Given to high school students, career assessments can provide guidance on what type of careers may match their interests and abilities, easing decisions regarding whether to pursue higher education and what majors they may wish to pursue. An increasing number of corporations, on the other hand, use career assessments as a tool to recruit candidates who will be a good fit for the employment setting as well as to promote within the company. In addition, vocational rehabilitation counselors use career assessments to support individuals who have developed a disability that does not allow them to return to their previous careers investigate potential future career fits. And as Erford and Crockett (2012) reveal, career assessments have also quickly gained importance in many counseling settings as high rates of unemployment and work-related stressors have a significant impact on mental health concerns. Fortunately, many of the tests we discuss below do not require advanced training to administer. However, as mentioned in Chapter 5, counselors need to ensure they can appropriately select, administer, score, and report assessment results. Furthermore, counselors should not rely on a single test to assist clients in choosing a career.

ASSESSING INTERESTS AND VALUES

Interests and values are often used interchangeably in the literature, which can result in confusion. While there is some overlap in the concepts, values and interests are not the same. Super (1995) defines **values** as "the result of further refinement through interaction with the environment, both natural and human. . . . The need for help thus becomes love, and the need to help becomes altruism" (p. 54). According to Super, **interests** are "the activities within which people expect to attain their values and thus satisfy their needs" (p. 54). Compared to interests, values are generally defined, and they describe the qualities sought.

Interest inventories are widely used in counseling and play a major role in the career decision-making process. Interest inventories allow counselors to assess a client's interest and provide a wealth of knowledge of the client's likes or dislikes. Researchers demonstrate that interests and self-estimates of ability predict occupational choice (Tracey & Hopkins, 2001). Furthermore, for individuals with many abilities, interests rather than aptitude predict a person's occupational choice. As a result of the potential for predicting occupational choice, interest inventories are used in a variety of arenas. As Lynch, Seery, and Gordon (2011) point out, students' interests have also been correlated with educational success in higher education. Because of this, interest inventories are often given to high school students to support them in making informed decisions about the career paths they may wish to take. For example, an interest inventory provided to a junior in high school will produce results which may enable him or her to make informed decisions about a course of study. Because of this inventory, the student will gain additional knowledge about what other individuals with similar interests are doing for an occupation.

Given their prominence in high schools as a means of supporting students with narrowing down potential career choices, employers have followed suit in using interest inventories. Swanson (2012) notes that in an attempt to fill the void associated with the inability to hire and retain foreign language teachers in numerous parts of the world, interest inventories were provided to current foreign language teachers and compared to stress levels. The similarities associated with interest scores among individuals with lower stress levels provided an interest profile of candidates who could likely be recruited as a fit for similar positions. In addition to use by educators and employers, interest inventories may also be used as valuable tools by counseling professionals. As in the case of high school students, interest inventories may be used with clients to guide their career decisions. Beyond their usefulness in establishing potential career choices, Nauta (2010) argues that interest inventories are often used by counselors to gain insight into an individual's personality. For example, an interest inventory which reveals that an individual would be suited for a position such as a nurse demonstrates the value that the client places on helping others. With this insight, the counselor may be able to make a connection to the presenting issue.

Values play an important role in job satisfaction, and several inventories have been developed to help counselors assess clients' values. Compared to interests, values are more highly correlated with job satisfaction. In career counseling, we often talk about two types of values: **work-related values** and **general values**. Work-related values inventories (e.g., Work Values Inventory) measure values associated with job satisfaction and success. These inventories are often used to assist clients in determining which occupations might meet their needs and provide additional career exploration information. General values inventories (e.g., Values Scale) measure a broad range of values besides those associated with job success. General values inventories are often used to explore what clients may want out of life. Like interest inventories, **values inventories** are used in a variety of environments. According to Lutrell and Richard (2011), values inventories are often administered to individuals transitioning to high school and college. Not only do the results help students prepare for their future, but they may also identify areas which could prevent future success. For example, an individual who reveals higher values on income and lower values on academic achievement may not be suited for a position which requires a 4-year degree but does not pay very much. Corporations, on the other hand, administer values inventories to prospective employees and for purposes of promotion in order to identify an individual who shares similar values to the company mission. An individual who is identified as establishing high values for supervision and low values for independence and challenge, for example, would likely not be identified as an appropriate manager for an organization which values cutting-edge ideas and quick reaction times. Finally, counselors may administer values inventories to clients who are questioning a career move or trying to make a career decision. After administering the test to the client, the counselor can support him or her with evaluating the results and addressing any additional apprehensions that the client may possess in order to assist in making an informed decision. As a result, clients can make informed decisions about job choices which meet their interests. We will now turn our attention to discussing popular interests and values inventories.

INTEREST INVENTORIES

Strong Interest Inventory

The **Strong Interest Inventory** is one of the most widely used inventories, with over 80 years of research demonstrating its validity. It was originally published in 1927 and is based on the work of Edward K. Strong Jr., who developed the Strong Vocational Interest Blank (SVIB). Strong believed that if you asked an individual about his or her likes or dislikes concerning occupations, areas of study, leisure activities, and personality, you could gain a sense of his or her vocational interests. Strong then wanted to discover how people in current occupations would answer the same questions. He used what is referred to as empirical keying to compare individuals' responses to those of people currently working in certain occupations. By empirical keying, he discovered a fit between the individual and the occupations. Since then, the assessment has undergone several revisions and as of 2004 is referred to as the Strong (see Case Illustration 12.2).

The current version of the **Strong** consists of 291 items that are divided into six sections: occupations, subject areas, activities, leisure activities, people, and characteristics. The first five sections of the test ask individuals to use a 5-point Likert scale (*strongly like, like, indifferent, dislike, strongly dislike*) certain occupations, people, characteristics, or topics. For the remaining two sections, individuals use a 5-point scale (*strongly like me, like me, don't know [if can't decide], unlike me, strongly unlike me*) to indicate the degree to which the characteristic is like them. The Strong measures interests reported on four scales: General Occupational Themes, Basic Interest Scales, Occupational Scales, and Personal Style Scales. Each of these scales is discussed below.

CASE ILLUSTRATION   12.2

The Strong Interest Inventory has been in use since 1927; however, the instrument is frequently updated to be relative to individuals working in today's job market as job trends, skills, duties, and occupations have changed significantly over the past decades. In 2004 the Strong Interest Inventory

(Continued)

(Continued)

underwent a major revision, which resulted in changes in all four of its scales and the administrative indexes. At that time, the Strong added 130 female and 130 male occupational scales. The scales were revised using the same method as the original Strong, which included comparing the answers of the people answering the Strong to the answers provided by individuals working successfully in a chosen career. This is done to keep the Strong Interest Inventory as current as possible, so counselors can be assured when using the Strong that they are giving their clients information that will be relevant to them in today's job market.

Source: Herk & Thompson (2012).

General Occupational Themes (GOTs)

The **General Occupational Themes (GOTs)** measure six categories of interest based on John H. Holland's theory. After years of frustrations as a vocational counselor, Holland began his research into how personality appeared to influence individual differences, soon linking these personal differences to vocational interests. Through careful evaluation and fueled by frustrations associated with other measures attempting to link individual differences to vocational preferences, Holland developed his own model. Published originally in 1959, Holland's theory has evolved based largely in part to his focus on establishing empirical evidence to support his model (Nauta, 2010). Preceded by his Vocational Preference Inventory (VPI), Holland's theory proposed that an individual's employment selection was a product of his or her personality (Ohler & Levinson, 2012). As you may recall from Chapter 9, many personality assessments were established as having applications in career counseling. These are based on Holland's assumptions regarding the connection between personality and job satisfaction, including the belief that people can be categorized as one of six personality types: Realistic, Investigative (referred to as Intellectual until 1966), Artistic, Social, Enterprising, or Conventional (RIASEC). In addition, Holland argued that there were six environment types that correspond to the six personality types. People search out an environment that allows them to express their skills, abilities, attitudes, and values. An individual's behavior is then determined by the interaction of both the personality and the environment (Holland, 1997).

Specifically, Holland noted that realistic individuals enjoy working with objects as opposed to working with individuals. This is due to their desire to work with concrete physical objects and situations. These individuals are often hands-on and prefer the ability to work with machines and tools. They often seek work which is more physically demanding. Because they prefer concrete ideas and activities, they are less likely to enjoy activities which require artistic abilities. Individuals who are realistic can often be found working as auto mechanics, construction workers, plumbers, repair technicians, mechanical engineers, landscapers, and even cooks. These individuals are often described by terms such as *practical, persistent,* and *hardheaded.* Famous individuals who were likely in this category include Thomas Edison and Amelia Earhart.

Investigative individuals, on the other hand, enjoy the ability to work alone. This is due to their desire for exploration. These individuals are abstract thinkers and problem solvers. They seek knowledge for knowledge's sake and excel in areas of math and science. Individuals in this category seek to manipulate ideas, numbers, and symbols as opposed to concrete objects. Individuals who are investigative can often be found working as researchers, biologists, surgeons, veterinarians, and airline pilots. They are often found in settings such as hospitals, laboratories, and universities. These individuals are often described as *introverted, intellectual,* and *methodical*. Famous investigative types include Sigmund Freud and Albert Einstein.

Artistic individuals seek opportunities which allow them to utilize their creativity. As a result, they avoid situations and environments which are too structured. Often these individuals are visible through their work in music, writing, acting, and art due to their expressiveness. Individuals who are artistic can often be found in a variety of environments, including theaters, studios, and newspapers. They often work as writers, artists, actors, photographers, dancers, architects, singers, songwriters, designers, and publicists. *Original, emotional,* and *idealistic* are terms often used to describe them. Famous artistic types include Mark Twain and Laura Ingalls Wilder.

Social individuals prefer the ability to work with people over objects. They are often compassionate and seek the opportunity to help others. They seek knowledge in intrapersonal and interpersonal interactions. These individuals value the ability to be introspective and to talk as well as to listen. Individuals who are social can often be found in the social service and healthcare fields, especially in hospital, social service, counseling, and school settings. They often hold jobs such as nurses, counselors, teachers, clergy, and daycare workers. *Understanding, warm,* and *patient* are words often used to describe individuals in this category. Famous social types include Abraham Lincoln and Martin Luther King Jr.

Enterprising individuals prefer working with others due in part to their strong persuasive skills. These individuals seek the ability to be leaders in order to influence others and are not afraid of taking risks. They enjoy recognition and often seek environments which will provide them with it. Individuals in this category often enjoy subjects such as economics and politics. They can often be found working as politicians, salespeople, real estate or insurance agents, lawyers, advertisers, and managers. They often work in political offices, car dealerships, insurance agencies, and law firms. These individuals are often described as *domineering* and *energetic*. Famous enterprising individuals include Walt Disney and Bill Gates.

Finally, conventional individuals enjoy activities in which they can follow directions. They prefer organization and often can be found indoors. These individuals prefer routines and set deadlines. Individuals in this category are often good with computer work and have good mathematics skills. They can often be found working as database operators, secretaries, accountants, medical coders or billers, proofreaders, and bankers. They often work in financial firms, business offices, and software firms. These individuals are often described as *careful* and *practical*. Famous conventional types include Sandra Day O'Connor and John D. Rockefeller.

Guided Practice Exercise 12.1 gives you the opportunity to take the Holland Code Career Test and reflect on your results.

GUIDED PRACTICE EXERCISE 12.1

Prior to class, go to the website www.truity.com/test/holland-code-career-test. It contains a free Holland Code Career Test. Follow the directions and mark your areas of interest for each activity listed. After you have completed all questions, click on the "Score It" button. Review your results. Did your results surprise you? Why or why not? Based on your interest profile, the website suggests careers that might be well suited to you. Were any of those listed career paths ones that you had considered previously? Be prepared to discuss your results and experiences in small groups or with the entire class.

In order to illustrate this theory, Holland developed a hexagon model in 1969 that shows the circular relationships between the types; the types next to each other are the most similar (see Figure 12.1). For example, social types are most similar to enterprising and artistic types, less similar to conventional and investigative types, and least similar to realistic types. As a result, it would be more likely for an individual with a social personality type to experience job satisfaction in an enterprising environment as opposed to a realistic environment. Understanding this connection will help individuals make informed decisions about career choices.

Since its original publication, Holland's theory has undergone several revisions. The first significant revision included integration of the **Environmental Assessment Technique (EAT)**,

Figure 12.1 Holland's Personality Type Hexagon

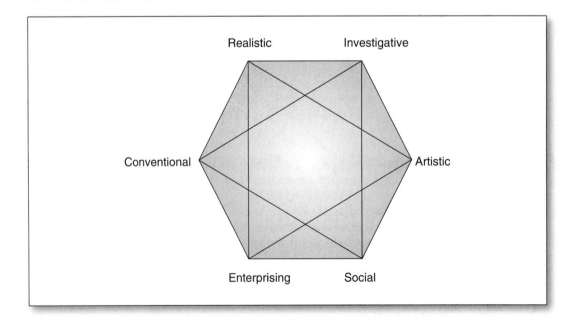

which provided the means to measure the environment as well as more complete information regarding types. These comprehensive typologies were later expanded in detail in 1973 (Nauta, 2010). Two final revisions, the most recent in 1997, further integrated empirical evidence, including notations regarding the effects of intellectual demands of environments, abilities of individuals, and the potential impact of cultural variables in associations.

On the GOTs report, individuals receive a standardized score and a chart which displays the results from greatest to least level of interest (see Figure 12.2). Each theme is presented with a description of interests, work activities, potential skills, and values. For example, those with a Social theme show interest in people and teamwork, enjoy work activities such as teaching and caring for others and encompass potential skills such as people skills, listening, understanding, value cooperation, and service to others. Standard scores are reported as a T score of 50 and standard deviation of 10. However, these standardized scores combined working women and men, and thus have implications when relating the results. For example, men in the normed sample averaged .5 to .1 standard deviation above women on the Realistic GOT.

Basic Interest Scales (BISs)

The **Basic Interest Scales** (BISs) measure clusters of interests in 30 broad areas related to the GOTs. Individuals are given a list of their top five interest areas as well as areas of least interest. Results in a chart further show an individual's interest under each Holland theme (see Figure 12.3). For example, under Social, one's basic interest in Religion and Spirituality, Counseling and Helping, Teaching and Education, Human Resources and Training, Social Sciences, and Healthcare Services is reported as a standard score. A standard T score of 50 and standard deviation of 10 is used to compare individuals' scores against average scores for gender.

Occupational Scales (OSs)

The **Occupational Scales** (OSs) measure how similar an individual's interests are to those of people of the same gender who are working in and are satisfied with their occupation. Individuals receive a report that indicates the top 10 occupations aligned with their interests (see Figure 12.4). This report is followed by an additional list illustrating the individual's scores for all 130 occupations. Standard scores are reported as T scores with a mean of 50 and standard deviation of 10. In addition, a graph indicates dissimilar results (e.g., 29 or below shares few interests with others in occupation and would not enjoy the work), midrange results (e.g., 30–39 shares some interests and probably would enjoy some of the work), and similar results (e.g., 40 and above shares interest and would probably enjoy the work). To further explore the occupations, individuals can use the O*NET database to see summaries of the occupation of interest.

Personal Style Scales (PSSs)

The **Personal Style Scales** (PSSs) use bipolar scales to measure an individual's comfort level in activities such as Work Style (high score: enjoys helping others; low score: enjoys data and ideas), Learning Environment (high score: prefers academic environments; low

Figure 12.2 GOT Sample Report

JANE SAMPLE | F | Page 3

GENERAL OCCUPATIONAL THEMES

SECTION 1

The General Occupational Themes (GOTs) measure six broad interest patterns that can be used to describe your work personality. Most people's interests are reflected by two or three Themes, combined to form a cluster of interests. Work activities, potential skills, and values can also be classified into these six Themes. This provides a direct link between your interests and the career and education possibilities likely to be most meaningful to you.

Your *standard scores* are based on the average scores of a combined group of working adults. However, because research shows that men and women tend to respond differently in these areas, your *interest levels* (Very Little, Little, Moderate, High, Very High) were determined by comparing your scores against the average scores for your gender.

THEME DESCRIPTIONS

THEME	CODE	INTERESTS	WORK ACTIVITIES	POTENTIAL SKILLS	VALUES
Social	S	People, teamwork, helping, community service	Teaching, caring for people, counseling, training employees	People skills, verbal ability, listening, showing understanding	Cooperation, generosity, service to others
Artistic	A	Self-expression, art appreciation, communication, culture	Composing music, performing, writing, creating visual art	Creativity, musical ability, artistic expression	Beauty, originality, independence, imagination
Enterprising	E	Business, politics, leadership, entrepreneurship	Selling, managing, persuading, marketing	Verbal ability, ability to motivate and direct others	Risk taking, status, competition, influence
Conventional	C	Organization, data management, accounting, investing, information systems	Setting up procedures and systems, organizing, keeping records, developing computer applications	Ability to work with numbers, data analysis, finances, attention to detail	Accuracy, stability, efficiency
Investigative	I	Science, medicine, mathematics, research	Performing lab work, solving abstract problems, conducting research	Mathematical ability, researching, writing, analyzing	Independence, curiosity, learning
Realistic	R	Machines, computer networks, athletics, working outdoors	Operating equipment, using tools, building, repairing, providing security	Mechanical ingenuity and dexterity, physical coordination	Tradition, practicality, common sense

YOUR HIGHEST THEMES	YOUR THEME CODE
Social, Artistic	**SA**

THEME	CODE	STANDARD SCORE & INTEREST LEVEL	STD SCORE
Social	S	HIGH	62
Artistic	A	MODERATE	45
Enterprising	E	LITTLE	41
Conventional	C	LITTLE	40
Investigative	I	VERY LITTLE	34
Realistic	R	VERY LITTLE	32

The charts above display your GOT results in descending order, from your highest to least level of interest. Referring to the Theme descriptions provided, determine how well your results fit for you. Do your highest Themes ring true? Look at your next highest level of interest and ask yourself the same question. You may wish to highlight the Theme descriptions above that seem to fit you best.

Figure 12.3   Basic Interest Scales Report

Strong Interest Inventory® Profile   JANE SAMPLE I F I Page 4

BASIC INTEREST SCALES   SECTION 2

The Basic Interest Scales represent specific interest areas that often point to work activities, projects, course work, and leisure activities that are personally motivating and rewarding. As with the General Occupational Themes, your interest levels (Very Little, Little, Moderate, High, Very High) were determined by comparing your scores against the average scores for your gender.

As you review your results in the charts below, note your top interest areas and your areas of least interest, and think about how they relate to your work, educational, and leisure activities. Take time to consider any top interest areas that are not currently part of your work or lifestyle and think about how you might be able to incorporate them into your plans.

YOUR TOP FIVE INTEREST AREAS

1. Religion & Spirituality (S)
2. Counseling & Helping (S)
3. Teaching & Education (S)
4. Writing & Mass Communication (A)
5. Politics & Public Speaking (E)

Areas of Least Interest

Programming & Information Systems (C)

Protective Services (R)

Visual Arts & Design (A)

SOCIAL — High

BASIC INTEREST SCALE	STD SCORE & INTEREST LEVEL	STD SCORE
Religion & Spirituality	VH	67
Counseling & Helping	VH	66
Teaching & Education	H	65
Human Resources & Training	M	56
Social Sciences	M	51
Healthcare Services	VL	35

ARTISTIC — Moderate

BASIC INTEREST SCALE	STD SCORE & INTEREST LEVEL	STD SCORE
Writing & Mass Communication	H	63
Culinary Arts	M	59
Performing Arts	M	47
Visual Arts & Design	VL	32

ENTERPRISING — Little

BASIC INTEREST SCALE	STD SCORE & INTEREST LEVEL	STD SCORE
Politics & Public Speaking	H	58
Management	M	50
Marketing & Advertising	S	40
Sales	VL	36
Law	VL	34
Entrepreneurship	VL	32

CONVENTIONAL — Little

BASIC INTEREST SCALE	STD SCORE & INTEREST LEVEL	STD SCORE
Office Management	M	53
Finance & Investing	VL	36
Taxes & Accounting	VL	33
Programming & Information Systems	VL	31

INVESTIGATIVE — Very Little

BASIC INTEREST SCALE	STD SCORE & INTEREST LEVEL	STD SCORE
Research	L	39
Mathematics	L	37
Science	VL	35
Medical Science	VL	35

REALISTIC — Very Little

BASIC INTEREST SCALE	STD SCORE & INTEREST LEVEL	STD SCORE
Nature & Agriculture	L	41
Athletics	L	37
Military	VL	36
Computer Hardware & Electronics	VL	33
Mechanics & Construction	VL	32
Protective Services	VL	31

INTEREST LEVELS: VL = Very Little I L = Little I M = Moderate I H = High I VH = Very High

Figure 12.4 Occupational Scales Report

Strong Interest Inventory® Profile

JANE SAMPLE | F | Page 6

OCCUPATIONAL SCALES

SECTION 3

SOCIAL — Helping, Instructing, Caregiving

THEME CODE	OCCUPATIONAL SCALE	DISSIMILAR / MIDRANGE / SIMILAR	STD SCORE
SA	Speech Pathologist		62
S	Mental Health Counselor		59
S	Special Education Teacher		59
S	Elementary School Teacher		58
SA	Social Worker		58
SE	School Counselor		57
S	Secondary School Teacher		55
S	Career Counselor		54
SE	Community Service Director		54
S	Instructional Coordinator		53
S	Middle School Teacher		53
SA	University Administrator		53
SEA	School Administrator		47
SEA	Human Resources Manager		46
SAE	Training & Development Specialist		46
SC	Customer Service Representative		45
SA	Rehabilitation Counselor		45
S	Religious/Spiritual Leader		43
SAI	University Faculty Member		43
SEA	Bartender		42
SAE	Human Resources Specialist		42
SE	Parks & Recreation Manager		40
SCE	Loan Officer/Counselor		38
SA	Recreation Therapist		35
SAC	Management Analyst		34
SAR	Occupational Therapist		34
SE	Personal Financial Advisor		34
SI	Registered Nurse		22
SIR	Physical Therapist		3

Similar results (40 and above)
You share interests with women in that occupation and probably would enjoy the work.

Midrange results (30–39)
You share some interests with women in that occupation and probably would enjoy some of the work.

Dissimilar results (29 and below)
You share few interests with women in that occupation and probably would not enjoy the work.

For more information about any of these occupations, visit O*NET™ online at http://www.onetonline.org

ARTISTIC — Creating or Enjoying Art, Drama, Music, Writing

THEME CODE	OCCUPATIONAL SCALE	DISSIMILAR / MIDRANGE / SIMILAR	STD SCORE
A	Librarian		59
AE	Public Relations Director		57
ASE	English Teacher		56
AE	Broadcast Journalist		54
AE	Advertising Account Manager		50
A	Translator		50
A	Reporter		45
ASE	Attorney		42
A	Arts/Entertainment Manager		39
ASI	ESL Instructor		38
ARE	Photographer		37
A	Editor		35
AIR	Technical Writer		32
AER	Public Administrator		31
AR	Artist		30
AI	Urban & Regional Planner		27
A	Musician		26
ASE	Art Teacher		20
ACI	Computer/Mathematics Manager		19
A	Graphic Designer		8
AIR	Medical Illustrator		-4
ARI	Architect		-20

Source: Consulting Psychologists Press (2009). Modified and reproduced by special permission of the Publisher, CPP, Inc., Mountain View, CA 94043 from Strong Interest Inventory® Profile Sample Report by CPP, Inc. Copyright 2004, 2012 by CPP, Inc. All rights reserved. Further reproduction is prohibited without the Publisher's written consent.

score: prefers practical learning environments), Leadership Style (high score: prefers direct-ing others to doing the job alone; low score: prefers to do the job rather than directing others), Risk Taking (high score: likes risk taking; low score: dislikes risk taking), and Team Orientation (high score: prefers working on teams, enjoys problem solving; low score: pre-fers accomplishing tasks independently). Results are compared to a combined group of men and women; clear scores (below 46 and above 54) indicate a clear preference for one style versus another, and midrange scores (46–54) indicate some characteristics on each side apply to the individual. Individuals also receive their five personal style scales prefer-ences (e.g., You likely prefer working with people; see Figure 12.5).

Individuals also receive a Profile Summary of the previous reports (see Figure 12.6). It includes the individual's highest themes (e.g., Social Artistic), theme code (e.g., SA), top five areas of interest, three areas of least interest, top 10 strong occupations, and personal style scales preferences.

Reliability and validity of the Strong are sound. Internal consistency reliabilities are high on all the scales, with estimates ranging from .90 to .95 for the GOTs, .82 to .92 for BISs, and .82 to .87 for PSSs (Consulting Psychologists Press, 2009). It should be noted that internal consistency reliability was not reported for OSs because the scales include items of hetero-geneous content, thus making it not appropriate to determine internal consistency. In terms of validity, researchers reveal that GOTs predict work-related variables (Rottinghaus, Lindley, Green, & Borgen, 2002), BISs effectively distinguish occupations (L. M. Larson & Borgen, 2002), PSSs show evidence of validity through correlations with the Skills Confi-dence Inventory and Myers Briggs Type Indicator (Hammer & Kummerow, 1996), and OSs predict the occupations individuals will eventually enter (Dirk & Hansen, 2004).

Self-Directed Search (SDS)

In 1971, John Holland developed the **Self-Directed Search (SDS)**, which is based on Holland's Theory of Types. Since then, the SDS has been revised and is currently in its fourth edition.

Four forms of the SDS are available: Form R (Regular), to be used with high school stu-dents, college students, and adults; Form E (Easy-to-Read), designed at a fourth-grade reading level for high school students and adults who may have limited reading ability; Form CE (Career Explorer), appropriate for middle school and junior high students; and Form CP (Career Planning), designed to focus on long-term planning and occupations with upper levels of responsibility and educational requirements. We will briefly discuss the SDS Form R.

Although the majority of the SDS items assess interests, this instrument also assesses competencies and self-estimates of abilities. Individuals complete five categories of the SDS: Daydreams, Activities, Competencies, Occupations, and Self-estimates. Daydreams ask the individual to list the careers he or she has dreamed of or discussed with others. For Activities, individuals read 66 statements and are asked to select "like" for those activities they would like to do and "dislike" for those they would dislike doing or would show indifference toward. Activities are related to the RIASEC model. Examples include "Read scientific books or magazines" (investigative activity), "Write novels or plays" (artis-tic activities), and "Work for charity" (social activity). On the Competencies section of the

Figure 12.5 Personal Styles Scale Report

Strong Interest Inventory® Profile   JANE SAMPLE | F | Page 9

PERSONAL STYLE SCALES   SECTION 4

The Personal Style Scales describe different ways of approaching people, learning, and leading, as well as your interest in taking risks and participating in teams. Personal Style Scales help you think about your preferences for factors that can be important in your career, enabling you to narrow your choices more effectively and examine your opportunities. Each scale includes descriptions at both ends of the continuum, and the score indicates your preference for one style versus the other.

Your scores on the Personal Style Scales were determined by comparing your responses to those of a combined group of working men and women.

YOUR PERSONAL STYLE SCALES PREFERENCES

1. You likely prefer working with people.
2. You seem to prefer to learn through lectures and books.
3. You probably prefer to lead by taking charge.
4. You may dislike taking risks.
5. You probably enjoy both team roles and independent roles.

Clear Scores
(Below 46 and above 54)
You indicated a clear preference for one style versus the other.

Midrange Scores (46–54)
You indicated that some of the descriptors on both sides apply to you.

PERSONAL STYLE SCALE			STD SCORE
Work Style	Prefers working alone; enjoys data, ideas, or things; reserved	Prefers working with people; enjoys helping others; outgoing	73
Learning Environment	Prefers practical learning environments; learns by doing; prefers short-term training to achieve a specific goal or skill	Prefers academic environments; learns through lectures and books; willing to spend many years in school; seeks knowledge for its own sake	62
Leadership Style	Is not comfortable taking charge of others; prefers to do the job rather than direct others; may lead by example rather than by giving directions	Is comfortable taking charge of and motivating others; prefers directing others to doing the job alone; enjoys initiating action; expresses opinions easily	58
Risk Taking	Dislikes risk taking; likes quiet activities; prefers to play it safe; makes careful decisions	Likes risk taking; appreciates original ideas; enjoys thrilling activities and taking chances; makes quick decisions	30
Team Orientation	Prefers accomplishing tasks independently; enjoys role as independent contributor; likes to solve problems on one's own	Prefers working on teams; enjoys collaborating on team goals; likes problem solving with others	48

Figure 12.6   Profile Summary

Strong Interest Inventory® Profile   JANE SAMPLE | F | Page 10

PROFILE SUMMARY   SECTION 5

YOUR HIGHEST THEMES	YOUR THEME CODE
Social, Artistic	**SA**

YOUR TOP FIVE INTEREST AREAS

1. **Religion & Spirituality (S)**
2. **Counseling & Helping (S)**
3. **Teaching & Education (S)**
4. **Writing & Mass Communication (A)**
5. **Politics & Public Speaking (E)**

Areas of Least Interest

Programming & Information Systems (C)

Protective Services (R)

Visual Arts & Design (A)

YOUR TOP TEN STRONG OCCUPATIONS

1. Speech Pathologist (SA)
2. Librarian (A)
3. Mental Health Counselor (S)
4. Special Education Teacher (S)
5. Elementary School Teacher (S)
6. Social Worker (SA)
7. Public Relations Director (AE)
8. School Counselor (SE)
9. English Teacher (ASE)
10. Secondary School Teacher (S)

Occupations of Dissimilar Interest

Architect (ARI)

Athletic Trainer (RIS)

Physicist (IRA)

Veterinarian (IRA)

Medical Illustrator (AIR)

YOUR PERSONAL STYLE SCALES PREFERENCES

1. **You likely prefer working with people.**
2. **You seem to prefer to learn through lectures and books.**
3. **You probably prefer to lead by taking charge.**
4. **You may dislike taking risks.**
5. **You probably enjoy both team roles and independent roles.**

RESPONSE SUMMARY   SECTION 6

This section provides a summary of your responses to the different sections of the inventory for use by your career professional.

ITEM RESPONSE PERCENTAGES

Section Title	Strongly Like	Like	Indifferent	Dislike	Strongly Dislike
Occupations	4	21	3	2	71
Subject Areas	11	15	13	7	54
Activities	2	36	7	4	51
Leisure Activities	52	11	11	4	22
People	13	25	44	6	13
Your Characteristics	33	44	0	11	11
TOTAL PERCENTAGE	10	24	9	4	53

Note: Due to rounding, total percentage may not add up to 100%.

Total possible responses: 291   Your response total: 290   Items omitted: 1   Typicality index: 21 — Combination of item responses appears consistent.

CPP, Inc. | 800-624-1765 | www.cpp.com
© Full copyright information appears on page 1.

SDS, individuals read 66 statements and indicate "yes" for activities they do well or completely and "no" for activities they never performed or performed poorly. Example statements include "I can use algebra to solve mathematical problems" (investigative competency) and "I find it easy to talk with all kinds of people" (social competency). The Occupations component assesses feelings and attitudes about many kinds of work. Individuals read 84 statements and select "yes" for the occupations that interest or appeal to them and "no" for the occupations they dislike. An example is "Marriage Counselor" (social occupation). Individuals then complete 12 Self-estimate rating scales, indicating on a 7 point Likert Scale from 1 (*low*) to 7 (*high*) their abilities (i.e., manual skills, math ability, music ability, understanding of others, managerial skills, office skills).

After completing the SDS, individuals receive a three-letter Holland summary code (e.g., SIA). The three RIASEC types with the highest scores from the SDS yield the three-letter code called the Holland code. The Holland code aligns individuals' strengths with descriptions of Holland's six categories (RIASEC). For example, with a code of SAI a person most resembles the social type, then the artistic type, and then the investigative type. Figure 12.7 is an example of an SDS report. The **Occupations Finder**, a classification system that includes over 1,300 common occupations in the United States, is then used to generate a

Figure 12.7   SDS Report

Interpretive Report

by
Robert C. Reardon, PhD,
and PAR Staff

General Information

Name:	Evelyn Rose
Client ID:	
Reference Group:	Adult
Test Date:	06/30/2013
Age:	33
Gender:	Female

Realistic:	**11**	Social:	**43**
Investigative:	**22**	Enterprising:	**20**
Artistic:	**23**	Conventional:	**13**

Summary Code: SAI

Introduction

To get the most from your Self-Directed Search (SDS) results, read this report carefully. The report answers some of the questions most frequently asked about the SDS; it also provides lists of possible career options for you to consider as you think about your future. The report concludes with suggestions and resources to assist you with your educational and career planning.

What is the Self-Directed Search (SDS)?

The SDS is a guide to educational and career planning. It was first developed by Dr. John Holland in 1971 and subsequently has been revised three times. The SDS and this Interpretive Report are based on extensive research about how people choose careers. The SDS is the most widely used interest inventory in the world.

What is the SDS Interpretive Report based upon?

The SDS Interpretive Report helps you learn about yourself and your educational and life/career choices. It is based upon the theory that people can be loosely classified into six different groups: Realistic, Investigative, Artistic, Social, Enterprising, and Conventional (RIASEC). Important information about these six types is presented below. Think about yourself as you read about the RIASEC types.

Which types are most like you?

Realistic (R) people like realistic careers such as auto mechanic, aircraft controller, surveyor, electrician, and farmer. The **R** type usually has mechanical and athletic abilities, and likes to work outdoors and with tools and machines.

The **R** type generally likes to work with things more than with people. The **R** type is described as conforming, frank, genuine, hardheaded, honest, humble, materialistic, modest, natural, normal, persistent, practical, shy, and thrifty.

Investigative (I) people like investigative careers such as biologist, chemist, physicist, geologist, anthropologist, laboratory assistant, and medical technician. The I type usually has math and science abilities, and likes to work alone and to solve problems.

The **I** type generally likes to explore and understand things or events, rather than persuade others or sell them things. The I type is described as analytical, cautious, complex, critical, curious, independent, intellectual, introverted, methodical, modest, pessimistic, precise, rational, and reserved.

Artistic (A) people like artistic careers such as composer, musician, stage director, dancer, interior decorator, actor, and writer. The **A** type usually has artistic skills, enjoys creating original work, and has a good imagination.

(Continued)

Figure 12.7 (Continued)

The **A** type generally likes to work with creative ideas and self-expression more than routines and rules. The **A** type is described as complicated, disorderly, emotional, expressive, idealistic, imaginative, impractical, impulsive, independent, introspective, intuitive, nonconforming, open, and original.

Social (S) people like social careers such as teacher, speech therapist, religious worker, counselor, clinical psychologist, and nurse. The **S** type usually likes to be around other people, is interested in how people get along, and likes to help other people with their problems.

The **S** type generally likes to help, teach, and counsel people more than engage in mechanical or technical activity. The **S** type is described as convincing, cooperative, friendly, generous, helpful, idealistic, kind, patient, responsible, social, sympathetic, tactful, understanding, and warm.

Enterprising (E) people like enterprising careers such as buyer, sports promoter, television producer, business executive, salesperson, travel agent, supervisor, and manager. The **E** type usually has leadership and public speaking abilities, is interested in money and politics, and likes to influence people.

The **E** type generally likes to persuade or direct others more than work on scientific or complicated topics. The **E** type is described as acquisitive, adventurous, agreeable, ambitious, attention-getting, domineering, energetic, extraverted, impulsive, optimistic, pleasure-seeking, popular, self-confident, and sociable.

Conventional (C) people like conventional careers such as bookkeeper, financial analyst, banker, tax expert, secretary, and radio dispatcher. The **C** type has clerical and math abilities, likes to work indoors and to organize things.

The **C** type generally likes to follow orderly routines and meet clear standards, avoiding work that does not have clear directions. The **C** type is described as conforming, conscientious, careful, efficient, inhibited, obedient, orderly, persistent, practical, thrifty, and unimaginative.

Sometimes the RIASEC letters are used to describe the areas that a person's interests most resemble. For example, we could say that one person is most like a Realistic, or **R**, type. Another person might be more like a Social, or **S**, type. Furthermore, a person often resembles several types, not just one.

How are the six types similar or different?

A six-sided figure—called a hexagon—is used to show the similarities and differences among the six types. Types that are next to one another on the hexagon are most similar. The hexagon presented earlier in Figure 12.1 shows the relationships among the six types. For example, Realistic and Investigative types tend to have similar interests, but Realistic and Social types tend to be most different. Conventional types are most closely related to Enterprising and Realistic types, somewhat less similar to Social and Investigative types, but tend to be most different from Artistic types, and so on.

What does my three-letter summary code mean?

Completing the SDS helped you describe what you like--your favorite activities and interests. The three RIASEC types with the highest SDS Summary Scores are your three-letter Holland summary code. Your summary code is a brief way of saying what you like—your combination of interests.

Your interests are mostly a combination of S, A, and I. The first letter of your code shows the type you most closely resemble; the second letter shows the type you next most closely resemble, and so on. The types not in your three-letter code are the types you least closely resemble.

Your summary scores on the SDS were R = 11, I = 22, A = 23, S = 43, E = 20, C = 13. You might think of your interests as a RIASEC pie, with the size of the six slices being equal to the size of your scores on the SDS. The larger the slice, the greater your interest in that area. Score differences of less than 8 points can be considered as similar. Sometimes summary codes have tied scores, which means they are about equally interesting to you.

Can RIASEC letters be used to classify jobs and other things?

Yes. Jobs, occupations, fields of study, and leisure activities can be grouped into RIASEC areas. It is helpful to think of these as environments that are more comfortable, friendly, and beneficial for some Holland types than for others. For example, if you are a Social type, you will probably like a social environment most because social jobs require activities, values, abilities, and self-views that you have or prefer. In general, people who find environments that match their type are likely to be the most satisfied and successful.

What is included in this report?

The SDS Interpretive Report has taken your code and searched lists of 1,379 occupations, over 750 fields of study, and over 700 leisure activities in order to print examples of each for your report.

All combinations of the letters of your Holland summary code were used to build this Interpretive Report. This was done to increase your awareness of potentially satisfying occupations, and to provide you with a better understanding of your future possibilities. Remember, every code is different, and Interpretive Reports vary in the numbers of possibilities printed.

What careers have you daydreamed about?

When you completed the SDS you were asked to list the occupations you have considered in thinking about your future. You were asked to list the careers you have daydreamed about as well as those you have discussed with others. The occupations you selected are listed in the table below along with the Holland code that corresponds to each occupation.

What occupations might interest me?

The SDS Interpretive Report has created a list of occupations based on the letters in your summary code. Next to each occupation, the O*NET™ code can be found. These codes are from the *Occupational Information Network (*http://online.onetcenter.org) database that provides

(Continued)

Figure 12.7 (Continued)

detailed descriptions of occupations. The corresponding descriptions for each occupation listed in this report can be directly accessed by clicking on the O*NET code in the report. In the last column, the numbers listed under the Education Level (ED) heading have the following meaning:

5 means that an advanced degree (e.g., graduate school) is necessary
4 means that college training (e.g., a 4-year degree) is necessary
3 means that some college, technical, vocational, or business training is necessary
2 means that a high school diploma or GED is necessary
1 means that elementary school training or no special training is required

Note: "*" in the O*NET Code column indicates there is currently no corresponding code for that occupation.

Code: SAI

	Occupation	O*NET Code	ED	
	Acquisitions Librarian	25-4021.00	5	
	Librarian	25-4021.00	5	
	Marriage and Family Therapist	21-1013.00	5	
	Speech-Language Pathologist	29-1127.00	5	
	Dental Assistant	31-9091.00	3	
	Dental Hygienist	29-2021.00	3	

What does my code mean?

Some people find it easy to see which types they are like and to find useful possibilities to explore. For example, the three letters of their code may all be next to one another on the hexagon (e.g., SEA); the first letter of their code may have a summary score much higher than the second letter; or the first two code letters are adjacent on the hexagon.

Other people find it difficult to match themselves to any of the RIASEC types, and they feel that their interests are less clear or stable. For example, the letters of their code are separated by less than 8 points, and can be viewed as about the same. They are about equally interested in several areas.

Your interests are a result of what you have learned and experienced up to this point in your life. You may develop new interests related to the RIASEC types by trying out new things. Also, a person's type may become clearer as he or she grows older or has more life experiences.

Source: Reproduced by special permission of the Publisher, Psychological Assessment Resources, Inc., 16204 North Florida Avenue, Lutz, Florida 33549, from the Self—Directed Search® Interpretive Report by Robert C. Reardon, Ph.D. and PAR Staff, Copyright 1985, 1987, 1989, 1994, 1996, 1997, 2001, 2010, 2013. Further reproduction is prohibited without permission from PAR, Inc.

list of occupations and educational requirements based on the Holland code. For example, the Holland code SAI includes occupations such as marriage and family therapist, speech-language pathologist, and acquisitions librarian. Next to each occupation, the O*NET code is provided. Individuals can use these codes to look up detailed job descriptions. We will cover O*NET in more detail later in the chapter. Guided Practice Exercise 12.2 allows you to brainstorm possible occupations that may fit with your client's code on the General Occupation Themes.

GUIDED PRACTICE EXERCISE 12.2

You are a counselor working in a community counseling center in a large city. Among the services you offer are career counseling and assessment. You have a young adult client who has started several degree programs at several of the local colleges and universities in the area, only to quit because he lost interest in the subjects he was studying. He has come to you for help with career assessments and counseling in order to try to find a career path that is truly right for him in terms of his interests and personality. You administer the General Occupational Themes based on Holland's theory. Your client gets a code of ASE (artistic, social, and enterprising). In small groups, brainstorm possible occupations that might fit that code.

POSSIBLE ANSWERS:

Teacher (art, drama, English), interior designer, actor or performer, advertising director or manager, journalist or reporter, museum curator, photographer, graphic designer, counselor, therapist, social worker, or entrepreneur, to name a few.

Kuder Career Search With Person Match (KCS)

In the 1970s, Kuder challenged Holland's theory. If you recall, Holland's interest inventory uses likes and dislikes to produce a personality code that is matched to occupational environments. Kuder (1977), however, did not believe in categorizing people by stereotypical prototypes. Furthermore, recall that on the Strong Interest Inventory, an individual's final score is compared to normed occupational groups rather than to individuals in general. In other words, the individual's interests resemble the interests of the individuals in the occupation. Kuder believed interest inventories could better match people to jobs if individuals were matched to people who were satisfied and enthusiastic about their work and scored the same on the interest inventory. This technique became known as person matching. The **Kuder Career Search With Person Match (KCS)** is essentially a person match inventory in which individuals "learn which 25 persons from the criterion pool have activity preference patterns most similar to their own" (Zytowski, 2001, p. 233).

The KCS is often used to foster career exploration with individuals who may have limited knowledge about occupational possibilities (Zytowski, 1997). The KCS takes approximately 20 minutes to complete online and includes an inventory of activity preferences, the Kuder Career Clusters, and the Person Match. The activity preferences are art, communications, computations, human services, mechanical, music, nature, office detail, sales/management, and science/technical. The Kuder Career Clusters are art/communication, business detail, outdoor/mechanical, sales/management, science/technical, and social/personal services. Individuals receive a report that includes scores on the Activity Preference Profile, the Kuder Career Clusters, and the top 25 Person Match. The report also includes steps for continuing career exploration.

The individual's scores are compared to a pool of over 2,000 responders in the KCS database who have at least 3 years of work experience and are satisfied in their work. Thus, scores on the KCS resemble the degree of fit between the individual's interests and the interest patterns of those from a pool of satisfied employed individuals. Based on the two highest career clusters, individuals receive 14 narratives from individuals in the pool for whom matches have occurred. These narratives include descriptions of careers and lifestyles (e.g., how they chose their career, likes/dislikes, future career aspirations). The narratives can be used to improve career decision making, generate a list of occupational possibilities, and foster career exploration. Case Illustration 12.3 gives an example of using the Kuder Career Search With People Match in counseling.

CASE ILLUSTRATION 12.3

Antonia Gonzales is a school counselor in a high school in El Paso, Texas. She works with a large population of students who have immigrated to the United States from Mexico and for whom English is their second language. For many of her students, career options in the United States were not high on their priority list until recently as their U.S. educational experiences opened new doors and insights for them in terms of the world of work. However, many of these students are not sure how to go about choosing or identifying a career path or occupation for themselves. One assessment instrument that Ms. Gonzales likes to use with this group of students is the Kuder Career Search With People Match. She likes this assessment because she can administer it in Spanish as well as in English. The assessment doesn't take much time, so students are motivated throughout the process to complete it. Results can be shared through social media outlets such as Facebook and Twitter. Students can share their results with friends and family still living in Mexico, which Ms. Gonzales has found to be important for these students. Ms. Gonzales often does outcome surveys of her graduates who go on to pursue a career option identified by the Kuder. She has found that many students go on to live happy, healthy, satisfied lives in terms of their career choices.

Source: Kuder (2014).

Campbell Interest and Skill Survey (CISS)

The **Campbell Interest and Skill Survey** (CISS) emerged from David Campbell's work on the Strong-Campbell Interest Inventory. The CISS measures vocational interests (e.g., attraction/how much one likes the specific occupation) and skills (e.g., how confident one feels about performing the activity). A unique feature of the CISS skills scale is that it measures an individual's confidence in performing different occupational activities. The CISS requires a sixth-grade reading level, but it is most often used with people interested in pursuing a college education because the assessment focuses on careers that require postsecondary education.

The CISS consists of 320 items on a 6-point Likert scale from *very positive* to *very negative*. Levels of interests are assessed in 200 academic and occupational items: 85 occupations, 43 school subjects, and 72 activities. Level of skill is assessed in 120 occupational activities. High scores do not reflect actual ability; instead, high scores in level of skill suggest one has confidence about performing the activity. Scores on level of interest and skill are reported on the following scales: 7 Orientation Scales, 29 Basic Interest and Skills Scales, 60 Occupational Scales, and 3 Special Scales (Academic Focus, Extraversion, and Variety). The 29 Basic Interest and Skills Scales are divided among the 7 Orientation Scales: Influencing, Organizing, Helping, Creating, Analyzing, Producing, and Adventuring. These orientations correspond with the six Holland scales on the Strong. *Note:* Holland's Realistic scale is made up of the Producing and Adventuring scales on the CISS.

Individuals receive a report concerning the Orientation Scales (e.g., seven broad themes of interests and skills), Basic Interest and Skill Scales (detailed subscales of the Orientation Scales), and Occupation Scales, which allows them to compare their interests and skills with those of workers in the occupation. In addition, the report includes narrative comments if the individual should pursue (high interest, high skill), develop (low skill, high interest), explore (high skill, low interest), or avoid (low interest, low skill) specific vocations (Pearson, 2012b). Figure 12.8 is a sample report for the CISS.

Jackson Vocational Interest Inventory

Unlike the previously discussed interest inventories, the **Jackson Vocational Interest Inventory** (JVIS) consists of 34 basic interest scales that represent work roles (preference for activities associated with occupations) and work styles (preference for certain work environments; see Case Illustration 12.4). The JVIS requires a seventh-grade reading level and was developed for career and educational planning for high school and college students, as well as adults. Individuals read 289 pairs of statements regarding work roles or work styles and indicate which item in the pair they prefer. Work Roles basic interest scales are Life Science, Medical Service, Personal Service, Adventure, Performing Arts, Physical Science, Nature-Agriculture, Family Activity, Elementary Education, Engineering, Author-Journalism, Creative Arts, Law, Social Science, Skilled Trades, Mathematics, Dominant Leadership, Sales, Social Services, Teaching, Business, Office Work, Supervision, Finance, Human Relations, Technical Writing, and Professional Advising. Work Styles basic interest subscales are Job Security, Independence, Accountability, Interpersonal Confidence, Academic Achievement, Planfulness, and Stamina.

The JVIS often appeals to individuals because it is inexpensive compared to other interest inventories, generates several reports, and can be taken directly online at www.jvis .com. Individuals receive a Basic Report which includes (a) percentiles on the 34 Basic Interest Scales, (b) 10 General Occupational Themes (e.g., Inquiring, Expressive, Practical, Helpful), (c) an Academic Satisfaction score which shows the similarity between the individual and an average university student enrolled in a course of study, (d) a Similarity to

Figure 12.8 CISS Sample Report

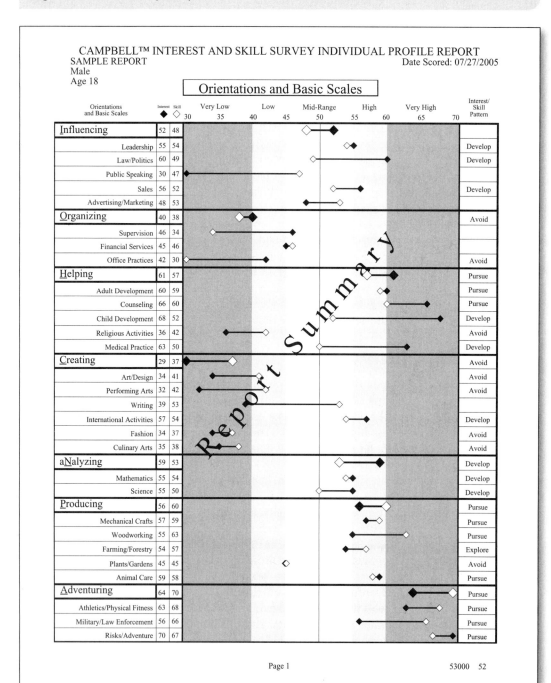

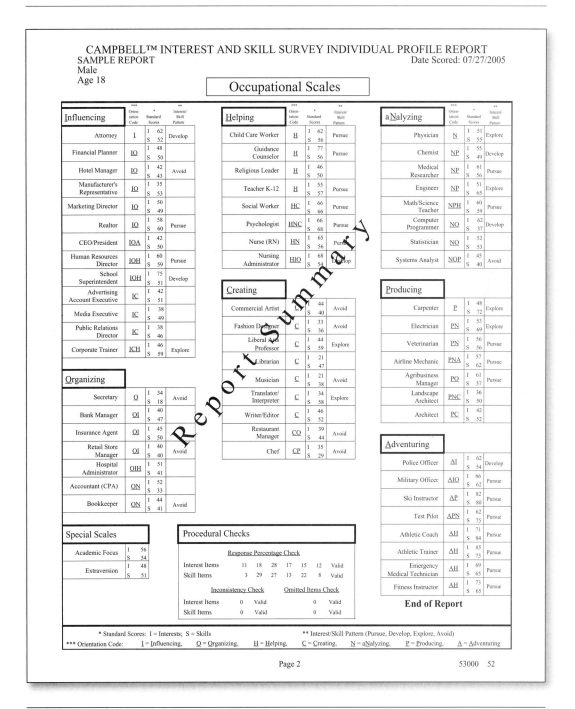

CAMPBELL™ INTEREST AND SKILL SURVEY INDIVIDUAL PROFILE REPORT
SAMPLE REPORT   Date Scored: 07/27/2005
Male
Age 18

Occupational Scales

Influencing

Occupation	Orientation Code	Standard Scores	Interest/Skill Pattern
Attorney	I	I 62 / S 52	Develop
Financial Planner	IO	I 48 / S 50	
Hotel Manager	IO	I 42 / S 43	Avoid
Manufacturer's Representative	IO	I 35 / S 53	
Marketing Director	IO	I 50 / S 49	
Realtor	IO	I 58 / S 60	Pursue
CEO/President	IOA	I 42 / S 50	
Human Resources Director	IOH	I 60 / S 59	Pursue
School Superintendent	IOH	I 75 / S 51	Develop
Advertising Account Executive	IC	I 42 / S 51	
Media Executive	IC	I 38 / S 49	
Public Relations Director	IC	I 38 / S 46	
Corporate Trainer	ICH	I 46 / S 59	Explore

Organizing

Occupation	Orientation Code	Standard Scores	Interest/Skill Pattern
Secretary	O	I 34 / S 18	Avoid
Bank Manager	OI	I 40 / S 47	
Insurance Agent	OI	I 45 / S 50	
Retail Store Manager	OI	I 40 / S 40	Avoid
Hospital Administrator	OIH	I 51 / S 41	
Accountant (CPA)	ON	I 52 / S 33	
Bookkeeper	ON	I 44 / S 41	Avoid

Helping

Occupation	Orientation Code	Standard Scores	Interest/Skill Pattern
Child Care Worker	H	I 62 / S 56	Pursue
Guidance Counselor	H	I 77 / S 56	Pursue
Religious Leader	H	I 46 / S 50	
Teacher K-12	H	I 55 / S 57	Pursue
Social Worker	HC	I 66 / S 66	Pursue
Psychologist	HNC	I 66 / S 68	Pursue
Nurse (RN)	HN	I 65 / S 56	Pursue
Nursing Administrator	HIO	I 68 / S 54	Develop

Creating

Occupation	Orientation Code	Standard Scores	Interest/Skill Pattern
Commercial Artist	C	I 44 / S 40	Avoid
Fashion Designer	C	I 33 / S 36	Avoid
Liberal Arts Professor	C	I 44 / S 59	Explore
Librarian	C	I 21 / S 47	
Musician	C	I 21 / S 38	Avoid
Translator/Interpreter	C	I 34 / S 58	Explore
Writer/Editor	C	I 46 / S 52	
Restaurant Manager	CO	I 39 / S 44	Avoid
Chef	CP	I 35 / S 29	Avoid

aNalyzing

Occupation	Orientation Code	Standard Scores	Interest/Skill Pattern
Physician	N	I 51 / S 55	Explore
Chemist	NP	I 55 / S 49	Develop
Medical Researcher	NP	I 61 / S 56	Pursue
Engineer	NP	I 51 / S 65	Explore
Math/Science Teacher	NPH	I 60 / S 59	Pursue
Computer Programmer	NO	I 62 / S 37	Develop
Statistician	NO	I 52 / S 53	
Systems Analyst	NOP	I 45 / S 40	Avoid

Producing

Occupation	Orientation Code	Standard Scores	Interest/Skill Pattern
Carpenter	P	I 48 / S 72	Explore
Electrician	PN	I 53 / S 69	Explore
Veterinarian	PN	I 56 / S 56	Pursue
Airline Mechanic	PNA	I 57 / S 62	Pursue
Agribusiness Manager	PO	I 61 / S 57	Pursue
Landscape Architect	PNC	I 36 / S	
Architect	PC	I 42 / S 52	

Adventuring

Occupation	Orientation Code	Standard Scores	Interest/Skill Pattern
Police Officer	AI	I 62 / S 54	Develop
Military Officer	AIO	I 66 / S 62	Pursue
Ski Instructor	AP	I 82 / S 80	Pursue
Test Pilot	APN	I 62 / S 75	Pursue
Athletic Coach	AH	I 71 / S 84	Pursue
Athletic Trainer	AH	I 85 / S 73	Pursue
Emergency Medical Technician	AH	I 69 / S 65	Pursue
Fitness Instructor	AH	I 73 / S 65	Pursue

End of Report

Special Scales

	Standard Scores
Academic Focus	I 56 / S 54
Extraversion	I 48 / S 51

Procedural Checks

Response Percentage Check

Interest Items	11	18	28	17	15	12	Valid
Skill Items	3	29	27	13	22	8	Valid

	Inconsistency Check		Omitted Items Check	
Interest Items	0	Valid	0	Valid
Skill Items	0	Valid	0	Valid

* Standard Scores: I = Interests; S = Skills   ** Interest/Skill Pattern (Pursue, Develop, Explore, Avoid)
*** Orientation Code: I = Influencing,   Q = Organizing,   H = Helping,   C = Creating,   N = aNalyzing,   P = Producing,   A = Adventuring

Page 2   53000   52

Source: Pearson (2012a). *Peabody Individual Achievement Test-Revised-Normative Update (PIAT-R/NU).* Copyright © 1998 NCS Pearson, Inc. Reproduced with permission. All rights reserved.

College Students report that shows the individual's pattern of interest compared to students in the field of interests on 17 broad academic clusters (e.g., Science, Education, Engineering, Business), (e) a Similarity to Job Groups report which shows the similarity of an individual's interest to those working in 32 job groups (e.g., Social Welfare, Law and Politics, Writing), and (f) Administrative Indices. You probably noticed that the JVIS differs from the Strong in that academic interest and occupations are described in terms of clusters rather than specific occupations.

In addition, the JVIS is linked to O*NET listings. Individuals receive Top Job Group, Second Job Group, and Third Job Group reports that list O*NET group jobs, activities, and professional organizations to become involved in. If you are wondering what O*NET is, do not worry; we will discuss O*NET in detail soon. While the JVIS may be helpful for providing a framework for career planning, it should not be used alone to provide feedback on career plans. At the end of the chapter, we will discuss the importance of assessing for career readiness.

CASE ILLUSTRATION   12.4

The Jackson Vocational Interest Survey was established in 1967 by Douglas N. Jackson II (1929–2004). He graduated from Cornell University in 1951 with a degree in clinical psychology and went on to teach at Pennsylvania State University, Stanford University, and the University of Western Ontario, where he spent 32 years. In addition to holding many other distinguished titles, Dr. Jackson was a founding member of the Association of Test Publishers; chair of the American Psychological Association's (APA) Committee on Psychological Tests and Assessment; president of the APA's Division of Evaluation, Measurement, and Statistics; and president of the Society of Multivariate Experimental Psychology. He had over 200 publications in scientific journals and wrote numerous book chapters. Dr. Jackson's Vocational Interest Survey has helped millions of people find satisfying careers for themselves.

Source: Jackson (1999).

VALUES INVENTORIES

Super's Work Values Inventory (SWVI-R)

Donald Super (1970) originally developed the Work Values Inventory. Since the 1970s the assessment has undergone multiple revisions; the most recent version, developed by Zytowski (2006), is called the **Super's Work Values Inventory-Revised (SWVI-R)**. The SWVI-R consists of 12 scales measuring the relative importance of work-related value dimensions: Achievement, Co-Workers, Creativity, Income, Independence, Lifestyle, Challenge, Prestige, Security, Supervision, Variety, and Workplace. Each scale contains six items, for a total of 72 items. A 5-point Likert scale response format (ranging from *Not important at all. Not a factor in my job selection* to *Crucial. I would not consider a job without it*) is used to measure the degree of importance of each value. SWVI-R values can be used to generate an occupation list. Because Zytowski aligned the 20 values on the SWVI-R with the 20 O*NET work values, a list of O*NET occupations can be created. The list provides clients with occupations in which their values may be satisfied and that these values are typically associated with. Furthermore, counselors can use the SWVI-R to assist clients in making a hierarchy of values. The hierarchy can help clients assess which values are important to them, engage in career planning, and identify values of strength. If you recall from earlier in the chapter, the SWVI-R is part of the Kuder Career Planning System and thus is often administered with the Kuder Skills Assessment and the Kuder Career Search.

Values Scale

In the late 1970s, Donald Super initiated the **Work Importance Study (WIS)**, which was an international consortium of research teams. One of the goals of the WIS was to examine the values people seek through their work and various life roles. Super worked with Dorothy Nevill and other psychologists to develop instruments that would measure values cross-culturally. During this time the Values Scale (VS) and the Salience Inventory (Nevill & Super, 1986) were developed.

The VS can help clients assess the general values they seek to satisfy though various life roles. Because the VS allows clients to identify which values are important and a priority to them, counselors may find the VS helpful when working with clients who are uncertain about a career direction or contemplating a career change. The VS is easy to administer and takes approximately 30–45 minutes to administer. The VS consists of 106 items and measures 21 values: Ability Utilization, Achievement, Advancement, Aesthetics, Altruism, Authority, Autonomy, Creativity, Economic Rewards, Life Style, Personal Development, Physical Activity, Prestige, Risks, Social Interaction, Social Relations, Variety, Working Conditions, Cultural Identity, Physical Prowess, and Economic Security (Nevill & Kruse, 1996). The 21 values each contain five items that clients rate using a 4-point Likert scale ranging from 1 (*of little or no importance*) to 4 (*very important*). The VS requires an eighth-grade reading level and is appropriate for high school, university, and adult populations. The authors of the Values Scale recommend using an ipsative interpretation, that is, comparing traits within the same individual instead of comparing a person to other individuals who took the instrument. For example, after scores are obtained on each scale, counselors can help clients rank values to create a values hierarchy.

Salience Inventory

The **Salience Inventory** is based on Super's lifespan theory of career development. **Super's Life-Career Rainbow** (Super, 1990) is a graphic display showing how roles may vary during a person's lifetime. These six roles are child, student, leisurite, citizen, worker, and homemaker. The salience of these different life roles changes as a person moves throughout the developmental stages of growth, exploration, establishment, maintenance, and disengagement. The Salience Inventory measures five of the six roles: student, leisurite, citizen, worker, and homemaker (spouse and parent). The assessment is composed of 170 items and uses a 4-point scale to assess each of the five roles from three perspectives:

participation, commitment, and value expectation. These three components of role salience in turn produce the Participation Scale (person's participation in each role), Commitment Scale (person's attachment to each role), and Value Expectations (expectation that values will be met in the five roles). The Salience Inventory can provide clients with opportunities to explore differences in role salience, identify role changes over time, discuss the values one hopes to find in different life roles, and understand role conflicts. Part of Super's basic assumption was that satisfaction depends on the availability of outlets for needs, values, and interests and that work and life satisfaction depend on how well one's values are met. Similar to the other assessments that measure values, the Salience Inventory can facilitate discussion to assess the fit between a person's values and work outcomes. In other words, "Does my work fit my vision of me?"

MULTIAPTITUDE AND SPECIFIC APTITUDE TESTING

If you recall from previous chapters, we conceptualized different aptitude tests in the following four categories: (a) cognitive ability, (b) intellectual and cognitive functioning, (c) specific aptitude, and (d) multiaptitude. In Chapter 7, we discussed intellectual and cognitive functioning tests, and in Chapter 8, we focused on cognitive ability tests. In these chapters, we discussed the importance of both cognitive functioning tests and cognitive ability tests in scholastic environments. Application of aptitude tests, however, is not limited to educational environments. As we turn our focus toward discussing the last two categories of aptitude testing, specific aptitude tests and multiaptitude tests, we explore their usefulness for career planning and employment success.

Specific Aptitude Tests

Specific aptitude tests focus on one aspect of ability. These tests are often used to determine how well a person might perform in a particular employment profession or the likelihood of success in a specific vocation. Educational institutions and hiring departments use these tests as a screening process. For example, to name just a few, there are mechanical aptitude tests, artistic aptitude tests, and clerical aptitude tests. **Mechanical aptitude** tests measure the ability to learn mechanical principles and use reasoning skills to solve mechanical problems. Such tests include the Bennet Mechanical Comprehension Test, the Mechanical Aptitude Test (MAT-3C), and the Wiesen Test of Mechanical Aptitude (WTMA). People often have to take these tests to qualify for employment in positions such as welders, automotive and aircraft mechanics, electricians, carpenters, and truck operators. Technical institutes, businesses, and government agencies often administer these tests in selecting apprentices, trainees, or other candidates before training them. **Artistic aptitude tests** evaluate artistic talent (e.g., music, drawing, creative expression); examples include the Primary Measures of Music Audition, Intermediate Measures of Music Audition, and Graves Design Judgment Test. **Clerical aptitude tests** are frequently used to screen job applicants for clerical jobs. Two popular assessments are the Minnesota Clerical Test (MCT) and Clerical Test Battery (CTB2). Table 12.1 summarizes some of the most popular tests used to measure mechanical, artistic, and clerical aptitude. However, it is

Table 12.1   Measures of Specific Aptitude Testing

Mechanical Aptitude Tests
Bennet Mechanical Comprehension Test (BMCT) (Pearson, 2012a)
Measures ability to apply mechanical and physical principles in practical situations. Consists of 68 items, requires sixth-grade reading level, and takes approximately 30 minutes to complete. Two forms are available, S and T, which can be individually or group-administered. English or Spanish and online, written, or audio versions are available. Those applying to industrial, technical, or repair jobs (e.g., electrician, carpenter, automotive mechanic, welder) are required to take this test.
Mechanical Aptitude Test (MAT-3C) (Ramsay, 2013)
Measures ability to learn production and maintenance job activities. Consists of 36 multiple-choice items covering the following content items: household objects, hand and power tools, work production and maintenance, and school (science and physics). Takes approximately 20 minutes to complete and is useful for those applying for apprenticeships or trainee programs for maintenance jobs.
Wiesen Test of Mechanical Aptitude (WTMA)
Designed to minimize racial, ethnic, and gender bias. Measures ability to use and maintain equipment and machinery, and predicts performance for occupations involving the operation, maintenance, repair, and servicing of mechanical equipment and machinery. Consists of 60 items measuring broad mechanical and physical concepts, including basic machines, movement and objects, gravity and center of gravity, basic electricity, transfer or heat, and basic physical properties of matter. English or Spanish version is available.
Artistic Aptitude Tests
Primary Measures of Music Audition (PMMA) and Intermediate Measures of Music Audition (IMMA)
PMMA measures music potential in kindergarten through third grade, and IMMA for first through sixth grade. Each test is divided into two parts, Tonal and Rhythm, and each part takes approximately 25 minutes. The tests require children to listen to a tonal CD and rhythm CD; they decide if the tonal or rhythm pairs they hear are the same or different and then answer questions on an answer sheet using pictures rather than numbers or words.
Graves Design Judgment Test (Graves, 1948)
Measures certain components of aptitude for the appreciation and production of art structure. Participants are shown 90 slides in black, white, and green, which contain abstract and regular figures that vary in unity, symmetry, and balance. For each pair of slides, participants are asked to indicate their aesthetic preference and select the best set.
Clerical Aptitude Tests
Minnesota Clerical Test (MCT)
Assesses clerical aptitude by measuring elements of perceptual speed and accuracy in two tasks: number comparison (8 minutes) and name comparison (7 minutes). Both tasks contain 200 items each. Participants are presented with pairs of numbers or names, and they must select the identical pairs. Takes approximately 15 minutes and requires a second-grade reading level. Used as a screening tool for positions such as administrative assistants, typists, data processors, cashiers, and bank tellers.
Clerical Test Battery (CTB2)
Assesses abilities needed for a wide range of clerical jobs. Consists of Verbal Reasoning, Numerical Ability, Perceptual Speed and Accuracy (clerical checking), and Spelling Ability. The complete battery can be administered or each test can be given individually, and it takes 27 minutes to administer.

important to note that there are many more specific assessments beyond the scope of this textbook. You should refer to the resources we mentioned in Chapter 5 for identifying additional assessments.

Guided Practice Exercise 12.3 asks you to consider which career assessments might be useful in helping a client determine which career paths may suit him.

GUIDED PRACTICE EXERCISE 12.3

You are a counselor working for a vocational rehabilitation agency. You are working with a veteran of the Iraq War whose job was that of a sniper and who is now being treated for posttraumatic stress disorder as a result of his military service. Your client entered the military at the age of 18 and just retired from service at the age of 39. He now wants to go into the private sector to start a new career, but doesn't think any of his military skill set will transfer. Based on what you have learned about the many career assessments in this chapter, which one would be most useful for this client in helping him determine career paths that might suit him? There is no one right answer to this question, but be prepared to defend your answer in terms of why you selected that particular assessment for this client.

Multiaptitude Tests

Multiaptitude tests measure several aspects of ability. Rather than determining the likelihood of success in a vocation, these tests provide information on the likelihood of success in several vocations. Some of the most popular multiaptitude batteries are the Armed Services Vocational Assessment Battery (ASVAB), the Differential Aptitude Test (DAT), and the O*NET Ability Profiler. The ASVAB, DAT, O*NET Ability Profiler were developed from trait-and-factor theory.

Multiaptitude tests have been used in various environments. Although high school students may take the ASVAB to help them make a decision about military participation, they may also take multiaptitude tests to help them make scholastic and career decisions. For example, a high school student who is working with a school counselor will likely be administered a multiaptitude test to help the student identify jobs of interest and jobs in which he or she has the ability to be successful. Although an individual's interest inventory may have identified mechanic and electrician as two careers of interest, multiaptitude tests are necessary to determine if the individual has the ability to perform the functions necessary for these types of careers. Just because someone likes to sing does not mean that he or she has the voice to be the next singing superstar. Just like other career assessments, multiaptitude tests have also been used by employers in recruitment of qualified individuals. In addition to an interview, an employer may administer a multiaptitude test. Performance on this test may then be used to compare candidates. An individual who performs mediocre in the interview but surpasses other candidates on the multiple aptitudes necessary for the position may be chosen over candidates who perform better on the interview because the results of the aptitude test reveal a strong possibility that the individual is likely to perform well on the job. Additionally, as with other career assessments, multiaptitude tests are integrated into the counseling relationship. A counselor who is working with an individual who is no longer able to perform in a previous career may administer a multiaptitude test to determine potential new careers. The therapeutic relationship would then be utilized to evaluate the results and to support the client in making choices about the path he or she wishes to follow.

In 1909, Frank Parsons published *Choosing a Vocation,* in which he described his concept of vocational guidance that later contributed to the development of trait-and-factor theory. If you recall from your Career Assessment course, traits are stable characteristics of a person that can be measured over time through testing, while factors are characteristics that are required for successful job performance. When we use the terms *trait* and *factor,* we are simply referring to characteristics of the person and the job. According to trait-and-factor theory, the closer one can match his or her traits with the traits required by the occupation, the more likely it is that he or she will have successful job performance and personal satisfaction. In other words, "Do they fit?"

Let's take a closer look at the ASVAB and DAT. We will discuss the O*NET Ability Profiler in more detail when we cover career measurement packages that include interests, values, and aptitudes.

MULTIAPTITUDE TESTING

Armed Services Vocational Aptitude Battery (ASVAB) Career Exploration Program

The **Armed Services Vocational Aptitude Battery (ASVAB) Career Exploration Program** (CEP) is a multiaptitude battery that consists of the ASVAB aptitude test and the Find Your Interest (FYI), which is an interest inventory. In addition, the ASVAB CEP includes online career exploration tools, which help participants identify occupations and careers that fit their aptitude, interests, and plans for the future. The ASVAB CEP is available for free for high schools throughout the country.

The **Armed Services Vocational Aptitude Battery (ASVAB)**, designed by the U.S. Department of Defense, is primarily used for recruitment and testing by the armed services to assess the potential and qualifications of armed services enlistees and to assign applicants to military jobs. In addition, school counselors frequently use the ASVAB as an educational and vocational counseling tool to help students in 10th grade and above explore job opportunities and training for civilian and armed services careers. The ASVAB consists of eight power subtests, which measure aptitudes in four domains: Verbal, Math, Science and Technical, and Spatial. The eight individual subtests are General Science, Arithmetic Reasoning, Word Knowledge, Paragraph Comprehension, Mathematics Knowledge, Electronics Information, Mechanical Comprehension, and Auto and Shop Information. Guided Practice Exercise 12.4 allows you to take a practice exam of the Armed Services Vocational Aptitude Battery and become more familiar with the questions on each of the eight subtests.

GUIDED PRACTICE EXERCISE 12.4

Prior to class, go to the 4Tests website at www.4tests.com/exams/examdetail.asp?eid=67, where you can take a practice exam of the Armed Services Vocational Aptitude Battery. The exam has questions in the area of arithmetic reasoning (20 questions), auto and shop information (15 questions), electronics information (15 questions), general science (15 questions), mathematics knowledge (20 questions), mechanical comprehension (15 questions), paragraph comprehension (15 questions), and word knowledge (20 questions). Explore the exam to view the types of questions asked in the eight subtests. Be prepared to discuss your results and experiences in small groups or with the entire class.

Standard scores for the eight subtests, three Career Exploration Scores, and a Military Entrance Score are calculated and provided on a score sheet. The individual scores on the eight subtests are summed in various combinations to form three Career Exploration composite scores: Verbal Skills, Math Skills, and Science and Technical Skills. The Career Exploration Scores allow students to see how their verbal, math, science, and technical skills compare to those of students enrolled in the same grade level. The Military Entrance Score, also referred to as the Armed Forces Qualification Test (AFQT), is used to assess one's qualifications and predict how well one might perform in training and occupations in the U.S. Armed Forces. See Figure 12.9 for a sample ASVAB score sheet.

After completing the ASVAB, the next step of the CEP is completing the FYI inventory. The FYI is based on Holland's RIASEC personality types. Participants respond to 90 items with a 3-point Likert-type scale in which they indicate if they like, are indifferent to, or dislike the activity. Upon completing the FYI, participants receive results indicating their highest interests and three highest codes. The FYI results and the Holland code can be used to explore careers that match their interests. If you recall from earlier, the Holland code can be used to search for career information on the O*NET database.

The final step of the CEP involves exploring careers through the career exploration tools, such as the OCCU-Find and Career Clusters. The OCCU-Find is linked to O*NET OnLine, the Occupational Outlook Handbook, and the website www.careersinthemilitary.com. The OCCU-Find allows participants to search information based on occupational titles, Career Clusters, Interests Codes, and skills. The U.S. Department of Education developed 16 Career Clusters based on skill sets, interests, abilities, and activities (e.g., Government and Public Administration, Health Science). Each of the clusters contains subgroupings known as Career Pathways. Valuable information such as the skills, training, or education requirements for certain occupations can be found using the above resources.

Differential Aptitude Tests (DAT)

The **Differential Aptitude Tests (DAT), Fifth Edition**, is a series of eight tests most commonly used in educational counseling and career guidance with high school students and adults to measure the ability to learn or succeed in several different areas.

Figure 12.9 ASVAB Score Sheet

ASVAB SUMMARY RESULTS

Student
12th Gr. Female (Form 23G)
SSN: XXX-XX-9999
Test Date: Jul 11, 2006
Old Dominion H.S.
Hometown DC

Print No. XXXXX

ASVAB Results

	Percentile Scores			12th Grade Standard Score
	12th Grade Females	12th Grade Males	12th Grade Students	
Career Exploration Scores				
Verbal Skills	97	95	96	65
Math Skills	22	17	19	42
Science and Technical Skills	81	48	64	53
ASVAB Tests				
General Science	91	81	86	61
Arithmetic Reasoning	43	30	37	47
Word Knowledge	98	95	96	66
Paragraph Comprehension	92	91	91	62
Mathematics Knowledge	14	12	13	37
Electronics Information	13	10	11	38
Auto and Shop Information	53	21	37	45
Mechanical Comprehension	95	76	85	59

Military Entrance Score (AFQT) 57

12th Grade Standard Score Bands

EXPLANATION OF YOUR ASVAB PERCENTILE SCORES

Your ASVAB results are reported as percentile scores in the three highlighted columns to the left of the graph. Percentile scores show how you compare to other students – males and females, and for all students – in your grade. For example, a percentile score of 65 for an 11th grade female would mean she scored the same or better than 65 out of every 100 females in the 11th grade.

For purposes of career planning, knowing your relative standing in these comparison groups is important. Being male or female does not limit your career or educational choices. There are noticeable differences in how men and women score in some areas. Viewing your scores in light of your relative standing in both men and women may encourage you to explore areas that you might otherwise overlook.

You can use the Career Exploration Scores to evaluate your knowledge and skills in three general areas (Verbal, Math, and Science and Technical Skills). You can use the ASVAB Test Scores together information on specific skill areas. *Together, these scores provide a snapshot of your current knowledge and skills.* This information will help you develop and review your career goals and plans.

EXPLANATION OF YOUR ASVAB STANDARD SCORES

Your ASVAB results are reported as standard scores in the above graph. Your score on each test is identified by the "X" in the corresponding bar graph. You should view these scores as *estimates* of your true skill level in that area. If you took the test again, you probably would receive a somewhat different score. Many things, such as how you were feeling during testing, contribute to this difference. This difference is shown with gray score bands in the graph of your results. Your standard scores are based on the ASVAB tests and composites based on your grade level.

The score bands provide a way to identify some of your strengths. Overlapping score bands mean your true skill level is similar in both areas, so the real difference between specific scores might not be meaningful. If the score bands do not overlap, you probably are stronger in the area that has the higher score band.

The ASVAB is an aptitude test. It is neither an absolute measure of your skills and abilities nor a perfect predictor of your success or failure. A high score does not guarantee success, and a low score does not guarantee failure, in a future educational program or occupation. For example, if you have never worked with shop equipment or cars, you may not be familiar with the terms and concepts

assessed by the Auto and Shop Information test. Taking a course or obtaining a part-time job in this area would increase your knowledge and improve your score if you were to take it again.

USING ASVAB RESULTS IN CAREER EXPLORATION

Your career and educational plans may change over time as you gain more experience and learn more about your interests. *Exploring Careers: The ASVAB Career Exploration Guide* can help you learn more about yourself and the world of work, to identify and explore potential goals, and develop an effective strategy to realize your goals. The *Guide* will help you identify occupations in line with your interests and skills. As you explore potentially satisfying careers, you will develop your career exploration and planning skills.

Meanwhile, your ASVAB results can help you in making well-informed choices about your future high school courses.

We encourage you to discuss your ASVAB results with a teacher, counselor, parent, family member or other interested adult. These individuals can help you to view your ASVAB results in light of other important information, such as your interests, school grades, motivation, and personal goals.

USE OF INFORMATION

Personal identity information (name, social security number, street address, and telephone number) and test scores will not be released to any agency outside of the Department of Defense (DoD), the Armed Forces, the Coast Guard, and your school. Your school or local school system can determine any further release of information. The DoD will use your scores for recruiting and research purposes for up to two years. After that the information will be used by the DoD for research purposes only.

MILITARY ENTRANCE SCORES

The Military Entrance Score (also called AFQT, which stands for the Armed Forces Qualification Test) is the score used to determine your qualifications for entry into any branch of the United States Armed Forces or the Coast Guard. The Military Entrance Score predicts in a general way how well you might do in training and on the job in military occupations. Your score reflects your standing compared to American men and women 18 to 23 years of age.

Use Access Code: 123456789X

(for online Occu-Find and FYI)

Access code expires: Jul 15, 2007

Explore career possibilities by using your Access Code at

www.asvabprogram.com

SEE YOUR COUNSELOR FOR FURTHER INFORMATION

Source: http://asvabprogram.com/downloads/ASR_Poster.pdf

School counselors often use the DAT to help students decide what areas they might excel in and if they attend college. Employers also use the DAT for hiring purposes to identify client strengths, weaknesses, and aptitude for learning new skills. The DAT includes eight subtests: Verbal Reasoning, Numerical Reasoning, Abstract Reasoning, Perceptual Speed and Accuracy, Mechanical Reasoning, Space Relations, Spelling, and Language Usage. The complete battery takes approximately 2.5 hours. A score is generated for each subtest plus a Total Scholastic Aptitude Score, yielding nine test scores. Each of the scores has relevance to different occupational and educational domains. There are two levels of the DAT available: one and two. Level one is designed for students in Grades 7–9; Level two is recommended for students in Grades 10–12. Either level can be used with adults.

Although the DAT can be used alone, it is often used in conjunction with the **Career Interest Inventory (CII)** to provide a comprehensive picture of a client's interests and aptitudes. The CII measures students' interest in 15 occupational groups: Social Science, Clerical Services, Health Services, Agriculture, Customer Services, Fine Arts, Mathematics and Science, Building Trades, Educational Services, Legal Services, Transportation, Sales, Management, Benchwork, and Machine Operation. Similar to the DAT, two levels of the CII are available; however, it is recommended that only Level II of the CII be used with adults.

Career Occupational Preference System (COPSystem)

Now that we have discussed common instruments used to assess interests, values, and aptitudes, let's turn our attention to a career measurement package that is often used by school counselors and in a variety of settings to assess interests, values, and abilities. The **Career Occupational Preference System (COPSystem)** contains three instruments that provide a comprehensive measure of interests, values , and abilities. Table 12.2 briefly summarizes each of the three instruments that constitute the COPSystem. They can be administered as three separate career inventories, although the combined approach is favored as

Table 12.2 COPSystem Assessments

Assessment	Measures	Time	Target Population
Career Occupational Preference System Interest Inventory (COPS)	Interests related to 14 career clusters	20–30 minutes	Grades 7–12, college, and adult
Career Orientation Placement and Evaluation Survey (COPES)	Values related to eight dichotomous bipolar scales: • Investigative vs. Accepting • Practical vs. Carefree • Independence vs. Conformity	20–30 minutes	Grades 6–12, college, and adult

Assessment	Measures	Time	Target Population
Career Ability Placement Survey (CAPS)	• Leadership vs. Supportive • Orderliness vs. Flexibility • Recognition vs. Privacy • Aesthetic vs. Realistic • Social vs. Reserved Abilities across eight dimensions: • Mechanical Reasoning • Spatial Relations • Verbal Reasoning • Numerical Ability • Language Usage • Word Knowledge • Perceptual Speed and Accuracy • Manual Speed and Dexterity	5 minutes per test	Grades 6–12, college, and adult

it provides not only a more comprehensive idea of what the individual likes to do, what work values are important, and what the individual can do, as do other assessments discussed in this chapter, but also an idea of what positions may be available once an individual receives the necessary training or experience. Case Illustration 12.5 describes the use of the COPSystem by a school counselor.

CASE ILLUSTRATION   12.5

Juanita Martinez is a high school counselor who works with juniors and seniors to help guide them in determining their future studies or career path. She frequently uses the Career Occupational Preference System (COPSystem) with students due to its brevity and ease of use and because it evaluates students' interests, values, and abilities and matches those to specific career fields. Ms. Martinez finds the COPSystem useful for students who have a variety of reading levels because it was designed to be used with students with reading skills as low as a fourth-grade level. So Ms. Martinez is confident that most of her juniors and seniors will be able to use this instrument. Students like the summary report, which uses icons to indicate how their interests, abilities, and values line up with specific career fields. The interest icon is a smiley face, the abilities icon is a light bulb, and the values icon is a heart. When an occupation field has all three icons, it indicates a strong possibility that particular career opportunity would be a good match for the student. The COPSystem also determines skill gaps in the areas of academics, job skills, and planning skills to help students adequately prepare to enhance their job marketability. Students going on to college can use this information to improve their skills in the identified areas.

Source: Career Occupational Preference System Summary (2013); EdITS Online (2012).

Career Occupational Preference System Interests Inventory (COPS)

The **Career Occupational Preference System Interest Inventory (COPS)** is helpful in promoting exploration of one's job activity interests as they relate to different career clusters. The COPS interests inventory contains 168 items and is designed for those in seventh grade through adult. There are several forms of the COPS interest inventory based on one's reading level and ability, including the **COPS II (Intermediate Inventory)**, which is for those in Grades 6–12 who may have a learning disability and operate at a fourth- to fifth-grade reading level; the **COPS Inventory-R**, which is for Grades 6–12 and requires a sixth-grade reading level; and the **COPS Inventory-P**, which is an advanced version intended for college students and adults who are considering professional occupational options only. If clients are unable to read or have difficulties in reading, the **COPS-PIC** (Picture Inventory), which contains only pictures to assess interests, can be administered.

On all forms except the COPS-PIC, participants read a series of statements regarding work-related activities and respond using a 4-point scale: L (*like very much*), l (*like moderately*), d (*dislike*), D (*dislike very much*). Examples of statements include "Solve math problems in chemical research," "Be in charge of designing a space shuttle," and "Make custom drapes or window coverings." The client's job activity interest scores are related to 14 occupational clusters and are graphed on a profile form. Raw scores are then converted to percentile ranks and allow the individual to compare his or her score with the scores of people at the same educational level and within occupational groupings (e.g., science professional, clerical, communication, technology professional). A higher score reflects a higher level of interest in that particular group compared to others who have taken the assessment. Most clients will have one or two high scores on the occupational areas. Counselors can use the COPSystem Comprehensive Career Guide to assist clients in exploring these areas (e.g., nature of the occupation, required training). Figure 12.10 is an example summary profile sheet for the COPS.

Career Orientation Placement and Evaluation Survey (COPES) (Values)

The **Career Orientation Placement and Evaluation Survey (COPES)** is a helpful aid for exploring the importance of clients' values for occupational choice and job satisfaction as well as assisting clients in examining the relationship between their values and type of career. The assessment comprises 128 items and measures work values on eight dichotomous bipolar scales (see Table 12.2). Participants read through a series of statements representing opposite ends of each scale, marking either (a) or (b). For example, "I value activities or jobs in which I . . . "

1. (a) use existing methods or (b) discover new methods

2. (a) spend money for enjoyment or (b) spend money on useful things

3. (a) take orders from others or (b) don't have to take orders from others

Number 1 represents an item pair on the Investigative vs. Accepting scale. Number 2 represents an item pair on the Practical vs. Carefree scale. And Number 3 represents an item pair on the Independence vs. Conformity scale.

Figure 12.10 COPS Profile Sheet

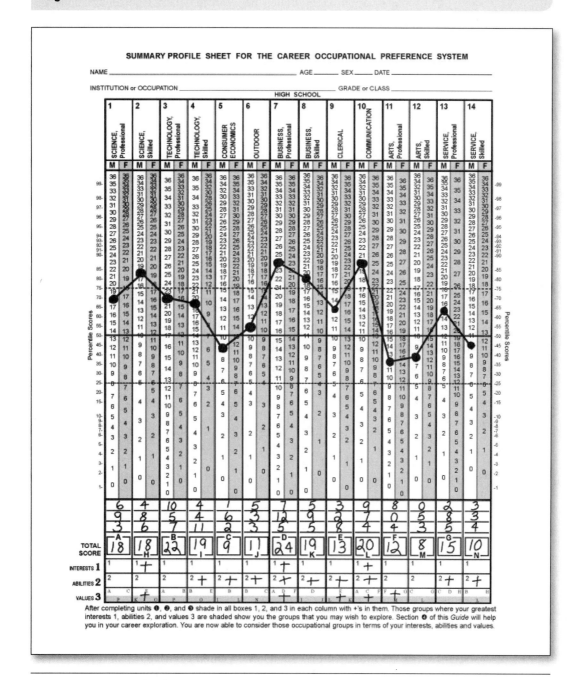

Source: Career Occupational Preference System Summary (2013).

COPES scores are then keyed to the 14 COPSystem Career Clusters in Figure 12.10, which provide a representation of the match between the client's personal values and various occupational areas.

Career Ability Placement Survey (CAPS)

The **Career Ability Placement Survey (CAPS)** measures vocational abilities related to occupations and consists of eight 5-minute ability tests: Mechanical Reasoning, Spatial Relations, Verbal Reasoning, Numerical Ability, Language Usage, Word Knowledge, Perceptual Speed and Accuracy, and Manual Speed and Dexterity. The CAPS is often used to help clients identify occupations in which their abilities match the requirements of the job. The instrument can also be useful in providing insight about which of the client's abilities may need to be developed or areas in which the client may require additional training to purse the occupation. The instrument may be used with sixth-grade students through adults and is available in an English or Spanish version.

Two methods are typically used to interpret CAPS results. First, the client's raw score, which measures his or her ability in the eight dimensions mentioned above, is obtained. The raw score is then converted to a stanine score on a profile form. If you recall from Chapter 2, stanines range from one to nine. The stanine score indicates the client's abilities relative to others' abilities at the same educational level. In the second method, the client's scores on the eight ability measures are linked to the 14 occupational clusters.

O*NET System and Career Exploration Tools

The **Occupational Information Network (O*NET)** is a comprehensive career classification system developed by the U.S. Department of Labor, Employment and Training Administrations, currently listing over 800 different careers provided by occupational analysts (Walmsley, Natali, & Campbell, 2012). O*NET, which replaced the Dictionary of Occupational Titles in the 1990s, provides occupational information used by students, career counselors, school counselors, vocational rehabilitation counselors, and people who are changing careers or seeking first or new jobs. Several components of the O*NET system are discussed below.

The O*NET database is free to the public and contains information on hundreds of occupations in the United States (visit www.onetcenter.org). The O*NET Content Model, which was developed to provide the most important information about work, describes each occupation in terms of six content characteristics: Work Characteristics (e.g., abilities, occupational interests, work values, work styles), Worker Requirements (e.g., basic skills, cross-functional skills, knowledge, education), Experience Requirements (e.g., experience and training, basic skills-entry requirements, cross functional skills-entry requirements, licensing), Occupation-Specific Information (e.g., tasks, tools, technology), Workforce Characteristics (e.g., labor market information, occupational outlook), and Occupational Requirements (e.g., generalized work activities, detailed work activities, organizational context, work context; National Center for O*NET Development, n.d.-b).

The **Occupational Information Network (O*NET) OnLine** is a web application used for exploring occupations with the O*NET database. O*NET OnLine allows individuals to find occupations by a keyword search, browsing groups of similar occupations, advanced searches to focus on occupations that use specific tools or need the individual's skills, or to use Crosswalks, which converts other classifications to the O*NET classifications.

Occupational Information Network (O*NET) Career Exploration Tools were designed by the O*NET team and are based on what they refer to as the *whole-person* concept. This set of career exploration assessments include the Ability Profiler, Interest Profiler, Computerized Interest Profiler, Interest Profiler Short Form, Work Importance Locator, and Work Importance Profiler. With these assessments individuals can explore occupations that identify with their work-related interests, values, and abilities. While each of these tests can be administered on a stand-alone basis or with other instruments, the National Center for O*NET Development (n.d.-b) says that these tests were designed based on the whole-person concept and thus recommends using them together for career exploration, planning, and counseling. In Guided Practice Exercise 12.5, you can explore O*NET further.

GUIDED PRACTICE EXERCISE 12.5

Prior to class, go to the O*NET OnLine website at www.onetonline.org. This is a wonderful resource to explore possible career options for yourself or for clients. Go to the "Occupation Search" that has an icon that looks like a key. Searching by keyword, look up five occupations that you are curious about (e.g., counselor, psychologist, teacher). The website will give you a list of what skills, abilities, and interests are needed to be successful in that career, such as tasks, tools and technology, knowledge, work activities, work context, job zone, education, interests, work styles, work values, related occupations, and wages and employment trends. What did you learn about your chosen occupations that surprised you? Under "interests" the Holland Code is given for that occupation (e.g., SIA: social, investigative, and artistic). Does this correlate to your score from the Holland Code Career Test that you took earlier? Be prepared to discuss your results and experiences in small groups or with the entire class.

Interest Profiler

The **Occupational Information Network (O*NET) Interest Profiler** is used as a career exploration tool to assist individuals in learning about broad interests and exploring occupations they might like (National Center for O*NET Development, n.d.-a). A computerized version is also available called the O*NET Computerized Interest Profiler. The Interest Profiler and Computerized Interest Profiler measure six types of occupational interests including: Realistic, Investigative, Artistic, Social, Enterprising, and Conventional. The assessment is composed of 180 items that describe work activities and takes approximately 30 minutes to complete. Individuals then receive a Master List where careers organized by interests as well as preparation required (e.g., job zones) are listed.

Work Importance Profiler

The **Occupational Information Network (O*NET) Work Importance Profiler (WIP)** is used with clients to help identify satisfying occupation by matching their work values and the characteristics of the occupation. The O*NET Work Importance Profiler is administered by computer, and the paper-and-pencil version is known as the O*NET Work Importance Locator (WIL). Six types of work values are assessed for both forms: Achievement, Independence, Recognition, Relationships, Support, and Working Conditions. Individuals first read 21 work need statements (e.g., "On my ideal job it is important that I could do something different every day," "On my ideal job it is important that I could do things for other people") and then rank order the statements based on importance. After ranking the 21 statements, individuals rate the work need. The assessment takes 15–45 minutes to complete. After completing the assessment, the computer ranks the six values and focuses on the two highest scale scores. These Work Values scores identify satisfying occupations, or Job Zones, based on the similarity between the individual's work values and the characteristics of the occupation.

Job Zones are used to identify the amount of preparation required to enter an occupation and range from one to five. Job Zone One occupations include those in which little or no preparation is needed. Job Zone Two lists jobs in which some preparation is needed. Job Zone Three lists jobs in which medium preparation is needed. Job Zone Four comprises jobs for which considerable preparation is needed. And Job Zone Five contains a list of jobs requiring extensive preparation. These results are then linked to over 800 occupations in O*NET OnLine. Individuals can search through the occupations to determine which fit their strengths. Case Illustration 12.6 illustrates how counselors can use O*NET OnLine in their discussion of career choices.

CASE ILLUSTRATION   12.6

Quintin DeMarcus works as a career information and assessment expert. He helps his clients assess their personality traits, work environment preferences, values and beliefs, interests, and abilities and helps guide them in finding a career. It is Mr. DeMarcus's personal belief that if an individual isn't happy in his or her chosen profession, then workplace unhappiness will often carry over into other aspects of the person's life. One tool that Mr. DeMarcus frequently uses with his clients is the O*NET database. Both he and his clients like O*NET because it is easy to use and it allows users to search for job information on variables that are important to them.

For example, Mr. DeMarcus had a client last week, Ms. Meyers, who really wanted a career in a "green" field. Her personal values were that she did not want to work in an occupation that added to the "destruction of the earth's resources." By starting with the "Find Occupations" drop-down menu at O*NET OnLine and clicking on "Green Economy Sector," then linking to other values Ms. Meyer's held (e.g., wants to work outdoors, loves animals, has computer and technology skills, has a bachelor's degree in biology, has good communication and conflict resolution skills), she found a career field that seemed a good match: Game Warden. This career field also had the RIASEC code of RI (realistic and investigative). Ms. Meyers's RIASEC code was RIC.

What Mr. DeMarcus and Ms. Meyers also learned through this process is that Ms. Meyers would need some on-the-job training through an apprenticeship. With the help of Mr. DeMarcus, an internship was arranged. In exploring this career option through O*NET, Ms. Meyers also saw that it would be helpful for her to have a background in fishing and fisheries sciences and management, natural resources management and policy, and wildlife science and management. She then enrolled in her local community college, which offered classes in these areas, in order to strengthen her opportunities in this field.

Ability Profiler

The **Occupational Information Network (O*NET) Ability Profiler**, which replaced the General Aptitude Test Battery, is used in career counseling to help clients explore and identify occupations that fit their strengths, identify areas in which they may need more training and education, and plan their work lives. The *O*NET Ability Profiler Administrator Training Manual* makes it very clear that the Ability Profiler cannot be used for personnel selection, but rather, it should be used for career exploration, career counseling, and career planning purposes.

The Ability Profiler measures nine abilities: Verbal, Arithmetic Reasoning, Computation, Spatial, Form Perception, Clerical Perception, Motor Coordination, Finger Dexterity, and Manual Dexterity. The Ability Profiler can be administered individually or in a group setting, but it is recommended that it be administered to two or more examinees. In order to take the assessment, a person must have a sixth-grade reading level or above and be at least 16 years of age. The assessment is available in paper-and-pencil format and has optional apparatus parts and computerized scoring. The Ability Profiler, both the paper-and-pencil format and optional apparatus parts, takes approximately two to three hours to complete.

Once an individual completes the Ability Profiler, the O*NET Ability Profiler Scoring Program Software, which uses Occupational Ability Profiles, relates his or her abilities to the abilities important in performing certain occupations. On the individual score report, occupations for all five job zones are provided. These results are linked to over 800 occupations in O*NET OnLine. Individuals can search through the occupations to see which ones fit their strengths.

Now that we have covered interests, values, and abilities assessments, let's turn our focus to assessing career readiness.

ASSESSING CAREER READINESS

Career readiness is often called career maturity when referring to adolescents and career adaptability when discussing adults. **Career maturity** is defined as the attitudinal and cognitive readiness to make decisions about one's vocational and/or educational choices (Crites, 1971). Career maturity results from the interaction between the person and the environment. Noticing the variability in degree of career development with adults in comparison to adolescents, Super and Knasel (1981) coined the term *career adaptability* to describe the career development among adults. Savickas (1997) proposes that career adaptability replace career maturity. Savickas reasons that Super (1955) identified maturation in terms of adolescent career development and career maturity, which is not as useful for understanding career development in adults. Savickas defines **career adaptability** as "the readiness to cope with the predictable tasks of preparing for and participating in the work role and with the unpredictable adjustments prompted by changes in the work and working conditions" (p. 254).

While the interests inventories previously mentioned can be helpful in describing a client's general occupational interest and assisting with vocational choices, they are useful only if clients have the requisite attitudes and competencies to make occupational decisions. Throughout the remaining portion of this chapter, we discuss measures of client readiness. Note that in the literature, there is limited information on assessments that measure career development in elementary school children.

CAREER DEVELOPMENT INVENTORY

The **Career Development Inventory (CDI)** is currently the best measure of career choice competencies (Savickas & Porfeli, 2011). By administering the CDI before the interest inventory, counselors assess the client's readiness to make occupational choices. In some cases counselors will administer the CDI with an interest inventory to help decide how to interpret the results.

The Career Development Inventory is based on Super's model of career choice readiness among adolescents and young adults (Super, Thompson, Lindeman, Jordaan, & Myers, 1988). Super believed that the readiness to make career choices started in childhood and then further developed in adolescence. In order to choose an occupation, one must possess the requisite readiness and resources. Super believed that career choice readiness is dependent on career choice attitudes and competencies. **Career choice attitudes** describes the amount of thought or planning one has given to the occupational choice, while **career choice competencies** describe the client's ability to apply his or her knowledge to the world of work. Super's model of readiness focuses on four variables: the two career choice attitudes of planfulness (e.g., future orientation, awareness of choices to be made) and exploration (e.g., curiosity of world of work) and the two career choice competencies of one's knowledge of the world of work (e.g., knows requirements and has detailed knowledge about occupation interested in) and decision-making competence (e.g., applies decision making to vocational choices or educational choices).

Two versions of the CDI are available: the CDI school form, which is for students in Grades 8-12, and the CDI college form for college students. The CDI is broken up into two parts. Part I consists of 80 items across four subscales: Career Planning (CP), Career Exploration (CE), Decision Making (DM), and knowledge of the World of Work (WW). Career Development Attitudes are measured by the CP and CE subscales, while Career Competencies are measured by the DM and WW subscales. Part II measures one's particular fields through use of a fifth subscale: Knowledge of Preferred Occupation (PO). The manual clearly states that the PO subscale should not be administered to students enrolled below the 11th grade. Part II should not be administered to those who may not have the knowledge or maturity to answer the questions. In addition to the four subscale scores from Part I and the PO score in Part II, three composite scores can be calculated: Career Development Attitudes (combination of CP and CE), Career Decision Knowledge (combination of DM and WW), and Career Orientation Total (i.e., total vocational maturity; combination of CP, CE, DM, WW). The composite scores provide additional information on the attitudes and knowledge of the world of work. The Career Orientation Total score based on the four subscale scores provides a comprehensive measure of career maturity. The CDI is available at www.vocopher.com.

Table 12.3 provides a brief summary of the interpretation of CDI results. Consult the manual for a more extensive interpretation. The use of the CDI in a counseling situation is the topic of Case Illustration 12.7.

Table 12.3   Interpretation of Career Development Inventory Scales

Part I

Career Development Attitude Scales

Career Planning (CP)

- High: has awareness of occupational decisions, displays sense of curiosity about world of work, actively engages in career planning; high score may indicate readiness to narrow choices and engage in deeper exploration

- Low: may not be serious or has given little thought to future occupational and educational choices, may benefit from discussing plans with others, becoming part of community activities, discovering what one does in the field of interest, applying for part-time job

Career Exploration (CE)

- High: has gathered information important to future choice and uses resources to explore information about available career opportunities; high score may indicate readiness to explore the world of work the client is attracted to

- Low: has not actively gathered information important for future occupations, may consider gathering quality information relevant to future occupational choices and exploring these different fields

Career Competency Scales

Decision Making (DM)

- High: has skills for making effective vocational decisions, may be ready to now match interests and abilities with occupations

- Low: lacks ability to apply effective decision making to vocational issues, may benefit from practicing effective decision making (e.g., identify problem)

World of Work (WW)

- High: has information to support career decision choices, may benefit from gathering information about occupational choices before deciding on a specific choice

- Low: lacks knowledge about the requirements and routines of occupation in which one is interested as well as detailed knowledge about the occupational group, before making career decisions or occupational choice may benefit from gathering more information about occupational fields and tasks

Part II

Knowledge of Preferred Occupation (PO)

- High: has detailed knowledge and information on preferred occupation, may be ready to narrow down choices to a couple occupational fields

- Low: may need more information on preferred occupation and this information may come from professionals working in the preferred occupation, career counselors, etc.

CASE ILLUSTRATION 12.7

Rose is a 23-year-old who has been out of high school for 5 years. During those 5 years, she attended two semesters of college with a major in history at the state university. Rose flunked both semesters because she quickly lost interest in her major and got too involved with the social aspects of living on a university campus. After a brief period of time, Rose then went a semester at a local community college with a major in education. However, she did not stay to finish the semester.

Rose has become increasingly frustrated with having to find a "career." Since leaving school, she has worked in retail as a sales clerk, in a restaurant as a server, in a financial institution that gives loans in exchange for car titles, as a photographer's assistant, and in a day care facility. Rose has discovered that she really likes working with children and thinks she might want to be a teacher, but does not really want to go to college.

Due to increased pressure from her parents, who tell her she has to do something to support herself, Rose went to the career center at her local community college for guidance and help. After hearing Rose's story, the career counselor suggested some assessments, which included a career readiness assessment. Ms. Combs, the career counselor, decided to give Rose the Career Development Inventory (CDI) College Form. Ms. Combs chose the CDI because it can provide knowledge about Rose's attitudes, competencies, and knowledge related to how much thought she puts into planning potential career choices. The CDI is composed of the subscales of Career Planning, Career Exploration, Decision Making, and Knowledge of the World of Work, with a total score called Preferred Occupation.

Rose obtained a low score on Career Planning, indicating she has not given a lot of thought or planning to career decisions. She also received a low score on Career Exploration, which was not a surprise to either Rose or Ms. Combs. Rose scored high on Decision Making, which indicates she has the cognitive maturity to make good decisions for herself. However, her score on World of Work was low, indicating that she does not have a large fund of knowledge regarding occupations that might interest her.

Rose also had an overall low score on the Preferred Occupation scale, which indicates that she needs to do more exploration and gain further knowledge toward her stated interest in working with children. Although Rose was able to identify this interest, she indicated that she does not have enough information about possible occupations that work with children to make an informed choice.

After interpreting this assessment with Rose, Ms. Combs recommended that Rose take an interest inventory to explore other vocations that might interest her in addition to working with children. Ms. Combs also recommended that Rose start talking to individuals who work in occupations that interest her to get a better understanding of the requirements for each occupation. Rose indicated she does not want to go to college, so Ms. Combs recommended that Rose focus on those careers that do not require a college degree. Ms. Combs also directed Rose to O*NET so she could gain further information about possible careers that match her interests.

ADULT CAREER CONCERNS INVENTORY

The **Adult Career Concerns Inventory (ACCI)** was originally developed by Super and his colleagues (Super et al., 1988) and evolved from the CDI. The ACCI consists of 61 items and takes approximately 20 minutes to complete. The items assess current level of career concerns associated with Super's theory of developmental career stages (exploration, establishment, maintenance, decline) and substages (crystallizing, specifying, implementing, stabilizing, consolidating, advancing, holding, updating, innovating, deceleration, retirement planning, retirement living). Items are rated on a 5-point scale ranging from 1 (*no concern*) to 5 (*great concern*). The client's highest score indicates the greatest concern. Typically, a client's highest score appears in the career stage related to his or her age.

Even though the ACCI evolved from the CDI, the ACCI focuses strictly on Super's planning dimension and focuses on assessing adults' needs for career planning and adaptation. While researchers have shown that the ACCI is reliable and valid, counselors should note that using the designated age ranges within the stages may not be helpful in determining career patterns for clients who have had multiple careers. Remember that Super's stages are not related solely to age. For example, a client who has already had multiple careers may recycle or go through the stages at different times. Furthermore, because the ACCI focuses on career planning, counselors should not administer it if they are looking to assess career competencies.

Career Maturity Inventory-Revised (CMI-R)

The **Career Maturity Inventory-Revised (CMI-R)**, originally known as the Vocational Development Inventory (VDI), was the first test to measure vocational development. Crites's (1965) original version of the VDI was based on Donald Super's Career Pattern Study, which assessed the process (e.g., attitudes, competencies) of forming career decisions. The original version was used with adolescents, but in 1995, CMI item content pertaining to Grades 5–12 was removed to create an adult version (Savickas & Porfeli, 2011). Today, the CMI-R is widely used by counselors to assess the degree to which an individual is ready to make career decisions (Savickas & Porfeli, 2011). In addition to screening for client readiness, the CMI-R is also used to assist in clarifying interest scores.

The CMI-R consists of the Attitude Test and the Competence Test. The Attitude Test comprises 25 questions that measure one's attitudes and feelings toward career decisions. The Competence Test contains 25 questions that measures one's knowledge about decisions needed in choosing a career. Individuals read statements or narratives and indicate "agree" if they agree or mostly agree with the statement or "disagree" if they disagree or mostly disagree with the statement. There is no time limit, but the test typically takes about 45 minutes to administer. The CMI-R generates three scores: Attitude Scale, Competence Test, and Career Maturity. After an individual completes the CMI-R, the counselor can use the Career Developer (CDR) supplement to "teach the test." When we use the phrase "teach the test," we mean the counselor has the opportunity to teach the process of career decision making and career maturity. Individuals reflect on their responses on the CMI-R and then fill in the answer on the CDR. Individuals are provided with an explanation based on their answer as to what a more mature response entails.

Career Maturity Inventory-Form C

Recently, Savickas's career construction theory was applied to Crite's inventory, and as a result, a new **Career Maturity Inventory-Form C (CMI-Form C)** was created (Savickas & Porfeli, 2011). Career adaptability is a major component to career construction theory. Career adaptability is defined as "a multidimensional construct that characterizes an individual's psychosocial readiness and resources for coping with current and imminent vocational development tasks, occupational transitions, and work traumas" (Savickas & Porfeli, 2011, p. 357). As a client's adaptability increases, his or her readiness to make occupational choices also increase. The CMI-Form C includes four scales: Concern, Curiosity, Confidence, and Consultation. Figure 12.11 is an example of the CMI-Form C. Individuals read 24 statements that they respond to by indicating "agree" or "disagree."

After completing the assessment, a total score of career choice readiness is calculated. The total career choice readiness is based only on the 18 items in the Concern, Curiosity, and Confidence scales. Individual scores for the Concern, Curiosity, and Confidence scales are reported, and a fifth score for the Consultation scale is calculated. Table 12.4 briefly describes each scale and provides interventions that may fit the needs of clients who score

Figure 12.11 CMI-Form C

Career Maturity Inventory—Counseling Form C
John O. Crites and Mark L. Savickas

1. There is no point in deciding on a job when the future is so uncertain.
2. I know very little about the requirements of jobs.
3. I have so many interests that it is hard to choose just one occupation.
4. Choosing a job is something that you do on your own.
5. I can't seem to become very concerned about my future occupation.
6. I don't know how to go about getting into the kind of work I want to do.
7. Everyone seems to tell me something different; as a result I don't know what kind of work to choose.
8. If you have doubts about what you want to do, ask your parents or friends for advice.
9. I seldom think about the job that I want to enter.
10. I am having difficulty in preparing myself for the work that I want to do.
11. I keep changing my occupational choice.
12. When it comes to choosing a career, I will ask other people to help me.
13. I'm not going to worry about choosing an occupation until I am out of school.
14. I don't know what courses I should take in school.
15. I often daydream about what I want to be, but I really have not chosen an occupation yet.
16. I will choose my career without paying attention to the feelings of other people.
17. As far as choosing an occupation is concerned, something will come along sooner or later.
18. I don't know whether my occupational plans are realistic.
19. There are so many things to consider in choosing an occupation, it is hard to make a decision.

20. It is important to consult close friends and get their ideas before making an occupational choice.
21. I really can't find any work that has much appeal to me.
22. I keep wondering how I can reconcile the kind of person I am with the kind of person I want to be in my occupation.
23. I can't understand how some people can be so certain about what they want to do.
24. In making career choices, one should pay attention to the thoughts and feelings of family members.

Response format = Agree—Disagree

Scoring key
Concern = 1(D), 5 (D), 9(D), 13(D), 17(D), 21(D)
Curiosity = 2(D), 6(D), 10(D), 14(D), 18(D), 22(D)
Confidence = 3(D), 7(D), 11(D), 15(D), 19(D), 23(D)
Consultation = 4(D), 8(A), 12(A), 16(D), 20(A), 24(A)

Source: Savickas & Porfeli (2011).

Table 12.4 Career Maturity Inventory-Form C

Scale	Measures
Concern	Degree to which the individual is involved in the process of making career decisions; low score: interventions that increase awareness and involvement in decision making process
Curiosity	Degree to which the individual explores the world of work and seeks occupational requirements; low score: interventions that focus on increasing interest in exploring the future and investigating appealing occupations, discuss intrinsic and extrinsic motivations, encourage participation in exploratory experiential activities
Confidence	Degree to which individual believes in his or her abilities to make realistic occupational decisions; low score: interventions that develop self-esteem and increase decisional self-efficacy, connect current behavior to future goals, affirm clients strengths, role modeling, active problem solving
Consultation	Degree to which individual seeks assistance by requesting information and advice; scores should be interpreted using the cultural formation model
Total Score	Degree of adaptability in career decision making and readiness to make occupational choices

Source: Savickas & Porfeli (2011).

low on these scales. Although high scores on the Concern, Curiosity, and Confidence scales indicate advanced development, Savickas and Porfeli (2011) urge counselors to use the cultural formulation model when interpreting these results. Interpretation of the consultation scale scores must be assessed in the cultural context.

Childhood Career Development Scale

The **Childhood Career Development Scale (CCDS)** is based on Super's (1990) growth stage of career development and was designed by Schultheiss and Stead (2004) to assess career progress in students enrolled in Grades 4–6. The CCDS consists of 52 items (e.g., "I know people who have my favorite job"); the student reads a statement and scores the statement using a 5-point Likert scale ranging from 1 (*strongly agree*) to 5 (*strongly disagree*). Eight subscale scores are generated from the 52 items: Information, Curiosity, Interests, Locus of Control, Key Figures, Time Perspective, Planning, and Self-concept. School counselors and teachers often use this instrument as a needs assessment to create activities, design academic lessons, and identify student needs in terms of career development. Furthermore, the CCDS is often used to evaluate career development programs.

COUNSELORS' ROLE IN CAREER ASSESSMENT

Counselors in the school system as well as private practice use career assessments to facilitate career counseling and to explore and discover career identity among clients. Since many individuals seek career counseling to aid in selection of or adjustment to an occupation, counselors must not only be familiar with different career assessments but have knowledge of descriptions of the occupation, qualifications required, working conditions, job duties, education level required, and where to seek additional information. If you recall in the beginning of the chapter, we stated that career assessment is a multifaceted process consisting of the assessment of both content (e.g., values, interests, aptitudes) and process (e.g., career readiness). As we discussed in previous chapters, counselors should be competent in administering, scoring, and interpreting assessment results. In addition to the American Counseling Association (2014) *Code of Ethics*, counselors would benefit from becoming familiar with the National Career Development Association (2007) *Code of Ethics*, which serves as a guide for career practitioners. Section E: Evaluation, Assessment, and Interpretation discusses the use of appropriate career and other psychological assessment instruments. The key to remember is that test results should be interpreted in concert with other available information about the applicant to ensure that the decisions made based on the available information are informed and reliable.

KEYSTONES

- Career assessment is a multifaceted process. We assess both the content (e.g., values, interests, aptitude) and the process (e.g., career readiness).
- Counselors should compile a comprehensive profile that includes relevant constructs, such as personality, interests, values, and abilities rather than relying on a single construct.
- Interest inventories allow counselors to assess a client's interest and provide a wealth of knowledge of client likes and dislikes. Common interest inventories explored in this chapter include the Strong, SDS, KCS, CISS, and JVIS.

- Values play an important role in job satisfaction. Values inventories discussed in this chapter include the SWVI-R, VS, and Salience Inventory.
- The COPSystem and the O*NET System and Career Exploration tools are two comprehensive career information systems whose instruments measure interests, abilities, and values.
- Specific aptitude tests focus on one aspect of ability, while multiaptitude tests provide information on the likelihood of success in several vocations. Some of the most popular multiaptitude batteries discussed here are the Armed Services Vocational Assessment Battery (ASVAB), Differential Aptitude Tests (DAT), and O*NET Ability Profiler.
- Before administering an interest inventory, consider the client's career readiness. Common career readiness assessments discussed in this chapter include the CDI, ACCI, CMI-R, CMI-Form C, and Childhood Career Development Scale.

KEY TERMS

Adult Career Concerns Inventory (ACCI)

Armed Services Vocational Aptitude Battery (ASVAB)

Armed Services Vocational Aptitude Battery (ASVAB) Career Exploration Program

artistic aptitude tests

Basic Interest Scales

Campbell Interest and Skill Survey

Career Ability Placement Survey (CAPS)

career adaptability

career assessment

career choice attitudes

career choice competencies

Career Development Inventory (CDI)

Career Interest Inventory (CII)

career maturity

Career Maturity Inventory-Form C (CMI-Form C)

Career Maturity Inventory-Revised (CMI-R)

Career Occupational Preference System (COPSystem)

Career Occupational Preference System Interest Inventory (COPS)

Career Occupational Preference System Interest Inventory (COPS-II) Intermediate Inventory

Career Occupational Preference System Interest Inventory-P (COPS-P)

Career Occupational Preference System Interest Inventory-Picture Inventory (COPS-PIC)

Career Occupational Preference System Interest Inventory-R (COPS-R)

Career Orientation Placement and Evaluation Survey (COPES)

Childhood Career Development Scale (CCDS)

clerical aptitude tests

Differential Aptitude Tests (DAT), Fifth Edition

Environmental Assessment Technique (EAT)

General Occupational Themes (GOTs)

general values

interest inventories

interests

Jackson Vocational Interest Inventory

Kuder Career Search With Person Match (KCS)

mechanical aptitude tests

Occupational Scales

Occupational Information Network (O*NET)

Occupational Information Network (O*NET) Ability Profiler

Occupational Information Network (O*NET) Career Exploration Tools

Occupational Information Network (O*NET) Interest Profiler

Occupational Information Network (O*NET) OnLine

Occupational Information

Network (O*NET) Work Importance Profile (WIP)

Occupations Finder

Personal Style Scales

Salience Inventory

Self-Directed Search (SDS)

Strong

Strong Interest Inventory

Student Vocational Self

Analysis

Super's Life-Career Rainbow

Super's Work Values Inventory-Revised (SWVI-R)

values inventories

values

Work Importance Study (WIS)

work-related values

ADDITIONAL RESOURCES

- "100 Years of Career Guidance—Honoring Frank Parsons"

  http://ww2.kuder.com/news/vol6_no3/Parsons.html

This article was written by Dr. Don Zytowski, the director of research for Kuder. It gives the history of career or vocational guidance for the last 100 years.

- A-Z List of Careers

  http://www.bls.gov/ooh/a-z-index.htm

This U.S. Department of Labor website lists some of the more popular or prominent career options in alphabetical order. Each career option is a link. When readers click on the link it takes them to that career's page in the Occupational Outlook Handbook (OOH). The OOH gives a summary of that career's options such as median pay, entry-level education or on the job training needed, job outlook information for this decade, typical work environment, and similar occupations to the one chosen. In addition, there is a link to O*NET to direct future exploration.

- Careers.org

  http://assessments.careers.org

This website is a resource for individuals looking for a career. It provides a list of career and assessment resources. It offers occupational and industry profiles for thousands of career opportunities, helps readers locate colleges that offer an education in specific fields, and offers advice for career planning.

- Guide to Holland Code

  http://www.wiu.edu/advising/docs/Holland_Code.pdf

This handout helps explain the Holland Code of RIASEC and explains in detail how the codes are used along with possible career options for different combinations of the code.

- National Career Development Association

  http://ncda.org/aws/NCDA/pt/sp/home_page

This website is a resource for finding career counseling, professional development, or continuing educational opportunities, and has a resource page to provide tools for career planning.

- O*NET Online

  http://www.onetonline.org

On this website, readers can do an occupational search and investigate career options. Readers can find occupations that fit specific criteria such as careers with a bright outlook, those in the "green" economy sector, or those within a STEM discipline. Readers can also search by general occupational abilities, interests, knowledge, skills, work activities, work contexts, and work values.

Student Study Site: Visit the Student Study Site at **www.sagepub.com/watson** to access additional study tools, including quizzes, web resources, and journal articles.

SECTION III

Applications and Issues

CHAPTER 13

Clinical Assessment

LEARNING OBJECTIVES

After reading this chapter, you will be able to

- Describe the role clinical assessment plays throughout the counseling process
- Identify the primary decision-making models used in conducting clinical assessments
- Describe the *Diagnostic and Statistical Manual of Mental Disorders—5th Edition*
- Describe the various types of data collection methods used in clinical assessment
- List the components of an intake assessment
- Differentiate between a structured, semistructured, and unstructured clinical interview
- Explain the function of a mental status examination and how it contributes to an accurate clinical diagnosis
- Discuss the components of an effective suicide assessment
- Describe the clinical activities included in forensic assessment
- Discuss the importance of addressing culture and diversity in the clinical assessment process

Although counselors assess clients for a variety of reasons, the primary type of assessment conducted is a clinical assessment. Clinical assessment is an important part of the counseling process. It is through clinical assessment procedures that counselors are able to evaluate, diagnose, and treat their clients effectively. Traditionally, counselors begin the assessment process by interviewing the client to gather a basic understanding of the presenting problem. A wide variety of questions may be asked to determine the true scope and nature of the problem. From there, the counselor determines the next steps to take, including whether additional assessments may be warranted. The goal is to narrow in on the specific issue or problem that will need to be addressed with the client. If you were to visualize the clinical assessment process, it would look like a funnel. The counselor begins with a great deal of information and begins organizing it and moving from general to specific in order to arrive at an accurate diagnosis of the client's problem (similar to the process a physician uses when a new client presents in an office or in a hospital emergency department).

In this chapter you will learn the basics of clinical assessment and how this process can be used to guide the work you do with your clients or students, regardless of the setting in which you work. In addition, you also will be introduced to the concepts of suicide assessment, forensic assessment, and the emerging field of neuropsychological assessment. Each of these elements is becoming an increasingly common part of the clinical assessment process and can be used by counselors to further understand clients and their needs for counseling.

WHAT IS CLINICAL ASSESSMENT?

A common misconception many beginning counselors have is that clinical assessment is a specific technique or intervention to be applied with a client. On the contrary, clinical assessment is more a continuous process than a singular event. Counselors conducting clinical assessments are always collecting new information about clients to refine their understanding of the clients' issues and needs. As such, **clinical assessment** can best be defined as a multifaceted process whereby counselors gather information from, and about, a client to make informed decisions related to diagnosis, treatment planning, and documenting therapeutic efficacy. In fact, the information counselors obtain through clinical assessment informs the work they will be able to do with their clients at each stage of the counseling process. The process through which the presenting problems of clients are conceptualized, diagnoses are determined, treatment goals are established, progress is monitored, and outcomes are evaluated depends on the information counselors are able to obtain from their clients through clinical assessment. Therefore, it should not come as a surprise that the ability to conduct a thorough clinical assessment is a skill that all counselors, regardless of work setting, should possess and be able to effectively implement.

Although clinical assessment serves multiple purposes, one of its primary functions is to help counselors assess for the potential presence of a mental disorder. Mental disorders are created constructs that allow counselors to label or put a name to the subjective experiences of a client. Examples of common mental disorders counselors might encounter in their work with clients include major depression, bipolar disorder, posttraumatic stress disorder, schizophrenia, and borderline personality disorder. Mental disorders are differentiated from other problems or issues a client may present by their severity and impact on the client's life. Disorders often are more pervasive and extend beyond an acute period of time. While there are hundreds of documented mental disorders, some features are common to all of them. According to the *Diagnostic and Statistical Manual of Mental Disorders* (5th ed.; American Psychiatric Association [APA], 2013) a mental disorder can generally be defined as a condition in which each the following elements is present:

1. A clinically significant disturbance in an individual's cognition, emotion regulation, or behavior that reflects a dysfunction in the psychological, biological, or developmental processes underlying mental functioning.

2. Significant distress or disability in social, occupational, or other important activities (must not be merely an expectable or culturally approved response to a common stressor or loss).

3. The disorder must not be primarily a result of social deviance or conflicts with society. (p. 20)

The ability of counselors to accurately identify and diagnose mental disorders is becoming more and more critical. According to Kessler, Chiu, Demler, and Walters (2005), approximately one in four American adults (ages 18 and older) suffer from a diagnosable mental disorder in a given year. Furthermore, 4 million children and adolescents suffer from a serious mental disorder that causes significant functional impairment either at home, at school, or with peers (U.S. Department of Health and Human Services, 1999). Given these numbers, it is likely that counselors working in all settings (including mental health agencies; elementary, secondary, and postsecondary schools; rehabilitation centers; hospitals; and private practices) will be called on to conduct a clinical assessment. When conducting a clinical assessment, counselors can guide their work using one of two primary decision-making models: the clinical judgment model and the statistical decision-making model.

Clinical Judgment Model

In the **clinical judgment model**, counselors integrate information gathered through observation as well as subjective and objective data to reach a logical conclusion on a diagnosis for a client based on existing evidence. This information is supplemented with knowledge the counselor has accumulated through interactions with previous clients, personal experiences, and any relevant research and theory related to the presenting problem (Strohmer & Leierer, 2000). Decisions regarding a client's diagnosis and subsequent treatment plan are then made intuitively based on what "feels right" for a particular client and situation. As a result, the clinical judgment model is viewed as largely individual in nature.

To effectively implement the clinical judgment model, counselors are required to possess specific skills and training. Counselors who make decisions based on their clinical judgment often have sound judgment and analytical reasoning skills, a strong understanding of counseling theory and research, and a keen awareness of client and self. While some of these skills are innate, others develop and strengthen over time. There is a strong maturational effect in the development of clinical judgment skills. As you gain more experience working with clients, your clinical judgment skills will improve.

Because assessments made using this model are based largely on the unique experiences and background of the individual counselor, the results are often quite subjective and exhibit poor reliability. Counselor bias is a known deficit of the clinical judgment model. Such bias may be intentional or unintentional. Counselors' past personal and professional experiences could influence their conceptualization as much as their adherence to a particular theoretical orientation or overlooking certain pieces of information. While this approach does not lend itself to generalizing information or comparing the reported symptom patterns of a client to other individuals known to have a particular mental disorder, it does have heuristic value. The personalized nature of this approach is often well received by clients as it focuses on them more as people than as clinical subjects. The intuitive nature of this approach compels counselors to focus more on their clients and truly hear their story in order to pull out all of the subtle nuances that make them unique.

Statistical Decision-Making Model

Although the clinical judgment model has its place, there are times when a more formal and structured assessment is needed to produce a valid diagnosis. In these situations, the statistical decision-making model is the preferred option. The **statistical decision-making model** is an approach whereby counselors move from hypothesis to conclusion using a number of analytic techniques such as statistical inference, probability, and sampling. Counselor intuition is replaced by scientific inquiry. As a result, diagnoses made using this model are more reliable and valid than those using the other approach. In a meta-analysis of the literature reviewing both the clinical judgment and statistical decision-making models, Ægisdóttir and her colleagues (2006) found that the statistical decision-making model led to a more accurate diagnosis in nearly 95 % of all clinical cases.

The improved diagnostic capabilities of this approach are based on how information is collected and analyzed. Rather than basing clinical decisions on their own experiences and understanding of human behavior, counselors employ instruments that allow them to objectively assess clients and compare their noted symptoms to profiles of individuals diagnosed with a particular mental disorder. On these instruments, cut scores are defined that differentiate between those likely to meet criteria for a mental disorder and those that do not. This approach derives its name from the fact that criteria for each disorder are assigned using statistical analyses conducted to identify those symptoms most commonly associated with a disorder. To make decisions using this model, specific diagnostic criteria are needed for each disorder. In the following section we will discuss the classification systems used by counselors to diagnose mental disorders under the statistical decision-making model. In the meantime, Guided Practice Exercise 13.1 is included to help you begin thinking about the different ways you can apply the clinical judgment and statistical decision-making models in your counseling practice.

GUIDED PRACTICE EXERCISE 13.1

Clinical Judgment Model or Statistical Decision-Making Model?

In a small group, discuss the benefits of the clinical judgment model and the statistical decision-making model. Identify as many counseling situations as you can in which each of these approaches would be the better model to employ in making a clinical diagnosis.

CLASSIFICATION SYSTEMS USED TO DIAGNOSE MENTAL DISORDERS

To help mental health professionals across disciplines communicate with each other using a consistent language, classification systems are used to diagnose mental disorders. These classification systems ensure that all practitioners are talking about the same conditions and client experiences when they describe the mental disorders of their clients. The primary classification system professional counselors use in their clinical work is the *Diagnostic and Statistical Manual of Mental Disorders* (DSM).

DSM-5

The **DSM-5** is the current edition of the *Diagnostic and Statistical Manual of Mental Disorders* and was published by the American Psychiatric Association in 2013. It includes concise and explicit criteria for a number of disorders and is intended to facilitate the objective assessment of symptom presentation in a variety of clinical settings (American Psychiatric Publishing, 2014). Over the past 60 years, the DSM has become the most commonly used resource for mental health professionals in assessing and diagnosing mental disorders. The DSM-5 is 947 pages long (by contrast, the first edition of the DSM, published in 1952, was only 145 pages long) and is divided into three sections. Section I highlights the updates made to the manual and describes how it should be used as a tool in the diagnostic process. Section II includes information related to all of the disorders listed in the DSM-5. Over 300 mental disorders are organized into 22 chapters in this section (see Table 13.1 for a list of chapters in the DSM-5). Section III describes the conditions that are in need of additional research before they can be considered for full inclusion in future editions of the DSM, as well as a glossary of terms used throughout the manual.

In many ways, the DSM-5 represents the first major revision to the diagnostic manual in nearly 30 years. As such, there are several noticeable changes in this new edition that will require changes in the way counselors historically have used the manual. One of the first changes you will find is in the title of the manual. In the past, APA used roman numerals (I, II, III, and IV) to differentiate between editions of the DSM. Beginning with DSM-5, Arabic numbers are now being used. The reason for the change is twofold. First, the new numbering system allows for the manual to be updated (e.g., 5.1, 5.2, 5.3) more expeditiously as science and research increase our understanding of mental disorders. The second reason is more practical in nature. As the DSM becomes a more prominent resource for mental health professionals worldwide, this change was made because Arabic numbers are more globally recognized than roman numerals.

A second major change in the DSM-5 has to do with the organization of the manual. Chapters have been restructured based on the apparent relatedness of disorders to one another (similar symptoms and underlying vulnerabilities). The manual also is now organized based on developmental and lifespan considerations (APA, 2013). In other words, diagnoses identified in early childhood are presented first (e.g., neurodevelopmental and schizophrenia spectrum disorders), followed by diagnoses identified in adolescence and early adulthood (e.g., bipolar, depressive, and anxiety disorders) and then adulthood and later in life (e.g., neurocognitive disorders). In addition to chapters being organized based on developmental factors, individual disorders included in each chapter are listed in a similar fashion. A new section titled "Development and Course" is included for each disorder and offers such information as: age at which typical symptoms present, a detailed description of symptom presentation specific to each age group (including a discussion of how these presentations change over the lifespan), and an estimated trajectory of how disorders may evolve into other disorders over time. The inclusion of both risk and prognostic factors at different ages will help counselors better identify symptoms and tailor treatments to their clients.

A third major change is the elimination of the multiaxial diagnostic system introduced in the previous version of the DSM (DSM-IV). Using this system, a multifaceted diagnosis was made for clients along five individual axes:

- Axis I—All clinical syndromes or conditions not attributable to a mental disorder except for personality disorders and mental retardation
- Axis II—Personality disorders and mental retardation
- Axis III—General medical conditions
- Axis IV—Psychosocial and environmental stressors contributing to the disorder
- Axis V—Global Assessment of Functioning (GAF) score

The multiaxial diagnostic system was eliminated to make the DSM-5 more compatible with the World Health Organization's International Classification of Diseases (ICD) coding system. Along with the DSM diagnostic codes for each disorder, you will see the corresponding ICD-10 code. The ICD codes began being used in place of the DSM codes in 2014. Under the new approach, nonaxial documentation will be used to indicate the presence of any disorders that previously would have been included on Axes I–III. Only information related to these three former axes is needed as they represent the only codable information. Psychosocial and contextual factors (formerly Axis IV) and disability (formerly Axis V) will be indicated through separate notation as they still will have utility in goal setting and treatment planning with clients. Section III of the DSM-5 includes the World Health Organization Disability Assessment Schedule (WHODAS 2.0) with the intent that it will soon be used in place of the former Global Assessment of Functioning (GAF) scale in the DSM-IV (see Guided Practice Exercise 13.2).

A fourth major change is the shifting of the DSM-5 to a more dimensional approach. This change was made to highlight the fact that there is significant overlap among the disorders listed in the DSM. In some chapters, disorders are now grouped together and discussed as spectrum disorders (e.g., autism spectrum disorder, mild and major neurocognitive disorders). In addition, dimensional assessments also have been included in the DSM-5. These assessments were designed to assist counselors in making accurate diagnoses and documenting changes in client presentation as a response to treatment provided. Counselors now are able to document client insight as well as the severity of the presenting disorder.

A fifth change you will notice in the DSM-5 is the removal of the *not otherwise specified* (NOS) diagnosis. In its place, the DSM-5 now includes diagnoses of *other specified* and *unspecified* mental disorders. These new diagnoses are included to assist counselors who are unable to make an accurate diagnosis of a client following an acute observation or assessment. Rather than having to narrow the presentation of a client to a specific category (e.g., Psychosis NOS), counselors can use the unspecified mental disorder diagnosis until additional information can be obtained and a more informed diagnosis can be made. This approach also is in line with the manner in which diseases and other physical illnesses are coded in the ICD-10.

Table 13.1 DSM-5 Chapters

Neurodevelopmental Disorders

Schizophrenia Spectrum and Other Psychotic Disorders

Bipolar and Related Disorders

Depressive Disorders

Anxiety Disorders

Obsessive-Compulsive and Related Disorders

Trauma- and Stressor-Related Disorders

Dissociative Disorders

Somatic Symptom and Related Disorders

Feeding and Eating Disorders

Elimination Disorders

Sleep-Wake Disorders

Sexual Dysfunctions

Gender Dysphoria

Disruptive, Impulse-Control, and Conduct Disorders

Substance-Related and Addictive Disorders

Neurocognitive Disorders

Personality Disorders

Paraphilic Disorders

Other Mental Disorders

Medication-Induced Movement Disorders and Other Adverse Effects of Medication

Other Conditions (V-Codes)

GUIDED PRACTICE EXERCISE 13.2

Implications of Changing From a Multiaxial to a Nonaxial Diagnostic Model

With the publication of the DSM-5, APA has eliminated the use of the multiaxial diagnostic system introduced with the DSM-IV. What do you see as the major implications for counseling practice that this change will have?

As a counselor, regardless of your work setting, you will likely benefit from a familiarity with the DSM-5. In addition, it will be helpful for you to have a strong working knowledge of the various assessment strategies that can be used to obtain clinical information from your clients that will be useful in making an accurate diagnosis and developing a relevant treatment plan. The following section examines common diagnostic interviewing strategies you might need to use in your work as a counselor.

DIAGNOSTIC INTERVIEWING STRATEGIES

There are many different interviewing strategies counselors can use to assist in accurately diagnosing the presenting issue of a client. Counselors should recognize that the various interview approaches all differ in purpose, focus, and duration (Craig, 2005). Choosing the correct strategy requires counselors to consider the specific needs of their client and match those needs to the strategy that appears to have the best chance of being effective. In this section we will introduce you to a number of diagnostic interviewing strategies. While it is true these strategies have several common features, there are distinctive differences between them that dictate when each should be used. Although the following list is by no means exhaustive, it does represent the most common diagnostic interviewing strategies counselors can expect to use.

Intake Interview

Before you can begin formulating a plan for helping your clients, you will need to know more about who they are and what problems they are currently experiencing that led them to the decision to seek counseling. The more informed you are as a counselor, the more effective you will be at helping your clients reach their treatment goals. Generally speaking, the intake interview is an assessment technique that provides counselors with information about clients' past functioning and how it relates to their current situation and the problems they are facing. In addition to helping counselors identify, evaluate, and explore their clients' presenting issues, intake interviews also aid counselors in identifying clients' interpersonal style, interpersonal skills, and personal history so that an appropriate level of care can be identified. Although a single standard format does not exist, most intake interviews include questions in several common core areas. These areas are important to assess because they provide information that can help a counselor better understand the nature and scope of a client's presenting problem. In total, the following eight core areas are most often addressed in an intake interview using a series of open-ended questions:

Demographic information. This section collects basic descriptive data about clients, including name, gender, age, marital status, race, ethnicity, employment status, and living situation.

Referral reasons. This section solicits information from clients about why they are currently seeking counseling, including the symptoms experienced that led them to believe it was time to get help. Knowing what led clients to seek counseling now, as opposed to last week or two weeks from now, can help counselors understand how the problem may be exceeding their current coping strategies.

Current situation. Clients are asked to provide a brief description of how the problem currently factors into their lives. How often they are troubled by the problem, how they cope with the problem when it emerges, and what impact the problem has had on their quality of life are all questions asked of clients to better understand the current situation. The approach a counselor takes with a client who has been dealing with a problem for 3 or 4 weeks would be markedly different than the approach taken with a client who has been dealing with the same problem for over 2 years.

Previous counseling experience. The questions in this section are designed to ascertain whether clients have ever sought professional help for their problems in the past. Clients are asked to report on all forms of help they may have sought, including individual therapy, group therapy, family therapy, medication, outpatient programs, and inpatient hospitalization. Here it is helpful to get as much information as possible, including any specific information (dates, locations, treatment providers) on these past treatment attempts. This information allows counselors to see what approaches may have been effective in the past. These strategies could be replicated, and those that have proved to be ineffective could be avoided. Additionally, there may be a need in the future to contact and consult with previous providers, so knowing who was seen and for what purpose is useful information to have.

Birth and developmental history. In this section questions are asked of clients to understand their past. Specifically, counselors inquire about whether there were any noteworthy issues or complications surrounding the client's birth or whether any significant developmental milestones may have been missed. This information potentially can help to explain the current functioning and abilities of a client. If clients do not know the answers to these questions, they could ask family members to help provide the requested information.

Family history. Clients are asked to describe their family constellation. Who is in their immediate family, and with which extended family members do they maintain active relationships? The questions in this section also help counselors explore whether members of the client's family may have experienced the same presenting problem as well. Several of the mental disorders clients present with have a strong genetic component to them. Knowing what illnesses run in a client's family may help identify particular disorders that should be screened for or ruled out.

Medical history. Clients share information related to past or current medical conditions and any treatment sought for those conditions. Additionally, clients are asked to describe any past surgeries or major illnesses and any known drug allergies they may have. In assessing a client's medical history, counselors should identify any medications a client may be taking currently as these medications may be contraindicated with any medications that might be prescribed to help deal with the current issue for which the client is seeking counseling.

Educational and/or vocational background. Questions typically found in this section of the intake interview include the following: What is the highest grade completed or degree earned by the client? What kind of student is/was the client? Is the client currently employed, and if so, who is the employer, what is the job the client performs, and how long has the client been employed in this position? Any prolonged absences from the workforce should be noted also.

Conducting an effective intake interview requires counselors to establish rapport with their clients (Ivey, Ivey, & Zalaquett, 2010). When a trusting relationship is established, clients feel more comfortable sharing personal information, and the counselor is able to gain a much richer understanding of what the client is experiencing. Counselors should take time to explain to clients what the interview will cover and how the information gathered will be used to help them in the counseling process. Different settings may have their own policies and procedures for how and when intake interviews are to be administered. Alternately, counselors may even be given the freedom to develop their own personal intake interview protocol (see Guided Practice Exercise 13.3). As a result, counselors should check with their supervisors to see what format should be followed at their place of employment.

GUIDED PRACTICE EXERCISE 13.3

Personalizing Your Own Intake Interview Questionnaire

While there are several common components to an intake interview, there is no set format for how this evaluation should be conducted. Imagine that you are opening your own private counseling practice and need to create an intake instrument to use with new clients. What types of questions would you ask in your interview? Is there information you would focus on more as a result of the types of clients with whom you will work?

In addition to needing to establish rapport with their clients, counselors also need time to conduct an intake interview. By its very nature, the intake interview is designed to be inclusive. Information is gathered across many dimensions. While the focus of the intake interview may seem at first glance to be quite broad in scope, all of the information acquired by the counselor could prove to be essential to the overall success of the counseling process. Because of the inclusive nature of the interview, it is not uncommon for the process to stretch out over multiple sessions (Zunker, 2008). The exact length of time it takes to administer an intake interview depends on the format of the interview and the characteristics of the client (e.g., age, cognitive ability, presenting problem) being assessed.

Clinical Interviews

One of the best methods you can use to gather the information you need to make informed decisions about your clients' current functioning and to help them reach their goals is the clinical interview. Generally speaking, a **clinical interview** is an action-oriented intervention in which a counselor solicits information about a client and the client's past using a series of questions, assesses the client's verbal and nonverbal responses to those questions, and uses that information to formulate a diagnosis for the client. In other words, the clinical interview is used to assess and provide treatment for the symptoms the client reports experiencing. Depending on the purpose of the interview, counselors have multiple types of interview formats from which to choose, including structured, semistructured, and unstructured.

Structured interviews. One type of clinical interview format a counselor can use is the structured interview. In this type of interview the counselor follows an established protocol when communicating with a client. Structured clinical interviews define what a counselor should ask, how it should be asked, and the ordered sequence in which questions should be asked. According to Edelbrock and Costello (1990), structured clinical interviews have become useful tools for describing the current distress and impairments being experienced by a client and diagnosing potential mental disorders in a reliable and valid manner. In general, structured clinical interviews share many common features. They all consist of a list of relevant behaviors, symptoms, and events to be addressed during an interview; guidelines for conducting the interview; and procedures for recording and analyzing the data that are obtained (Vacc & Juhnke, 1997). Counselors who choose to use a structured clinical interview should be sure that the instrument is appropriate for their client and the situation or setting, and will allow them to obtain the data they need to better understand their client.

Advantages of a structured interview include the following:

- Counselors are able to gain a better understanding of a client's presenting problem by asking direct questions that lead clients toward providing a deeper explanation of what they are experiencing. Many clients may not know how to verbalize what it is that they are experiencing, so these types of questions help them put words to their various thoughts and feelings.
- The standardized format of these interviews requires that all clients be asked the same questions in the same exact manner. This type of administration typically leads to the counselor obtaining more reliable information that can easily be replicated. Additionally, structured interviews allow counselors to compare the responses of their client to others who may have a particular diagnosis.
- The information provided in a structured interview can serve as the foundation for further exploration in specific areas. Additional assessment techniques such as in-depth interviews or observations can be used to follow up on the results gained from the initial structured interview.

Disadvantages of structured interviews include the following:

- Structured interviews can be time-consuming. Depending on the instrument used, the interview could last anywhere between 60 and 90 minutes. In some settings, counselors do not have that much time to spend with their clients. As such, this type of approach would have limited appeal.
- The quality of the responses the client provides is a direct result of the quality of the questions asked. Because a standard protocol is used in these interviews, counselors need to ask questions as they are worded and in the order they are listed in the interview manual. Counselors should make sure that they choose instruments that are of high quality and appropriate for their client population prior to introducing them in the counseling process.
- The structured nature of these interviews may be a challenge when used with a client who is less verbal or is apprehensive about the counseling process. Counselors should ensure that they have established good rapport with their clients before conducting a structured clinical interview. Clients need to know that they can trust their counselor before they will be willing to share their personal, and sometimes sensitive, information.

The popularity of structured clinical interviews can be attributed to the American Psychiatric Association's release of the DSM-III in 1980. In the DSM-III, for the first time, counselors were provided with a differentiated taxonomy of mental health disorders that were explicit in their criteria. Structured interviews allowed counselors to gather relevant information that supported clinical diagnoses. Since that time, various structured clinical interviews have been developed for use with clients of all ages. These instruments can be used to assess for a specific diagnosis or across a broad spectrum of disorders. Examples of structured clinical interviews are the Diagnostic Interview Schedule (DIS) and Diagnostic Interview Schedule for Children (DISC-IV), published by the National Institute of Mental Health.

Semistructured interviews. A semistructured interview is a less formal interviewing technique that allows counselors some leeway in shaping the content and direction of the interview. While a set of predetermined questions is used, counselors are able to vary the order and wording of the questions (Power, Campbell, Kitcoyne, Kitchener, & Waterman, 2010). The benefit of this type of interview is that counselors are able to gain a deeper understanding of clients and their presenting problems by allowing clients to expand on their responses. Semistructured interviews begin with counselors using a standard interview protocol that includes many open-ended questions. The responses clients provide to the interview questions then determine the direction the interview takes and what additional questions may be asked. In this type of interview format, the number and types of questions asked of each client will vary. For example, a client who indicates having had thoughts of harming self or others would likely be asked additional follow-up questions related to intent and whether a specific plan was in place. Clients who do not indicate having any thoughts of harming themselves or others would not be asked these additional risk assessment questions.

When using a semistructured interview, the counselor is given the freedom to tailor the interview to the specific client. Questions can be repeated or stated differently to help clients better understand what is being asked. In addition, counselors are able to choose which components of the interview protocol need to be included and which can be omitted. There may be certain areas that are not relevant to the current situation and would not add much to the counselor's conceptualization. As a result, additional time need not be spent addressing areas in which the client is not experiencing any distress or disability. For the counselor, this type of interview allows for the exploration of issues that arise spontaneously (Berg, 2009). For clients, this type of interview allows them to feel heard and understood, as questions target the specific areas in which they report having the most problems.

A number of semistructured interview protocols are available for counselors to use. Popular examples are the Structured Clinical Interview for DSM Disorders. A separate form exists to assess for Axis I disorders (SCID-CV) and Axis II disorders (SCID-II). Despite their name, these instruments are classified as semistructured interviews because they allow counselors to deviate from the standard protocol and probe further when it is apparent that a client is experiencing noticeable distress in a particular area. Since the DSM-5 no longer uses the multiaxial diagnostic system, these instruments need to be revised to better align with DSM-5 criteria. According to the APA, these instruments are currently in revision and are slated for release in 2014. Another example of a semistructured clinical interview is the **Semistructured Clinical Interview for Children and Adolescents (SCICA)**. The SCICA is a part of the Achenbach System of Empirically Based Assessment instruments and is designed to assess the cognitive and interpersonal functioning of children ages 6–18. Topics addressed in the SCICA include activities, school, job, friends, family relations, fantasies, self-perceptions, feelings, problems reported by the parent or teacher, and performance on achievement tests. Responses to interview questions are scored on a 4-point scale with values of 0 (*no occurrence*), 1 (*very slight or ambiguous occurrence*), 2 (*definite occurrence with mild to moderate intensity and a duration of less than three minutes*), and 3 (*definite occurrence with severe intensity and a duration of more than three minutes*). The self-report form includes 114 items and takes 60–90 minutes to administer.

Unstructured interviews. Unstructured interviews are some of the most common types of interviews used by counselors in a clinical setting (Craighead & Nemeroff, 2004). As their name implies, these interviews have no established form or structure. Unstructured interviews often start with a broad, open-ended question (e.g., What brings you here today?). Subsequent questions are then asked based on client responses (Holloway & Wheeler, 2010). This approach allows for the interview process to take on more of a conversational tone. Although flexibility is a hallmark of the unstructured interview, these interviews are not completely devoid of structure. Questions are not asked of clients in a haphazard manner, jumping from topic to topic with no apparent rationale. Instead, counselors using this approach typically follow an interview guide based on themes. For example, a counselor may ask several questions related to the current mood state of a client.

Interpreting the information gathered from an unstructured interview can be challenging. According to Summerfeldt and Antony (2002), counselors are fully responsible for deciding what questions to ask and how to analyze client responses in order to arrive at a clinical diagnosis. As such, counselors using unstructured interviews should have a strong working knowledge of the DSM symptoms and diagnostic criteria. Additionally, counselors should be able to identify themes in client responses and group like responses. In an unstructured interview, the counselor may ask questions related to the present as well as past functioning of the client to gain a better perspective of the problem and how it affects the client. Despite the issues of poor validity associated with unstructured interviews, this type of assessment intervention is most often used to establish a mental health diagnosis in the clinical setting (Craig, 2005).

Each of the approaches listed in this section has its own inherent advantages and disadvantages. Counselors should take into account client characteristics, setting, and purpose for interviewing the client when choosing an interview format. Guided Practice Exercise 13.4 asks you to consider the situations and settings in which each of these interview formats would be most helpful to you as a counselor.

GUIDED PRACTICE EXERCISE 13.4

Choosing the Appropriate Clinical Interview Format

Identify two advantages each for structured, semistructured, and unstructured interviews. With which types of clients would you recommend using each? With which types of clients would you not use each interview style? Consider a variety of client characteristics and work settings as you formulate your responses.

Mental Status Examination

Another commonly used clinical assessment interview is the mental status examination. The **mental status examination** (MSE) is a structured interview designed to objectively assess the emotional, behavioral, and cognitive functioning or mental state of a client at the time of the interview. An MSE can be administered at various times throughout the counseling process. When used as part of the intake process, the MSE can be a useful tool for counselors as they begin to conceptualize their clients' functioning into a diagnosis and focus treatment efforts. When used during the working stages of the counseling process, the MSE is helpful in assessing the course of a disorder and its response to treatment efforts. Regardless of when the MSE is administered, consideration is given to all aspects of mental functioning.

Several versions of the MSE are available for counselors to use. While there is some variation in what sections are included on the examination, there are some general guidelines for how these assessments are structured. Trzepacz and Baker (1993) note that the standard MSE is generally organized into the following categories: (1) appearance, attitude, and activity; (2) mood and affect; (3) speech and language; (4) thought process, thought content, and perception; (5) cognition; and (6) insight and judgment. As you can see, an MSE protocol typically includes a description of the individual across multiple domains using information gathered through either interview or observation (see Table 13.2). Collectively, these domains contribute to the counselor's understanding of a client's presenting problems in terms of clinical diagnosis and severity (Erford, 2013). Below we will look at the various domains that are commonly assessed in the standard MSE along with possible descriptors of each domain.

- **Appearance**—Assess the client's gait, posture, clothing, grooming.
- **Behavior**—Assess the client's mannerisms, gestures, psychomotor activity, expression, eye contact, ability to follow commands and requests, or compulsions.
- **Attitude**—Assess whether the client is cooperative, hostile, open, secretive, indifferent, irritable, agitated, focused, easily distracted, anxious, distant, or apathetic.
- **Level of Consciousness**—Assess whether the client is vigilant, alert, drowsy, lethargic, stuporous, asleep, comatose, confused, or fluctuating.
- **Orientation**—Assess how oriented the client is to time, place, and identity. Questions asked to assess orientation typically include: What is your full name? Where are you right now? What is today's date? What month is it? Who is the current president of the United States?
- **Speech and Language**—Assess the client's speech and language in terms of quantity (talkative or poverty of speech), rate (fast or slow), volume (loud, soft, or monotone), and fluency and rhythm (clear with good articulation or hesitant and slurred).
- **Mood**—Assess the inner feelings of the client. Questions to ask include: How are you feeling today? How are your spirits? What has your mood been like in the past few days?

- **Affect**—Assess the client's affect in terms of appropriateness to the current situation (consistent with mood or not), fluctuations (labile or even), range (broad or restricted), intensity (blunted, flat, or normal intensity), and quality (sad, angry, hostile, irritable, euphoric, elated, or anxious).
- **Thought Processes or Form**—Does the client appear to be thinking in a logical, linear, and coherent fashion? Are responses to specific questions appropriate and formulated in a correct manner?
- **Thought Content**—Possible questions to ask to assess thought content include: What do you think about when you are sad or angry? What has been on your mind lately? Do you find yourself ruminating or obsessing about things more lately? Are you worried more than usual? Do you think that there are people out there who are trying to get you? Do you ever see/smell/hear/taste/feel things that are not really there, such as voices or visions? Does it seem like people may be trying to steal your ideas or place unwanted thoughts in your mind?
- **Suicidal and Homicidal Ideation**—Ask clients if they are having any thoughts of harming either themselves or others. If so, further assessment should examine both intent and means.
- **Insight and Judgment**—Does the client know why he or she is presenting for counseling today? Ask if the client knows what the problem is, how the problem is impacting his or her life, how the client sees his or her role in perpetuating the problem, and what the client would like to see happen as a result of counseling.
- **Attention**—Can the client concentrate and attend to the task at hand, or is the client easily distracted? Attention can be assessed through a series of small exercises, including digit span (have the client repeat a recited set of numbers both forward and backward), spelling (have the client spell the word *world* both forward and backward), serial calculations (have the client start with 100 and count backward by 7s), and simple mathematical calculations (have the client either add three numbers together [e.g., 12 + 20 + 31] or multiply two numbers [e.g., 20 × 4]).
- **Memory**—Assess the client's immediate, recent, and long-term memory. Immediate memory can be assessed by asking the client to remember three simple words (usually colors, animals, shapes, or objects in the room) and repeat them to you after a period of 5 minutes. Recent memory can be assessed by asking the client what your name is, what time his or her appointment was for today, and what medications were taken today. Long-term memory can be assessed by asking the client to recall details of significant past personal events (graduations, marriages, and birthdays) or historical events.
- **Intellectual Ability**—Assess the client's knowledge of information and vocabulary as well as abstraction ability. When formulating questions for this section, keep in mind the client's age, fluency, and education level.

Scoring will depend on the version of the mental status examination you use. A point value is assigned to the response to each item. These points are then summed for the entire instrument and compared to established cut scores. How clients score in relation to these

Table 13.2   Components of a Mental Status Examination

Dimension	Method Used to Assess
Appearance	Observation
Behavior	Observation
Attitude	Observation
Level of consciousness	Observation
Orientation	Client inquiry
Speech and language	Observation
Mood	Client inquiry
Affect	Observation
Thought process/form	Observation and/or client inquiry
Thought content	Observation and/or client inquiry
Suicidality and homicidality	Client inquiry
Insight and judgment	Observation and/or client inquiry
Attention span	Observation and/or client inquiry
Memory	Observation and/or client inquiry
Intellectual functioning	Observation and/or client inquiry

preestablished cut scores determines how their mental status is assessed and whether they are competent enough to participate in counseling and make decisions for themselves. As with all other forms of assessment, the results of this single test should be considered in context and compared to other information the counselor may already have or be able to readily collect using alternative data gathering techniques.

Suicide Assessment

Suicide, defined as the act of taking one's own life on purpose, has become a major public health concern in the United States. According to data collected by the Centers for Disease Control and Prevention (2013), 38,364 suicides were reported in 2010, making suicide the tenth leading cause of death for Americans. An estimated 11 attempted suicides occur per every suicide death (National Institute of Mental Health, 2013). Although the number of deaths by suicide continues to increase each year, suicide is a wholly preventable occurrence. Given the high prevalence of suicidal behavior and its impact on the mental health treatment community, it is important that mental health counselors have access to state-of-the-art information related to the assessment of suicide risk (J. R. Rogers, 2001). This knowledge, along with clinical experience and training, is what allows counselors to effectively assess for suicide risk (see Case Illustration 13.1).

Table 13.3   Suicide Risk Assessment Instruments

Child and Adolescent Psychiatric Assessment (CAPA)

Diagnostic Interview Schedule for Children (DISC)

Child Suicide Potential Scales (CSPS)

Suicidal Behaviors Interview (SBI)

Adolescent Suicide Interview (ASI)

Suicide Behaviors Questionnaire-Revised (SBQ-R)

Beck Scale for Suicidal Ideation (BSI)

Reasons for Living Inventory (RFL)

Suicidal Ideation Questionnaire (SIQ)

Inventory of Suicide Orientation-30 (ISO-30)

A suicide assessment can be conducted using formal techniques such as standardized instruments and questionnaires, informal techniques such as observations and interview protocols, or a combination of both (Granello, 2010). Several assessment tools for general use or for use with specific client populations are commercially available (see Table 13.3). While these instruments do assist counselors in assessing suicide risk in their clients, Granello and Granello (2006) assert that the unstructured interview is still the most commonly used assessment method in suicide risk assessment. According to Shea (2009), a sound suicide risk assessment interview should comprise the following three key components:

- Gathering information related to the risk factors, protective factors, and warning signs of suicide. Suicide risk assessment and management have proved to be far more viable than suicide prevention efforts (Westefeld et al., 2000). A list of empirically derived risk factors is included in Table 13.4.
- Collecting information related to the client's current suicidal ideation, planning, behaviors, desire, and intent. This is where counselors probe to determine the level of severity of a client's thoughts and intentions. Among the questions counselors should seek to answer are the following: Does the client have a specific plan for how he or she would take his or her own life (e.g., taking pills, running in traffic, using a gun)? What is the lethality of the means verbalized in that plan? Does the client have readily available access to those means? Keep in mind, the more detailed the plan, the more likely it will be that the client will act on that plan.
- Making a clinical formulation of risk based on the information obtained related to the two areas noted above. Counselors consider all information they have and make informed decisions regarding the appropriate level of care needed to ensure the client's safety and to prevent a tragedy from occurring.

Table 13.4 Suicide Risk Factors

Family history of suicide

Family history of child abuse or mistreatment

Previous suicide attempt(s)

History of mental disorders

History of alcohol and substance abuse

Feelings of hopelessness

Impulsive or aggressive tendencies

Cultural and religious beliefs

Local epidemics of suicide

Isolation or feelings of being cut off from other people

Barriers to accessing mental health treatment

Loss (relational, social, work, or financial)

Physical illness

Easy access to lethal methods

Unwillingness to seek help because of mental health stigma

CASE ILLUSTRATION 13.1

To assist counselors in assessing individuals for immediate suicide risk, the mnemonic "Is Path Warm?" can be used. Each letter in this sentence corresponds to a risk factor noted as frequently experienced or reported within the last few months before a suicide (Juhnke, Granello, & Lebrón-Striker, 2007).

I	Suicidal **I**deation
S	**S**ubstance Abuse
P	**P**urposefulness
A	**A**nger
T	**T**rapped
H	**H**opelessness
W	**W**ithdrawing
A	**A**nxiety
R	**R**ecklessness
M	**M**ood Change

COUNSELING ASSESSMENT IN FORENSIC SETTINGS

Since the 1990s there has been a growing interest in the area of forensic assessment. According to Burke (1999–2009), **forensic assessment** is an evaluation of cognition, mood, personality, or behavior conducted by a licensed mental health practitioner for the purpose of assisting attorneys or the court in legal matters. The objectives of this type of assessment are to clarify possible psychopathology, needs, risk of reoffending, and possibilities of treatment for an identified client (Duits, van der Hoorn, Wiznitzer, Wettstein, & de Beurs, 2012). While the counselor conducting the forensic assessment does not specifically address the legal question before the court (i.e., render a decision on a person's guilt or innocence), he or she does provide critical information to the court that can be helpful in reaching a just verdict or settlement. In this section we will examine how forensic assessment differs from traditional forms of counseling and assessment and look at some of the more common areas in which counselors working with the judicial system are asked to conduct assessments and report their findings to the court.

Although both use many of the same techniques and interventions, there are fundamental differences between traditional counseling assessment and forensic assessment. In a traditional counseling setting, the goals of a counselor's assessment activities are to identify a client's presenting problem, gauge the severity of the problem, and determine the appropriate level of care (individual therapy, outpatient care, inpatient hospitalization, etc.) that the client may need. This process typically takes time, as counselors must first work to establish rapport and build a trusting relationship with their clients. Typically, clients are encouraged to actively participate in the counseling process because the ultimate goal is to help them address and deal with their presenting problems.

Forensic assessment, by nature, takes on a much different feel and approach. When conducting a forensic assessment, the counselor's goal is to collect factual information that can be used by the Court to rule on a pending criminal or civil case. In this situation, counselors are not interested in helping clients address their problems, only how the existence of their problems may factor into their culpability in the ongoing case. As such, little attention is paid to building a therapeutic relationship with the client. Counselors conducting forensic assessments will typically be more direct and less empathic than if they were working with the client in a counseling relationship. When engaging in forensic activities, counselors need to remember the role they are being asked to fill and for whom they are working. Most forensic counselors are hired by legal counsel or commissioned by the courts. A counselor retained for the purpose of conducting a forensic assessment should not have any existing or past therapeutic relationship with the defendant on trial.

A common misconception is that all counseling activities that take place in the context of the legal system are considered a part of forensic assessment. On the contrary, many activities counselors might find themselves engaged in would not be considered a part of traditional forensic practice. For example, a counselor's testimony in court regarding the provision of counseling services that does not include clinical opinion would not ordinarily be considered forensic practice. Generally speaking, forensic assessment activities are employed to gather information used to make decisions in three main areas: (1) competency to stand trial, (2) mental status at time of defense, and (3) prediction of an individual's likelihood of being a danger to self or others and risk for future offending (Miller, 2013).

Competency to Stand Trial

Evaluations to assess competency to stand trial (CST) are some of the most common forensic assessments performed. Bonnie and Grisso (2000) note that between 50,000 and 60,000 cases each year involve an assessment of CST. Assessing competency is an important element because competency is required for a defendant to be arrested, waive Miranda rights, consent to search, enter a plea, stand trial, and be sentenced (Miller, 2013). To assist in correctly identifying whether an individual is competent, a set of standard criteria is needed. In 1960, the U.S. Supreme Court established the criteria used to determine CST following the case of *Dusky v. United States*. Since then, these criteria have come to be used as the standards for all federal and state courts.

According to Bonnie (1992), there are two distinct parts to a comprehensive CST evaluation: the assessment of basic and decisional competency. **Basic competence** refers to the individual's ability to understand the charges brought against him or her and work effectively with his or her defense counsel. In other words, does the defendant understand the legal proceedings in which he or she is involved and the basic elements of courtroom decorum? Defendants must be deemed competent enough to participate in the upcoming courtroom proceedings before a trial can begin. **Decisional competence** focuses on the quality of the defendant's reasoning abilities. Here the question is whether the defendant understands the penalties if convicted and is making decisions that are in his or her own best interest. Following a CST evaluation counselors must assess the individual and determine whether he or she is competent to proceed, temporarily incompetent to proceed, or permanently incompetent to proceed.

To assist counselors in conducting a CST evaluation, several informal and commercially available instruments can be used. Two published instruments that are useful in evaluating CST are the MacArthur Competence Assessment Tool-Criminal Adjudication (MacCAT-CA) and the Evaluation of Competency to Stand Trial-Revised (ECST-R). While both appear to have sound psychometric properties, they do require advanced training to fully understand the administration, scoring, and interpretation procedures. The successful integration of these instruments into a counselor's forensic evaluation protocol requires advanced study of the measures, experience administering them, and a careful consideration of their clinical utility on a case-by-case basis (Acklin, 2012).

Mental Status/Legal Sanity

A second type of forensic assessment counselors engage in is the evaluation of an individual's mental status for the purpose of determining legal sanity (also known as criminal responsibility). **Sanity** refers to the soundness of a person's mind and whether he or she is able to think rationally and function as a member of society. It is important to note that *sanity* is a legal term and not a counseling term. Whereas the focus of a CST assessment is on the defendant's mental status at the time of trial, legal sanity assessments are concerned with the defendant's mental status at the time the alleged offense took place.

In all U.S. jurisdictions with an insanity defense, there is a specific standard that must be met for an individual to be found not guilty by reason of insanity. For an insanity defense to effectively be argued, Reid (2006) states that there must be a diagnosable mental deficit that causes a problem in perception or behavior severe enough to interfere with criminal intent at the time of the alleged criminal act. Additionally, the individual's disease or mental defect cannot be diagnosed based solely on his or her documented criminal or antisocial behavior. Despite the popularity of insanity defenses seen being argued in movies and television shows, the defense is actually employed in a relatively small number of cases. In actuality, the insanity defense is used in less than 1% of all criminal proceedings and is successful in only one quarter of those cases (Hooper & McLearen, 2002).

Counselors tasked with assessing a defendant's sanity often conduct a series of three interviews. The first interview is designed to assist the counselor in gathering historical information about the defendant. The second interview attempts to assess the defendant's mental state at the time the alleged crime was committed. The final interview assesses the defendant's current mental state. The information collected from these interviews is then compared to existing evidence, police reports, witness testimony, and information obtained from speaking to other involved parties. After analyzing all of the evidence, the counselor's goal is to assess whether the defendant understood the nature and quality of the criminal act he or she is being accused of committing and whether he or she recognized the act as wrong. While defendants can be tried multiple times on the grounds of competency, they can be tried only once for insanity. As a result, sanity evaluations are much more in depth and take longer to conduct than CST evaluations. Because of the importance that the results of this type of evaluation can have for the defendant and his or her legal defense, counselors should ensure that they have gathered useful information from multiple sources so that they can make an informed assessment.

Risk Assessment

The third category of forensic assessment counselors engage in involves assessing the client's potential for harmful or violent behavior. These types of assessments, commonly referred to as **risk assessments**, are often used to evaluate the likelihood of an individual becoming a reoffender upon his or her release. The results of these assessments factor into probation, parole, and civil commitment decisions, as well as conditional releases of individuals who were declared not guilty by reason of insanity or mental defect. The primary focus of a risk assessment is to identify the individual and situational risk factors correlated with the occurrence of target behaviors identified for the client. Examples of risk factors include impulsivity, negative emotionality, antisocial attitudes, alcohol and substance abuse, and unstable interpersonal relationships (Miller, 2013). For some cases there is a finite time frame associated with the assessment (probations and parole). In other cases (conditional releases) ongoing assessments for an extended period of time are mandated.

According to Barbara McDermott and her colleagues (2008), researchers who have followed forensic patients who had been conditionally released found revocation rates ranging between 35% and 50%. Because the likelihood for reoffending is high, the risk assessments conducted by forensic counselors are important for safeguarding the public and helping those most at risk for reoffending continue to receive the help they need. To assist in the assessment process, counselors may choose to use an instrument such as the **Historical Clinical Risk Management-20 (HCRM-20)**. The HCRM-20 comprises 20 probing questions that elicit qualitative information a counselor can use to assess the probability of a person engaging in harmful or violent behavior in the future. Questions are grouped into three main areas: historical, clinical, and risk management (see Table 13.5). Items are coded using scores of 0 (*not present*), 1 (*possible, less serious*), or 2 (*definite, serious*). The higher the total score (sum of each individual item), the more likely the individual's propensity for violence.

Table 13.5 HCRM-20 Content Areas

Historical

Previous violence

Young age at first violent incident

Relationship instability

Employment problems

Substance use problems

Major mental illness

Psychopathy (personality traits deviant from societal norms)

Early maladjustment or exposure to family discord that led to problems with coping

Personality disorders

Previous treatment noncompliance

Clinical

Lack of insight or difficulty understanding cause and effect

Negative attitudes

Active symptoms of a major mental illness

Impulsivity

Unresponsiveness to treatment

Risk Management

Plans lack of feasibility

Exposure to destabilizers (lack of a support system, access to drugs and/or alcohol)

Lack of personal support

Refusal to attend counseling or take prescribed medications

Stress

Despite the knowledge that recidivism rates are high, there is no current statutory guidance for conducting risk assessment evaluations like there is for the evaluations of competence or legal sanity (Gowensmith, Murrie, & Boccaccini, 2013). As a result, counselors should be cautious when engaging in these types of assessments because of the high stakes associated with their evaluations. Collectively, the information obtained should allow for the counselor to inform criminal and mental health–related decisions based on the best available clinical estimates of risk of violence (see Guided Practice Exercise 13.5).

GUIDED PRACTICE EXERCISE 13.5

Understanding the Application of Forensic Assessment

Counselors in all settings are called on to participate in forensic evaluations. Consider the setting in which you currently work or aspire to one day work, and think about the ways you might be asked to contribute to a forensic evaluation. What types of evaluations would you likely need to conduct, and how would you use the results of these evaluations?

ADDRESSING DIVERSITY IN CLINICAL ASSESSMENT

Throughout your career as a professional counselor, you likely will have the opportunity to work with clients from a number of different backgrounds. As a counselor, you should keep in mind that the rich cultural background and personal experiences of your clients contribute greatly to how they present for counseling and their needs from the process. In a clinical assessment, where the results often have meaningful implications for a client (e.g., access to care, types of treatments applied), counselors must consider culture and diversity when assessing their clients. To assist in this endeavor, the Association for Assessment and Research in Counseling (2012) has created the *AACE Standards for Multicultural Assessment,* which outlines how counselors should account for cultural diversity in the selection, administration, scoring, and interpretation of assessment instruments. The more informed you become as a counselor, the less likely you will be to misdiagnose a client based on cultural misunderstandings.

KEYSTONES

- Clinical assessment has become an important aspect of the counseling profession.
- Clinical assessment practices help counselors determine whether clients meet diagnostic criteria for a mental disorder.
- Counselors can diagnose their clients using either the clinical judgment or statistical decision-making model. Both have their advantages and disadvantages, and it is the responsibility of the counselor to choose the appropriate method to use in each situation.
- The diagnostic criteria used to assess mental disorders most used by professional counselors are included in the *Diagnostic and Statistical Manual of Mental Disorders* (DSM-5).
- Several data gathering assessment strategies can be used in a clinical setting, including intake interviews; structured, semistructured, and unstructured interviews; mental status examinations; and suicide risk assessments.
- The role of counselors in forensic settings has increased in recent years. Counselors now play an important role in evaluating client cognition, mood, personality, and behavior and preparing reports on these assessments for use in courtroom settings.

- When assessing clients and evaluating psychopathology, counselors need to consider client diversity and account for cultural factors when making a clinical diagnosis about a client's current mental state.

KEY TERMS

basic competence

clinical assessment

clinical interview

clinical judgment model

decisional competence

Diagnostic and Statistical

Manual of Mental Disorders (DSM-5)

forensic assessment

Historical Clinical Risk Management-20 (HCRM-20)

mental status examination

risk assessments

sanity

Semistructured Clinical Interview for Children and Adolescents (SCICA)

statistical decision-making model

suicide

ADDITIONAL RESOURCES

- American Psychiatric Association *DSM-5* Development
  http://www.dsm5.org/Pages/Default.aspx
- National Association of Forensic Counselors
  http://www.nationalafc.com/
- Suicide Assessment Five-Step Evaluation and Triage (SAFE-T) Screening Information
  http://www.integration.samhsa.gov/images/res/SAFE_T.pdf

Student Study Site: Visit the Student Study Site at **www.sagepub.com/watson** to access additional study tools, including quizzes, web resources, and journal articles.

CHAPTER 14

Outcome Assessment and Program Evaluation

LEARNING OBJECTIVES

After reading this chapter, you will be able to

- Define the term *counseling outcome* and identify various types of outcomes than can be assessed in the counseling process
- Discuss the concept of effect size and explain how effect size factors into counseling outcome research
- Describe the various outcome research design strategies counselors can employ to evaluate treatment effectiveness
- Articulate how the results of counseling outcome research can be applied to the practice of counseling
- Describe the components of an effective program evaluation
- Explain how the results of a program evaluation can be used for accountability purposes

$\mathbf{A}$s counselors we have the ability to help our clients in a variety of ways. Throughout your counselor training program, you will be introduced to a number of theoretical orientations and taught how to apply an even larger number of techniques and interventions. But do these approaches and interventions really work? Is counseling effective? Is one approach really better to use than another? Questions such as these form the basis of counseling outcome research. Since the early formative years of the counseling profession, outcome questions have been of particular interest to counseling researchers and practitioners. In recent years, the interest in counseling outcomes has expanded as the profession moves more to an evidence-based practice model. This trend has resulted in substantial research that has explored the effectiveness of numerous practices among various counseling fields (Whiston, Tai, Rahardja, & Eder, 2011). Increasingly, counselors are being asked to not only use counseling approaches that have been empirically validated and are known to be effective in helping clients, but also conduct their own research and contribute to the expanding research literature.

There are several reasons why counseling has shifted toward a more evidence-based practice model. For one, it represents an ethical approach to the counseling process. Counselors have an ethical responsibility to function in the best interest of their clients and apply effective treatments designed to promote client welfare. In addition to this ethical mandate, counselors today also find themselves working in an era of increased accountability. This means that counselors are coming under increased pressure to be able to document that the work they do is effective and has therapeutic value. If the counseling profession cannot prove its effectiveness, there may be less need for its services (Stone, 2012). In this chapter we will look at how counselors can assess counseling outcomes and substantiate the work they do with their clients and the communities in which they serve. In addition, we will introduce program evaluation and explain how counselors can use this assessment approach to substantiate the viability and success of the various treatment programs they provide to their communities.

DEFINING COUNSELING OUTCOMES

An **outcome** can best be defined as the end result or consequence of an action. If you study for a test, the likely outcome will be that you perform well on the test. However, in counseling, outcomes are not as easy to identify. Unlike other professions and industries, counseling does not produce a tangible product that readily can be seen and measured (Leibert, 2006). Absent this end product, how then do counselors substantiate that what they do works? According to Bachelor and Horvath (1999), the key may be to look to our clients for answers. In their research, Bachelor and Horvath found that clients are far more accurate at evaluating the effectiveness of treatment and predicting outcomes than counselors are. As such, any planned evaluation of treatment effectiveness should take into account the outcomes desired by clients.

By now you have no doubt learned that individuals seek counseling services for a variety of reasons. Each client presents with a different set of issues and concerns that are of varying degrees of severity. For some clients, they seek counseling for support or guidance on a specific issue. Perhaps they are having difficulties in a current relationship or experiencing school- or job-related stress. For other clients, their decision to present for counseling is motivated by more serious concerns. The symptoms these clients exhibit may point to the presence of a mental disorder that is having a negative impact on their functioning and overall quality of life. Although these clients each present for counseling with differing needs, the outcome for them all essentially is the same—change.

In the counseling profession the outcome most often sought is change. Many clients who seek counseling services do so because they have problem areas in their lives that they would like to see changed or improved. Through counseling they hope to achieve a reduction in symptoms and an improvement in psychosocial functioning. Additionally, change is sought by third-party interests as well. Reimbursement for counseling services is often predicated on the ability of the counselor to evoke positive change (Erford, 2010). No matter which theoretical orientation you choose to follow or the interventions you opt to employ, the common goal of all counseling treatment approaches should be creating measureable change in the lives of our clients. The treatment strategies and interventions counselors use, in addition to being research-based and empirically sound, should be capable of producing desired changes. After all, absent change there really would be no apparent therapeutic value to the work we as counselors do with our clients.

Effect Size and the Magnitude of Change

Effect size is a statistical term that refers to the family of indices used to measure the magnitude of a treatment effect. In the context of counseling and therapeutic outcome research, effect size refers to the numerical expression of the difference between the means of two or more compared groups as measured by an outcome measure (Timulak, 2009, p. 18). The reporting of effect sizes in outcome research has grown in popularity in recent years. In addition to being easy to calculate, readily understood, and applicable to any number of measured outcomes, effect sizes also promote a more scientific approach to the accumulation of knowledge (Coe, 2002). Researchers can now move beyond the simple question of whether a treatment works, and address the far more sophisticated question of how well it works in a range of contexts and settings.

The calculation of effect size begins with a comparison of means between two groups (usually through a t-test analysis). Comparisons can be made either within a group or between groups. A within-group comparison measures observed change in clients before and after the administration of a counseling intervention. This pretest/posttest design allows the counselor to determine the impact a particular intervention has on clients. A between-groups comparison measures the difference in observed change between clients exposed to different treatment approaches. In this model, the goal is to identify whether there is a significant difference between the two treatment approaches that would support the use of one over the other. Once the treatment condition has been applied, results are collected from the two groups and the means of the two groups are then compared.

Following the mean comparison test, counselors can further their inquiry and examine effect size. In counseling outcome research, the effect size measure most often used is Cohen's *d* (J. Cohen, 1988). Conceptually, Cohen's *d* is simply the difference in the means of the two groups being compared divided by the average of their standard deviations. Mathematically speaking, Cohen's *d* can be computed using the following formula:

$$ES = \frac{\bar{X}_t - \bar{X}_c}{S}$$

In the above formula, $\bar{X}_t$ represents the mean of the treatment group, $\bar{X}_c$ represents the mean of the control group, and S represents the average standard deviation of the two groups together. In the past, effect sizes were computed only when a statistically significant difference was noted between the treatment and control group. However, current practices appear to allow for the computation of effect sizes despite statistical nonsignificance. To aid in the process of interpreting effect size measures in social sciences research, Cohen suggested the following categorizations: an effect size (*d* value) of 0.2 would be considered a small effect size, 0.5 a medium effect size, and 0.8 a large effect size. This indicates that if the means of the two groups being compared do not differ by at least 0.2 standard deviation, the difference between them will be trivial at best, regardless of statistical significance (see Case Illustration 14.1).

$$ES = \frac{15-11}{8} = 0.50$$

CASE ILLUSTRATION   14.1

A counselor is attempting to evaluate the impact of adding motivational enhancement therapy (MET) to an existing substance abuse treatment program. A treatment group was established to pilot the new MET component. Individuals receiving the existing treatment constitute the control group. Following a 14-day treatment program, clients were administered a symptom checklist to evaluate how effective treatment had been at reducing the number of symptoms they experience. The treatment group, which received the traditional treatment model as well as the MET component, had an average mean score of 11 (on a scale of 0–20) on the symptom checklist. The mean score for the control group, which received the traditional treatment model only, was 15. The pooled standard deviation for the two groups was computed to be 8. Using this data the counselor computes an effect size for this study of 0.50. Based on this result, the counselor concludes that the addition of the MET component had a medium effect.

Now you know how to compute an effect size, but what does this statistic really tell you? What does it mean to say that a study has a small, medium, or large effect? To understand the value of the effect size measure, think of it as a determination of practical significance. When comparing two groups, counselors may find a statistically significant difference, but that difference may exist only on paper and not be felt in real-world applications. Statistical significance is largely influenced by the number of participants in your study and how homogenous those participants are. With a large number of participants, statistical significance is not hard to achieve. To address this issue, effect size can be a useful alternative to help you see how different treatments actually impact your clients. A large effect size indicates that a substantial difference between the two groups being compared exists. The impact of the treatment being evaluated would be readily apparent to all parties involved. On the other hand, when smaller effect sizes are computed, it means that the true difference between the two groups is quite small and may not necessitate any changes in treatment delivery. To confidently state that a treatment is related to positive outcomes, counselors prefer large effect sizes.

ASSESSING COUNSELING OUTCOMES

Historically the assessment of counseling outcomes has been the focus of researchers and not practicing counselors (Walton, 2012). These researchers focused their efforts on studying the treatment efficacy of various counseling approaches to identify the salient characteristics of counseling that best predicted positive outcomes. Knowing which interventions are the most effective is a significant benefit to mental health counselors (Bradley, Sexton, & Smith, 2005). However, in this era of increased accountability, counselors are being asked to assume a more active role in the process of identifying best practices in counseling. As Erford (2010) notes, counselors must be held personally accountable in their provision of empirically proven therapeutic interventions so clients and other stakeholders can be confident that the services they receive are valid, valuable, and effective. In this section we will examine the methods counselors can use to assess change and document the efficacy of their counseling efforts.

Client Satisfaction Surveys

Satisfaction surveys are a quick and easy way to gather feedback regarding services provided (Steenbarger & Smith, 1996). These surveys can be administered in one of three ways: during counseling, at termination, and as a follow-up after counseling has concluded. Assessing client satisfaction during the counseling process allows a counselor to make adjustments that might benefit the client while there is still time. Assessments conducted at termination allow counselors to understand clients' immediate feelings about the experience they just had and how well they felt it helped. Follow-up surveys of client satisfaction provide the opportunity to assess clients after they have had a chance to distance themselves from the process and see how the gains made in the counseling process actually translate to their day-to-day life. Because of their varied utility, client satisfaction or feedback surveys have become quite popular in mental health settings (see Guided Practice Exercise 14.1).

Despite their utility, client satisfaction surveys used as outcome measures of treatment efficacy present several noted disadvantages. Although professionally useful, satisfaction surveys are scientifically problematic, as noted by Barker, Pistrang, and Elliott (1994). For one, these surveys are often created for service agencies and are geared specifically to the services they provide. Few surveys are actually constructed using sound test construction principles. Furthermore, these surveys collect data self-reported by the client, a data collection approach with noted reliability issues. Combined, these features contribute to the general weakness of attribution and causation between counseling satisfaction and the results these surveys are able to make (Fischer & Valley, 2000). Examples of empirically tested satisfaction surveys that can be used to assess client perceptions on the value of services received include the Client Satisfaction Questionnaire (CSQ-8; Larsen, Attkisson, Hargreaves, & Nguyen, 1979; see Figure 14.1) and the Service Satisfaction Scale-30 (SSS-30; Greenfield & Attkisson, 2004).

Figure 14.1 Client Satisfaction Questionnaire (CSQ-8)

CSQ-8 English

CLIENT SATISFACTION QUESTIONNAIRE
CSQ-8

Please help us improve our program by answering some questions about the services you have received. We are interested in your honest opinions, whether they are positive or negative. *Please answer all of the questions.* We also welcome your comments and suggestions. Thank you very much. We appreciate your help.

CIRCLE YOUR ANSWERS

1. How would you rate the quality of service you received?

4 *Excellent*	3 *Good*	2 *Fair*	1 *Poor*

2. Did you get the kind of service you wanted?

1 *No, d*	2 *No, not really*	3 *Yes, generally*	4 *Yes, d*

3. To what extent has our program met your needs?

4 *Almost all of my needs have been met*	3 *Most of my needs have been met*	2 *Only a few of my needs have been met*	1 *None of my needs have been met*

4. If a friend were in need of similar help, would you recommend our program to him or her?

1 *No, d*	2 *No, I don't think so*	3 *Yes, I think so*	4 *Yes, d*

5. How satisfied are you with the amount of help you received?

1 *Quite dissatisfied*	2 *Indifferent or mildly dissatisfied*	3 *Mostly satisfied*	4 *Very satisfied*

6. Have the services you received helped you to deal more effectively with your problems?

4 *Yes, they helped a great deal*	3 *Yes, they helped somewhat*	2 *No, they really didn't help*	1 *No, they seemed to make things worse*

7. In an overall, general sense, how satisfied are you with the service you received?

4 *Very satisfied*	3 *Mostly satisfied*	2 *Indifferent or mildly dissatisfied*	1 *Quite dissatisfied*

8. If you were to seek help again, would you come back to our program?

1 *No, definitely not*	2 *No, I don't think so*	3 *Yes, I think so*	4 *Yes, definitely*

Source: Attkisson (1979, 1989, 1990, 2013). Instrument reproduced with permission of C. Clifford Attkisson.

GUIDED PRACTICE EXERCISE 14.1

Constructing a Client Satisfaction Survey

In a small group (three to four students) create a brief client satisfaction survey that could be used to assess clients' perceptions of how beneficial counseling was for them. Before developing the questions to be included in your survey, decide as a group on the counseling setting (clinical, school, college, or vocational) where this survey will be used. Also consider the age of the clients you likely would serve in this setting.

Global Measures of Outcomes

Global measures of counseling outcomes are used to assess clients across a broad spectrum of diagnoses. Many common disorders include general symptoms that can easily be detected by a global measure instrument (Leibert, 2006). These are especially useful to counselors who work with clients who may be dually diagnosed or present for counseling with issues that do not reach the clinical threshold for a formal diagnosis to be made. Global measure instruments typically include normative information that can be used to compare a client's results to those of individuals who have sought counseling services in the past as well as those who have never received counseling services. Counselors can compare how clients score in relation to these norm groups and assess whether progress is being made. In addition, these measures allow counselors to assess symptom reduction in clients.

Two global outcome measures frequently used in clinical practice are the **Symptom Checklist-90-Revised** (SC-90-R; Derogatis, 1994) and the **Outcome Questionnaire-45.2** (OQ-45.2; Lambert et al., 1996). The SC-90-R is a self-report instrument that is used to evaluate a broad range of psychological problems and symptoms of psychopathology as well as measure the progress and outcome of mental health treatment. Scores are obtained along nine primary symptom scales and three global distress indices (see Table 14.2). Due to the strong reliability and validity of the instrument, it is widely used in both clinical practice and research. The OQ-45.2 is another self-report measure that provides clinicians with feedback related to their clients' progress and predictable outcomes. In addition to an overall composite score, the OQ-45.2 provides scores along three subscales that address depression and anxiety (Symptom Distress scale), problems in relationships (Interpersonal Relations scale), and levels of conflict in isolation and interpersonal relationships (Social Role scale). According to Doerfler, Addis, and Moran (2002), the OQ-45.2 meets psychometric standards that warrant its usage in both practice and research settings.

Specific Measures of Outcomes

When counselors are more interested in assessing client progress in relation to specific treatment goals, a more narrowly focused instrument is often preferred. These instruments are designed to assess the presence of symptoms of a particular disorder. An example of a

Table 14.2 Symptom Checklist-90-Revised (SCL-90-R) Scales

Symptom Scales

Somatization (SOM)

Obsessive-Compulsive (O-C)

Interpersonal Sensitivity (I-S)

Depression (DEP)

Anxiety (ANX)

Hostility (HOS)

Phobic Anxiety (PHOB)

Paranoid Ideation (PAR)

Psychoticism (PSY)

Global Indices

Global Severity Index (GSI)—designed to measure overall psychological distress

Positive Symptom Distress Index (PSDI)—designed to measure the intensity of symptoms

Positive Symptom Total (PST)—Reports number of self-reported symptoms

specific outcome measure is the Beck Depression Inventory-II (BDI-II; Beck, Steer, & Brown, 1996). Because these instruments focus on a single outcome only, they are typically more sensitive to change and can be used throughout the counseling process to monitor client improvement. These measures are often used to assess treatment progress and symptom relief as counseling services are being provided.

School-Based Outcome Assessment

Although the aforementioned outcome measures are widely applied in a number of clinical and other counseling settings, they are seldom used by school counselors in school settings. Even though these measures are not routinely used, the school counselor must still collect data related to outcomes. As noted in the *ASCA National Model*, "counselors analyze student achievement and counseling-program-related data to evaluate the counseling program, conduct research on activity outcomes, and discover gaps that exist between different groups of students that need to be addressed" (American School Counselor Association, 2003, p. 44). To meet this practice standard, school counselors can use a number of sources of data. In addition to student achievement data (grade point averages, test scores), school counselors can look at attendance records, behavioral records, and referrals for disciplinary action. Other stakeholders can also be assessed to determine their perceptions of the success of a particular program. Administrators, teachers, parents, and community members can each provide feedback the school counselor could find useful in evaluating the effectiveness of a school guidance program and making changes necessary to address stakeholder concerns.

STRATEGIES FOR CONDUCTING OUTCOME RESEARCH

The assessment methods discussed in the previous section are useful to counselors evaluating the success of their work with clients. However, this is not the only assessment of counseling outcomes that takes place. Counselors also may find themselves engaged in research efforts to document the effectiveness of various treatment approaches. As the counseling profession continues to build its research foundation and identify strong, empirically based treatment approaches, counseling outcome research becomes increasingly important. Counseling outcome research can be carried out in a number of ways. Kazdin (1991) outlines seven research strategies that can be employed to assess treatment outcomes. The choice as to which strategy to use will depend on the needs of the counselor and the specific question of interest to be addressed. The strategies identified by Kazdin are the treatment-package, dismantling, constructive, parametric, comparative outcome, client-counselor variation, and process (see Table 14.3). A brief description of each of these strategies is presented in the following section.

Treatment-Package Strategy

In the treatment-package strategy the counselor attempts to determine whether a particular treatment approach has an effect for a specific clinical problem or disorder. To achieve this goal, a counselor compares the results of a group of clients treated with a particular approach (e.g., cognitive behavioral therapy) to the results collected from an

Table 14.3 Treatment Outcome Research

Treatment Outcome Research Strategy	Research Question Addressed
Treatment-Package	Does treatment work?
Dismantling	What part of treatment works?
Constructive	What could be added to an effective treatment to make it even better?
Parametric	What element of treatment could be changed to make treatment work better?
Comparative Outcome	Which treatment approach is best?
Client-Counselor Variation	With which type of counselor or client is treatment most likely to be effective?
Process	How does the process of treatment impact outcome?

Source: Adapted from Kazdin (1991).

established control group. The participants in the control group receive no treatment. Often these control group participants are potential clients who are on a waiting list to see a counselor. Except for the treatment received, the counselor does not manipulate any other conditions or clients variables. At the end of the study period, the counselor compares the results of the treatment and control groups. Any difference noted between the groups is called a **treatment effect**. Using the treatment-package evaluation strategy, a counselor is able to address the question of whether the application of a treatment approach is more effective than receiving no treatment at all.

Dismantling Strategy

The dismantling strategy is used to identify the specific components of a treatment approach responsible for therapeutic success after the approach has been determined effective (Plante, 2011). To conduct a dismantling research study, the counselor establishes multiple treatment groups. Each group receives a different aspect of the treatment approach. Some may receive the entire treatment condition, while others may receive only a partial variation of the approach. For example, a counselor could use the dismantling strategy to determine which components of an inpatient substance abuse rehabilitation program are most effective in helping clients. One group may receive the complete treatment package and be exposed to each and every treatment intervention the program offers, another group may participate in all that the program offers except for psychoeducational groups, while a third group may not participate in individual therapy sessions with a counselor. Through this design, the counselor is able to identify which components of the inpatient rehabilitation program have therapeutic value and which might be dropped in the future. If similar outcomes are achieved by clients who participate in the entire program and those who participate in activities except for psychoeducational groups, the decision may be made to remove these groups from the treatment protocol.

Constructive Strategy

The constructive strategy is used to assess the impact that inclusion of additional treatment components might have on a treatment approach already deemed effective. In other words, this research design helps counselors identify how existing programs might be made even better. A treatment group receiving the established treatment approach is compared to another group receiving the established approach as well as an additional treatment component. These groups are compared to see if the added component results in any significant increase in therapeutic effectiveness. To help you understand the utility of the constructive strategy, consider the treatment of adult attention deficit hyperactivity disorder (ADHD). Although research (Advokat, 2010) shows that the use of stimulant medications is effective in improving attention and concentration of adults with ADHD, the combination of cognitive behavioral therapy (CBT) and medication has proved to be an even more effective treatment strategy (Davidson, 2008; S. P. McDermott, 2010). By adding new components and then evaluating the impact of these additions, counselors are able to provide the best possible care and treatment to their clients.

Parametric Strategy

In the parametric strategy the counselor attempts to identify the impact that changes in treatment parameters have on the overall effectiveness of a treatment. A **parameter** is the quantity or magnitude of a treatment component. Instead of determining whether the presence of a particular treatment component is effective, the goal in this design is to determine the optimal amount of the component that is needed to produce a successful outcome. To design a parametric study, a counselor would compare two groups of clients that each are exposed to the same treatment intervention. The only difference between the two groups is the amount of the treatment intervention to which they are exposed. At the end of the evaluation period, the groups are compared to see what results varying the levels of treatment exposure had on the clients.

For example, Kazdin (2001) notes that Power Solving Skills Training (PSST-P) has shown to decrease deviant behavior and increase prosocial behavior in children diagnosed with conduct disorder. Employing a parametric strategy, a counselor could identify the optimal number of sessions required for this treatment approach to be successful. For some strategies and interventions, it may be that clients need to be exposed to a greater amount of the treatment component before successful outcomes can be achieved.

Comparative Outcome Strategy

The comparative outcome study is used when the counselor wants to compare two or more treatments to determine which approach is most effective. For example, would a counselor be more effective in treating a client's social anxiety using cognitive techniques, behavioral techniques, or a combination of the two (CBT)? A separate treatment group would be established for each condition. At the end of the study period, outcome results would be compared to determine what the most effective treatment approach was. The comparative outcome strategy can be used as an exploratory approach when the counselor does not have any existing evidence to suggest which approach would be more effective. Although this approach is most often used in exploratory inquiries, it also can be used to compare a number of approaches that have existing empirical support for their use. Such a design would be employed to determine the best approach among several effective approaches.

Client-Counselor Variation Strategy

The client-counselor variation strategy allows counselors to assess the impact that changes in certain client and/or counselor variables might have on overall treatment outcomes. Even treatment approaches that have proved to be effective may not always result in positive therapeutic outcomes. A number of individual differences could affect how well a treatment is delivered and received. For example, an experienced counselor may be more successful using a treatment approach than one who is a novice in the field or who has limited experience using the approach. Similarly, client motivation plays a pivotal role in determining how successful counseling will be. Using this research design, counselors are able to ascertain how individual variables (ethnicity, race, gender, age, experience) or combinations of variables (counselor's age and client's motivation) might impact the overall effectiveness of a treatment approach. For example, consider a situation in which treatment is only effective when the counselor and client are of the same gender. In a study of Finnish clients who were being treated for substance abuse–related issues, Kuusisto and Artkoski (2013) found that female clients who worked with female counselors expressed a greater sense of overall satisfaction with their therapy.

Process Strategy

The final outcome research design is the process strategy. In this design, counselors attempt to identify which aspects of the counseling process are associated with positive treatment outcomes. Here, counselors focus more on therapeutic conditions rather than specific treatment components. For example, does a strong therapeutic alliance predict successful outcomes? This line of research is helpful because it identifies certain conditions that are conducive to clients benefiting from the counseling process. Guided Practice Exercise 14.2 asks you to consider how you could implement these various outcome research designs in your work with clients.

GUIDED PRACTICE EXERCISE 14.2

Selecting Outcome Research Designs

Imagine that you are a marriage and family counselor and you have recently been asked to start a premarital counseling group for young couples. Conceptually, you envision the purpose of the group to be helping couples build a strong and healthy relationship that will enable them to have a stable and satisfying marriage. Choose two of the outcome research strategies discussed in this chapter and describe how they can help you not only construct the most effective group program, but also evaluate its overall effectiveness.

PROGRAM EVALUATION

In addition to helping evaluate individual client success, counselors also can use their assessment skills to evaluate existing programs that serve clients. Whereas research is intended to help build a knowledge base, evaluation is intended to guide the use and application of a program. When we use the term **program**, we are doing so to describe the focus of counselors' evaluation efforts. Programs can include any type of action or intervention designed to improve outcomes for whole communities, specific sectors (e.g., agencies, schools, work settings), or specific client populations (e.g., adjudicated youth, individuals who are suicidal, clients presenting with career concerns). There are many different programs offered to help people with their mental health and wellness. In your career as a counselor, you likely will find yourself participating in a number of counseling programs. For each of these programs, evaluation is an important element.

Effective treatment programs are the result of advanced planning, intentional decision making, and a sound program evaluation strategy. The **program evaluation** process allows counselors to systematically collect and analyze information about a program and determine its merit, worth, or significance. Evaluations are

Table 14.4   Common Counseling Programs

Psychotherapy (individual and group)

Psychoeducational

Medication management

Day treatment

Intensive outpatient

Inpatient hospitalization

Medically monitored detoxification

Community outreach

Advocacy

Prevention

typically carried out using established research methods and allow for the collection of information from multiple sources using a variety of data-gathering methods. There are several reasons why counselors might conduct a program evaluation (see Table 14.4). Generally speaking, though, the process of program evaluation allows counselors to make informed decisions about the efficiency, effectiveness, and impact of a counseling program. According to the Centers for Disease Control and Prevention (2012), a strong evaluation approach should ensure that the following questions are answered:

- What will be evaluated?
- What aspects of the program will be considered when judging program performance?
- What standards must be reached for the program to be considered successful?
- What evidence will be used to indicate how the program has performed?
- What conclusions regarding program performance are justified by comparing the available evidence to the selected standards?
- How will the lessons learned from the inquiry be used to improve program effectiveness?

When it comes to evaluating counseling programs, there is not a standard template that describes what a program evaluation should look like. The program evaluation plan a counselor uses in a federally funded clinical mental health center would look markedly different than the plan used by a counselor in a private practice setting or a school counselor working with sixth through eighth graders at the local middle school. In the following section we will look at the steps taken by counselors to form the basis of a sound program evaluation.

BASIC ELEMENTS OF PROGRAM EVALUATION

Program evaluation is a process. Through this process counselors gather information, analyze that information, and make decisions based on the information gathered. This process generally includes six connected steps, which are ordered in such a way that the information gathered in earlier steps can be used to guide future steps. The steps are engaging stakeholders, describing the program, focusing the evaluation design, gathering credible evidence, justifying conclusions, and using results to improve services.

Engaging stakeholders. For a program to be successful, there needs to be community buy-in. The individuals and consumer groups who will be involved in, or affected by, the program should be consulted throughout the development process to ensure that the program designed is one that will be well received by the community as a whole. Consumer groups may include mental health providers, secondary related agencies (those who make referrals to mental health services), high-risk individuals (those most likely to participate in these programs), community and civic groups, community leaders and government officials, and members of the community at large. One way to engage the community is to conduct a needs assessment. The perspective of numerous consumer groups is typically taken into account in a needs assessment. As a result, a needs assessment can be a great way to gauge the opinions, assumptions, key issues, needs, and assets of a defined community.

The information obtained through a needs assessment allows counselors to make informed programming decisions based on the service gaps, needs, and priorities of a given community (see Guided Practice Exercise 14.3). When conducting a needs assessment, counselors must differentiate between needs, wants, and desires. A need is not something we hope will happen or something that would make our lives more convenient; these are wants and desires. By contrast, a need represents the gap between the current situation and the optimal situation. For example, whereas an individual may *need* a job to help support a family, an individual may *desire* a job that pays really well, has excellent benefits, and offers a flexible schedule.

Ideally, the information gathered through a needs assessment should come from various groups using a combination of both quantitative and qualitative methods of data collection. Focus group interviews, public forums, client interviews, community surveys, and secondary data analysis are all examples of data-gathering tools that can be employed by counselors conducting a needs assessment. To ensure the validity of the information collected, counselors need to make sure they ask the right questions appropriate to each consumer group. Knowing when the services are needed and should be offered is information that should be obtained from service providers and high-risk individuals. On the other hand, determining what zoning issues may need to be addressed related to the building of a community mental health center in a particular part of town is a question that should be posed to local officials.

Although needs assessments are most often thought of as the preliminary stage of a program evaluation, they can occur at other times in the process as well. For example, a needs assessment might be a good way to determine whether the need for a particular program still exists or if changes in the community may have rendered the program obsolete. A program that is designed to help individuals seek employment may be needed when the economy is sluggish, but the demand may wane when the economy is performing well. A needs assessment could help counselors determine whether programs should shift focus or disband entirely.

GUIDED PRACTICE EXERCISE 14.3

Planning a Community Needs Assessment

Imagine that you have been asked by your administrator to create a wellness program for students at your school. The administrator has read that holistic wellness is positively correlated to increased academic performance and would like you to use your newly created program to help improve student test scores. Trusting in your abilities as a counselor, the administrator leaves it up to you to determine the focus and structure of the new school wellness program. For your first step, you decide to conduct a needs assessment. How would you identify the needs of the school community? Who would you include in the assessment? What types of data collection methods would you use to collect the information you need?

Another way to engage stakeholders is to create an asset map. Asset mapping is an activity that often is performed in concert with a needs assessment. Whereas a needs assessment identifies the service gaps in a community, an asset map helps to identify the strengths and resources of a community. Assets need not be tangible items only. A community's resources might also include people, associations, and institutional customs. The results of a needs assessment and an asset map can be compared to better understand how the existing resources in a community can be used to help counselors in structuring programs aimed at addressing current needs. Asset mapping is designed to promote connections or relationships between individuals, between individuals and organizations, and between organizations. An understanding of these relationships will allow you to see where resources are located and how they can best be accessed (see Case Illustration 14.2). Doing so engages community members and enables them to become invested in seeing the program become successful.

CASE ILLUSTRATION   14.2

A local community mental health center is developing an afterschool program for at-risk adolescents. The aim of the program is to provide these youth with a safe place to go after school where they can talk to staff counselors and learn how to make better choices in life. The mental health center has faced many budget cuts recently, so the counselor placed in charge of setting up this new program decides to construct an asset map for the community to see what resources may already be available. She finds that there are two philanthropic foundations located in the community that might be willing to help provide financial assistance. She also learns through the chamber of commerce that local businesses would be interested in partnering with the mental health center to provide computers, school supplies, and athletic equipment for the youth to use in the afterschool program. Although internal funding was not available, the counselor was able to identify existing resources in the community and establish connections with those resources to help make the program more of a reality.

Describing the program. For counselors to be able to assess whether a program has been successful, there first must be an agreed-upon description of what the program should look like and what it is intended to accomplish. The accuracy of an evaluation depends on the amount of detail placed in the description of the program at the onset. Counselors should determine the specific need the program has been designed to address, the goals and objectives of the program, the activities to be included in the program as well as a rationale for their inclusion, and the logical outcomes that could be expected by participants and other stakeholders (Joint Committee on Standards for Educational Evaluation, 1994).

Focusing the evaluation design. Once the program has been defined and objective goals have been established, counselors can turn their attention to developing an evaluation design. This evaluation design will serve the basic purpose of answering the question: Does this program work? When it comes to evaluating the program, there are two basic types of assessments that can be conducted: formative and summative. Formative evaluations are used to assess the process through which a program is being administered. Specifically, formative evaluations are used to evaluate how individual program activities are being delivered and whether the program is operating and being implemented as originally planned. This type of evaluation is useful as it provides information that allows counselors to

- paint a clear and compelling picture of the population targeted with each strategy,
- reach important target audiences and stakeholders,
- provide data for program improvement efforts, and
- distribute the information through as many channels as possible to reach the target audience. (Substance Abuse and Mental Health Services Administration, 2013)

Counselors conducting formative evaluations use more qualitative data collection methods. Interviews and participant self-report measures are frequently employed strategies.

The results of a formative evaluation allow counselors to see how well the program is resonating with the intended target population, identify barriers that may be preventing the successful implementation of the program, and determine what structural changes may need to be made to a program to better meet the needs of the target audience. Structural changes that may need to be made include adding or eliminating staff members, changing service delivery hours, switching locations, or improving the marketing and publicity of the program.

In addition to assessing how well the program is functioning, counselors also will need to assess the overall efficacy of the program. In other words, did the program have a positive impact for its clients? The process of summative evaluation is used when the counselor is interested in assessing how well a program achieved its goals at the end of the program operating cycle. Whereas the results of a formative evaluation are typically used to determine how to best revise, modify, or improve an existing program, summative evaluation results are used to help determine whether a program should be adopted, continued, or modified for improvement (see Guided Practice Exercise 14.4). Since the results of a summative evaluation are often used to establish the impact of an intervention or program, data are collected using quantitative rather than qualitative methods. Therapeutic outcomes are compared to established standards to

Table 14.5   Outcome Measures Collected in a Summative Evaluation

Changes in attitudes, knowledge, or behavior

Changes in morbidity or mortality rates

Number of people participating in or being served by a program

Cost-benefit analysis

Cost-effectiveness analysis

Changes in policies

Impact assessments

determine how well the program achieved its goals. Examples of therapeutic outcomes that can be assessed as part of a summative evaluation are included in Table 14.5.

When developing a program evaluation plan, counselors should incorporate both formative and summative evaluation methods as the combination of the two provides counselors with ongoing feedback related to the overall functioning of the program as well as an opportunity to review overall progress on major program goals and objectives. Case Illustration 14.3 provides an example of how this integration of evaluation methods can effectively be combined.

CASE ILLUSTRATION   14.3

A counselor is running a support group for children of divorced parents. At any given time, the group includes 8–10 children between the ages of 10 and 13. The goals of the group are to (1) minimize the emotional and behavioral problems the children experience related to the divorce in their families, (2) increase the children's ability to identify and appropriately express their divorce-related feelings, and (3) increase the children's coping abilities affected by familial divorce. Conducting a formative evaluation, the counselor could speak to the children individually after group one day and ask how they feel about their participation in the group. Questions the counselor might ask include the following: What do you see as being the best part of this group? What do you see as being the worst part? Do you believe the group is helping you better manage your feelings related to your parents' divorce? As a summative evaluation, the counselor could assess students using objective measures related to the program goals. Instruments like the Reynolds Child Depression Scale-2nd Edition and the Children's Coping Questionnaire could be used to quantitatively assess how participation in the program is helping children cope more effectively with the familial divorce.

GUIDED PRACTICE EXERCISE 14.4

Formative Versus Summative Evaluation

As a school counselor you recently established an anti-bullying program at your school. The program includes the creation of a safe zone where students can report bullying behavior, an afterschool group for students who have been victims of bullying, and an anti-bullying classroom guidance program which includes three video-based lessons on bullying behavior. Identify two methods you could use to collect formative assessment data and two methods you could use to collect summative assessment data. Which approach do you anticipate being the more difficult to implement?

Gathering credible evidence. For both the formative and summative evaluations, data collected need to be credible for valid interpretations to be made. Determining the credibility of the data obtained can be challenging. Counselors should gather as much information as possible before reaching a conclusion to ensure that they are fully informed. By using multiple sources of data, counselors can determine whether the individual reports support one another. A client may report an improvement in mood, but the results of a Beck Depression Inventory-II and discussion with the client's spouse indicate that an improvement in mood might not really exist. As you begin collecting information, you should ask yourself the following questions: Do these data make sense? Does this individual have anything to gain from presenting false information? What is the treatment history of this client? Are there any inherent biases in the data collection method I used? Intentionality will help you focus on collecting and interpreting information that is both accurate and credible.

Justifying conclusions. Following the collection and analysis of data, counselors need to be sure that the claims they make regarding a program are supported by the available data. Conclusions need to be linked to evidence collected. For a counselor to say that a program had a positive impact on a client's functioning, there needs to be substantive evidence to support that claim. When deriving conclusions counselors should be cautious. For one, conclusions need to be generalized appropriately. Counselors should limit their conclusions to situations, time periods, contexts, and purposes for which the findings are applicable (Joint Committee on Standards for Educational Evaluation, 1994). Additionally, recommendations made regarding the operation of a program or its impact should be consistent with conclusions reached and supported by existing data. When counselors are able to justify their conclusions with available data, they are operating in an ethical manner.

Using results to improve services. At this stage of the evaluation process, counselors are ready to share their results with the appropriate stakeholders. A report summarizing the findings of the program evaluation should be disseminated so all can see how the program performed and whether it ultimately proved to be effective. Keep in mind that the results of a program evaluation are intended to be action-oriented. They should inform the next stage of the process, which includes the modification or continued offering of a program. If the results indicate that the clients did not find their counselor to be particularly helpful, this situation needs to be examined and substitution for a new counselor should be made before the next set of clients come through the program.

CHALLENGES IN CONDUCTING PROGRAM EVALUATIONS

Conducting a program evaluation is not without its challenges. Issues related to the counseling personnel involved in the evaluation process, logistics related to the instrumentation and data collection methods selected, and the support of program consumers and stakeholders all can prove problematic to conducting an effective program evaluation.

Counseling personnel issues. In terms of the counseling personnel involved in the evaluation process, personal biases could skew results obtained. A counselor may have a vested interest in the program being successful and may focus on results that affirm the effectiveness of the program while neglecting or failing to include results that may indicate the program is not as effective as anticipated. Additionally, human error could play a role in the process. Counselors may make errors in analyzing and interpreting data. While these mistakes are inadvertent, they still change the overall results and perceptions of the viability of a program. To avoid contaminating results, counselors should make sure they are not letting their own personal biases influence their professionalism and double-check their work to make sure errors in interpretation were not made, especially when results indicate a significant impact on program participants.

Data collection logistics. Counselors should carefully review how data are collected to ensure that data are credible and valid. Were psychometrically sound instruments used? Were any standardized administration protocols followed? Did the information collected relate to program goals and objectives in a way that would allow for the determination of whether they have been met? These are all questions counselors will need to address for themselves so that they can be confident that the results they present are accurate.

Consumer and stakeholder support. For a program evaluation to be successful, there must be a certain level of investment among those who will be affected by a program. When these parties are invested, they tend to provide richer feedback that can be used either to develop a more targeted program or to make specific changes to an existing program. When individuals are not involved in the process of determining the scope and direction of the program, they have less of an investment in its overall success. Consequently, counselors should make a conscious effort to solicit feedback from multiple stakeholders and design a program that is both responsive to the needs of the community and established to make a sustained positive impact.

KEYSTONES

- Assessing client outcomes is an important component of the counseling process that helps demonstrate accountability.
- The most important outcome in counseling is change. Counselors should continuously assess their work with clients to ensure that they keep working toward creating positive change for their clients.
- Evaluating the impact of a counseling approach goes beyond pure statistical significance. To document treatment effectiveness, counselors should report measures of effect size as it refers more to the magnitude of the change.

- Counselors can use outcome assessment in their own work with clients to gain insight into what works with individual clients. Outcome measures counselors might use include satisfaction surveys, global outcome measures, and specific outcome measures.
- Several strategies for conducting counseling outcome research exist. Each strategy is designed to address a specific research question.
- Program evaluation is becoming an increasingly common practice for counselors. Through program evaluation, counselors are able to develop targeted programs that are responsive to the needs of a community and appropriate for the resources and potential consumers in the community.
- When conducting program evaluation, counselors need to be aware of several potential factors that might prove challenging throughout the evaluation process. Awareness of these potential issues will allow counselors to be proactive and minimize the impact they might have on the overall evaluation of the program.

KEY TERMS

effect size

outcome

Outcome Questionnaire-45.2

parameter

program

program evaluation

Symptom Checklist-90-Revised

treatment effect

ADDITIONAL RESOURCES

- Center for Mental Healthcare and Outcomes Research

  http://www.hsrd.research.va.gov/centers/cemhor.cfm

This U.S. Department of Veterans Affairs website has information on a good deal of policy-relevant and clinically relevant health services research.

- *Counseling Outcome Research and Evaluation*

  http://www.sagepub.com/journals/Journal201967/manuscriptSubmission

This is the official journal of the Association for Assessment in Counseling and Research.

- Ronald H. Fredrickson Center for School Counseling Outcome Research & Evaluation

  http://www.umass.edu/schoolcounseling/surveys-for-program-evaluation-and-review.php

This site includes a variety of resources and sample assessment instruments that school counselors can use to conduct program evaluations.

Student Study Site: Visit the Student Study Site at **www.sagepub.com/watson** to access additional study tools, including quizzes, web resources, and journal articles.

Assessment Issues With Diverse Populations

LEARNING OBJECTIVES

After reading this chapter, you will be able to

- Explain diversity
- Discuss issues in multicultural assessment
- Describe the goal of culture-fair tests and identify current culture-fair tests used in the counseling profession
- Discuss issues in addressing individuals with disabilities
- Identify standards for assessment for working with diverse populations

$\mathbf{U}$p to this point in the textbook, we have discussed the importance of assessment in the field of counseling, the areas evaluated through these assessments, and most recently, the application of assessments related to various environments. By this time, you have hopefully identified the fundamental importance of assessment in the fields of counseling and education. What also may be obvious based on the previous chapters is the diversity that exists with the assessment tools available in these settings. From the different structure of available assessment tools, to the constructs that the assessments measure, and even the environments in which the assessments are administered, thousands of assessments are available for potential implementation.

In this chapter, we will focus on elements of diversity, not necessarily in terms of the specific assessments but in terms of the populations to which tests may be administered. In this chapter, our goal is to illustrate the complexity of cultural diversity and the impact of this diversity on conducting relevant testing procedures. Specifically, we will cover potential biases associated with the assessment of diverse individuals either through the structure of the test or from the test taker or test evaluator; attempts to develop culturally unbiased assessments, including illustration of a selection of these tests; considerations associated with testing individuals with disabilities; and standards linked with the delivery of these assessments. Although cultural diversity is a complex phenomenon worthy of its own textbook, this will support you in evaluating the elements of assessments and determining the credibility of the results regarding the construct of measurement and the particular client or clients of interest.

UNDERSTANDING DIVERSITY

Variance in cultural characteristics within the population results in the presence of complex personal identities in the social science field. Although differences regarding primary characteristics of culture (e.g., race, ethnicity, sex, religion) have historically been the focus of research studies and education on cultural diversity, Fischer (2012) assesses that **culture** and therefore **diversity** extend far beyond primary characteristics to other factors such as personal experiences. Adding to characteristics of race, ethnicity, sex, and religion other factors such as gender, age, disability status, presence of a mental illness, and military status, for example, has the potential to influence the ways in which individuals think, believe, and behave. When considering the impact that these differences have on individuals, it is clear that diversity exists in the ways in which individuals view and understand the world.

The complexities of individual identity associated with the blending of cultural variables (e.g., middle-aged, African American female) result in individual formations of a worldview. Johnson, Hill, and Cohen (2011) argue that **worldview**, the totality of psychological, thought, and emotional components of behaviors and decision making, comprises six fundamental components. Specifically, Johnson et al. note that research has defined these components as ontology (theology, cosmology, and metaphysics), epistemology (reasoning), semiotics (symbols and gestures), axiology (values and ethics), teleology (beliefs about afterlife), and praxeology (social norms). Although specific cultural characteristics may appear to affect specific worldview components, the presence of multiple cultural variables in a single identity is likely to increase worldview complexity. For an example of the types of differences in individuals from the same ethnicity, see Case Illustration 15.1.

CASE ILLUSTRATION   15.1

NaPing is a 45-year-old Chinese national who has lived in the United States for the last 10 years. He spent 10 years in prison in China due to his role in the rebellion in Tiananmen Square in 1989. Recently, NaPing was successful in becoming a naturalized citizen of the United States and has now renounced his Chinese citizenship. NaPing identifies as a gay male, a Buddhist and Taoist, and he works in the computer industry. He is not currently in a relationship.

Carl is a 21-year-old U.S. citizen who was born in the United States and is of Chinese ethnicity. His grandparents were immigrants to the United States; he and his parents were born here. Carl currently is a sergeant in the U.S. Marines and has been deployed to Afghanistan two times. Prior to enlisting in the Marines he worked in the computer industry. Carl identifies as heterosexual, is married to his childhood sweetheart, and has a 1-year-old daughter. Carl identifies as a Buddhist.

While both men share some commonalities, they also have many important differences. These cultural dynamics would need to be considered when choosing an assessment. Complete Guided Practice Exercise 15.1 to explore these dynamics in more detail.

GUIDED PRACTICE EXERCISE 15.1

For this exercise, please get into pairs or small groups for a discussion. Now that you have read about NaPing and Carl, what are some of the possible cultural dynamics they might share? What are some clear differences that might shape their views about the world differently?

POSSIBLE ANSWERS

Similarities: They both share Chinese ethnicity, religious practice in Buddhism, and U.S. citizenship (although NaPing has only recently acquired that status). They may both have some possible issues with trauma due to their roles in conflict (NaPing as a protester in China who was then incarcerated, Carl as a veteran of the war in Afghanistan). Both are male and both have worked in the computer industry.

Differences: English is probably NaPing's second language, whereas English is probably Carl's first. Carl may or may not also know Chinese. They are of different ages, and their primary development occurred in different historical periods, which can play a role in worldview. They also have different sexual orientations and relationship statuses. They also may experience differences in practice of their religious beliefs. NaPing formed his Buddhist practices as a citizen of China and also practices Taoism, whereas Carl developed his Buddhist practice in the United States and does not identify also as a Taoist.

The fluidity of many aspects of cultural identity and merging of competing elements of self are two elements that affect an individual's worldview. According to Silva, Campbell, and Wright (2012), instances occur when two conflicting cultural variables must be reconciled by developing a third, unique, cultural variable, also known as **assimilation**. Although individuals may be forced to assimilate to the blending of cultural characteristics, the compromise between ideals may also be made voluntarily by the individual. For example, an individual with strong Catholic ideals may marry an individual of Jewish faith. Given the differences in the fundamental elements of these religions, the couple may compromise to develop religious beliefs which are independent of the two ideals.

Whereas assimilation results in the development of a new cultural identity, not all culturally diverse interactions result in substantial changes in an individual's concept of self. **Acculturation**, a process in which individuals encounter culturally diverse characteristics beyond their own identity, includes assimilation or negotiation of new cultural ideals, varying integration of components of the newly introduced cultural characteristics, and in some cases no change in cultural identity. As Yoon et al. (2013) note, the uncertainty associated with variable rates of acculturation produces within-group differences and further complicates cultural diversity. The uniqueness of individual cultural identity and worldview caused by the complexity of cultural characteristics results in the need for considering the ways that individuals are assessed (Association for Assessment in Counseling and Education, 2012).

ISSUES IN MULTICULTURAL ASSESSMENT

Diversity in culture and worldview has caused inaccuracies in assessment outcomes. According to Schroeder, Plata, Fullwood, Price, and Dyer Sennette (2013), research outcomes have demonstrated decreased performance among culturally diverse groups on a variety of assessments, resulting in overpathology of symptoms or underdiagnosis of disorders. As a result of these challenges in accurate assessment outcomes, professional standards have been developed that highlight expectations for integrating aspects of diversity in assessment.

The Association for Assessment in Counseling and Education (2012), now known as the Association for Assessment and Research in Counseling, notes that the first step in developing assessments which are applicable to diverse populations is awareness of where biases exist. **Bias** occurs when aspects of the test or test delivery unfairly penalize test takers due to personal characteristics. Whereas some biases may be more evident, other biases may be more hidden. The following sections provide information regarding three specific areas of bias: the test, the test taker, and the examiner. In order to ensure that the results of the assessment are a clear reflection of the test taker's performance on a specific construct, these areas must be evaluated.

Test Bias

Content bias. In Chapter 4, you learned about different types of validity. One of the questions you will want to ask yourself as you select an assessment is: Does this test measure what it purports to measure for examinees across different cultural groups? There are several ways to evaluate test bias, including content validity, criterion-related validity, and construct validity. According to C. R. Reynolds, Lowe, and Saenz (1999),

> An item or subscale of a test is considered to be biased in content when it is demonstrated to be relatively more difficult for members of one group than another when the general ability level of the groups being compared is held constant and no reasonable theoretical rationale exists to explain group difference on the item or subscale in question. (p. 564)

When **content bias** occurs, testing materials are more familiar to one group than another. There are several sources that may account for content bias, including but not limited to test language (i.e., wording of questions is unfamiliar), test items asking for information that those from a different culture may not have had equal opportunity to learn, lack of clarity in testing instructions, or inappropriate and faulty scoring of the items.

Content bias should be addressed during the development of the instrument, thus you always want to evaluate the procedures the authors used to create the assessment and check to see if **differential item functioning (DIF)** analysis was conducted. DIF is a phenomenon that occurs when individuals have a similar ability on the construct being assessed, but score differently due to the format of specific items (H. J. Rogers, 2005). Specifically, test developers use DIF analysis to look for DIF items (i.e., items in which people from different groups with the same underlying ability have a different probability of giving certain responses due to group membership) in order to evaluate equivalence in item content across groups that vary by culture.

Predictive bias. Test bias can also be evaluated in terms of criterion-related validity. In Chapter 4, you learned that criterion-related validity assesses whether a test reflects a certain set of abilities. To measure the criterion validity of an instrument, test scores are compared to a known standard or outcome measure. This standard or outcome measure is referred to as a *criterion*. A criterion is typically a score on a separate test or instrument that purports to measure the same construct or set of abilities as the test in question. Under the heading of criterion-related validity, you learned that there are two different approaches to obtaining validity evidence: concurrent validity and predictive validity. Furthermore, you learned that a sound criterion is free from bias.

Predictive bias concerns the degree to which scores predict the criterion measure performance equally well among different groups. For example, in Chapter 8 you learned that SAT scores along with high school GPA are used to predict performance in undergraduate studies, and universities often use SAT scores as part of admission decisions. The SAT may be nonbiased in criterion-related validity if it predicts freshman GPA equally well for freshmen from different ethnic backgrounds. However, if we found the opposite (i.e., test scores are not equally predictive of an outcome for two groups) and the SAT predicts freshman GPA better for some groups compared to others, then we might question whether the SAT has predictive test bias. Test developers should report both concurrent and predictive validity among different groups, especially when results are being used to make decisions about individuals from a given culture. According to Standard 7.1 in the *Standards for Educational and Psychological Testing*,

> When credible research reports that test scores differ in meaning across examinee subgroups for the type of test in question, then to the extent reasonable, the same forms of validity evidence collected for the examinee population as a whole should also be collected for the relevant subgroup. Subgroups may be found to differ with respect to appropriateness of test content, internal structure of test responses, the relation of test scores to other variables, or the response processes employed by the individual examinees. Any such findings should receive due consideration in the interpretation and use of scores as well as in subsequent test revisions. (American Educational Research Association, American Psychological Association, & National Council on Measurement in Education, 1999, p. 80)

Bias in internal structure. Counselors should be cautious about cultural bias that may be evident in the internal structure of assessments. **Internal structure** refers to the correlations between items and the total test score and describes the pattern of correlations. Bias in internal structure occurs when the factor structures for the groups are inconsistent or scores across groups yield different relationships due to instrumentation. Because bias in internal structure may be due to norming factors, counselors must consider the norming process of the instrument. Developers of the assessment should report in the manual any differences that exist among test takers. Psychometric procedures, including evaluating item difficulties, total correlations, and factor analyses, are often used to evaluate the internal structure of tests for bias. In fact, Higgins et al. (2011) identify that failure to address the potential impact of internal bias results in either the overestimation or underestimation of an individual's performance on a measured construct. For practice in reviewing whether an assessment is biased toward a cultural group, read the case of Aaron in Case Illustration 15.2 and then participate in the Guided Practice Exercise 15.2.

CASE ILLUSTRATION   15.2

Aaron is a 15-year-old Israeli boy who recently moved to the United States when his father became the ambassador from Israel. Aaron speaks English, but it is his second language; his first is Hebrew. He was referred for testing by his school counselor after teachers noted a possible learning disorder in terms of Aaron's academic abilities. Aaron's difficulties in the classroom do not appear to be cultural, nor the result of an intellectual deficit, but rather seem to be due to an observed difficulty, possibly dyslexia. In order to properly diagnose Aaron for a learning disability, he must be given an intelligence test. The IQ test given to him was administered in English, and while it was normed on different cultural groups, the norming population did not include the Jewish or Israeli cultures.

GUIDED PRACTICE EXERCISE 15.2

Now that you have read about the different ways a test can be biased against a cultural group or an individual, and now that you have read the case about Aaron above, get into small groups or pairs and discuss whether you believe the assessment administered to Aaron was biased. Review and consider the many ways a test can be biased, and determine which ways might apply to Aaron. Back up your perceptions from the information in this chapter.

Test Taker Bias

Language Barriers. As our society becomes more multiculturally diverse, the number of nonnative English speakers continues to grow. One's **language,** the means by which either written or spoken information is communicated, is an important factor of assessment bias to consider. Overlooking this variable in the assessment process can cause harm and have damaging effects. In schools, there is a large increase in students who require special support services and have been identified as English language learners (ELL) or limited English proficient (LEP). According to the National Center for Education Statistics (2010), from 1979 to 2008, there was an increase from 3.8 to 10.9 million in the number of school-age children (5 to 17 years old) that spoke a language other than English at home. For an example of a student who might have a language barrier, see the case of Luís in Case Illustration 15.3.

CASE ILLUSTRATION 15.3

Luís is a Latino male who recently came to the United States to escape the drug violence between the cartels in his city. Luís was nearing the end of his basic education in Mexico, but U.S. educators are not sure where he might fit into the U.S. educational system. The school counselor of the school district where Luís now resides has decided to assess him on several dimensions to provide the best placement for him. Having lived in a U.S./Mexico border city, Luís speaks English fluently; however, the school counselor knows that there may be vast differences between an individual's language abilities, specifically between his expressive (speaking) and receptive (understanding when others speak) language ability. Therefore, she decides to administer both the Test of Nonverbal Intelligence (TONI-4) and another standardized assessment of intelligence that was written in English. What are your thoughts about why she may have decided to do this?

As the test administrator, you will need to be aware of the level of English proficiency that is required and whether your client has this proficiency. Even though a test may be offered in another language besides English, you want to make sure the translation has been normed. If the translated test has not been normed, then the test is not valid. If you decide to use a translator to aid in the assessment process, you must decide if a meaningful assessment can take place and consider the potential effects of using the translator when you interpret the results.

Test familiarity. A common source of bias in psychological testing is the examinee's familiarity with the materials/stimuli on the assessment. In Chapter 10, you learned about the Thematic Apperception Test, in which the examinee is shown stimulus material consisting of 31 cards (30 are black-and-white picture cards, and 1 card is blank), and the pictures are used to gather information about the examinee's drives, emotions, conflicts, and complexity of personality. The scenes on these pictures come from a Western orientation. Imagine the implications of giving this assessment to an examinee that has no experience with Western culture. As noted above and in Chapter 7, in the 1940s Cattell tried to minimize test familiarity by using geometric stimuli. However, it is important to realize that, depending on someone's educational experience, he or she might have less familiarity with geometric figures. Recall from Chapter 3 that test-retest is often used to test for method equivalence.

Motivation. One's perceived performance can have an impact on test-taking **motivation**. Duckworth, Quinn, Lynam, Loeber, and Stouthamer-Loeber (2011) reveal that factors such as paid performance or instances in which individuals were seeking employment were associated with higher perceived performance, concluding that motivation may be more a product of perceived outcome as opposed to individual effort. You can imagine that the more familiar you are with the items, the higher your test-taking motivation might be. When giving an assessment, we assume that the individual is giving his or her best effort to respond correctly and that the test taker's performance accurately represents his or her ability. As the test administrator, it is important to be aware when individuals may be representing invalid performances. For example, a client may be inattentive, distracted, or fatigued. The individual might not care about the assessment and might be disengaged from responding correctly. He or she might be malingering, which in assessment means is motivated to perform poorly and pretending to have deficits in a convincing manner. Many assessments have included items to measure one's truthfulness and reduce invalid assessments. For an example of how a test taker's external circumstances can affect his or her motivation or test performance, see the case of Mary in Case Illustration 15.4.

CASE ILLUSTRATION 15.4

Mary is a 35-year-old widowed mother of three. She was a housewife for nearly all of her marriage until she lost her husband to cancer. Mary and her family have been financially supported by the life insurance benefits of her husband. However, Mary knows she needs to find employment in order to continue providing for her children. Mary has been diligently working on her marketable skills and has recently been scheduled to undergo assessment for an employment company in order for them to help provide services and guidance to find Mary employment.

The night before Mary was to do her assessment battery, her 12-year-old son who has autism had a difficult night and Mary was up all night trying to comfort her distraught child. Mary arrived for her assessment exhausted. She found she had difficulty concentrating and had to keep reading the questions and prompts over and over again. Mary quickly became frustrated and discouraged with the process due to her fatigue. The assessment administrator noticed these changes in Mary's demeanor and upon questioning her, determined that Mary's assessment needed to be rescheduled as the results would not be valid in terms of assessing Mary's true abilities due to her current context.

Examiner Bias

In addition to considering test and test taker biases, counselors must consider **examiner biases** and how the examiner's beliefs and values may be impacting the assessment process. Even though you may select a standardized assessment that has high validity and high reliability, and was normed on the population you are working with, your bias may influence the assessment results (Liu, 2011).

Whether intentionally or unintentionally, the way you treat the individual examinee can influence their responses. As you continue through your counseling courses, it is important to consider and recognize your own biases and stereotypes when it comes to working with different people. Understanding these biases is instrumental in ensuring that participants are given an equal opportunity for optimal performance.

CULTURE-FAIR TESTS

Presence of biases in the current structure of many counseling assessments produces the potential for some cultures to have either an unfair advantage or disadvantage when it comes to scoring of the test. In fact, Carjuzaa and Ruff (2010) argue that tests based on traditional standards are contradictory to the fundamental tenets of promoting a culturally diverse society. Recognition of the inconsistencies between tests founded on the ideals of Western society and the goals of multicultural competency ultimately resulted in a movement within the counseling field to develop testing which is free of these biases. Fox and Mitchum (2013) have established that the goal of developing **culture-free tests**, which are intended to involve questions and processes providing all individuals with an equal familiarity or footing, have been most prominent in the field of intelligence testing.

Mayer and Hanges (2003) traced the development of culture-free tests to the 1930s, when intelligence test developers attempted to negate the cultural impact of language by removing it from intelligence testing. Cattell (1940), for example, proposed a culture-free intelligence test, which focused solely on fluid intelligence, while negating aspects of crystallized intelligence. By controlling against the impact of potential cultural characteristics associated with disadvantages in performance, proponents of culture-free testing argue that results will demonstrate measurement of the intelligence construct. Unfortunately for these proponents, Fox and Mitchum (2013) note that despite the idea of culture-free tests surfacing for several decades, an assessment measure which is truly free of cultural impact has not materialized.

Although attempts to develop culture-free assessments have been unsuccessful, identification of the potential deficiencies in traditional standardized tests has resulted in an increased understanding of the cultural impact of test measures. **Cultural loading**, a process in which test questions reflect an expectation of previous development of knowledge, has the potential to affect testing results. Although noting that the majority of traditional tests are culturally loaded to benefit performance of Westernized ideals, Landau, Greenberg, and Rothschild (2009) identify the potential for tests to be developed based on other cultural norms and knowledge. For example, a test could be developed to increase performance for individuals belonging to lower socioeconomic statuses if questions were asked to reflect knowledge pertinent to this cultural characteristic. A question reflecting on slang terms for housing, for example, is likely to be more culturally loaded toward lower socioeconomic classes as this population uses many terms to refer to this concept.

Awareness of the potential effects of cultural loading on test performance coupled with the inability to develop a culture-free test has resulted in a new effort within the profession to minimize the effects of culture in testing. **Culture-fair tests**, tests designed to minimize as opposed to eliminate biases in the test-taking procedures and interpretation of the results, are often synonymous with recently developed tests of intelligence. The National Center for Fair and Open Testing (www.fairtest.org) was developed in 1985 as an attempt to address the disadvantages present in testing procedures. With focus in the areas of education and employment, FairTest seeks to ensure that all tests are fair and valid, open, and used appropriately. In addition, ensuring that multiple tests are provided to students over a period of time to eliminate the potential for a single test used in isolation to have a major impact on educational success and providing alternative assessments serve as overall principles of developing and delivering culture-fair tests.

Developed by the American Educational Research Association, American Psychological Association, and National Council on Measurement in Education (1999), the *Standards for Educational and Psychological Testing* provide a collaborative framework for numerous professionals conducting testing procedures to follow. Although these collaborative bodies agree that the establishment of culture-free tests is impossible, notation is provided that fairness in testing is expected. What promotes fairness in testing practice, however, has been the source of subjectivity and potential contempt within the field. The overall divisiveness regarding the construct of fairness in testing may overshadow the consensus that has been obtained on specific components regarding what it means to be fair. Specifically, the *Standards* identify fairness in testing as the presence of a lack of bias, equal treatment of participants, equal opportunity in outcomes, and an opportunity to learn. Based on these standard elements of fairness, culture-fair tests must be developed with a clear understanding of potential cultural factors.

Despite the goal of reducing bias in testing through culture-fair tests, Landau et al. (2009) argue, in an attempt to reduce the impact of cultural bias, culture-fair intelligence tests actually have reduced the accuracy of these tests to measure the construct of intelligence. In effect, elimination of the cultural elements of intelligence tests results in the inability to assess measures of intelligence. Given the cultural implications of many constructs such as intelligence, questions have arisen as to whether culture-fair tests accurately measure the intended constructs. As such, implementation of these tests must be accompanied by a clear understanding of the scope of testing results.

Attempts to eliminate disadvantages associated with testing procedures for specific populations and associated questions with the accuracy of tests given accommodations have resulted in the formulation of procedures to separate those tests taken with standard expectations and those in which accommodations are provided. **Flagging**, the process of establishing when accommodations have been made to standardized assessments, has been highly controversial due to questions regarding whether identification unfairly labels individuals who need accommodations. As such, tests designed to be culturally fair as opposed to those allowing for accommodations have gained increasing focus.

You are already familiar with several culture-fair tests such as the TEMAS (Chapter 10), and Goodenough-Harris Drawing Tests (Chapter 10). Let's now turn our attention to discussing additional culture-fair tests: Cattell's Culture Fair Intelligence Test, Naglieri Nonverbal Ability Test, and Columbia Mental Maturity Scale.

Cattell's Culture Fair Intelligence Test

Designed by R. B. Cattell, the **Culture Fair Intelligence Test (CFIT)** is a nonverbal test used to measure fluid ability. Recall from Chapter 7 that Cattell viewed fluid intelligence as an inherited (innate) quality that refers to problem-solving and information-processing ability, uninfluenced by culture or education.

The CFIT was designed to measure intelligence independent from culture as Cattell designed the material to be unfamiliar to all subjects regardless of the culture they identified with. The CFIT is a paper-and-pencil test and comes in two parallel forms with three ability scales: Scale I for ages 4–8 and mentally disabled adults, Scale II for ages 8–12 and adults of average intelligence, and Scale III for high school–age and adults of above-average intelligence. Scale I includes eight subtests consisting of mazes, copying symbols, identifying drawings that are similar, and nonverbal tasks. Scales II and III consist of four types of nonverbal items: (1) series items (i.e., examinee is presented with incomplete progressive series and must select the figure that completes the series), (2) classification (i.e., select figure that is different from other or identify multiple figures that are different from others), (3) matrices (i.e., complete the design or matrix presented), and (4) topological conditions (i.e., of five choices, select which one duplicates the condition). To gain your own experience of a culture-free IQ assessment, participate in Guided Practice Exercise 15.3.

GUIDED PRACTICE EXERCISE 15.3

Go to the following website prior to class and take the free culture-fair IQ assessment: www.delosis.com/surveys. This IQ assessment is based on two subtests of the Culture Fair Intelligence Test (CFIT). It will take you approximately 6 minutes to complete it. Taking this IQ assessment will also facilitate the research of John Rogers, a PhD student at University College London.

Once you have taken the assessment and are back in class, get into small groups or pairs and discuss your perceptions of this intelligence test. What are your thoughts as to why this is deemed a culture-fair test? Do you agree or disagree? What did you experience while taking this assessment? Were you surprised by your IQ results? Why or why not? (*Note:* You do not have to share your results with other students, just your perception of whether this assessment captured your IQ.)

Naglieri Nonverbal Ability Test

If you recall in Chapter 7, we discussed standardized measures of ability that do not involve language, such as the Universal Nonverbal Intelligence Test (UNIT) and the Test of Nonverbal Intelligence (TONI). Similar to the UNIT and TONI, the **Naglieri Nonverbal Ability Test, Second Edition (NNAT-2)** provides a culturally neutral evaluation of general ability and does not require the child to read, write, or speak. Although the NNAT-2 is widely used to screen students for gifted and talented programs, it can also be used to evaluate children with limited motor skills, hearing impairments, or color vision impairments. The test is also ideal for non-English speakers or people who are learning English for the first time.

The test is appropriate for children ages 4–18 in prekindergarten through 12th grade and can be administered online or by paper and pencil. There are seven test levels, each of which contains 38 questions. Levels are based on grade, and children have 30 minutes to complete the assessment. The NNAT-2 consists of nonverbal picture questions based on progressive matrices with shapes and designs. Skills tested by the NNAT-2 include analogous reasoning, patterns and sequences, sorting and classification, memory, and spatial reasoning. There are four categories of questions: pattern completion (i.e., complete pattern by determining the design of a missing part), reasoning by analogy (i.e., recognize the relationship between geometric shapes), serial reasoning (i.e., recognize a sequence of shapes and change in the sequence), and spatial visualization (i.e., determine how two designs will appear when combined).

Because the NNAT-2 was normed on a 2011 sample, it is one of the most recently normed ability tests. Raw scores are converted into a Naglieri Ability Index, percentile ranks, stanines, and normal curve equivalents by age (Pearson Education, 2014b). The **Naglieri Nonverbal Ability Test-Individual Form** (**NNAT-I**; Naglieri, 2003) is another version that is a particularly useful assessment for those with motor problems when administering a timed performance test would not be appropriate.

The NNAT-2 is considered to be a culturally neutral evaluation of general ability compared to the Cognitive Abilities Test (CogAT-7). If you recall from Chapter 7, the CogAT-7 includes verbal and quantitative batteries in addition to the nonverbal battery. Giessman, Gambrell, and Stebbins (2013) compared the performance of 4,038 kindergartners, first graders, and second graders who took the NNAT-2 with 5,833 second graders who took the CogAT-6 as part of a screening for a gifted program. Giessman et al. found the "CogAT-6 Nonverbal score appeared to identify as many or more high-ability students from underrepresented groups as the NNAT-2" (p. 101). This study is worth noting as it highlights the importance of gifted programs not relying solely on the NNAT-2 to address minority underrepresentation.

Columbia Mental Maturity Scale

The **Columbia Mental Maturity Scale** (**CMMS**; Burgemeister, Blum, & Lorge, 1972), originally designed for children with cerebral palsy, measures general reasoning ability for children ages 3 years, 6 months to 9 years, 11 months. The test is suitable for children with sensory, motor, or speech deficits, including children with cerebral palsy or brain damage, intellectual disabilities, hearing loss, visual handicaps, speech impairment, or lack of proficiency in English. The assessment takes approximately 15–20 minutes to administer, does not require verbal responses, does not require the child to read or speak English, and uses minimal motor responses. The assessment consists of 92 pictorial items, which are presented on 6- by 19-inch cards containing three to five drawings each. The child is asked to look at all the pictures on the card and identify which drawing is unrelated and does not belong in the set and to point to it. The bases for pictorial discrimination are according to color, size, clarification, missing parts, number, or symbolic concept.

The CMMS yields an Age Deviation Score with a mean of 100 and standard deviation of 16. In addition, raw scores are converted to percentile ranks, stanines, and Maturity Index Scores. The CMMS was normed on 2,600 children and was stratified according to geographic region, race, sex, and parental occupation. Split-half reliability coefficients are high (.85 to .91) for most age groups, and test-retest reliability coefficients range from .86 at age 4 to .84 at ages 5 and 6. The CMMS shows concurrent validity with the Stanford Achievement Test, the Otis-Lennon Mental Ability Test, and the Stanford-Binet Intelligence Test. Although the CMMS is considered a culture-fair assessment, the sample used to standardize the assessment was collected in the 1960s and 1970s. Because the assessment is based on 1960s U.S. Census data, the CMMS is in need of a revised standardized sample.

Although not discussed here, there are several additional culture-fair tests such as Raven's Progressive Matrices, Culture-Free Self-Esteem Inventories, and the Learning Potential Assessment Device, which are known for reducing language and cultural content.

ISSUES IN ASSESSING INDIVIDUALS WITH DISABILITIES

Nearly 1 in 5 people in the United States has a disability. According to Brault (2012), approximately 56.7 million people (18.7%) of the 303.9 million in the noninstitutionalized U.S. population reported a disability and 38.3 million (12.6%) indicated they had a severe disability in the 2010 U.S. Census. In terms of visual, hearing, motor, and cognitive impairments, the U.S. Census Bureau (2012) highlights that 8.1 million people have difficulty seeing; 2.0 million are blind or unable to see; 7.6 million people experience difficulty hearing; 30.6 million had difficulty walking or climbing stairs, or used a wheelchair, cane, crutches, or walker; and 7.0 million adults indicated that feelings of depression and anxiety interfered with their daily activities.

If you recall from Chapter 8, we discussed that in 1975, the Education for All Handicapped Children Act (PL94-142) required that all public schools that receive federal funds provide handicapped children and adults ages 3–21 with an education in the "least restrictive environment," meaning they must be educated with other children who are not handicapped to the maximum possibility. The act was revised and renamed the Individuals with Disabilities Education Improvement Act (IDEIA). According to this law, if a child is suspected of having a learning disability, he or she has the right to be tested at the school's expense. Before a child becomes eligible for special education programs, an extensive evaluation must take place and certain criteria must be determined, such as whether a child has a physical or mental disability that substantially limits learning, the possible causes of the child's disability, and the educational diagnosis category that best describes the child's disability. Furthermore, Section 504 of the Rehabilitation Act of 1973 indicates that modifications are to be made for students with disabilities.

Depending on the individual's disability, accommodations or modifications may need to be made. There are several different forms of modifications, including but not limited to (a) the form or presentation of the test, (b) response format, (c) modifications to timing and scheduling, (d) modifications to the physical environment, and (e) modifications to the interpersonal environment. Let's discuss each of these briefly.

Modification of the presentation format may include changing test instructions or test items. For example, a client who is hearing impaired may be given the test in sign language or in writing, while a client who is visually impaired may need the directions read verbally or printed in larger print or in Braille. Sometimes the response format must be modified for students who are unable to respond according to the standardized format. For example, a client with a speech impairment may be allowed to write out his or her responses rather than answer orally or have someone record them, while a client with motor impairments may be allowed to verbally answer rather than mark responses. Other modifications to format responses include allowing the client to write directly on the test or booklet, use a computer, or use an interpreter to record answers in English. Extended time is the most requested modification for those with a disability. Modification of timing and scheduling may involve allowing additional time to complete the test or sections of the test, offering additional breaks, administering the test on different days or in multiple sessions rather than in one sitting, and modifying the order of the items. For example, a student diagnosed with sensory disorders may be granted additional time on the SAT. The individual may be given certain parts on different days rather than all in one sitting. The SAT is administered in a group. Modifying the physical environment would include allowing the student to take the test individually rather than in a group setting. Sometimes modifications to the interpersonal environment are needed. For example, an individual may require a service dog. In order to determine which form of modification is most suitable, it is important that you gather information from a range of sources, interviews with family, friends, teachers (if the client is a student); records of previous assessments, including psychoeducational or other professional evaluations; live observations; and individuals' past use of testing accommodations.

As a counselor, you will be required to focus on various aspects of accommodations, such as methods of test administration, documentation, score comparability, and even the motivation of test takers to request modifications. Before you make a decision about accommodations, you must carefully consider the meaning of the scores as well as the validity of the data that will be derived from the modified assessment. According to the American Counseling Association (2014) *Code of Ethics*, standard E.7.a,

> When assessments are not administered under standard conditions, as may be necessary to accommodate clients with disabilities, or when unusual behavior or irregularities occur during administration, those conditions are noted in the interpretation, and the results may be designated as invalid or questionable validity. (p. 11)[*]

Let us now briefly discuss some types of disabilities such as vision, hearing, motor, cognitive, and emotional impairments.

Vision Impairments

Although many people may think blindness refers to complete loss of vision, this form is rare. Many people have permanent loss of some eyesight but not all. According to the Centers for Disease Control and Prevention (2009) and the American Foundation for the Blind (2013), **blindness** is defined as having visual acuity with best correction worse or equal to 20/400 or a visual field of 20 degrees or less, while **vision impairment** is having 20/40 or worse vision even with corrective eyeglasses. It is important for one to note that vision loss can vary widely and thus lead to varying degrees of vision impairment.

A number of assessments are available for those with vision impairments. Some assessments are adaptations of instruments that are commonly used, and they examine verbal IQ, performance IQ, or both. Other instruments have been developed specifically for persons with physical challenges such as the Blind Learning Aptitude Test (measures learning potential), the Cognitive Test for the Blind (assesses cognitive function), and the Intelligence Test for Visually Impaired Children (measures intelligence).

Several of the intelligence tests you read about in Chapter 7 are used with people who are blind or have partial sight. If you recall, the Slosson Intelligence Test-Revised Third Edition is a verbal intelligence test often used in schools and clinics with children and adults ranging from 4 to 65 years of age. You also learned that David Wechsler designed a series of individually

---

administered intelligence tests to measure intellectual abilities from preschool to adulthood, with the most common and currently used being the Wechsler Adult Intelligence Scale-Fourth Edition (WAIS-IV) for ages 16 to 90 years, 11 months and the Wechsler Intelligence Scale for Children-Fourth Edition (WISC-IV) for ages 6 through 16 years, 11 months. The verbal WAIS and the verbal scale tests on the WISC are usually the only ones administered to the visually impaired. The mean scores for visually impaired people on the WAIS and WISC have been shown to be equivalent with those of the sighted.

In Chapter 8, you became familiar with achievement tests such as the Woodcock Johnson III (WJ III), the SAT, and the GRE. The WJ III is available in large print, Braille, and tactile editions from the American Printing House for the Blind. Also available in larger print and Braille editions are the SAT and the GRE.

There are several common accommodations for those with vision impairments. When the individual is partially blind, it is important that the room have few distractions and the lighting be modified for optimal vision and appropriate writing instruments and materials be available. For example, the individual may need thicker writing pens or pencils and the test may need to be administered in Braille, larger print, or audio. One should note that reading in Braille takes 2.5 times as long, thus the examinee will need more time for testing. Other time modifications might include additional time for reading directions, slower reading instructions, or testing over several days.

Hearing Impairments

Deafness and **hearing impairment** refer to the total or partial inability to hear. Sound is measured by its loudness or intensity (measured in decibels) and its frequency or pitch (measured in hertz). Those with hearing impairments may experience loss in both areas. The magnitude of hearing loss can range from slight, mild, moderate, severe, to profound among the deaf or hard of hearing. As a counselor, it will be important for you to find out which mode of communication (i.e., signed, written, verbal) your client prefers, and assessments should always be administered in the client's preferred mode of communication.

Several instruments, with which you are already familiar, have been normed on those who are deaf or hard of hearing. However, it is important to note that some of them are only partially useable, such as the use of only the performance section. Because hearing is related to language acquisition, verbal IQ assessments are rarely used. Instead, performance subtests are considered the most accurate measure of intelligence or cognitive ability with people who have hearing impairments (Remine, Brown, Care, & Rickards, 2007). Widely used cognitive and intelligence assessments include the Universal Nonverbal Intelligence Test, the Wechsler Intelligence Scale for Children-Fourth Edition (WISC-IV), the Kaufman Assessment Battery for Children (K-ABC), the Test of Nonverbal Intelligence-Third Edition (TONI-III), and the Comprehensive Test of Nonverbal Intelligence, Second Edition (CTONI-2). Widely used personality assessments administered to individuals with hearing impairments include the Kinetic House-Tree-Person Drawings and the Children's Apperception Test.

Depending on the severity and fluctuation of the hearing impairment, modifications will differ. For example, an individual who has mild hearing impairment may be allowed to use an electronic device to amplify the examiner's voice. An individual with a severe hearing impairment may need written instructions or an interpreter to sign the instructions, test questions, and responses.

Motor Impairments

Clients with **motor impairments** may experience partial or total loss of function of a body part. Such loss may result in muscle weakness, lack of muscle control, or paralysis. Motor impairment is often seen in clients with cerebral palsy, multiple sclerosis, Parkinson's disease, or stroke. As a counselor, you may need to assess a client's gross and fine motor skills, intelligence, general ability, or another construct with individuals with motor impairments and/or make modifications to the assessment process based on the impairment.

A **motor test** is an assessment used to evaluate a person's mobility and ability to move parts of the body. The **Bruininks-Oseretsky Test of Motor Proficiency, Second Edition (BOT-2**; Bruininks & Bruininks, 2005) and the **Movement Assessment Battery for Children-Second Edition (Movement ABC-2**; Henderson, Sugden, & Barnett, 2007) are two widely used individually administered tests designed to assess gross and fine motor skills. One of the most widely used assessments that identifies neurological deficits is the **Bender Visual-Motor Gestalt Test, Second Edition (Bender-Gestalt II)**. It is important to note that the qualification for the BOT-2 and Movement ABC-2 is Level B, and the Bender-Gestalt II requires a Level C qualification. One should have appropriate training and skills before administering the aforementioned tests.

The BOT-2 is used for screening, diagnosing motor impairments, determining educational placement, and evaluating motor training programs. The assessment can be administered to individuals 4–21 years of age, and there are four testing options: Complete Form, Short Form, select composites, and select subtests. The Complete Form has four components (Fine Manual Control, Manual Coordination, Body Coordination, and Strength and Agility) and eight subtests. In the manual, strong inter-rater reliability and test-retest reliability for the subtests are reported as well as good construct validity (Bruininks & Bruininks, 2005). It is important to note that scoring can be time-consuming, and there are many tables and transferring of numbers that may lead to increased error in scoring.

The Movement ABC-2 is used with children 3–16 years of age to identify, describe, and help plan treatment interventions for motor impairment (Pearson Education, 2014a). The Movement ABC-2 Intervention Manual includes a guide for assisting children in learning new skills. Raw scores are converted into total standard scores and percentiles. The Movement ABC-2 Checklist is available and can be administered individually or as a group. The checklist is appropriate for children 5–12 years of age and is used to assess the child's attitudes and feeling about motor tasks.

The Bender-Gestalt II, named after Lauretta Bender, was first published in 1938 and since then has undergone revisions, with the most current version published in 2003. The Bender-Gestalt II is considered an expressive, projective measure that provides information about a client's neuropsychological functioning. The assessment is often used to discern whether brain damage has occurred or the degree of maturation of the nervous system. The original assessment consisted of nine cards, each of which had a printed design. Bender (1938) believed perceptual maturation and neurological impairment could be assessed using the designs. Today, people ages 4 and older are still shown a series of nine template cards, each displaying a unique, geometric figure, and are asked to draw the nine figures. However, seven additional cards have been added. Children ages 4 years to 7 years, 11 months have four additional cards to replicate, and individuals ages 8 and older have three additional cards to replicate. The Bender-Gestalt has no time limit but usually takes around 5–10 minutes to administer. The Bender-Gestalt II was normed on 4,000 individuals ages 4 to 85+ and included special populations such as those with cognitive impairments, learning disorders, and autism as well as gifted individuals. Test-retest reliability, internal consistency, inter-rater reliability, and validity were reported in the manual. It is important to note that the Bender-Gestalt II should never be used alone to make a diagnosis and requires advanced training beyond a master's degree.

If you recall from Chapter 7, many IQ tests include verbal and motor components. You should try to select a test that does not need to be modified due to an individual's impairment or requires minimal modifications. In Chapter 7, you learned about the CTONI-2, a popular nonverbal, norm-referenced intelligence instrument that is ideal for those with language or motor impairments. Picture vocabulary tests, such as the **Peabody Picture Vocabulary Test-Fourth Edition (PPVT-4**; Dunn & Dunn, 2007) and the **Expressive Vocabulary Test, Second Edition (EVT-2**; Williams, 2007), are commonly used when assessing intelligence and general ability with individuals who have motor impairments. The PPVT-4 assesses vocabulary acquisition and can be administered to ages 2 years, 6 months to 90 years and older. Examinees are presented with four full-color pictures on a page. The examiner says a word aloud, and the examinee points to the picture that best illustrates the word's meaning. The administration of the PPVT-4 requires no reading or writing and is untimed, thus any problems associated with motor coordination are eliminated. The EVT-2, a complimentary tool to the PPVT-4, requires no reading or writing and quickly assesses expressive vocabulary. When an individual with motor impairments is administered an assessment which requires paper-and-pencil tasks—unlike the EVT-2, PPVT-4, or CTONI-2—a common modification includes using a writer who is available to enter the responses which require coordination.

Hidden Impairments

Whereas disabilities such as vision, hearing, and motor impairments may be more apparent to the test administrator, numerous other **"hidden" disabilities** also have the potential to impact test performance. According to Manalo, Ede, and Wong-Toi (2010), a significant proportion of individuals with a disability are often indistinguishable from the population of individuals without a disability. Hidden disabilities include a wide variety of psychological, cognitive, physical, behavioral, and emotional disorders and diagnoses, varying in severity. The combination of invisibility and variance of disability characteristics results in various limitations in the potential to affect test interpretation. We will discuss issues of cognitive and emotional impairments here in more depth.

Cognitive impairments, including those caused by neurological disorders, circulatory issues, environmental toxicity, oxygen deprivation, and infection, are often referred to as intellectual disabilities. The presence of these impairments has the potential to affect the ways in which individuals are able to learn and process information, including slower processing speeds, reduced memory retention, and language deficits. Specifically, Buffum, Hutt, Chang, Craine, and Snow (2007) define cognitive impairments as the presence of deficits in perception of information as well as the ways in which this information is coded, stored, and used in practical applications. These deficiencies can grossly affect the results of standardized assessments in which directions and processes are developed for individuals without such deficits. As such, examiners must take into consideration the potential impact of cognitive impairments and make necessary accommodations to address these limitations.

If you recall from Chapters 7 and 8, we discussed numerous instruments used to assess cognitive abilities. Cullen, O'Neill, Evans, Coen, and Lawlor (2007) reviewed 39 screening tools used for the establishment of cognitive impairments. Each tool was reported to address different areas of cognitive disability. Although Cullen et al. note promising findings, including high reliability and validity estimates of several scales, they also note that completion of any test is not sufficient to provide a differential diagnosis. Instead, a complete psychological evaluation comprising multiple tests is necessary. Given the invisibility of cognitive impairments in many settings, failure to address the potential presence of a cognitive impairment will result in inaccurate test results. In cases where a cognitive disability has been established, test administers must evaluate potential accommodations which will not interfere with the test purpose.

Emotional impairments, including psychological and behavioral manifestations, are categorized by issues caused by factors unrelated to physical or cognitive causes. According to the National Dissemination Center for Children with Disabilities (2010), emotional impairments encompass mental health disorders (i.e., mood disorders, anxiety disorders, eating disorders, and conduct disorders), which have the potential to affect test performance. Attention deficit hyperactivity disorder (ADHD), for example, is categorized by inattention and/or impulsivity in a variety of environments. The presence of ADHD-associated symptoms has the potential to affect the time required to complete a test as well as the accuracy of tests to measure the intended constructs. Although other contributors to emotional impairments including depression and anxiety vary in symptomology, these, too, have the potential to affect test results.

As with the presence of cognitive impairments, the relative invisibility of emotional impairments complicates the potential integration of accommodations for test takers. Cullen et al. (2007) note that assessment of impairments requires the use of multiple assessment tools with established reliability and validity estimates for the issue being evaluated. Given the variance in factors associated with emotional impairment, the list of potential assessment tools is varied. According to the National Institute of Mental Health (n.d.), however, no single test should be used independently to diagnose an individual. Once these issues have been identified, test administrators must review whether specific accommodations will affect the validity of test results. For a description of an individual who might need an accommodation for a disability, read the case of LaShonda in Case Illustration 15.5, then participate in Guided Practice Exercise 15.4 to explore ways you might accommodate her if you were the person doing her assessment.

CASE ILLUSTRATION   15.5

LaShonda is a 25-year-old female who is partially blind and deaf on her left side due to a stroke she suffered as the result of a car accident 2 years ago. Since that time, LaShonda has also been treated for severe depression. She used to be a professional athlete prior to her accident and has had a difficult time adjusting to her injuries and the loss of her identity as an athlete. LaShonda's doctor is concerned about her cognitive functioning and has referred her for assessment.

GUIDED PRACTICE EXERCISE 15.4

Now that you have read about the different types of accommodations that can be made for an individual with a disability, get into small groups or pairs and discuss what kinds of accommodations might need to be made if you were assessing LaShonda (see Case Illustration 15.5).

STANDARDS FOR ASSESSMENT WITH DIVERSE POPULATIONS

Throughout previous chapters, we discussed assessment competencies required of professional counselors, including those spelled out in the *Code of Fair Testing Practices in Education* (Joint Committee on Testing Practices, 2004), *Responsibilities of Users of Standardized Tests* (Association for Assessment in Counseling, 2003a), *Standards for Qualifications of Test Users* (Association for Assessment in Counseling, 2003b), and *Rights and Responsibilities of Test Takers: Guidelines and Expectations* (Joint Committee on Testing Practices, 2000). In addition to these standards, the Association for Assessment and Research in Counseling (AARC), the Council for Accreditation of Counseling and Related Educational Programs (CACREP), the Council on Rehabilitation Education (CORE), the American Counseling Association (ACA), and the International Test Commission (ITC) have outlined standards specific to multicultural assessment. These standards are briefly discussed below.

AACE

In 1992, the Committee on Diversity in Assessment collaborated with AARC, previously known as the Association for Assessment in Counseling and Education (AACE), to create the first set of standards that addressed multicultural competence in assessment. Since 1992, these standards have undergone revisions and are currently referred to as the **Standards for Multicultural Assessment, Fourth Revision** (AACE, 2012). The newest standards emphasize the role of social advocacy in assessment as well as the importance of selecting, administering, and interpreting assessments. The standards are grouped into five main categories: (1) Advocacy; (2) Selection of Assessments: Content and Purpose, Norming, Reliability, and Validity; (3) Administration and Scoring of Assessments; (4) Interpretation and Application of Assessment Results; and (5) Training in the Uses of Assessments. It is important that you take time to read through the standards to enhance your professional knowledge and carefully consider how the selection of assessment, administration, scoring, and interpretation impact cultural diverse groups.

CACREP and CORE

The CACREP (2009) standards and the CORE (2010) standards acknowledge the importance of cultural competence. For example, in the CACREP standards for Clinical Mental Health Counseling, Standard H.1 states, "Selects appropriate comprehensive assessment intervention to assist in diagnosis and treatment planning, with an awareness of cultural bias in the implementation and interpretation of assessment protocols" (p. 33). One should note that the CACREP standards are currently undergoing a revision process, and the new standards will be out in 2016.

In 2013, CORE became a corporate affiliate of CACREP. Together, CACREP and CORE released the newly adopted Clinical Rehabilitation Counseling Standards (CIRC) to be used by counseling programs seeking to gain accreditation in clinical rehabilitation counseling (CACREP, 2013). Specifically, CIRC Standard I.4 states, "Identifies standard screening and assessment instruments that are psychologically appropriate for people with disabilities" (p. 5), while Standard I.8 states, "Understands the relevance and potential biases of commonly used diagnostic and assessment tools with multicultural populations" (p. 5).

ACA

Although we have already discussed in detail the ACA (2014) *Code of Ethics* and Section E, which relates to evaluation, assessment, and interpretation, it is important to review Standards A.2.c (Developmental and Cultural Sensitivity), E.5.b (Cultural Sensitivity), and and E.8. (Multicultural Issues/Diversity in Assessment) as these standards directly apply to multicultural assessment. According to Standard E.8, "Counselors select and use with caution assessment techniques normed on populations other than that of the client" (ACA, 2014, p. 12). It is your responsibility to familiarize yourself with these standards in order to demonstrate cultural competence in the area of assessment.

ITC

The **International Test Commission (ITC)** is widely known internationally for its Guidelines on Adapting Testing. ITC, a not-for-profit organization, is considered an "association of national psychological associations, test commissions, publishers, and other organizations committed to promoting effective testing and assessment policies and to the proper development, evaluation, and uses of educational and psychological instruments" (ITC, 2008, para. 1). ITC holds regular international meetings, conferences, and produces publications related to ethically sound use of tests in the official journal of ITC, *International Journal of Testing*. It has developed four sets of guidelines: (a) the ITC Guidelines on Adapting Tests, (b) the ITC Guidelines on Test Use, (c) the ITC Guidelines on Computer-Based and Internet-Delivered Testing, and (d) the ITC Guidelines on Quality Control in Scoring, Test Analysis, and Reporting of Test Scores. ITC is currently working to develop two additional sets of guidelines: (a) Guidelines on Test Security and (b) Guidelines on Testing in Non-Native Languages. Each of the guidelines can be downloaded from the ITC website at www.intestcom.org/guidelines. These guidelines, similar to the standards mentioned above, serve as another resource to help you develop multicultural competence for assessment in counseling. We hope you will take the time to review each of them carefully and reflect on the skills necessary to practice competent assessment in the multicultural world.

KEYSTONES

- Diversity in cultural characteristics is associated with different worldviews. Factors of acculturation and assimilation combined with various cultural characteristics result in complex individual identities. Such differences result in the need for consideration in assessment.
- Counselors must be aware of potential bias in an instrument across diverse groups. Test, test taker, and examiner biases should be evaluated to ensure that the results of the assessment are a clear reflection of the test taker's performance on a specific construct.
- Attempts to eliminate cultural bias in assessment have included culture-free tests and culture-fair tests. Efforts to eliminate disadvantages for culturally diverse individuals have resulted in identified concerns about the effects of culture-fairness on the scope of results.
- There are several different forms of modifications, including modifications to the form or presentation of the test, response format, timing and scheduling, physical environment, and the interpersonal environment. Counselors must carefully consider the meaning of the scores as well as the validity of the data that will be derived from the modified assessment.
- Widely known culture-fair tests that are designed to be free of cultural bias include the TEMAS, Wechsler Nonverbal Scale of Ability, Goodenough-Harris Drawing Tests, Cattell's Culture Fair Intelligence Test, Naglieri Nonverbal Ability Test, Columbia Mental Maturity Scale, and Raven's Progressive Matrices.
- In addition to the *Code of Fair Testing Practices in Education*, *Responsibilities of Users of Standardized Tests*, *Standards for Qualifications of Test Users,* and *Rights and Responsibilities of Test Takers: Guidelines and Expectations*, there are several standards and guidelines that specify multicultural competence for assessment in counseling, including AACE Standards for Multicultural Assessment, ACA *Code of Ethics*, ITC Guidelines on Adapting Tests, ITC Guidelines on Test Use, ITC Guidelines on Computer-Based and Internet-Delivered Testing, and ITC Guidelines on Quality Control in Scoring. Furthermore, CACREP and CORE include standards specific to diversity in assessment.

KEY TERMS

acculturation

assimilation

Bender Visual-Motor Gestalt Test, Second Edition (Bender-Gestalt II)

bias

blindness

Bruininks-Oseretsky Test of Motor Proficiency, Second Edition (BOT-2)

cognitive impairments

Columbia Mental Maturity Scale (CMMS)

content bias

cultural loading

culture

Culture Fair Intelligence Test (CFIT)

culture-fair tests

culture-free tests

differential item functioning (DIF)

diversity

emotional impairments

examiner biases

Expressive Vocabulary Test, Second Edition (EVT-2)

flagging

hearing impairment

hidden disabilities

internal structure

International Test Commission (ITC)

language

motivation

motor impairments

motor test

Movement Assessment Battery for Children-Second Edition (Movement ABC-2)

Naglieri Nonverbal Ability Test-Individual Form (NNAT-I)

Naglieri Nonverbal Ability Test, Second Edition (NNAT-2)

Peabody Picture Vocabulary Test-Fourth Edition (PPVT-4)

predictive bias

Standards for Multicultural Assessment, Fourth Revision

vision impairment

worldview

ADDITIONAL RESOURCES

- American Educational Research Association

  http://www.aera.net

This national research association focuses on educational research and has resources for working professionals and students. It promotes the use of research to improve education and is composed of 12 divisions encompassing multiple facets of education.

- Association for Assessment in Research and Counseling

  http://aarc-counseling.org

This association has membership that encompasses counselors, educators, and researchers with the goal of promoting best practices in counseling in assessment, research, and counseling. It also provides resources for test reviews.

- *International Journal of Testing*

  http://www.tandfonline.com/loi/hijt20#.UqZb_Ljn94s

This journal is dedicated to advancing the theory of testing and assessment construction and encompasses many diverse disciplines ranging from education to human resource management. The journal publishes original articles on testing- and assessment-related topics.

- International Test Commission

  http://www.intestcom.org

This organization is dedicated to providing policies to govern effective testing and assessment and is composed of psychologists, test commissioners, and test publishers. The commission works on problems related to test construction, distribution, and test use. It publishes guidelines on test adaptation, test use, testing via the Internet, and controlling the quality of test administration and its process.

- *Journal of Multicultural Counseling and Development*

  http://www.jmcdonline.org

This is the journal of the Association of Multicultural Counseling and Development and publishes research related to multicultural issues in counseling.

- National Center for Fair and Open Testing

  http://www.fairtest.org

This organization is dedicated to protecting standardized testing from improper use and ensuring that "evaluation of students, teachers and schools is fair, open, valid and educationally beneficial." The website also provides fact sheets pertaining to standardized testing.

- National Institute of Mental Health

  http://www.nimh.nih.gov

This institute is dedicated to funding and disseminating research on mental health issues. The website contains the latest information regarding most mental health disorders such as ADHD/ADD, anxiety, autism spectrum disorder, and others. It also has a link to provide resources for finding treatment.

- *Standards for Educational and Psychological Testing*

  http://www.apa.org/science/programs/testing/standards.aspx

This site provides access to the *Standards for Educational and Psychological Testing* and provides an overview of the standards.

Student Study Site: Visit the Student Study Site at **www.sagepub.com/watson** to access additional study tools, including quizzes, web resources, and journal articles.

CHAPTER 16

Ethical and Legal Issues in Assessment

LEARNING OBJECTIVES

After reading this chapter, you will be able to

- Define ethics and articulate their intended purpose
- Identify the moral principles on which professional counseling ethics are based
- List available resources counselors could consult to ensure that they are practicing sound and ethical assessment
- Review the relevant standards related to assessment and evaluation in the ACA *Code of Ethics*
- Describe the steps in the ethical decision-making model and articulate how the model can be applied to assist you in making ethical choices for you and your clients
- Discuss important legislative issues governing the practice of counseling assessment
- Introduce important court cases that have created legal precedents relevant to testing and assessment practices
- Describe the importance of becoming informed regarding both state and federal laws governing the counseling profession

Counseling is a unique profession. The clients who counselors work with each present with their own unique set of circumstances and problems. This uniqueness requires counselors to be flexible in their assessment approaches. Plainly speaking, there is no

Note: Throughout this chapter, excerpts from the American Counseling Association's *Code of Ethics* are reprinted from 2014 ACA *Code of Ethics.* © (2014) The American Counseling Association. Reprinted with permission. No further reproduction authorized without written permission from the American Counseling Association.

one-size-fits-all assessment approach that can be applied universally to all clients. Additionally, developing a set of rules and regulations governing the practice of counseling assessment in all situations across all settings in which counselors may work would be a near-impossible endeavor. Instead, counselors have available to them several resources that help describe appropriate practices that should be used with clients. In this chapter we will introduce you to the ethical principles and legislative issues related to the practice of counseling assessment. Becoming familiar with these standards will help ensure that you are best meeting the needs of your clients and respecting their rights and dignity.

ETHICS DEFINED

Generally speaking, **ethics** refers to the philosophical discipline concerned with human conduct and moral decision making. Ethics establishes which actions are considered right and which actions are considered wrong. In other words, ethics define what one should or should not do in various situations. Ethical standards are typically developed by professional associations and serve to guide the behavior of those who are members of that profession. Counselors are held accountable to the ethical standards for counselors, but not to the ethical standards set forth for doctors, lawyers, or teachers. In the counseling profession there are several sources of ethical standards. Which standards you abide by in your counseling practice depends on several factors, including your work setting, client demographics served, and any state or national licenses or certifications you may hold. A few of the more common sources of ethical standards are discussed below.

American Counseling Association (ACA) *Code of Ethics*

The ACA *Code of Ethics* (ACA, 2014) is perhaps the most widely referenced source of ethical standards in the counseling profession. It represent a set of mandatory ethics and is designed to protect the well-being of those served by counselors and advance the work of the profession. Many of the ethical codes established by ACA divisions and other counseling organizations are based on the ACA *Code of Ethics*. As a result, it is the ACA *Code* that we will discuss in detail here.

The ACA *Code of Ethics* was first published in 1961. Since that time, it has been revised six times: 1974, 1981, 1988, 1995, 2005, and 2014. The current version, released in 2014, is four times larger than the 1961 version, reflecting the progress the profession has made and the complexity counselors face (Francis, 2013). The ACA *Code of Ethics* serves the following main purposes:

1. The *Code* sets forth the ethical obligations of ACA members and provides guidance intended to inform the ethical practice of professional counselors.

2. The *Code* identifies ethical considerations relevant to professional counselors and counselors-in-training.

3. The *Code* enables the association to clarify for current and prospective members, and for those served by members, the nature of the ethical responsibilities held in common by its members.

4. The *Code* serves as an ethical guide designed to assist members in constructing a course of action that best serves those utilizing counseling services and established expectations of conduct with a primary emphasis on the role of the professional counselor.

5. The *Code* helps to support the mission of ACA.

6. The standards contained in this *Code* serve as the basis for processing inquiries and ethics complaints concerning ACA members. (p. 3)

The foundation of the ACA *Code of Ethics* is Kitchener's (1984) five moral principles of autonomy, justice, beneficence, nonmaleficence, and fidelity. **Autonomy** refers to the concept of independence and relates to the ability of clients to make decisions on their own based on their best interests (freedom of choice). **Justice** speaks to the counselor's need to treat clients fairly. This does not mean that all clients need to be treated the same, just that they are each given the same level of care and professionalism. **Beneficence** means always striving to do what is good and acting in the best interests of the client. As counselors, our actions should always be based on what is most beneficial for our individual clients (see Case Illustration 16.1). The concept of **nonmaleficence** refers to the belief that counselors should not cause their clients any harm. Our work with clients should not cause them any undue stress or hardship. In addition to not inflicting any intentional harm on our clients, we also should refrain from actions that might risk harm to them. The final principle is **fidelity** and it involves the concept of loyalty. Counselors should always remain loyal to their clients, honoring any and all commitments made. Fidelity is based on trust and is an important component needed for counselors to be effective in their work with clients. A faithful counselor is one who guards the client's trust and does not threaten the therapeutic relationship.

CASE ILLUSTRATION   16.1

George is an 8-year-old third grade student at the local elementary school. He has been referred to the school administrator four times in the past 2 weeks for disruptive behavior in class. The administrator asks the school counselor to please help begin the process of having George transferred to the alternative school. After spending some time getting to know George, the counselor begins to suspect that George may have a learning disability. All of George's behavioral problems occur during reading class. George relates to the counselor that he is embarrassed to read in front of the class and fears the other students will make fun of him, so he acts out to be sent out of class before he would have to get up and read before the class. Rather than processing the transfer paperwork to the alternative school, the school counselor works to have George tested to see if he indeed may have a learning disability. In this scenario, the counselor is acting in a beneficent manner because his actions are aimed at helping and benefiting George, not punishing him and removing him from the school.

The *Code of Ethics* consists of nine main sections covering the following areas: The Counseling Relationship (section A); Confidentiality and Privacy (section B); Professional Responsibility (section C); Relationships With Other Professionals (section D); Evaluation, Assessment, and Interpretation (section E); Supervision, Training, and Teaching (section F); Research and Publication (section G); Distance Counseling, Technology, and Social Media (section H); and Resolving Ethical Issues (section I). Each section describes what a counselor should aspire to do with regard to ethical behavior and responsibility in that area. For the purposes of this book, we will explore the standards related to assessment that are included in section E in further detail.

Section E contains ethical standards that relate to the practices of evaluation, assessment, and interpretation. The standards describe counselor responsibilities related to the use of standardized and nonstandardized assessment activities. In total there are 13 standards in this section related to all aspects of the assessment process: protecting client welfare; counselor training and credentialing; appropriate test selection, administration, scoring, and interpretation; and forensic evaluation. The subsections included in section E are presented below along with a discussion of how these standards influence and can be incorporated into your assessment practices. The text that appears in italics has been taken verbatim from the ACA *Code of Ethics* (reprinted with permission of ACA, all rights reserved).

Section E: Evaluation, Assessment, and Interpretation

Introduction. Counselors use assessment instruments as one component of the counseling process, taking into account the clients' personal and cultural context. Counselors promote the well-being of individual clients or groups of clients by developing and using appropriate educational, psychological, and career assessment instruments.

E.1. General

E.1.a. Assessment. The primary purpose of educational, mental health, psychological, and career assessment is to gather information regarding the client for a variety of purposes, including, but not limited to, client decision making, treatment planning, and forensic proceedings. Assessment may include both qualitative and quantitative methodologies.

E.1.b. Client Welfare. Counselors do not misuse assessment results and interpretations, and they take reasonable steps to prevent others from misusing the information provided. They respect the client's right to know the results, the interpretations made, and the bases for counselors' conclusions and recommendations.

In these statements we see that counselors are responsible for choosing quality assessments in their work with clients. Whether the assessments are interviews, observations, or tests, counselors have an obligation to their clients to share how the decision to use various assessment methods was made, the characteristics of the assessment approach that made it the best possible option, and how results obtained from the assessment will be used both in the immediate counseling relationship and in the future. In terms of tests, counselors should ensure that the tests they employ have strong psychometric properties (reliability, validity, generalizability) and are appropriate for use with the population in which they find themselves working. Resources like the *Mental Measurements Yearbook* (discussed in Chapter 5) are a good place for counselors to look to find tests and assessments that will help them meet the spirit of these ethical standards.

E.2. Competence to Use and Interpret Assessment Instruments

E.2.a. Limits of Competence. Counselors use only those testing and assessment services for which they have been trained and are competent. Counselors using technology-assisted test interpretations are trained in the construct being measured and the specific instrument being used prior to using its technology-based application. Counselors take reasonable measures to ensure the proper use of assessment techniques by persons under their supervision.

E.2.b. Appropriate Use. Counselors are responsible for the appropriate application, scoring, interpretation, and use of assessment instruments relevant to the needs of the client, whether they score and interpret such assessments themselves or use technology or other services.

E.2.c. Decisions Based on Results. Counselors responsible for decisions involving individuals or policies that are based on assessment results have a thorough understanding of psychometrics.

GUIDED PRACTICE EXERCISE 16.1

Select a common issue you might expect to encounter in your work as a counselor: anxiety, depression, grief and loss, stress, and so on. Identify three different instruments that can be used to assess that construct. Choose one Level A test, one Level B test, and one Level C test. Which appears to be the best choice?

Standard E.2 describes the training counselors are required to have in order to use various assessment instruments. In earlier chapters we talked about the different administration levels (A, B, C) assigned to many tests and assessments. These levels describe the training, experience, and competencies that counselors are required to demonstrate before they are allowed to use a particular assessment (see Guided Practice Exercise 16.1). Before selecting an assessment to use, counselors should educate themselves in the proper usage of that test. In addition, counselors should always seek to update their skills and knowledge base. In order to remain current in their knowledge, counselors should continually engage in professional development opportunities related to assessment practices. Attending conferences, workshops, or local trainings are all good ways to learn the latest practice trends.

In standards E.2.b and E.2.c, counselors are required to use tests in an appropriate manner. To ensure appropriate usage, counselors should be well versed in the various tests and assessments they plan to use. Identifying the populations for which an instrument is intended and evaluating the existing research supporting the instrument are both good steps to take before introducing an assessment approach into the counseling relationship.

Although information is available to help counselors make informed decisions, ultimately the responsibility for the selection decisions that are made rests with the counselor. When in doubt the ethical counselor should seek guidance or consultation. Additionally, resources such as the *Responsibilities of Users of Standardized Tests-3rd Edition (RUST-3*; Association for Assessment in Counseling [AAC], 2003a), *Code of Fair Testing Practices in Education* (Joint Committee on Testing Practices, 2004), and *Standards for Educational and Psychological Testing* (American Educational Research Association, American Psychological Association, & National Council of Measurement in Education, 1999) all contain guidelines for the appropriate selection and use of tests and assessments.

E.3. Informed Consent in Assessment

E.3.a. Explanation to Clients. Prior to assessment, counselors explain the nature and purposes of assessment and the specific use of results by potential recipients. The explanation will be given in terms and language that the client (or other legally authorized person on behalf of the client) can understand.

E.3.b. Recipients of Results. Counselors consider the client's and/or examinee's welfare, explicit understandings, and prior agreements in determining who receives the assessment results. Counselors include accurate and appropriate interpretations with any release of individual or group assessment results.

Counselors who wish to incorporate tests into the counseling process must first obtain informed consent from the client. This requires the counselor to fully divulge to the client all that is involved in the testing process and why this particular intervention would be advantageous at that time. When it comes to educating clients on the testing process, there are several topics that will need to be addressed before informed consent can be obtained. A list of these can be found in Table 16.1. Additionally, counselors also may choose to provide their clients with a copy of the *Rights and Responsibilities of Test Takers: Guidelines and*

Table 16.1 Topics to Cover in the Informed Consent Process Prior to Testing

Purpose of the test

Skills to be measured or assessed

Criteria used for choosing the test

Test administration process (what the client will be expected to do)

Testing conditions made available

Sample questions the client can expect to see

Scoring methods (including any standardization or norming)

How scores are interpreted and what results mean

Who should have access to the test results

Expectations (Joint Committee on Testing Practices, 2000). This document details what clients can expect from the testing process and also what they will be tasked with doing in the process. After providing this document to a client, the counselor should plan to go over it with the client in session to address any questions the client may have and set up the arrangements for testing to begin. When describing the testing process to your clients, it is important to keep in mind their age and cognitive level. Using terms that they are familiar with will help them better understand what they are being asked to participate in and the benefits they can expect to realize (see Guided Practice Exercise 16.2).

GUIDED PRACTICE EXERCISE 16.2

Imagine that you are working with a young child (3–5 years of age) and you want to perform an assessment on that child. How would you describe the assessment process to the child's parents in order to obtain their informed consent? What information would be important to share with the parents?

E.4. Release of Data to Qualified Professionals

Counselors release assessment data in which the client is identified only with the consent of the client or the client's legal representative. Such data are released only to persons recognized by counselors as qualified to interpret the data.

This standard actually addresses two issues. First, counselors are bound to maintain client confidentiality. This extends to the communication of test results. Clients have the expectation that their test results will not be communicated to any other party without their expressed written consent. In the case of a minor, the consent of the parent or legal guardian is required to release any information on assessments performed or data collected. The second issue addressed here is evaluation of the credentials of the recipient of any test results. There are countless examples in the counseling literature and in the media in which test results were interpreted incorrectly by individuals who lack the requisite skills and training needed to properly interpret test data. As a result, counselors are strongly encouraged to have potential third-party recipients verify their credentials before the release of any test results (Welfel, 2006).

E.5. Diagnosis of Mental Disorders

E.5.a. Proper Diagnosis. Counselors take special care to provide proper diagnosis of mental disorders. Assessment techniques (including personal interview) used to determine client care (e.g., locus of treatment, type of treatment, recommended follow-up) are carefully selected and appropriately used.

E.5.b. Cultural Sensitivity. Counselors recognize that culture affects the manner in which clients' problems are defined and experienced. Client's socioeconomic and cultural experiences are considered when diagnosing mental disorders.

E.5.c. Historical and Social Prejudices in the Diagnosis of Pathology. Counselors recognize historical and social prejudices in the misdiagnosis and pathologizing of certain individuals and groups and strive to become aware of and address such biases in themselves or others.

E.5.d. Refraining from Diagnosis. Counselors may refrain from making and/or reporting a diagnosis if they believe it would cause harm to the client or others. Counselors carefully consider both the positive and negative implications of a diagnosis.

The stigma of mental illness is a profound social problem with a long history, and it is widely believed that diagnostic labels cause or contribute to such stigmatization (Ruscio, 2004). Furthermore, assigning diagnostic labels to a client's problem or presenting issue can have both powerful and negative psychological effects (Welfel, 2006; see Case Illustration 16.2). Because of the weight diagnostic labels carry, counselors should assign them judicially. When considering potential diagnostic categories, counselors should strive for parsimony. In other words, counselors should try to identify the least stigmatizing label that still accurately reflects the lived experience of their clients. In addition, the proper diagnosis of a client also requires counselors to be sensitive to the diverse backgrounds of their clients. As Whiston (2009) contends, counselors should consider contextual factors such as the clients' cultural and socioeconomic experiences when making a clinical diagnosis.

A unique inclusion in the ACA *Code of Ethics* that is not found in the ethical codes of other mental health professions is standard E.5.d, which states that counselors can refrain from making a diagnosis. For many counselors, the practice of diagnosing disorders in clients runs counterintuitive to their understanding of the purpose of counseling. More in line with the developmental underpinnings of the counseling profession, counselors may choose to avoid labeling a client's pathology and instead focus on more positive terminology that encourages clients to build on their strengths (Dougherty, 2005).

CASE ILLUSTRATION 16.2

In their 2004 book *Misdiagnosis and Dual Diagnoses of Gifted Children and Adults,* Webb and his co-authors note that a significant percentage of gifted and talented children and adults are misdiagnosed by mental health professionals. The most common misdiagnoses given to these individuals are attention deficit hyperactivity disorder, oppositional defiant disorder, obsessive compulsive disorder, and mood disorders such as cyclothymic disorder, dysthymic disorder, depression, and bipolar disorder. According to Webb et al., many of these incorrect diagnoses are made because the professionals diagnosing these individuals have not been adequately trained to recognize specific social and emotional characteristics of gifted individuals. As a result, these characteristics are often mistakenly seen as signs of pathology.

E.6. Instrument Selections

E.6.a. Appropriateness of Instruments. Counselors carefully consider the validity, reliability, psychometric limitations, and appropriateness of instruments when selecting assessments and, when possible, use multiple forms of assessment, data, and/or instruments in forming conclusions, diagnoses, or recommendations.

E.6.b. Referral Information. If a client is referred to a third party for assessment, the counselor provides specific referral questions and sufficient objective data about the client to ensure that appropriate assessment instruments are utilized.

When counselors opt to include testing as part of the counseling process, they assume responsibility for ensuring that the tests used are appropriate for the client and situation. Identifying whether a test is appropriate requires the counselor to have knowledge of the test as well as of the client. When selecting a test, questions to ask yourself include the following: What information do I need to gather? What information do I already have? How will this information allow me to better understand my client? What are the psychometric properties of the test? (Is it reliable? Is it valid?) Has normative data been collected for the client population in which I intend to use the test? Addressing these questions at the beginning of the process will help you eliminate tests that are not appropriate for your current need and narrow your list of potential options to a small sample of tests. To assist you in making your final decision, resources such as the *RUST-3* (AAC, 2003a) should be consulted for additional guidance on accurate test selection and usage.

E.7. Conditions of Assessment Administration

E.7.a. Administration Conditions. Counselors administer assessments under the same conditions that were established in their standardization. When assessments are not administered under standard conditions, as may be necessary to accommodate clients with disabilities, or when unusual behavior or irregularities occur during the administration, those conditions are noted in interpretation, and the results may be designated as invalid or of questionable validity.

E.7.b. Provision of Favorable Conditions. Counselors provide an appropriate environment for the administration of assessments (e.g., privacy, comfort, freedom from distraction).

E.7.c. Technological Administration. Counselors ensure that technologically administered assessments function properly and provide clients with accurate results.

E.7.d. Unsupervised Assessments. Unless the assessment instrument is designed, intended, and validated for self-administration and/or scoring, counselors do not permit unsupervised use.

Adhering to the standardized administration protocol outlined in a test manual is important because it allows you to make more reliable comparisons between a client and the test norms or between a client and other clients. When the administration conditions are the same for all test takers, the influence of outside error is mitigated. Differences in client test scores become more representative of differences in the construct being assessed than any unexplained, extraneous variable. As a result, counselors are better able to state whether treatment is effective.

As the counselor, you are responsible for ensuring that the administration protocol is applied in the same fashion to each client. The same responsibility exists for tests that are administered on a computer or by a colleague or trainee. Counselors should always make sure that the correct test materials are present, all clients are afforded the same testing opportunities, any computer or other technology to be used is functioning properly, and any client needs are addressed before testing begins. Should a situation arise in which a disparity in the testing conditions is noted, counselors should make note of the disparity and factor it into their interpretations. For example, the power may go out during the administration of a test for one client but not for others. This unplanned event may have negatively impacted the client's performance and caused him or her to be assessed differently. Apart from noting these discrepancies in the test report, counselors also should inform their clients directly of any disparities observed and give them the opportunity to have the test administered a second time under more standardized conditions.

E.8. Multicultural Issues/Diversity in Assessment

Counselors select and use with caution assessment techniques normed on populations other than that of the client. Counselors recognize the effects of age, color, culture, disability, ethnic group, gender, race, language preference, religion, spirituality, sexual orientation, and socioeconomic status on test administration and interpretation, and they place test results in proper perspective with other relevant factors.

When working with diverse populations, the culturally competent counselor's best course of action is to select tests and assessments that were specifically designed for the groups with whom he or she is working (Sedlacek & Kim, 1996). Unfortunately, this is not an option that is always available. Many existing tests were created using homogenous normative samples that were not very diverse. As you evaluate tests, make sure you make note of the characteristics and demographics of the norm group and recognize any potential limitations to using the test that might arise when working with other populations (Remley & Herlihy, 2010). Failure to do so may result in you having invalid test results that really do not tell you anything useful about the client that can be used in the counseling process.

E.9. Scoring and Interpretation of Assessments

E.9.a. Reporting. When counselors report assessment results, they consider the client's personal and cultural background, the level of the client's understanding of the results, and the impact of the results on the client. In reporting assessment results based on quantitative data, counselors indicate reservations that exist regarding validity or reliability due to circumstances of the assessment or the inappropriateness of the norms for the person tested.

E.9.b. Instruments With Insufficient Empirical Data. Counselors exercise caution when interpreting the results of research instruments not having sufficient empirical data to support respondent results. The specific purposes for the use of such instruments are stated explicitly to the examinee. Counselors qualify any conclusions, diagnoses, or recommendations made that are based on assessments or instruments with questionable validity or reliability.

E.9.c. Assessment Services. Counselors who provide assessment scoring and interpretation services to support the assessment process confirm the validity of such interpretations.

They accurately describe the purpose, norms, validity, reliability, and applications of the procedures and any special qualifications applicable to their use. At all times, counselors maintain their ethical responsibility to those being assessed.

Numbers can be misleading if not placed in their proper context. When interpreting scores from an assessment, it is important for counselors to understand what the numbers mean and how they were derived (see Case Illustration 16.3). When possible, try to supplement test data with other pieces of information you have about the client. Do the results seem to validate how you conceptualized the client, or do they paint a completely different picture? Information from other sources or the administration of other tests can help develop a holistic picture of the client and his or her presenting problem. The more information you have, the more accurate your diagnosis will likely be.

CASE ILLUSTRATION   16.3

A client recently was administered the Strong Interest Inventory to gauge her career interests. The counselor presents her with the following results: Social 64, Artistic 48, Enterprising 43, Conventional 40, Investigative 36, and Realistic 32. What do these scores mean? Without much context, they probably mean very little to the client. Did she score above average or below average? What type of career would be best for her? In this scenario the counselor did not follow ethical practice in reporting test scores. The counselor should have included additional information to help the client better understand what her scores mean. Additional information that would have been helpful includes the range of scores, averages and standard deviations, cut scores used to denote high levels of interest, percentiles, and more. Without any of these pieces of information, the client's raw scores exist only in a vacuum.

E.10. Assessment Security

Counselors maintain the integrity and security of tests and assessments consistent with legal and contractual obligations. Counselors do not appropriate, reproduce, or modify published assessments or parts thereof without acknowledgment and permission from the publisher.

Counselors have both an ethical and legal obligation to protect the integrity of the tests they use (Remley & Herlihy, 2010). Testing materials should be stored in a secure location that is not accessible by those who are not authorized or trained to administer the tests. When tests are not kept in secure locations, there is a risk that copies of a test may circulate, potentially biasing the results of those who now have access to the test before they take the test. As a general rule, counselors should take extra precautions to ensure that all testing materials are kept in a safe and secure location to not only protect the integrity of the test but also maintain client confidentiality. These extra precautions may include using locked storage cabinets or password-protecting computer-based assessment programs and results.

E.11. Obsolete Assessments and Outdated Results

Counselors do not use data or results from assessments that are obsolete or outdated for the current purpose (e.g., noncurrent versions of assessments/instruments). Counselors make every effort to prevent the misuse of obsolete measures and assessment data by others.

Occasionally, commercially available tests undergo revisions. These revised versions improve on their predecessors in many fundamental ways. As a counselor, you must make sure you are using the most current version of the instrument. As you go through the process of selecting a test to use, make sure that it is one that is still currently used by professionals in the field. In addition, double-check that the version to which you have access is the latest version and no revisions or updates have been released (see Case Illustration 16.4).

CASE ILLUSTRATION   16.4

In 1989 a revised version of the Minnesota Multiphasic Personality Inventory-2 (MMPI-2) was released. One of the major changes in the revised version was the inclusion of a more diverse normative sample. For the normative sample used to create the original MMPI, individuals from minority ethnic or racial groups were not included. Use of this first version in practice today, when clients represent more and more diverse backgrounds, would most likely result in many invalid profiles that had little to no practical or clinical value.

E.12. Assessment Construction

Counselors use established scientific procedures, relevant standards, and current professional knowledge for assessment design in the development, publication, and utilization of assessment techniques.

Counselors who choose to develop their own instruments should follow the principles of sound test design. These include operationally defining all constructs, selecting an appropriate question style (forced-choice or open-choice) and item response set (variable response or Likert-type scale), identifying an appropriate and representative normative sample, and establishing measures of reliability and validity. As the administration of tests becomes a more popular activity in mental health treatment, the level of sophistication involved in their development will only increase.

E.13. Forensic Evaluation: Evaluation for Legal Proceedings

E.13.a. Primary Obligations. When providing forensic evaluations, the primary obligation of counselors is to produce objective findings that can be substantiated based on information and techniques appropriate to the evaluation, which may include examination of the individual and/or review of records. Counselors form professional opinions based on their professional knowledge and expertise that can be supported by the data gathered in evaluations. Counselors define the limits of their reports or testimony, especially when an examination of the individual has not been conducted.

E.13.b. Consent for Evaluation. Individuals being evaluated are informed in writing that the relationship is for the purposes of an evaluation and is not therapeutic in nature, and entities or individuals who will receive the evaluation report are identified. Counselors who perform forensic evaluations obtain written consent to be evaluated from those being evaluated or from their legal representative unless a court orders evaluations to be conducted without the written consent of individuals being evaluated. When children or vulnerable adults who lack the capacity to give voluntary consent are being evaluated, informed written consent is obtained from a parent or a guardian.

E.13.c. Client Evaluation Prohibited. Counselors do not evaluate current or former clients, clients' romantic partners, or clients' family members for forensic purposes. Counselors do not counsel individuals they are evaluating.

E.13.d. Avoid Potentially Harmful Relationships. Counselors who provide forensic evaluations avoid potentially harmful professional or personal relationships with family members, romantic partners, and close friends of individuals they are evaluating or have evaluated in the past.

Forensic counseling is a growing specialty area that involves the application of assessment and intervention services in legal settings (see Chapter 13 for more information related to forensic assessment). Counselors who participate in this activity usually do so at the request of the court or criminal justice system. Their goal is to obtain information that can be used to assist in competency evaluations, sentencing recommendations, custody hearings, and expert witness court testimony. Because of the unique relationship that develops between the assessor and individual being assessed, the ACA decided to include a section in the ethical guidelines that deals with how this relationship differs from a traditional counseling relationship. As you can see in the standards listed above, counselors should never engage in a dual relationship with individuals they are evaluating in a forensic setting. As this practice continues to grow in popularity and more counselors begin working in this area, the need for counselors to clearly discuss with their clients how the roles of counselor and forensic evaluator differ and how the two should never cross paths will become increasingly important.

ADDITIONAL SOURCES OF ETHICAL CODES

While we have spent a great deal of time discussing ethical standards related to testing and assessment that are included in the ACA (2014) *Code of Ethics*, they do not represent the only source for information on ethical conduct. Similar ethical codes you might come across in your counseling career are the National Board of Certified Counselors' (2005) *NBCC Code of Ethics*, the American School Counselor Association's (2010) *Ethical Standards for School Counselors*, and the American Mental Health Counselors Association's (2010) *AMHCA Code of Ethics*. Each replicates many of the ethical principles found in the ACA *Code of Ethics*. Where they differ is in the specificity they include related to working with various client populations in various settings (see Guided Practice Exercise 16.3).

GUIDED PRACTICE EXERCISE 16.3

Review the American Mental Health Counselors Association and American School Counselor Association ethical codes and compare them to the ACA *Code of Ethics*. What similarities do you see? What are some of the more noteworthy differences between them? How would you reconcile the differences between them in your work as a practicing counselor?

Although professional counseling codes of ethics speak to various issues, counselors should recognize that these codes are purposefully designed to be broad in scope. They will never be able to address each and every potential ethical issue facing counselors today. Consequently, professional codes of ethics are necessary but not sufficient for exercising ethical responsibility (Welfel, 2006). Counselors may still be held accountable when potential ethical breaches occur, even if ethical codes do not contain information on a particular issue. In the absence of a clear answer in the ethical code, counselors should employ an ethical decision-making model to determine their next course of action.

ETHICAL DECISION-MAKING MODEL

The ethical decision-making model (Forester-Miller & Davis, 1995) represents a practical, sequential, step-by-step approach toward ethical decision making. The authors note that their conceptualization of the model was derived from several existing ethical decision-making models. Using Forester-Miller and Davis's (1995) model, counselors are better able to assist their clients in an ethical and legal manner. Their model consists of seven steps. Case Illustration 16.5 demonstrates the application of this model.

Step 1: Identify the problem. You should focus on gathering as much information as possible to clearly understand the situation and any dilemmas that may be faced. In so doing, you should be as specific and objective as possible in describing the dilemma. Facts should be separated from opinion and conjecture so that an accurate representation of the current situation can be examined.

Step 2: Apply the ethical guidelines. Here is where you want to consult the ACA *Code of Ethics*. Specifically, you should determine whether the particular issue identified in Step 1 is addressed in any of the codes or standards. At this point you are faced with two options. When the current issue is addressed in the *Code*, you should follow the prescribed course of action as it is laid out. If the current issue does not clearly fit into any of the existing codes, or if it appears to be covered in conflicting standards, you will need to proceed to the next step in the ethical decision-making model.

Step 3: Determine the nature and dimensions of the dilemma. It is incumbent on you as the counselor to make sure that you have thoroughly reviewed the situation from all angles and considered all possibilities. This often requires you to reach out and use other sources. In this step you should research the existing professional literature to see if any guidance can be ascertained. You also could consult with colleagues and supervisors.

Sometimes a fresh perspective will shed light on an element of the situation that previously may have been overlooked. Finally, you might consider consulting with professional associations in which you are a member. ACA and many of the state branches have standing ethics committees in place to help members work through potential ethical dilemmas. Armed with the information gained in this step, you can now move on to Step 4.

Step 4: Generate potential courses of action. Many times there is more than one way to proceed in your work with a client. A variety of theoretical orientations can be applied, and several different techniques and interventions can be employed. At this point you should consider all available alternatives for you and your client. Select approaches that appear to fit most with your current needs and the presentation of the client.

Step 5: Consider the potential consequences of all options and determine a course of action. Once you have identified all possible solutions to the current problem, you should consider the consequences associated with each of these solutions. What would be the result of each of the solutions, should it be applied? Would the client benefit or be subjected to additional pain or stress? Each solution identified in Step 4 will have advantages and disadvantages. The goal is to select the solution that overall has the potential to benefit the client the most.

Step 6: Evaluate the selected course of action. By this point in the process you have brainstormed several potential courses of action and examined the advantages and disadvantages of each option. Once you select an option, you need to reassess the situation to determine if the implementation of this new course of action could potentially give rise to any other ethical dilemmas. A good way to assess your chosen course of action is to evaluate against the moral principles we discussed earlier. If the chosen solution satisfies the principles, you can confidently move toward implementing the solution.

Step 7: Implement the course of action. In this final step in the model, you implement the chosen course of action. This step frequently arouses a lot of anxious energy in counselors. The unknown may be quite anxiety-provoking for you. You may even ask yourself questions such as "Did I make the right choice?" or "Was this really the best option for my client?" Knowing that you progressed through the steps in this model should help you feel more comfortable with the decision you made. After you implement your solution, you should regularly check in with your client to assess whether your actions had the anticipated effect. Follow-up will help you be better prepared and more informed in the future.

CASE ILLUSTRATION   16.5

Mrs. James is the school counselor at the local middle school. She has been working with an 11-year-old student named Becky for the past few months related to Becky's feelings about the recent news that her parents are divorcing. The divorce has become contentious and Becky feels torn between both parents. Mrs. James receives a subpoena to provide testimony in a child custody case involving Becky and her parents. In the court papers, Mrs. James sees that she is being asked to disclose information she considers confidential. To determine what she should do, Mrs. James applies the ethical decision-making model. In addition, she consults with a colleague at another school. Together they weigh the advantages and disadvantages of sharing the requested information and how it would benefit Becky to do so or not. Considering all available data, Mrs. James is then able to make an informed choice.

LEGAL ISSUES IN ASSESSMENT

In addition to following ethical standards of practice, counselors also should be familiar with the legal issues related to assessment. **Laws** are rules that address proper conduct that have been codified and enacted by local, state, or federal legislation. Laws are more prescriptive than ethical standards and typically carry greater sanctions or penalties for failure to comply. A counselor who violates an ethical standard might be censured by a local state licensing agency, but a counselor who breaks a law risks being fined, arrested, or even incarcerated.

There are a number of laws that impact the work of counselors who engage in testing and assessment practices. Though the laws were not created with the expressed intent of regulating the practice of counseling assessment, the work of counselors is affected in a variety of environments as a result of their passage (Whiston, 2009). A common feature of all of these laws is that they include language designed to safeguard and protect individual rights. In the following section we will examine some of the legislatively enacted federal statutes and court-adjudicated case laws that regulate the testing and assessment practices of professional counselors.

FEDERAL STATUTES

Family Educational Rights and Privacy Act of 1974

The Family Educational Rights and Privacy Act (FERPA), also known as the Buckley Amendment, was enacted into law by Congress in 1974 as the major piece of legislation that established parameters on accessibility and disclosure of student records. Under FERPA, a student and his or her parents have the right to access the student's educational records, challenge any of the content of the educational record, and restrict access or release of the educational records or any personally identifiable information (e.g., name, address, social security number, any other information that would make the student's identity easily traceable) to third parties. Included in the educational record are any assessment or test scores the student may have as well as any counseling records. Parents and students have access to these documents and can request to view them at any time. What is not included, and what students and parents do not have access to, are personal notes maintained as personal memory aids to recall comments made by parents, teachers, administrators, or other students about the student seeking counseling services. The guidelines on what constitutes personal notes are complex. Counselors are encouraged to check the guidelines before keeping any notes or documents separate from the student's file.

Education of All Handicapped Children Act of 1975

The Education of All Handicapped Children Act was signed into law in 1975. The law requires that fair and equitable access to education be provided to everyone. As such, it is the responsibility of school staff to identify students in need and provide them with the specialized learning tools that represent the least restrictive method. While this law initially covered the education of only school-aged children, the passage of Public Law 99-457 in 1986 extended the scope of the earlier law to now include all children above 3 years of age, providing coverage for children in preschool.

Americans with Disabilities Act of 1990

The Americans with Disabilities Act requires employers to provide reasonable and appropriate testing accommodations for individuals with documented disabilities covered under the law. The key word here is *reasonable*. Counselors should use professional judgment when determining what constitutes reasonable accommodations. Although the ACA *Code of Ethics* directs counselors to maintain uniform testing conditions for all test takers, you will recall that a provision was included that allowed for alterations and accommodations to be made for clients who may require special assistance (standard E.7.a). When it comes to clients who have documented disabilities, counselors can now work with those clients and their limitations and practice in an ethical and legal manner.

Civil Rights Act of 1991

The Civil Rights Act was first passed into law in 1964. Title VII of that law specifically prohibited discrimination in the workplace on the basis of race, color, religion, gender, pregnancy, or national origin. Challenges to the original law led to several amendments through the years, the most recent occurring in 1991. The 1991 Civil Rights Act has had a direct impact on assessment practices. Under the amended law, employers are prohibited from using assessment instruments to make employment decisions when the instrument may have an adverse impact on the hiring, evaluation, and promotion of individuals in classes protected by Title VII. Use of such assessments will be deemed discriminatory unless the test can measure a reasonable measure of job performance.

Health Information Portability and Accountability Act of 1996

The Health Information Portability and Accountability Act (HIPAA) was passed into law by Congress in 1996. There are three basic rights individuals have under HIPAA. First, clients have a right to access their medical records and are entitled to see and copy their records. They also have the ability to request that amendments be made to the record. Second, clients have a right to request that a restriction be placed on the disclosure of their protected health information for the purposes of treatment, payment, or healthcare operations. Finally, covered entities (medical facilities, doctors, counselors, mental health professionals) are required to provide clients with a clear, written explanation of how protected health information can be used and disclosed. Although clients have a right to access their records, it is up to the individual institution to determine the policy by which this access is granted. Some facilities require so many hours, or days, of advance notice before access is granted. Other facilities may charge a per-page fee for any copies of the record requested.

Individuals with Disabilities Education Improvement Act of 2004

The Individuals with Disabilities Education Improvement Act (IDEIA) was established to increase the services and access to educational opportunities available to students with disabilities. Specifically, when counselors diagnose clients as having specified learning disabilities (SLDs), they are required to use a multidimensional approach. A single test can no longer serve as the sole criterion for placement in special education programs. These new multidimensional approaches must include evidence-based assessments that assess for cognitive and behavioral factors. In response to these new placement guidelines, many schools are revamping their curriculum to better meet the needs of students with SLDs. Models such as Responsiveness to Intervention (RtI) have gained in popularity since the passage of the 2004 version of IDEIA. Through RtI, school counselors and educators are able to address the specific needs of a student using a level of care that is uniquely designed for that student.

CASE LAWS

Griggs v. Duke Power Company (1971)

Prior to 1965, Duke Power Company had engaged in a longstanding practice of segregating its workforce. According to company policy, separate labor classifications were created for White and Black employees. The jobs available to African American employees were often the most labor intensive and lowest paying. This practice changed with the passage of the Civil Rights Act of 1964. Under Title VII of the law, discrimination in the workplace became illegal. To comply with the new federal law, Duke Power Company removed its segregation policy and opened its jobs to all applicants. Despite this change, African American workers at the company still experienced restrictions. Duke Power Company had amended its hiring practices to now require all applicants to positions outside of its labor division to have a high school diploma and achieve a satisfactory score on two aptitude tests, the Wonderlic Test and the Bennett Mechanical Comprehension Test. Essentially, these new requirements were put into place to block transfers of employees without high school diplomas, the majority of whom were African American, from the labor division to other departments.

Believing that the new job requirements essentially served as a new form of racial segregation, Willie Griggs filed a class action lawsuit on behalf of himself and 12 other African American employees at Duke Power Company's Dan River hydroelectric plant in Draper, North Carolina. Their argument was that the company was engaging in practices that went against Title VII, specifically citing its use of the two aptitude tests as a condition of employment. The bar for satisfactory performance on the tests was set as the national median score for high school graduates. As many African Americans at the time had not completed high school, their scores were noticeably lower than those of White applicants who had completed high school. Although the court that reviewed the case found the tests to have a cultural bias, it sided in favor of the defendant, ruling that the use of these tests did not reflect any discriminatory intent on behalf of Duke Power Company. The ruling was appealed and eventually made its way to the U.S. Supreme Court in 1970. After months of deliberation the Court ruled in favor of Griggs, overturning the decision of all lower courts. In delivering the Court's ruling, Chief Justice Warren Burger noted that Duke Power Company had made no attempt to determine the validity of these aptitude test scores as predictors of work performance. While the tests themselves were not considered illegal, the use of them in hiring decisions for jobs in which the test content did not pertain to expected job skills or performance was illegal.

The outcome of *Griggs v. Duke Power Company* has had a direct impact on assessment practices. The Court's ruling brought about a stronger focus on the validity of tests especially when they are used to make placement decisions. Essentially, if an instrument has an adverse or disparate impact on a certain group of people, an employer must demonstrate how the instrument is job-related. In other words, the employer holds the burden of proof for establishing how the information collected from these tests relates to the ability of applicants to perform the job duties required of the position for which they are applying. The disparate impact standard established in this 1971 ruling was further codified into federal law with the passage of the Civil Rights Act of 1991.

For counselors, the result of *Griggs v. Duke Power Company* highlights the importance of choosing tests and assessments appropriately. Instruments should be well researched prior to being implemented with clients to ensure that they can produce valid results that will be useful in the counseling process. When counselors need to make high-stakes decisions regarding placement and treatment care, test results should be integrated with additional information about the client and his or her presenting problem.

Larry P. v. Riles (1979)

Larry P. v. Riles was a case filed against the State of California challenging the state's current practice of classifying students with learning disabilities. In the 1970s, children who had documented learning disabilities were classified as having educable mental retardation (EMR). Because of their disability, these children were unlikely to be successful in the traditional classroom setting. As a result, special EMR classrooms were established to work with these students. Placement in these special classes was based on a student's IQ score obtained from the administration of a standardized intelligence test. Larry P. was an African American child whose parents argued that the school's system of placing students in the EMR classrooms appeared to be culturally biased. Their initial complaint led to the filing of this class action lawsuit.

During the trial, data were presented that seemed to support the parents' claim of inequity. According to state records, during the 1968–1969 school year, African Americans constituted 9% of the total school population in California. However, these records also indicated that African Americans made up 27% of the student population in the school's EMR programs. The plaintiffs argued that the larger percentage of African American students being classified as EMR was evidence that the IQ tests were discriminatory. The 9th Circuit U.S. Court of Appeals ruled in favor of Larry P., stating that the IQ tests, which were designed and standardized on an all-White population, were in fact culturally biased. As a result, placement in special education programs could not be made using an IQ score. A more versatile approach that included the collection of data from numerous sources was put in place to ensure that no one group was being unfairly affected.

The results of the *Larry P. v. Riles* case continue to have an influence on the assessment activities of counselors today, especially those working in school settings. In addition to establishing the legal precedent that states intelligence tests administered to minority children must be validated for use with that population, the impact of the Larry P. case has expanded throughout the years. Although the original ruling applied specifically to standardized intelligence tests, many standardized speech and language tests used by counselors also fall under the Larry P. mandate because they either directly or indirectly purport to measure IQ or their construct validity is partially or fully determined through correlations with intelligence tests (Novak, Hamaguchi, & McCullough, 2003). As society continues to increase in diversity, school counselors should continue to assess whether the tests used in their schools have been normed on and are appropriate for the students with whom they work.

Debra P. v. Turlington (1981)

Debra P. v. Turlington is another case that involved the appropriate use of high-stakes testing. In 1978 the Florida state legislature approved an amendment to the Educational Accountability Act of 1976 that required all public school students in the state to pass a functional literacy examination in order to receive their high school diploma. The rationale behind this amendment was government officials' desire to hold the education system more accountable and ensure that students graduating from public schools in Florida possessed the basic skills necessary to become positive and productive members of society. Beginning in the 1978–1979 academic year, students were required to take the Florida State Student Assessment Test, Part II (SSAT II) at the conclusion of their senior year, with a passing score being a requirement for students to receive their high school diploma. Almost immediately the instructional validity of the SSAT II was called into question.

In 1981 a group of Hillsborough County students, led by Debra P., filed suit against the state, challenging the constitutionality of the SSAT II. The U.S. District Court sided with the students and ruled that the test was unconstitutional and could not be used as a criterion for graduation in the state of Florida. The decision focused on two key points: due process and test validity (Lunenberg, 2010). The SSAT II was implemented in the 1978–1979 academic year. Students graduating that year were not given advance notice of the test, nor were they informed about what the test would look like. Without sufficient advance notice, students were unable to adequately prepare for the test. The second key point dealt with the validity of the test. A review of the test statistics highlighted a significant disparity in the pass rates for African American and White students. The pass rate for White students was 98%, while only 80% of African American students were passing the test. A closer review revealed that the content of the test was not based on material being taught in all schools. Prior to desegregation, students of color were taught in separate schools. The curriculum offered in these schools was often inferior to what students in the White schools were learning. As many of these now high school students had most likely spent an early portion of their education in segregated schools, they were at a disadvantage in terms of having had equal access to the material on which they now were being tested. In its ruling, the court prohibited the state from using the SSAT II test for a period of 4 years so as to ensure that students being tested would all have matriculated through their education under desegregated conditions (Lunenberg, 2010). Moving forward, the state would have to collect data to demonstrate curricular validity for the test.

Sharif v. New York State Department of Education (1989)

In the 1970s, the state of New York awarded academic scholarships designed to recognize and reward superior high school achievement and to encourage New York's brightest students to attend college in the state. Over 26,000 merit-based scholarships were awarded on an annual basis. Beginning in 1977 the criteria for these scholarships changed. Scholarship recipients were now selected based solely on their performance on the SAT. There were several issues with using the SAT as the award criterion. For one, the test included only two sections; one assessing verbal aptitude and the other mathematical aptitude. Knowledge of other subjects taught in high school was not assessed. Second, by design the test is meant to assess potential for success in college and not measure high school success. Finally, the test has a known gender bias, with female test takers scoring lower than their male counterparts. Based on these several shortcomings, the validity of the state's decision to use the SAT was called into question.

In 1989 a group of 10 female high school students filed suit against the state department of education as well as the publishers of the SAT. Their argument was based on the disparate impact clause in Title VII of the Civil Rights Act of 1964. The U.S. District Court ruled in favor of the plaintiffs and ceased the state's use of the SAT as the sole criteria for the awarding of scholarships. The award process was changed to incorporate a combination of markers, including standardized test score and high school grade point average. Counselors can learn from this case by remembering the importance of assessing whether they are using the results of tests in a manner consistent with their intended purpose. While some instruments may assess the presence of symptoms, describe a mood state, or construct a personality profile, these may not be appropriate sources of information for making clinical diagnoses.

Soroka v. Dayton Hudson Corporation (1991)

The Dayton Hudson Corporation is a holding company that owns and operates several Target department stores throughout California. Applicants for the position of store security officer (SSO), as a condition of employment, were asked to complete a psychological test known as Psychscreen as part of the application process. The executives at Dayton Hudson Corporation included the Psychscreen because they felt good judgment and emotional stability were important job skills for SSOs and wanted to screen out those who were not emotionally able to handle the job. The Psychscreen is a combination of items from the Minnesota Multiphasic Personality Inventory-2 and California Psychological Inventory personality tests. A total of 704 questions are on the Psychscreen. Although the majority of applicants successfully passed this initial screening, one applicant raised questions about the use of the screening tool.

Despite passing the screening and being hired as an SSO, Sibi Soroka objected to the use of the Psychscreen based on the content of its questions. Several of the questions were either religious or sexual in nature. Having little luck seeking resolution in the administrative process, a lawsuit against the parent company was filed. The plaintiffs claimed that Psychscreen violated applicants' privacy and asked questions that were completely unrelated to the job duties required of the position for which they were applying. After hearing testimony on both sides, the California State Superior Court issued an initial order denying injunctive relief on the ground that the plaintiffs had failed to establish that Target had based its hiring decisions on religious beliefs or sexual traits or that the questions were designed to reveal such information. The initial ruling was appealed and the California Court of Appeals reversed the order denying relief. The court struck down the individual questions as violating privacy rights, focusing on the test questions themselves and dis-regarding the lower court's factual findings that Target never received the test answer sheets and that the answers had no meaning except in their cumulative power to identify certain emotional traits. However, the court did hold that questions that violate privacy must be directly and narrowly related to the nature of the employee's duties. If a cogent relationship can be demonstrated, questions such as those on the Psychscreen can be used. This case illustrates another example of the importance of content and construct validity.

STATE LAWS AND REGULATIONS

In addition to federal mandates, counselors also should become familiar with the local laws that govern the counseling profession in the state in which they practice. With the adoption of a counselor licensure law in California in October 2009, all 50 states now have licensure laws in place. In addition, all 50 states also have laws that are used to regulate the school counseling profession. These laws describe the practice of counseling as it is defined in that state, including the type of education and experience required and the scope of practice within which counselors are able to provide counseling services. Laws vary by state, so counselors should research what they may or may not be able to, including assessment-related activities, in the state in which they are employed. The American Counseling Association regularly publishes information related to the state laws applicable to counselors and counseling licensure. These can be viewed on the ACA website or by ordering hard copies of these reports. Since laws may change, counselors are encouraged to update their understanding of what they can and cannot do as a counselor in their state on a regular basis. Doing so demonstrates your professionalism and will help prevent you from practicing outside the law.

KEYSTONES

- The practice of counseling assessment is regulated by several ethical and legal principles.
- Ethical standards related to assessment practices can be found in the ACA *Code of Ethics*.

- When counselors find themselves confronted with ethical dilemmas, the ethical decision-making model can be followed to determine the best course of action to take in almost any counseling situation. Using the model is seen as professional practice for counselors.
- Several important pieces of federal legislation have had a direct impact on counselors and their assessment practices. These legislative items include elements that relate to the assessment work counselors do in both clinical and school-based counseling settings.
- Each of the legal precedents related to counseling and assessment that we have today came about due to litigation surrounding the inappropriate use of tests and other forms of assessment. As a result, testing and assessment practices are highly regulated today and require counselors to be both knowledgeable and competent.

KEY TERMS

autonomy	fidelity	nonmaleficence
beneficence	justice	
ethics	laws	

ADDITIONAL RESOURCES

- American Counseling Association *Code of Ethics*

  http://counseling.org/docs/ethics/2014-aca-code-of-ethics.pdf?sfvrsn=4

In addition to the *Code of Ethics* document, this section of the ACA Knowledge Center has information on how counselors can request a free and confidential ethical/professional practice consult.

- American Counselor Association Knowledge Center

  http://www.counseling.org/knowledge-center/licensure-requirements

This resource offers updated information on state licensure and certification information for mental health counselors and school counselors. Counselors can look here to see what the laws specific to the practice of counseling are in their state.

- American School Counselor Association Ethical Standards

  http://www.schoolcounselor.org/school-counselors-members/legal-ethical

These are the ethical standards applicable to school counselors.

- Commission on Rehabilitation Counselor Certification Code of Ethics

  http://www.crccertification.com/pages/crc_ccrc_code_of_ethics/10.php

This ethical practice resource is for certified rehabilitation counselors.

- National Board for Certified Counselors Code of Ethics

  http://www.nbcc.org/Ethics

This is the code of ethics that NBCC applicants and certificants are expected to adhere to in their counseling practice.

Student Study Site: Visit the Student Study Site at **www.sagepub.com/watson** to access additional study tools, including quizzes, web resources, and journal articles.

Glossary

accommodation   The process of modifying existing schemas or creating new ones to deal with new information.

acculturation   A process in which individuals encounter culturally diverse characteristics beyond their own identity, includes assimilation or negotiation of new cultural ideals, varying integration of components of the newly introduced cultural characteristics, and in some cases no change in cultural identity.

achievement tests   Instruments designed to measure how much someone has learned or mastered in a given context.

ACT   A widely used achievement test measuring skills and knowledge taught in high school that is used as an entrance exam for undergraduate studies.

activity-based learning   A type of learning which occurs in children as they gain knowledge through their experiences and the process of constructing and reconstructing knowledge.

adaptation   A term used to describe an individual's ability to adjust to the environment.

Adult Career Concerns Inventory (ACCI)   An instrument used to assess an individual's current level of career concerns associated with Super's theory of developmental career stages and substages.

analogue observation   Process by which an observer creates a simulated environment that replicates the client's natural surroundings and observes how the client behaves in that created environment.

analytic intelligence   A type of intelligence which includes executive processes such as analyzing, comparing, and evaluating.

apperceive   A verb meaning to perceive in terms of past events.

arithmetic mean   The sum of all scores in a distribution divided by the total number of scores.

Armed Services Vocational Aptitude Battery (ASVAB)   A multiaptitude test designed by the U.S. Department of Defense which is primarily used for recruitment and testing by the armed services to assess the potential and qualifications of armed forces enlistees and assign applicants to military jobs.

Armed Services Vocational Aptitude Battery (ASVAB) Career Exploration Program   A multiaptitude test battery that consists of the Armed Services Vocational Aptitude Battery and the Find Your Interest inventory.

Army Alpha   Test that measured the verbal ability, numerical ability, ability to follow directions, and knowledge of information of military recruits.

Army Beta   Nonverbal counterpart to the Army Alpha that was used to evaluate the aptitude of illiterate, unschooled, or non-English-speaking recruits.

artistic aptitude tests   Specific aptitude tests used to evaluate an individual's artistic talents.

assessment   A process that integrates test information with information from other sources including information obtained from other tests as well as the individual's social, educational, employment, health, or psychological history.

assessment report   A document that outlines the presenting problem that led the client to seek counseling, summarizes the services provided, and addresses the outcomes of those services that were provided.

assimilation   The process of incorporating new objects into present schema.

association techniques   Techniques in which respondents are presented with visual or auditory stimuli and asked to respond with the first association that comes to mind.

authentic assessment   Assessment tasks that evaluate student abilities by measuring how well the student performs in real-life contexts.

autonomy   Independence; the ability of clients to make decisions on their own based on their best interests (freedom of choice).

bar graphs   Graphs used to represent nominal data. The bars in a bar graph do not touch to illustrate the discrete aspects of the nominal data.

bar-on model of emotional social intelligence   A model of emotional intelligence defined by an individual's ability to understand oneself and others, ability to relate with others, and ability to adapt to immediate surroundings effectively.

basal levels   An individual's entry-level score on an assessment.

basic competence   An individual's ability to understand the charges brought against him or her and to work effectively with his or her defense counsel.

Basic Interest Scales   A section of the Strong which measures clusters of interest in 30 broad areas related to the General Occupational Themes.

behavior   The range of actions exhibited by an individual.

Behavior Assessment System for Children, 2nd Edition (BASC-2)   A screening system designed to assess behavioral and emotional strengths and weaknesses in children and adolescents and to assist counselors in diagnosing emotional and behavioral problems and designing effective treatment plans.

Behavior Rating Profile, 2nd Edition (BRP-2)   A norm-referenced, ecological, integrated behavior assessment system comprising six elements which, when used collectively, provide counselors with a more ecological view of an individual's behavioral functioning.

behavioral assessment   Process that includes the identification and measurement of meaningful response units (including overt behavior, feelings, and cognitions) and their controlling variables (both environmental and organismic) for the purposes of understanding and altering human behavior.

behavioral interview   A structured interview that is used to collect information about past behavior.

Bender Visual-Motor Gestalt Test, Second Edition (Bender-Gestalt II)   An expressive, projective measure that provides information about a client's neuropsychological functioning; often used to discern whether brain damage has occurred or the degree of maturation of the nervous system.

beneficence   Always striving to do what is good and acting in the best interest of your client.

bias   A condition which occurs when aspects of the test or test delivery unfairly penalize test takers due to personal characteristics.

Big Five   A model of personality which proposes that personality is composed of five domains (neuroticism, extraversion, openness, agreeableness, and conscientiousness).

bimodal   A distribution where two scores share the distinction of being the highest score obtained.

blindness   A condition in which visual acuity with best correction is worse than or equal to 20/400 or a visual field of 20 degrees or less.

Boehm Test of Basic Concepts-3 (Boehm-3)   A standardized assessment that measures children's understanding of basic relational concepts important for language and cognitive development; appropriate for students in kindergarten through second grade.

Boehm Test of Basic Concepts-3 Preschool (Boehm-3 Preschool)   A standardized assessment which is an extension of the Boehm Test of Basic Concepts-3; appropriate for children age 3 years to 5 years 11 months.

Bruininks-Oseretsky Test of Motor Proficiency, Second Edition (BOT-2)   An instrument used for screening, making diagnoses of motor impairments, determining educational placement, and evaluating motor training programs.

California Achievement Tests   Widely used assessments of basic academic skills among children from kindergarten through 12th grade.

California Psychological Inventory   A criterion-constructed assessment used to measure more normal characteristics of personality and to emphasize positive aspects of personality in individuals ages 13 and older.

California Psychological Inventory 260   A shorter version of the California Psychological Inventory often used in leadership development and management training programs.

Campbell Interest and Skill Survey   A tool developed from the Strong-Campbell Interest Inventory which measures vocational interests and skills as well as the individual's confidence in performing certain occupational activities.

Career Ability Placement Survey (CAPS)   One of three components of the Career Occupational Preference System which measures vocational abilities related to occupations and consists of eight 5-minute ability tests (Mechanical Reasoning, Spatial Relations, Verbal Reasoning, Numerical Ability, Language Usage, Word Knowledge, Perceptual Speed and Accuracy, and Manual Speed and Dexterity).

career adaptability   An individual's ability to adapt to the adjustments associated with career development and workplace changes.

career assessment   A multifaceted assessment process in which counselors assess an individual's aptitudes, achievements, interests, values, and personalities through testing and interviewing.

career choice attitudes   The amount of thought or planning one has given to occupational choice.

career choice competencies   The individual's ability to apply his or her knowledge to the world of work.

Career Development Inventory (CDI)   The best measure of career choice competencies used to assess the individual's readiness to make occupational choices.

Career Interest Inventory (CII)   An interest inventory that measures students' interests in 15 occupational groups and is often used in conjunction with Differential Aptitude Tests to provide a comprehensive picture of an individual's interests and aptitudes.

career maturity   The attitudinal and cognitive readiness to make decisions about one's vocation and/or educational choices.

Career Maturity Inventory-Form C (CMI-Form C)   A vocational development instrument based on the theories of Mark Savickas and John Crites that assesses an individual's career choice readiness, career adaptability, and relational style in forming occupational choices.

Career Maturity Inventory-Revised (CMI-R)   A widely used instrument, originally known as the Vocational Development Inventory, used to assess the degree to which an individual is ready to make career decisions.

Career Occupational Preference System (COPSystem)   A career measurement package often used by school counselors and in a variety of settings to assess interests, values, and abilities.

Career Occupational Preference System Interest Inventory (COPS)   One of three components of the Career Occupational Preference System used in a variety of settings to assess an individual's interests as they relate to different career clusters.

Career Occupational Preference System Interest Inventory (COPS-II)   Intermediate Inventory A version of the Career Occupational Preference System Interest Inventory administered to individuals in Grades 6–12 who may have a learning disability and operate at a fourth- to fifth-grade reading level.

Career Occupational Preference System Interest Inventory-P (COPS-P)   An advanced version of the Career Occupational Preference System Interest Inventory intended for college students and adults who are considering professional occupations only.

Career Occupational Preference System Interest Inventory-Picture Inventory (COPS-PIC)   A version of the Career Occupational Preference System Interest Inventory which can be administered to individuals who are unable to read or have difficulties in reading.

Career Occupational Preference System Interest Inventory-R (COPS-R)   A version of the Career Occupational Preference System Interest Inventory administered to individuals in Grades 6–12; requires a sixth-grade reading level.

Career Orientation Placement and Evaluation Survey (COPES)   One of three components of the Career Occupational Preference System which serves as a helpful aid for exploring the importance of individuals' values for occupational choice and career satisfaction as well as assisting individuals in examining the relationship between their values and type of career.

carryover effect   Occurs when an experimental treatment continues to affect a participant long after the treatment is administered and the scores on the first administration of a test influence the scores obtained on subsequent administrations of the same test.

case conceptualization   A method and clinical strategy for obtaining and organizing information about a client, understanding and explaining the client's situation and maladaptive patterns, guiding and focusing treatment, anticipating challenges and roadblocks, and preparing for successful termination.

Cattell-Horn-Carroll (CHC) model   A model of intelligence which integrates Carrol's Three Stratum theory with Cattell and Horn's Gf-Gc theory, which also consists of three hierarchies (general ability, group factors, and primary cognitive abilities).

Cattell-Horn *Gf-Gc* **model**   A model of intelligence developed by John Horn which expanded Cattell's fluid and crystallized intelligence to nine broad abilities: crystallized intelligence (Gc), quantitative knowledge (Gq), reading/writing (Grw), fluid intelligence (Gf), visual-spatial thinking (Gv), auditory processing (Ga), long-term retrieval (Glr), short-term retrieval (Gsm), and processing speed (Gs)

central tendency   A statistical measure that indicates the center or the middle of the distribution.

checklist   A list of potential target behaviors that observers are asked to identify and note the number of times each behavior occurs during the course of an observation period.

Child Behavior Checklist System 6-18 (CBCL 6-18)   A component of the Achenbach System of Empirically Based Assessment used for evaluating both maladaptive behavioral and emotional problems. The current version of the questionnaire allows parents, teachers, or other individuals who know the child well to provide descriptive data on the competencies and problem behaviors of children and adolescents between the ages of 6 and 18.

Childhood Career Development Scale (CCDS)   An instrument used to assess career progress in students enrolled in Grades 4–6.

Children's Apperception Test (CAT)   A story construction test consisting of 10 animal cards used for describing personality or emotional disturbance in children ages 3 to 10 years.

Children's Apperception Test, Human Form (CAT-H)   An alternate form of the Children's Apperception Test which contains pictures of humans rather than animals.

Children's Apperception Test, Supplemental Form (CAT-S)   An alternate form of the Children's Apperception Test which contains pictures of family situations.

clerical aptitude tests   Specific aptitude tests used to screen applicants for clerical jobs.

clinical assessment   A multifaceted process whereby counselors gather information from, and about, a client to make informed decisions related to diagnosis, treatment planning, and documenting therapeutic efficacy.

clinical interview   An action-oriented intervention in which a counselor solicits information about a client and the client's past using a series of questions, assesses the client's verbal and nonverbal responses to those questions, and uses that information to formulate a diagnosis for the client.

clinical judgment model   An approach in which information gathered through observation as well as subjective and objective data are integrated to reach a logical conclusion on a diagnosis for a client based on existing evidence.

Cognitive Abilities Test, Form 7 (CogAT-7)   The most recent version of a group-administered ability test for students in kindergarten through Grade 12 used to assess students' general and specific abilities in reasoning and problem solving through verbal, nonverbal, and quantitative batteries.

Cognitive Abilities Test (CogAT-7) Screening Form   An abbreviated form containing one subtest of each of the three batteries of the CogAT7 used when the complete assessment cannot be administered.

cognitive ability   A term often used in place of the construct of intelligence.

cognitive ability tests   Instruments designed to measure cognitive ability and focus on cognitive skills.

Cognitive Development theory   A theory proposed by Jean Piaget that children move through four stages of cognitive development as a result of the interaction between biological factors and learning.

cognitive impairments   The presence of deficits in perception of information as well as the ways in which this information is coded, stored, and used in practical applications.

Columbia Mental Maturity Scale (CMMS)   An instrument originally designed for children with cerebral palsy which measures general reasoning ability for children ages 3 years, 6 months to 9 years, 11 months.

Common Core State Standards   A set of standards developed by the National Governors Association and the Council of Chief State School Officers to identify the expectations of achievement for individuals in kindergarten through Grade 12 in both language arts and mathematics in order for students to be appropriately prepared for success in college and workforce training programs.

Comprehensive System (CS)   The most commonly used Rorschach scoring system in which responses are scored based on 100 characteristics in three areas (content, location, and determinants).

Comprehensive Test of Nonverbal Intelligence, Second Edition (CTONI-2)   A popular nonverbal, norm-referenced intelligence instrument that is ideal for those with language or motor ability impairments.

concurrent validity   Validity assessment obtained when a test score and criterion performance measure are collected at approximately the same time.

Conners Rating Scales, 3rd Edition (Conners-3)   An integrated behavioral rating assessment system designed to assess for attention deficit hyperactivity disorder as well as other comorbid disorders such as oppositional defiant disorder and conduct disorder in children ages 6 years to 18 years, 11 months.

construct   An abstraction that cannot be seen directly but is valued because it helps organize the myriad of potential observations in the real world.

construct validity   The extent to which a test may be said to accurately and thoroughly measure a particular construct or trait.

constructivist learning   An adaptive type of learning which involves individuals utilizing real-life experiences to challenge schemas, integrate information into previous knowledge, and develop new ideas.

content bias   A condition which occurs when testing materials are more familiar to one group than another.

content validity   The ability of an instrument to fully assess or measure a construct of interest by sufficiently sampling from the entire universe of items for which the instrument was designed to sample.

content validity ratio   A ratio of the number of raters who evaluate an item and the number of raters who deem an item to be an essential component of the construct being measured.

contextual perception   The way an individual perceives a specific stimulus depending on the context of the occurrence.

continuous data   Data that can be subdivided infinitely as they are more of an approximation based on available data.

continuous recording   Assessment process that involves documenting the number of times a specific behavior occurs over a defined period of time.

convergent validity   A form of validity whereby scores on a test are compared to scores obtained on other tests believed to measure the same construct.

Coopersmith Self-Esteem Inventory (SEI)   A tool used to measure attitudes toward the self in social, academic, family, and personal areas of experience in children.

core subtests   Subtests within an assessment tool which are required to be administered in order to obtain a composite score.

correlation   A statistical technique used to measure and describe a relationship between two variables.

correlation coefficient   A numeric value that indicates the strength of the relationship between two variables.

creative intelligence   A type of intelligence which involves creating, inventing, or designing new ways of solving problems when individuals are faced with an unfamiliar situation.

criterion   A score on a separate test or instrument that purports to measure the same construct or set of abilities as the test in question.

criterion-related validity   A measure of the degree to which a test or instrument reflects a certain set of abilities applicable to the real world.

crystallized intelligence   Skills and knowledge acquired over the course of one's lifetime based on formal learning and experiences, which does not decrease over time.

cultural loading   A process in which test questions reflect an expectation of previous development of knowledge; has the potential to affect testing results.

culture   Any aspect of an individual's identity with the potential to impact the way the individual thinks, feels, or behaves.

Culture Fair Intelligence Test (CFIT)   A culturally fair nonverbal test used to measure fluid ability.

culture-fair tests   Tests designed to minimize as opposed to eliminate biases in the test-taking procedures and interpretation of the results.

culture-free tests   Assessments intended to involve questions and processes providing all individuals with an equal familiarity or footing.

decisional competence   Assessment of the quality of a defendant's reasoning abilities.

descriptive statistics   Set of statistical analyses that can be used to organize and describe the characteristics of a set of data.

Developmental Age Score   A score calculated from the Gesell Developmental Observation-Revised which identifies a child's individual development and associated abilities relative to typical growth patterns.

deviation IQ   An age-based index of general mental ability, which has a mean of 100 and a standard deviation of 15.

diagnosis   The process of learning more about the client for the purpose of understanding the client's presenting issue and potentially identifying the presence of a mental disorder.

diagnostic achievement tests   Instruments used in conjunction with intelligence tests to diagnosis a learning disability and assess learning difficulties.

Diagnostic and Statistical Manual of Mental Disorders (DSM-5)   A manual that includes concise and explicit criteria for a number of disorders and is intended to facilitate the objective assessment of symptom presentation in a variety of clinical settings.

Differential Aptitude Tests (DAT), Fifth Edition   A series of eight tests most commonly used in educational counseling and career guidance with high school students and adults to measure one's ability to learn or succeed in several different areas.

differential item functioning (DIF)   A phenomenon that occurs when individuals have a similar ability on the construct being assessed, but score differently due to the format of specific items.

discrete data   Variables or units of measurement that cannot be divided or broken down into smaller units.

discriminant validity   A form of validity whereby scores on a test are contrasted with scores obtained on other tests believed to measure alternate constructs.

diversity   Variety in cultural identity.

Draw-A-Family   A technique developed by Hulse which often produced stiff images of families.

Draw-A-Man task   A brief projective assessment developed by Goodenough which is widely used to assess intelligence maturation in children.

duration recording   Assessment of the length of time over which a behavior occurs.

Education for All Handicapped Children Act   A public law passed in 1975 which required that all public schools that receive federal funds provide handicapped children and adults ages 3–21 with an education in the "least restrictive environment."

effect size   Statistical term that refers to the family of indices used to measure the magnitude of a treatment effect.

emotional impairments   Psychological and behavioral manifestations caused by factors unrelated to physical or cognitive causes.

emotional intelligence   A type of intelligence defined and measured by four branches (one's ability to perceive emotion, utilize emotions to facilitate thought, understand emotion, and manage emotion).

empirically based assessments   Also referred to as evidenced-based assessment, in which the assessment is developed based on research studies selected based on established norms.

Environmental Assessment Technique (EAT)   A technique integrated in the first major revision of Holland's theory which provides the means to measure the environment as well as more complete information regarding types.

ethics   The philosophical discipline concerned with human conduct and moral decision making.

examiner biases   The degree to which the test administrator's beliefs and values may be impacting the assessment process.

Expressive Vocabulary Test, Second Edition (EVT-2)   A complimentary tool to the PPVT-4 that requires no reading or writing and quickly assesses expressive vocabulary and is used with individuals with motor impairment.

extraversion   Half of the first dichotomy identified in the Myers-Briggs Type Indicator used to describe individuals who direct energy outward and use less energy toward inner activity.

face validity   Assesses whether an instrument appears to look like it measures what it is meant to measure.

factor analysis   A statistical technique used to determine how well items mathematically group together, thus indicating similarity and the measurement of a common construct.

factor-analytic theories   Theories in which factor analysis is used to determine the underlying relationship between a set of variables such as test scores.

fatigue   A situation where clients tire from multiple administrations of a test and their performance decreases as they grow weary of the testing process.

feeling   The second half of the third dichotomy identified in the Myers-Briggs Type Indicator used to describe individuals who are concerned with the impact of their judgment and others' well-being.

fidelity   Loyalty; honoring any and all commitments made to clients.

Figure-Drawing Test   A projective assessment in which the client produces a drawing.

fixed interval time sampling   Observational approach in which the observation period is divided into equal intervals.

flagging   The process of establishing when accommodations have been made to standardized assessments.

fluid intelligence or fluid reasoning (Gf)   An inherited quality that refers to problem-solving and information-processing ability, uninfluenced by culture or education, which increases from birth until it reaches its peak before declining.

forensic assessment   An evaluation of cognition, mood, personality, or behavior conducted by a licensed mental health practitioner for the purpose of assisting attorneys or the court in legal matters.

formal techniques   Standardized assessments which are data driven to measure a specific construct or series of constructs.

formative evaluation   Real time assessments conducted during the counseling process to determine the efficacy of a given treatment or intervention as it is being implemented.

frequency distribution   A graphic that orders a set of disorganized raw scores and summarizes the number of times each of the different scores occurs within a sample of scores.

frequency polygon   Variation of a histogram where rather than a series of vertical bars, a line is drawn to connect the midpoint for each of the different measured variables in the distribution.

full scale IQ (FSIQ)   A term used to describe an individual's overall general intelligence score.

g **factor**   A measure of general intelligence that underlies performance on a wide variety of tasks.

general ability factor (*g* factor)   A measure of general intelligence that underlies performance on a wide variety of tasks.

General Ability Index   A fifth index score of the Wechsler Adult Intelligence Scale which is computed using the Verbal Comprehension and Perceptual Reasoning Indexes.

General Occupational Themes (GOTs)   A category of scales which measure six areas of interest (Realistic, Investigative, Artistic, Social, Enterprising, or Conventional) based on Holland's theory that personality is associated with job satisfaction.

general values   A broad range of values besides those associated with job success.

Gesell Developmental Observation-Revised (GDO-R)   A criterion-referenced test that measures a child's behavior through direct observation and through surveying parents and teachers to make a determination of a child's developmental readiness.

Gesell Early Screener (GES)   An abbreviated version of the Gesell Developmental Observation-Revised used to provide a quick evaluation of the development capacities of children aged 3–6.

Goodenough-Harris Draw-A-Person Test (GHDAP)   An extension of Goodenough's Draw-A-Man Task that includes components such as Draw-A-Woman and Draw-A-Self; appropriate for ages 3 to 15.

GRE revised General Test   A widely used scholastic aptitude test used in evaluating an applicant for graduate admissions.

graphs   Pictorial representations of the data and information that one would normally find in a frequency distribution table.

group intelligence tests   Intelligence tests which can be administered in groups to reduce costs or when a limited amount of time is available.

grouped frequency distribution   A distribution in which individual X-values are combined into sets known as intervals. Frequencies are then counted for each of these intervals.

hearing impairment   A condition associated with the total or partial inability to hear.

hidden disabilities   A wide variety of psychological, cognitive, physical, behavioral, and emotional disorders and diagnoses, varying in severity, that are indistinguishable from the population of individuals without a disability.

high-stakes testing   A term used to describe a situation in which the results of a single assessment are used to make an important decision.

histogram   Graph that uses vertical bars to represent the frequencies of a set of variables. The measured values found within the distribution are listed on the horizontal axis (x-axis) and frequency counts are placed on the vertical axis (y-axis).

Historical Clinical Risk Management-20 (HCRM-20)   A risk assessment instrument that includes a list of 20 probing questions designed to elicit qualitative information a counselor can use to assess the probability of a person engaging in harmful or violent behavior in the future.

House-Tree-Person drawing test (HTP)   A projective assessment in which individuals are given three sheets of paper and asked to draw a house, a person, and a tree.

inclusive range   A measure of variability calculated by subtracting the lowest score in a distribution from the highest score in the distribution and adding 1.

Individuals with Disabilities Education Improvement Act (IDEIA)   The revised version of the Education for All Handicapped Children Act which allows all children suspected of having a learning disability to be tested at the school's expense.

inferential statistics   Set of statistical analyses used to draw inferences from a smaller group of data (sample) that then can be applied to a larger group (population).

informal techniques   Assessments used to evaluate performance and skill levels without making use of standardized instruments or procedures.

information-processing theories   Theories which focus on how information is processed and the mental processes that make up the construct of intelligence.

intake interview   An assessment technique that provides counselors with information about a client's past functioning and how it relates to his or her current situation and the problems he or she is facing.

intellectual and cognitive functioning tests   Assessments which measure an individual's overall intellectual ability, memory, processing ability, and perceptual ability.

intelligence   A measure of one's ability to acquire and apply knowledge.

intelligence ceiling   The highest level of intelligence that the instrument reportedly measures.

intelligence floor   The lowest level of intelligence that the instrument reportedly measures.

intelligence quotient (IQ)   Ratio between the mental age and chronological age of an individual.

interactionism   A concept used to describe the interaction between one's heredity and environment and the influence this has on intelligence.

interest inventories   Tests widely used in counseling and career assessment which evaluate a client's interest, provide a wealth of knowledge of a client's likes or dislikes, and gain insight into an individual's personality.

interests   Preferred activities influenced by an individual's values which also can provide information about potential career choices.

internal consistency   A measure of reliability which evaluates how strongly items in an assessment are related in a single administration.

internal structure   The correlations between items and the total test score, including the pattern of correlations.

International Test Commission (ITC)   A widely known international organization which develops guidelines on adapting testing.

interpersonal intelligence   Intelligence defined by an individual's ability to relate to other people.

interval   Scale used to categorize, rank order, and arrange data so that an equal interval unit appears between each of the scores.

interval recording   Observational approach in which an observer establishes a period of time during which observations will occur and divides that time period into a collection of equal intervals.

intrapersonal intelligence   Intelligence defined by an individual's ability to self-reflect.

introversion   The second half of the first dichotomy identified in the Myers-Briggs Type Indicator used to describe individuals who direct energy inward and less energy for outward activity.

intuition   Second half of the second dichotomy identified in the Myers-Briggs Type Indicator used to describe individuals who prefer to use their insight while minimizing the value of experience.

InView   A group intelligence test consisting of verbal reasoning, sequences, analogies, and quantitative reasoning that assesses cognitive abilities in students in Grades 2 through 12.

Iowa Test   A standardized test that measures basic skills and educational development for children in kindergarten through 12th grade.

Iowa Test of Basic Skills (ITBS)   The most widely used comprehensive achievement battery which includes assessments in vocabulary, word analysis, listening, reading comprehension, language, math, social studies, and science.

Iowa Test of Educational Development (ITED)   A high school achievement battery for Grades 9–12.

item analysis   A series of statistical tests and procedures that can be used to assess for homogeneity in a test.

Jackson Vocational Interest Inventory (JVIS)   A career and development planning tool developed for use with high school and college students as well as adults with a minimum of a seventh-grade reading level.

judging   First half of the last dichotomy identified in the Myers-Briggs Type Indicator used to describe individuals who like to make a plan and stick to the plan, finish one project before beginning another, and follow rules and schedules.

justice   Treating all clients fairly and working with them in a manner that is appropriate based on their presenting situation and condition.

Kaufman Adolescent and Adult Intelligence Test (KAIT)   An individually administered test that measures both fluid and crystallized intelligence for individuals between the ages of 11 and 85 years of age.

Kaufman Assessment Battery for Children, Second Edition (KABC-II)   An assessment of cognitive ability for children 3 to 18 years of age based on a dual theoretical foundation that uses the Luria neuropsychological model or the Cattell-Horn-Carroll approach, providing the administrator with options for children who may not be mainstreamed in the culture or language.

Kaufman Brief Intelligence Test, Second Edition (KBIT-2)   An intelligence test developed by Allen and Nadine Kaufman that is helpful in obtaining a quick estimate of intelligence in people from 4 to 90 years of age.

Kaufman Test of Educational Achievement, Second Edition (KTEA-II)   An individually administered academic achievement test that measures reading, math, written language, and oral language.

KeyMath 3 Diagnostic Assessment   An individually administered achievement test used to assess mathematics concepts and skills.

Kindergarten Readiness Test (KRT)   An instrument used to assess the levels of maturity and development of children ages 4 to 6 to determine if they are developmentally ready to begin kindergarten.

Kinetic Drawing System for Family and School (KDS)   A projective assessment used to evaluate children and adolescents who have difficulty in verbal communication in order to explore personality and attitudes and assess a child's perception of relationships.

Kinetic Family Drawing (KFD)   A test designed by Burns and Kaufman which asks participants to draw their family doing something in order to reduce the stiffness associated with the Draw-A-Family technique.

Kinetic House-Tree-Person (KHTP)   A projective assessment which varies slightly from the House-Tree-Person Drawing test as individuals are given a single sheet of paper and asked to draw a house, tree, and person.

Kinetic School Drawing (KSD)   An adaptation of the Kinetic Family Drawing in which a participant is asked to draw a picture of himself or herself interacting with relevant school figures.

Kuder Career Search With Person Match (KCS)   A person-match inventory used to foster career exploration with individuals who may have limited knowledge about occupational possibilities.

kurtosis   The peakness or flatness of a frequency distribution.

language   The means by which either written or spoken information is communicated.

latency recording   Assessment of the amount of time it takes a client to begin exhibiting a target behavior.

laws   Rules that address proper conduct that have been codified and enacted by local, state, or federal legislation.

Luria-Nebraska Neuropsychological Battery   A screening tool used by clinicians to determine if significant brain injury or psychological impairments are present or to distinguish between brain damage and mental health disorders.

Machover's Draw-A-Person Test   A projective assessment in which individuals are given a sheet of paper and instructed to draw a person and then analyzed on elements such as location placement of the figure, size of the figure, and characteristics of the figure.

managed care companies   Organizations with the goal of reducing healthcare costs while increasing the quality of services.

Mayers's Gravely Disabled Sentence Completion Task   A sentence completion test used with individuals who are unable to complete a standard battery due to the extent of their mental status in order to identify individuals with a severely impaired mental status.

measures of variability   Statistics that describe the amount of variation in a distribution.

mechanical aptitude tests   Instruments used to measure the ability to learn mechanical principles and use of reasoning skills to solve mechanical type problems.

median   A measure of central tendency that is defined as the middle score or the score that divides a distribution exactly in half.

mental ability model   A model developed to reflect the four branches of emotional intelligence (perceiving emotions, using emotions to facilitate thought, understanding emotions, and managing emotions).

Mental Measurements Yearbook   A collection of consumer-oriented test reviews designed to promote informed test selection that is published every few years by the Buros Center for Testing at the University of Nebraska.

mental retardation   A developmental disorder present prior to the age of 18 in which an individual has an intelligence quotient significantly lower than average (below 70) and difficulty in adaptive functioning.

mental status examination   A structured interview designed to objectively assess the emotional, behavioral, and cognitive functioning or mental state of a client at the time of the interview.

mental test   Process by which a series of tests could be administered to assess the intellectual level of an individual.

Metropolitan Readiness Tests, Sixth Edition (MRT)   An instrument used to assess beginning reading, story comprehension, and quantitative concepts and reasoning in preschoolers, kindergarteners, and first graders.

Miller Analogies Test (MAT)   A norm-referenced standardized test accepted by many graduate schools for admission that measures analytical ability and content by requiring examinees to solve problems stated as analogies.

Millon Adolescent Personality Inventory (MAPI)   A widely used personality assessment appropriate for ages 13–18 years old with at least a sixth-grade reading level composed of three scale dimensions (personality styles, expressed concerns, and behavioral patterns).

Millon Index of Personality Styles-Revised (MIPS Revised)   An instrument used with individuals 18 and older to assess different personality styles among adults within normal functioning who may experience difficulties in work, family, or social relationships.

Minnesota Multiphasic Personality Inventory (MMPI)   A test developed using empirical criterion keying that is used to assist in the diagnosis of psychological disorders.

Minnesota Multiphasic Personality Inventory-2 (MMPI-2)   The revised version of the Minnesota Multiphasic Personality Inventory published in 1989 that addressed concerns of cultural bias in the initial norming process by using current census data in the standardization process.

Minnesota Multiphasic Personality Inventory-2 Restructured Form (MMPI-2-RF)   A shorter version of the Minnesota Multiphasic Personality Inventory consisting of 338 items as opposed to the 567 of the MMPI.

Minnesota Multiphasic Personality Inventory-Adolescent (MMPI-A)   An alternative assessment to the Minnesota Multiphasic Personality Inventory-2 that measures psychopathology in adolescents between 14 and 18 years old.

mixed ability model   A model of intelligence which focuses on five emotional intelligence constructs of leadership (self-awareness, self-motivation, self-regulation, empathy, and adeptness in relationships), developed by Daniel Goleman.

mode   A measure of central tendency that represents the score with the greatest frequency in a distribution.

motivation   A reason or incentive for an individual to perform in a particular way.

motor impairments   A condition characterized by partial or total loss of function of a body part.

motor test   An assessment used to evaluate one's mobility and ability to move parts of the body.

Movement Assessment Battery for Children-Second Edition (Movement ABC-2)   An instrument used with children 3 to 16 years of age to identify, describe, and help plan treatment interventions for motor impairment.

multiaptitude tests   Type of aptitude test which measures more than one aspect of ability.

multilevel survey achievement batteries   Assessments composed of a series of subtests used to measure achievement in certain areas at once.

multimodal   A distribution where three or more scores share the distinction of being the most commonly reported score.

Myers-Briggs Type Indicator (MBTI)   The most popular and widely used personality assessment around the world for normal functioning individuals.

Naglieri Nonverbal Ability Test-Individual Form (NNAT-I)   A version of the Naglieri Nonverbal Ability Test that is a particularly useful assessment for those with motor problems when administering a timed performance test would not be appropriate.

Naglieri Nonverbal Ability Test, Second Edition (NNAT-2) A culturally neutral evaluation of general ability that does not require the child to read, write, or speak widely; used to screen students for gifted and talented programs.

naturalistic observation Observation and recording of client behaviors as they occur without any manipulation of the environment by the observer.

negatively skewed A distribution where the majority of scores fall on the upper end of the distribution and the asymmetrical tail extends into the negative side of the graph.

NEO Five-Factor Inventory-3 (NEO-FFI-3) A shorter version of the NEO Personality Inventory-3 consisting of 60 questions appropriate for individuals 12 years and older.

NEO inventories Instruments that provide a comprehensive and concise measure of adult and adolescent personality based on the five major dimensions, or domains, of personality known as the Five Factor Model. Current versions of the NEO inventories are NEO Personality Inventory-3 (NEO-PI-3), Revised NEO Personality Inventory (NEO PI-R), and NEO Five-Factor Inventory-3 (NEO-FFI-3).

NEO Personality Inventory-3 (NEO-PI-3) A modification of the Revised NEO Personality Inventory appropriate for individuals ages 12 years and older.

neuropsychological assessments A type of assessment consisting of interviewing and a battery of tests used to identify neurological deficits associated with specific parts of the brain.

neuropsychology A field of psychology developed by Aleksandr Luria which evaluates how learning and behaviors are associated with specific areas of the brain.

New SAT Also known as the SAT Reasoning Test.

nominal Scale used to classify or categorize data into groups that have different names but are not related to each other in any other systematic way.

nonmaleficence The belief that counselors should not cause any harm to their clients.

nonverbal IQ A measure of intelligence associated with an individual's ability to perform tasks which require little to no language.

norm-referenced test A type of assessment which measures individual performance compared to a larger representative sample in order to rank individual performance relative to the larger group performance.

normal curve A theoretical distribution of scores where the mean, median, and mode all share the same value and an equal percentage of scores fall on either side of the distribution. Also called a bell-shaped curve based on the visual form this type of distribution takes when graphed.

objective assessments Structured assessments which require individuals to respond to a fixed set of questions or items typically in a forced-choice format.

observation The most common informal technique used to assess a particular construct consisting of watching an individual act in a prescribed environment.

observer bias A situation that occurs when raters respond to an item due to extraneous factors unintended by the instrument.

observer drift A situation that occurs when at some point in the observation process the criteria the rater is using to respond to each item changes.

observer fatigue   A situation in which observers become less focused or miss observations when observing behaviors over an extended period of time or when the behaviors being observed occur briefly or infrequently.

Occupational Information Network (O*NET)   A comprehensive career classification system developed by the U.S. Department of Labor, Employment and Training Administrations, which currently lists over 800 different careers.

Occupational Information Network (O*NET) Ability Profiler   An instrument used in career counseling to help individuals explore and identify occupations that fit their strengths, identify areas in which they may need more training and education, and plan their work lives.

Occupational Information Network (O*NET) Career Exploration Tools   A set of career exploration assessments based on the whole-person concept to assist individuals in career exploration.

Occupational Information Network (O*NET) Interest Profiler   A career exploration tool used to assist individuals in learning about broad interests and exploring occupations they may like.

Occupational Information Network (O*NET) OnLine   A web application used for exploring occupations with the O*NET database.

Occupational Information Network (O*NET) Work Importance Profile (WIP)   An instrument used with clients to help identify satisfying occupations by matching their work values and the characteristics of the occupation.

Occupational Scales (OSs)   A section of the Strong used to measure how similar an individual's interests are to people of the same gender who are working in and are satisfied with their occupation.

Occupations Finder   A classification system that includes 1,300 common occupations in the United States which is used to generate a list of occupations and educational requirements based on the Holland three-letter code.

ordinal   A scale used to rank order data along some type of continuum so that each value on the scale has a unique meaning and appears in an ordered relationship to every other value on the scale in terms of size and magnitude.

organization   A term used to describe how individuals organize mental processes.

Otis-Lennon School Ability Test, Eighth Edition (OLSAT 8)   A cognitive ability test that assesses a student's verbal, nonverbal, and quantitative ability.

outcome   The end result or consequence of an action.

Outcome Questionnaire-45.2   A self-report measure that provides clinicians with feedback related to their clients' progress and predictable outcome. In addition to an overall composite score, scores are provided along three subscales that address depression and anxiety, problems in relationships, and levels of conflict in isolation and interpersonal relationships.

parameter   The quantity or magnitude of a treatment component.

partial interval recording method   An approach whereby an observer is interested in whether an individual exhibits target behaviors at any point, and for any length of time, during a defined observation interval.

Peabody Individual Achievement Test-Revised/Normative Update (PIAT-R/NU)   An individually administered achievement test that was designed to evaluate students referred to special education.

Peabody Picture Vocabulary Test-Fourth Edition (PPVT-4)   An instrument which assesses vocabulary acquisition and can be administered to people ages 2 years, 6 months to 90 years and older with motor impairments.

perceiving   One of the preferences identified in the fourth dichotomy of the Myers-Briggs Type Indicator to describe individuals who are more open to obtaining information in the moment in order to make decisions as opposed to preferring an already laid-out plan.

percentage   A portion in relation to the whole. A ratio between two dichotomous outcomes.

percentile score   Numeric value that indicates the percentage of people in a reference group that fall at or below the individual's raw score.

Personal Style Scales (PSSs)   A section of the Strong which uses bipolar scales to measure an individual's comfort level in activities such as Work Style, Learning Environment, Leadership Style, Risk Taking, and Team Orientation.

personality   A psychological characteristic or blend of characteristics that make a person unique.

personality assessment   The measurement and evaluation of psychological traits, states, values, interests, motives, individual religious values and beliefs, and cognitive and behavioral styles.

Personality Assessment Inventory (PAI)   A widely used self-report, objective inventory used to assess psychopathology, some personality disorders, and interpersonal traits in adults 18 years and older.

Personality Assessment Screener (PAS)   An abbreviated version of the Personality Assessment Inventory often used in triage settings and college health settings as a quick personality screen to assess potential behavioral or emotional problems that might require follow-up testing and evaluation.

Piers-Harris Children's Self Concept Scale (2nd Edition)   A popular measure of self-concept for children and adolescents ages 7 to 18 which covers six subscales (physical appearance and attributes, intellectual and school status, happiness and satisfaction, freedom from anxiety, behavioral adjustment, and popularity).

positively skewed   A distribution where the majority of scores fall on the low end of the distribution and the asymmetrical tail extends into the positive side of the graph.

practical intelligence   An assessment developed by Louis and Thelma Thurstone to measure the seven primary mental abilities proposed by Thurstone's Primary Mental Abilities theory.

practice effect   A situation in which individuals improve their scores across test administrations as a result of increased familiarity and comfort with a test and the content that is being assessed.

predictive bias   The degree to which scores predict the criterion measure performance equally well among different groups.

predictive validity   Validity assessment obtained when a criterion performance measure is collected in the future, after test scores have already been collected.

Preliminary Scholastic Aptitude Test/National Merit Scholarship Qualifying Test (PSAT/NMSQT)   A standardized test many students take as practice for the Scholastic Assessment Test in their sophomore or junior year of high school.

primary abilities   Independent factors of mental functioning that constitute intelligence. The primary abilities include word fluency, verbal comprehension, spatial visualization, number facility, associative memory, reasoning, and perceptual speed.

Primary Mental Abilities Test (PMA)   The first of six established categories of interest proposed by Holland used to describe individuals who have a desire to work with concrete physical objects and situations.

program   The focus of counselors' evaluation efforts. Programs can include any type of action or intervention designed to improve outcomes for whole communities, specific sectors (agencies, schools, work settings), or specific client populations (adjudicated youth, individuals who are suicidal, clients presenting with career concerns).

program evaluation   A process that allows counselors to systematically collect and analyze information about a program and determine its merit, worth, or significance.

projective arrangement   A technique in which examinees either arrange or select certain presented visual stimuli based on their order of preference.

projective assessments   Unstructured assessments in which stimuli presented are ambiguous or incomplete and responses are not limited to specific given response choices.

projective techniques   Qualitative approaches which allow for greater flexibility in response and greater subjectivity in analysis.

psychological core   The representation of the "real" person which typically develops in early childhood and comes from parents, teachers, and caregivers.

psychological test   An objective, standardized measure of behavior.

qualitative variables   Variables that are nonnumeric in nature and are defined using nominal or categorical data.

quantitative variables   Variables defined using numeric values or scores.

range   A measure of variability that represents the difference between the highest and the lowest value in a distribution.

rating scales   Assessment techniques designed to quickly and effectively collect data about a client's presenting behaviors and their functionality across multiple settings using a standardized methodology.

ratio   Scale in which the value of zero represents the absence of the variable being measured.

ratio IQ   A measure of intelligence based on mental age or the age level at which the individual appears to be functioning intellectually, which is computed by taking the mental age divided by the chronological age multiplied by 100.

readiness assessments   Instruments which measure an individual's readiness for moving forward which are often administered with kindergarten students to ensure they are ready to move to first grade.

reliability   Refers to the ability of test scores to be interpreted in a consistent and dependable manner across multiple test administrations.

Revised NEO Personality Inventory (NEO PI-R)   A self-administered measure of personality which contains 240 statements based on a 5-point Likert scale.

risk assessments   Interventions used to evaluate the likelihood of an individual becoming a reoffender upon his or her release.

Roberts Apperception Test for Children: 2 (Roberts-2)   A narrative storytelling formatted assessment used with children 6–18 years of age to assess adaptive and maladaptive social perceptions.

role-related behavior   The ways in which an individual acts in a particular situation, usually gained through modeling and social learning experiences.

Rorschach Inkblot Test   The most widely used projective personality assessments in which respondents are shown 10 bilaterally symmetric inkblots and asked to identify what they see, think of, or what it means to them.

Rotter Incomplete Sentence Blank, Second Edition (RISB-2)   One of the most popular standardized sentence completion tests available for clinicians; used in college and university settings as well as medical, military, education, and research settings.

routing test   A pretest or subtest used to direct a test taker to a suitable level of testing.

Salience Inventory   An instrument which measures five of the six roles proposed by Super (child, student, leisurite, citizen, worker, and homemaker) on three perspectives (participation, commitment, and value expectation).

sanity   The soundness of a person's mind and whether he or she is able to think rationally and function as a member of society.

SAT Reasoning Test   One of two components of the Scholastic Assessment Test-I (SAT-I) that includes three main sections (reading, writing, and math), which are each scored on a 200- to 800-point scale for a possible total score of 2400.

SAT Subject Tests   Tests consisting of five broad category subjects (English, history, mathematics, science, and languages) which are required by some colleges in addition to the SAT Reasoning Test.

schema   A term developed by Jean Piaget to describe a cognitive structure that grows with life experiences that helps people understand and leads to knowledge.

scholastic aptitude tests   Tests used by schools and universities in making decisions about admission, course placement, and scholarship offers for students.

Scholastic Assessment Test-I (SAT-I)   A common scholastic aptitude test given at the secondary level which is usually taken in the spring of the junior year or fall of the senior year in high school and is used by colleges to determine placement.

school ability tests   Group intelligence tests administered in a school setting.

Self-Directed Search (SDS)   An assessment developed by John Holland which assesses interests, competencies, and self-estimates of abilities.

self-monitoring   The practice of observing and recording one's own behaviors.

Semistructured Clinical Interview for Children and Adolescents (SCICA)   A part of the Achenbach System of Empirically Based Assessment instruments that is designed to assess the cognitive and interpersonal functioning of children ages 6–18.

semistructured interview   A less formal interviewing technique that allows counselors some leeway in shaping the content and direction of the interview.

sensing   First half of the second dichotomy identified in the Myers-Briggs Type Indicator used to describe people who prefer to observe through the physical senses.

sentence completion tests   Verbal completion projective personality techniques that are considered semistructured in which a participant is required to finish a sentence for which the first word or words are provided.

severe and profound mental retardation   A term used to describe individuals who have an IQ that falls below 40 and who can master basic self-care and communication skills, often with support and training.

short-term memory   Limited capacity in the brain which stores information for easy recall but which can be lost with distraction or the passage of time.

simultaneous processing   One of two processes of intelligence proposed by Aleksandr Luria by which individuals process information. In simultaneous processing, individuals simultaneously integrate information at one time.

Sixteen Personality Factor (16PF), Fifth Edition   An instrument developed through factor analysis which is widely used to measure normal adult personality on 16 factors identified to be the basic elements of personality.

Slosson Intelligence Test-Primary (SIT-P)   A brief, standardized instrument available to screen and provide quick estimates of a child's intelligence as well as identify children who may need further testing.

Slosson Intelligence Test-Revised Third Edition (SIT-R3)   An instrument used to measure six components of verbal intelligence (general information, comprehension, quantitative, similarities and differences, vocabulary, and auditory memory) in children and adults aged 4 to 64 years.

Smarter Balanced Assessment Consortium   Organization that specifies guidelines for assessments measuring the Common Core standards.

smooth curves   Graph used to display the distribution of numeric scores obtained from either an interval or ratio scale. Instead of a series of straight lines between data points, a continuous line is created to connect scores.

Spearman-Brown Prophecy Formula   An adjusted version of the correlation coefficient formula used to account for the fact that the correlation is being computed between two halves of a test rather than two full-length versions of a test.

specific aptitude tests   A type of aptitude test which focuses on one aspect of ability.

standard age score   Standard score used to compare an individual's performance on a test to individuals of the same age.

standard deviation   A measure of variability that represents the average amount by which individual scores in a distribution vary from the mean.

standard error of measurement   The standard deviation of a normal distribution. SEM is used to assess whether the standard deviation of the normal distribution is the same for each member of the treatment group tested.

standard scores   Numeric value that indicates the distance an individual's raw score is above or below the mean of the reference group in terms of standard deviation units.

standardization   The process of establishing uniform procedures for using an assessment so that the observation, administration, equipment, materials, and scoring rules remain the same for all who are administered the test.

Standards for Multicultural Assessment, Fourth Revision   The most recent set of standards developed by the Committee on Diversity in Assessment and the Association for Assessment and Research in Counseling (AARC) that address multicultural competence in assessment.

Stanford Achievement Test Series, Tenth Edition (Stanford 10)   The latest edition of the Stanford Achievement Test; appropriate for students in kindergarten through 12th grade, which aligns to the Common Core State Standards and meets federal requirements for accountability under No Child Left Behind.

Stanford-Binet Intelligence Scale   An American version of the Binet-Simon Scale published by Lewis Madison Teman to measure intelligence.

stanine   A set of normalized standard scores that divides a data distribution into one of nine possible scores with 1 being the lowest and 9 being the highest, which have a distribution of 2 and mean of 5.

state   A temporary expression of a personality characteristic in relation to an environmental trigger or cue.

statistical decision-making model   Approach whereby counselors move from hypothesis to conclusion using a number of analytic techniques such as statistical inference, probability, and sampling.

statistics   A set of tools and techniques used for describing, organizing, and interpreting data or information.

Sternberg Triarchic Abilities Test (STAT)   A multiple-choice test which uses verbal, quantitative, and figural items to measure three aspects of Sternberg's triarchical intelligence on different scales.

story construction test   A projective assessment in which a respondent constructs a story based on a picture shown by the examiner.

Strong   The most recent revision of the Strong Interest Inventory which consists of 291 items that are divided into six sections (occupations, subject areas, activities, leisure activities, people, and individual characteristics).

Strong Interest Inventory   One of the most widely used inventories with over 80 years of research demonstrating its validity.

structured assessments   Another term used to describe an objective assessment.

structured interview   An interviewing technique where the counselor follows an established protocol when communicating with a client. Structured clinical interviews define what a counselor should ask, how it should be asked, and the ordered sequence in which questions should be asked.

Student Vocational Self Analysis   The first noted career assessment intended for use with 10th-grade students in public schools as a means of establishing potential career paths.

successive processing   One of two processes of intelligence proposed by Aleksandr Luria in which individuals process information in sequential or serial order.

suicide   The act of purposefully taking one's own life.

summative evaluations   Assessment conducted at the end of the counseling process to evaluate outcomes.

Super's Life Career Rainbow   A graphic showing how roles may vary during a person's lifetime.

Super's Work Values Inventory-Revised (SWVI-R)   The most recent revision of the Work Values Inventory which measures the relative importance of work-related values dimensions, including achievement, co-workers, creativity, income, independence, lifestyle, challenge, prestige, security, supervision, variety, and workplace.

supplemental subtests   Subtests which provide additional information or can be used to replace unnecessary or inappropriate subtests.

Symptom Checklist-90-Revised   A self-report instrument that is used to evaluate a broad range of psychological problems and symptoms of psychopathology as well as measure the progress and outcome of mental health treatment.

systematic error   A situation that occurs when a test being used consistently measures a domain other than the trait it was designed to assess.

Szondi Test   A projective personality technique similar to the Rorschach except that it uses the projective arrangement or selection technique.

Tell-Me-A-Story (TEMAS)   A story construction test in which individuals are given cards that depict a range of psychosocial situations and asked to provide a complete story around the pictures from beginning to end.

Tennessee Self-Concept Scale, 2nd Edition (TSCS:2)   One of the most famous measures of self-concept in children, adolescents, and adults; provides a total of 15 scores.

TerraNova, Third Edition Tests (TN3)   The most recent version of the California Achievement Test consisting of a series of standardized achievement tests designed to assess student achievement in reading, language arts, mathematics, science, social studies, vocabulary, spelling, and other areas for students in kindergarten through 12th grade.

test familiarity   An examinee's familiarity with the materials/stimuli on the assessment.

Test of Cognitive Skills, Second Edition (TCS/2)   A group-administered test of cognitive abilities that was originally designed to be an equivalent to the Stanford-Binet.

Test of Nonverbal Intelligence, Fourth Edition (TONI-4)   A 15- to 20-minute test used to measure intelligence, aptitude, abstract reasoning, and problem solving in individuals ages 6 to 89 years.

test scores   The numerical results of a test administration.

Tests   Reference guide published by Pro Ed that includes information on over 2,000 tests from more than 164 publishers in the areas of psychology, education, and business.

Tests in Print   A bibliography of all known commercially available tests currently in print in the English language published by the Buros Center for Testing.

Thematic Apperception Test (TAT)   The most widely used story construction test in which respondents are asked to construct stories after seeing one of 31 possible cards.

theory of Multiple Intelligences   A theory of intelligence developed by Howard Gardner which establishes seven intelligences (linguistic, musical, logical-mathematical, spatial, bodily kinesthetic, interpersonal, and intrapersonal).

theory-based assessments   A type of assessment developed based on theory as opposed to empirical research, often referred to as neuropsychological assessment.

thinking   First half of the third dichotomy identified in the Myers-Briggs Type Indicator used to describe individuals who analyze readily, are considered rational, and focus on logical problem solving.

Three Stratum theory   A model of intelligence developed by John Carroll which combines the elements of the g and Gf-Gc model. This model consists of three levels (general, broad, and specific).

time sample recording   Observation approach in which an observation period is defined and that period is then divided into smaller intervals.

Total Self-Concept (TOT) Score   A score obtained from the Tennessee Self-Concept Scale which is considered to be the most important score as it indicates whether the client typically has positive and consistent or negative and variable self-view.

trait characteristics   The enduring components of personality which can be represented as attitudes, behaviors, or dispositions.

trait model of emotional social intelligence   A model of emotional intelligence used to describe an individual's self-perception of his or her abilities as opposed to actual abilities.

treatment effect   Any measureable difference observed between a treatment and control group.

treatment plan   A written outline for the counseling process that allows both counselor and client to understand how they will proceed from their point of origin (the client's presenting concerns and underlying difficulties) to their destination, alleviate any troubling or dysfunctional symptoms and patterns, and establish improved coping.

triarchic theory of intelligence   A theory developed by Sternberg to measure three types of reasoning processes that people use to solve problems (analytic, creative, and practical).

type   A collection of traits.

typical responses   The ways individuals usually adjust.

Universal Nonverbal Intelligence Test (UNIT)   A relatively new nonverbal instrument that requires no language on the part of the counselor or the client; used among low-functioning populations.

unstructured assessments   Another term used to describe projective assessments.

unstructured interview   An interview that has no established form or structure. Unstructured interviews often start with broad open-ended questions and include follow-up questions based on client responses.

unsystematic error   The collection of factors that contribute to the variation in scores noted across administrations of a test or instrument. Also referred to as random error.

validity   The degree to which evidence and theory support the interpretations of test scores entailed by proposed uses of tests.

validity coefficient   Numeric value representative of the relative strength of an assessment's validity.

values   A set of beliefs or ideas developed throughout an individual's life which are important to him or her and are likely to predict the type of career the individual will enjoy.

values inventories   Instruments used to assess an individual's work-related or general values.

variability   A quantitative measure that describes the degree to which scores in a distribution are spread out or clustered together.

variable   A construct that can assume multiple values, qualitative or quantitative.

variable interval time sampling   Observational approach whereby the observation period is divided into random and unpredictable time intervals.

variance A measure of variability that represents the mean of all squared deviation scores.

verbal IQ A measure of intelligence which involves an individual's ability to analyze information and solve problems using language based reasoning.

Vernon's theory of intelligence A four-level hierarchical theory of intelligence proposed by Vernon. The first and highest level consists of general intelligence for which there is the greatest variability between people, the second level consists of major group factors of intelligence, the third level consists of minor group factors, and the fourth level consists of specific factors of intelligence.

vision impairment A condition defined as having 20/40 or worse vision even with corrective eyeglasses.

Visual Processing (Gv) A measure of an individual's ability to visualize, remember, and translate mental images.

Washington University Sentence Completion Test (WUSCT) One of the most validated sentence completion forms available to date with excellent reliability and construct validity.

Wechsler Abbreviated Scale of Intelligence A brief measure of intelligence used in educational, clinical, and research settings as a screening tool to determine if more thorough intelligence testing is warranted.

Wechsler Adult Intelligence Scale-Fourth Edition (WAIS-IV) The most recent Wechsler instrument used to measure intelligence in individuals from 16 years to 90 years and 11 months.

Wechsler Bellevue Intelligence Scale An intelligence test consisting of six verbal subtests and five performance subtests developed by David Wechsler to include aspects of nonverbal intelligence in addition to measures of verbal intelligence.

Wechsler Individual Achievement Test, Second Edition (WIAT-II) An individually administered measurement tool used for achievement assessment, learning disability diagnosis, and special education placement for individuals aged 4 to 85 and grades pre-kindergarten through 16.

Wechsler Intelligence Scale for Children-Fourth Edition (WISC-IV) An instrument used to assess intellectual ability in children ages 6 years to 16 years and 11 months which yields an FSIQ and four index scores (verbal comprehension index, perceptual reasoning index, working memory index, and processing speed index).

Wechsler Preschool and Primary Scale of Intelligence (WPPSI-IV) A comprehensive, standardized intelligence test for children ages 2 years and 6 months to 7 years and 7 months.

whole interval recording method Approach whereby an observer is interested in whether an individual exhibits target behaviors during the entire observation interval.

Wide Range Achievement Test 4 (WRAT4) An instrument which measures basic academic skills in reading, sentence comprehension, spelling, and math computation which is often used to assess a potential learning disability.

Wonderlic Cognitive Ability Test The most current version of the Wonderlic Personnel Test available in three versions (Wonderlic Cognitive Ability Pretest, Wonderlic Contemporary Cognitive Ability Test, and Wonderlic Classic Cognitive Ability Test).

Wonderlic Personnel Test   An assessment often given by human resources, especially in business during the hiring process to measure a potential employee's cognitive ability.

Woodcock-Johnson III Normative Update (WJ III NU) Complete   A measurement tool used to aid in diagnosing learning disabilities, plan IEPs, and determine discrepancies between achievement and ability testing.

Woodcock-Johnson III Tests of Achievement (WJ III ACH)   One of two batteries which compose the Woodcock-Johnson III Normative Update Complete, used to determine if students are eligible for accommodations.

Word Association Test (WAT)   A test influenced by the work of Jung in which respondents are provided with a list of 100 words from a standardized list and asked to say the first thing that comes to mind after hearing the word.

Work Importance Study (WIS)   An international consortium of research teams initiated by Donald Super with the goal of examining the values people seek through their work and various life roles.

work-related values   Values associated with job satisfaction and success that can assist individuals in determining which occupations might meet their needs and provide additional career exploration information.

worldview   The totality of psychological, thought, and emotional components of behaviors and decision making.

References

Achenbach, T. (2001). *Child Behavior Checklist for Ages 6–18.* Burlington: University of Vermont.

Acklin, M. W. (2012). The forensic clinician's toolbox I: Review of competency to stand trial (CST) instruments. *Journal of Personality Assessment, 94*(2), 220–222. doi:10.1080/00223891.2011.6 27970

ACT. (2007). *ACT Assessment technical manual.* Iowa City, IA: Author. Retrieved from http://www.act .org/aap/pdf/ACT_Technical_Manual.pdf

Advokat, C. (2010). What are the cognitive effects of stimulant medication? Emphasis on adults with attention-deficit/hyperactivity disorder (ADHD). *Neuroscience & Behavioral Reviews, 34,* 1256–1266. doi:10.1016/j.neurbiorev.2010.03.006

Ægisdóttir, S., White, M. J., Spengler, P. M., Maugherman, A. S., Anderson, L. A., Cook, R. S. . . . Rush, J. D. (2006). The meta-analysis of clinical judgment project: Fifty-six years of accumulated research on clinical versus statistical prediction. *The Counseling Psychologist, 34,* 341–382.

AGS. (2004). *Kaufman Test of Educational Achievement-Second Edition, Comprehensive Form (KTEA-II).* Circle Pine, MN: Author.

American Counseling Association. (2014). *ACA code of ethics and standards of practice.* Alexandria, VA: Author.

American Dental Association. (2012). *Dental Admission Test (DAT) 2013 program guide.* Chicago, IL: Author. Retrieved from http://www.ada.org/sections/educationAndCareers/pdfs/dat_examinee_ guide.pdf

American Educational Research Association, American Psychological Association, and National Council on Measurement in Education. (1999). *Standards for educational and psychological testing* (4th ed.). Washington DC: American Psychological Association.

American Foundation for the Blind. (2013). *Living with vision loss.* Retrieved from http://www.afb.org/ section.aspx?FolderID=2&SectionID=93?

American Mental Health Counselors Association. (2010). *AMHCA code of ethics.* Alexandria, VA: Author.

American Psychiatric Association. (2013). *Diagnostic and statistical manual of mental disorders* (5th ed.). Arlington, VA: American Psychiatric.

American Psychiatric Publishing. (2014). *DSM.* Retrieved from http://www.appi.org/Pages/DSM.aspx

American Psychological Association. (1966). *Standards for educational and psychological tests and manuals.* Washington, DC: Author.

American School Counselor Association. (2003). *The ASCA national model: A framework for school counseling programs.* Alexandria, VA: Author.

American School Counselor Association. (2010). *Ethical standards for school counselors.* Alexandria, VA: Author.

Anastasi, A., & Urbina, S. (1997). *Psychological testing* (7th ed.). Upper Saddle River, NJ: Prentice Hall.

Association for Assessment in Counseling. (2003a). *Responsibilities of users of standardized tests (RUST).* Alexandria, VA: Author.

Association for Assessment in Counseling. (2003b). *Standards for qualifications of test users.* Alexandria, VA: Author.

Association for Assessment in Counseling and Education. (2012). *AACE standards for multicultural assessment* (4th ed.). Retrieved from http://aarc-counseling.org/assets/cms/uploads/files/AACE-AMCD.pdf

Association for Assessment and Research in Counseling & American School Counselor Association. (1998). *Competencies in assessment and evaluation for school counselors*. Alexandria, VA: Authors.

Atlanta Public Schools. (n.d.). *Screening and referral frequently asked questions*. Retrieved from http://www.atlanta.k12.ga.us/cms/lib/GA01000924/Centricity/Domain/2747/FAQ%20Screening%20and%20Referral%2012-13.pdf

Attkisson, C. (2013). *Client Satisfaction Questionnaire CSQ-8*. Mill Valley, CA: Tamalpais Matrix Systems.

Bachelor, A., & Horvath, A. (1999). The therapeutic relationship. In M. A. Hubble, B. L. Duncan, & S. D. Miller (Eds.), *The heart and soul of change: What works in therapy* (pp. 133–178). Washington, DC: American Psychological Association.

Bahreinian, M., Ahi, M., & Soltani, F. (2012). The relationship between personality type and leadership style of managers: A case study. *Mustang Journal of Business and Ethics, 3,* 94.

Bailey, J. S., & Burch, M. R. (2002). *Research methods in applied behavioral analysis*. Thousand Oaks, CA: Sage.

Barber, B. L., Paris, S. G., Evans, M., & Gadsden, V. L. (1992). Policies for reporting test results to parents. *Educational Measurement: Issues and Practice, 11,* 15–20.

Barker, C., Pistrang, N., & Elliott, R. (1994). *Research methods in clinical and counseling psychology*. Chichester, UK: John Wiley & Sons.

Baron, I., & Leonberger, K. (2012). Assessment of intelligence in the preschool period. *Neuropsychology Review, 22,* 334–344. doi:10.1007/s11065-012-9215-0

Bartholomew, D. J. (2006). *Measuring intelligence: Facts and fallacies*. Cambridge, UK: Cambridge University Press.

Bausell, R. B. (1986). *A practical guide to conducting empirical research*. New York, NY: Harper & Row.

Beck, A. T., Steer, R. A., & Brown, G. K. (1996). *Manual for the Beck Depression Inventory-II*. San Antonio, TX: Psychological Corporation.

Bellak, L. (1975). Intercultural studies in search of a disease. *Schizophrenia Bulletin, 1*(12), 6–9.

Bender, L. (1938). *A visual-motor gestalt test and its clinical use* (Research Monograph No. 3). New York, NY: American Orthopsychiatric Association.

Benson, E. (2003). Intelligent intelligence testing. *APA Monitor, 34*(2), 48.

Berg, B. I. (2009). *Qualitative research methods for the social sciences* (7th ed.). Boston, MA: Allyn & Bacon.

Bernard, J. M., & Goodyear, R. K. (2009). *Fundamentals of clinical supervision*. Upper Saddle River, NJ: Pearson.

Binet, A., & Simon, T. (1905). Methodes nouvelles pour le diagnostic du niveau intellectual des anormaux [New methods for the diagnosis of abnormal intellectual level]. *L'Année Psychologique, 11,* 191–244.

Boehm, A. E. (2008). *Technical report Boehm-3 Preschool Boehm Test of Basic Concepts Third Edition*. San Antonio, TX: Pearson Education.

Bolliger, D. U., & Erichsen, E. A. (2013). Student satisfaction with blended and online courses based on personality type. *Canadian Journal of Learning and Technology, 39*(1), 1–23.

Bonnie, R. (1992). The competence of criminal defendants: A theoretical reformulation. *Behavioral Sciences and the Law, 10,* 291–316. doi:10.1002/bsl.2370100303

Bonnie, R., & Grisso, T. (2000). Adjudicative competence and youthful offenders. In T. Grisso & R. Schwarz (Eds.), *Youth on trial: A developmental perspective on juvenile justice* (pp. 73–103). Chicago, IL: University of Chicago Press.

Borsboom, D., Mellenbergh, G. J., & Van Heerden, J. (2004). The concept of validity. *Psychological Review, 111,* 1061–1071. doi:10.1037/0033-295X.111.4.1061

Bracken, B. A., & McCallum, R. S. (1998). *The Universal Test of Nonverbal Intelligence.* Chicago, IL: Riverside.

Bradley, L. J., Sexton, T. L., & Smith, H. B. (2005). The American Counseling Association practice research network: A new research tool. *Journal of Counseling and Development, 83,* 488–491. doi:10.1002/j.1556-6678.2005.tb00370.x

Bradley-Geist, J. C., & Landis, R. S. (2012). Homogeneity of personality in occupations and organizations: A comparison of alternative statistical tests. *Journal of Business and Psychology, 27*(2), 149–159. doi:10.1007/s10869-011-9233

Brault, M. W. (2012). *Americans with disabilities: 2010.* Retrieved from http://www.census.gov/prod/2012pubs/p70-131.pdf

Bridgeman, B., Burton, N., & Cline, F. (2008). *Understanding what the numbers mean: A straightforward approach to GRE predictive validity.* Princeton, NJ: Educational Testing Services. Retrieved from http://www.ets.org/Media/Research/pdf/RR-08-46.pdf

Brown, L., & Hammill, D. D. (1990). *Behavior Rating Profile* (2nd ed.). Austin, TX: PRO-ED.

Brown, L., Sherbenou, R. J., & Johnsen, S. K. (2010). *Test of Nonverbal Intelligence-Fourth edition (TONI-4).* Austin, TX: PRO-ED.

Brown, L. H., & Unger, M. A. (1998). *PAR comprehensive catalog.* Odessa, FL: Psychological Assessment Resources.

Bruininks, R. H., & Bruininks, B. D. (2005). *Bruininks-Oseretsky Test of Motor Proficiency: Examiners manual* (2nd ed.). Circle Pines, MN: AGS.

Bryan, L., & Gast, D. (2000). Teaching on-task and on-schedule behaviors to high-functioning children with autism via picture activity schedules. *Journal of Autism and Developmental Disorders, 30,* 553–567.

Buck, J. (1948). The H-T-P test. *Journal of Clinical Psychology, 4,* 151–159.

Buck, J., & Hammer, E. (Eds.). (1969). *Advances in the House-Tree-Person technique: Variations and applications.* Los Angeles, CA: Western Psychological Services.

Buffum, M. D., Hutt, E., Chang, V. T., Craine, M. H., & Snow, A. L. (2007). Cognitive impairment and pain management: Review of issues and challenges. *Journal of Rehabilitation Research and Development, 44,* 315–350. doi:10.1682/JRRD.2006.06.0064

Burgemeister, B. B., Blum, L. H., & Lorge, I. (1972). *Columbia Mental Maturity Scale* (3rd ed.). New York, NY: Harcourt Brace Jovanovich.

Burke, H. L. (1999–2009). *Benefits of forensic assessment/consultation.* Retrieved from http://www.brain-injury-therapy.com/services/witness.htm

Burley, J. B. (1957). Psychodiagnostic limitations of Szondi interseries changes. *Journal of Clinical Psychology, 13,* 396–399.

Burns, R. (1987). *Kinetic House-Tree-Person drawings (K-H-T-P): An interpretative manual.* New York, NY: Brunner/Mazel.

Burns, R. C., & Kaufman, S. H. (1970). *Kinetic family drawings (K-F-D): An introduction to understanding children through kinetic drawings.* Ann Arbor, MI: Brunner/Mazel.

Burns, R. C., & Kaufman, S. H. (1972). *Actions, styles, and symbols in Kinetic Family Drawings (K-F-D).* New York, NY: Brunner/Mazel.

Buros Center for Testing. (2014). *History of the Buros Center for Testing.* Retrieved from http://buros.org/history

Butcher, J. N. (2005). *Minnesota Multiphasic Personality Inventory-2, user's guide: The Minnesota report: Adult Clinical System-Revised, 4th edition.* Minneapolis: Regents of the University of Minnesota.

Butcher, J. N., Graham, J. R., Ben-Porath, Y. S., Tellegen, A., Dahlstrom, W. G., & Kaemmer, B. (2001). *MMPI-2 Minnesota Multiphasic Personality Inventory-2 Manual for administration, scoring and interpretation* (2nd ed.). Minneapolis: University of Minnesota Press.

Butler, R. J., & Gasson, S. L. (2005). Self esteem/self concept scales for children and adolescents: A review. *Child and Adolescent Mental Health, 10*(4), 190–201. doi:10.1111/j.1475-3588.2005.00368.x

Callahan, C., & Eichner, H. (2008). *IQ tests and your child.* Retrieved from http://www.nagc.org/index .aspx?id=960

Career Occupational Preference System Summary. (2013). Retrieved from http://www.edits.net/support/ self-scoring-tutorial.html

Carjuzaa, J., & Ruff, W. G. (2010). When Western epistemology and an indigenous worldview meet: Culturally responsive assessment in practice. *Journal of the Scholarship of Teaching and Learning, 10*(1), 68–79.

Carroll, J. B. (1997). The three-stratum theory of cognitive abilities. In D. P. Flanagan, J. L. Genshaft, & P. L. Harrison (Eds.), *Contemporary intellectual assessment: Theories, tests, and issues* (pp. 122–130). New York, NY: Guilford Press.

Cattell, R. B. (1940). A culture-free intelligence test. I. *Journal of Educational Psychology, 31*(3), 161–179. doi:10.1037/h0059043

Cattell, R. B. (1963). Theory of fluid and crystallized intelligence: A critical experiment. *Journal of Educational Psychology, 54*, 1–22. doi:10.1037/h0046743

Cattell, J. M., & Bryant, S. (1889). Mental association investigated by experiment. *Mind, 14,* 230–250.

Centers for Disease Control and Prevention. (2009). *Why is vision loss a public health problem?* Retrieved from http://www.cdc.gov/visionhealth/basic_information/vision_loss.htm

Centers for Disease Control and Prevention. (2012). *A framework for program evaluation.* Retrieved from http://www.cdc.gov/evaL/framework/index.htm

Centers for Disease Control and Prevention. (2013). *Suicide and self-inflicted injury.* Retrieved from http://www.cdc.gov/nchs/fastats/suicide.htm

Coe, R. (2002, September). *It's the effect size, stupid. What effect size is and why it is important.* Paper presented at the Annual Conference of the British Educational Research Association, Exeter, England. Retrieved from http://www.leeds.ac.uk/educol/documents/00002182.htm

Cohen, J. (1988). *Statistical power analysis for the behavioral sciences* (2nd ed.). Mahwah, NJ: Lawrence Erlbaum.

Cohen, R. J., & Swerdlik, M. E. (2005). *Psychological testing and assessment: An introduction to tests and measurements* (6th ed.). Columbus, OH: McGraw-Hill.

College Board. (2013). *Scores and reviews.* Retrieved from http://www.collegeboard.com/student/testing/ psat/scores.html

Columbia Center for New Media Teaching. (2002–2003). *Validity and reliability.* Retrieved from http:// ccnmtl.columbia.edu/projects/qmss/measurement/validity_and_reliability.html

Commission on Rehabilitation Counselor Certification (CORE). (2010). *Code of professional ethics for rehabilitation counselors.* Schaumburg, IL: Author.

Conners, C. K. (2008). *Conners, 3rd edition.* North Tonawanda, NY: Multi-Health Systems.

Connolly, A. (2012). *KeyMath3 diagnostic assessment.* Retrieved from http://psychcorp.pearsonassess- ments.com/HAIWEB/Cultures/en-us/Productdetail.htm?Pid=PAaKeymath3

Consulting Psychologists Press. (2009). *Validity of the Strong Interest Instrument.* Retrieved from https://www.cpp.com/Pdfs/smp284108.pdf

Coopersmith, S. (2002). *Coopersmith Self-Esteem Inventories: Manual, instrument sample, and scoring guide.* Menlo Park, CA: Mind Garden.

Costantino, G., Malgady, R. G., & Rogler, L. H. (1988). *TEMAS (Tell-me-a-story) test manual.* Los Angeles, CA: Western Psychological Services.

Council for Accreditation of Counseling and Related Educational Programs. (2009). *CACREP stan- dards.* Retrieved from http://www.cacrep.org/wp-content/uploads/2013/12/2009-Standards.pdf

Council for Accreditation of Counseling and Related Educational Programs. (2013). *Clinical rehabilita- tion counseling standards.* Retrieved from http://www.cacrep.org/wp-content/uploads/2014/01/ Clinical-Rehabilitation-Counseling-Standards.pdf

Council of Chief State School Officers. (2011, June). *Moving forward with kindergarten readiness assessment efforts.* Retrieved from http://www.ccsso.org/Documents/CCSSO_K-Assessment_Final_7-12-11.pdf

Craig, R. J. (2005). The clinical process of interviewing. In R. J. Craig (Ed.), *Clinical and diagnostic interviewing* (2nd ed., pp. 21–41). Lanham, MD: Jason Aronson.

Craighead, W. E., & Nemeroff, C. B. (2004). *The concise Corsini encyclopedia of psychology and behavioral science* (3rd ed.). Hoboken, NJ: John Wiley & Sons.

Crites, J. O. (1965). Measurement of vocational maturity in adolescence. *Psychological Monographs, 79*(595).

Crites, J. O. (1971). *The maturity of vocational attitudes in adolescence.* Washington, DC: American Personnel and Guidance Association.

Cronbach, L. J., & Meehl, P. E. (1955). Construct validity in psychological tests. *Psychological Bulletin, 52,* 281–302. doi:10.1037/h0040957

Crusan, D. (2010). *Assessment in the second language writing classroom.* Ann Arbor: University of Michigan Press.

CTB/McGraw-Hill. (2014). *TerraNova Third Edition Complete Battery.* Retrieved from http://www.ctb.com/ctb.com/control/ctbProductViewAction?p=products&productFamilyId=449&productId=733

Cullen, B., O'Neill, B., Evans, J. J., Coen, R. F., & Lawlor, B. A. (2007). A review of screening tests for cognitive impairments. *Journal of Neurology, Neurosurgery, and Psychiatry with Practical Neurology, 78,* 790–799. doi:10.1136/jnnp.2006.095414

Dana, R. H. (Ed.). (2000). *Handbook of cross-cultural and multicultural personality assessment.* Mahwah, NJ: Lawrence Erlbaum.

Davidson, M. A. (2008). ADHD in adults: A review of the literature. *Journal of Attention Disorders, 11,* 628–641. doi:10.1177/1087054707310878

Dechant, L. (2013, August 28). Whiz kid, 11, navigates college life. *ABC News.* Retrieved from http://abcnews.go.com/blogs/lifestyle/2013/08/whiz-kid-11-navigates-college-life

Dental Admission Testing Program. (2012). *Dental Admission Test (DAT) validity study, 2009–2010 data.* Chicago, IL: Author. Retrieved from http://www.ada.org/sections/educationAndCareers/pdfs/dat_validity_study.pdf

Derogatis, L. R. (1993). *Brief Symptom Inventory: Administration, scoring, and procedures manual.* Minneapolis, MN: NCS Pearson.

Derogatis, L. R. (1994). *Symptom Checklist-90-R: Administration, scoring, and procedures manual* (3rd ed.). Minneapolis, MN: NCS Pearson.

Dimitrov, D. M. (2012). *Statistical methods for validation of assessment scale data in counseling and related fields.* Alexandria, VA: American Counseling Association.

Dirk, B. J., & Hansen, J. C. (2004). Development and validation of discriminant functions for the Strong Interest Inventory. *Journal of Vocational Behavior, 64*(1), 182–197.

Doerfler, L. A., Addis, M. E., & Moran, P. W. (2002). Evaluating mental health outcomes in an inpatient setting: Convergent and divergent validity of the OQ-45 and BASIS-32. *Journal of Behavioral Health Services & Research, 29,* 394–403. doi:10/1007/BF02287346

Dougherty, J. L. (2005). Ethics is case conceptualization and diagnosis: Incorporating a medical model into the developmental counseling tradition. *Counseling and Values, 49,* 132–140. doi:10.1002/j.2161-007X.2005.tb00259

Drummond, R. J., & Jones, K. D. (2010). *Assessment procedures for counselors and helping professionals* (7th ed.). Upper Saddle River, NJ: Pearson/Prentice Hall.

Duckworth, A. L., Quinn, P. D., Lynam, D. R., Loeber, R., & Stouthamer-Loeber, M. (2011). Role of motivation in intelligence testing. *Proceedings of the National Academy of Science of the United States of America, 108,* 7715–7720. doi:10.1073/pnas.1018601108

Duits, N., van der Hoorn, S., Wiznitzer, M., Wettstein, R. M., & de Beurs, E. (2012). Quality improvement of forensic mental health evaluations and reports of youth in the Netherlands. *International Journal of Law and Psychiatry, 35,* 440–444. doi:10.1016/j.ijlp.2012.09.018

Dunn, L. M., & Dunn, D. M. (2007). *Peabody Picture Vocabulary Test* (4th ed.). Minneapolis, MN: Pearson.

Dykeman, D. D., & Roebuck, P. (2008, March). *Navajo emergence in Dinétah: Social imaginary and archaeology.* Paper presented at the meeting of the Society for American Archaeology, Vancouver, British Columbia, Canada. Retrieved from http://drarchaeology.com/publications/navajoemergence.pdf

Edelbrock, C., & Costello, A. J. (1990). Structured interviews for children and adolescents. In G. Goldstein & M. Hersen (Eds.), *Handbook of psychological assessment* (2nd ed.). Elmsford, NY: Pergamon.

EdITS Online. (2012). *COPS Interest Inventory.* Retrieved from http://www.edits.net/component/content/article/40/18-cops.html

Educational Testing Service. (2012). *GRE guide to use of scores 2012–2013.* Princeton, NJ: Author. Retrieved from http://www.ets.org/s/gre/pdf/gre_guide.pdf

Educational Testing Service. (2013). *About the GRE revised General Test.* Retrieved from http://www.ets.org/gre/revised_general/about/content/

Edwards, O. (2006). Special education disproportionality and the influence of intelligence test selection. *Journal of Intellectual and Developmental Disability, 31,* 246–248. doi:10.1080/13668250600999178

Ellers, R. A., Ellers, S. L., & Bradley-Johnson, S. (1989). Stability reliability of the Behavior Rating Profile. *Journal of School Psychology, 27,* 257–263. doi:10.1016/0022-4405(89)90040-X

Elliott, R., & Zucconi, A. (2006). Doing research on the effectiveness of psychotherapy and psychotherapy training: A person-centered/experiential perspective. *Person-Centered and Experiential Psychotherapies, 5,* 82–100. doi:10.1080/14779757.2006.9688398

Erford, B. T. (2006). *Counselor's guide to clinical, personality, and behavioral assessment.* Boston, MA: Houghton Mifflin/Lahaska Press.

Erford, B. T. (2010). Accountability in counseling. In B. Erford (Ed.), *Orientation to the counseling profession: Advocacy, ethics, and essential professional foundations* (pp. 361–389). Upper Saddle River, NJ: Pearson.

Erford, B. T. (2013). *Assessment for counselors* (2nd ed.). Boston, MA: Cengage Learning.

Erford, B. T., & Crockett, S. A. (2012). Practice and research in career development—2012. *Career Development Quarterly, 60,* 329–332. doi:10.1002/j.2161-0045.2012.00024.x

Erford, B. T., Vitali, G. J., & Slosson, S. W. (1999). *Manual for the Slosson Intelligence Test-Primary (SIT-P).* East Aurora, NY: Slosson Educational.

Evans, R., Ferguson, N., Davies, P., & Williams, P. (1975). Reliability of the Draw-a-Man Test. *Educational Research, 18,* 32–36. doi:10.1080/0013188750180104

Ewing, M., Huff, K., Andrew, M., & King, K. (2005). *Assessing the reliability of skills measured by the SAT.* New York, NY: College Board. Retrieved from http://research.collegeboard.org/sites/default/files/publications/2012/7/researchnote-2005-24-reliability-skills-measured-sat.pdf

Exner, J. E. (1993). *The Rorschach: A comprehensive system, Volume 1: Basic foundations* (3rd ed.). New York, NY: John Wiley & Sons.

Exner, J. E. (2001). *A Rorschach workbook for the comprehensive system* (5th ed.). Asheville, NC: Rorschach Workshops.

Eysenck, H. J. (1987). Personality and aging: An exploratory analysis. *Journal of Social Behavioral Personality, 3,* 11–12.

FairTest. (2013). *Schools that do not use SAT or ACT scores for admitting substantial numbers of students into bachelor degree programs.* Retrieved from http://www.fairtest.org/university/optional

Feldt, L. S., & Brennan, R. L. (1989). Reliability. In R. L. Linn (Ed.), *Educational measurement* (3rd ed., pp. 105–146). New York, NY: American Council on Education and Macmillan.

Fernandez-Berrocal, P., & Ruiz, D. (2008). Emotional intelligence in education. *Journal of Research in Educational Psychology, 15,* 421–436.

Fischer, R. (2012). Intersubjective culture: Indeed intersubjective or yet another form of subjective assessment? *Swiss Journal of Psychology, 71*(1), 13–20. doi:10.1024/1421-0185/a000067

Fischer, R. L., & Valley, C. (2000). Monitoring the benefits of family counseling: Using satisfaction surveys to assess the clients' perspective. *Smith College Studies on Social Work, 70*(2), 271–286. doi:10.1080/00377310009517592

Fiske, S. (1978). Rules of address: Navajo women in Los Angeles. *Journal of Anthropological Research, 34*(1), 72–91.

Fitts, W. H., & Warren, W. L. (1997). *Tennessee Self-Concept Scale: Second edition (TSCS:2)*. Los Angeles, CA: Western Psychological Services.

Flanagan, D. P., & Caltabiano, L. F. (2004). *Psychological reports: A guide for parents and teachers*. Bethesda, MD: National Association of School Psychologists. Retrieved from http://www.nasponline.org/resources/principals/nasp_reports.pdf

Foley, H. (2004). Carryover effect. In M. Lewis-Beck, A. Bryman, & T. Liao (Eds.), *Encyclopedia of social science research methods* (p. 90). Thousand Oaks, CA: Sage.

Forbey, J., & Lee, T. (2011). An exploration of the impact of invalid MMPI-2 protocols on collateral self-report measure scales. *Journal of Personality Assessment, 93*, 556–565. doi:10.1080/00223891.2022.608757

Forester-Miller, H., & Davis, T. E. (1995). *A practitioner's guide to ethical decision making*. Alexandria, VA: American Counseling Association.

Fox, M. C., & Mitchum, A. L. (2013). A knowledge-based theory of rising scores on "culture-free" tests. *Journal of Experiential Psychology: General, 142*, 979–1000. doi:10.1037/a0030155

Francis, P. C. (2013). *Overview of the revisions to the American Counseling Association 2005 Code of Ethics*. Retrieved from http://www.counseling.org/docs/ethics/introduction_to_the_code_of_ethics

Frank, L. K. (1948). *Projective methods*. Springfield, IL: Charles C Thomas.

Freeburg, M. N., & Van Winkle, J. L. (2011). *Increasing intake interview skills: A creative approach*. Retrieved from http://counselingoutfitters.com/vistas/vistas11/Article_33.pdf

Freud, S. (1911). *General Psychological Theory: Papers on Metapsychology*. New York, NY: Collier Books.

Frick, P. J., Barry, C. T., & Kamphaus, R. W. (2010). *Clinical assessment of child and adolescent personality and behavior*. New York, NY: Springer.

Furnham, A., Boo, H. C., & McClelland, A. (2012). Individual differences and the susceptibility to the influence of anchoring cues. *Journal of Individual Differences, 33*(2), 89–93. doi:10.1027/1614-0001/a000076

Galton, F. (1879). Psychometric experiments. *Brain, 2*, 149–162.

Garb, H. N., Lilienfeld, S. O., Nezworski, M. T., Wood, J. M., & O'Donohue, W. T. (2009). Can quality improvement processes help psychological assessment meet the demands of evidence based practices. *Scientific Review of Mental Health Practice, 7*(1), 17–25.

Gardner, H. (1999). *Intelligence reframed: Multiple intelligences for the 21st century*. New York, NY: Basic Books.

Gardner, H. (2006). *Multiple intelligence: New horizons*. New York, NY: Basic Books.

Gardner, H. (2011). *Frames of mind: Theory of multiple intelligences*. New York, NY: Basic Books.

Garrett, J. W., Balkin, R., Devlin, J. M., Erford, B., Flamez, B., Mendoza, S., . . . Wall, J. (2011). *Marriage, couple and family assessment competencies*. Retrieved from http://aarc-counseling.org/assets/cms/uploads/files/AACE-IAMFC.pdf

Gast, D. L. (2009). *Single subject research methodology in behavioral sciences*. New York, NY: Routledge.

Geisinger, K. F. (2000). Psychological testing at the end of the millennium: A brief historical review. *Professional Psychology: Research and Practice, 31*, 117–118. doi:10.1037//0735-7028.31.2.117

Gesell Institute of Child Development. (2013). *Gesell Developmental Observation-Revised and Gesell Early Screener technical report*. Available from http://www.gesellinstitute.org

Giessman, J. A., Gambrell, J. L., & Stebbins, M. S. (2013). Minority performance on the Naglieri Nonverbal Ability Test, second edition, versus the Cognitive Abilities Test, Form 6: One gifted program's experience. *Gifted Child Quarterly, 57*(2), 101–109. doi:10.1177/0016986213477190

Goleman, D. (1995). *Emotional intelligence: Why it can matter more than IQ.* New York, NY: Bantam Books.

Goleman, D. (1998). *Working with emotional intelligence.* New York, NY: Bantam Books.

Goodenough, F. (1926). *Measures of intelligence by drawings.* New York, NY: World Book.

Gough, H. G. (1987). *California Psychological Inventory administrator's guide.* Palo Alto, CA: Consulting Psychologists Press.

Gough, H. G., & Bradley, P. (2002). *CPI manual* (3rd ed.). Mountain View, CA: Consulting Psychologists Press.

Gowensmith, N. W., Murrie, D., & Boccaccini, M. T. (2013). Forensic mental health evaluations: Reliability, validity, quality, and other minor details. *Jury Expert, 25,* 40–44.

Graham, J. R., & Naglieri, J. A. (2002). *Handbook of assessment psychology.* New York, NY: John Wiley & Sons.

Graham, K. J., & Wells, S. (2001). Aggression among young adults in the social context of the bar. *Addiction Research, 9*(3), 193–219. doi:10.3109/16066350109141750

Graham-Day, K. J., Gardner, R., & Hsin, Y.-W. (2010). Increasing on-task behaviors of high school students with attention deficit hyperactivity disorder: Is it enough? *Education and Treatment of Children, 33*(2), 205–221.

Granello, D. H. (2010). The process of suicide risk assessment: Twelve core principles. *Journal of Counseling & Development, 88,* 363–370. doi:10.1002/j.1556-6678.2010.tb00034.x

Granello, D. H., & Granello, P. F. (2006). *Suicide: An essential guide for helping professionals and educators.* Columbus, OH: Pearson.

Graves, M. (1948). *Design Judgement Test.* San Antonio, TX: Psychological Corporation.

Greenfield, T. K., & Attkisson, C. C. (2004). The UCSF Client Satisfaction Scales: II. The Service Satisfaction Scale-30. In M. Maruish (Ed.), *The use of psychological testing for treatment planning and outcome assessment* (3rd ed., pp. 813–838). Mahwah, NJ: Lawrence Erlbaum.

Gregory, R. J. (2007). *Psychological testing: History, principles, and applications* (5th ed.). Boston, MA: Allyn & Bacon.

Groth-Marnat, G. (2009). *Handbook of psychological assessment.* New York, NY: John Wiley & Sons.

Hammer, A. L., & Kummerow, J. K. (1996). *Strong and MBTI career development guide* (Rev. ed.). Mountain View, CA: Consulting Psychologists Press.

Hammill, D., Pearson, N. A., & Wiederholt, J. L. (2009). *Comprehensive Test of Nonverbal Intelligence examiner's manual—Second edition.* Austin, TX: PRO-ED.

Harrington, T., & Long, J. (2013). The history of interest inventories and career assessments in career counseling. *Career Development Quarterly, 61,* 83–92. doi:10.1002/j.2161-0045.2013.00039.x

Harris, D. (1963). *Children's drawings as measures of intellectual maturity.* New York, NY: Harcourt Brace Jovanovich.

Haynes, S. N. (2001a). Clinical applications of analogue behavioral observation: Dimensions of psychometric evaluation. *Psychological Assessment, 13,* 73–85. doi:10.1037/1040-3590.13.1.73

Haynes, S. N. (2001b). Introduction to the special section of clinical applications of analogue behavioral observation. *Psychological Assessment, 13,* 3–4. doi:10.1037/1040-3590.13.1.3

Haynes, S. N., Heiby, E. M., & Hersen, M. (2003). *Comprehensive handbook of psychological assessment, behavioral assessment: Volume 3.* San Francisco, CA: John Wiley & Sons.

Henderson, S. E., Sugden, D. A., & Barnett, A. (2007). *Movement Assessment Battery for Children-2, 2nd edition (Movement ABC-2), Examiner's manual.* London, UK: Pearson Assessment.

Heppner, P. P., Wampold, B. E., & Kivlighan, D. M. (2008). *Research design in counseling* (3rd ed.). Belmont, CA: Thomson.

Herk, N. A., & Thompson, R. C. (2012). *Strong Interest Inventory manual supplement.* Mountain View, CA: Consulting Psychologists Press. Retrieved from https://www.cpp.com/PDFs/8402.pdf

Higgins, P. T., Altman, D. G., Gøtzsche, P. C., Jüni, P., Moher, D., Oxman, A. D., . . . Sterne, A. C. (2011). The Cochrane Collaboration tool for assessing risk of bias in randomised trials. *British Medical Journal, 343.* doi:10.1136/bmj.d5928

Hojnoski, R. L., Morrison, R., Brown, M., & Matthews, W. J. (2006). Projective test use among school psychologists: A survey and critique. *Journal of Psychoeducational Assessment, 24,* 145–159.

Holaday, M., Smith, D. A., & Sherry, A. (2000). Sentence completion tests: A review of literature and results of survey of members of the Society of Personality Assessment. *Journal of Personality Assessment, 74,* 371–383.

Holland, J. L. (1994). *Self-directed search.* Odessa, FL: Psychological Assessment Resources.

Holland, J. L. (1997). *Making vocational choices: A theory of vocational personalities and work environments* (3rd ed.). Odessa, FL: Psychological Assessment Resources.

Holloway, I., & Wheeler, S. (2010). *Qualitative research in nursing and healthcare* (3rd ed.). Oxford, UK: Wiley-Blackwell.

Hood, A. B. (2001). *Communicating assessment results in the counseling interview* (Report No. CG 031-161). (ERIC Document Reproduction Service No. ED457438)

Hood, A. B., & Johnson, R. W. (2009). *Assessment in counseling: A guide to the use of psychological assessment procedures* (5th ed.) Alexandria, VA: American Counseling Association.

Hooper, J., & McLearen, A. M. (2002). Does the insanity defense have a legitimate role? *Psychiatric Times, 39.* Retrieved from http://www.psychiatrictimes.com

Hoyt, W. T., Warbasse, R. E., & Chu, E. Y. (2006). Construct validation in counseling psychology research. *The Counseling Psychologist, 34,* 769–805. doi:10.1177/0011000006287389

Hubley, A. M., & Zumbo, B. D. (2011). Validity and the consequences of test interpretation and use. *Social Indicators Research, 103,* 219–230. doi:10.1007/s11205-011-9843-4

Hulse, W. G. (1951). The emotionally disturbed child draws his family. *Quarterly Journal of Child Behavior, 3,* 151–174.

Hulse, W. G. (1952). Childhood conflict expressed through family drawings. *Quarterly Journal of Child Behavior, 16,* 152–174.

Hunsley, J., & Bailey, J. M. (1999). The clinical utility of the Rorschach: Unfilled promises and an uncertain future. *Psychological Assessment, 11,* 266–277.

Hunter, J. E., & Schmidt, F. L. (2004). *Methods of meta-analysis: Correcting error and bias in research findings* (2nd ed.). Thousand Oaks, CA: Sage.

Hy, L. X., & Loevinger, J. (1996). *Measuring ego development* (Rev. ed.). Mahwah, NJ: Lawrence Erlbaum.

Industrial Organizational Solutions. (2010). *Standards for demonstrating content validity evidence.* Westchester, IL: Author. Retrieved from http://www.iosolutions.org/uploadedFiles/IOS/IO_Solutions/Research_and_Resources/Agency_Resources/White_Papers/Standards%20for%20Demonstrating%20Content%20Validity%20Evidence.pdf

International Test Commission. (2008). *ITC home.* Retrieved from http://www.intestcom.org

Ivey, A. E., Ivey, M. B., & Zalaquett, C. P. (2010). *Intentional interviewing and counseling: Facilitating client development in a multicultural society* (7th ed.). Belmont, CA: Brooks/Cole, Cengage Learning.

Jackson, D. N. (1999). *JVIS: Jackson Vocational Interest Survey.* Retrieved from http://www.sigmaassessmentsystems.com/resources/presentations/jvis.pdf

Johnson, K. A., Hill, E. D., & Cohen, A. B. (2011). Integrating the study of culture and religion: Toward a psychology of worldview. *Social & Personality Psychology Compass, 5*(3), 137–152. doi:10.1111/j.1751-9004.2010.00339.x

Joint Committee on Standards for Educational Evaluation. (1994). *Program evaluation standards: How to assess evaluations of educational programs* (2nd ed.). Thousand Oaks, CA: Sage.

Joint Committee on Testing Practices. (2000). *Rights and responsibilities of test takers: Guidelines and expectations.* Washington, DC: Author.

Joint Committee on Testing Practices. (2004). *Code of fair testing practices in education.* Washington, DC: Author.

Jolly, J. L. (2010). Florence L. Goodenough: Portrait of a psychologist. *Roeper Review, 32*(2), 98–105. doi:10.1080/02783191003587884

Jongsma, A. E., & Peterson, M. L. (2006). *The complete adult psychotherapy treatment planner* (4th ed.). Hoboken, NJ: John Wiley & Sons.

Juhnke, G. A., Granello, P. F., & Lebrón-Striker, M. A. (2007). *IS PATH WARM? A suicide assessment mnemonic for counselors* (ACAPCD-03). Alexandria, VA: American Counseling Association.

Jung, C. G. (1907). On psychophysical relations of the associative experiment. *Journal of Abnormal Psychology, 1*(6), 247–255. doi:10.1037/h0073328

Jung, C. G. (1910). The association method. *American Journal of Psychology, 21,* 219–269. doi:10.2307/1413002

Jung, C. G. (1964). *Psychological types* (Trans. H. G. Baynes). London, England: Pantheon. (Original work published 1921)

Kane, M. T. (2001). Current concerns in validity theory. *Journal of Educational Measurement, 38,* 319–342. doi:10.1111/j.1745-3984.2001.tb01130.x

Kaufman, A. S., & Kaufman, N. L. (2004). *KBIT-2 manual: Kaufman Brief Intelligence Test, 2nd edition.* Minneapolis, MN: NCS Pearson.

Kazdin, A. E. (1991). *Research design in clinical psychology.* Upper Saddle River, NJ: Pearson.

Kazdin, A. E. (2001). Conduct disorder. In H. S. Friedman (Eds.), *Disorders: Specialty articles from the encyclopedia of mental health* (pp. 131–146). Burlington, MA: Academic Press.

Kessler, R. C., Chiu, W. T., Demler, O., & Walters, E. E. (2005). Prevalence, severity, and comorbidity of twelve-month DSM-IV disorders in the National Comorbidity Survey Replication (NCS-R). *Archives of General Psychiatry, 62,* 617–627.

Kitchener, K. S. (1984). Intuition, critical evaluation and ethical principles: The foundation for ethical decisions in counseling psychology. *Counseling Psychologist, 12,* 43–55. doi:10.1177/0011000084123005

Kline, T. J. B. (2005). *Psychological testing: A practical approach to design and evaluation.* Thousand Oaks, CA: Sage.

Knoff, H. M., & Prout, T. H. (1985). *Kinetic Drawing System for Family and School: A handbook.* Los Angeles, CA: Western Psychological Services.

Kuder, F. (1977). *Activity interests and occupational choice.* Chicago, IL: Science Research Associates.

Kuder. (2014). *Research-based assessments.* Retrieved from http://www.kuder.com/our-unique-approach/research-based-assessments

Kuncel, N. R., & Hezlett, S. A. (2007). Standardized tests predict graduate students' success. *Science, 315*(5815), 1080–1081.

Kuncel, N. R., Hezlett, S. A., & Ones, D. S. (2004). Academic performance, career potential, creativity, and job performance: Can one construct predict them all? *Journal of Personality and Social Psychology, 86*(1), 148–161.

Kuusisto, K., & Artkoski, T. (2013). The female therapist and the client's gender. *Clinical Nursing Studies, 1*(3), 39–56. doi:10.5430/cns.v1n3p39

Lahti, M., Räikkönen, K., Lemola, S., Lahti, J., Heinonen, K., Kajantie, E., . . . Eriksson, J. G. (2013). Trajectories of physical growth and personality dimensions of the Five-Factor Model. *Journal of Personality and Social Psychology, 105*(1), 154–169. doi:10.1037/a0032300

Lambert, M. J., Hansen, N. B., Umphress, V., Lunnen, K., Okiishi, J., Burlingame, G., . . . Reisinger, C. S. (1996). *Administration and scoring manual for the outcome questionnaire* (OQ-45.2). Wilmington, DE: American Professional Credentialing Services.

Landau, M. J., Greenberg, J., & Rothschild, Z. K. (2009). Motivated cultural worldview adherence and culturally loaded test performance. *Personality and Social Psychology Bulletin, 35,* 442–453. doi:10.1177/0146167208329630

Larsen, D. L., Attkisson, C. C., Hargreaves, W. A., & Nguyen, T. D. (1979). Assessment of client/patient satisfaction: Development of a general scale. *Evaluation and Program Planning, 2,* 197–207. doi:10.1016/0149-7189(79)90094-6

Larson, L. M., & Borgen, F. H. (2002). Convergence of vocational interests and personality: Examples in an adolescent gifted sample. *Journal of Vocational Behavior, 60,* 91–112.

Larson, S. L., & Vitali, G. J. (1988). *KRT Kinder readiness test manual.* East Aurora, NY: Slosson Educational.

Latham, S. (2006). Some limits of decision-theory in bioethics: Rights, ends, and thick concepts. *American Journal of Bioethics, 6*(3), 56–58.

Law School Admission Council. (2013). *LSAT scores as predictors of law school performance.* Retrieved from http://www.lsac.org/jd/pdfs/lsat-score-predictors-of-performance.pdf

Lawshe, C. H. (1975). A quantitative approach to content validity. *Personnel Psychology, 28,* 563–575. doi:10.1111/j.1744-6570.1975.tb01393.x

Legg, S., & Hutter, M. (2006). A collection of definitions of intelligence. In B. Goertzel & P. Wang (Eds.), *Advances in artificial general intelligence: Concepts, architectures, and algorithms, Volume 57 of Frontiers in Artificial Intelligence and Applications* (pp. 17–24). Amsterdam, Netherlands: IOS Press.

Leibert, T. W. (2006). Making change visible: The possibilities in assessing mental health counseling outcomes. *Journal of Counseling and Development, 84,* 108–113. doi:10.1002/j.1556-6678.2006.tb00384.x

Leppma, M., & Jones, K. D. (2013). Multiple assessment methods and sources in counseling: Ethical considerations. In G. R. Walz, J. C. Bleuer, & R. K. Yep (Eds.), *Ideas and research you can use: VISTAS 2013.* Retrieved from http://counselingoutfitters.com/vistas/vistas13/Article_37.pdf

Lewis-Palmer, T., Reed-Schindler, H., & Ingram, K. (2005). Behavioral assessment interviews. In M. Hersen, J. Rosqvist, A. Gross, R. Drabman, G. Sugai, & R. Horner (Eds.), *Encyclopedia of behavior modification and cognitive behavior therapy: Volume 3, Educational applications* (pp. 1174–1177). Thousand Oaks, CA: Sage.

Lilienfeld, S. O., Wood, J. M., & Garb, H. N. (2000). The scientific status of projective techniques. *Psychological Science in the Public Interest, 1,* 27–66. doi:10.1111/1529-1006.002

Lindzey, G. (1959). On the classification of projective techniques. *Psychological Bulletin, 56,* 158–168. doi:10.1037/h0043871

Liu, O. (2011). Do major field of study and cultural familiarity affect TOEFL iBT reading performance? A confirmatory approach to differential item functioning. *Applied Measurement in Education, 24,* 235–255. doi:10.1080/08957347.2011.580645

Loevinger, J. (1976). *Ego development.* San Francisco, CA: Jossey-Bass.

Loevinger, J. (1998). Reliability and validity of the SCT. In J. Loevinger (Ed.), *Technical foundations for measuring ego development* (pp. 29–40). Mahwah, NJ: Lawrence Erlbaum.

Loevinger, J., & Wessler, R. (1970). *Measuring ego development: 1. Construction and use of a sentence completion test.* San Francisco, CA: Jossey-Bass.

Lohman, D. F. (2011). Introducing CogAT Form 7. *Cognitively Speaking, 7,* 1–9.

Lopez, E. C. (1997). The cognitive assessment of limited English proficient and bilingual children. In D. P. Flanagan, J. L. Genshaft, & P. L. Harrison (Eds.), *Contemporary intellectual assessment: Theories, tests, and issues.* (pp. 503–516). New York, NY: Guilford Press.

Lunenberg. F. C. (2010). State-mandated performance testing: Legislation and litigation. *Schooling, 1,* 1–4.

Luria, A. R. (1966). *Human brain and psychological processes.* New York, NY: Harper & Row.

Lutrell, V. R., & Richard, D. C. S. (2011). Development of the higher education value inventory: Factor structure and score reliability. *Psychology, 2*, 909–916. doi:10.4236/psych.2011.29137

Lyman, H. B. (1998). *Test scores and what they mean* (6th ed.). Needham Heights, MA: Allyn & Bacon.

Lynch, R., Seery, N., & Gordon, S. (2011). Student interests and undergraduate performance: The importance of student-course alignment. *Irish Educational Studies, 30*, 345–363.

Machover, K. (1949). *Personality projection in the drawing of a human figure*. Springfield, IL: Charles C Thomas.

Maddox, T. (2008). *Tests: A comprehensive reference for assessment in psychology, education, and business* (6th ed.). Austin, TX: PRO-ED.

Maloney, M. P., & Ward, M. P. (1976). *Psychological assessment: A conceptual approach*. New York, NY: Oxford University Press.

Manalo, E., Ede, J., & Wong-Toi, G. (2010). Provision of learning support for university students with learning, mental health, and other forms of hidden disabilities. *Open Rehabilitation Journal, 3*, 23–33.

Martella, R. C., Nelson, R. J., Marchand-Martella, N. E., & O'Reilly, M. (2012). Preliminary considerations. In *Comprehensive behavior management: Individualized, classroom, and schoolwide approaches* (2nd ed., pp. 212–246). Thousand Oaks, CA: Sage.

Martin, D. C. (1990). The Mental Status Examination. In H. K. Walker, W. D. Hall, & J. W. Hurst (Eds.), *Clinical methods: The history, physical, and laboratory examinations* (3rd ed., Ch 207). Boston, MA: Butterworths. Retrieved from http://www.ncbi.nlm.nih.gov/books/NBK320/

Martínez Pons, M. (1997). The relation of emotional intelligence with selected areas of personal functioning. *Imagination, Cognition and Personality, 17*, 3–13. doi:10.2190/68VD-DFXB-K5AW-PQAY

Mayer, D. M., & Hanges, P. J. (2003). Understanding the stereotype threat effect with "culture-free" tests: An examination of its mediators and measurement. *Human Performance, 16*, 207–230.

Mayer, J. D., & Salovey, P. (1997). What is emotional intelligence? In P. Salovey & D. Sluyter (Eds.), *Emotional development and emotional intelligence: Implications for educators* (pp. 3–31). New York, NY: Basic Books.

Mayers, K. S. (1991). A sentence completion task for use in the assessment of psychotic patients. *American Journal of Forensic Psychology, 9*, 19–30.

McAleavey, A. A., Nordberg, S. S., Hayes, J. A., Castonguay, L. G., Locke, B. D., & Lockard, A. J. (2012). Clinical validity of the Counseling Center Assessment of Psychological Symptoms-62 (CCAPS-62): Further evaluation and clinical applications. *Journal of Counseling Psychology, 59*, 575–590. doi:10.1037/a0029855

McCallum, R. S., & Bracken, B. A. (1997). The Universal Nonverbal Intelligence Test. In D. P. Flanagan, J. L. Genshaft, & P. L. Harrison (Eds.), *Contemporary intellectual assessment: Theories, tests, and issues* (pp. 268–280). New York, NY: Guilford Press.

McCrae, R. R., & Costa, P. T. (2010). *NEO Inventories for the NEO-PI3, NEO-FFI-3, NEO PI-R Professional Manual*. Lutz, FL: Psychological Assessment Resources.

McDermott, B. E., Scott, C. L., Busse, D., Andrade, F., Zozaya, M., & Quanbeck, C. D. (2008). The conditional release of insanity acquittees: Three decades of decision-making. *Journal of American Academy of Psychiatry and the Law, 36*, 329–336.

McDermott, S. P. (2010). Clinical application of research on cognitive-behavioral therapies for adults with ADHD. In J. K. Buitelaar, C. C. Kan, & P. Asherson (Eds.), *ADHD in adults: Characterization, diagnosis, and treatment* (pp. 254–270). Cambridge, UK: Cambridge University Press.

McGoey, K., Cowan, R., Rumrill, P., & LaVogue, C. (2010). Understanding the psychometric properties of reliability and validity in assessment. *Work: A Journal of Prevention, Assessment, and Rehabilitation, 36*(1), 105–112.

McQuaid, J. R., Marx, B. P., Rosen, M. I., Bufka, L. F., Tenhula, W., Cook, H., & Keane, T. M. (2012). Mental health assessment in rehabilitation research. *Journal of Rehabilitation Research & Development, 49*, 121–137. doi:10.1682/JRRD.2010.08.0143

Merrell, K. W. (2008). *Behavioral, social, and emotional assessment of children and adolescents* (3rd ed.). New York, NY: Lawrence Erlbaum.

Messick, S. (1989). Validity. In R. L. Linn (Ed.), *Educational measurement* (3rd ed., pp. 13–103). New York, NY: Macmillan.

Miller, L. (2013). Psychological evaluations in the criminal justice system: Basic principles and best practices. *Aggression and Violent Behavior, 18,* 83–91. doi:10.1016/j.avb.2012.10.005

Millman, J., & Greene, J. (1993). The specification and development of tests of achievement and ability. In R. L. Linn (Ed.), *Educational measurement* (pp. 335–366). Phoenix, AZ: Oryx Press.

Millon, T. (2003). *MIPS Revised manual.* Minneapolis, MN: Pearson Assessments.

Miltenberger, R. G. (2012). *Behavior modification: Principles and procedures* (5th ed.). Belmont, CA: Wadsworth.

Morey, L. C. (2007). *Personality Assessment Inventory professional manual* (2nd ed.). Lutz, FL: Psychological Assessment Resources.

Morgan, C. D., & Murray, H. A. (1938). Thematic Apperception Test. In H. A. Murray (Ed.), *Explorations in personality: A clinical and experimental study of fifty men of college age* (pp. 530–545). New York, NY: Oxford University Press.

MostExtreme.org. (2012). *Highest IQ in the world.* Retrieved from http://mostextreme.org/highest_iq.php

Multi-Health Systems. (2009). *Conners 3 update.* Retrieved from http://downloads.mhs.com/conners/C3-Supplement.pdf

Murray, H. A. (1943). *Thematic Apperception Test manual.* Cambridge, MA: Harvard University Press.

Mushquash, C. J., & Bova, D. L. (2007). Cross-cultural assessment and measurement issues. *Journal of Developmental Disabilities, 13,* 53–65.

Naglieri, J. A. (2003). Current advances in assessment and intervention for children with learning disabilities. In T. E. Scruggs & M. A. Mastropieri (Eds.), *Advances in learning and behavioral disabilities, Volume 16: Identification and assessment* (pp. 163–190). New York, NY: JAI.

Naglieri, J. A., & Goldstein, S. (2009). *Practitioner's guide to assessing intelligence and achievement.* New York, NY: John Wiley & Sons.

National Board of Certified Counselors. (2005). *NBCC code of ethics.* Greensboro, NC: Author.

National Career Development Association. (2007). *Code of ethics.* Retrieved from http://association database.com/aws/NCDA/asset_manager/get_file/3395/code_of_ethicsmay-2007.pdf

National Center for Education Statistics. (2010). *The condition of education 2010.* Washington, DC: U.S. Department of Education. Retrieved from http://nces.ed.gov/pubs2010/2010028.pdf

National Center for O*NET Development. (n.d.-a). *O*NET career exploration tools.* Retrieved from http://www.onetcenter.org/tools.html

National Center for O*NET Development. (n.d.-b). *The O*NET content model.* Retrieved from http://www.onetcenter.org/content.html

National Dissemination Center for Children with Disabilities. (2010). *Disability.* Retrieved from http://nichcy.org/disability

National Institute of Mental Health. (2013). *Suicide in the U.S.: Statistics and prevention.* Retrieved from http://www.nimh.nih.gov/health/publications/suicide-in-the-us-statistics-and-prevention/index.shtml

National Institute of Mental Health. (n.d.). *Mental health information.* Retrieved from http://www.nimh.nih.gov/health/topics/index.shtml

Naugle, K. A. (2009). Counseling and testing: What counselors need to know about state laws on assessment and testing. *Measurement and Evaluation in Counseling and Development, 42*(1), 31–45. doi:10.1177/0748175609333561

Nauta, M. M. (2010). The development, evolution, and status of Holland's theory of vocational personalities: Reflections and future directions of counseling psychology. *Journal of Counseling Psychology, 57*(1), 11–22. doi:10.1037/a0018213

Nelson, R. O., & Hayes, S. C. (1979). Some current dimensions of behavioral assessment. *Behavioral Assessment, 1,* 1–16.

Neukrug, E. S., & Schwitzer, A. (2006). *Skills and tools for today's professional counselors and psychotherapists: From natural helping to professional counseling.* Belmont, CA: Brooks/Cole.

Nevill, D. D., & Kruse, S. J. (1996). Career assessment and the values scale. *Journal of Career Assessment, 4,* 383–397.

Nevill, D. D., & Super, D. E. (1986). *The Values Scale: Theory, application, and research: Manual (research ed.).* Palo Alto: CA: Consulting Psychologists Press.

Novak, J. M., Hamaguchi, P., & McCullough, J. (2003, April). *CSHA Task Force: Guidelines for evaluation and treatment of central auditory processing disorders.* Paper presented at the California Speech-Language Hearing Association Conference, Monterey, CA.

O'Connor, D. P. (2014). Stanine distribution [image]. Retrieved from http://grants.hhp.uh.edu/doconnor/pep6305/Topic%20005%20Normal%20Distribution.htm

Ohler, D., & Levinson, E. (2012). Using Holland's theory in employment counseling: Focus on service occupations. *Journal of Employment Counseling, 49*(4), 148–159. doi:10.1002/j.2161-1920.2012.00016.x

Onwuegbuzie, A. J., & Daniel, L. J. (2002). A framework for reporting and interpreting internal consistency reliability estimates. *Measurement and Evaluation in Counseling and Development, 35,* 89–103.

Oster, G. D., & Crone, P. G. (2004). *Using drawings in assessment and therapy: A guide for mental health professionals.* New York, NY: Routledge.

Patterson, B. F., & Mattern, K. D. (2013). *Validity of the SAT for predicting first-year grades: 2010 SAT validity sample* (College Board Statistical Report No. 2013-2). New York, NY: College Board. Retrieved from http://research.collegeboard.org/sites/default/files/publications/2013/4/statisticalreport-2013-2-validity-sat-1st-yr-gpa-2010-sample.pdf

Paul, G. L. (1967). Strategy of outcome research in psychotherapy. *Journal of Consulting Psychology, 31,* 109–118. doi:10.1037/h0024436

Pearson. (2012a). *Bennett Mechanical Comprehension Test (BMCT).* Retrieved from http://www.pearsonassessments.com/talentassessment/products/100000410/bennett-mechanical-comprehension-test-bmct-bmct.html?Pid=015-8341-430&Mode=summary

Pearson. (2012b). *Campbell Interest and Skill Survey (CISS).* Retrieved from http://psychcorp.pearsonassessments.com/HAIWEB/Cultures/en-us/Productdetail.htm?Pid=PAg115

Pearson. (2012c). *Kaufman Test of Educational Achievement, Second Edition (KTEA-II).* Retrieved from http://www.pearsonassessments.com/HAIWEB/Cultures/en-us/Productdetail.htm?Pid=PAa32215

Pearson. (2012d). *PIAT-R/NU technical information.* Retrieved from http://images.pearsonclinical.com/images/Products/PIAT/piat.pdf

Pearson. (2012e). *Wechsler Individual Achievement Test-Second Edition (WIAT-II).* Retrieved from http://www.pearsonassessments.com/HAIWEB/Cultures/en-us/Productdetail.htm?Pid=015-8983-505

Pearson. (2013). *Miller Analogies Test candidate information booklet.* Retrieved from http://psychcorp.pearsonassessments.com/hai/Images/dotCom/milleranalogies/pdfs/MAT2011CIB_FNL.pdf

Pearson Education. (2014a). *Behavior Assessment System for Children, Second Edition (BASC-2).* Retrieved from http://www.pearsonclinical.com/psychology/products/100000658/behavior-assessment-system-for-children-second-edition-basc-2.html?Pid=PAa30000#tab-details

Pearson Education. (2014a). *Movement Assessment Battery for Children-Second Edition (Movement ABC-2).* Retrieved from http://www.pearsonclinical.com/therapy/products/100000433/movement-assessment-battery-for-children-second-edition-movementabc2.html?pid=015-8541-308

Pearson Education. (2014b). *Naglieri Nonverbal Ability Test Online-Second Edition (NNAT-2 Online).* Retrieved from http://www.pearsonassessments.com/learningassessments/products/100000690/naglieri-nonverbal-ability-test-online—second.html?Pid=NNAT2_online&Mode=summary

Phillips, S. E. (1993). *Legal implications of high-stakes assessments: What states should know.* Oak Brook, IL: North Central Regional Educational Laboratory.

Piaget, J. (1954). *The construction of reality in the child.* New York, NY: Basic Books.

Plante, T. G. (2011). *Contemporary clinical psychology.* New York, NY: John Wiley & Sons.

Ponsoda, V., Abad, F. J., Francis, L. J., & Hills, P. R. (2008). Gender differences in the Coopersmith Self-Esteem Inventory: The incidence of differential item functioning. *Journal of Individual Differences, 29,* 217–222. doi:10.1027/1614-0001.29.4.217

Power, Z., Campbell, M., Kitcoyne, P., Kitchener, H., & Waterman, H. (2010). The hyperemesis impact of symptoms questionnaire: Development and validation of a clinical tool. *International Journal of Nursing Studies, 47*(1), 67–77. doi:10.1016/j.ijnurstu.2009.06.012

Psychological Assessment Resources. (2012). *Wide Range Achievement Test 4 (WRAT4).* Retrieved from http://www4.parinc.com/Products/Product.aspx?ProductID=WRAT4

Ramsay. (2013). *Mechanical Aptitude Test MAT-3C.* Retrieved from http://www.ramsaycorp.com/catalog/view/?productid=25

Rapaport, D., Gill, M. M., & Schafer, R. (1945–1946). *Diagnostic psychological testing* (2 vols.). Chicago, IL: Year Book.

Regulation implementing Education for All Handicapped Children Act of 1975 (PL94-142). (1977). *Federal Register, 42*(163), 42474–42518.

Reid, W. H. (2006). Sanity evaluations and criminal responsibility. *Applied Psychology in Criminal Justice, 2*(3), 114–146.

Reitman, K. M., & Noell, G. (2003). *Practitioner's guide to empirically based measures of school behavior.* New York, NY: Kluwer Academic.

Remine, M., Brown, P., Care, E., & Rickards, F. (2007). The relationship between spoken language ability and intelligence test performance of deaf children and adolescents. *Deafness & Education International, 9*(3), 147–164.

Remley, T. P., & Herlihy, B. (2010). *Ethical, legal, and professional issues in counseling* (3rd ed.). Upper Saddle River, NJ: Pearson.

Resnick, J. L. (2005). Evidence-based practice for treatment of eating disorders. *Journal of College Student Psychotherapy, 20,* 49–65. doi:10.1300/J035v20m01_05

Reynolds, C. R., & Kamphaus, R. W. (2004). *BASC-2: Behavior assessment system for children, second edition manual.* Circle Pines, MN: American Guidance Service.

Reynolds, C. R., Lowe, P. A., & Saenz, A. L. (1999). The problem of bias in psychological assessment. In C. R. Reynolds & T. B. Gutkin (Eds.), *The handbook of school psychology* (pp. 549–595). New York: John Wiley & Sons.

Reynolds, S. (2000). Evidence-based practice and psychotherapy research. *Journal of Mental Health, 9,* 257–266. doi:10.1080/713680248

Reynolds, W. M., & Kobak, K. A. (1998). *Reynolds Depression Screening Inventory.* Odessa FL: Psychological Assessment Resources.

Rindermann, H. (2007). The bigg-factor of national cognitive ability. *European Journal of Personality, 21,* 767–787. doi:10.1002/per.658

Riverside. (n.d.). *CogAT-7 sample items.* Retrieved from http://www.riverpub.com/products/cogAT7/pdf/CogAT7SampleItems.pdf

Riverside. (2002). *Cognitive Abilities Test: A short guide for teachers.* Chicago, IL: Author.

Roberts, G. E., & Gruber, C. (2005). *Roberts-2.* Los Angeles, CA: Western Psychological Services.

Rogers, H. J. (2005). Differential item functioning. In B. S. Everitt & D. C. Howell (Eds.), *Encyclopedia of Statistics in Behavioral Sciences* (pp. 485–490). Colchester, UK: John Wiley & Sons.

Rogers, J. R. (2001). Suicide risk assessment. In E. R. Welfel & R. E. Ingersoll (Eds.), *The mental health desk reference* (pp. 259–264). New York, NY: John Wiley & Sons.

Rorschach, H. (1921). *Psychodiagnostik*. New York, NY: Hans Huber.

Rossier, J., Meyer de Stadelhofen, F., & Berthoud, S. (2004). The hierarchical structures of the NEO PI-R and the 16PF5. *European Journal of Psychological Assessment, 20*(1), 27–38. doi:10.1027/1015-5759.20.1.27

Rotarescu, V., & Ciurea, A. V. (2010). The brain—The organ of the psychic (The lesions/the defense mechanisms). *Journal of Medicine & Life, 3*, 221–228.

Rotter, J. B., Lah, M. I., & Rafferty, J. E. (1992). *The Rotter Incomplete Sentences Blank, second edition manual*. New York, NY: Psychological Corporation.

Rotter, J. B., & Rafferty, J. E. (1950). *The Rotter Incomplete Sentences Blank manual*. New York, NY: Psychological Corporation.

Rottinghaus, P. J., Lindley, L. D., Green, M. A., & Borgen, F. H. (2002). Educational aspirations: The contribution of personality, self-efficacy, and interests. *Journal of Vocational Behavior, 61*, 1–19.

Rubio, D. (2005). Content validity. *Encyclopedia of Social Measurement* (Vol. 1). New York, NY: Elsevier.

Rudner, L. M. (2013). *What we know about integrated reasoning six months after launch*. Retrieved from http://officialgmat.mba.com/2013/03/01/what-we-know-about-integrated-reasoning-six-months-after-launch/

Ruscio, J. (2004). Diagnoses and the behaviors they denote: A critical evaluation of the labeling theory of mental illness. *Scientific Review of Mental Health Practice, 3*(1). Retrieved from http://www.srmhp.org

Russell, M., & Karol, D. (2002). *16PF Fifth Edition administrator's manual*. Champaign, IL: Institute for Personality and Ability Testing.

Salkind, N. J. (2006). *Tests and measurements for people who think they hate tests and measurement*. Thousand Oaks, CA: Sage.

Salovey, P., & Mayer, J. D. (1990). Emotional intelligence. *Imagination, Cognition, and Personality, 9*, 185–211. doi:10.2190/DUGG-P24E-52WK-6CDG

Sampson, J. P. (2000). Using the Internet to enhance testing in counseling. *Journal of Counseling and Development, 78*, 348–356. doi:10.1002/j.1556-6676.2000.tb01917.x

Santelli, J., Klein, J., Graff, C., Allan, M., & Elster, A. (2002). Reliability in adolescent reporting of clinician counseling, health care use, and health behaviors. *Med Care, 40*, 26–37. doi:10.1097/00005650-200201000-00005

Sattler, J. (2001). *Assessment of children: Cognitive applications* (4th ed.). San Diego, CA: Jerome M. Sattler.

Savickas, M. L. (1997). Career adaptability: An integrative construct for Life-Span, Life-Space theory. *Career Development Quarterly, 45*, 247–259.

Savickas, M. L., & Porfeli, E. J. (2011). Revision of the Career Maturity Inventory: The adaptability form. *Journal of Career Assessment, 19*, 355–374. doi:10.1177/1069072711409342

Sax, G. (1997). *Principles of educational and psychological measurement and evaluation* (4th ed.). Belmont, CA: Wadsworth.

Scalise, K., & Gifford, B. (2006). Computer-based assessment in e-learning: A framework for constructing "intermediate constraint" questions and tasks for technology platforms. *Journal of Technology, Learning, and Assessment, 4*(6). Retrieved from http://ejournals.bc.edu/ojs/index.php/jtla/index

Schaubhut, N. A., & Thompson, R. C. (2011). *MBTI Step II manual supplement*. Mountain View, CA: Consulting Psychologists Press.

Schilling, D., & Schwartz, I. (2004). Alternative seating for young children with autism spectrum disorder: Effects on classroom behavior. *Journal of Autism and Developmental Disorders, 34*, 423–432. doi:10.1023/B:JADD.0000037418.48587.f4

Schrank, F. A., Miller, D. C., Wendling, B. J., & Woodcock, R. W. (2010). *Essentials of WJ III Cognitive Abilities Assessment* (2nd ed.). Hoboken, NJ: John Wiley & Sons.

Schroeder, J. L., Plata, M., Fullwood, H., Price, M., & Dyer Sennette, J. (2013). Increasing the cultural competence of assessment professionals via online training. *National Forum of Multicultural Issues Journal, 10*(1), 1–13.

Schulte, M. J., Ree, M. J., & Carretta, T. R. (2004). Emotional intelligence: Not much more than g and personality. *Personality and Individual Differences, 37,* 1059–1068. doi:10.1016/j.paid.2003.11.014

Schultheiss, D. E. P., & Stead, G. B. (2004). Childhood Career Development Scale: Scale construction and psychometric properties. *Journal of Career Assessment, 12,* 113–134.

Schultz, D. S., & Loving, J. L. (2012). Challenges since Wikipedia: The availability of Rorschach online and internet users' reactions to online media coverage of the Rorschach-Wikipedia debate. *Journal of Personality Assessment, 94*(1), 73–81. doi:10.1080/00223891.2011.627963

Sedlacek, W. E., & Kim, S. H. (1996). Multicultural assessment. *ERIC Digest.* Greensboro, NC: ERIC Clearinghouse on Counseling and Student Services, University of North Carolina. (ERIC Document Reproduction Service No. ED391112)

Seligman, D. (2002). Good breeding. *National Review, 54*(1), 53–54.

Seligman, L. (1996). *Diagnosis and treatment planning in counseling.* New York, NY: Basic Books.

Seligman, L., & Reichenberg, L. W. (2012). *Selecting effective treatments: A comprehensive, systematic guide to treating mental disorders* (4th ed.). Hoboken, NJ: John Wiley & Sons.

Shapiro, E. S., & Skinner, C. H. (1990). Principles of behavioral assessment. In C. R. Reynolds & R. Kamphaus (Eds.), *Handbook of educational and psychological assessment of children: Personality, behavior, and context* (pp. 342–364). New York, NY: Guilford.

Shea, S. C. (2009). Suicide assessment. *Psychiatric Times, 26*(12), 1–6. Retrieved from http://www.suicideassessment.com/pdfs/PsychiatricTimesArticleparts1-2PDF.pdf

Silva, L. C., Campbell, K., & Wright, D. W. (2012). Intercultural relationships: Entry, adjustment, and cultural negotiations. *Journal of Comparative Family Studies, 43,* 857–870.

Smith, T. B., Rosenstein, I., & Granaas, M. M. (2001). Intake screening with the self-rating depression scale in a university counseling center. *Journal of College Counseling, 4,* 133–141. doi:10.1002/j.2161-1882.2001.tb00193.x

Solano-Flores, G. (2011). Assessing the cultural validity of assessment practices: An introduction. In M. del Rosario Basterra, E. Trumbull, & G. Solano-Flores (Eds.), *Cultural validity in assessment: Addressing linguistic and cultural diversity* (pp. 3–21). New York, NY: Routledge.

Soto, C. J., & John, O. P. (2009). Using the California psychological inventory to assess the Big Five personality domains: A hierarchical approach. *Journal of Research in Personality, 43,* 25–38.

Sparrow, S. S., & Davis, S. M. (2000). Recent advances in the assessment of intelligence and cognition. *Journal of Child Psychology and Psychiatry, 41,* 117–131. doi:10.1111/1469-7610.00552

Spearman, C. (1927). *The abilities of man: Their nature and measurement.* New York, NY: Macmillan.

Sperry, L. (2005). Case conceptualization: A strategy for incorporating individual, couple, and family dynamics in the treatment process. *American Journal of Family Therapy, 33,* 353–364. doi:10.1080/01926180500341598

Sperry, L. (2010). *Core competencies in counseling and psychotherapy: Becoming a highly competent therapist.* New York, NY: Taylor & Francis.

Sperry, L., & Sperry, J. (2012). *Case conceptualization: Mastering this competency with ease and confidence.* New York, NY: Routledge.

Spriggs, A. D., Gast, D., & Ayres, K. M. (2007). Using picture activity schedule books to increase on-schedule and on-task behaviors. *Education and Training in Developmental Disabilities, 42,* 209–223.

Sprinkle, S. D., Lurie, D., Insko, S. L., Atkinson, G., Jones, G. L., Logan, A. R., & Bissada, N. N. (2002). Criterion validity, severity cut scores, and test-retest reliability of the Beck Depression Inventory-II in a university counseling center sample. *Journal of Counseling Psychology, 49,* 381–385. doi:10.1037/0022-0167/49/3/381

Stanton, A. L., Revenson, T. A., & Tennen, H. (2007). Health psychology: Psychological adjustment to chronic disease. *Annual Review of Psychology, 58,* 565–592. doi:10.1146/annurev.psych.58.110405.085615

Steenbarger, B. N., & Smith, B. H. (1996). Assessing the quality of counseling surveys: Developing accountable helping systems. *Journal of Counseling and Development, 75,* 145–150.

Stephen Hawking. (n.d.). Retrieved from http://www.hawking.org.uk/

Sternberg, R. J. (1988). *The triarchic theory of intelligence.* New York, NY: Viking.

Sternberg, R. J., & Grigorenko, E. L. (2000–2001). Guilford's structure of intellect model and model of creativity: Contributions and limitations. *Creativity Research Journal, 13,* 309–316. doi:10.1207/S15326934CRJ1334_08

Stone, D. (2012). *Accountability and outcomes in the counseling profession.* Retrieved from http://psychological-musings.blogspot.com/2012/02/accountability-and-outcomes-in.html

Strohmer, D. C., & Leierer, S. J. (2000). Modeling rehabilitation counselor clinical judgment. *Rehabilitation Counseling Bulletin, 44,* 3–9, 38. doi:10.1177/003435520004400102

Substance Abuse and Mental Health Services Administration. (2013). *Using process evaluation to monitor program implementation.* Retrieved from http://captus.samhsa.gov/access-resources/using-process-evaluation-monitor-program-implementation

Summerfeldt, L. J., & Antony, A. M. (2002). Structured and semi-structured diagnostic interviews. In A. M. Antony (Ed.), *Handbook of assessment and treatment planning for psychological disorders* (pp. 3–37). New York, NY: Guilford Press.

Super, D. E. (1955). The dimensions and measurement of vocational maturity. *Teachers College Record, 57,* 15-1163.

Super, D. E. (1970). *Work Values Inventory.* Boston, MA: Houghton Mifflin.

Super, D. E. (1990). A life-span, life-space approach to career development. In D. Brown & L. Brooks (Eds.), *Career choice and development: Applying contemporary theories to practice* (2nd ed., pp. 197–261). San Francisco, CA: Jossey-Bass.

Super, D. E. (1995). Values: Their nature, assessment, and practical use. In D. E. Super & B. Sverko (Eds.), *Life roles, values, and careers: International findings of the Work Importance Study* (pp. 54–61). San Francisco, CA: Jossey-Bass.

Super, D. E., & Knasel, E. G. (1981). Career development in adulthood: Some theoretical problems. *British Journal of Guidance and Counseling, 9,* 194–201.

Super, D. E., Thompson, A. S., Lindeman, R. H., Jordaan, J. P., & Myers, R. A. (1988). *Adult Career Concerns Inventory.* Palo Alto, CA: Consulting Psychologists Press.

Swanson, P. B. (2012). The congruence of vocational interests and the workplace environment: Reducing the language teacher shortage. *Language Teaching Research, 16,* 519–537. doi:10.1177/1632168812455588

Szondi, L. (1947). *Experimentelle triebsdiagnostik* [Experimental operation diagnostics]. Bern, Switzerland: Verlag Hans Huber.

Texas Education Agency. (2013). *STAAR resources.* Retrieved from http://www.tea.state.tx.us/student.assessment/staar

Thurstone, L. L. (1938). Primary mental abilities. *Psychometric Monographs,* No. 1.

Thurstone, L. L., & Thurstone, T. G. (1941). *Factorial studies of intelligence. Psychometric Monographs,* 2. Madison, WI: Psychometric Society.

Timulak, L. (2009). *Research in psychotherapy and counseling.* Thousand Oaks, CA: Sage.

Tracey, T. J. G., & Hopkins, N. (2001). Correspondence of interests and abilities with occupational choice. *Journal of Counseling Psychology, 48,* 178–189.

Trinidad, D. R., Unger, J. B., Chou, C. P., & Johnson, C. A. (2004). The protective association of emotional intelligence with psychosocial smoking risk factors for adolescents. *Personality and Individual Differences, 36,* 945–954. doi:10.1016/S0191-8869(03)00163-6

Trzepacz, P. T., & Baker, R. W. (1993). *The psychiatric mental status examination.* New York, NY: Oxford University Press.

Turner, S. M., DeMers, S. T., Fox, H. R., & Reed, G. M. (2001). APA's guidelines for test user qualifications. *American Psychologist, 56,* 1099–1113. doi:10.1037/0003-066X.56.12.1099

Urbina, S. (2004). *Essentials of psychological testing.* Hoboken, NJ: John Wiley & Sons.

U.S. Census Bureau. (2012). *Nearly 1 in 5 people have a disability in the U.S., Census Bureau Reports.* Retrieved from http://www.census.gov/newsroom/releases/archives/miscellaneous/cb12-134.html

U.S. Department of Health and Human Services. (1999). *Mental health: A report of the Surgeon General.* Rockville, MD: U.S. Department of Health and Human Services, Substance Abuse and Mental Health Services Administration, Center for Mental Health Services.

Vacc, N. A., & Juhnke, G. A. (1997). The use of structured clinical interviews for assessment in counseling. *Journal of Counseling and Development, 75,* 470–480. doi:10.1002/j.1556-6676.1997.tb02363.x

Van Rooy, D. L., & Viswesvaran, C. (2004). Emotional intelligence: A meta-analytic investigation of predictive validity and nomological net. *Journal of Vocational Behavior, 65,* 71–95. doi:10.1016/S0001-8791(03)00076-9

Vaughn, S., Bos, C. S., & Schumm, J. S. (2000). *Teaching exceptional, diverse, and at-risk students in the general education classroom* (2nd ed.). Boston, MA: Allyn and Bacon.

Vernon, P. E. (1984). Intelligence, cognitive styles, and brain lateralization. *International Journal of Psychology, 19,* 435–455. doi:10.1080/00207598408247540

Volpe, R. J., & McConaughy, S. H. (2005). Systematic direct observational assessment of student behavior: Its use and interpretation in multiple settings: An introduction to the mini-series. *School Psychology Review, 34,* 451–453.

Walmsley, P. T., Natali, M. W., & Campbell, J. P. (2012). Only incumbent raters in O*NET? Oh yes! Oh no! *International Journal of Selection and Assessment, 20,* 283–296. doi:10.1111/j.1468-2389.2012.00600.x

Walton, R. (2012). *Measuring therapy progress, effectiveness and outcomes.* Retrieved from http://behavioralhealthmatters.blogspot.com/2012/08/measuring-therapy-progress.html

Waterhouse, L. (2006). Inadequate evidence for multiple intelligences, Mozart Effect, and emotional intelligence theories. *Educational Psychologist, 41,* 247–255. doi:10.1207/s15326985ep4104_5

Watson, J. C., & Sheperis, C. J. (2010). *Counselors and the right to test: Working toward professional parity* (ACAPCD-31). Alexandria, VA: American Counseling Association.

Webb, J. T., Amend, E. R., Webb, N. E., Goerss, J., Beljan, P., & Olenchak, F. R. (2004). *Misdiagnosis and dual diagnoses of gifted children and adults: ADHD, bipolar, OCD, Asperger's, depression, and other disorders.* Scottsdale, AZ: Great Potential Press.

Wechsler, D. (1939). *The measurement of adult intelligence.* Baltimore, MD: Williams & Wilkins.

Wechsler, D. (1967). *Manual for the Wechsler Preschool and Primary Scale of Intelligence.* New York, NY: Psychological Corporation.

Weinberg, R. A. (1989). Intelligence and IQ: Landmark issues and great debates. *American Psychologist, 44,* 98–104. doi:10.1037/0003-066X.44.2.98

Weiner, I. B. (1998). *Principles of Rorschach interpretation.* Mahwah, NJ: Lawrence Erlbaum.

Weis, R., Toolis, E. E., & Cerankosky, B. C. (2008). Construct validity of the Rotter Incomplete Sentence Blank with clinic-referred and nonreferred adolescents. *Journal of Personality Assessment, 90,* 564–573. doi:10.1080/00223890802388491

Weiss, D. S., Zilberg, N. J., & Genevro, J. L. (1989). Psychometric properties of Loevinger's Sentence Completion Test in an adult psychiatric outpatient sample. *Journal of Personality Assessment, 53,* 478–486. doi:10.1207/s15327752jpa5303_6

Welfel, E. R. (2006). *Ethics in counseling and psychotherapy: Standards, research, and emerging issues* (3rd ed.). Pacific Grove, CA: Brooks/Cole.

Westefeld, J. S., Range, L. M., Rogers, J. R., Maples, M. R., Bromley, J. L., & Alcorn, J. (2000). Suicide: An overview. *The Counseling Psychologist, 28,* 445–510.

Whiston, S. C. (2009). *Principles and applications of assessment in counseling* (3rd ed.). Belmont, CA: Wadsworth/Thomson Learning.

Whiston, S. C., Tai, W. L., Rahardja, D., & Eder, K. (2011). School counseling outcome: A meta-analytic examination of interventions. *Journal of Counseling and Development, 89,* 37–55. doi:10.1002/j.1556-6678.2011.tb00059.x

Whitcomb, S. A., & Merrell, K. W. (2012). *Behavioral, social, and emotional assessment of children and adolescents* (4th ed.). New York, NY: Routledge.

Wicherts, J. M., & Dolan, C. V. (2010). Measurement invariance in confirmatory factor analysis: An illustration using IQ test performance of minorities. *Educational Measurement: Issues and Practices, 29*(3), 39–47. doi:10.1111/j.1745-3992.2010.00182.x

Williams, K. T. (2007). *Expressive Vocabulary Test, Second Edition.* Circle Pines, MN: AGS.

Wilson, F. R., Pan, W., & Schumsky, D. A. (2012). Recalculation of the critical values for Lawshe's content validity ratio. *Measurement and Evaluation in Counseling and Development, 45*(3), 197–210. doi:10.1177/0748175612440286

Wood, J. M., & Lilienfeld, S. O. (1999). The Rorschach Inkblot test: A case of overstatement? *Assessment,* 6341–349.

Wood, J. M., Lilienfeld, S. O., Nezworski, M. (2010). Validity of Rorschach Inkblot scores for discriminating psychopaths from nonpsychopaths in forensic populations: A meta-analysis. *Psychological Assessment, 22,* 336–349. doi:10.1037/a0018998

Yoon, E., Chang, C., Kim, S., Clawson, A., Cleary, S., Hansen, M., & . . . Gomes, A. M. (2013). A meta-analysis of acculturation/enculturation and mental health. *Journal of Counseling Psychology, 60*(1), 15–30. doi:10.1037/a0030652

Zimmerman, I. L., & Woo-Sam, J. M. (1978). Intellectual testing today: Relevance to the school age child. In L. Oettinger (Ed.), *The psychologist, the school, and the child with MBD/LD* (p. 51). New York, NY: Grune & Stratton.

Zucker, S. (2004). *Administration practices for standardized assessments.* San Antonio, TX: Pearson. Retrieved from http://www.pearsonassessments.com/NR/rdonlyres/3E4B7986-D815%E2%80%934960-BCBF-A8E599C81FD8/0/AdministrationPractices.pdf

Zunker, V. G. (2008). *Career, work, and mental health: Integrating career and personal counseling.* Thousand Oaks, CA: Sage.

Zytowski, D. G. (1997). *Kuder Career Search Schedule: User's manual.* Adel, IA: National Career Assessment Services.

Zytowski, D. G. (2001). Kuder Career Search with person match: Career assessment for the 21st century. *Journal of Career Assessment, 9,* 229–241.

Zytowski, D. (2006). *Super's Work Values Inventory–Revised: Technical manual* (Version 1.0). Retrieved from www.Kuder.com/PublicWeb/swv_manual.aspx

Index

About the Authors

Joshua C. Watson, PhD, LPC, NCC, ACS, is an associate professor of counselor education at Texas A&M University–Corpus Christi. He has more than 15 years of clinical experience working in a variety of community mental health and private practice settings. In addition to his teaching, Dr. Watson has authored over 60 publications and has presented at several state, national, and international professional counseling conferences. In recognition of his scholarship, Dr. Watson has received numerous awards, including the Ralph F. Berdie Memorial Research Award, the Herb Handley Memorial Research Award, the American College Counseling Association's Distinguished Research Award, and the Mississippi Counseling Association's Distinguished Research Award. A past president of the Association for Assessment in Research and Counseling (AARC), Dr. Watson also is an active member of the American Counseling Association (ACA), serving as an elected member of the Association's Governing Council and managing editor of the *Journal of College Counseling.* Dr. Watson currently resides in Corpus Christi, Texas, with his wife April and their two daughters, Kaylee and Cara.

Brandé Flamez, PhD, LPC, NCC, is a professor in the counselor education and supervision program at Walden University. She has over 100 national and international presentations and has authored or coauthored several book chapters and referred articles. She is the author of the upcoming textbook *Diagnosing and Treating Children and Adolescents: A Guide for Mental Health Professionals.* She serves on the American Counseling Association (ACA) Governing Council, is chair of the ACA Publications Committee, and serves as the president of the Association for Humanistic Counselors (AHC). She is the recipient of numerous national awards, including the ACA Wrenn Award for a Humanitarian and Caring Person, International Association for Marriage and Family Counselors Distinguished Mentor Award, and AHC Humanistic Clinician Award.

⑤SAGE research**methods**

The essential online tool for researchers from the world's leading methods publisher

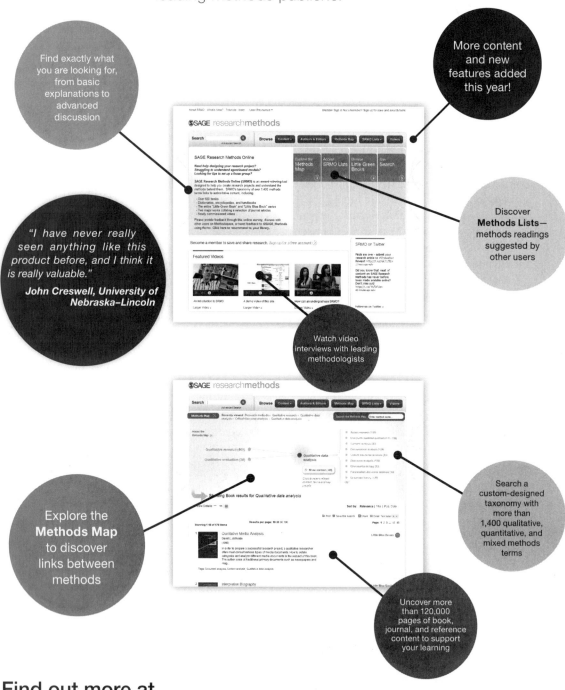

Find exactly what you are looking for, from basic explanations to advanced discussion

More content and new features added this year!

"I have never really seen anything like this product before, and I think it is really valuable."

John Creswell, University of Nebraska–Lincoln

Discover **Methods Lists**— methods readings suggested by other users

Watch video interviews with leading methodologists

Explore the **Methods Map** to discover links between methods

Search a custom-designed taxonomy with more than 1,400 qualitative, quantitative, and mixed methods terms

Uncover more than 120,000 pages of book, journal, and reference content to support your learning

Find out more at
www.sageresearchmethods.com